In America

ALSO BY GEERT MAK

An Island in Time: The Biography of a Village

Amsterdam: A Brief Life of the City

In Europe: Travels Through the Twentieth Century

The Bridge: A Journey Between Orient and Occident

Geert Mak

In America

Travels with John Steinbeck

TRANSLATED
FROM THE DUTCH
BY
LIZ WATERS

Harvill Secker
LONDON

Published by Harvill Secker 2014

2 4 6 8 10 9 7 5 3 1

First published with the title *Reizen zonder John: Op zoek naar Amerika* in 2012
by Uitgeverij Atlas Contact, Amsterdam

First published in Great Britain in 2014 by
Harvill Secker
Random House, 20 Vauxhall Bridge Road
London SW1V 2SA

www.vintage-books.co.uk

Addresses for companies within The Random House Group Limited can be found at: www.
randomhouse.co.uk/offices.htm

The Random House Group Limited Reg. No. 954009

A CIP catalogue record for this book is
available from the British Library

ISBN 9781846557026 (hardback)
ISBN 9781846557033 (trade paperback)

The publisher gratefully acknowledges the support of the
Dutch Foundation for Literature

N **ederlands**
   letterenfonds
dutch foundation
for literature

Grateful thanks to Chester Music Ltd trading as Dash Music Co. and Redwood Music for
permission to reprint 'When the Lights Go On Again (All Over the World)', words and music
by Edward Seiler, Bennie Benjamin and Sol Marcus © 1942 Porgie Music Corporation and
Redwood Music Ltd; Houghton Mifflin Harcourt for 'Chicago' from *Chicago Poems* by Carl
Sandburg © 1944 by Carl Sandburg; the Wylie Agency for 'Howl' by Allen Ginsberg © 2006
The Allen Ginsberg Trust; Chappell-Morris for 'Route 66' by Bob Troup © Edwin Morris & Co.

Map by Rolf Weijburg

Typeset in Joanna MT by Palimpsest Book Production Limited,
Falkirk, Stirlingshire

Printed and bound in Great Britain by
Clays Ltd, St Ives plc

In memory of Edith and Louis Laub

Contents

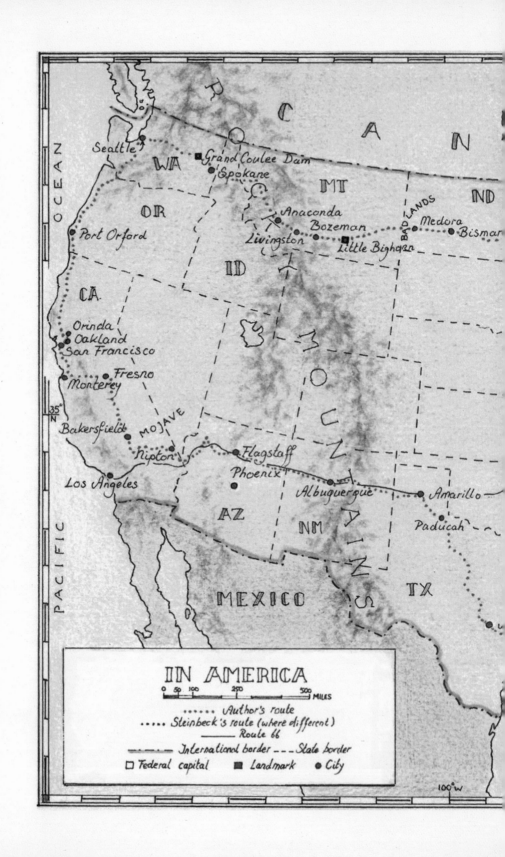

Seattle

WA

Grand Coulee Dam
Spokane

MT

ND

OR

Port Orford

Anaconda
Bozeman
Livingston
Little Bighorn

BAD LANDS
Medora
Bismar

ID

CA.

Orinda
Oakland
San Francisco

Fresno

Monterey

35°
N

Bakersfield

MOJAVE

Kipton

Flagstaff

Phoenix

Los Angeles

Albuquerque
Amarillo

Paducah

AZ

NM

TX

MEXICO

OCEAN

PACIFIC

IN AMERICA

0 50 100   250   500
MILES

.... Author's route
.... Steinbeck's route (where different)
———— Route 66
–·–·– International border – – – State border
▢ Federal capital   ■ Landmark   ● City

100°W

PART ONE

Sag Harbor

'When the lights go on again all over the world
And the ships will sail again all over the world
Then we'll have time for things like wedding rings and
free hearts will sing
When the lights go on again all over the world.'

VERA LYNN

One

NO ONE COULD SAY EXACTLY when the great celebration erupted. There were those who claimed it kicked off as soon as the war was over, straight after the Japanese surrender on 14 August 1945, when everyone danced in the streets and a Jewish refugee, Alfred Eisenstaedt of *Life* magazine, took the photograph of his life on Times Square: a sailor, delirious with joy, kissing a nurse on the lips.

These were the months when GIs returned from all corners of the globe, the years when people suddenly had money in their pockets. Even in America, luxuries had been scarce and rationed for years; now you could buy washing machines again, and radios, and the latest Chevrolet. General Electric flooded the country with luxury gadgets: food processors, toasters, floor-polishing machines, FM radios, electric blankets, and so on. These were all products promoted by that epitome of the television salesman Ronald Reagan, a popular actor whose work in advertising eventually taught him to sell himself, too. Traditional ideals were put on hold and 'selling out' became a catchphrase – you accepted a job that gave you no satisfaction because the pay was good. These were the months and years when British singer Vera Lynn touched American hearts with 'A kiss won't mean "Goodbye" but "Hello to love"'. Yes, that's when it started, with that kiss on Times Square.

Others say it was rather less romantic than that. It began right at the point when people had to pick up everyday life again. 'You should start your story with that brilliant invention by the Levitts,' I was told. 'That's what really got it all going.'

Bill Levitt, his brother Alfred and their father Abraham were the first to mass-produce prefabricated homes, an invention no less significant than Henry Ford's assembly line in 1913. With an ingenious design and brilliant planning, Bill Levitt was able to build a simple, sturdy house for less than 8,000 dollars. The basic model, with its two bedrooms plus an attic, was just the thing for a young family. It was the Model T Ford of houses, sure, but a good bit of luxury was included all the same: the living room had a fireplace and a built-in television set; the kitchen was equipped with a fridge, a stove and a Bendix washing machine. For an extra 250 dollars you could have a car as well; the buyer of that package was all set for the future.

The Levitts erected their first houses in a huge potato field in Hempstead, twenty miles from Manhattan, in 1946. Within two years the place had become a town in its own right. By July 1948, 180 houses were being manufactured every week, and just three years later 82,000 people were living on the old potato field in 17,000 prefab dwellings. Most of those drawn to the brand-new Levittown were GIs, each with a generous discharge payment in his pocket. The ads didn't exaggerate; the instalment plan was generous: 'Uncle Sam and the world's largest builder have made it possible for you to live in a charming house in a delightful community without having to pay for them with your eyeteeth', 'All yours for $58. You're a lucky man, Mr Veteran.' The homes sold hand over fist.

In that strange, intermediate world between country and city, men and women forged countless alliances, exploring peace together. 'In front of almost every house along Levittown's 100 miles of winding streets sits a tricycle or a baby carriage,' a report for Time magazine noted in the summer of 1950. 'In Levittown, all activity stops from 12 to 2 in the afternoon; that is nap time.'

Levittown marked the start of the explosive growth of suburbia, a concept that stands for an entire culture, a specific kind of life and society. To countless GIs suburbia was the beginning of modern life, of 'time for things like wedding rings', a safe adventure that united all newcomers. These were young families no longer fearful of getting into debt: avid consumers since they possessed almost nothing; children of poor Irish, Italian, Jewish and other immigrants convinced that all their dreams for the future were about to come true. Levittown and communities like it nurtured a social change that was to turn traditional America on its head:

the start of the move to the suburbs, the end of the old city and the old countryside.

Another beginning, an elderly American once told me, was the advent of new cars. For him it all started with the cars, or rather their colours. He traced it back to the autumn of 1954, when he noticed people thronging in front of local car showrooms. Something extraordinary was going on. Models had always been different each year, but consistently solid and square, usually black or dark green. Suddenly a completely new generation was on gleaming display – wider and softer than ever.

I've looked at the advertisements for that year. The earthy colours of previous decades were replaced by pastels, pinks and pale blues. The Chevrolet Bel Air and the Pontiac Star Chief, with their Strato-Streak V8 engines, were available in 'Avalon Yellow' as well as 'Raven Black'. The new models had rounded, panoramic windscreens and, in the case of the new Cadillac, a strange rear end with tail fins like a fighter plane. Sales soared, rising by thirty-seven per cent between 1954 and 1955 alone. People were no longer so concerned about technology and durability; it was more about shape and style. A new era truly has dawned, was the feeling those cars gave you.

At some point in that decade, American society changed abruptly in tone and mentality. Instead of being preoccupied above all with survival, it became a consumer society. A world of toil was transformed into a world of enjoyment.

Domestic interiors were still full of things from the 1930s and 1940s, but amid the brown furniture and crocheted rugs a different lifestyle was emerging, with all the features of the old austerity but a cheerful sense of amazement as well. 'What sort of fairyland is this we suddenly find ourselves in?' was the general mood.

These were the years of what became known as the 'baby boom'. The birth rate shot up by almost fifty per cent and stayed high until the end of the 1950s. In 1957, at the peak of the boom, 123 in every 1,000 women gave birth – a figure unprecedented in American history – and all those children were brought up in far greater prosperity than their parents had known. 'There never was a country more fabulous than America,' wrote

British historian Robert Payne after a visit in 1949. 'She bestrides the world like a colossus: no other power at any time in the world's history has possessed so varied or so great an influence on other nations . . . Half the wealth of the world, more than half the productivity, nearly two-thirds of the world's machines are concentrated in American hands; the rest of the world lies in the shadow of American industry.' It was the American Century, and so it would remain.

A few more statistics, which speak for themselves. At the start of the twentieth century, the average life expectancy for white Americans was barely fifty, and for black Americans it was roughly thirty-five. Americans spent almost twice as much on funerals as they did on pharmaceuticals; half a century later, the reverse was the case. By then, average life expectancy was around seventy, the black population included.

National income rose by close to a third in the 1950s. In 1956 American teenagers had a weekly income of ten dollars and fifty-five cents, more than the disposable income of the average household in 1940. The middle class – that segment of the population able to spend money on non-utilitarian products – accounted for almost half of all American households.

On the face of it, life was God-fearing and respectable. Almost sixty per cent of American families owned their own homes, an unprecedented figure. The divorce rate was remarkably low, at 8.9 couples per thousand all told in 1958. According to Gallup polls, in 1940 a third of American adults went to church every week; by 1955 the proportion had risen to around half. To the 'happiness question', more than half of all Americans answered 'very happy' in 1957. Never had there been so much quantifiable happiness, and never would there be so much again.

Anyone wishing to be catapulted back into the America of those years should take a look on YouTube at the home movie *Disneyland Dream*, filmed in the summer of 1956 by enthusiastic amateur filmmaker Robbins Barstow, who recorded his family's experiences year after year. He did so in such an entertaining and original manner that his films have gradually become classics.

In *Disneyland Dream*, the family – father, mother, and three children aged between four and eleven – enters a competition sponsored by the then-new Scotch tape. The winners are to be treated to a trip – by airplane! – to the recently opened Disneyland in Anaheim, California. Lo and behold the youngest child, Danny, wins first prize with the indomitable slogan: 'I like "Scotch" brand cellophane tape because when some things tear then I can just use it.'

Excitement all round, and the Barstows' neighbours step out into their front gardens to wave the family off. Then comes the thrilling nine-hour flight to California aboard a TWA Super Constellation, with room for no fewer than sixty-four passengers. Next we see the simple funfair of the original Disneyland. At the hotel, the Barstows are jubilant that the chic swimming pool is open to them. Yes, the days when such luxury was reserved for the stylish elite are over. The family deals with its budgetary constraints by not eating in restaurants but picnicking outdoors.

There is no hint of any doubt or cynicism. Every minute of the movie is filled with sun, innocence and boundless enthusiasm. It's true, Barstow says at the end, Walt Disney is right: Disneyland is 'the happiest place on earth'. The entire family is 'forever grateful to Scotch brand cellophane tape' for the experience.

The closing chorus of this charming cantata to America comes through loud and clear: from now on we all belong together, and anyone can make it in these new times.

We Europeans heard that tune from afar. To the children of small-town Europe, America was a dreamland with a freewheeling lifestyle, fragments of which occasionally blew across the ocean. Shortly after the fall of the Berlin Wall, I stayed with a family in Armenia. For years the girls had collected empty Chanel and Lancôme perfume bottles. The bathroom was full of them. Somewhere deep inside those bottles, the aroma of the rich West still lingered. That's exactly how we European children of the 1950s experienced America: through a few glossy magazines, or toy cars made of soft but tough plastic – even the steering wheel was of astonishing quality – or a free copy of Donald Duck that fell through the letter box one autumn day, featuring a lottery with a thousand wristwatches (a thousand iPads in today's youth economy) to give away. Not to mention the content. Donald Duck as a teacher. The nephews squash an ice cream onto their weary uncle's forehead. Wasting a whole ice cream without a second thought!

At some point, from that same America, packets of green-and-white powder arrived that a housewife could instantly transform into a pan of soup. 'California', the concoction was called. 'California,' we whispered. California. In the provincial town where I grew up, we lugged the cabbage, lettuce and potatoes we'd grown on our allotment past several new factories on the Marshallweg, a road named after a general who, as I understood it, had paid to set up all those manufacturing companies: America! With our pocket money we bought flat packets of chewing gum, beautifully wrapped, that included a picture of a movie star – we collected those – and it all smelled strange and rosy: America! On short-wave radio an army station crackled into the room, with an announcer who might start talking right over a swing band: America! Lionel Hampton came to the Netherlands in September 1953 and his saxophonist lay on his back onstage and carried on playing. Hampton abandoned his vibraphone to play drums for a while and to do an improvised dance to 'Hey-Ba-Ba-Re-Bop'. De Gelderlander, our provincial newspaper, wrote: 'How vast must be the emptiness of those hearts that have lost any longing for values more exalted than those of Negro moaning.' But the audience, unaccustomed to any of this, went wild: America!

The high point of this whirring, pale-blue era was 1960. The average American earned more than 5,000 dollars a year; a newly built house cost 12,500 dollars, a car 2,600, a pair of shoes 13, a litre of gasoline 6.7 cents.

The tail fins on the new Cadillac Eldorado were the largest and sharpest ever seen. In April, the world's first weather satellite was launched. In the Philippines, the Japanese government tried in vain to coax the last two Japanese soldiers out of the jungle – they refused to believe the war was over. Xerox put the first commercial photocopier on the market. Chubby Checker started a new dance craze, the twist. Frank Sinatra, cigarette in hand, stood and sang in a short film called Music for Smokers Only, taking a drag at the end of each line: 'I get no kick from champagne . . .'

National Airlines was the first company to fly jets from New York to Miami, in barely three hours, charging fifty-five dollars a ticket. The construction of the Interstate Highway System, the largest motorway network in the world, had been in full swing for four years.

The mechanical cotton picker had taken over the South. The arrival of air conditioning allowed housebuilders to throw up suburbs even in the desert. The countryside moved to the city, the overcrowded inner cities moved to suburban avenues, the black South moved to the factories of the North.

On 9 May – Mother's Day – the first contraceptive pill, Enovid, was declared safe and approved for sale. Dr John Rock, champion of the pill, rejoiced that humanity's rampant sex drive would finally be stripped of its consequences: 'The greatest menace to world peace and decent standards of life today is not atomic energy but sexual energy.' The Cold War resumed at full intensity after an American U-2 spy plane was shot down over the Soviet Union. War hero Dwight D. Eisenhower was still president; it was his last year in office. The election campaign was a neck-and-neck race between man of the people Richard Nixon and rich kid Jack Kennedy.

Nineteen sixty is the year in which this story begins.

Two

THIS BOOK IS AN ACCOUNT of two journeys: one undertaken in 1960 and the other in 2010. The eyes that looked at America in 1960 were those of the writer John Steinbeck and his dog Charley. Together they travelled around the country in a green GMC pickup truck called Rocinante. It was named after Don Quixote's horse because everyone had decided this was a similar kind of expedition: a foolish, elderly knight setting out alone to free the country of savage, dangerous windmills. The eyes of 2010 are my own.

In 1960 John Steinbeck was a fairly tall, greying man of fifty-eight. His face, as he writes, had been marked by time with 'scars, lines, furrows and erosions'. He had a moustache and a beard, and he felt happiest in working clothes: short Wellington boots, khaki cotton trousers, a hunting jacket, and a faded-blue British naval cap. He'd been given that cap during the war by the captain of a torpedo boat that was itself torpedoed shortly afterwards. As could be said of countless other men, remnants of the war years were lodged in all the cracks and seams of Steinbeck's existence.

He was married to Elaine Anderson, a cultivated Texan lady who bore a certain resemblance to Lady Bird Johnson, wife of the influential senator and future president. The two women were good friends. When Lady Bird became a public figure, Elaine shopped for her regularly and even bought her clothes, since they had precisely the same measurements. John and Elaine spent most of their time in Sag Harbor, an old fishing port on the east coast between the crocodile jaws of Long Island, two hours north-east of New York City.

In those days, Sag Harbor was a small manufacturing town, a

blue-collar place. Bulova had a watchcase factory there, Grumman built aircraft, and on the shore were several shipyards. At one time, in around 1840, it had been among the world's roughest whaling ports. In the Old Burying Ground, dating back to 1767, are the graves of the town's first inhabitants: fighters in the American Revolution, French merchants, Portuguese sailors, and Irish and English whalemen. There are tales of the crews of some ships not daring to go ashore at Sag Harbor: the countless bars and brothels presented too much of a risk.

It was also one of the richest of ports, as is clear to this day from the opulent rustic villas, built in the nineteenth century, which stand among the trees just outside the centre of town. They feature large balconies and verandas, Greek pillars, leaded windows, and no end of other ornamentation. Most of the houses have been taken over and restored by rich New Yorkers in recent years, but in 1960 a good many were in a neglected state.

In 1955 the Steinbecks bought a small house in the town. It soon became John's favourite place. He wrote four books and countless letters there, fretted about the state of the world and about his life, suffered a crisis and pulled himself out of it again. Their house stood, and still stands, on Bluff Point, a green slope leading down to an arm of the Atlantic, surrounded by stately old oaks, with its own jetty for the boat Steinbeck had always dreamed of owning. From the house you look out across the lawn, then over the calm water of the bay as far as the town and the harbour.

John's life followed an established pattern: up early, drive to Main Street with Charley beside him in the passenger seat to fetch the mail, buy a paper, drink coffee in the fishermen's bar, Black Buoy, and purchase a few items at Bob Barry's hardware store. Steinbeck was crazy about all things technical. 'Tools, mechanisms, he couldn't get enough of them,' old friends of his told me. 'Fitting out that camper, Rocinante – that was precisely the kind of thing he enjoyed.' Then it was home to write, and in the afternoon down to the harbour again for a few drinks with Barry and other friends at the bar of the Upper Deck.

The rugged John and the distinguished Elaine were the perfect match. Friends say they differed fundamentally on only one point: Elaine loved New York; John hated it. For him there was only one city: San Francisco.

Sag Harbor was the ideal compromise. John had a circular writing pavilion built at the edge of the garden, and for Elaine a tiny swimming pool, although it was soon appropriated by the ducks. The place was small but comfortable, pleasant and peaceful.

It's not hard to see why Steinbeck instantly fell for Sag Harbor. He was a child of the other ocean: of the west coast, of California. He grew up in Salinas, the centre of a prosperous agricultural district in the middle of the state, some two hours south of San Francisco. His mother was an ambitious and cultivated schoolteacher, his father a quiet adventurer of the kind you often find out west, accustomed to making his own way in difficult circumstances. In his personal affairs Steinbeck's father was none too happy, almost drowning in worry about money and family matters, yet his son always carried his picture with him, and a character like him pops up in all of Steinbeck's books. 'He was a man intensely disappointed in himself,' John later wrote about his father.

Steinbeck attended a handful of lectures at Stanford – on marine biology – but soon left, determined to educate himself in real life. He failed in New York, returned to California and camped with a friend called Toby Street over two long winters, looking after an empty summerhouse on the shores of Lake Tahoe, surrounded by wilderness. He then lived for years beside the ocean in Pacific Grove, half an hour from Salinas, close to the stinking sardine industry on the piers of Monterey.

There he got to know Ed Ricketts, a marine biologist who earned his living by collecting every imaginable kind of sea creature for university laboratories. Ricketts' own lab was the centre of an intense social life, with many friends, especially girlfriends, and enormous quantities of cheap drink. Ricketts became the best friend Steinbeck would ever have, the older brother who taught him to accept himself, with all his pretensions and shortcomings.

In those years John started writing a series of short novels that became famous all over the world, including the Eastern Bloc: *Tortilla Flat* (1935), *Of Mice and Men* (1937), *The Red Pony* (1937), *Cannery Row* (1945) – which featured Ed Ricketts in the romantic role of 'Doc' – and *The Pearl* (1947). The stories were mostly set in California, and they were always about simple lives and hard-won happiness, about fate and the tenacity of survivors.

He had a good feel for titles. The two real classics among his books are *The Grapes of Wrath* (1939), a novel about the miserable fate of those driven from their land in the Midwest by the great drought of the 1930s, and *East of Eden* (1952), an almost biblical drama about a struggle between two brothers that was loosely based on his own family history in Salinas.

The Grapes of Wrath had a particularly far-reaching influence. Steinbeck's description of the hardships faced by the victims of the Dust Bowl and how they were exploited by their fellow Americans was fiercely attacked in the right-wing press. In his native region he was unable to show his face for years. At the same time, no one could escape the book's tough message. In the words of playwright Arthur Miller: 'The Joads [the central characters] became more vividly alive than one's next-door neighbor, and their sufferings emblematic of an age. His picture of America's humiliation of the poor was Steinbeck's high achievement, a picture which for a time challenged the iron American denial of reality.'

To literary historians, Steinbeck's work is an important link in the chain that is the American storytelling tradition, in which the ordinary man is central, which started with Mark Twain and Walt Whitman and continues to this day. Steinbeck consistently refused to follow the literary fashion for understatement and hidden narratives. A dialogue must sparkle with life.

He was always a storyteller. As E. L. Doctorow wrote, 'Steinbeck's genius was to perceive a story that would accommodate all the chaos and almost universal misery of America in the 1930s.'

John married three times. His first wife was his childhood sweetheart Carol, his second a failed actress, Gwyn, with whom he had a turbulent relationship in the war years and who bore him two sons, Thomas and John. Steinbeck regularly toured the European front lines as a correspondent for the *New York Herald Tribune*, and towards the end of their marriage Gwyn tormented him time and again with the 'confession' that John Jr was not really his son. The issue even became the central theme of the play *Burning Bright*. It was nonsense; the likeness between father and son was all too obvious in later years, but at the time Steinbeck could not be completely certain.

He saw the boys regularly, spent endless holidays with them, but

somehow the relationship between father and sons was always problematic, both close and distant at the same time. All the same, as he once
wrote to a friend, there was a 'deep and wordless love' that filtered
through 'from both sides of the barricade'.

The couple divorced when Steinbeck was in his mid-forties and Gwyn
skilfully fleeced him. Poor and embittered, he withdrew to the old family
home in Pacific Grove. Men and women ought to avoid one another, he
decided in those days, 'except in bed', the only place 'where their natural
hatred of each other is not so apparent'. Within a year he had met a new
love, Elaine.

Steinbeck led a double life. He lived part of the time in Manhattan, in a
brownstone at 209 East 72nd Street. He would suddenly disappear, said
his friends in Sag Harbor. He might be in New York, or perhaps abroad.
'Elaine kept those lives strictly separate,' they said. He was large and small
at the same time: himself while in Sag Harbor, and a public figure in
that damned New York and the rest of the world. In photographs, especially in his later years, John looks like an intractable, rather surly man,
clearly convinced he is right. The image that emerges from his letters,
which were eventually published, is very different — that of a man who,
despite all his success, continually doubted himself and the value of his
work, an obsessive writer who nevertheless felt insecure about his achievements. 'The great crime I have committed against literature is living too
long and writing too much, and not good enough,' he wrote in 1958 to
his friend Elia Kazan. 'But I like to write. I like it better than anything.
That's why neither theatre nor movies really deeply interest me.'

He was not after fame and immortality, although they came to him
along the way. At heart he was a solitary craftsman, a word-carpenter. He
rarely, if ever, performed in public. When an interviewer asked how he
saw himself as an author, he had no answer: 'I have never looked upon
myself as an author — I don't think I have ever considered myself an
author. I've considered myself a writer, because that's what I do. I don't
know what an author does.'

He grew to become one of the most famous of American writers. By
the time he was forty, his status was impregnable; every new book from
his pen was an event. Within a month of its publication in 1942, his

novel about the occupation of Norway, *The Moon is Down*, had sold half a million copies. In the late 1950s, based on the number of books sold and titles translated, he was number three in the world.

He was also seriously underrated. 'Once I read and wept over reviews,' he wrote in 1954. 'Then one time I put the criticisms all together and I found that they canceled each other out and left me nonexistent.' That was indeed the standard pattern. He was either praised to the skies for his beautiful use of words, his brilliant storytelling and his humanity, or reviled for his supposedly filthy and despicable language (by the right) or his sentimentality and cartoonish characters (by the left).

He never did make much of an impression on the more academic critics, a fate he shared with other fine storytellers. In the 1930s, when he came to fame with tales of tramps, prostitutes and poor migrant labourers, he was quickly dismissed as too 'proletarian' and too much of a 'realist'. Later his work was thought too naive and above all too romantic, a verdict that has echoed down the decades. 'The extraordinary thing about John Steinbeck is how good he can be when so much of the time he's so bad,' Robert Gottlieb opined in the *New York Review of Books* as recently as 2008.

Yet Steinbeck, both at home and abroad, remained an exceptionally popular writer, year after year. 'I have seen my father dolefully staring up at me from strange wastebaskets, his likeness celebrated on fifteen-cent stamps,' wrote his son John Jr in his own inimitable style. 'In a drunken or drugged state I have seen his name fly by me on papers in the wind, and bumped into statues of him while innocently looking for a quiet, private place to vomit.'

What the literati failed to see was Steinbeck's great value as a chronicler of his time. He was hugely successful at reaching the audience he had in mind, and his readers recognised themselves and their world in the tales he told. He managed to express, in words and stories, exactly what they were feeling.

Steinbeck is still very much with us, in a way that few living writers can match. 'Want to learn about the plight of unemployed workers during the Great Depression? Head to Amazon.com and order John Steinbeck's Depression-era epic *The Grapes of Wrath*,' wrote columnist Ezra Klein in September 2011. Lyrics by The Band, a rock group that reflected the lives of ordinary Americans like no other, were inspired by Steinbeck. The elegant Penguin mass-market paperbacks of his work still sell in their hundreds of thousands every year, reprint after reprint after reprint. His books remain required reading at countless American schools. 'Reason for your visit?' the Chinese-American passport-stamper at San Francisco airport asked me in the summer of 2010. 'Archival research.' 'Into what?' 'John Steinbeck.' His face lit up. 'Ah, *Of Mice and Men*, I wrote a paper about that.'

In later life Steinbeck increasingly doubted the quality of his work, Elaine and his friends would recall. Every time he published a book he was subjected to fierce attacks, often by prominent reviewers. For all his solitude, these criticisms affected him deeply – it began to seem as if in his heart he believed the critics were right. He'd often wondered why no writer ever survived the success of a bestseller. Only later, he said, did he understand it. 'One gets self-conscious and that's the end of one's writing.'

By the 1950s he had an impressive oeuvre to his name, but he questioned all that success: Am I really worth this? Do I really mean anything? The subject of his writing was 'restless America', but he was himself a prime example of it – always searching, always wrestling with his own thoughts. Then again, he was able to drown all that out with a form of bluster.

John 'seemed to want to expand himself physically', Arthur Miller wrote in his memoirs, 'to present a strong and able and heartily Western image'. In a commemorative volume of recollections of John Steinbeck, Miller paints a wonderful portrait of the man as he knew him. In the 1950s Steinbeck was world famous, he was a 'celebrity whose life was filled with famous friends and the powers that come with fame'. Close up, however, Miller was surprised by Steinbeck's insecurity, sensitivity and shyness – especially since he was so celebrated, and so outspoken in his opinions.

He'd read a great deal of philosophy, knew his literary classics and, others say, was a popular guest at dinners held by Miller and his then wife, Marilyn Monroe. Marilyn and John had a deep respect for each other. She saw in him the True Artist, and she made a tremendous effort to be entertaining and intelligent; he saw a Star, with a sexy glamour from which even a man as gnarled as he couldn't possibly shy away. Yet John's heart clearly lay elsewhere. There was something simple about him, and according to Miller he became truly enthusiastic only when talking about life on the land or in a small town. 'As a native New Yorker, I couldn't help seeing in John a grownup country boy,' Miller wrote.

The spirit of the times worked against Steinbeck as well. The late 1950s were years of an excessive patriotism inconceivable to us today. The contest with the Soviet Union was at its height and Steinbeck, who had started his career as a progressive writer, clearly felt caught between the beliefs that had once defined his life and the now-dominant mentality. Arthur Miller wrote: 'To be honest about it, I often felt Steinbeck, in the last part of his life, was feeling much of the time like a displaced person, rather than a cosmopolitan at home anywhere. But it is a very rare thing for an American writer to stay at home.'

Steinbeck did indeed continue to travel, mainly in Europe and Mexico. He also took refuge in a kind of spiritual exile. Each year he spent months in Europe, rented a magnificent house in Paris, continually complained about money worries while at the same time driving around in a Jaguar, and wrote about Spain, France, Ireland and Italy for *Collier's*, *Saturday Review* and the travel magazine *Holiday*. Gradually, however, he was shutting himself up in the Middle Ages, writing *The Acts of King Arthur and His Noble Knights*, an ambitious attempt to make *Le Morte d'Arthur*, the classic fifteenth-century history by Thomas Malory, accessible to a broad contemporary audience.

He had already engaged in a failed attempt to write an American version of *Don Quixote*, called *Don Keehan* – no, the name Rocinante was not plucked out of thin air. But with *Arthur* he went further than a simple reworking. He identified with the fifteenth-century author as if hoping to become a contemporary Malory. He was seeking a completely new way of telling the story, of making it fit the modern world, although in fact the development of the story wasn't the most important thing. In the words of his biographer, Jackson Benson: 'He was in love with the magical evocations of the language, the sense of being in history that the sound and the sight of the words conveyed.'

In February 1959, John and Elaine rented a humble farm cottage in

Somerset, in England's West Country, to enable him to work in the closest possible proximity to his medieval heroes and heroines. From his study he looked out over rolling hills and ancient oaks, with 'nothing in sight that hasn't been here since the 6th century'. There was a Roman fort nearby, which he believed might actually be Camelot, Arthur's mythical castle. In those months he rewrote the medieval story completely, reconstructing it, as it were, for use by modern Americans.

It became one great lump of kitsch, the same kind of kitsch as all those fake-medieval cathedrals and castles scattered across Europe and America. His agent and confidante Elizabeth Otis did what a good agent and publisher should, and told him the bitter truth: this doesn't work, this won't do, it lacks the poetry and rhythm of the original, there's no life in it.

He continued working on the book all summer, and then he stopped. Tellingly, he abandoned the project at the point when his great hero, Lancelot, finally falls for Arthur's wife, the beautiful Guinevere, and betrays everything: his lord, his religion and his oaths of allegiance.

To a drinking buddy, journalist Joe Bryan, he wrote: 'A man must write about his own time no matter what symbols he uses. And I have not found my symbols nor my form. And there's the rub.' Deeply disappointed, he sailed back to America in October 1959.

Illustrative of Steinbeck's impasse was the interior of that writing pavilion in Sag Harbor. In his biography, Jackson Benson describes it in detail: an easy chair in the middle with tables and bookshelves around it, a stunning view, instruments for the boat strewn about as well as things for the garden, news clippings, notes, gardening books, history books, dictionaries, dog books, boat books – the most diverse things. He'd sorted it all into ingeniously arranged drawers and other systems of storage with labels such as 'Matters of Rubber' and 'Extraordinary Things'.

Benson writes that Steinbeck had created the ideal workplace. But the work itself did not return from England with him. He had lost it somewhere along the way.

At this point Steinbeck was fifty-seven years old. He'd always been a healthy, robust man, but after the failure of his Arthur project he started to ail. He became ill, even having a mild stroke in December 1959, and took a short holiday to consider how things stood. 'We are getting to the age when the obit pages have a great deal of news,' he wrote to his older buddy Toby Street. Elaine and he had always been heavy drinkers; now they tried to limit their drinking to weekends.

Then, as often happens with older men who feel their powers fading, there came a sudden explosion of activity. On the morning of Easter Sunday in 1960 he went to sit in his little summerhouse and wrote the first lines of a new novel, *The Winter of Our Discontent*. The plot was based on a light-hearted short story he'd written in 1956 called 'How Mr Hogan Robbed a Bank', about an upright citizen who finds a way to steal money from the local bank. In this expanded version, everything gets out of hand. As ever, Steinbeck worked to the schedule of an office clerk. He usually produced some 800 words a day, but now he pushed the number up to more than double that. The action takes place in exactly the same period as the writing process, between Easter 1960 and 6 July 1960, the day before Steinbeck completed the first draft: unique, he felt.

His letters, preserved in the library of Stanford University, written in pencil on yellow legal paper in compact handwriting, show evidence of this race to the finish. To Elizabeth Otis he wrote on 24 June 1960: 'My book is tearing me to pieces now. The callus on my first finger from the pencil is big as an egg.' And, a week later: 'Here is a thing of interest, perhaps only to me. I am writing not only about the present but the exact present.' To his old friend Toby Street he wrote on 6 July: 'I have lost time in a bucket of water. My winterbook became obsessive. What I had thought would be about 60,000 words will be near 140,000. I'm just now in the very last part of the first draft. I don't know what I have, but it is not ordinary. It has grown like a tree with its roots in dark water.'

In the spring he'd seized upon another plan. While still immersed in *Winter* he ordered a special truck for a great trip around America. He wanted to renew his acquaintance with 'this monster of a land'. He had a feeling that fundamental changes had taken place, in its mentality as much as anything. He planned to travel through the north of the country from the east coast to the west, then down the west coast from Seattle and Oregon, then eastwards again through Arizona, Texas and the Southern states. The trip would take about three months. He wanted to avoid large

cities and he was eager to see mainly small towns, to look at the countryside, to hang around in bars and hamburger joints for hours, and to
attend church every Sunday. Holiday magazine was prepared to publish his
reportage in instalments. A book might perhaps come of it.

Steinbeck wanted to travel alone and anonymously. His agent even
suggested using the name 'J. S. America'. 'I have to go alone, and I
shall go unknown,' he wrote to friends. 'I just want to look and listen.
What I'll get I need badly – a re-knowledge of my own country, its
speeches, its views, its attitudes and its changes. It's long overdue –
very long. New York is not America.' He'd said the same to Elaine, on
many occasions. He asked her for one favour: he wanted to take their
poodle Charley with him.

In an auction catalogue for Steinbeck's belongings I came upon Charley's
pedigree and discovered that he was probably born in 1951 and that he'd
once had a different name: Anky de Maison Blanche. He was originally
from the Paris suburb of Bercy and, although his owner claimed he later
acquired a good bit of poodle English, he always responded more quickly
to orders in French. When I spoke to Bob Barry's daughter Gwen
Waddington in Sag Harbor, she could still clearly remember Charley. As
a toddler she'd been taken on boat trips that Steinbeck made with her
father, and sometimes she'd had to stay in the cabin with Charley. She
was frightened of the burly animal, but Steinbeck said every time: 'Tell
him stories. That always helps.'

Steinbeck named his project 'Operation America'. Elaine and Elizabeth
Otis, who were vehemently opposed to it because of his precarious state
of health, soon redubbed it 'Operation Windmills'. It was indeed a thoroughly romantic plan. Steinbeck, or so his son Thom said, had never
camped in his life; the planned itinerary was on the tight side and the
cold of autumn was quickly approaching. John had in fact done something
similar in 1936, as part of his preparations for writing The Grapes of Wrath.
On that occasion he bought a baker's van, a 'pie wagon' as he called it,
which he converted into a travelling writer's room. This time he fitted
out his truck as a kind of land-bound ship, with all sorts of tools, ropes,
fishing rods, rifles, writing equipment and maps, as well as an encyclopaedia and dozens of other reference works, a block-and-tackle, and a
tank that could hold thirty gallons of water.

Half a century later I saw Rocinante at the National Steinbeck Center in Salinas. It was a redoubtable four-wheel-drive pickup with a heater effective enough for the traveller to brave a polar winter. In the bed of the truck, a structure made of white-painted aluminium had been added, the interior of which was indeed rather like a ship: a cosy, wooden cabin with a large table and two brown-leather sofa beds, a white sink, a stove and a fridge, green-and-brown curtains, a few action pictures of hunters and dogs, and the rest of the walls covered with hatches and cupboard doors. The cab in which the driver sat all day was, by contrast, one big metal rattletrap − the norm then for utility vehicles. It was little more than a simple workspace with a hard, grey row of front seats, heavy pedals, and no power steering or any other kind of luxury.

According to his friends, John was as excited as a schoolboy. In that same letter to Toby Street he wrote: 'I have what you call a lorry with a tiny apartment on it, rather like the cabin for a small boat. Wherever I stop, I will be at home. It has a stove, a bench, a desk and a refrigerator. Charley will go with me. This is very necessary to me. I must see how the country looks and smells and sounds.'

In short, it was to be the classic journey of the lonesome hero, with Charley as Sancho Panza, his squire, although the poodle's sober commentary was confined to the lifting of his leg, all across America, on a thousand and one trees.

Three

ON THE CLEAR FRIDAY MORNING of 23 September 1960, John
Steinbeck and Charley set off together, with the yellow-brown of autumn
already in the air. There was a vague sense of unease – in Steinbeck's
case, that is; Charley thought everything was just fine as long as he could
sit next to his boss in the front seat. Sure enough, their expedition had
all the hallmarks of a quixotic undertaking, galloping into battle against
the windmills.

As for me, half a century later, I felt just as much of a fool. Steinbeck's
travel account appeared in 1962 as *Travels with Charley*, and it was followed
in 1966 by a series of interesting afterthoughts entitled *America and
Americans*. The whole project has always fascinated me. I found *Travels*
gripping the first time I read it, full of colours and human voices,
witty and nimble. The story jumps about, like the thoughts and associations of someone who has been sitting behind the wheel day after
day. You drive through an autumnal landscape, then a memory plays
around in your head; an hour or so later you're sitting in a diner
between a couple of silent farmers, the rain pelts down, and before
long you find yourself relaxing in the evening sun beside a quiet river.
Meanwhile you read the land.

What an irresistible book. It made me think I ought to go on a tour
of inspection like that around Europe. I took a full year over that trip,
and it was a very different project, but it all started with *Travels*. When it
was done I asked myself whether someone shouldn't repeat Steinbeck's
journey some time, with today's eyes and ears. But was that a task for
me, a European journalist?

We Europeans, enjoying new comforts and prosperity, had taken a similar course to the Americans, albeit with rather less extravagance, numerous slight differences and carrying the ballast of two devastating world wars. The pace of change was slower. When the Steinbecks stayed in Somerset in 1959 they encountered a way of life in England that seemed untouched by the passage of time. There were hardly any cars, the baker and grocer came door to door, the postman did his rounds on a bicycle, the houses were heated only by coal fires and no one had a fridge, let alone a washing machine. The Steinbecks grew vegetables in the garden and cut the grass with a scythe; mains electricity had only recently been connected and running water was installed that summer. In 1960 the age of prosperity in Western Europe was only just beginning, and for most Eastern Europeans it would not appear on the horizon until decades later.

America fascinated us as Europeans, naturally. Intensely, in fact. It was the future, it was the way to live, with that American spunk and that enviable flair. As far back as the early nineteenth century, the young French aristocrat Alexis de Tocqueville wrote a visionary travel account about the then refreshingly new America. He had travelled all over the country between May 1831 and February 1832 with his friend Gustave de Beaumont, officially to study the American prison system but really to gain an impression of the New World and its peculiar democracy, in which everyone was equal.

His great work, Democracy in America, became a classic, but as a source the letters, notes and journal entries written by the two young men along the way are pure gold. They were acute and witty observers, and they heard and saw a great deal precisely because they were outsiders. As Tocqueville wrote: 'A stranger frequently hears important truths at the fire-side of his host, which the latter would perhaps conceal from the ear of friendship.'

Tocqueville and Beaumont had worthy European successors, from the British ambassador James Bryce, who followed Tocqueville's route precisely and in 1888 produced a classic of his own, The American Commonwealth, to the Swede Gunnar Myrdal with his legendary study of race relations, An American Dilemma (1944), and the Brit Jonathan Raban, who with Bad Land (1996) wrote a delightful mini-history of the farmers who worked tiny patches of land on the endless prairie.

There were dozens of others, along with countless Americans of course.

If there was ever a country in which people were continually writing and thinking about their own identity and role in the world, then it was America. What could I possibly add?

Still, let me honestly admit that America had been my secret love for decades. Like many Europeans, I had a complex relationship with our cousins across the ocean, and with the uncle we shared, the powerful, secretly wealthy Scrooge McDuck. That far-off country was an inexhaustible source of stories and ideas, and nothing was ever the way you thought it was. I'd travelled around America in the 1980s and 1990s, lumbering from east to west and back again by train. I'd reported on elections and drug wars, endlessly talked and interviewed, befriended peace activists, schoolteachers and police chiefs, immersed myself in rodeo festivals and PEN congresses, and I always ended up sitting at the kitchen table with my American second mother – because sometimes Americans can easily become family. Edith was her name, Edith Laub.

The kitchen of the house where Edith lived with her husband Lou was the first American kitchen I saw, and at their breakfast table I engaged in my first American discussions. In their home I experienced American hospitality and generosity for the first time. I was taken totally by surprise, that chilly morning in August 1978 when we first met.

I'd never been to the United States before. With two friends, I booked a cheap and absurdly long flight. On the plane we drank too many Cuba Libres, purely because we found the name so funny, and after almost twenty hours we stumbled into the house of a friend of a friend in Berkeley. There was not enough space, so a few phone calls were made and I was transferred to the house of yet more friends of friends, the way it went in those years. They pushed me up a narrow staircase and I fell exhausted onto a bed and slept like a log, almost around the clock.

The first thing that struck me the following morning was the light. To us, from the always slightly misty Netherlands, that astonishing, clear-as-glass Californian light is a miracle. I couldn't get enough of it. Then there was the typical scent of a wooden American house, mixed with the smell of the thousands of books stowed away in the rooms and attics. Through it all rose the spicy aroma of Edith's famous scrambled eggs, and somehow or other I was home. It was a happiness that never left me, revived every time I called by to see them: the light, the smells, the warmth.

I jumped out of bed, pulled on my clothes, went downstairs to the kitchen, and there we began to talk, to debate and to laugh – Edith, Lou and me. It was seven in the morning, and suddenly it was one o'clock, and so began a close friendship.

Lou died in the mid-1980s. Edith became a dignified elderly lady. Although unsteady on her feet, she carried on working in a small library for devotees of Marxist theology. On Sunday afternoons we would sometimes sit looking at old photos, dug out from under the bed in which she was already spending a good deal of her time by then. I couldn't believe it. 'Jeepers Creepers! Where'd ya get those peepers? Jeepers Creepers! Where'd ya get those eyes?' That was the song I associated with the young Edith, who'd met Lou in New York on one of those summer evenings in 1945 when everyone danced in Times Square. A beautiful Jewish girl, sharp and witty. No one else could laugh the way she did.

At sixteen she'd wanted to become a movie star, and with those eyes she could have done. One evening an uncle came to visit, a prominent Mafioso but to her a member of the family like any other. 'What do you want to be when you grow up?' he asked Edith. 'I want to go to Hollywood,' she said firmly. 'Okay,' said the uncle. 'Here's a thousand dollars to get you started, but you have to leave right now!' He counted the banknotes out onto the table. The room fell silent. Edith didn't hesitate for a second. She grabbed the cash, and ran down the stairs and out into the street. A little while later her father and brothers had to drag her away from the bus-stop sign, which she was clinging to, shouting in anger.

Sixty years later we sat watching hit TV shows together. She did leave for California when the time came, ending up in a second-hand bookstore that she ran with Lou. She brought up two sons and became a fairly staunch leftist – we sometimes argued about the Soviet Union a little – but she was always mad about the great glamour shows. She was an American to the core, that second mother of mine, full of American ideals and the American Dream, which was precisely why she was so critical of her own country. Edith was eighty-six when she died in 2007.

Perhaps it was her death that set me thinking once more about the Steinbeck project. Why not? I read *Travels* for a second time, now with more of an eye to the practical side of the project. Steinbeck's journey was meticulously planned. It would be no problem at all to follow the same route. And what could be better than to make the trip precisely fifty years later, in the autumn of 2010, with John and Charley next to me in my imagination, and with the same question in mind: What has happened over recent decades to this 'monster of a land'?

That close and yet so strange America had an enormous influence on us Europeans, but how much did we actually know about it? How much did we not know? What was reality, semblance, myth? Now that the glorious American century, the twentieth, was over, what would happen next? What kind of a place was twenty-first-century America? Were the Americans still showing us the way to the future?

I decided to go. Without many pretensions, with open eyes and an empty head, purely for reasons of my own. Windmills or not, what did I care?

In 1960 John Steinbeck had every reason to head out and investigate. His old America had changed at an astonishing pace, slipping away from him even as he watched.

A year earlier in Moscow, on 24 July 1959, during the American National Exhibition, a historical confrontation had taken place, an unexpected political duel between the Republican vice-president Richard Nixon and the Soviet premier Nikita Khrushchev, in which the triumph of the American century was demonstrated once again. It was an almost surreal scene, that great conversation between communism and the flashy America of the 1950s – the two great ideologies shaping the world at that moment – and all in front of the kitchen counter of an American show home built for the event.

Everyone had gaped at the luxury, and the Soviet press had written derisively of what it called the 'Taj Mahal', saying the house was as representative of ordinary America as the Taj Mahal was of domestic life in India. Not so, said Nixon. With instalments of a hundred dollars a month, a steelworker could easily afford a house like that. Khrushchev bluffed in turn: 'You need dollars in the United States to get this house, but here all you need is to be born a citizen.'

The two men stood facing each other, the thickset peasant from Ukraine and the son of a man who ran a gas station in California. Nixon waved his finger at Khrushchev as he summed up the American successes of the 1950s: between them the forty-four million families living in America owned fifty-six million cars, fifty million television sets and 143 million radios, and so it went on. 'What these statistics demonstrate is this,' Nixon declared. 'That the United States, the world's largest capitalist country, has from the standpoint of distribution of wealth come closest to the ideal of prosperity for all in a classless society.' Then Nixon pressed a bottle of Pepsi-Cola into Khrushchev's hands and the Soviet leader was recorded for posterity holding it – a decisive victory for Pepsi and for America.

Of course it didn't all simply fall into the Americans' laps. In the first post-war years the nation was in a less-than-triumphant mood. Its joy was accompanied by a sense of humility. Wartime events had been so overwhelming, had touched so many families, often changing them forever, that daily cares meant nothing in comparison to that devastating conflict.

'When you look from today back to 1945, you are looking into a different cultural epoch, across a sort of narcissism line,' conservative commentator David Brooks wrote more than sixty years later. 'Humility, the sense that nobody is that different from anybody else, was a large part of the culture then.' Such modesty persisted for a while in the Europe of the 1950s; in America it disappeared fairly quickly.

Adult Americans driving around in their pale-blue Chevys in the 1950s had experienced the battle for survival during and after the Great Depression, when families were sometimes on the verge of starvation, and it determined their attitude to life. Even in the 1920s, roaring or not, more than forty per cent of city dwellers lived in poverty.

I remember Lou talking about his childhood. In 1920 he was living in Manhattan's Lower East Side, a member of a large Jewish family. All his life he was hard of hearing, the legacy of a bout of yellow fever in his early years, and he had a slight limp from another old illness. His father gambled. He could recall the hunger. When he went to fetch bread on Yom Kippur he would secretly nibble at it a little, thinking: there can't be a God who'd let a child go hungry and then strike him with lightning for such a tiny bit of bread.

Even most of the idols of the 1950s, from President Eisenhower to Elvis Presley, knew all about living on the edge. Dwight D. Eisenhower grew up in a remote town in the Midwest: Abilene, a place without sealed roads or paved sidewalks. When it rained, even Main Street became a quagmire. His father did menial work for the railroad, having fallen into poverty because of an agricultural crisis. At home there was never a cent to spare and everyone worked their fingers to the bone. As far as possible they grew their own food in the garden.

Elvis Presley was born in a wooden cabin built by his father in the poorest part of the cotton-growing region of Mississippi. Presley Sr was jailed for altering a cheque, and in desperation the family moved to Memphis. Elvis said later: 'We were broke, man, broke.' Vice-President Richard Nixon's father went bankrupt and later ran a grocery store with a gas station attached, roping in the entire family to help. Nixon's wife Pat grew up in a miner's hut in Nevada.

As for John Steinbeck, from a respectable bourgeois family, during his years in Monterey with Ed Ricketts he had earned almost nothing. 'In our group of denizens, we had no envy for the rich,' he would say later. 'We didn't know any rich. We thought everyone lived the way we lived, if we thought of that at all.'

These austere lifestyles were accompanied by an ideal of equality. In the first half of the twentieth century, most Americans liked to see themselves as members of a more or less uniform middle class. 'The rich man smokes the same sort of cigarettes as the poor man, shaves with the same sort of razor, uses the same sort of telephone, vacuum cleaner, radio and TV set,' Harper's Magazine wrote with satisfaction in 1947. With this ideal came a sense of proportion; you didn't always need to seem the best or to stand out. As Steinbeck wrote to one of his friends: 'When the invasion barges started for the beaches during the last war – full of huddled frightened men, the sergeants and officers did not address soldiers saying – "Go forth and fight for glory and immortality!" No, they said, "Hit the surf! Do you want to live forever?"'

Yet even that equality within the American middle classes had started to erode. The new models of car, for example, were categorised by rank and status. For those starting out there was the Chevrolet, next came the Pontiacs, Oldsmobiles and Buicks, while the seriously rich drove Cadillacs. Not only that; buying and consuming were increasingly a social norm. You had to drive a new Pontiac, and by 1959 anyone still riding around in a 1956 model was a loser. A new car was the reward for years of self-denial and hard work, as the Cadillac ads were constantly making clear: 'Here is the man who has earned the right to sit at this wheel.'

Most families gradually let go of their traditional puritan sobriety. Historian William Leach described the development of a 'culture of desire that confused the good life with goods'. His colleague David M. Potter complained as early as 1954 that modern society expected a man 'to consume his quota of goods – of automobiles, of whiskey, of television sets – by maintaining a certain standard of living, and it regards him as a "good guy" for absorbing his share, while it snickers at the prudent, self-denying, abstemious thrift that an earlier generation would have respected'. This too signified a breach between the old society of survival and the consumer society; getting into debt, always regarded as a burden and possibly a disgrace, was suddenly perfectly normal, even encouraged.

I need to be careful about using the word 'breach'. In a sense there was continuity as well. Back in the 1920s, America had already begun to develop a kind of luxury culture, and in 1928 Herbert Hoover actually campaigned for the presidency under the slogan 'Two cars in every garage'. Just before the stock-market crash, he declared: 'We in America today are nearer to the final triumph over poverty than ever before in the history of any land.' After twenty years this thread was picked up again.

But it was about rather more than that. The vast majority of Americans, young and old, had embraced a completely new way of thinking. After so many years of anxiety, danger and hardship, they thoroughly enjoyed every form of excess and superficial happiness. This was their reward for all those generations of hard labour, this was the promise of America finally being fulfilled. This was what life ought to be like from now on.

In those same years the Americans were confronted with another phenomenon that had a far-reaching influence on their society. Robert Kennedy once said that when he was young the American child had three reference points: home, school and church. In the 1950s they were joined by a fourth: television.

In 1941 hardly anyone in Sag Harbor owned a television set, but those few who did sat up and took notice on 1 July. New York television station WNBT interrupted its normal programming to show, for a full ten seconds, a quietly ticking watch. A Bulova! From their very own Bulova factory in Sag Harbor! At the end of the ten seconds the picture faded away. That was all. It was the world's first television commercial.

By 1947 there were just 44,000 television sets in the country. Only local programming was possible then, but new broadcasting techniques were soon introduced; the first national networks came into being and, after that, developments followed each other with lightning speed. For the 1952 presidential campaign Eisenhower created a series of one-minute spots and deployed them against his opponent Adlai Stevenson. They were the first ever political advertisements. Quite a few people felt it was undignified to 'sell the presidency like cereal'.

Eisenhower won. Stevenson, however, who went on to fight another unsuccessful presidential campaign against Eisenhower in 1956, retained the affection of his intellectual following precisely because of his refusal to give in to modern technology. Steinbeck was a great friend of Stevenson's and sometimes wrote speeches for him. The novelist and his political friends regarded the campaign of 1952 as a final knightly joust, a last upsurge of old-fashioned eloquence, even as new ways of engaging in politics were casting shadows before them.

By 1953 television had already overtaken radio. Americans owned more televisions than radios, and one episode of The Ed Sullivan Show drew more than fifty million viewers. Soap operas, frequently interrupted by commercials from soap manufacturers because of the number of housewives watching, were more and more the subject of conversation. David Halberstam describes a young viewer – he may mean himself – who was fascinated by the fact that a child in one such series was 'sent upstairs to his room' as a punishment. At that point he could only dream of living in a house that had an upstairs, let alone a room of his own. But the message of every soap manufacturer, repeated over and over again, was 'tomorrow you too can live like this'.

Mass television-viewing had some rather less desirable effects on Americans as well. Graphs for those years show a clear change of direction: Americans read fewer books, did less voluntary work, grew fatter and spent more time at home. The house and the immediate family became central, to the detriment of public life.

In the suburbs, new homes were built with gardens, swimming pools and other comforts of family life at the back; at the front there was only a garage. Residents turned away from the street. Advertising slogans and political messages were no longer aimed at the crowd outside but instead at the family at home. The statistics speak volumes; Americans went to the cinema and theatre less often, attended fewer meetings and gatherings, spent less time at sports fixtures, in bars and cafés, or with their neighbours. Funerals, which had always been village or neighbourhood events, were increasingly a private matter.

John Ward, one of the older residents of Sag Harbor, told me that Steinbeck had always helped him with the traditional Independence Day fireworks display. 'He was crazy about it; as soon as he heard something go bang he'd come and join in.' But even the Fourth of July, always a typical street party with parades, flags and firecrackers, became a more private affair in the 1950s, a holiday increasingly devoted to family outings, picnics and barbecues. Nada Barry, widow of Bob Barry, had first arrived in Sag Harbor to carry out some sociological research. One of her observations, even back then, was that the typical American porch culture, whereby a family would sit on the large veranda at the front of the house in the evenings and chat with every passer-by, had disappeared completely in Sag Harbor by the end of the 1950s.

The great story of post-war America revolves around the adjustment to this totally new way of living together. Within a period of less than ten years, the basic values of the dominant culture were turned on their head. Americans switched from a culture in which they had to deal with deprivation – with all the rigour and tenacity that required – to one in which the enjoyment of abundance, and the ever-increasing enjoyment of ever-greater abundance, was central.

This quiet social revolution, this fundamental change of priorities, this evaporation of American values such as thrift, frugality and solidarity, made quite a few Americans feel insecure. They sensed that the festivities surrounding washing machines, pink Buicks and fresh petticoats marked a clear cultural change. Victory over the world of scarcity was a historical accomplishment of the first order, but they also realised that the domain of plenty would bring new problems, of a nature and extent at which they could only guess.

It's a classic tale of generational change. The first generation struggles up out of poverty, the second generation acquires wealth, the third generation becomes spoilt and goes off the rails. Yet something else was going on here as well, something that concerned the very foundations of society. In a culture of survival, people have little choice, whereas now there were alternatives, more and more of them. Almost all the traditional norms and values, which had their roots in a 'world of necessity', were suddenly up for discussion.

In all sorts of ways, the American society of the 1950s was in a state of fermentation: black citizens wanted equal rights; students and artists were experimenting in a bid to find alternatives to the consumer society; conservatives were carrying out experiments of their own in an attempt to hold on to their religion and traditions; and women had begun to realise they were suffocating in the pretty-pretty life of the suburbs.

'What happened to us came quickly and quietly, came from many directions and was the more dangerous because it wore the face of good,' John Steinbeck wrote in *America and Americans*. 'Leisure, which again had been the property of heaven, came to us before we knew what to do with it and all of these good things falling on us unprepared constitute calamity. We have the things and we have not had time to develop a way of thinking about them. We struggle with our lives in the present and our practices in the long and well-learned past.'

PART TWO

New York – Connecticut – Massachusetts – Vermont – New Hampshire – Maine

'We shall be as a city upon a hill,
The eyes of all people are upon us.'

SERMON BY JOHN WINTHROP
1630

One

MY ROCINANTE WAS A JEEP, a silver Liberty. It was brand new, a robust automatic with cruise control and power steering, yet not too big, by American standards at least. I put it through its paces on a stretch of concrete next to JFK airport, and once I'd filled out a few forms it was mine for ten weeks or more. It had 189 miles on the clock. Everything smelled of fresh plastic and new metal.

I had a couple of bags and suitcases with me, and a good deal of reading material – Steinbeck, of course, plus copies of all the letters he's known to have written along the way. I also took several other travel accounts by writers and journalists who had made comparable journeys. There were the collected columns of Ernie Pyle, for instance, a friend of Steinbeck's and a prominent war reporter, who criss-crossed the country tirelessly in the 1930s for various daily papers.

I lugged the fat *Inside U.S.A.* by John Gunther with me as well. Between November 1944 and late 1945 he visited all forty-eight American states and compiled a systematic inventory of the country, full of tables and useful bits of information. Gunther was one of the most famous journalists of his generation and Steinbeck knew him from the New York circuit. It was a still-austere America that Gunther travelled through in 1945: fifteen per cent of draftees could neither read nor write; only one in ten families had an annual income above 4,000 dollars; forty per cent of homes had no bath or shower, and thirty-five per cent lacked even an indoor toilet.

Again from the 1940s, I took with me the revealing character studies of *The Americans* by anthropologist Geoffrey Gorer, and from the 1980s and 1990s I had the historic conversations with all and sundry conducted by

Studs Terkel. There was the incisive *Blue Highways* by William Least Heat-Moon, also from the 1980s, and from the final year of the century a disturbing travel account by Robert Kaplan called *An Empire Wilderness*, plus more along similar lines.

My wife kept me company – a happy necessity, since together, as we'd learned on previous expeditions, we quickly become a well-oiled travelling machine. I'd also secured the services of Sandy; that was the name of the voice that told me the way, speaking from a small device stuck to the dashboard. Whatever American address I typed in, she reliably guided me there. She also knew of all possible motels and restaurants in the vicinity. Hers was a miraculous little box that would undoubtedly have sent Steinbeck into ecstasies fifty years earlier, with his fascination for gadgets of all kinds. He had taken a thick file of maps with him, yet still he regularly got lost. That wasn't going to happen to me. I did have the hefty 1960 edition of the *National Geographic Atlas of the Fifty United States* on the back seat, so that I could tell exactly which route Steinbeck would have followed. Many of the interstate highways had yet to be built in his day.

It was a warm September afternoon when we swung away from the airport onto the leafy Southern State Parkway, the sun at our backs, heading for the easternmost tip of Long Island. The road was congested and everyone was pushing relentlessly ahead, out of the city towards the weekend. Sandy issued her cheerful instructions, the radio sang a song, my beloved kept an eye on the traffic lights and upcoming intersections: 'Now switch lanes, quick, that's it, yes, very good. Stick in this lane. Watch out for that semi-trailer, it's about to pass on your right. In a mile from now you'll hit the junction with the twenty-seven.' Our travelling machine was working as smoothly as ever.

We passed Levittown off to our left. It's still a thriving suburb, even though successive generations have adapted and tinkered with the houses so much that, out of the thousands of Levitt homes, only a handful remain in something close to their original state. The stream of hurrying vehicles was with us for an hour or more but, by Sunrise Highway, New York had burned itself out: the woods to left and right were lonelier, the traffic more courteous and good natured. At Bridgehampton we turned off north, up through gently rolling countryside. For a moment you think you're driving through an English village with a few small lakes and ponds, but in fact they're the offshoots of a sequence of bays and inlets that stretches for miles, all grandchildren and great-grandchildren of the Atlantic Ocean. Then you roll down out of the hills into Sag Harbor.

The broad Main Street of the harbourside town has a dignity and peacefulness that seem almost a thing of the past. An elegant shopping street, it runs down in a gentle curve from the more expensive suburbs to the Custom House and the dilapidated, brown windmill that Steinbeck helped to build for the Old Whalers' Festival.

Most of the houses are made of wood and painted white or blue. The few cars travel at walking pace, stopping immediately for anyone wanting to cross. At the harbour is the little office of the *Sag Harbor Express* (since 1859), 'Combined with *The Corrector* (1822) and *The News* (1909)'. From eight in the morning until deep in the night, the elegant American Hotel functions as the town's living room. From the gardens further along comes the scent of firs and larches. There's a constant chirping of crickets.

In the 1950s Sag Harbor was still much like a nineteenth-century town, where the dogs might lie sleeping in the middle of the road. During the lunch break, after the factory sirens had sounded, everyone would prom-enade along Main Street. The rest of the day was generally quiet, aside from the sweep of a broom and exhaust noise from the occasional car. The town had not yet fully recovered from the crisis of the 1930s; even on Main Street some of the shops were boarded up. Many people would have been unable to manage without the soup kitchens. 'You went fishing,' I heard people say. 'You shot deer in the hills. You could still live off the land to some extent if necessary. Until the Sixties, hunting and fishing trips like that were perfectly normal if you didn't have a job.'

There were no tourists. Everyone you met on the street was someone you already knew, or an acquaintance of someone you knew. Attention would be inexorably drawn to outsiders by Mrs Rose Heatley in the *Sag Harbor Express*: 'Mr and Mrs Joe Velsor entertained Mrs Velsor's uncle, Mr L.W. Telro of Atlanta, at dinner Wednesday evening.'

This kind of peace was exactly what Steinbeck was after. Fifty years later it's not hard to track down old comrades of his. 'John didn't want

anyone bothering him. There were four or five young men here that he
went around with every day,' says John Ward, now eighty-eight. 'We'd go
to parties, I always helped him with his boat, but we didn't ever do much
talking. We fished.'

With Dave Lee, an elderly watchmaker, Steinbeck was always at loggerheads. 'John was a socialist to his bootstraps, whereas I'd left England in
the Forties precisely because of that miserable socialism. Up to a point
he believed that everyone, simply by being born, has a right to everything,
even if we conservatives had to pay for it. He always looked at the world
from the point of view of the workers. He was fascinated by the effect
of rationing on our food-supply situation in Britain, for example; the
results were impressive. When he talked about the workers and about
improvements in their lives, his eyes would sparkle with pleasure.' No,
they'd never had a serious quarrel.

'John and Bob did the strangest things, racing naked through the
swimming pools at night, that kind of stuff,' says Nada Barry. 'The police
knew us all, so that was never a problem. It was literally an old boys'
network here. John and a handful of others were the driving force
behind the Sag Harbor Old Whalers' Festival, something we dreamed
up to bring a bit of life to the place.' Her daughter Gwen adds: 'Elaine
was very different; she was a real theatre lady, a show person. If she
didn't feel like going somewhere she'd always say, "Sorry dear, I don't
feel too good, I probably had a bad oyster." She taught that excuse to
my mother too. "A bad oyster. Works every time."' Except that Elaine
forgot she'd ever talked about her trick with Nada and Gwen. She failed
to show up at Gwen's wedding. 'A bad oyster . . .' The ladies still felt
sore about that.

John Ward told me: 'He was a writer; he had one of those huts in his
backyard and that's where he wrote. You weren't to bother him. If a
tourist asked where he lived we played dumb.' As for Dave Lee: 'John was
one of the better people I've known in my life. But all that stuff he wrote
. . . We hardly ever read anything by him.'

In Steinbeck's day there were a couple of bars on Main Street, a cinema,
the Paradise Restaurant, the Relay-Matic for electrical goods, Mr Youngs'
bicycle shop with gas station attached, Bohack's grocery store, Bob Barry's
hardware supplies, a bank, the Ideal (since 1863) for gifts and stationery,

and the Variety Store (since 1922) for soap, ice creams, toys, keys and everything not sold elsewhere. Together they formed the backdrop to *The Winter of Our Discontent*.

The small businesses of those days still look in fairly good shape. The Ideal, the bank, Schiavoni's Market, Bob Barry's hardware business, the Variety Store – they're all still there. In every other respect this forbidding old factory town has changed utterly in character over the past half-century. The Black Buoy is now a burger bar, the cinema is a gallery, bakeries and grocery stores have been converted into restaurants or diving gear outlets, the café terraces are full, and the harbour is white with sailing boats whose owners you rarely see because all the work is done by Mexicans and Filipinos. The houses where the fishermen and factory foremen used to live are advertised in the papers as 'Sag Harbor Traditional' or 'Sag Harbor Village Classic' and go for around 2,195,000 and 1,950,000 dollars respectively. In the parking spaces along Main Street you no longer see Dodges or GMCs but mainly Japanese and European cars: BMWs, Mercedes, Volvos, Toyotas, Jaguars and the odd Range Rover. When withdrawing cash from the ATM at the Capital One bank you can choose between four languages: English, Spanish, Russian and Chinese. The Colossus that Robert Payne wrote about, the giant that bestrode the world, no longer exists. Steinbeck, even in his most enlightened mood, could not have predicted it all.

The story of his travels with the poodle Charley begins with a storm, a wild heroic epic on garden-pond scale. Steinbeck had originally intended to leave right after Labour Day, the first Monday in September and unofficial end of the summer season. But that week the approach of Hurricane Donna sabotaged his plans. Sag Harbor had been hit by fierce storms several times before and all over town preparations were thorough. On Main Street the storefronts were boarded up by the weekend. All night long, the *Sag Harbor Express* reported, you could hear boats chugging past in search of a safe place to moor, and by early morning everyone was busy pulling his boat – or his neighbour's boat – ashore or making it fast.

On Monday 12 September, at ten o'clock in the morning, it started to rain heavily. The wind soon got up. A window at the Ideal was smashed and the phone lines went down. At four o'clock gusts were measured at almost 125 miles an hour. In the words of the newspaper: 'A mile wide wall of water, about two foot deep, rushed over the dunes at Napeague, completely covering the Montauk Highway.' Trees were felled by the wind.

From his house Steinbeck watched the hurricane strike. It hammered 'like a fist'. The entire top of an oak tree crashed to the ground and the next gust stove in one of the big windows. Craft tore loose from their moorings and rammed each other. He saw his own beloved *Fayre Eleyne* get caught between boats that had dragged anchor. It was carried off downwind 'fighting and protesting' before being forced up against the next jetty. 'We could hear her hull crying against the oaken piles.'

Steinbeck had once written that storms and other extreme weather conditions made a weak start to a book, but in *Travels* he disregards that notion and relishes describing how, despite pleas from Elaine, he went out and leapt onto the flooded jetty to save his 'whining' boat. Elaine hurried after him in the lashing rain and watched, astounded, as he made his way through the waves, cut the lines of the other vessels so that they floated free, fumbled his way aboard his own boat, managing to start the engine 'at a touch', and edged her off into clear water further out. That was not the end of the adventure, since now he had to get back to land. Desperate, he jumped into the water again and finally reached the shore by clinging to a length of floating branch.

This event sets the tone: just as the hero-narrator, running on pure adrenaline, plunges into the waves like a fool to save his beloved *Eleyne*, so he begins his journey with a similar recklessness. *Travels with Charley* has an undertone of bravura: watch me drink and live rough, camp alone, wallow in the mud under Rocinante to change a tyre, drive hard all day and all night to find a vet for Charley. The lightness and irony of books like *Cannery Row* are nowhere to be found.

In reality, as we now know, Steinbeck had serious health problems. His speech sometimes slurred and his fingers regularly turned numb, making it hard for him to pick certain things up. After the seizure of December 1959 he'd lain unconscious for a while, even starting a small fire with his cigarette. He was kept in hospital for about ten days. Of his once so robust constitution, little was left by 1960.

Elaine had been horribly shocked by that last seizure. She no longer thought it sensible for him to go out on the *Fayre Eleyne* alone and decided she ought to learn to work the boat herself. In fact she hardly dared leave him on his own at all. Two friends described to Jackson Benson the many arguments the couple had around that time:

'The doctor told me you can't go out . . . I can't let you out in that boat alone . . .'

'Bullshit.'

'John . . .'

'Bullshit.' At that point John turned to his friends and said: 'I'll be God damned if I am going to become some kind of a cripple. She is not going to learn to drive the boat. I am going to get a truck. I am going to drive all of this country by myself. I am going to leave her here. I am a man, I will not be a boy, and she's not going to be taking care of me all the time. If you don't watch Elaine, she can do that, you know.'

This was the less romantic motive for Operation America; John wanted to escape being cosseted by his wife, if only for one final time. The whole project was a last attempt to drown out his decline, his old age and increasing dependence. It's a subject that keeps cropping up in his letters. In *Travels with Charley* he proudly describes his turbulent past, his physical strength, the hard work. He refused to give all that up just to be able to live a couple of years longer: 'My wife married a man; I saw no reason why she should inherit a baby.'

Of course the project was not simply a sudden flight. It had been preying on his mind for years, ever since he heard Ed Ricketts talk about a walking trip he'd made through the South in his youth. Steinbeck's next seizure might well be the end; he knew that better than anyone. It was his last possible chance to make this trip for real, to reconcile himself with his country, with this new world.

Steinbeck manages to pack just about everything into the description of Hurricane Donna and the wild rescue of the *Fayre Eleyne* that begins his travel account: nature, the raging elements, the challenge, the madness, the man, the unpredictable outcome, the shouting wife, the victory and the homecoming. And, yes, recklessness and courage. Benson is correct in writing that if you look back over Steinbeck's life, this book was more than anything an act of courage. Desperate courage, perhaps, but courage nonetheless.

Exactly fifty years later there was no Donna, but there was an Earl. Sag Harbor once again set all its emergency planning in motion as the Category 4 hurricane approached. The atmosphere was the same as half a century earlier: the windows of houses and shops were boarded up, boats were dragged ashore or secured away from the coast by three, four, perhaps five anchors, and flashlights and basic rations were placed at the ready. There were even evacuation plans for the lower-lying districts. If necessary, 800 people would be able to shelter in the Pierson Gymnasium. Older residents like John Ward and Dave Lee, who had seen such events at intervals throughout their lives, knew it might not get too bad; if a hurricane makes landfall a few degrees further east, the wind at Sag Harbor is no stronger than in a serious storm. But the difference is subtle, and during Hurricane Gloria in 1985, the first in Sag Harbor since Donna, the water lapped up against the building that houses the American Legion.

By the time we arrive Earl has moved off again beyond the horizon. It had been less disastrous than anticipated. 'No more than a good practice drill,' the police chief says. In New York City there was a huge mess, trucks were blown over, 30,000 households were without power for several hours, but in Sag Harbor just one tree fell. The office of the *Sag Harbor Express* is flooded – the carpets are still wet when we get there – but the weekly print run of 5,000 copies has been produced and distributed without difficulty.

I have an appointment with Bryan Boyhan, the paper's editor-in-chief and publisher, an enthusiastic storyteller with a red face and tired eyes. No, he assures me, everything's okay here. The American press is in deep trouble, but local papers like this are holding their own just fine. Bryan laughs. 'You can read all about the war in Afghanistan on the internet, but if you want to know what the school board has decided about a new sports field you have to turn to us.'

The weekly deadline is approaching and in the editorial office – stacks of cuttings and old newspapers, an ancient printing press in one corner: everything as it should be – four of his colleagues are typing screenful after screenful of news reports about a quarrel over the name of a hamburger joint, about the town's new judge, Andrea Schiavoni, and even about John Steinbeck. The fact that he started his journey across America half a century ago has not escaped the attention of the *Sag Harbor Express*.

Despite his deadline, Bryan takes the time to reveal to me the anatomy of Sag Harbor, because it's not just a town, it's a phenomenon. He's seen it all himself: the transformation from Sag Harbor the factory town into Sag Harbor the haven of rest and recreation, the explosive growth of the Old Whalers' Festival that Steinbeck invented and Bryan chaired for fifteen years, and the forces they thereby unwittingly unleashed.

'A typical family town,' he calls the old Sag Harbor. 'Steinbeck's friends, men like John Ward and Bob Barry, were all local businessmen, and all family men, too. Together they dreamed up that festival, with a competition for whalers, using fake whales of course. Great fun.' It was a huge success and every year more people came, until it got completely out of hand. 'A quarter of a century ago only a few big yachts called in here. Now Sag Harbor is a fixed stop on Atlantic cruises for all those expensive ships.' Money follows money, so house prices shot up and the population looks quite different from a few decades ago. 'There's something quite tragic about it,' Bryan tells me. 'Steinbeck and his friends knew they had to do something to promote Sag Harbor, but they let the genie out of the bottle.'

I ask Bryan Boyhan about the latest economic crisis and what it meant for Sag Harbor. After mumbling a few words of optimism he tells me what he's been hearing everywhere on the street over the past few years: frustration and jealousy. Social tensions between the haves and have-nots are increasing rapidly, he says. Many of the old families have adjusted wonderfully to the new situation, but not all of them. 'Quite a few of our more elderly residents don't understand this town any more. They feel lost, also in a financial sense. The changes haven't been kind to them. The middle class has been driven out, for the most part, and in its place an unimaginable amount of money has come in. It's a big effort for the original residents not to get hugely jealous of everything they see passing on Main Street.'

So has local solidarity gone, along with the middle class? 'In Steinbeck's day the community spirit was still very much alive,' says Bryan. 'That's no longer the case today.' The town collects a great deal of money for good causes all the same, and when a young man from Sag Harbor died recently in Iraq it shook everyone. Still, people experience the local community in different ways. 'For the old families, who have always lived here, the community consists of a tight group of friends and relations, people they've always known. The newcomers see things differently. They often have an idealised view of Sag Harbor. Their notion of what our community's like is often unrealistic, full of nostalgia.' He impresses upon me that no matter how beautiful his town might be, it is not the real America. 'These days this is one of the most other-worldly places in the country.'

Then he has to get going; one more piece about Steinbeck. The newspaper is about to be put to bed. He springs to his feet. 'You either change or die. Life is a moving target.' In the newspaper on sale the next day I read about the sun that 'seems be setting on the "progress" Steinbeck saw dawning in 1960', about the financial meltdown, 'massive home foreclosures', poverty statistics that were 'the worst since the Great Depression', and about 'this little village by the bay' that 'gave him great comfort'.

We take a walk down Main Street, then up onto the hill, a mile or so along leafy lanes in the direction of Bluff Point and the house where Steinbeck lived. The street is quiet. The elegant wooden verandas are empty. American flags are flying everywhere – it looks like a national holiday, but it isn't. As long as there's a war there are flags, especially in this rich part of America where support for the boys and girls overseas is expressed in a profusion of flapping fabric. The sun is still hot, squirrels dash back and forth along the branches, the gardens are past their best. Here and there you can hear the tapping of a woodpecker. One of the houses is being restored by a crew of Mexicans. Other Mexicans work in the gardens and the only voices you hear are speaking Spanish. Quite a few of the houses are up for sale.

A boy and a girl walk towards us, down the middle of the road. The boy has an open, friendly face, but his girlfriend looks rather dejected.

He's in fine spirits, that's clear. He'll cheer her up; his whole life long he'll make every effort to do that. It will become his main goal in life to catch a smile from this girl, and she'll never be content.

Steinbeck's house stands grey and modest under tall trees. It now belongs to Elaine's sister, and from time to time it's rented out. I surreptitiously slip into the backyard. There's no one around. On the lawn is the swimming pool built for Elaine, and you can still make out the text he wrote in the cement: '. . . in thee I find my earthly joy'. A couple of crickets are chirruping away while the traffic drones on in the distance. It's an unusually peaceful place.

Near the water stands Steinbeck's old writing hut, empty now because the papers and books were suffering from damp, and in a corner is the shabby-looking garage where Steinbeck kept his handyman's things. The walls are lined with Californian wallpaper he bought in Salinas, with a grape motif. The shelves and drawers still bear Steinbeck's labels: 'Knives, Chisels and Bladey Things', 'Screws (Anybody)', 'Glory! Nails, In Excelsis', 'Exotics'.

I didn't see those with my own eyes, incidentally. I'm borrowing from the New York Times. Their reporter is the only one allowed to walk around the house this week – officially to mark the fiftieth anniversary of Steinbeck's American journey; in reality because behind the scenes a feud has been raging for years about Steinbeck's estate. The current owner could use some positive publicity. Steinbeck's surviving son, Thomas, is still pursuing a case against Elaine's family. He believes the estate should pass to the writer's direct blood relations. Elaine is said to have left everything to her own family in her last will, contrary to Steinbeck's wishes. In a little over two weeks the case will come to court again.

So much for peace in this place. But I'm getting ahead of my story.

I cast my mind back to The Winter of Our Discontent. It is almost unavoidable this afternoon, since the novel is set among these houses and behind these front doors. Many residents were clearly identifiable as characters in the book, according to local chaplain John P. Drab at any rate: 'Maybe I have a good imagination.' New Baytown in the book is a microcosm of America, sales clerk Ethan Allen Hawley is the average American of

1960 and, if you ask me, the shop run by the Schiavonis on Main Street was the model for the grocery store where the main character gnaws away at his frustrations.

It's not one of Steinbeck's best novels – in fact Elaine later confessed that she simply detested it – yet the set-up, despite all the book's obvious weaknesses, is far cleverer and more effective than is generally recognised. It's a complex tangle, involving all kinds of machinations, about the dismantling of ideals both personal and American.

In essence, *Winter* comes down to the following. The hero of the book, Ethan Allen Hawley, is a virtuous, well-brought-up man, happily married and the father of two growing children. The Hawleys were once among the richest middle-class families in the little town, but through his own stupidity Ethan has thrown away the old grocery business. He still works there, but now as a sales clerk under the new owner, Alfio Marullo. The elderly Italian has every faith in Ethan, as does everyone else in town. Despite his economic downfall he's a beacon of decency and integrity, always standing aloof from the quest for money and power. The cashier at the First National Bank, for example, jokingly reveals to him when and how he could rob the bank without being caught. He picks up rumours about all kinds of transactions and power shifts, and discovers that his boss has been resident in America illegally all his life.

During a sleepless night, Ethan comes to the conclusion that his self-important efforts to be a Good Person have made him lose sight of all manner of dark goings-on around him. He decides that he's going to start playing the game, and will rob the bank and rebuild the family fortune.

Everything comes together at the end of the book. Ethan doesn't go through with the bank theft, but he does manage to trick a drunken old friend out of a crucial bit of land that is of great value to speculators. He plays hardball in politics, gets everything he wants, starts a sweaty relationship with the local available woman, and betrays Marullo's secret to the municipal authorities. When Marullo is eventually deported, he gives the store to Ethan, the only truly honest man he has ever met. 'One guy didn't try to cheat him, didn't steal, didn't whine, didn't chisel.' In the end Ethan loses all faith in himself and, with his pockets full of dishonestly earned money, tries to kill himself – but he seems to fail even at that.

In short, this is the story of the moral decline of Ethan Allen Hawley, and along with him the American ideal. The book is littered with pet names and terms of affection, surprising perhaps from the rugged Steinbeck, but they become increasingly platitudinous, gradually forming a blanket over everything, just as the countless civilities of modern America create not closeness but distance.

One event is the final straw for Ethan: his own son turns out to have been corrupted. Ethan Allen Jr takes part in a national essay competition on the subject 'I Love America' and receives an honourable mention. Money, respect and fame are just around the corner; television shows compete for his favours. But then it emerges that he's lifted every single sentence from a handful of patriotic writers, even including Thomas Jefferson and Abraham Lincoln. It's the complacency he sees in Ethan Jr that shocks Ethan most of all: 'Everybody does it.' His despair is complete.

The plot of *Winter*, too, closely reflects the reality of the time. Steinbeck uses young Hawley's plagiarism to weave the early excesses of the new phenomenon of television into the story, specifically a quiz-show scandal that was the talk of America in late 1959.

It all started with the overwhelming success of a new TV game show, *Twenty-One*, in which the champion appeared week after week until defeated. The challenger was asked to pick a point value to play for, with harder questions scoring more points. Each contestant tried to get to twenty-one before the other.

The show immediately became the subject of daily conversation. It held out the prospect of a huge fortune and a glittering future. The contestants appeared to be perfectly ordinary Americans – they could have been your neighbours in Levittown or Sag Harbor – some of whom had great hidden talents.

In the background, major interests were at stake in *Twenty-One*. For the main sponsor, Revlon, this was a golden age. Some days the show drew more than forty-seven million viewers. The programme-makers quickly realised that its huge appeal lay not with the participants' command of general

knowledge, but with the show's value as theatre and the emotional responses
it evoked. In practice, therefore, contestants were selected as potential heroes
or villains, as if they were auditioning for roles in a soap opera. Winners
who came over as unpleasant would be given more difficult questions in
subsequent rounds, to manoeuvre them swiftly out of the contest.

All this went swimmingly for a couple of months, until a penniless
student stepped into the arena. Herb Stempel was a typical nerd. He
was small and squat and from a humble background but, as his family
and friends put it, he was a 'walking encyclopaedia' with a photo-
graphic memory. In the first few tests his score was astonishing, and
he would have been the ideal contestant had he not been so unat-
tractive. The producers decided to make a virtue out of necessity, and
for theatrical purposes they made Stempel into an 'unpleasant person'.
He was helped in all kinds of ways (by being asked the same questions in the quiz as he'd been asked during one of the rehearsals, for
example) and he gratefully played his role, winning thousands of
dollars plus admiring looks from all the girls at City College, where
he was a mature student. But the script dictated that he would have
to take a fall at some point. His ultimate role was that of a loser.

To defeat 'bad guy' Stempel, a polar opposite was required: a 'good
American', a 'hero'. He was found in the person of Charles Van Doren,
a young English lecturer at Columbia University. Van Doren was precisely
the man they were looking for: attractive, white, friendly, slightly shy,
well balanced, and at the same time hyper-intelligent. His family background, moreover, was impeccable. The name Van Doren signified an
old American family of Dutch origin, intellectuals with an unimpeach-
able reputation, natural members of the American liberal elite. Charles,
his contemporaries said, was actually a precursor to John Kennedy – he
was just like him, with the same kind of aura.

Charles Van Doren performed splendidly. In no time he became a real
TV star, one of the first. He crushed all his opponents and at the same
time he retained a kind of lightness, a boyish innocence. He earned a
fortune and *Time* put him on its cover. He personified the hope of a new,
wiser America after all the dark years. As his father, with some surprise,
wrote to a friend: 'About fifteen million people have fallen in love with
him – and I don't use the word lightly.'

But Charles Van Doren was part of the act. In reality he knew exactly what questions were going to be asked. He learned to leave pauses and even to stammer, as if unsure of the correct answer. Herb Stempel found all this difficult to take. 'I felt that here was a guy, Van Doren, that had a fancy name, Ivy League education, parents all his life, and I had just the opposite, the hard way up,' he said later. All the same, he played his sad role of 'loser' to the end. On the night of 5 December 1956 he was due, according to the secret script, to take a dive. He'd been asked to respond incorrectly to a question to which he knew the answer: Which film won the Academy Award in 1955? The correct answer was *Marty*.

Stempel was crazy about that picture. He'd seen it three times. But now his role had run its course. Van Doren was the great hero; proposals poured in, NBC took him under contract for three years and he was even offered professorships. Stempel gambled away his winnings in failed investments, became increasingly bitter and began to approach journalists. When one of the contestants in a new television quiz on CBS got hold of another contestant's notebook with all the prepared answers for the next show, the scandal broke.

The resulting commotion led to an investigation by a special committee of Congress. Charles Van Doren insisted he was innocent. The members of the committee treated the popular hero with all due respect, but eventually he had to take the stand. Before a deeply shocked America, he announced on 2 November 1959: 'I've learned a lot about good and evil. They are not always what they appear to be. I was involved, deeply involved, in a deception.'

The whole business, both the quiz and the consternation it caused, says a great deal about America in the 1950s. One of the show's producers later acknowledged that they'd had no inkling of the enormous influence moving pictures were having on families sitting watching at home. They were still playing with the new phenomenon of television as if it were radio. The fierce, deeply felt indignation about the lapse also says something about the relative innocence of the average American in those years – and the relative trust people still had in leading figures in the media, in business and politics, and in each other. For some this scandal was the beginning of the end for the society based on mutual trust that America had once been.

When Charles Van Doren admitted he'd been taking everyone for a ride, Elaine and John had just got back from England. Somerset had a popular quiz of its own; a small radio station put difficult questions to listeners, and if you gave the right answer you won a pound. Steinbeck regarded hyped-up quizzes like Twenty-One as absurd, but he was deeply shocked to hear it was fraudulent. He knew the Van Dorens as an exemplary family, and cheating with quiz questions was to him the ultimate symptom of the moral cancer that was taking hold of the soul of America: in the name of progress you can appeal to people's worst instincts; the end always justifies the means. It made him feel ill.

Three days after Van Doren's confession, Steinbeck wrote to his friend Adlai Stevenson: 'Someone has to reinspect our system and that soon. We can't expect to raise our children to be good and honorable men when the city, the state, the government, the corporations all offer the highest rewards for chicanery and dishonesty. On all levels it is rigged, Adlai. Maybe nothing can be done about it, but I am stupid enough and naively hopeful enough to want to try.'

In her flourishing garden, in the evening sunlight, Nada Barry pours glasses of wine to mark our parting. She is almost eighty now, with strikingly alert eyes, a broad face and long grey hair. She starts asking questions right away: how far have I got and what do I think about her old friend John, and about Sag Harbor? 'John would never have come to live in Sag Harbor the way it is today,' her daughter says. 'No,' says Nada. 'He wouldn't have come here now. But he would have stayed and grown old here.'

She has few memories of the Charley project. There was a masculine atmosphere in those days and she was fifteen years younger than her husband Bob. 'John was not a simple man. Oh no. He was very shy. You never knew quite what he was thinking. But he was a very good listener.' She liked him. She could have a good talk with him about ordinary things. 'All those men were staunch Republicans and John was a true liberal, so they did sometimes clash, but usually they talked about local politics, about the laying of a sewer, say, and they could talk about things like that endlessly.'

She says that if he were alive now he'd probably hang out at the

American Hotel, but she's not completely sure. 'We rarely went to restaurants or places like that. We entertained ourselves at home, we had parties, Elaine and I cooked, we played hostess. That was our role, but we joined in everything along with the men and that was still unusual in Sag Harbor in those days.'

Was John really the outdoorsman he so badly wanted to be? I tell her about his son Thomas, who describes how on all those proud fishing trips his father showed little interest in the fishing itself. 'Instead he considered a line in the water as a perfect cover for reading or daydreaming.' Nada laughs. 'He didn't even have holders for the rods on his boat. Fishing was just something he talked about.' But he was keen on the simple tasks in life, wasn't he? 'John good with his hands? No way! He'd ring Bob for the slightest thing, sometimes three times in one day.' So did he always want to be different from the man he was? 'He wanted to be a macho man, like the others, and he wasn't. In fact he was very sensitive.'

We move on to the subject of Steinbeck's stories and the question of how much truth there is in his account of the journey he took. Anyone looking closely at the details will start to have doubts, and the book regularly diverges from the places and dates given in the letters he wrote along the way. The scenes are sometimes too good to be true, the dialogues too straightforward, too rounded and complete. In the South he describes long conversations with three different hitchhikers – a white racist, a black radical and a moderate black man – all three the result of improbable chance meetings. What's more, I know from Toby Street, who rode with him for a few days, that Rocinante made such a racket it was impossible to have a proper conversation in the cab.

I tell Nada what John Jr wrote about *Travels with Charley*: 'Thom and I are convinced that he never talked to any of those people . . . He just sat in his camper and wrote all that shit.' Nada bursts out laughing. 'I'm on the best of terms with all my exes. But they're all dead. As are their friends. There's no one left I can ask.' Again she laughs. 'Only John, as far as that goes . . . When we read *Travels with Charley* we thought: Oh, John. Now, now, now. He did sometimes blow things out of proportion, you know. He was great at blowing bubbles . . .'

Two

JOHN AND CHARLEY'S EXPEDITION BEGAN that September morning in 1960 at about nine. Their departure was fast and fleeting. Elaine 'exploded' away to her beloved New York and John, with Charley beside him, drove calmly to the Shelter Island ferry, the first in a series of three ferry crossings that connect Sag Harbor to mainland Connecticut via Greenport and Orient Point. He wanted to avoid the New York traffic and, as he admitted, the accompanying sense of 'gray desolation'. It was a feeling that would catch up with him.

They were a great duo, Charley and John. Charley loved riding in the truck. He was a tall dog and his head was almost as high in the cab as Steinbeck's. He would press his nose close to his boss's ear and make a sort of whistling sound with his teeth and lower jaw: ftt. It was usually a sign that he wanted to mark the route, in his own way.

The newspapers that day were dominated by the General Assembly of the United Nations, the grand political theatre that had just started, with leading roles played by figures including the Yugoslav president Tito, Egyptian leader Nasser, Indonesian president Sukarno (who made a big impression with a clever speech about the new role of the Third World), Fidel Castro from Cuba, whom everyone ignored, and Nikita Khrushchev, who was regarded as so dangerous that he was allowed to see little more of New York than the inside of the Soviet Embassy.

The *Sag Harbor Express* mentions a radio message from President Eisenhower, the first to be broadcast coast to coast, using a man-made satellite to reflect the signal. It was conceivable that one day 'active' satellites would circle the earth, capable of beaming down television pictures, but scientists still regarded that as in the distant future. The paper's society column features a roast-beef party held by Mr and Mrs Malloy, a boat trip by Teddy Smith, guests who stayed with the Hirsch family for the weekend, and the return of the Duncans after a brief holiday. According to Philip Morris, cigarettes were cleaner than ever before: 'Every bit of tobacco in the new king-size Philip Morris Commander is gently vacuum-cleaned and rolled in air in a newly invented machine – the Mart VIII.'

Exactly fifty years later, on 23 September 2010, the local papers cover the story of a man of thirty-six arrested with marijuana in his pocket, of Richie Cox (23), spotted on Main Street riding a stolen green Raleigh bicycle, and of climate change and rising sea levels and what it could all mean for Sag Harbor and the surrounding district: 'Around $1 billion in property was at risk.'

It's a beautiful late-summer morning with patchy cloud, the start of a hot day. Some way south of here the weather has been breaking temperature records all week; the August heat is dragging on. There's no sign of autumn. The trees are big, leaden and solidly green. The crickets are in full throat, a few birds too, but otherwise deathly silence prevails at Steinbeck's old house at the end of Bluff Point Lane.

This must be the start of my journey: at the old hobby shed with its many cupboards and drawers and Steinbeck's ingenious rock-polishing machine; at Elaine's rusty greenhouse; at the wooden fence, behind which the heirs are sharpening their knives for the latest legal proceedings concerning the author's estate. There is nothing further to interest me here.

We drive away across the gravel, around the bay, along a leafy lane called John Street, then out to Main Street. No need for directions. The sky is clear. The little ferry to Shelter Island laps back and forth from the weathered mooring posts behind Sag Harbor to the wooded far bank, surrounded by the quiet waves of the landlocked sea and its sandy beaches, the places where Bob Barry taught his friend John to fish. Everywhere – on the ferry boats, on the ships and in front of the houses – flies the proud American flag.

From a distance Shelter Island looks unspoilt, as if nothing has changed since Native Americans paddled between these bays and islands. Close up it turns out to be one big park, full of old trees and smooth lawns, and scattered among them one colonial villa after another, like white confectionery. It's one of those rich and rustic places that can be found within reach of any of the world's major cities, too heavenly to be true.

'Who ever heard of Orient Point?' noted Ernie Pyle. He waited on the jetty for this same ferry for two hours on 6 July 1936. 'How obscure some places can be, and how contented and peaceful.' There was hardly anyone around. A gentle breeze. Two or three children stood fishing at the end of the pier. That was all.

More than twenty years later his old friend John waited on the wooden jetty in a similar mood. He bought two postcards of the lighthouse, one for his agent Elizabeth Otis and one for Elaine. He was planning to take the 11.30 boat, and Charley, he wrote, had just 'slashed' his America project onto the beach. I found the postcard to Elaine in the Stanford archives. Scribbled down one side was a minuscule sum: '300 x 40 = 12,000'. The number of miles he aimed to cover per day, the number of days on the road and the total distance he planned to travel? 'Suddenly the United States became huge beyond belief and impossible ever to cross,' he wrote of that first morning. 'I wondered how in hell I'd got myself mixed up in a project that couldn't be carried out. It was like starting to write a novel.'

An 'oily tub' served as a ferry in those days, an old naval landing craft with a new superstructure welded on. In the early 1980s William Least Heat-Moon made the crossing on the same boat, but a month later it was at last replaced by a new ferry, specially designed for this stretch of water. This was the craft on which I made the crossing.

Steinbeck and Least Heat-Moon both describe in detail the lighthouse on the far bank, about an hour away, and then the first houses of New London with their grassy waterfront gardens, the shipyards belonging to the Electric Boat Company and the nuclear submarines moored there – it was an important naval base during the Cold War.

Both travellers saw a 'dagger of a shadow' in the distance and philosophised with their fellow passengers about the submarines, packed with missiles and nuclear warheads, the 'dreadnoughts of the next war'. Steinbeck's interlocutor, a young man with eyes reddened by the stiff wind, told him with some excitement that the latest class could stay under water for three months. 'I know them. I'm on them.'

When William Least Heat-Moon saw the new nuclear-powered Trident submarine waiting in readiness at the shipyards, he wondered how something so huge could move under water. The man standing next to him at the railing worked on the docks as an engineer. 'The *Ohio* will carry twenty-four missiles, each one with a dozen warheads: two hundred eighty-eight atomic explosions. One hell of a bitch with twelve sisters coming along behind at a billion dollars each.' He grumbled that it was no longer fashionable to believe in military power, but 'it will be again, and when that happens, people will love those exploding cigars'.

In both their accounts, the Second World War is still very much present. The man who chatted with Least Heat-Moon had spent the war in what he called the 'hooligan Navy', which did the dirty work. 'I can still hear the blue whispers coming at us. A little streak of blue smoke and a hiss and you were gone.' Steinbeck was torn. On the one hand he thought the submarines beautiful, on the other hand he felt once again the fear of those lurking, dark things when you were crossing the Atlantic on a troop ship and remembered 'burned men pulled from the oil-slicked sea'.

All those worries are forgotten in 2010. True, on the ferry, along with the usual announcements about life jackets and lifeboats, we are earnestly requested to report 'any suspicious activity' to the authorities. This country is in a permanent state of war. But the Red Peril has evaporated and practically nothing is left of all that hectic naval activity. The water is full of pleasure craft, and so we sail into the old town of New London.

We drive off into the hot afternoon, clattering along the winding streets of the central district, and suddenly it's as if we're home. The town was founded by the British in the mid-seventeenth century, and like all new colonists they started by replicating every aspect of their old country in the New World. Nothing here is straight or square, as it is elsewhere in America. Instead there's a street pattern familiar from almost all European towns. We'll encounter more such places, like Hartford and Springfield – not for nothing is this called New England. Their elegant church towers, which stuck high above everything when Steinbeck made this trip, are hemmed in by immense, glass office blocks. Although still

extant, they look rather shy, like elderly aunts at a birthday party where
they don't really fit in.

The route takes us northwards, past the same cosy houses and gardens
my precursor drove by fifty years ago, past the same stalls selling fruit,
pumpkins and the fattest potatoes I've ever seen, along the same leafy
roads, past the same Kentish woods – which here are starting to show a
dash of autumn.

Steinbeck and Charley passed a liquor store set back from the road
and stopped to take on board a substantial supply of spirits: bourbon,
scotch, gin, vermouth, vodka, brandy and applejack (the American
calvados), as well as a case of beer. All this with an eye to the puritanical
drinking laws in some states, but also because he was planning to invite
all sorts of people into his travelling home along the way. That was how
he intended to gauge the mood of the nation. In the end, though, little
came of it.

He drove on to Deerfield, where his younger son was at Eaglebrook,
a prestigious boarding school for children of the wealthy. In *Travels* he
doesn't waste many words on that visit: 'It can be imagined what effect
Rocinante had on two hundred teen-age prisoners of education just
settling down to serve their winter sentence.'

The school is still there, an elegant cluster of low buildings in the
woods, and on the nearby paths you find little groups of outspoken and
happy children, a world away from the tormented youngsters Steinbeck
describes. To judge from his first letter to Elaine, he had a good time. He
arrived in the middle of the annual 'Pow-Wow', a ritual designed to
absorb new boys into the two 'tribes' in the school, with a big fire and
a speech by the headmaster, who dressed up as a war leader for the
occasion. Rocinante was admired by all the teachers, John Jr passed around
cups of coffee like the perfect host, and they talked about his academic
progress. Steinbeck stood on the touchline during soccer practice and
that evening father and son ate a bad steak together at a 'doleful' roadside
eatery. He had a good feeling as they parted: 'We liked each other and
were easy together and that's the best.'

How can fathers and sons be so mistaken about one another, or at least
about the image they have of one another? In his autobiography *The Other*

Side of Eden, published years later, John Jr describes at some length his time at Eaglebrook. He experienced the school as a luxurious 'holding tank', a dumping ground for the children of the very rich, provided with the most beautiful parks and sports fields purely to salve the consciences of parents who spent all their time at work and at play. By then, John Jr writes, he had realised that 'my father was an asshole . . . He was into his Great Writer Bubble, so it wasn't like having a dad around, but instead having the Great Writer present.'

What John Jr did not realise, however, was that in Steinbeck's universe the Great Son also played a central role. Friends like Ed 'Doc' Ricketts appear time and again in his novels as the ideal figure, poor but wise and authentic, rough but straight as a die, a luminous and purifying counterpoint to the depravity of America. That idealised image dated back to the 1930s, and his sons were going to have to comply with it. Whenever they fell short he was deeply disappointed.

Perhaps this had something to do with his own father's failure, a humiliation that must never be repeated. All the same, Steinbeck's attitude was typical of America. He saw before him a classic dream of the ideal American childhood, which it was down to you to create, just as 'the American' in the American self-image is a conscious creation. Being an American is not your fate, it's a choice, a deliberate act. In American films and literature of the 1940s and 1950s, in much-loved novels of growing up such as *Revolutionary Road* (1961) by Richard Yates, the main characters all dream of a life that means something, that makes a difference – life as an act of will. This is reflected in the ads for present-day boarding schools: 'Solid competence in the active command of language, in writing and speaking with conviction.' 'Mastery of social etiquette and manners.' 'Physical training, specifically aimed at personal grace, health, beauty and self-discipline.' 'Demanding challenges such as caring for a horse, a hundred-mile cycle ride, setting up a business,' and so on.

Living life gloriously. That was typical of Steinbeck. The boys must become what they were not; their father demanded it of them, but the American ideal demanded it too. John Jr must get to know the simple life. But he was at a boarding school only the very richest could afford, sharing a room with the son of the director of Trans World Airlines. Steinbeck's other son, Thomas, sat in his room for years on end, obediently building model airplanes – although his brother suggests he enjoyed sniffing the glue.

'I never understood much about his relationship with his sons,' Nada Barry said during the conversation I had with her before leaving Sag Habor. 'It was always tense; there was never a close bond. Of course when it came down to it, Steinbeck was a very tight-lipped man.'

No matter how young they were, Steinbeck systematically treated the two boys as adults-to-be, as his letters demonstrate time and again. He'd grown up in an America where children were more or less regarded as miniature adults, like in most other countries. As soon as they could hold a broomstick they had to help out: in their parents' store, on the farm, in the household. That tradition lingered for a long time. Delivering newspapers, washing cars and doing other odd jobs – for boys especially, such chores remained an essential part of the proper American upbringing for decades to come.

The basic attitude of parents to their offspring changed fundamentally in the years when Steinbeck's sons were growing up. The constantly repeated message of the 1950s had been: 'our children will have better lives than we did, we who lost our early years to war and economic depression, in fact we're going to make sure they have better lives, whatever it takes'. The new prosperity made it possible for one breadwinner – almost always the man – to earn all the money while his spouse devoted her time and attention to the household and the children. That was the new ideal around which Levittown was built, and indeed all those other suburbs. The child became central – not just to the family but to society – more so than ever before in history.

There is something contradictory about that whole development. On the one hand, all the new choices and products available brought a new sense of freedom, individual freedom, and often the start of permissiveness, even in family relationships. On the other hand everything, more than ever, was aimed at protecting the young. To put it another way, men and women no longer needed to sacrifice themselves for each other, that was outdated, but they must be prepared to do everything for their children.

These contradictory feelings come to the fore regularly in Steinbeck's correspondence when he mentions the boys. Nothing could be allowed to impede his craving for freedom – he immersed himself in writing projects, repeatedly took long foreign trips, was eternally out of reach for his sons – yet at the same time they were the focus of grand gestures, ambitious plans and great expectations. Gwyn, the boys' mother, demanded a similar freedom in her own way, with her wild partying and drinking. Eaglebrook School meant the couple could buy their way out of all the problems that resulted.

John Jr's book has a decidedly aggrieved tone. That's understandable enough, but it also says something about his generation. When the baby boomers were children, they had no idea how privileged they were, certainly compared to earlier generations. To them it was all perfectly natural and self-explanatory, because that's how things are to children. As historian Henry William Brands writes, they grew up with a sense of entitlement, a sense that the world existed to satisfy them. That feeling, which is after all still an aspect of the American self-image, was stronger in them than in any previous generation.

Three

MY FRIEND JOSEPH AMATO ONCE WROTE a local history of America based entirely on sounds. He started with the sounds of nature, the murmur of rivers, the wind rustling the trees and the dry grass of the plains – 'Even if there is no wind you can hear the wind,' the Native Americans said – the buzz of insects above pools of water, the howling of wolves, the thundering of bison, the croaking of frogs, the cackling of geese and ducks, the calls of hundreds of birds, a waterfall, and now and then a falling branch, or a voice.

Alexis de Tocqueville, who walked through one of America's virgin forests in the summer of 1831, wrote of a sound 'something like a long sigh' that you could hear in the heat of the day, 'a plaintive cry lingering in the distance'. It was the last breath of wind. 'Then everything around you falls back into a silence so deep, a stillness so complete, that the soul is invaded by a kind of religious terror.'

After many centuries, new sounds had suddenly been introduced by the coming of the first European pioneers. The dull boom of gunfire in the fields. Horses' hooves. The murmur of the ever-restless racoons and the cooing of doves attracted by the new farms. The bleating of sheep, the clucking of chickens, the lowing of cattle. The chirping of sparrows and the endless chatter of starlings – both European imports. The different tone of the newcomers, the strange names and words, the new music. Within a few decades there was a completely new world of sounds.

The farms themselves made noises: the creaking of doors, the sweeping of brooms, the grinding of wagon wheels, the sounds of building and hammering, the squeak of a well-crank, the clatter of buckets and churns. Then came the first machines: a pump, a tractor engine. This was a tapestry of hundreds of sounds, in which silence played its own part. Silence was a way of showing respect, whether you were in a church, a courtroom or a graveyard.

The first towns brought more human voices, and as well as sawing and hammering there were the sounds of tree trunks being split, of carts, of women beating carpets, sometimes of a piano. Speeches, church bells: America liberated itself from the British. Singing floated from open schoolroom windows; a band marched along the street (the cultural pride of any new community). In the evenings came the sound of young men on the sidewalks, their conduct described in police reports as 'drunken, noisy and disorderly'. In outlying districts you could hear the sharp crack of modern shotgun cartridges.

Then, like a clarion call, came the whistle of the first steam train. Now the sounds were loud and shrill: wheezing and hissing from steam pipes, grinding wheels, squealing brakes, steel on steel. The doors slammed. In the chapter of *Walden* entitled 'Sounds', Henry David Thoreau (1817–62) describes how the train tore open the landscape of sound here in Massachusetts, previously made up of the calling of owls, the barking of dogs, the croaking of frogs and the jolting noise of a few carts. 'The whistle of the locomotive penetrates my woods summer and winter, sounding like the scream of a hawk sailing over some farmer's yard, informing me that many restless city merchants are arriving within the circle of the town.'

Thoreau wondered whether the coming of the railroad had made people act and think more quickly. It was the start of a new way of life, he realised, and there would be no going back. Time was now measured not by the rising and setting of the sun but by the whistle of the train, and so the rhythm of life was adjusted accordingly. The train, Joseph Amato writes, brought the city into the countryside, in fact it *was* the city in the countryside. It was the herald of all the new sounds inundating America: the din of the steelworks, the thud of the printing press, the rattle of the assembly line. 'The train led the parade of vehicles that would come to speed through modern life . . . The train marked the beginning of the machine's acoustic tyranny over the landscape.'

That is roughly what must have happened in Deerfield. The houses are wedged between the buildings and sports fields of Eaglebrook and at least another four boarding schools. This is still a dumping ground for rich children, but that's not all that makes the place special. Deerfield has become a museum village, one of the most important in the area, and it has won back its silence. The railroad track running past the rear of the village is rusty and neglected.

Deerfield used to be at the edge of the known world, where the maps quickly went blank and had no more to say. It was founded in 1669, almost half a century after the famous 1620 landing by pious English Pilgrims at Plymouth Rock, and the first steps taken on Manhattan by small groups of Dutch colonists in 1624. To the south, on the coast of Virginia, the English had begun establishing colonies as early as 1607, as had the French in the north, on the east coast of what became Canada.

In Deerfield little has changed over the past century, it seems. Old Main Street is quiet, lined with tall trees. Rays of sunlight fall through the foliage, yellow and orange leaves flutter down, squirrels run busily along the branches – winter is on its way and they fear nothing and no one. The layout of the roads and paths and the parcels of grazing land are much as they were when all this started. The two plane trees in front of the town hall are at least 300 years old. Most of the houses date from the eighteenth century, a few are a little more recent, but it is above all the tranquil atmosphere that makes the place unique.

Credit for all this goes to a well-to-do couple who bought and renovated house after house over the course of the twentieth century, dwellings once occupied by farming families, sometimes a weaver, shoemaker, cooper, schoolmaster or church minister. As in farming communities all over the world, almost everyone had some kind of business on the side. Generation by generation, prosperity increased. It's a process that can be traced through countless details in today's Deerfield: the first crude dwellings with a single room that housed everything; the homes built later with three or more separate spaces, one for cooking, one for eating, and one or more for sleeping; then at last, after 1700, a best room in which to receive guests. We inspect everything that came to embellish the houses after that: expensive wooden ornamentation, hearths and stoves that replaced open fires, furniture, and dressers used to present evidence of life's latest luxuries.

Even in the seventeenth century the residents of the old pioneers' village of Deerfield owned beautiful French mirrors and gloves. You can find enchanting eighteenth-century British pottery, and in one of the houses I even came upon a dish and six plates from eighteenth-century Holland, covered in political slogans. '*Vivat Oranje*' they said in rough lettering. And: '*Ik brand ligt / voor de Pruis z'n nigt / En ook de Oranje-Spruit / Die het niet wil zien / Die blaast het uit*', meaning something like: 'I burn a light / for the Prussian niece / and also for the Orange sprig / Whoever does not wish to see it / blows it out.' Trading links between Deerfield and Europe were strong, that much is clear. From the late seventeenth century onwards, the new land had excellent craftsmen, more than enough to produce a stream of luxury goods. The quality of American furniture was high, and glass-fronted cabinets were built to display the most refined of eighteenth-century American silverware.

As historian Daniel Boorstin remarked about this period: 'Whereas Europe is a land with too much history and not enough geography, America has little history and plenty of geography.' It presented the European pioneers with an unprecedented opportunity to reinvent themselves. When the immense territory of North America was discovered by Europeans, it was probably home to between five and ten million people, whereas Europe, with its hundred million inhabitants, was already struggling with over-population in places, and the resulting famine and destitution.

Those first pioneers could find no words to describe the abundance of the place: immense forests; valleys filled with oaks, walnut trees and wild vines; endless beds of giant mussels along the coast; and 'in lakes and rivers a tremendous wealth [of] fish so big that one held [them] at first for tree trunks', as one pioneer put it. There was so much game everywhere that they thought themselves in paradise.

Abundance would help to shape the American mentality; *People of Plenty* was the title that historian David Potter gave his book about the Americans. Yet they managed not to become trapped in the classic cycle whereby the increasing wealth of a country eventually leads to laziness, weakness, decadence and ruin. In fact in America the husbanding and exploitation of the land's abundance, combined with an endless supply of new immigrants, resulted if anything in precisely the opposite: a mentality of setting to, of stepping up, and indeed restlessness, since the grass might prove even greener beyond the horizon.

Individualism was the norm. Everyone had come to find, stake out and cultivate a place of their own in this new world. Progress and innovation, with all their attendant risks, were taken for granted. Amid such abundance, enterprise was often richly rewarded. Education was of vital importance from the start, since it would enable the next generation to progress even further.

Of course the pioneering life in the fields and woods around places like Deerfield was far from easy. The New England climate was fairly cool compared to the South, and here you had to work harder for less. There were very few slaves or servants, but the soil on the hills was fertile and everyone could labour on his own property and expand from there. In that early America it was possible to work your way up to a reasonable degree of prosperity within one or two generations.

Less than twenty years after the Pilgrim Fathers' arduous beginnings, their successors were doing so well that in Cambridge they were able to build their first college, for thirty students, based around the library of the late Reverend John Harvard. These seventeenth-century colonists ate far more meat than the Europeans, according to the earliest statistics. They lived much healthier lives and suffered less from famine, while epidemics – not unusual in Europe in the same period – were rare. In short, in those years they already had a higher standard of living than the population of any European country, and it was a fact they made known. By the time Deerfield was founded, around 100,000 colonists were living in America. A little over a century later, in about 1775, there were some two and a half million.

The houses of Deerfield tell a classic American success story, and it fills today's groups of visitors – eighty per cent grey, a hundred per cent white – with contentment, tranquillity and mutual courtesy. In fact there's more to it. The history of those pious and courageous pioneers who escaped the suffocating Old World, who seized their opportunities here and so, chosen by God, found great prosperity – that oft-repeated story forms the core of the American self-image. The first settlers symbolise like nothing else the high ideals of American nationalism, the American Creed: freedom, enterprise, individualism, democracy, respect for the law and the Constitution, religion without compulsion, independent people united as like-minded citizens.

The actual history is not so simple, even here in Deerfield. I see an old door hacked and scored from top to bottom, a reminder of a raid on these peaceful houses by a group of Native Americans in 1704. In the balmy evening I walk across an old graveyard with hundreds of low headstones, beginning at Joseph Bernard (died 1695) and Martha Allen (1696), then on past families called Arms (nineteen graves), Hawks (twenty-four graves), Wells (nineteen graves) and Williams (twenty-two graves), all the way to the remains of Justin Ball, who died on 5 June 1795. 'Tender were his feelings / The Christian was his faith / Honest were his dealings / And happy was his End.' Bruce Springsteen blasts out from one of the nearby dormitories. Then I spot a small memorial plaque bearing a few lines about the drama of Elisabeth Corse, 'captured February 29, 1704, on the March to Canada, aged 34'. Her children, James and Elisabeth, were also taken to Canada as captives, 'and never came back'.

What happened?

American historians who have studied local history abandoned long ago the triumphant tale of the uniqueness of America, since they are confronted time and again with the price paid by the original inhabitants, and by the original environment, for its intensive colonisation. Was this place really such a wilderness before the Europeans came to put things in order? Was there really only a thin scattering of natives to be found and did they really lead such peripatetic lives? What about the losers in this great American story, the countless pioneers who, far from becoming successful, perished from hunger or disease, or were killed in one of the many skirmishes? Of the 102 Pilgrims, for example, only half survived the first winter. What about the indigenous peoples whose territories were taken and who, in their hundreds of thousands, died of previously unknown diseases brought across by the Europeans, such as smallpox and measles? The Pilgrims survived only because they were able to take over an abandoned native settlement, with well-tended fields, where most of the original inhabitants had died in the smallpox epidemic of 1618–19. What about the story of the black slaves, masses of whom were brought from Africa in the eighteenth century to compensate for the shortfall in native labour, so important for the plantations of the South?

'Losers far outnumbered winners,' writes historian John Murrin, in 'a tragedy of such large proportions that no one's imagination can easily encompass it all'. The few available statistics speak for themselves. Despite a huge influx of newcomers, the total population of North America declined between 1492 and 1776. In the America of 1776, with its revolution in the name of freedom and democracy, one in five people were slaves. Of the estimated five to ten million 'Indians' who once made a living north of Mexico, only around 300,000 were still alive by 1830. As a colonist in these parts reported in 1620, the natives 'died on heapes, as they lay in their houses, and the living; that were able to shift for themselves, would runne away, and let them by, and let their carkases ly above the ground without buriall . . . And the bones and skulls upon the severall places of their habitations, made such a spectacle after my coming into those partes, that as I travailed in the Forrest, near the Massachusetts [Bay], it seemed to mee a new found Golgotha.'

In short, the people of Deerfield were not so pious, hard working and blessed as the traditional American story would have us believe. The social and political situation in the seventeenth and eighteenth centuries was in reality quite complicated, and the same goes for the early years of the United States in general.

Rather than one overarching narrative, there are at least three tales to be told, and they differ greatly: a European story, a Native American story and an African-American story. They are set in two quite distinct places, where two different cultures developed that divided the nation – and politics – for centuries: the South and the North.

The South, where the first wave of immigrants consisted largely of the same kind of fortune seekers as the Spanish conquistadors who went in search of gold in Mexico and Peru (Alexis de Tocqueville writes, quoting from William Stith's History of Virginia, of 'unprincipled young men of family, whom their parents were glad to ship off, discharged servants, fraudulent bankrupts, or debauchees'), and where society was later shaped mainly by slaves, plantation owners, great poverty and vast wealth; and the North, where the first immigrants were true pioneers – decent, sober, knowing neither extreme wealth nor extreme poverty, often driven by religious ideals.

Within those major narratives lie all kinds of smaller stories, again offering totally different perspectives. For example, within the European arc are the stories of the British, Swedes, Finns, Germans, French Huguenots and Dutch, and the British stories can be further divided into Puritan, Scottish and Irish. If there is an example anywhere of a complex and chaotic reality lying behind a beautiful and heartening tale, then it is the history of the colonisation of North America.

'Colonial societies did diverge from their mother countries – but in a more complex and radical manner than imagined within the narrow field of vision once traditional to colonial history,' writes Alan Taylor in a revealing account of the early years of this new world called *American Colonies*. 'The biggest difference was the unprecedented mixing of radically diverse peoples – African, European, and Indian – under circumstances stressful for all.'

Most contemporary American historians have therefore expanded their research and shifted their focus. The Native Americans are no longer the shadowy inhabitants of a 'wilderness' to which the colonists brought order and civilisation. They now play the main role in the early history of America. In the initial phase at least, there was close cooperation. The Pilgrims were actually saved in that first winter by two friendly Natives, Samoset and Tisquantum. Without that help they would never have made it.

There has been a similar shift when it comes to the slaves, who were always regarded as marginal. The slave was essential to the economy and society of early America, at least in the South. In the eighteenth century, for every one free immigrant, three slaves entered the country. 'The colonial intermingling of peoples – and of microbes, plants, and animals from different continents – was unparalleled in speed and volume in global history,' Taylor writes. 'Everyone had to adapt to a dramatic new world wrought by those combinations.'

Deerfield had to survive within this 'dramatic' new world for the first half-century of its existence, when it was an outpost. The graveyard, for example, where those families called Arms, Hawks, Wells and Williams lie, was once a Native burial ground. The surrounding 'wilderness' the colonists consistently talked of was far more cultivated than they realised, like many places in New England. Whatever the classic tale might suggest, the Native Americans did not in fact live by hunting alone. Their horticulture seems strange to our eyes – they used a clever combination of plants that stimulated each other's growth – but it was extremely efficient and productive. The fields were covered in small mounds, each of which had maize at the centre, pumpkins at the edges and beans trailing down the sides. These provided by far the largest proportion of their food.

In the seventeenth century, the area around Deerfield was occupied and cultivated by the Pocumtuc people. To get their hands on the land, the British colonists drew up a contract that was duly signed by a Native man called Chaulk. He had no authority to do so, and probably no idea what he was doing, since the Native Americans had no concept of contractual agreements, nor even of private property. In their nomadic existence, moving from camp to camp, they shared everything with their families and other members of the same tribe. They owned only a little clothing and a few tools. Theft was no less alien to them than property. That misunderstanding alone produced tensions in the New World with great regularity, and even wars.

Typical of this confusion is the famous 'purchase' of Manhattan by the Dutch in 1626. At the heart of the story is a letter from the States General of the United Netherlands in which a representative of the West India Company, Pieter Schagen, almost in passing, notes he has heard that 'the island of Manhattes' has been 'purchased from the wild people in exchange for goods worth 60 guilders; it is 11,000 morgens in size'. To any European this meant that the island was now Dutch 'property'. After its 'purchase' the Natives no longer had any business being there.

The Mahicans – for they were the 'wild people' concerned – saw the matter very differently. In their eyes the goods they had received were not the purchase price but simply a gift to confirm an alliance that would allow the Europeans to make use of Manhattan. Part of the agreement was a promise to come to each other's aid should either be attacked. They had no intention at all of leaving the island, and so, as a wide range of archival material makes clear, they continued to use it for many years afterwards.

The Native Americans regarded the colonists, as historian Allan Greer writes, 'not as conquering invaders, but as a new tribe negotiating a place for itself in the diplomatic webs of Native North America'. They believed they were operating from a position of strength and regarded themselves as far more intelligent and skilful than the Europeans. The warriors of the Abenaki and the Kahnawake peoples, who fought side by side with the French against the British in the area around Deerfield, were astonished, for example, at the way their allies fought. They were used to tracking and ambushing, but the French marched, in tight formation, straight towards the British artillery as they were being fired upon. The Native warriors thought their French allies astonishingly courageous, but at the same time foolish and suicidal, for allowing themselves to be slaughtered in the open like that.

The truth is that some 'Indians' were not anything like as 'wild' as people assumed. William Bradford, the first governor of the Plymouth colony, mentions in passing in his eyewitness report *Of Plymouth Plantation* that the Pilgrims were able to use the English language right from the start with their native helpers – just as they do in some cheap Hollywood films. The Pilgrims never needed to learn the complicated language of the Algonquians. Samoset had already picked up a few words and phrases from English fishermen who had been turning up regularly on the coast for years. Tisquantum – also known as Squanto – actually spoke the language fluently. He had probably visited the British Isles twice, once when he sailed back with an English captain in 1605 and once when he was taken to Spain as a slave and managed to escape via England. So this region was far from virgin and undiscovered in the early years of the seventeenth century.

The Dutch colonists on Manhattan, oblivious to all this, lurched from one conflict to the next. However proud the Dutch may be today about having founded New Amsterdam and about everything that followed from that, what they created was a kind of seventeenth-century Afghanistan. Unintentionally for the most part, the Dutch became combatants in, and indeed often the instigators of, the many wars and skirmishes between Native tribes.

Most frequently involved were the Mahicans and the Mohawks, the latter being one of the peoples of the Iroquois Confederacy, which gradually became the main trading partner of the Dutch. Unlike the French further north, Dutch merchants provided the Iroquois with large quantities of firearms in return for furs. This disturbed the shaky relationships between Native tribes fundamentally and permanently. The Iroquois became far stronger and more powerful than their neighbours the Huron, the Algonquin and the Montagnais. They raided their rivals' camps and trading convoys to rob them of furs, and then started attacking French trading convoys as well. They sold their spoils to the Dutch.

Even before the English arrived, the Pocumtuc of Deerfield suffered badly at the hands of the belligerent Mohawks with their Dutch guns. The fatal blow for both tribes came in 1634, when a sick Dutch child in the trading post of Albany infected them with smallpox. At least a third died, possibly half.

In Deerfield the cultural clash between Europe and the original America eventually led to a small pitched battle, the Battle of Bloody Brook. The Pocumtuc, furious at being driven from their lands, sought support from the colonists in New France, in what is now Canada. On 18 September 1675 they attacked a convoy of farmers' wagons that was carrying the harvest from Deerfield to neighbouring Hadley. This was during the time of the short but bloody 'King Philip's War', so called because of the nickname given to the leader of this major rebellion by the Native peoples of New England, in which almost half the new settlements were burned to the ground. In the attack on the farmers' convoy from Deerfield some sixty colonists were killed. The village was abandoned that winter and for a time Native families lived there again, but in the spring the pioneers and colonial troops returned. They took back the village, and on 19 May 1676 they organised a punitive expedition to a nearby Pocumtuc settlement. The inhabitants were slaughtered. There were some 200 fatalities in all, mostly women and children. The remaining Native Americans withdrew to New France, but they never forgot their humiliation. It was the start of a complex series of events leading up to that hacking of the old door, and to that small memorial in the graveyard to Elisabeth Corse and her lost children, 'captured February 29, 1704, on the March to Canada, aged 34'.

In the early years of the eighteenth century, from 1701 to 1714, events were shaped by the Spanish War of Succession, a ferocious encounter mainly between England and France, the latter supported by Spain. Officially the conflict was about who was to succeed to the Spanish throne. The French prince had an excellent claim, but a merging of the Spanish and French royal families might significantly upset the balance of power on the continent. So all the other major European powers – England, the Dutch Republic, Portugal, the Habsburg Monarchy – joined forces to prevent it. Other factors came into play too, especially the rise of Great Britain and the decline of Spain as a world power.

It was a widespread, bloody conflict, and hostilities between the colonies in North America went by the name of the Queen Anne's War. Here it was not so much about who would succeed to a throne in far-off Europe as about future power relations: which parts of the new continent would become British and which would fall to France. The Native tribes fought too, on the side of Britain, France or – in Florida, for example – Spain.

This major international conflict also sealed the fate, probably without their knowing it, of Elisabeth Corse and her two children, James and Elisabeth, who were captured by Natives. French troops had organised the attack on the British town of Deerfield on that infamous February day in 1704. They were helped by some 300 Pocumtuc, who had seized upon the Franco–British war as a chance to retake their old lands.

A thick blanket of snow covered the ground and in places it formed drifts so high that the attackers could easily slip over the palisade early the following morning. 'With horrid shouting and yelling', as the Reverend John Williams later wrote, they threw themselves 'like a flood' on the still-sleeping village. Within a few hours, forty-four villagers had been killed, including twenty-five children, two of whom belonged to the Reverend Williams: his son John, six years old, and his six-week-old daughter Jerusha, as well as their black maid, Parthena. The rest of the family was taken captive. In all, 109 villagers were led away northwards. Twenty died during that harsh, weeks-long trek of over 300 miles to Canada, most of them hacked to death when they were unable to go on. Williams' wife, only just out of confinement after bearing Jerusha, was one of the first to succumb. I found her headstone in the graveyard. She was killed by a Mohawk after she tripped while crossing a stream. Things would not have gone very differently for Elisabeth Corse.

Eventually the Reverend John Williams, after complex negotiations, managed to return to Deerfield. His daughter Eunice, ten years old, had ended up at a Jesuit mission post near Montreal and was adopted by a nearby Mohawk family, taking the place of a daughter who had died of smallpox. Her father tried to reach her after he was freed, but the French refused to hand her back. She was now a Mohawk child. An American mediator wrote in February 1707: 'Our spies . . . saw Mr Williams' daughter . . . she is in good health, but seems unwilling to return and the Indian not very willing to part with her.'

Eunice converted to Catholicism, changed her name to Marguerite in 1710 and married a prominent Mohawk in 1716. They had three children and Eunice lived the rest of her life under the Mohawk name Kanenstenhawi. She did keep in contact with her father and brothers, however. In vain they begged her to return. After 1740 she visited her family in Massachusetts three times, always accompanied by a guide and an interpreter, since she and her family spoke only Mohawk and French. She died in 1785 at the age of eighty-nine.

The daughter of Elisabeth Corse, also called Elisabeth, remained in Canada, although 'and never came back' turns out to be only half true. Just six years old when she was captured, Elisabeth left interesting traces in the French-Canadian archives. She died in 1766, aged sixty-eight, after two marriages and a generally busy and dramatic life. In 1705, when she was seven, she was baptised Elisabeth Casse in Montreal and adopted by a French couple. At seventeen she had an illegitimate child and that same year she married a man of around fifty, one Jean Dumontet. Neither the bride nor the groom was able to sign the marriage register. They had eight children, of whom only two sons and two daughters survived into adulthood. There must have been something attractive about Elisabeth, since within a few months of Dumontet's death, in the spring of 1729, she married a young man called Pierre Monet. With him she had another six children.

The younger Elisabeth always stayed in touch with her family in Deerfield, although she too resisted appeals to return. Documents show that she and her brothers all shared the inheritance from her mother: seventeen pounds and four shillings, three yards of lace, a child's jacket, and 'one box & what was in it'.

Four

STEINBECK WAS COLD, the night after his visit to Deerfield. In his correspondence he mentions temperatures just below zero. He drove further north, through the state of Vermont, before turning east towards New Hampshire, into the White Mountains, past the sweetest villages in all of America, their wooden houses all neatly painted white and, as he writes, 'unchanged for a hundred years except for traffic and paved streets'. In the mountains it quickly grew colder and the trees were starting to turn, the leaves astonishing reds and yellows. 'It isn't only color but a glowing,' he writes, 'as though the leaves gobbled the light of the autumn sun and then released it slowly.'

The small twin states of Vermont and New Hampshire are on the face of it fairly similar, but to the expert eye the differences are telling. New Hampshire, rugged and forested, was always an industrial state. Its soils are poor. The soil in Vermont is richer. It was traditionally a farming state, and when John Gunther drove around here in 1945, it looked as if the Industrial Revolution had failed to reach it. In New Hampshire he saw dilapidated farms everywhere, whereas in Vermont everything was tidy and manicured. The land was mostly given over to dairy farms, worked by their owners, often in the same family for generations. Vermont's neighbourliness was legendary, along with its self-esteem. 'People (including servants) don't work for you,' Gunther heard people say. 'They help you out.' He noted that people lived close to the soil. 'They know what two extra weeks of snow will do to the crops; they have an instinctive cognizance of weather, seasons, and the cruelties of flood and frost.'

Year after year, in late September, Vermont starts to ready itself for the winter. It's no different in 2010 in that respect than in 1945 and 1960.

The fields lie fallow. Next to the barns firewood is stacked high, and some shops even have their Christmas promotions outside already: 'Best Christmas Shop in Town'.

Meanwhile we drive on, through the endless forests of Vermont, uphill, down dale, green, yellow and orange as far as the eye can see. Close to Bradford a car is lying in a ditch on the far side of the road. It rolled just moments ago; a young woman and two children are standing next to it. The autumnal colours along Highways 91, 5 and 10 are as spectacular as ever, but the cold of half a century ago is absent. In fact it's still warm, like a summer's day. The intervening years have not left the villages untouched. Gas stations, chain stores, hamburger joints, large tourist hotels – the slapdash sprawl characteristic of all America has swept across here. But the landscape is as charming as ever, with countless traditional wooden houses and small farms, porches and white picket fences, gardens and orchards, and bright green spaces in between.

Near Lancaster in New Hampshire, as the day drew to a close, Steinbeck stopped on land belonging to an elderly farmer, beside a clattering stream. Rocinante's cabin revealed itself as a complete mess. After so much jolting about on the mountain roads, its inner space was strewn with loose papers and other belongings. The farmer knocked at the truck's door and they drank coffee together, with a generous dash of applejack against the cold, and talked for a while about life. At the General Assembly of the United Nations, Khrushchev, the farmer said, had pounded the desk with his shoe. That brought them onto the subject of the upcoming presidential elections, and the certainties with which everyone used to live. 'My grandfather knew the number of whiskers in the Almighty's beard. I don't even know what happened yesterday, let alone tomorrow.'

Steinbeck describes lying awake that night, worrying about the phenomenon of progress. Humanity had millions of years in which to master fire, for instance. Now far greater forces were at hand and we had barely any time to get used to them and think about them. Would we be able to cope with the side effects of such prosperity? As he travelled he had been amazed by the amount of garbage that seemed to be almost suffocating some towns. 'When an Indian village became too deep in its own filth, the inhabitants moved. And we have no place to which to move.' Only when the roosters started crowing did he finally fall asleep.

I too barely shut my eyes that September night and, yes, my insomnia has to do with the 'forces' Steinbeck described. He saw motels along his route that were trying to outdo each other by their modernity – or what passed for it in 1960. Near Bangor he even claims to have found a place where, to his amazement, everything you could possibly imagine was wrapped in cellophane. Even the drinking glasses were sealed 'for your protection' and everything was made of plastic, including the staff.

All those resting places turn out to have swelled into huge white fungi over the past half-century. 'Inns', 'spas' and 'resorts' five or seven storeys high have proliferated on mountain slopes, with conference facilities, swimming pools, and long corridors of rooms and suites, all featuring that same plastic and cellophane 'for your protection'.

The formula for success is obvious. The very thing we Europeans deplore has been a great plus point to the American traveller since the 1950s: wherever you stop, the rooms in a Holiday Inn and the taste of a McDonald's are precisely the same. The consistency and uniformity of the product – its dullness, if you like – are fundamental components of the formula. You could rely on that then as you can to this day. All the same, Steinbeck wondered, if people not only accept, but actually want their food flavourless but hygienic, what does that do to the emotional life of a country?

Years ago, on a camping trip in the hills of Oregon, I found myself beside a river on a beautiful Sunday afternoon. A lot of fishing was going on from small boats anchored in the current, and one trout after another was swung out of the water, glistening. Close to the bank was a floating restaurant, pleasantly busy. Ah, fresh fish, you think. But we were served neat blocks of Icelandic cod, filleted, pressed, packed and deep-frozen in huge factory ships. 'Well, that's what people here like to eat,' the owner said.

Or take the restaurant at the Mountain Club hotel in Lincoln, New Hampshire, where we find ourselves now, a typical product of the uniform culture all these chains offer, with remnants of a tough past hanging on the walls (snow shoes, ice saws), flickering television screens, immense sets of antlers above the fireplace, a bassist playing the same riff hour after hour, and slightly worn plastic Empire chairs in the dining room. The place is filled with a combination of smells, each displacing the others in turn: food, disinfectant, various powerful deodorants. Appropriate dishes appear on the table, including heritage port pâté, Tony G.'s clam chowder, a Black Diamond bacon cheeseburger, an eight-ounce skirt steak – there's no end to it. Only the waitress refuses to play the game and remains herself, with an awkward face and shy eyes.

Outside, the night is at last clear and cool. We take a short walk, and back in our room we throw open a window. The hills are silent; the pine trees rustle. Our neighbours return. A moment later you think a train is going past, or that some kind of mower has started up, but it's the inevitable air conditioning, which people turn on no matter how cold it is outside. The contraption drones away all night.

Machines seem to be the only things Americans trust. They don't feel safe unless they can hear a mechanical sound. In the end even the outdoor air is pre-packaged. It's like the way the buses on the pier at Orient Point leave their engines running for three-quarters of an hour, or the trucks I saw waiting patiently day after day, growling away until their drivers had finished their lunch. The senseless destruction of tranquillity, the colossal waste of energy – it's so insane as to be beyond comprehension, but everyone here seems to find it perfectly normal. It reminds me of Russian hotel rooms, with their eternally blazing-hot radiators, where you can adjust the temperature only by opening a window to the freezing cold, or by closing it again. It has something to do with abundance, with the generosity of this country, which must never end.

So I too lie awake, rereading yet again the conversation Steinbeck had with that elderly farmer. Nowadays it's almost impossible to imagine the fear, in both East and West, caused by the permanent threat of an atomic war that would destroy everything. The first Soviet nuclear test on 29 August 1949 ended the triumphant mood of the post-war years at a stroke. Now the communists had atomic bombs too. The fear was not unfounded. Thirteen years later, during the Cuban missile crisis, the world did indeed balance on the edge of the abyss. Fear made American society vulnerable to the political poison we know all too well: the campaigns of lies by the media and politicians, the hunt for scapegoats, the rumours and groundless suspicions.

Suddenly something occurs to me. Steinbeck and the farmer talked about these things too, if not in so many words. It's typical of the time. 'I think this might be the secretest election we ever had,' says the farmer. 'People just won't put out an opinion.' It never used to be like that. He remembers heated arguments in the past. Steinbeck agrees that it seems people don't dare to say what they think.

Did that cautious attitude have something to do with the after-effects of the anti-communist campaign by the Republican senator Joseph McCarthy? We can't be sure, although the stench of the people burned at the stake still hung in the air. Trading in fear, with a great sense of drama and theatrics, McCarthy unmasked 'red infiltrators' and 'communists' from the early 1950s onwards in every conceivable place: universities, the Pentagon and the State Department, Broadway, Hollywood, radio and television, later even at the United Nations. He made the best possible use of the new opportunities provided by television.

In the words of journalist and historian David Halberstam, it was 'a mean time . . . The nation was ready for witch-hunts.' Fifty years on, anyone reading the ledgers of newspapers from the autumn of 1960 will be impressed even now by the propaganda battles of the Cold War, front page after front page, day after day. China and Eastern Europe had been taken over by communist regimes, and the Berlin blockade and the defeat of the uprising in Budapest were still fresh in everyone's minds. In Korea the 'Red Peril' had been halted by a 'forgotten' war that demanded everything of American servicemen – more than 40,000 US troops and 100,000 Chinese and Koreans died. Little by little, America had fallen prey to a repressed moral panic – fertile ground for a firebrand like McCarthy.

The careers of countless innocent Americans were wrecked. Charlie Chaplin and many others went into exile. Steinbeck himself remained out of harm's way. His position was slightly ambivalent, but when Arthur Miller flatly refused to cooperate with McCarthy, Steinbeck was the only famous figure to stick up for him.

Joseph McCarthy was of Irish origin. He beat the drum for that typical American nationalism that occasionally displays almost religious traits: the belief that the American Creed is so self-evident and of such universal application that a failure by America must surely indicate either decadence or plotting by anti-American forces, be they communists, pinkos or intellectual liberals. Among the Irish and other poor whites, that message was received with enthusiasm.

One of McCarthy's predecessors was the popular broadcaster Father Charles Coughlin, who had built up a large following among Irish Catholics in the 1930s with his attacks on communists, Jews, liberals and the 'red' elite in general. The Irish had felt excluded for decades, both rightly and wrongly. Unlike the Jews and Italians, they rarely penetrated the top echelons of politics and economics. In cartoons they were depicted simply as idiots, as 'white niggers'.

Anti-communist hysteria, with its stress on the need for national unanimity, suddenly provided their bitterness with the perfect outlet. Through militant nationalism they could show they fully belonged, even though they were Catholics. At the same time, after all their humiliations they could finally take effective revenge on the Protestant elite and east coast intellectuals. Now every Catholic of Irish origin suddenly came through all kinds of screening, sight unseen; it was the Harvard people who were being investigated. The roles had been reversed.

In the end all those hearings were little more than a travelling circus, but the social impact was lasting and calamitous. McCarthy contributed nothing to the tracking-down of real spies, who did undoubtedly exist. His two main products were fear and headlines, writes David Halberstam: 'After a thousand speeches and a thousand charges, the last thing in the world he could probably have recognised was a real Communist or a real spy ring.' In the words of United Press International journalist George Reedy: 'He didn't know Karl Marx from Groucho.'

Yet McCarthy was allowed to have his way for years, because for most conservatives and Republicans he was a godsend. In their eyes, America had deviated wildly from its original mission since 1932. Okay, so Roosevelt had been a good wartime president, but they hated the New Deal and everything that flowed from it. Although they thought McCarthy a loathsome man, his hate campaign against all things progressive was perfectly timed. Their main concern was the New Deal. McCarthy's real value to them had nothing to do with spying.

McCarthy's campaign of hatred was indeed extremely effective. Even during the Vietnam War, fifteen years later, the Democrats were still doing all they could to prove they were not 'soft on communism'. For many years, meetings of the international writers' organisation PEN could not take place in the United States because some of its authors found it impossible to get a visa, purely as a result of their controversial political beliefs. Graham Greene was refused countless times, as was Iris Murdoch, and later Gabriel García Márquez. 'What kind of a free country is this?' Steinbeck would often grumble to his friends. He believed Socrates wouldn't have been let into the country either, because he'd associated with criminals. Sappho would have had even less of a chance, since she was a lesbian. It would transpire many years later, incidentally, that Steinbeck had a hefty FBI dossier of his own. The federal agents regarded his sympathetic descriptions of refugees, vagrants and other victims of the 1930s as material for Nazi and Soviet propaganda. They continually kept an eye on him.

For Joe McCarthy personally it was all over fairly quickly. In 1954 he had the audacity to attack the US Army. He'd overplayed his hand. During the hearing he failed to produce any evidence at all, and the television cameras recorded everything mercilessly. It was the army's lawyer, Joseph Welch, who struck the decisive blow with the historic words: 'Senator. You have done enough. Have you no sense of decency, sir, at long last?' McCarthy was censured by the Senate in 1954, his drinking worsened, and he died two and a half years later.

One question remains: what drove Joseph McCarthy? According to his biographer Richard Rovere, he was not out for political power. The idea of waging an anti-communist campaign was not even his. He was put onto it during a lunch with a priest, from whom he had asked advice about how to make himself famous. McCarthy was the kind of hellraiser that turns up quite regularly in history, the type who runs about causing endless agitation but does nothing constructive and is driven by narcissism.

In the real world his activities mainly caused political chaos and a great deal of personal misery. His 'success' was based purely on his magical slogans. The term had not yet been invented, but McCarthy was a master of 'framing', the technique of gaining control of a complicated and possibly threatening situation by means of a few turns of phrase, reducing it to a simple and attractive falsehood. The reporters loved him. Every day he furnished them with news and easily manageable quotations, and they swallowed everything, even when they knew better. 'McCarthy was a dream story,' one of them recalled later. 'I wasn't off page one for four years.'

Rovere writes that McCarthy was the most gifted demagogue in American history. He was a purely destructive force, a revolutionary without a vision, a rebel without a cause – and he had the spirit of the times on his side, times of modernisation, confusion and uncertainty.

Our departure from the Mountain Club hotel the following morning is virtually a flight. Not until half an hour has passed, during a pause at a viewing point deeper into the mountains, do I start to get the drone of all those air conditioners out of my head. The woods are peaceful, wide and green, speckled with tints of yellow and red. The trees slowly emerge from the blue morning mist as the day grows warmer. At places like this, Steinbeck allowed Charley to stake out the terrain while he sat on the back step of his Rocinante, poured himself a cup of coffee, and listened to the stream and the jumping of trout.

You can still do that here, but there is a difference. The drivers passing by and the people Steinbeck spoke to were all there for work: farmers, forestry men, the occasional travelling salesman. John Gunther, too, travelled through a land of workers, 'rugged, reticent, suspicious of outsiders, frugal, intensely individualistic, and with a great will to survive'.

That world seems to have gone. Everywhere now you see tourists, hikers and holidaymakers, transients concentrating mainly on seeing and enjoying, and in many places they are actually the majority. The roads are cluttered with four-wheel drives, even though there's not a mud track to be seen for miles around.

The 'scenic vista' where I'm standing was created to be consumed, rather than for the purpose of doing or making anything. The noticeboards tell me that the view has been presented to us by the Forest Service: 'The Forest you are visiting is indeed a planned, managed and nurtured place.' There follows an entire narrative about the various zones into which it is divided. Many visitors to the scenic vista act accordingly. They stay in their cars, stare at the landscape through their windscreens as if looking at a computer monitor, and then relocate to the next experience.

Further into New Hampshire the landscape slowly changes. Rolling fields look peaceful in the afternoon sun, punctuated by small woods and lines of trees. In between are farmhouses, their lawns taut with good intentions, the flag waving proudly from a pole. Here and there, near the barns, stand simple, community-built church halls, some dirty and dilapidated, their paths overgrown with weeds, others still neat and in use. This is the old America, in which religion thrived next to religion, sect next to sect, a result of reluctant tolerance, since in contrast to many European countries no particular denomination had the upper hand.

After the Pilgrims made their hazardous crossing, one group of religious colonists followed another: Scottish Presbyterians; Anglicans; English Puritans and Quakers; Dutch Calvinists; Norwegian, Swedish and German Lutherans; Dutch and German Baptists; Irish Catholics; Jews from the Low Countries, and with them adherents of innumerable small sects that fearlessly entered this new Zion as 'children of Israel'. By about 1750 there was one church for every 600 souls in New England, and elsewhere that figure was sometimes less than 500.

In Amsterdam I used to live just around the corner from the Barndesteeg, a narrow side street in the red-light district. While undertaking a small piece of historical research in the neighbourhood, I discovered that even in the early twentieth century the ruins of a sombre church building had stood there, 'a drab jagged hulk', according to someone who had seen it, 'a mouldering relic of a grim Puritan house of prayer, its crumbling walls greying as if from leprosy.' It had been the place of worship of a denomination known as the Brownists, a religious group that originally came from England. Several dozen Brownist families had settled in Amsterdam in the late sixteenth century.

It was a Pietistic movement, focused on the individual and the pure experience of faith, which had split from the Presbyterian Church in about 1575 under the leadership of one Robert Browne. He regarded the existing parishes as pools of ruination held hostage by the Antichrist himself. He believed it was the task of every Christian to achieve the greatest possible purity in life and faith. The Church establishment was corrupted by power and money, so in its place independent congregations must arise, in which anyone could preach and bear witness.

It was sects like these that emigrated to America in large numbers as early as the seventeenth century, quite often stopping in the relatively tolerant Netherlands on their way. Browne and his flock were harshly persecuted in England (Shakespeare even devotes a line in *Twelfth Night* to

them: 'I had as lief be a Brownist as a politician'). Brown moved to
Middelburg and later to Amsterdam, where he lived with his followers,
initially in deep poverty. In 1620 part of the group left on the *Mayflower*
with the Pilgrims, bound for the New World. Other members, who had
split from the main sect in 1609 and returned to England in 1611, helped
to found the Baptists, a movement that eventually gained a large following
in America.

The more the Brownists who remained in Europe strove after purity,
the fiercer the quarrels between them became – over the size of hat a
minister's wife should wear, for example, or the embroidery on her
sleeves. In the end most defected to the Dutch Reformed Church, or as
one of the Pilgrim Fathers put it, succumbed to the errors of the Low
Countries in which most buried themselves, along with their names. In
April 1701 the last five remaining Brownists dissolved their congregation
and in 1910 their church on Barndesteeg was demolished and erased
from history.

Another example of a group of religious pioneers are the so-called
Shakers or 'Shaking Quakers'. In their longing for purity they went further
even than the Puritans. Under the influence of their charismatic leader
Ann Lee ('Mother Ann'), they attempted to live in such a way that all
forms of sexuality were absolutely forbidden. Mother Ann had once been
married and she'd found conjugal duties far from fun. She invented her
own theology, believing that in heaven there is no marriage. Celibacy
was therefore the best way to prepare for the advent of the Kingdom of
God. The religious practices of the Shakers nevertheless involved a great
deal of ardour: singing, shouting, dancing, shaking, speaking in tongues
– anything went, in honour of 'the God of our salvation'.

Because members of the sect faced harassment all over England –
Mother Ann was regularly accused of being a witch – she and a number
of Shakers left for New England in 1774. Their message of total purity
found willing listeners. At the height of the movement there were more
than twenty Shaker settlements and, despite the onerous demands placed
on followers, they eventually managed to win some 20,000 souls for
their utopian and spiritual community.

The Shakers practised an early form of communism. Men and women
were completely equal. In that sense the Shakers were revolutionary,

although the two sexes were strictly separated and many Shaker buildings even featured separate men's and women's staircases. They formed pseudo-families. Since no babies were born they often adopted children, and the community was further replenished by new converts and by unattached people seeking shelter in the long or short term. They ate together, but in silence, as in some monasteries. Work was highly valued; in fact Mother Ann's admonitions included 'Put your hands to work, and give your hearts to God'. Ornamentation was taboo, since it represented worldly vanity. Plainness and cleanliness were central concerns, the broom an ever-present symbol.

In 1843 Charles Dickens described a brief visit to the Shaker community in New Lebanon, New York. 'We walked into a grim room, where several grim hats were hanging on grim pegs, and the time was grimly told by a grim clock which uttered every tick with a kind of struggle, as if it broke the grim silence reluctantly and under protest.'

Only during the Sunday service was all this turned on its head. The members, every one of them, went into raptures. In the time of Mother Ann, everyone was allowed to do whatever he or she liked while in a trance, but order was soon imposed. One of the brothers had seen angels walking in wide circles around God's throne in a vision, so from then on the Shakers reflected this in their dancing, the male outer circle leaping in one direction, the women, no less ecstatic, in the opposite direction, sometimes with two more circles inside them and at the centre a choir singing.

'The purity and virginity of which they were so proud were reflected in the sisters' Sunday gowns of white, with white caps, blue aprons and blue pointed high-heeled shoes, and the brethren's long-tailed blue coats and trousers,' I read in one of the most recent publications about the Shaker community. 'Before long the coats were discarded and the men danced in their shirtsleeves.'

Alexis de Tocqueville, who attended a service in 1831, was less enthusiastic. The most fanatical characters kept the rhythm by nodding, he wrote in a letter, 'which gave them somewhat the appearance of those porcelain Chinese figures with tilted heads on our grandmothers' mantelpieces.' The service lasted a total of two hours and the singing was 'ear-splitting . . . Two more spectacles like that one and I'll become a Catholic.'

In later years, members of the group were allowed to move away from the dancing circles, whirling around as they did so, and some Shakers reported extraordinary spiritual experiences, like the dervishes of the Sufi movement. But no man ever touched a woman.

All that striving for purity, all that spontaneous and emotional faith in God, set its stamp on early America. Of course, most colonial settlements had a commercial character as well. The trade in beaver pelts alone brought them gold. The narrative of economic honesty and thrift among American colonists tells only half the truth. In reality the colonisation of America was built on debt from the start, and hardly any enterprise could be financed without borrowing. Many of those early pioneers, as an abundance of court documents testify, led lives that were anything but retiring. Nevertheless the influence, in the broadest sense of the word, of the Puritan communities on today's American self-image is hard to exaggerate, despite their relatively modest size.

A sharp contrast between morality and everyday practice, sometimes to the point of absurdity, remains characteristic of American public debate. Like the Dutch Republic in the seventeenth century, America saw itself reflected in the biblical story of Israel. Americans were a chosen people that, after much hardship, had finally reached the Promised Land. In some regions you pass one biblical name after another. On my road map the place name Zion occurs five times, Bethel eight, Bethlehem seven.

God's New Israel was decidedly Protestant, a refuge for all those who were fleeing Catholic idolatry. The anti-Catholicism faced by Irish immigrants had deep roots. In other ways, too, living together was not always easy with so many different denominations and religious communities. A seventeenth-century Anglican minister described his parish as a 'soul destroying whirlpool of apostasy'. Harsh words were sometimes exchanged, but in America, in contrast to Europe, religious violence and persecution were almost unknown. Even my old atheist friend Edith, along with her mainly Jewish family, celebrated Thanksgiving, a commemoration of the feast held by the pious, Protestant Pilgrims after their first harvest in 1621. It has become a festival for all Americans.

As Alexis de Tocqueville wrote: 'The settlers of New England were at the same time ardent sectarians and daring innovators. Narrow as the limits of some of their religious opinions were, they were entirely free from political prejudices.' Whereas elsewhere in the world, certainly in Europe, religion and freedom were continually at loggerheads, the Americans managed to combine those two very different imperatives in a remarkable way. It gave the New World an unprecedented dynamism.

Each seeks his own kind. That old law of nature certainly applies to immigrants. There is a type of person who stays put and a type who dares to make the leap into the unknown. As far as non-Western emigrants are concerned, a clear and discernible difference exists between those who choose Europe – fewer opportunities, more certainties – and those who opt for the United States – more opportunities, fewer certainties. Mechanisms of that sort were already at work in the seventeenth and eighteenth centuries.

New England had a harsher climate than the colonies further south. The summers were short, but people stayed healthy. The Puritans thanked God that they had found a land that rewarded hard work. One of them wrote: 'If men desire to have a people degenerate speedily, and to corrupt their mindes and bodies too . . . let them se[e]cke a rich soile, that brings in much with little labour; but if they desire that Piety and Godlinesse should prosper . . . let them choose a Country such as [New England] which may yield sufficiency with hard labour and industry.'

According to Alan Taylor, in colonial America an extremely effective interplay quickly developed between land, people and religious values. The commercial success of New England was not symptomatic of the decay of Puritan values, he writes, but of their strength. As Mother Ann of the Shakers had preached, work was a way to honour God and anyone whose work paid off could be certain that God's blessing was upon him. 'Puritan values helped the colonists prosper in a demanding land. In the process, they developed a culture that was both the most entrepreneurial and the most vociferously pious in Anglo-America.' Everything people did, whether in the churches and schools or on the farms and at the counting houses and flourmills, was in the eyes of the Puritans a hymn of praise to God.

As well as being purifiers, the Puritans were therefore 'incorrigible doers'. Their souls depended on it. In Massachusetts in 1663 a law was introduced that made time-wasting a punishable offence: 'No person, householder or other, shall spend his time idly or unprofitably, under pain of such punishment as the court shall think meet to inflict.' With their powerful work ethic, however, they tied themselves in knots. On the one hand God rewarded the industrious and pious with prosperity, on the other hand those riches and those 'temptations of the flesh' must not distract them too much from their preparations for entering God's kingdom. So Puritan values involved a duty to give generously to pious, worthy causes and it was wrong to live too exuberantly, no matter how much wealth was to hand. This was what the Good Life ought to look like on earth. In biblical terms, it was one final attempt to escape Adam's curse.

As the philosopher and theologian Reinhold Niebuhr once put it, the American mentality contains 'a deep layer of Messianic consciousness'. These religious pioneers, for all their differences, shared a profound conviction that their strict communities and their harsh existence in the wilderness were bringing about a kind of purification, a new, clean page in the history of humanity. 'Every nation has its own form of spiritual pride,' Niebuhr writes. 'Our version is that our nation turned its back upon the vices of Europe and made a new beginning.'

Take Edward Johnson of Massachusetts, the author of the first history of New England, published in 1650. The title says it all: *Wonder-Working Providence of Zion's Saviour in New England*. In Johnson's eyes New England was the place 'where the Lord would create a new heaven and a new earth, new churches and a new commonwealth together'. Or take Thomas Jefferson, a man of the Enlightenment who came to the same conclusion: this was a new beginning in a corrupt world, an example of the power of 'nature's God'. Or the writer Herman Melville, in 1850: 'God has predestined, mankind expects, great things from our race; and great things we feel in our souls.'

It was 'a city upon a hill', John Winthrop preached, referring to his new land. 'For we must consider that we shall be as a city upon a hill. The eyes of all people are upon us.' Here lie the religious roots of what has been called American 'exceptionalism', the deep conviction that America is a country specially chosen and blessed by God, that American norms and values are universal, and that every person should think according to those values, since otherwise they will lag behind in their development. Such feelings are widespread. Six out of ten Americans believe their culture is superior to all others, as opposed to only three in ten French people, for example. According to this way of thinking, America has a unique moral status in the world and will therefore always play a unique role in history. Based on that notion, America can and must intervene time and again in world events.

This exceptionalism explains why in the American press 'American lives' are consistently treated as of a higher order than other lives, why important treaties and principles of international law are seen as invalid in the case of America, why most Americans find it perfectly natural that until recently 'their' dollar enjoyed an apparently inviolable status, and why the laws of history do not apply to them – or so they assume.

Woe betide the politician who, like Barack Obama, seems to doubt this, even for a moment. The rest of the inhabitants of our planet look on with astonishment and sometimes a degree of disquiet.

'Except in moments of aberration we do not think of ourselves as the potential masters, but as tutors of mankind in its pilgrimage to perfection,' wrote Reinhold Niebuhr in 1952, but at the same time he issued a severe warning against this misleading myth. All those years ago he was already drawing attention to 'our dreams of managing history', a tendency that may eventually prove fatal to the United States.

He was not alone. Twenty years later, in his much-read analysis of American culture, sociologist Philip Slater wrote about 'one of the oldest and deepest myths in the American psyche, the fantasy of being special'. Even former neo-conservatives, such as Robert Kagan and Francis Fukuyama, have gradually come to believe that American economics and politics rely too much on unearned privilege – or, as Fukuyama put it, on a 'belief in American exceptionalism that most non-Americans simply find not credible'. All these sensible words are to little avail. Reality or not, most Americans believe profoundly that they are special, perhaps now more than ever.

Five

THE SHAKER SETTLEMENT OF CANTERBURY is an empty shell today. The last Shakers to live here died in the late twentieth century. What remains is a museum. It consists of a few plain timber buildings, some simple furniture, and a handful of utensils of the kind I find hard to credit as already having the status of museum exhibits: scissors, needles, oven gloves, milk churns and a wooden wheelbarrow. The walls are white and chaste. Next to the barn you can watch a cider-pressing demonstration, and further on there's a special sale of Shaker apple tarts. Upstairs I hear a tape recording of Sister Mildred Barker (1897–1990) giving a rendition of old children's songs:

> Come little children, come to Zion
> Come little children, march along
> And your clothing and your dress
> Shall be a robe of righteousness.

In the shop the Shaker products, famous for their plain, almost Scandinavian design, are selling fast. A wooden box containing fish hooks with a fish painted on the lid: 95 dollars. A wooden fruit bowl: 275 dollars. A wooden well bucket: 395 dollars. They no longer have any association with ideals to live by, but you can still buy them, those purifying emotions, for 95, 275 or 395 dollars.

John Steinbeck was no puritan, but he did aim for a certain simplicity during his voyage, for reasons that had to do with his worldview. He was an old-fashioned American in that sense, with no faith in those ready-made things that stood gleaming at him. His Rocinante was a typical puritan vehicle, without chrome or tail fins, that eschewed fashion in every sense, made simply to function reliably for as long as possible.

The decision to drive a no-nonsense GMC truck, in those years especially, was a form of protest against the fledgling consumer society. The same applies to the multiplicity of tools he lugged around with him. Far from the throwaway generation, Steinbeck clearly belonged to the repair generation, accustomed to taking his fate in his own hands when faced with calamities large or small, knowing that it was possible to survive with little or no money by relying purely on his own strength and skill. To that extent he lived in the classic American tradition of independence, which runs all the way from the Puritans to today's Tea Party and can be summed up in two sentences: 'I'll fix it myself. Leave me alone!'

From Deerfield he drove northwards through Maine for two days, on his way to Deer Isle, another compulsory stopping point not to be missed, according to his trusty agent Elizabeth Otis. A place had been arranged for Rocinante to spend the night, with a certain Miss Eleanor Brace. The autumn air, he wrote, already had 'a sweet burn of frost'. Shooting resounded from the hills. The hunting season had begun.

Now that I'm following him, I notice how fast Steinbeck drove, in that rattling Rocinante of his. The first day he took it easy, as he had planned to do, but soon he was making good time. Even on those old roads he covered some 250 to 300 miles a day. He complained about the low maximum speed in some states; fifty miles an hour was simply annoying. Outside the cities there was hardly anyone else on the road. It soon began to rain. 'The roads are very long,' he wrote to Elaine. 'It's a big damn country. And I find I get tired in the behind over two hundred miles.' He had taken an inflatable boat seat with him, which helped a little. His main distraction was the crackly FM radio with its two round knobs in the middle of the dashboard. The top hit that autumn was 'Itsy Bitsy Teenie Weenie Yellow Polka Dot Bikini' and the singer, Brian Hyland, probably drove Steinbeck crazy with it.

Half a century later not a great deal has changed. From the speakers pour plaintive guitar girls and slow rock bands, hour after hour, an endless stream of wallpaper pap. The landscape has become more rugged now, as have the buildings. Alongside elegant timber villas and farmhouses I see wrecked caravans from time to time, and abandoned barns. The grassy meadows have gone, and we are driving across bare fields scattered with rocks as far as the eye can see. The forests are mainly conifer. It's colder here, too, much colder – but that's partly because the weather has turned.

Sunday comes around. In *Travels with Charley* Steinbeck goes to church just once. Somewhere in Vermont he put on a suit, polished his shoes and 'took [his] way with dignity' to a church of 'blindingly white ship lap'. No Steinbeck scholar has ever been able to determine quite where it was. Vermont, after all, is full of white wooden churches. The minister, 'a man of iron with tool-steel eyes and a delivery like a pneumatic drill' did make a profound impression, however. He 'spoke of hell as an expert, not the mush-mush hell of these soft days, but a well-stoked, white-hot hell served by technicians of the highest order'. It left Steinbeck with a delightful feeling of sinfulness that stayed with him for days. 'I hadn't been thinking very well of myself for some years, but if my sins had this dimension there was some pride left.'

Going to church was one of Steinbeck's ways of getting to know his country again, and it was a good idea. America is an extraordinarily religious place, and much of the congregation would have taken even the minister's hellfire sermon literally. Belief in hell has declined somewhat over recent decades, but heaven remains a real presence. For week after week as I retrace Steinbeck's journey, the book *Heaven is for Real: A Little Boy's Astounding Story of His Trip to Heaven and Back* is on the Amazon.com bestseller list. According to the latest surveys, nearly two-thirds of Americans believe in the devil and hell, almost three-quarters in heaven, and four out of five in a personal God who is actively present in their lives. As far as religion is concerned, Europe has changed a great deal over the past half-century. Barely half its citizens believe in God. It's an odd contradiction. The American Revolution and the Constitution that flowed from it are products of the Enlightenment through and through, yet there is hardly a single politician who will admit to being an atheist. Disputing the existence of God is political suicide; you'd be better off as a Muslim, or gay.

The striking religiosity of Americans, certainly in comparison to Europeans, undoubtedly has to do with the foundations of American nationalism, the sense of being part of an exclusive community, blessed and chosen by God. In countless customs and rituals – oaths, public holidays, or the pledge of allegiance that schoolchildren are forced to swear, hand on heart, every day – this notion is confirmed and reiterated. The rugged natural environment and the vagaries of gloves-off capitalism may have played a part as well, by making Americans more dependent on fate, on forces beyond their control, and therefore more submissive to God and religion. Steinbeck was an exception in that sense. In the rest of his story he doesn't mention any other church service, and I fear nothing further came of his good intentions with regard to churchgoing.

I want to improve on that. Churches here are social as well as religious communities, far more so than in Europe. When you see Americans in their churches, with all their community work and other social activities, you can hardly call them individualistic. In fact, quite the opposite. In contrast to Europe, participation in a community is not a simple fact, something handed to you by history, so to speak, but the result of a conscious choice. In the tradition of settlers, pioneers and immigrants, it doesn't simply go without saying that you'll continue to live in the neighbourhood or village where you grew up, remaining loyal to the old crowd and going to the church that your parents attended.

A quarter of Americans have changed their faith. Almost half of all Protestants switch churches at least once in their lives. You make that kind of choice yourself, and you can revisit it, just as you can start your life afresh here, time and again. In that respect, everything is a deal, a contract. Americans feel free to join a group or to move on, but as long as they are members it's for better and for worse. Some talk of a 'love it or leave it' rule. That, as sociologist Ann Swidler puts it, is 'America's brand of individualism', the idea that a person is free to choose his or her own community. It applies even to churches.

In Camden, a north-of-England-style factory town on the coast of Maine, I walk into a service for the first time on this trip. In the respectable Chestnut Street Baptist Church they've had little difficulty as yet with 'product refreshment'. It's not the kind of church I'm used to, however. It's all far more sociable. Almost half of actively religious Americans do regular voluntary work for the poor and homeless, compared to only one in six non-churchgoers. The same applies to all kinds of charity work.

Religious Americans spend, on average, twice as much money and energy on (even non-religious) good causes as non-religious Americans.

If you are feeling lost and forsaken in this country, go to a church. I'm not stared at for being a stranger here but welcomed from all sides, by the minister, by people sitting in nearby pews – in a continual round of introductions and handshakes – and by a deacon who soon invites me to lunch and hands me a welcome packet: 'Our service brings the best of all generations together – today's generation with that of long ago.'

We stand up and sing old hymns. I know most of them from my own Protestant past, so they must have crossed the Atlantic at some point and perhaps even back again. 'Holy, holy, holy, Lord God almighty . . .' The minister, his face round and friendly, bows his head and leads the prayers: for two newborn babies, for a man who fell off a roof and broke his leg, for a member of the congregation who had a heart attack last week – 'Praise the Lord, he's had surgery and is home again!' – for another member who is fighting his insurance company because he needs an operation and can't pay for it – 'Lord, guard his heart against bitterness.'

The sermon is no more than a gentle admonition. 'You wouldn't drive to California without a road map, would you? The Bible is our road map. Showing us the way to heaven!' The choir sings 'Seek Ye First', in parts, full and slow. 'That was truly beautiful,' the minister sighs when they finish. 'Can you imagine how the choirs in heaven will sing for us when we arrive there?' No, the Reverend Adam Kohlstrom does not resemble in the slightest the preacher of fire and brimstone that Steinbeck happened upon.

Deer Isle is half a day away. It's part of a coastal landscape of wooded islands and peninsulas that stretches for hundreds of miles along the Atlantic coast: clumps of trees in the grey sea, black-and-green islands with sandy beaches, the ground half grass and half moss, scattered with the last yellow and pale-blue wildflowers of autumn. Close to the water's edge is a stench of resin and rotting seaweed. The air is filled night and day with the rustle of pine trees, punctuated by a few gulls and far away the short blast of a ship's horn. Other than that, everything is deserted.

The hushed, almost magical atmosphere of this archipelago made a deep impression on Steinbeck. Deer Isle reminded him of Dorset or Somerset, the land of King Arthur. He arrived late, with no Sandy to tell him the way, getting lost in Bangor and later in Ellsworth before finally crossing the big iron bridge to the island, 'as high arched as a rainbow', and following a winding road through the pine forests. There stood the old house owned by Miss Brace. It was Monday evening, 26 September.

His visit was highly enjoyable, to judge by a letter to Elaine. Except that he had lost his ease of writing, as if *The Winter of Our Discontent* had sucked him dry. In his official account of the trip he describes above all the quality of the autumn light, so clear that each tree 'seems itself and separate'. In Stonington he finds a wonderful hardware store where he picks up an excellent kerosene lamp. Charley has a hard time, though. George, Miss Brace's grey cat, is a thoroughly unpleasant creature, full of animosity towards people and other animals.

Did Steinbeck omit one particular event? In his account he makes no mention of it, but according to a letter he wrote to Adlai Stevenson he was watching it at least part of the time. That same Monday evening, between half past nine and half past ten, just as Steinbeck was introducing himself at Miss Brace's, American history was made.

Everything turned on that first-ever live election debate, between Vice-President Richard M. Nixon and Senator John F. Kennedy. The confrontation occurred at a crucial moment. The country had been ruled for almost thirty years by three presidents, each of whom, in his own way, had set his stamp on the rise of America as an industrial and military imperial power. In the years that followed, the Civil Rights Movement erupted – and with it a full-on youth revolution. During the campaign of 1960, however, there was little sign of any of that.

In 1960 the two candidates were regarded very differently from the way we see them now. I have described them as 'man of the people' and 'rich kid', and that is how half of America saw them, but we might also interpret their battle as the courageous fight by an outsider – the Catholic Kennedy – against a vice-president – Nixon – who had been at the centre of power for over a decade already.

Richard Nixon was far from popular in liberal and progressive circles, but he was certainly not the notorious figure he has since become. John Kennedy, for his part, was not the statesman described in today's school textbooks. In fact the two candidates had a lot in common, or so people felt at the time. They were relatively young and brash. Their age was a break with tradition in itself, since they both belonged to the generation whose turn to lead the country had not yet come around. Nevertheless, during the campaign Nixon stressed his experience, and therefore the preservation of the status quo. Kennedy chose the slogan 'Moving Again', which expressed the restlessness that was characteristic of the period.

Nixon had been chosen as vice-president twice. He commanded respect for his astonishing energy, having fought his way out of a poverty-stricken environment. He was an excellent debater, and he had the support of big business and the incumbent president.

John F. Kennedy – Jack to those closest to him – was by contrast seen as a semi-playboy who had achieved nothing spectacular. For all the thirteen years he'd spent in the House of Representatives and the Senate, he did not have a single piece of important legislation to his name. The story filling the airwaves – and there is an obvious parallel here with the mythmaking surrounding the election of the 'Muslim' Barack Obama – was that if it elected Kennedy, America would in fact be run by the pope. Catholics like Kennedy, the reasoning went, believed the pope was infallible, and therefore they must obey him in everything.

Moreover, the name Kennedy was associated with the systematic buying of influence and political power. The Kennedys were typical parvenus. Father Joe had made a fortune on Wall Street in the 1920s and then spotted an opportunity to shepherd that fortune through the Crash and the Great Depression almost entirely intact. There are strong indications that he had contacts in criminal circles, although nothing has ever been proved. Despite his reputation, Roosevelt appointed him as the first chairman of the new Securities and Exchange Commission, the stock market watchdog. There, Joe Kennedy acquired a taste for public office. He decided to invest part of his fortune in power and prestige, for the whole family. By making a huge contribution to Roosevelt's campaign fund, he more or less bought the office of ambassador to Great Britain.

Kennedy and Roosevelt did not remain friends. The writer Gore Vidal heard years later from Eleanor Roosevelt that the presidential couple had invited Joe Kennedy, who was vacationing in America, to their country estate and that straight after his first face-to-face conversation with the president he was thrown out. Roosevelt, trembling and white with rage, said, 'I never want to see that man ever again as long as I live.' It was a unique event, not least because Roosevelt so rarely displayed anger.

Joe Kennedy was an appeaser who advocated doing a deal with Hitler, and it seems likely he was following a line of his own in London, against the express instructions of the Roosevelt administration. Eleanor never talked about the cause of the incident, but she did recall having to drive him around for hours before she could put him on the next train home. She described the episode – 'the most dreadful four hours of my life' – to Vidal, laughing as she did so, although after a pause she said she wondered whether 'the true story of Joe Kennedy will ever be known'.

Scepticism about John F. Kennedy among the older generation of polit-icians and opinion-formers, including Steinbeck, was therefore understand-able. Yet even before the election he was being compared to Franklin D. Roosevelt, Churchill and other great heroes. He undoubtedly had positive qualities, including pluck. His series of portraits of staunch American sena-tors, Profiles in Courage, had won him a Pulitzer Prize and during the Pacific War he acted with extraordinary bravery. But it was his charisma that made the difference in those uncertain times. 'He would seem at one moment older than his age, forty-eight or fifty, a tall, slim, sunburned professor with a pleasant weathered face, not even particularly handsome,' wrote Norman Mailer, who reported on the election of Kennedy for Esquire. 'Five minutes later, talking to a press conference on his lawn, three microphones before him, a television camera turning, his appearance would have gone through a metamorphosis, he would look again like a movie star, his coloring vivid, his manner rich, his gestures strong and quick, alive with that concentration of vitality a successful actor always seems to radiate.'

Neither candidate was entirely new and untainted. McCarthy was still around in some sense, if only in the background. Although a Democrat, old Joe Kennedy had always supported the hunt for communists whole-heartedly and McCarthy was a regular visitor to the Kennedy home: son

Robert had worked for him, the daughters went to social events with him, and even John never said a word against him. Richard Nixon, even more so than the Kennedys, had been directly involved in the crusade since 1948, when a well-known advisor to President Roosevelt by the name of Alger Hiss was accused of being a communist spy. As a young member of the House Committee on Un-American Activities, Nixon managed to produce more and more evidence, and eventually Hiss was charged with espionage (almost certainly with good reason in this instance, as we now know from Soviet sources) and convicted of perjury.

The Hiss affair represented a great breakthrough for Nixon and the new Republican story: Roosevelt, the president who had steered the country through the crisis and the war, had in reality bargained away America and Europe; the weak Democrat elite had been blind to the rising Red Peril; the moral values of ordinary America had been betrayed.

Nixon banged on along these lines for years, echoing McCarthy. He described leading Democrats such as Harry Truman, Dean Acheson and Adlai Stevenson as aiding the 'communist conspiracy' and did all he could to cast doubt on their patriotism. American politics had always been rough, but Nixon and McCarthy overstepped a boundary, throwing the entire system out of balance. They called into question not just their opponents' political beliefs but their love of their country, their identity as Americans.

The Democrats brooded for a long time on how to respond, until in October 1957 the Soviets became the first to fire a satellite, the Sputnik, into space. Shortly afterwards William Stuart Symington, a Democrat senator with a great talent for demagogic slogans, introduced the concept of a 'missile gap'. America's rocket technology was lagging hopelessly behind, he claimed, and in the foreseeable future the country would become easy prey to the advanced rockets built by the Soviets, with their unimaginably destructive atomic warheads. The term caught on immediately. The United States, wrote the *Washington Post*, was 'facing the greatest danger in its history'. John Kennedy quickly realised the value of the theme and recast the missile gap as a formidable weapon in the campaign: just look at how the Republicans have neglected our defences for years and how we, the Democrats, are stepping up to protect our fatherland.

President Eisenhower seethed with impotent rage. He could do nothing to stop this runaway argument. The missile gap was a myth, as he well knew. His U-2 spy planes were observing tortuously slow progress in Russian missile production and it was clear that the Soviets were way behind in the field of long-range missile technology. They could build powerful rockets capable of shooting lightweight satellites into space, but they did not have the accurate guidance systems necessary to send a missile to a military target on earth. The Americans, by contrast, had a whole new generation of Titan and Atlas rockets ready that did feature that technology.

All this information, however, was strictly secret, and in their bluffing propaganda the Soviets preferred to keep the truth under wraps as well. In fact the Sputnik had been launched partly to distract attention from the weaker aspects of their rocket technology. When Kennedy replaced Eisenhower, his staff soon realised that there was indeed a missile gap, but that the Russians were on the losing side. It turned out to have been in every sense a mock battle, yet in the 1960 election campaign it was one of the central themes.

How appearance and reality intermingled in that campaign, and how Americans like John Steinbeck saw the two candidates, is illustrated by a book that was passed around among Democrats that autumn. After a tip from someone who knows about these things, I managed to pick up a copy in a second-hand bookshop. It bears the title *Kennedy or Nixon: Does it make any difference?* and it was written by Arthur Schlesinger Jr, a historian who had already made his name with an excellent biography of President Roosevelt. Like Steinbeck, he had for years been a fervent supporter of Adlai Stevenson, for whom both men had written speeches. They moved in more or less the same political circles.

Where, Schlesinger asks himself, are the exciting figures we used to have, who got drunk and wept when the Spanish Republic fell, told of beautiful and foolish dreams about the perfectibility of mankind, and applauded Roosevelt? The two candidates, he writes, are both seen as 'cool cats', without any great passions or deep convictions. They are the apotheosis of the organisation man. He quotes journalist Eric Sevareid: 'The managerial revolution has come to politics, and Nixon and Kennedy are its first completely packaged products. The Processed Politician has finally arrived.'

From that point on Schlesinger takes aim primarily at Richard Nixon, the epitome of the new type of politician who, when it comes down to it, no longer believes in anything other than winning. In fact Nixon is a typical example of a new kind of American that sociologist David Riesman described in his American character study The Lonely Crowd (1950) as other-directed, a person who focuses entirely on the surrounding community, borrowing all his or her norms, values and goals from the group of people to which he or she wants to belong, in contrast to the more traditional inner-directed American, who discovers principles and life goals inside himself and is guided primarily by inner values.

Nixon, Schlesinger writes, has excellent antennae for the mood of the country. 'If it is a McCarthyite period, then he is prudently pro-McCarthy; if a liberal period seems to be coming along, then he is prudently pro-liberal.' Everyone had become so used to his chameleon-like behaviour that no one any longer asked whether his views were consistent. As a man without inner values, he had even become alienated from the history of his own country – it clearly didn't interest him, otherwise he wouldn't have violated the basic principles of American democracy as he did in the McCarthy period. But he was very adept at what Riesman called 'false personalization', the tendency to give offices of state and impersonal relationships a personal flavour by, for example, involving his wife and children in his work whether it suited them or not. Image is all that counted.

No, give us John Kennedy. Schlesinger did not have words enough to describe his favourite. Kennedy had all those characteristics that were so obviously lacking in Nixon: a sense of history, an interest in intellectual debate, and above all a determination to focus on real problems and realistic solutions. 'The commodity Kennedy seeks to sell is his program; the commodity Nixon seeks to sell is himself.'

Schlesinger's book remains sagacious half a century later, and here and there even prophetic when he describes the character of the 'new polit-ician'. At the same time it verges on the comical when he writes about Kennedy. Later, like his brother Robert, John Kennedy would indeed sometimes show true statesmanship, as he did during the Cuban missile crisis, but if there was ever a president who transformed the White House into an image factory, if there was ever a politician who used his family to polish that image further (and to conceal a less virtuous reality) then it was John F. Kennedy. As Gore Vidal once wrote of the Kennedys: 'They create illusions and call them facts.'

Under the leadership of Adlai Stevenson, the Democrats had been through a profound process of change, Schlesinger decided, and Kennedy was Stevenson's natural heir and successor. The American contentment of the early 1950s was over, and nowhere was that fact more obvious, he wrote, than in 1960 during the Democratic convention in Los Angeles, where speechmakers had the audacity to talk of perils, uncertainties, sacrifices and goals.

At the end of that convention, Kennedy gave his animated 'New Frontier' speech, in which he called upon his fellow Americans to explore fresh boundaries. 'We stand today on the edge of a New Frontier – the frontier of the 1960s, a frontier of unknown opportunities and perils, a frontier of unfulfilled hopes and threats.'

That evening, Joe Kennedy was visiting his friend Henry 'Harry' Luce, the publishing magnate who created the Time–Life magazine empire. In his authoritative work on the American press, The Powers That Be, David Halberstam describes their conversation. The two men talked about their sons. Luce was worried about young Hank. What was to be done with him? 'Why don't you just buy him a safe congressional seat?' Joe asked. Luce, despite having more or less seen it all, was appalled. 'What do you mean by that? You can't do that!' 'Come on, Harry,' said Joe. 'You and I both know how to do it. Of course it can be done.'

Behind the new language and the young faces, the old America of political networks and carefully channelled funding went on turning.

Aside from all kinds of practicalities, that scepticism may have been the main reason why Steinbeck did not think it worth the trouble to watch the whole debate on the evening of 26 September 1960. For Nixon he had only contempt ('He can hardly talk for unmelted butter in his mouth') and he did not share Schlesinger's enthusiasm for Kennedy. To the last he openly supported his old friend Stevenson. In Steinbeck's view this election was no longer about content but purely about image.

Yet history was written that night, if only television history. For Nixon things were not looking too good by late September. He was in bad shape. In fact in August he'd spent almost two weeks in hospital with an infection. It set his travel schedule back considerably – in an unguarded moment he'd promised to visit all fifty states – and the strain was starting to take its toll. Friends warned him that for a presidential campaign you needed as much physical stamina as an Olympic athlete. Nixon ignored all that and pelted on, criss-crossing the country.

Kennedy had a magnificently efficient team behind him. He took good care of himself, gave priority to carefully selected states and used an ingenious travel itinerary to make the best possible use of his energy. It was the first presidential campaign to be fought largely on television, and both candidates were aware of that. Nixon saw himself as an expert. He was one of the first politicians to have harnessed the new medium successfully. But Kennedy used television far more effectively. As a relatively unknown senator he would probably have had little chance without the cameras, as he was only too well aware.

Portable video recorders had just become available in 1960. They cost around 100,000 dollars, but Kennedy's staff had managed to get hold of one. Every appearance was recorded and carefully analysed, first of all by Kennedy himself. His team also continually monitored the response of the audience. In the Nixon camp there was no such initiative. Richard Nixon had always been a champion debater and he knew beyond doubt that he could easily win any argument with Kennedy on content. The people on Kennedy's team were convinced of something altogether different: 'Every time we get those two fellows on the screen side by side, we're going to gain and he's going to lose.' Both camps were proved right.

The debate that Monday evening took place in the VBBM-TV studio in Chicago. Nixon arrived first. His television advisor Ted Rogers was horrified: 'The candidate looked better suited for going to a funeral, perhaps his own, than to a debate. His face was sickly gray and seemed to sag. He was nearly exhausted.' Kennedy, unlike Nixon, was thoroughly prepared. He was well rested, and with his light tan he looked like a young athlete.

In both camps a heated discussion took place in the dressing room about the use of make-up. Nixon was particularly in need of it. He had naturally pale skin and heavy stubble, which would make a dreadful impression if nothing was done to rectify it. But both candidates strug-gled with the idea of cosmetics. They were 'real men' who did not powder their noses, and they were terrified the public would find out about it if they did. The last thing either of them wanted was to be seen as a 'sissy'. In the end Kennedy was persuaded by an assistant who had considerable experience in television; the man rushed out to a drugstore on the corner for a Max Factor Creme Puff compact. Nixon categorically refused. He merely used a little powder to mask his five o'clock shadow (brand: Lazy Shave), which only made his face look all the more grey. 'He [Nixon] just looks awful,' Kennedy mumbled to his press officer, Pierre Salinger, immediately before the countdown began. He knew then that he had won.

You can watch the debate on YouTube. The most striking thing half a century later is the sober setting: a few chairs, a lectern, a moderator, four people asking questions, no audience, no clever graphics. The tone is in keeping, quiet and respectful. Communism is the great evil on the horizon, but other than that the conversation is entirely about 'more and better': even more homes than the previous government, even better medical care for the elderly, even more hospitals, schools, hydroelectric power stations and freeways.

Anyone who listened to Nixon believed him. Anyone who saw him had growing doubts. When I watched the film again, Nixon's much-discussed appearance didn't seem too bad. It was mainly his facial expressions that were his downfall. He blinked, seemed to run his tongue along his lips all the time, looked away from the camera and started to sweat heavily in the hot studio, as if he was being pushed into a corner by Kennedy.

Behind the scenes, in the control room, goings-on were bizarre. The technicians, as well as the staff of both camps, saw the pictures and understood the consequences immediately. Every aspect of the broadcast had been agreed upon beforehand in detailed negotiations. They had even decided how many shots would be shown of each candidate while his rival was speaking. During the actual broadcast, all that was turned on its head. The Kennedy team wanted the cameras to keep focusing on the sweating Nixon, the more the better. Ted Rogers of the Nixon camp called for as many connecting shots of the unruffled Kennedy as possible, just as long as their candidate was kept off the screen.

In retrospect, that broadcast was decisive for the outcome of the election. On all fronts, image won out over content. Between sixty and eighty-five million Americans were watching, and to television viewers it was clear who had won. Nixon's great advantage, his eight years of experience as vice-president, was swept away in a single evening. 'My God,' exclaimed Dick Daley, boss of the famous Chicago party machine, 'they've embalmed him before he even died.' Nixon's mother called, worried, to check that he felt okay. Outside the studio a woman, apparently a supporter, broke through the cordon and cheered Nixon on: 'That's all right. You'll do better next time.' Her final, killer comment was not spontaneous, incidentally. The woman had been paid to say it by the dirty-tricks division of the Kennedy campaign.

For the seventeen million radio listeners, concentrating on the content, there was no clear winner or loser. They – and when I listened again I had the same experience – heard a Kennedy whose high-pitched voice made him come over as slightly stuck-up, whereas Nixon's deeper tones sounded extremely convincing. In Texas, Kennedy's running mate Lyndon B. Johnson sat listening to the radio feeling grim. He was convinced Kennedy had blown it: 'The boy didn't win.' Steinbeck, who followed the campaign from then on largely by listening to the radio and reading the newspapers, didn't know what to think. To Elaine he wrote that Kennedy had turned out to be a better debater than he'd expected, and that someone he knew – a Republican at that – was certain he was going to win. But the few people he spoke to on the subject were just as confused as he was.

There was one high-school student in a little town called Wheaton (near Chicago) for whom the outcome was clear. To the young Bob Woodward, soon to become one of the most important of American journalists, Richard Nixon was the born saviour of the fatherland. He thought Kennedy a weirdo, with that strange accent of his. The debate reassured him. America would never choose as its president a man who was so obviously a 'faggot' as John F. Kennedy.

Six

WE'RE DRIVING THROUGH the last September week of 2010. The *Boston Globe* reports that their city's Ford Lincoln dealership is being forced to close its showroom. You can't make a living from two car sales a week. The main rival, the Japanese Lexus Toyota, is selling thirteen times as many products. On the front page of the *Livermore Falls Advertiser*, Paul Beal – deep tan, Stetson – watches his pony perform at the annual Apple Pumpkin Festival. The *Coös County Democrat* reports that Sally Edmondson from Berlin went off the road trying to avoid a wapiti, a kind of deer that Americans call an elk. In the letters page of the *Rochester Democrat and Chronicle*, William Listra describes buying a new mixer: 'What do I see? A Black & Decker – can't get any more American than that. It is sturdy, and inexpensive. I think they used to make these in Brockport . . . Oops, Made in China. Next: China, China, China, Mexico, China . . .'

The potato harvest has begun. Mike Michaud, US Representative for Maine's 2nd congressional district, utters a cry of distress in the *Houlton Pioneer Times* ('The only newspaper in the world interested in Houlton, Maine') – in 2008 China passed the US as market leader in the paper industry. 'Having worked in a papermill in East Millinocket for nearly thirty years, I watched my hometown declining when the papermill shut down . . . When the mill shut down, the town didn't know if it would have enough money to keep the school running.'

Maine is a strange protuberance of the United States. As Steinbeck writes, it 'sticks up like a thumb into Canada'. On his trail we slowly trek along the east coast, northwards, passing little British and Scandinavian towns and crossing riverbeds, marshy fields and endless butter-coloured birch woods. From time to time someone passes in the other direction. The days are grey and it gets dark early now. We leave the coast, heading for Houlton, Presque Isle and Caribou. Now and then a gentle rain falls.

As ever, this is potato country, but the masses of Francophone Canadians who slipped over the border in Steinbeck's day to earn a few extra cents grubbing them up are gone. Here and there in the muddy fields large harvesting machines are at work. Hardly any humans are involved now. The houses and barns along the way become greyer and smaller. Often they look raggedy and neglected; in many places, one in every four or five houses has a 'For Sale' sign. 'We see the jigsaw puzzle of our lives, and we sit there in despair holding the loose pieces,' says a woman's voice on the radio. 'But God knows the final result. He knows where the last bits of that puzzle need to go. He guides your hand and says: "Your life will be great, and will serve the greatest of goals."'

Maine, I'm told, has two kinds of inhabitants: 'Natives' and 'From Aways'. If you don't happen to have been born close to where the conversation is taking place, then you're a From Away. The largest cities, Bangor and Portland, have no more residents than a small Dutch provincial town, and people here are indeed a little like people in the provinces of Friesland or Groningen: silent, extremely trustworthy (none of the houses are locked) and very helpful. Charging money for minor repairs is not done. As in outlying districts the world over these days, the young and clever leave for the cities. Nearby Boston is home to 645,000 people, half the population of the entire state of Maine. Those who have stayed are getting older and, on average, compared to the rest of New England, their level of education is low and declining.

This wet and muddy region is bristling with new plans, as peripheral areas often are: energy-saving schemes, the expansion of small communities, education of all sorts. There is a need for more self-confidence, writes the *Bangor Daily News*, but 'just as a hot dog stand doesn't compete with a white table cloth restaurant, Maine must accept and maximize its niche'. Some of the planners, warns the columnist, have a tendency to look in the mirror and think they are seeing Brad Pitt. 'Isn't it important for people to confront reality and to act accordingly?'

Robust election campaigning is underway all over the country this autumn, for the House of Representatives and the Senate, but also to elect governors, mayors, judges, sheriffs and other local public officials. In the rain, in between the 'For Sale' signs, election posters glide by, one in almost every front garden. Most are for a man called LePage. Yes, the Republican favourite for governor, Paul LePage, is coming to save Maine – the businessman who told the National Association for the Advancement of Colored People 'kiss my butt' and Obama to 'go to hell', and said that the only disadvantage to the toxic fumes given off by a certain sort of plastic was that 'some women may have little beards . . . and we don't want that'.

At Winter Harbor we happen upon a stretch of old road in the woods. The white lines are still just visible; the asphalt has been cracked by tree roots, the edges overgrown by bushes, grass and fungi. It's possible that Steinbeck drove along it in Rocinante, the rain drumming on the roof. In his letters to Elaine he complained of feeling exhausted and then having to look in the dark for a place to stop. 'There isn't a soul anywhere about, to invite to join me. You'd be amazed how deserted much of this north country is.'

We find beds in a tired-looking, timber hotel. Outside, the squirrels run around on an empty porch. Downstairs, in front of some leather chairs, a huge wood fire is burning. There are two other guests, two hunters. 'Coffee?' 'Mmm.' 'Deer?' 'Not bad.' 'The terrain?' 'Okay.' The silence is oppressive. The only sound comes from the pet parrot rattling its perch.

The owner joins us. He has no one but hunters to stay now. Next month they'll be shooting duck again, but no, it's not like it used to be. 'If you only knew what kind of paperwork it all involves. Permits, forms, we never used to have to deal with any of that. But some people here still live by hunting to some extent.' He wants to sell the hotel and asks whether I might be interested. He can't make a go of it here any longer. 'I earn twenty to thirty thousand a year. Two to four thousand of that goes in taxes. But someone who earns twenty or thirty million doesn't pay a cent. How can that be right?'

Does everyone think the same way about it? 'People blame Obama now, as if he didn't inherit a huge mess from George Bush. They seem to have forgotten that. And they're confused. One TV channel claims one thing, another the direct opposite.' As for him, he doesn't want to hear any more on the matter, from either party. 'The whole lot of them are in it together. They never live up to any of their promises.' His eyes harden. 'There's going to be a revolution here one day, I often tell myself. Perhaps even sooner than we think.'

There's another long silence. Outside the fog is thickening. The hunters mumble at the bar, the parrot screeches, a few dogs bark, a chair scrapes.

The next day the car radio suddenly picks up the calm voice of a typical British newsreader. Long live the CBC! We draw close to the Canadian border and then drive along it for a while, through a region of lakes, woods and marshes, with the grey-blue of mountains full of promise in the distance. On both sides of the road are Victorian villas, caravans and wooden huts, all jumbled together. The number of dilapidated structures increases rapidly: old garages, sheds, half-collapsed houses, a corroding piece of Canadian rolling stock, a blackened and burned-out gas station, even a church succumbing to subsidence. Outside its door is a large white noticeboard saying: 'God is like Scotch Tape. You can't see Him, but you know He's there.'

In the general store in Brookton, the only shop for miles around, I get talking with a couple of retired farmers. We chat about local history. From time to time, just as Steinbeck did, I've seen ramshackle houses that looked as if they'd been squashed by a Huge Evil Thumb from Above, pressed into the ground and broken open. Yes, it was indeed the snow that did that. 'Two years ago, for example, we had more than ten metres of snow, and the whole weight of it stayed lying all winter. Some houses, especially the rundown ones, can't take it. That's simply what it's like around here.'

My fellow customers begin to tell me, in detail, that this store is all that remains of a whole complex of shops and hotels that once stood here. They all went broke in the 1930s and were abandoned, like so many businesses in Maine. In the 1980s there was another wave of closures. Snow is not the only cause. 'Those collapsed houses. Some of them are ruins left over from the Great Depression.'

We drive on. It's starting to rain again. The rivers we cross are covered in foam and pieces of driftwood race past. Here and there the water flows over the road. The newspapers tell me that this is one of the poorest parts of the generally impoverished state of Maine. As in Europe, farming people are still around, but the farms have merged time and again. That was happening even when Steinbeck was here – every year some two per cent of American farmers called it a day. Between 1980 and 1990, however, the process gathered speed: in ten years the average size of farms doubled. Now there are hardly any small farmers left, and the consequences are obvious: smaller families, a greying population, shops, banks and cooperatives that have shut down, and empty churches.

At Kinney's Garage in Danforth I take the opportunity to fill the tank. Next to me is an elderly woman with bright blue eyes, grey hair and a snub nose. You can still see how beautiful and proud she once was. Her dark-green truck is muddy and dented, and she has an appearance to match: a gnarled body, her right arm maimed and bent by some atrocity or other. As the pump counts away the gallons she looks out over the hills, forgetting about time. The petrol overflows and startles her awake.

In *Travels with Charley* John Steinbeck describes a dreamlike scene in which he sits in the cabin of Rocinante with a few of those potato-grubbing Canucks, dispatching a bottle of good cognac – a cheerful, cosy evening of precisely the kind he'd envisaged. In his letters to Elaine, however, I find no trace of that gathering. He was mostly alone. In the roadside cafés men sat silently over their coffee as if they knew each other's stories already. 'It's very odd,' he writes. 'I haven't been very far from New York yet but I seem to have been on another planet. So much of Maine is solitary and deserted.'

Between seven and eight in the morning all over America, groups of men, plus the occasional woman, still gather in diners, cafés and other roadside restaurants to eat eggs, sausages, bacon, toast, baked beans and pancakes together. The quantities are lethal by European standards. Often the men are drivers, farmers or labourers, sometimes specialists with a job to do in the local district, and in rural areas in particular you regularly come upon established groups of pensioners.

The rooms where they dine are usually divided up by partitions, with Formica tables and brown or green leatherette seats. On the walls are diplomas, family photos, sometimes a hunting trophy, and without fail a colourful outdoor scene, perhaps of a big black bear cautiously crossing a forest stream. The waitresses are fabulous, women who exude a steely warmth, know everyone by name, don't make you wait for a second, and smile ceaselessly beneath their cheap make-up. They do all that from five o'clock in the morning, for four dollars an hour plus tips.

Like Steinbeck I quickly develop a habit of looking for one of these gathering places in the early morning as soon as I get up. It never takes more than a few minutes. Sometimes nothing comes of it. The sons and grandsons of the men Steinbeck wrote about still sit staring silently into their coffee cups; as far as that goes, nothing seems to have changed. But if you wait a while, something usually does happen. Even in Maine.

Take Al's Diner, in the little settlement of Mars Hill, where I find myself because we are sleeping at the Bear Paw Inn opposite. It's Wednesday 29 September at a quarter past seven. Large flocks of geese fly over, honking in the cool of the morning. Inside it's busy. A new pipeline to Alaska is being laid nearby and the workers gather here. As in the rest of the world, farmers sit with farmers, labourers with labourers, townspeople with townspeople. The men – chequered shirts, baseball caps – are as heavy as the potatoes they've pulled out of the ground all their lives. A farmer with a limp, wearing braces and dark glasses, stands up and comes over to shake hands with me, a stranger. 'He's the local millionaire,' the man next to me whispers, 'but he does a lot for the people around here.' The men eat their Super Sunrise breakfast and talk about the weather, the harvest, the taxes and other vicissitudes that can trouble a guy.

My neighbour at the bar is called David. He spent his life in the woods as a sawyer, and now he's retired. By chance, the results of the latest American census have just been published in the morning papers. David has seen the article. Of all the money earned in America, the richest twenty per cent of the population, those earning more than 100,000 dollars, get almost half the total, 49.4 per cent to be precise. The poorest 20 per cent get a thirtieth, 3.4 per cent. So the income ratio between the poorest and richest income groups is now 1 to 14.5. In 1968 it was 1 to 7.6.

'I've had to pay insurance all my life,' grumbles David. 'These farmers here, millionaires some of them, had almost nothing deducted because, supposedly, they gave people work. No one takes account of the fact that I was paid ten dollars an hour and my boss earned twenty-five from me.

They still get that reduction. It's like that with everything. All those extra tax cuts for the rich are still in place. If someone earns a lot, fine, but the fact that he gets tax breaks because of it while I have to pay the full whack, that's too crazy, isn't it? After eight years of Bush we were desperate for change. We all voted for Obama, but nothing happened.'

Another handful of facts: the number of households living on food stamps has risen by a good two million to 11.7 million; the number of married couples is falling, since people delay marriage when they have no work and are uncertain about their economic future; two-thirds of Americans expect their children to be worse off than they themselves are.

Is that the big difference between now and the 1960s? Yesterday I sat talking for a while with a retired couple. 'Everyone may have been poorer then,' the woman said, 'but the mood was completely different. If you went to college, you knew you'd get a job at the end of it. And if you had a job you knew you'd soon be able to buy a car.' The man was of the same mind: 'If you put aside a week's wages every month, you knew you could get enough money from the bank to buy a house. And you knew that after a few years you'd be able to buy a bigger house and that the old one would have risen in value. For our children, all those certainties have vanished.'

David says something similar: 'In 1960 I earned twenty-five dollars a week, and a family could live on that. Now men and women both have to work, practically everywhere, to keep their heads above water.' He goes on: 'If you worked for a good company, like mine, then you were insured and you had a decent pension. You could take that for granted. Until about ten years ago. Everything is on the slide now. You can't rely on anything.'

I ask how young people here are reacting. 'They feel insecure. We knew we were building something up and we took our time. Now everything has to happen at once, straight away, now, because tomorrow may be too late. And everything is running dry; there's no work any longer. In nineteen sixty we all worked in potatoes. At harvest time everyone had to get out into the fields. All that work has been taken over by machines, and machines don't get tired, don't complain, don't make demands.'

We talk about the village communities that are having a hard time in

these conditions, just as they are in Europe. Half the diner starts to join
in our conversation. 'It's really not too bad here at all,' David believes.
'We're a close-knit community. If someone needs help and the insurance
won't pay, then everyone comes together to hold fundraisers, sales, whatever they can think of. They don't let you down around here.'

'We're tough, you know,' says one of the other men. 'Even when we're
down in the dirt we think: this is only for a while; better times will
come. That always gets us back on our feet.' Some start to call out
comments about President Obama's new health insurance scheme. No
one likes the fact that healthcare will be free, not even an old working
man like David. 'If something is free, people will abuse it, that's inevitable,'
he says with great conviction. 'They'll go to the doctor far too often and
take far too much medication because it doesn't cost them anything. No,
it's not a good plan.'

There isn't actually all that much debate between left and right at these
tables. Most of the men are united by a collective anger at politics in
general and 'politicians' in particular. The greater the gap between rich
and poor becomes, the more intense the distrust seems to be.

'Hank,' says one of them. 'Just take Hank, a man we've known for
years. He used to come here regularly. Trustworthy guy. He goes into
politics and we all vote for him. After a year we have a small problem
here. We ring Hank. But, oh no, suddenly it's this rule and that rule and
we don't have any way in. Politics poisons everyone.' Another man says:
'We have more and more trouble with high diesel and gas prices, it's
starting to become a real problem. That's all politics, too.' I tell him that
in Europe it costs four times as much to fill the tank, but that doesn't
concern anyone. 'No, no, it doesn't have anything to do with scarcity.'

Now David starts telling me about a man in Houlton who invented a
carburettor thirty years ago that made it possible to drive a hundred miles
to the gallon. 'The oil companies bought the guy out, for a million dollars.
And every year he got a new car. That's how it went. Politics, all of it.'

Morning after morning, over eggs, bacon, beans and weak coffee, I watch
the optimism and certainties of an entire middle class disappear. In fact
I see the middle class itself going under. In the 1960s John Kennedy was
justified in declaring that 'a rising tide lifts all boats'. That was the

economic side of American exceptionalism: in America, the idea was that everyone who pulled up his sleeves could earn enough to have a family and support it. With a bit of luck, and if you worked extra hard, then even if you started out poor you could fairly quickly join the middle class. You might possibly get spectacularly rich: from newspaper boy to oil magnate. Anyone who behaved decently was guaranteed not to get any poorer.

That story held true, the general drift of it at least, from the eighteenth century, when the pioneer homes in Deerfield slowly filled with luxuries, through the nineteenth, when those items spread to the farthest reaches of the prairies, and into the twentieth with its cars, electrical goods and bigger and bigger houses – each generation had it better than the last, until the 1970s.

Then everything changed. It wasn't like the Great Depression; it happened more gradually. Wages stopped rising, American industry started to outsource work to low-wage countries, automation steadily destroyed jobs, and more women started to work.

Many of the people I spoke to described American society today as made up of haves and have-nots, and the majority by far put themselves in the latter category. The figures tell the same story. If you add everything up – wages, health insurance premiums, pensions, tax – the vast majority of American employees are worse off now than they were thirty years ago. It's difficult to let go of a dream, especially one so convincing and inspiring as the American Dream. For most Americans the past few decades have been a time of denial: no, we can maintain our living standards just fine, this is only temporary, capitalism is a blessing for us, not a curse. They managed by having more and more members of the family work longer and longer hours. I can't count the times I heard people say that in 1960 you could support a family on one wage whereas for the average worker that was practically impossible in 2010.

The figures for female participation in the workplace say a good deal about the emancipation of women, but they also say a lot about the need for a second source of income. In 1960 only one in five women with children to care for was in paid employment. In 2007 more than three in five went out to work. Between 1947 and 1973 the actual disposable income of the average American family doubled. Between

1973 and the start of the twenty-first century it rose by only a quarter, and that was mainly because both partners were now working outside the home. American families as a whole put in considerably more hours now than they used to, between two and a half and three months extra per year on average, with all the attendant worries and problems, such as childcare and the need for a good second car.

Another way out was to gamble on a better future, which after all was supposed to be just around the corner. The number of people without insurance for healthcare or unemployment rose quickly, and in the 1960s everyone began borrowing money. Savings for a rainy day, the traditional buffer against setbacks, disappeared. In 1980 Americans were still putting aside almost 10 per cent of their incomes; in 2005 the figure was only 1.5 per cent. 'The old thrift ethic had less meaning than ever,' wrote historian Daniel Boorstin back in 1973. 'For the American Standard of Living had come to mean a habit of enjoying things before they were paid for.'

So disillusion was postponed – until that became impossible when the bubble surrounding cheap family credit burst and the crises of 2007 and 2008 erupted. Day after day, people tell me stories of unemployment: friends, neighbours, wives, children, themselves. Suddenly the route to all that easy credit has been blocked. A study by the Pew Research Center in the summer of 2010 suggested that more than half of all employees had faced a period of unemployment, wage reduction or shorter hours over the previous thirty months. The dramatic drop in house prices and stock market values cost the average household a fifth of the value of all it owned. Compared to the parental households they came from, the standard of living of one in three Americans has declined.

All these problems can be read from the dead eyes of many silent breakfast eaters, the kind of eyes I saw in the streets of Russia shortly after the collapse of the Soviet Empire. Here in America the television screens in the diners chatter cheerfully on, showing happy men and women running across fields and beaches, laughing and able-bodied, mouths open, full of expectation for all the good things this country has to offer, their teeth dazzling white. There is always a gap between the collective fantasies a country lives by and the everyday reality, but here that gap is very wide indeed.

Although the main elements of the classic image America has of itself remain in place – the focus on the future that forms part of the American Dream, the powerful sense that life is determined not by fate but by you, the certain knowledge that everything is ultimately on the up – cracks are starting to show. In that sense, 2007 was a turning point. For the first time, more than half of all Americans who were asked said that life used to be better than it is now. By 2008 that had risen to almost two-thirds.

The self-conscious certainty that people here used to have about life is no more than a memory for a growing number. Researchers at Yale University have developed something called the Economic Security Index. It gives the percentage of Americans who have been affected over the past year by a combination of three disasters: the loss of a quarter or more of their income, large medical bills, and a lack of savings sufficient to deal with such setbacks. In America, where social provision is far more patchy and primitive than in Western Europe, the results can be dramatic, with the loss of job and house, and even complete dependency on family, neighbours and friends. The average fall in income is some forty per cent. At best it takes six to eight years for a family to recover, at least to some extent, and often recovery is impossible.

In 1984 the financial ground fell from under the feet of twelve per cent of the population. In 2001 it happened to seventeen per cent, and in 2008 to more than twenty per cent. The sense of economic insecurity has been increasing for years, the researchers write, for everyone including members of the middle class. Their report concludes: 'Looking forward, Americans appear extremely vulnerable to future economic shocks, in part because of the wearing down of their basic household "buffers" against economic risks, such as personal wealth and the potential to borrow from family and friends.'

'In all my travels I saw very little real poverty,' Steinbeck wrote to his editor Pat Covici after his America expedition. 'I mean the grinding terrifying poorness of the Thirties. That at least was real and tangible. No, it was a sickness, a kind of wasting disease. There were wishes but no wants. And underneath it all the building energy like gasses in a corpse. When that explodes, I tremble to think what will be the result.'

And now? The statistics and prognoses are grim. After my return home I checked the statistics. Almost 46.2 million Americans were living in poverty in 2011, more than fifteen per cent of the population. Among the black population the figure is as high as twenty-seven per cent. The poor are rapidly getting poorer, too; 44.3 per cent of them, 20.5 million people, now live in deep poverty, with an annual income lower than half the official poverty level, under 11,000 dollars per annum. And those percentages are increasing year on year.

Not since the Great Depression of the 1930s have there been so many jobless. It's approaching ten per cent of the working-age population, and if you add up all those looking for work – part-timers seeking full-time jobs, for instance – it's almost twenty per cent. For some sectors of the population the figures are simply disastrous. Of all black Americans who leave school early, almost seventy per cent face unemployment.

My American acquaintances, in contrast to Europeans, were always remarkably optimistic in times of personal misfortune. I found that an admirable quality, but it was realistic as well. The American economy lacks the buffers and safety valves of the European welfare states, but the system also recovers far more quickly after a crisis. Americans have always been able to rely on the fact that, after a period of unemployment, people would be taken on again in large numbers. This time it's not happening, and this is the great problem.

Although the American economy is clearly recovering and companies are making good profits again, hardly anywhere is this being translated into additional jobs. Between 1940 and 1999 the number of jobs in the United States grew every decade (with the exception of the agricultural sector) by an average of twenty-seven per cent. Over the past decade it declined for the first time, by 0.8 per cent. Since 2000, automation has eliminated 5.6 million jobs in manufacturing. America is famous for innovation, but that too has stopped working as a generator of employment opportunities. Not long ago, Apple took pride in manufacturing all its products in America, but ultimately the development of the iPod, iPhone and iPad created jobs mainly in China and elsewhere in Asia, some 700,000 in total. In America itself, Apple employs only 40,000 people, a tenth of the number of jobs provided by General Motors in the 1960s when it was the largest American company.

Economists talk of a jobless recovery and assume the phenomenon is here to stay. The country's social provision is not designed to cope. As one researcher wrote: 'We have a work-based safety net without any work.'

That is the sickness, those are Steinbeck's 'gasses in a corpse' in today's America. The American economy is three times the size it was thirty-five years ago, but quality of life for the average American is surprisingly low, at least by Western European standards. One in eight Americans – and one in four American children – relies on food stamps, a form of government provision that ensures poor people have enough to eat. Hardly anyone can afford to take more than two weeks' holiday a year, and there are always worries about healthcare costs and the uncertainties of old age. I'll never forget the cashier I saw at the Walmart in Phoenix. As she packed our shopping, I looked at her wrinkled, slightly trembling hands, then up at her face. She must have been approaching eighty.

Prosperity for all, which Kennedy talked about, the rising tide that lifts all boats – for an increasing number of Americans it's a promise that will never be fulfilled. And they know it.

Meanwhile the route, through Aroostook County, is becoming increasingly lonely. The road rises and falls like a roller coaster. Now and then a sharp rain shower hammers down and autumn leaves fly at the windscreen. For a moment you can see nothing, then there is brilliant sunlight again. To the left the rolling plain is covered in forest: yellow, orange, dark red, spectacular – almost too beautiful; at home all these images would surely be regarded as kitsch. On the horizon are mountains, grey in the clouds, like distant giants.

The rafts and tree trunks that Steinbeck saw bobbing in the rivers have gone, but the huge timber stores are still here, and this part of the country is intoxicated by the scent of resin. Away from the sawmills it is deathly quiet. You can drive for ten or twenty miles without seeing so much as a barn. Now and then a huge semi-trailer passes with a load of timber, and very occasionally we see a car. Everyone is calm and polite; time is still present and plentiful here. Then suddenly I'm slamming on the brakes as a large group of wild turkeys bustles across the road.

We don't go all the way north like Steinbeck. Instead we turn back in a wide arc through Portage, Squapan, Patten and then on towards New Hampshire via Millinocket, Guilford and Rumford. Here and there lie the ruins of farmhouses. The decline of the local retailers and tradespeople, which Steinbeck observed fifty years ago, has continued ever since. We pass a big abandoned sawmill, a village store with its windows smashed in, a huge country estate and a big field of yellow flowers. In a village called Sherwood Station a high proportion of the houses are empty, the porches have collapsed, the windows are broken. The still-inhabited houses look shabby and neglected.

We drive on across a quiet lakeland region, through nineteenth-century towns with a hint of decay: an abandoned factory, a villa built in 1869, an overgrown porch romantically draped in greenery beneath heavy trees that border a fast-flowing river. 'Just a dollar?' the radio shouts. 'I'm your dollar and I'm not just a dollar. So let me get out of your pocket and buy . . .' There follows a mouth-watering description of a special offer at some hamburger chain or other. But the busy little factory towns of Maine, where Steinbeck had to weave his way through the traffic, have grown as quiet as the surrounding countryside.

In Rick's Market in Wilton, three men are stocking up on cigarettes. They work in timber. What else is there to do here? 'We used to have a clothing manufacturer, and a shoe factory. All gone. Yep.' The conversation soon turns to the weather. That's changed a good deal too, even though they don't believe all those stories about the climate. The rivers almost dried up this summer, for example. No one had ever seen that before. Less than twenty years ago it could sometimes freeze hard at night in late August. This year it was sweltering hot, as if you were living in Texas. But now they're expecting a cold front very soon. 'If we don't need to clear the snow off our roofs in November, then it's a mild winter.'

We drive on through endless forests, beside a broad river with flecks of foam on the ripples. It's a dark afternoon. The trees are wet from the rain and there's an occasional ribbon of fog. The dead are never far away. From time to time, at the edge of a wood, a small field appears full of stone and colour, with king-sized graves for everyone. At the front are always the soldiers, the dead of the Second World War and Korea to the left, those who fell in more recent conflicts, often a further dozen or so, to the right. Everywhere in America little flags are set into the ground. The fresh graves are covered with bunches of weeping carnations.

Towards evening the wind gets up. The rain is lashing down now, as if someone is holding an enormous watering can over the mountains. The pounding of rain on the Jeep's roof drowns out everything else. Sandy directs us to a motel. Steinbeck camped in Rocinante somewhere here under the trees and for him, too, everything was clammy and wet – the weather reports in the old newspapers I hunted out mention little besides 'rain, showers and thundershowers' – but he just kept on driving. I'm still amazed by the distances he would cover in a single day. He barely allowed himself any time to look around or to chat. He must have driven for days through those astonishing autumn colours, yet he devotes only one sentence to them. He surely rolled into his bed each night exhausted.

In the archives at Stanford University I came upon the original of the long letter he wrote on 1 October 1960, at the end of the first week. He was lonely. He camped at a trailer park for 'Mobile Homes', inhabited by a new generation of Americans. He felt as if he was surrounded by Martians: 'They have no humor, no past, and their future is new models,' he wrote to Elaine. On that final page he tried to compose a poem for her, in messy and partly illegible French. The neat handwriting grows chaotic. He wrote it out again and it's still impossible to comprehend. The yellow paper is crumpled and splotchy.

John was cold, he missed Elaine, he drank.

PART THREE

New Hampshire – Vermont – Canada – Detroit

'When we are all hung for what we are now doing . . .'

BENJAMIN HARRISON, VIRGINIA DELEGATE TO THE
CONTINENTAL CONGRESS, DURING THE SIGNING OF
THE DECLARATION OF INDEPENDENCE
1776

One

NOW THAT WE'VE BEEN ON THE ROAD for a while and the rhythm of travel has got into our bones, now that our suitcases have become our furniture, I notice something strange about my thoughts and dreams. They are not here. They keep flying back over the ocean, returning home. On a trip like this it seems your mind is stimulated in an odd way, not so much by the things you experience as by everything that isn't there, by everyone you've left behind, by those cities and landscapes to which you turn out to be so profoundly connected.

Home. One of the things that has always amazed me about Americans is their concept of home. Nowhere is it more intensely cultivated, more reinforced by objects and rituals than in the United States. How beautifully my old friend Edith used to say it on the answering machine: 'This is the Laub home.' It made you feel warm all over, every time. Home is a wooden house with a porch, a lawn with trees, toys lying around, a garage for messing about in, a chimney that starts smoking gently as soon as the weather turns cold.

'Home' is the block and the neighbourhood where you live. It's the place where rules and norms are laid down, from 'Should my six-year-old daughter take piano lessons or should she learn Chinese, or both?' to 'At what point do we call the cops?' It's always the place that determines your status, since here like everywhere else in the world a neighbourhood and a house are the immediate and visible signs of a person's income. Home is often a dream, too, a future dwelling you'll one day call your own – home as fulfilment in life.

American interiors often suggest that a person has lived in a place for a lifetime, that their grandparents sat around that same kitchen table listening to Roosevelt's crackly radio broadcasts and that everything will remain unchanged for centuries. 'Coming home' was the key phrase during repatriation after the Second World War. Home was the place where the family would be reunited and put down roots, where everything would come right again.

Even the tumbledown, abandoned hulks we'd passed in Maine were once very much home. A number of times we stopped outside one of those ruins, walked through the overgrown front garden, picked our way carefully across a rotten porch, wriggled inside and stepped over holes in the living room floorboards. Birds flapped their way out of the kitchen, a rusty fridge sat tilted to one side, the floor was scattered with partially decomposed catalogues from Rene J. Fournier Farm Equipment Inc., scraps of net curtain hung at the windows like cobwebs, and the remains of floral wallpaper, once so carefully chosen, clung to the walls, wet and almost completely rotten.

There is a lively trade in the symbols of security and rootedness. Travelling through New England, Steinbeck spotted so many cluttered dealerships selling junk and antiques that he concluded everything colonial America had ever produced in the way of tables, chairs and crockery must be on sale there, and a lot more besides. If he wanted to do his as-yet-unborn great-grandchildren a favour, he wrote, he would pile up all the rubbish from the garbage dumps and mothball it, so that in a century from now his descendants would be 'the antique kings of the world'.

His prediction was close to the mark. In Ellsworth we spend an hour in the local antiques-shop-cum-junk-store. Sure enough, every item from the interiors of Steinbeck's day is on sale there as an antique: tables and chairs, card games, letter scales, brown furniture, doll's houses, coffee grinders, pipe racks, books with titles like *The Golden Widow*, *The Boy Allies with the Victorious Fleet* and *The Golden Boys on the River Drive*, a Domestic electric sewing machine, a photograph of a stern-looking forebear, a zinc washboard, a pram with enormous wheels, a biography of Abraham Lincoln, a rusty Raleigh bicycle and a home-made sailing boat.

The European concept of home is often broader. It may well include the familiar surroundings of your home town, often your entire home country. In Europe, 'home' stands for the nation as a whole, whereas in

America the focus is very much on the house and what it represents: the family. This gives home, or the family, huge political weight here, like a small-scale nation in its own right.

At the same time, America is the most restless country I know. Every year one in six Americans move house, compared to one in ten Dutch people or Germans. Between 1995 and 2000, 120 million Americans upped sticks and went to live somewhere else – forty per cent of the population. According to data put out by the United States Census Bureau, only one in four young people expect to continue living in the same town when they are adults. Americans switch jobs with similar frequency. The average Japanese will stay in the same job for over eleven years, the average German or Frenchman more than ten, the average American less than seven.

Those apparently solid homes often turn out on further inspection to be lightweight, temporary structures, at least when compared to the heavy brick buildings Europeans are in the habit of plonking down. On his trip around nineteenth-century America, Charles Dickens complained about the shopping streets of Boston, saying how temporary and provisional everything was, without a past to lend it some kind of context and value.

'It is strange to see with what feverish ardor the Americans pursue their own welfare,' wrote Alexis de Tocqueville after his 1831 journey. 'In the United States a man builds a house to spend his latter years in it, and he sells it before the roof is on: he plants a garden, and lets it just as the trees are coming into bearing: he brings a field into tillage, and leaves other men to gather the crops: he embraces a profession, and gives it up: he settles in a place, which he soon afterwards leaves, to carry his changeable longings elsewhere. If his private affairs leave him any leisure, he instantly plunges into the vortex of politics . . . Death at length over-takes him, but it is before he is weary of his bootless chase of that complete felicity which is forever on the wing.'

Such mobility points back to the practicalities of the nineteenth century. You could earn good money by it, since as soon as more settlers came, the land increased in value. A clever farmer would sell up, move west-wards, carve a new acreage of farmland out of the wilderness, sell up again after a few years and move on. Some might make such a leap five or six times.

Tocqueville sought a deeper explanation for the astonishing restlessness of the Americans. The main cause, he believed, was American social equality, which meant that 'laws and customs make no condition permanent' – in contrast to old, class-conscious Europe. Americans already had a certain level of equality, but 'they can never attain the equality they desire'. Freedom prevailed and in theory all options were open, so you saw people continually changing course 'for fear of missing the shortest cut to happiness'. Tocqueville looked upon it all with concern.

Other visitors found this lack of attachment extraordinarily liberating. They saw it as part of the irrepressible vitality of the nation. As the philosopher George Santayana, who chose to remain a Spanish citizen, once wrote: 'Americans don't solve problems, they leave them behind.' Perhaps that has to do with the old promise of abundance in the beckoning distance. If a situation no longer suits them, they move on, whether it's a matter of international politics or their own home environment.

According to Santayana, who lived most of his life in the United States and wrote one of the better analyses of the country, Americans are not driven to these measures by money and greed. If they were, they would take far better care of the things they own, whereas in fact they have a remarkably generous and relaxed attitude in that sense. Greed and miserliness can be found everywhere, but they are certainly not typical of America. Although Americans often talk about money, they spend it fairly easily, 'with a very light heart', as Santayana writes, because beneath lies a deeper imperative. 'To be an American is of itself almost a moral condition, an education and a career.'

In a night spent amid mobile homes in Vermont, Steinbeck was harshly confronted with this contradiction between connectedness and eternal restlessness, between home and the far horizon. His stay among the 'Martians' of the new America and their houses of aluminium and plywood unsettled him, even though he didn't really let this show in *Travels with Charley*. Such a way of life might mean the ultimate victory of restlessness, a definitive end to the concept of home. He reported at length to Elaine on the spacious caravans, which were considerably cheaper than houses. He compared their inhabitants to the White Leghorns on battery farms, waiting year after year for the new model and then trading theirs in like an automobile. 'It means you will throw away a house the way you consign a car to the junkyard.'

In *America and Americans* he returned to this experience. The word 'home', he wrote, can move any American to tears. 'Builders and developers never build houses – they build homes.' The dream dwelling is either in a small town or in a suburb where grass and trees create the illusion of countryside. 'It is a center where a man and his wife grow graciously old, warmed by the radiance of well-washed children and grandchildren.' Yet the average American moves house at least ten times in his or her life.

Along the way Steinbeck discussed the subject with Charley. Is restlessness an American character trait that initially arose through genetic selection? In the cities and villages they came from, emigrants were often the most dynamic of people. Are Americans restless by nature? There is surely more to it than that. The concept of 'home' may not be a solid reality, but it's a shared and deeply rooted illusion, an inseparable part of the national dream of all Americans. Steinbeck wrote that 'all dreams, waking and sleeping, are powerful and prominent memories of something real, of something that really happened'. In other words, 'home' may no longer exist, but it once did.

During his night in the trailer park, Steinbeck went outside to urinate. He looked at his neighbour's huge lighted window, which put him in mind of an architect's office. 'Dreadful!' he wrote to Elaine. 'A home accumulates. A home has a roof of hope and cellar of memories. That's our kind of home. But there's a new kind. That man meant it. That plywood and aluminum thing is his "home".'

John Steinbeck's sombre vision of the future did not accurately reflect reality. Americans in earlier times were driven not by their national dreams, as Steinbeck claimed, but by unemployment, poverty, drought, farm bankruptcies and other disasters. After the war, calamities of that kind were considerably fewer, and people immediately began staying put rather more. In 1960, despite all the new dynamism of their lives, they were remarkably settled, by American standards. The average American had no desire at all for a nomadic life as a 'Martian' in a mobile home made of aluminium and plastic.

Another lifestyle revolution passed Steinbeck by completely. For him 'the city' was still a nineteenth-century phenomenon, crowded, busy, dirty and criminal. He avoided cities as far as possible on his trip, in order to get to know the 'real' America. As a result he failed to notice that his fellow Americans had opted en masse to live in environments of a totally new kind called the suburbs: successors to Levittown, neither cities nor villages but large built-up patches of landscape, swiftly penned by developers, leafy and eternally green like a late-twentieth-century Deerfield. The formula used by Levitt and others had become hugely successful in the 1950s. More than four out of five new houses were constructed in a similarly vacant zone. Plans for major highways developed and implemented in the 1950s were inspired by the German autobahns, but in America they were intended not just to link cities but to reshape them into elements of the machinery of modern transport and to create new urban areas.

By 1970 more people were living in the suburbs than in cities, and at the end of the twentieth century ninety per cent of offices were being built in the suburbs, often in anonymous office parks beside the interstate highways. The population of Atlanta, for example, increased only slightly in those thirty years, by 20,000, but the suburbs surrounding the city grew by more than two million souls. The suburbs increasingly had a life of their own, breaking loose, as it were, from the classic city centres. You could find them scattered all over the country, white-and-green splashes in the dusty wilderness. They reflected the zeitgeist of the second half of the twentieth century. These were the neighbourhoods where the hippies grew up and where, a generation later, young urban professionals unwound; they were also a straitjacket that prompted more and more women to rebel.

In his analysis of twentieth-century America, Philip Slater wrote about the 'false illusion of autonomy'. Individualism, he claimed, is rooted in a denial of human beings' dependence on one another, on the earth, and on the rest of the universe. He was struck by the extent to which technology has had the effect of 'liberating' people from the necessity of normal human interaction over the past few decades, whether or not that was its intention. Life in the suburbs was the perfect example of this.

At the same time a trend arose in the opposite direction. Many suburbs developed into self-contained worlds of like-minded people, and in that

sense segregation in America markedly increased. Soon there were neighbourhoods in which the rasping voice of Bob Dylan drowned out the
din of cappuccino machines day after day and where front drives were
full of Volvos and Toyotas, and other neighbourhoods where McDonald's
was the centre of social life and country music blared across the swimming pools. You could choose almost anything between these two
extremes. Everyone you met would be on your wavelength, across the
whole spectrum from left to right.

Meanwhile the countryside and the old city fell behind. From 1950
until well into the 1960s, a million farmers a year abandoned their farms.
In that same period the inner cities, large and small, began to empty. In
the 1950s more than a million New Yorkers left the city for nearby suburbs.
Those suburbs, wrote John Brooks of the *New Yorker*, were 'draining downtown of its nighttime population, except for night watchmen and derelicts;
it was becoming a part-time city, tidally swamped with bustling humanity
every weekday morning when the cars and commuter trains arrived, and
abandoned again at nightfall when the wave sucked back − left pretty
much to thieves, policemen, and rats.'

Today the mobile home is still a symbol of freedom, but it increasingly
represents poverty. Driving around the country, you soon notice the
thousands of Americans for whom a 'recreational vehicle' (RV) is home.
The luxury models are inhabited by 'grey nomads', wealthy pensioners
who drive across America alone or in clusters, spending their summers
in the North and their winters in Florida and California, amusing themselves to death. For most of the rest, an RV is the last stop before the
gutter. 'If you want to see the poorest part of a city, you need to visit
the trailer courts,' my American friends told me. 'The new immigrants
gather there in RVs, and you can see all the people who've run aground
one way or another, all the failures.'

It makes me think of the dirt-poor villages in the deserts of Arizona
that I passed through on earlier trips, those huddles of white campers
and caravans, lonely in the quivering heat. There live the migrant workers
and the poor who want to be left in peace, retired people who have lost
their homes to medical fees and can afford only a caravan in a desert
village, and the sick who need clean air but could never afford a house
in the mountains. They all, without exception, live indoors, with an

air-conditioning unit running flat out on the roof and only an old television set to distract them.

On his travels around the country in the mid-1990s, Robert Kaplan
interviewed a Navajo called Cayce Boone, whose job it was to connect
and disconnect cable TV in the trailers and who was therefore one of the
few to enter homes of this sort regularly. What he encountered day and
night, he said, were dirty people who couldn't read, didn't talk to each
other, had few if any relatives or friends, could barely put food on the
table for their children, and were often just one unpaid bill away from
bankruptcy and homelessness. The little bit of money they had, they spent
on cable television. 'TV,' he said, 'is the whole existence for a new class
of silent people.'

Meanwhile our journey, like Steinbeck's, is growing cheerless, like a
persistently rainy holiday in the Ardennes. The colourful leaves, heavy
with moisture, are fluttering down wholesale now, the first bare trees are
emerging, the water in the rivers gushes past the piles of the wooden
bridges, and here and there parts of the road are flooded. Again we are
close to the Canadian border; the houses are neater, the lawns better
tended.

Hardwick's Main Street is not what it used to be. The chic Hardwick
Inn is empty, and some shops have been boarded up or turned into
second-hand stores. The Village Restaurant, right next to the raging river,
is bravely standing its ground. It's an old wooden structure that seems
to have changed little over the past half-century. Ordinary America often
makes an old-fashioned impression compared to Europe and there are
plenty of places that fail to bear out Steinbeck's fears about the rise of
plastic. The chairs and tables are ancient, and even the brass knobs on
the toilet doors gleam with age. We have no complaints about the food
in places like this: mother's home cooking.

It continues to rain, bucketing down, and the Caledonian Record is full of
alarming stories about floods and bursting rivers that might cross our
path. We decide to take a long break. In any case I have some serious
thinking to do. I have a problem. This autumn another journalist has set
out with precisely the same intention, the spirit of John Steinbeck next
to him on the front seat. In fact there is a third author, someone who

runs a website for dog lovers, and he is on the road too, accompanied by the spirit of Charley. My expedition is not, it turns out, unique.

Although we are following the same trail and the same route, I fail to spot any sign of them until I arrive in Lancaster, on the Connecticut River in New Hampshire. Lancaster is a small place and the iron bridge Steinbeck drove across – 'rattling the steel-tread plates' – is still there. Steinbeck spent the night nearby, on land surrounding an empty motel. He makes a nice little story out of it in *Travels with Charley*: everything was open, the lights were on, the pies and cakes were laid out under plastic covers ready for breakfast, except that there wasn't anyone around, not when he arrived and not when he left at half past nine the next morning. It was like a ghost motel.

No motel is in evidence now. I get out to fill the tank. In the shop attached to the gas station I broach the subject: Was there ever a motel here? 'Ah,' says a young man in a baseball cap from behind the till. 'John Steinbeck, eh? There was someone here yesterday asking after him, some journalist from Pittsburgh.' He refers me to a local historian who lives nearby and will be able to tell me more. The man isn't home so we drive on. We need to cover at least another 200 miles by nightfall.

The discovery is unsurprising. The idea of repeating the trip exactly fifty years later dropped into my lap fully formed; it was the kind of story that simply sits there and waits for a writer. In truth it was too obvious not to be picked up by someone else. During my preparations I'd soon realised there was a handful of particularly fanatical fans for whom Steinbeck's journey had roughly the same significance as a pilgrimage to Santiago de Compostela. Other writers had already repeated his trip and each had taken his own individual approach, as I was planning to do.

Bill Steigerwald is the name of the man who is marching with a heavy tread into my carefully constructed Steinbeck world. A former editor of the *Los Angeles Times* and the *Pittsburgh Tribune-Review*, he has written punchy columns against 'climate hysteria', the 'slavery' that resulted from the New Deal and liberal hobbies in general, and now, in retirement, he has a blog on the website of the *Pittsburgh Post-Gazette*. His intention is to repeat Steinbeck's journey asking the same question as I am: What has changed in this country over the past half-century? Along the way, Steigerwald will focus increasingly on Steinbeck himself, trying to reconstruct his travels as accurately as possible. Based on Steinbeck's letters, on news clippings, biographies, interviews, and of course *Travels* itself, he has put together a precise itinerary of all the places where our hero spent the night in 1960. He is now working through them, on his own, in a small rented Toyota in which he generally spends the night. As a libertarian, he thinks Steinbeck a good fellow. He will say later, 'I kind of like the old guy. He liked guns; he liked property rights.'

His travel plan turns out to be the same as mine. He too left on the morning of 23 September 2010 from Steinbeck's house in Sag Harbor, just a little earlier in the day. If we'd taken the ferry to the mainland an hour sooner, I would no doubt have bumped into him on the deck, notebook in hand like me. On that same boat, Steigerwald ran into his colleague John Woestendiek, a former journalist at the *Baltimore Sun*, who along with his dog Ace had started a similar Steinbeck project for the website Ohmidog.com. Later I find out that a woman from the *Washington Post* is travelling in Steinbeck's footsteps too – we weren't exactly going to be lonely, making this trip this year.

There is one difference between Steigerwald and all the rest, including Steinbeck and myself: the extremely austere nature of his trip. Steigerwald is the only one who is truly making the journey on his own, and he will seldom if ever take a hotel room, usually sleeping out in one of the huge parking lots outside a Walmart or a shopping mall (John Woestendiek likewise is sleeping in parking lots). In his blogs Steigerwald reveals himself to be a skilful practitioner of drive-by journalism. In Deerfield, for example, he asked around until he located the now-abandoned farm with the apple orchard where Steinbeck supposedly camped on his first night. In Lancaster he soon found the ghost motel Steinbeck wrote about, the Whip 'o Will, of which nothing but a shack remains.

I reassure myself. I'm concerned about quite different things, I think, travelling a day's journey behind. We won't tread on each other's toes.

The next day we have better weather. Like Steinbeck we pass St Albans, cross into New York State at Rouses Point and then drive along the Canadian border, through Malone and Watertown to Lake Ontario. It's warmer now, the autumn air is mild and carries the scent of earth, fungi and melancholy. Beside the country roads, the blue aster and chicory are still flowering profusely. In front of the houses stand proud rows of orange pumpkins. People have started dressing their ghosts and witches. Halloween is approaching.

In Altona a garage sale is underway, the standard means of ridding yourself of surplus belongings when you move. A little further on are two empty houses, the old contents still piled up against the front wall. The Main Street of Chateaugay is semi-deserted. A local restaurant offers truck drivers a discount 'until 3 o'clock', but it's boarded up.

This is a poor region of maize and pastureland, with dilapidated houses everywhere, tall empty barns, rusted silos, occasionally an abandoned farm. Looking at the houses you can see the creeping advance of poverty: first the peeling paint and poorly maintained roofs, next it's tarpaulins to cover leaks and rotting porches, then a final phase of smashed windows and kicked-in doorways. Further on there are suddenly neatly maintained neighbourhoods at the side of the road again. The transition is astonishingly swift and abrupt.

From over the border a Canadian radio show drifts into our Jeep. The jokes are old-fashioned but nevertheless make us laugh a great deal – maybe because the 1950s atmosphere is suddenly called back to life by a programme evoking the cosiness of 'let's all listen to the radio'. The centre of Potsdam seems to have been transplanted here from the Prussia of 1900, with its heavy brick *Hochschule*, the hall church and council office; even the old red-brown buttresses under the railway bridge look as though they've been hauled across from the *Heimat*. Half the stock of a cuddly-toy shop has been laid out along the sides of the road, bloodied and crumpled, an assortment of roadkill: hedgehogs, racoons, foxes and weasels. In Sandy Creek near Ellisburg, dozens of men in big cowboy hats are fishing in the midday sun.

Towards evening the wind gets up. Sandy guides us to Henderson Harbor, on a spur of Lake Ontario, to the door of the Captain's Cove motel. It's already getting dark. We are the only living souls here, other than the gloomy motel owner. Most of the boats have been brought ashore for the winter. The wind whistles through their stays, the jetties creak, pipes and drains gurgle in time with the slow rise and fall of the lake.

I read the Burlington Free Press, which I picked up along the way. Again a son of New England has been killed in action. Anthony Rosa from Swanton. The paper carries a detailed report of his funeral. Hundreds of people stood at the side of the road as he came past. 'The sort of guy you could count on to help push your car out of a ditch at 1 a.m.'

The bear-hunting season has started. Here they call it 'the bear harvest'. The number of bears keeps increasing; in Vermont alone, some 6,000 of them are ranging around, including quite a few notorious 'nuisance bears'. There's a fear of terrorist attacks in far-off Europe. The Burlington Free Press gives the threat a great deal of coverage. The security services are putting out bulletins and the United States has even issued a travel advisory. Americans are instructed to be extremely careful in European countries. As for me, I'm heading for Detroit (some 360 murders a year), Chicago (450) and New Orleans (170), but no one in authority has given me any warnings.

The next day we have breakfast with Fox News yet again, the channel everyone watches here. So what do you see at eight in the morning? All attention is focused on Europe, which suddenly seems to have become one of the most dangerous places on earth. News alerts flash across the screen, 'Europe specialists' give advice on how to avoid a possible attack, and our attention is drawn to particularly dangerous locations. I even spot the railway station at our very own Schiphol airport. My compatriots walk calmly with their bags and briefcases on their way to work or to take a vacation, but the excited voice of the newsreader rattles on without a pause: this is going to be a second Kabul, mark my words. There follows an advertisement for foldaway beds and another for a pill to treat depression that will set you right within three weeks.

Now the Fox commentators come into the studio. My goodness, how dangerous Europe has become; everyone, for all the variation in tone, agrees about that. Truth, in other words, has become social, no longer something sought by scientists, journalists and the like, as honestly, objectively and professionally as possible. Truth is now simply something about which we slap each other on the back. A warm feeling to share is all we're after. The truth is a social phenomenon. Investigation, persistent questioning, the eternal quest for objectivity characteristic of the Enlightenment – it all increasingly seems to have been replaced by hypnosis, exhibitionism and collective entertainment.

I switch to a Christian broadcaster. More news from the bad old world: an evangelical programme put out by the International Fellowship of Christians and Jews for the benefit of 'forgotten Jews in the former Soviet Union'. The campaign has a biblical motto, Isaiah 58, verse 10: 'And if thou draw out thy soul to the hungry, and satisfy the afflicted soul; then shall thy light rise in obscurity, and thy darkness be as the noon day.'

First of all we are shown a series of drab Ukrainian interiors with desperate mothers who can't even buy a hunk of bread after paying their medical fees. Viewers can help. For fifteen dollars this woman will receive a food parcel. 'Then suddenly someone arrives with food,' the mother says. 'An angel.' All donors will receive something in return: an Isaiah 58:10 prayer packet.

Halfway through, the tempo increases. This campaign is expertly compiled. Now they're showing images of the Holocaust, and an elderly lady in Kiev is describing how Jews are still persecuted there. 'We're just like the blacks in the United States.' The presenter turns to us: 'Do you want to receive God's blessing? Pick up the phone and be blessed! It's a marvellous experience to be a Christian . . . For only fifteen dollars a box, you can . . . Operation Isaiah 58 . . . Prayer packets . . .'

There is something magical about it. America is good; the rest of the world is evil and degenerate – and who wouldn't want to be an angel?

Two

WE'RE ACROSS THE NORTHERN BORDER of the United States before we fully realise it. At Niagara Falls several large bridges straddle the river, and beyond them the Canadians defend their country politely but firmly. Steinbeck, who wanted to drive along the quiet Canadian shore of Lake Erie to Detroit, was stopped in no man's land. Charley had not been vaccinated. That would be a serious problem if he wanted to get back into the United States.

Grumbling, he continued his journey on the American side of the lake, along a new road, the Interstate 90, 'a wide gash of a super-highway, multiple-lane carrier of the nation's goods'. A start had only just been made on laying the new Interstate Highway System and this was one of its first stretches. Drivers had yet to become accustomed to it, and the roadsides were plastered with warnings: 'Do not stop! No stopping! Maintain speed.'

Steinbeck didn't think much of this modern four-lane highway. There were no longer any stands selling squash at the roadside, no antiques stores. The staff in restaurants and diners had been replaced by vending machines. You needed to keep a close eye on the cars ahead and those alongside. He was driving into the wind and 'felt the buffeting, sometimes staggering blows of the gale' that he was helping to make. 'Trucks as long as freighters went roaring by, delivering a wind like the blow of a fist.' It was like driving inside a tube. 'When we get these thruways across the whole country, as we will and must, it will be possible to drive from New York to California without seeing a single thing.'

At this point I take the liberty of deviating from Steinbeck's route. We don't have a dog with us, so there is nothing to prevent us from making the Canadian excursion that Steinbeck had originally intended. It involves getting out at the border, going into a room with officials behind glass, waiting, and then answering a lot of serious questions: who are we, where do we want to go, what are we going to do, when will we be leaving the country again? You don't get into Canada with a nod and a stamp.

Then suddenly we drive into Europe. The municipal lawns are neatly manicured, every street corner is decorated with a planter full of flowers, petrol is fifty per cent more expensive and, oddly, discipline among road users has gone out of the window – no one sticks to the speed limit.

It's raining and the huge waterfalls are shrouded in soaking mist. Half of Japan and China seems to have turned out to observe this phenomenon, individually wrapped in the thin plastic raincoats you're given for free if you have the courage to go out on one of the little boats to almost directly under the falls. It's certainly impressive. With a huge roar the contents of three massive lakes crash down sixty metres, as if Our Dear Lord has personally flushed the toilet.

I can't help thinking of Oscar Wilde, who stood here in 1882 and regarded this wonder of the natural world as the epitome of pointlessness: 'Simply a vast unnecessary amount of water going the wrong way and then falling over unnecessary rocks.' He believed it would be a true miracle of nature only if the water were to fall upwards. You could easily find dozens of choice quotations, since the Falls were a compulsory item on the itinerary of practically every tourist in America from the earliest days. Charles Dickens, who passed this way in 1842, felt the need to capitalise everything he wrote about this Holy Place: Peace of Mind, Enchanted Ground, Calm Recollections of the Dead, Great Thoughts of Eternal Rest and Happiness. The legendary French actress Sarah Bernhardt, who visited in 1881, regarded the waterfalls primarily as an artwork, or rather as decor, since the real artwork was of course Bernhardt herself. To Steinbeck the phenomenon was more than anything a large version of the old Bond sign on Times Square, which was also a waterfall, only of light.

We walk back and forth through the rain, on the Canadian side, which offers the better view. All the big chains have built their tower-block hotels close to this boiling, primeval violence and you can experience the waterfalls in every imaginable way. The word 'experience' predominates, whether on one of the boats that travel back and forth across the whirlpools, through a tunnel system that runs behind the waterfalls, or in the super-cinema where the floor shakes and it even rains a little, or else in lifts, viewing towers and helicopters. You can even take a ride on a big wheel. I've never seen a wonder of creation so exhaustively exploited as these waterfalls.

A few miles further on lies Niagara-on-the-Lake, once the British military base of Butlersburg that the Brits only narrowly managed to keep out of American hands in the early nineteenth century. The town seems never to have quite recovered from the shock. It's less than half an hour's drive from the border, but the place is more British than Britain and the residents know it. Anyone driving onto the main street – not called Main Street here of course but Queen Street – is hit by a blast of English cosiness at hurricane force. Wherever possible – pavements, window ledges, lamp posts – exuberant flower displays stand or hang. The Prince of Wales Hotel (1863), the Bernard Shaw Festival Theatre, the shop that sells Christmas decorations, the souvenir stores, the candy stores – all those rosy little businesses are lined with floral wallpaper. In this strange little town no one ever seems to do anything, nothing is made here, nothing is real.

Some distance from Queen Street, normal life begins to take shape. We alight upon the Olde Angel Inn, a thoroughly English affair, brown and cosy, with warm beer, fish 'n' chips and shepherd's pie, and dominating it all that unmistakable smell of a British pub.

The Olde Angel Inn even has a resident ghost. He's called Captain Colin Swayze, a British officer who, during an invasion by the Yankees in May 1813, fled into the cellar at the inn, where he met his end. According to one version, he fought to his last breath to defend the residents, while another source claims it was to save his sweetheart. Captain Swayze haunts only the cellar, in his red jacket, but tradition has it that he'll come upstairs if the Union Jack is removed from the facade. The pub always flies the British flag.

Captain Swayze probably died – if any of this really happened at all – in one of the many raids that took place during what is known as the War of 1812, the epilogue to the War of Independence between the

Americans and the British that determined the shape of Canada. The 1812 war has been largely erased from the collective memory of Americans, since ultimately it gained them nothing at all, changing neither the border nor the politics of the two sides.

It was in every respect a bizarre affair. The British commanded an army of a quarter of a million men and a fleet of some 600 ships. The Americans had a standing army of at best 7,000 and a navy of sixteen warships plus a few other miscellaneous craft. The immediate cause of the conflict had been resolved before the war broke out, but that message failed to reach the Americans in time. In Alan Taylor's view the American War of Independence was essentially a civil war and this was its final flare. Both parties felt that the American continent could not permit itself two completely incompatible systems, the independent democratic republic of the United States, and Canada, a colony of an aristocratic empire. It was for that reason, Taylor writes, that the war was prosecuted and experienced as an extension of the American Revolution that had taken place a generation earlier. It was 'a civil war between competing visions of America: one still loyal to the empire and the other still defined by its republican revolution against that empire'.

Initially the same dividing line existed between American colonists. The First War of Independence started with a series of irritations and squabbles between the Americans and the British. The American population was growing rapidly (by 1775 it would reach 2.5 million), prosperity was increasing and the Americans were starting to demand treatment from London appropriate to the new status they had attained. But they were emphatically denied any say in the British parliament.

On 16 December 1773, in Boston, shooting broke out between civilians and British troops after the introduction of new taxes on paper, glass and tea. A British warship enforcing an unpopular trade blockade was set on fire and a cargo of tea with an estimated value of 10,000 pounds was thrown into Boston Harbor by activists. This was the famous Boston Tea Party. Events then escalated. The British sent occupying troops, the state of Virginia called the British occupation of Boston a 'hostile invasion', militias were drummed up and trained and in the autumn of 1774 the first Continental Congress gathered in Philadelphia, followed by a second in 1775. It was then that the War of Independence became a full-scale military conflict.

Despite all the animosity between them and the motherland, Britain, the rebellious colonists barely thought of themselves as Americans at first. They were proud to belong to the British Empire and appreciative of the trading opportunities it offered. For them, too, London was a political and cultural centre. Illustrative of this are the dozens of powder horns I saw at the local museum in Deerfield, skilfully worked cow horns in which the colonial soldiers kept their gunpowder. All sorts of slogans and scenes were carved into them, sometimes with great craftsmanship; works of art by ordinary soldiers who had marched through the American forests for years on end with their units. Until well into the second half of the eighteenth century, soldiers would generally carve curlicues and ornamentation on their powder horns, along with the coats of arms of the British regiments in which they were serving, with inscriptions such as 'John Corell, Horn Made at Ford Edward Oct 2nd 1758'.

But then suddenly there's a horn from 1775, belonging to one Stephen Upson, with the inscription 'Success to America!' And one from 1776, made by a certain Bartwich, heavily worked with heraldry and hunting scenes. At the place that would once have featured the king's coat of arms he had created a portrait of someone looking very much like George Washington. His horn also bears the words 'Success to America!'

The first skirmishes between the Yankees and the British took place in April 1775. On 4 July 1776 the United States declared itself independent, but the official document wasn't signed by most state representatives until 2 August, in Philadelphia. That solemn moment was later depicted in myriad ways. We commonly see a proud, almost exuberant gathering, but in reality the mood was if anything downcast. Everyone realised that in the eyes of the British, signing the declaration was an act of high treason, while the outcome of the struggle that lay ahead was not at all certain.

One of the signatories, a doctor called Benjamin Rush, later described in a letter the 'pensive and awful silence' in the room when the members of the Congress were called forward one by one 'to subscribe what was believed by many at that time to be our own death warrant'. One robustly built representative even made a morbid joke to a slimmer colleague, saying that he had a great advantage in that he would die within a few minutes, whereas the lighter man would 'dance in the air an hour or two . . . when we are all hung for what we are doing now'.

As of that moment, there was no way back. Another eight years of bloody fighting lay ahead before the British were to be defeated.

Letting go of Europe, economically and politically but also in language and mentality, was a more gradual matter than the handful of well-known dates might suggest. The American Revolution was not a simple leap from colonial status to a democratic system, it was a process of trial and error that took several generations. Americans were not born free, as is often claimed, nor was the American Revolution a change of direction comparable to the French or Russian revolutions.

American society was not heavily armed, either. In contrast to the prevailing myth, gun ownership was relatively uncommon in America before 1850. Everyone had the right to bear arms, but it was not customary to do so. Research into domestic inventories from 1765 and 1790 has shown that only fifteen per cent of the households studied were in possession of firearms. Government registers give a similar picture. The idea that Americans were firmly attached to their weapons from the start, and that the freedom to bear arms became a basic right for that reason, is a myth.

The period after the revolution, including that strange war of 1812, is therefore at least as interesting as the revolution itself. It was an open process, writes one of the experts in the field, Gordon Wood, in which 'the Americans of the Revolutionary generation had constructed not simply new forms of government, but an entirely new conception of politics'. That conception – and in this sense it differed from all other revolutionary systems – was self-correcting. With countless ways of adjusting and improving itself, it was a system of permanent reform. So the American Revolution was 'not delineated in a single book; it was peculiarly the product of a democratic society'.

Thomas Jefferson was only thirty-three when he composed the Declaration of Independence in 1776, one of the most beautiful state documents ever written. 'We hold these truths to be self-evident, that all men are created equal, that they are endowed by their Creator with certain unalienable rights, that among these are Life, Liberty and the Pursuit of

Happiness . . .' His starting point was a state in which citizens not only had the right to defend themselves against those in power, as was already the case in parts of Europe, but in which all sovereignty lay with the people.

The Constitution further elaborated upon that system. The United States of America would form a federation that shared power with the states and, ultimately, the American people. There would be a strict separation of powers, with the president in charge of the executive, with the Senate and the House of Representatives forming the legislature and with the Supreme Court as the highest body of a strictly independent judiciary. A Bill of Rights was coupled with the Constitution as its first amendment, guaranteeing freedom of religion and freedom of expression, the right to assemble and to petition, the right to property and other fundamental rights.

Long debates preceded the adoption of each of these documents, between federalists and anti-federalists for example, and between more and less democratically inclined factions. The history of their creation shows that the Declaration and the Constitution were not composed as unalterable, quasi-sacred texts, as many conservatives would claim. On the contrary, they were intended to be developed further. It was a dynamic system, and that was the great strength of this new revolution.

The young United States had countless allies, even in old Europe. The first foreign salute to the American flag was fired on 16 November 1776 from a Dutch fort on the Caribbean island of St Eustatius. The first representative of revolutionary America, future president John Adams, was received with open arms in Amsterdam and Paris, where he negotiated war loans worth millions. France, Spain and the Dutch Republic fully supported the rebellion against the British, if for the most part because it contributed to the weakening of Great Britain.

In many circles, America's fundamentally democratic stance was recognised and praised. Here the political ideas of the Enlightenment were being put into practice on a large scale for the first time. Here a new system and a new world could be seen emerging, of which the Europeans could only dream. The Americans were the first people in history to put the ideals of popular sovereignty into practice, and they were doing it brilliantly.

A kind of ideological reverberation soon resulted. The Europeans, especially the French, inspired the Americans with their Enlightenment philosophy, and the Americans in turn inspired the Europeans with their audacious political and social experiment.

Bold ventures on this scale never take place without fierce and lengthy political debates, and far from all American colonists supported the rebellion. The Orangist Dutch crockery I saw in Deerfield, with its aristocratic and anti-revolutionary message, presumably had political significance in America as well. At least half a million British subjects, amounting to a fifth of all American colonists, remained loyal to their king.

The American Revolution was as much as anything a civil conflict within America − a fact that was ignored for many years in traditional history writing. At least 19,000 'Loyalists' eventually fought on the side of the British against their fellow Americans. Native Americans were also divided, with the Mohawks, for example, supporting the British. The three most sparsely populated colonies in the north − Nova Scotia, Newfoundland and Quebec − also remained faithful to the British crown. They had no choice, being utterly dependent on British trade and protection.

Refugees began pouring into Canada. Almost 40,000 American colonists left for southern Canada during the revolution, settling in the region just beyond the border. To oblige these Loyalist newcomers, several new towns were built as perfect replicas of 'good old England', including the provincial capital, London. More than 20,000 black slaves took the opportunity to escape, among them two dozen owned by Enlightenment thinker Thomas Jefferson.

So the United States and the European colonies of Canada slowly grew apart.

The forgotten war of 1812 was a continuation of that process of separation. The cause lay in the fact that Britain refused to recognise former subjects who had emigrated − such as the countless Irish who were streaming into the United States − as American citizens. The British and the British colonists in Canada saw themselves as loyal subjects of the king of England and (in most cases) the Anglican Church. They preferred the old class-based society, the order imposed by God, and regarded

democratic rights as a source of republican ruin. They therefore blocked
all reform: elections, freedom of expression, freedom of the press. Even
transatlantic postal services were deliberately curtailed.

America, by contrast, turned all immigrants into Americans as quickly
as possible, whether they were German, Irish, French, British or Dutch.
The new American, of his own free will, was a citizen of a new land
with its own politics, culture and mentality. 'There, bustle, improvement
and animation fill every street,' noted a dejected Canadian shortly after
independence, looking out towards America across the Niagara River.
'Here dullness, decay and apathy discourage enterprise and repress
exertion.'

Yet Canada remained attractive to some American minorities. This was
especially true of the humble Quakers and the Pietistic Germans, who
felt more at home under the protection of a fatherly monarch than amid
that brisk mania for legislation displayed by the American democratic-
majority regimes. Canada had no black slaves and the Natives had more
freedom there. Americans regarded the 'Indians' as subjects, or indeed as
brutal wild creatures destined to die out, whereas the British saw them
as autonomous peoples living in their own territories. It was the start of
a uniquely Canadian policy that combined individual rights with the
protection of the rights of minorities, which explains why thousands of
Native Americans fought on the British side.

The war of 1812 was not a heroic conflict, incidentally, for all its high
ideals. Hostilities quickly degenerated into reciprocal bouts of murder
and looting, on both sides of the border. The American militias, imbued
with democratic and egalitarian rallying cries, had great difficulty abiding
by normal military discipline. The winter was wet and miserable – 'We
eat, drink and sleep in water,' a diarist claimed – and morale declined
with every month that passed. American soldiers regularly wasted ammunition by shooting around them at random, purely out of boredom. Their
commanders were confused: Brigadier General William Hull surrendered
with his whole army at Detroit without having fired a shot; the
commander-in-chief, Major General Stephen Van Rensselaer, believed deep
down that the whole war was nonsensical, and he crossed to the far side
of the Niagara River under a white flag to exchange courtesies with his
British colleagues.

After two years of war, on 24 December 1814 a peace treaty was signed in the Flemish city of Ghent. News that hostilities had ended did not reach Washington until 13 February 1815. Meanwhile, on 8 January the Americans took the opportunity to inflict a crushing defeat on British forces at New Orleans, if only with the help of an infamous pirate called Jean Lafitte and his gang. So a remarkable misunderstanding arose among the Americans. They believed they had won the war and laid down terms for peace. In reality hardly anything changed on the ground. Yet this second war of independence had far-reaching psychological and political consequences. America became more American, Canada more Canadian. The boundary between them was more clearly defined by the Canadians, and the influx of Americans was severely limited. The once-flourishing Canadian border region was comprehensively ravaged and plundered by Yankee militias. Bitterness lingered for generations.

Alan Taylor quotes an innkeeper, all of whose household effects were stolen by the Americans, even toys from the crib of his newborn child. He had developed a 'thorough detestation' of the Yankees and at the same time 'felt strongly the blessings of British protection'. The rift ran right through his family. He disinherited his eldest son for fighting on the enemy side. This was undeniably a civil war.

Canada did not become an independent state until 1931. As part of the British Empire it served mainly to keep the power of the United States in check. For many Americans it functioned as a kind of anti-country, without any great national goal beyond its own survival.

After the war of 1812, on the US side of the border, Uncle Sam appeared on stage, the invincible counterpart to Britain's John Bull. Uncle Sam became the symbol of a new, idealistic, purposeful nation, a unique historical experiment. Illustrative of these founding years is the well-known story of Rip Van Winkle, a fairy tale written in 1819 by Washington Irving. Van Winkle, a nice-but-dim Dutch farmer, runs into the ghosts of Henry Hudson and his men while out for a walk. The soldiers treat him to a seventeenth-century magic drink, which makes him fall asleep. When he wakes up, his rifle lies rotten and rusty beside him, his beard reaches to his feet and his village has changed out of all recognition. His sharp-tongued wife has died, his old friends have been killed in a strange war, and by introducing himself as a faithful subject of King George III he gets into serious trouble. But that's not all. The whole of society seems to have been affected: his beloved, peaceful village has grown immensely and instead of the usual calm there is a 'bustling disputatious tone'. He cannot even understand the language any longer; it is 'a Babylonish jargon' full of new terms like 'rights of citizens – elections – members of Congress – liberty'.

Rip Van Winkle, the personification of the traditional colonist, would indeed have woken in a different country after twenty years of sleep. Money had suddenly become very important. As a contemporary observed, wherever you found a church, a bar and a smithy, you would now also find a bank. In 1831 there were already more than 300 steamboats plying the American rivers. The 1,400 miles upstream from New Orleans to Louisville, which had once taken nine months of rowing, hunting for food along the way, could be covered by a steamer in just nine days.

In their letters home, Alexis de Tocqueville and Gustave de Beaumont regularly remarked on how fascinated Americans were by river steamboats, forever using them in competitions, stoking up their furnaces to maximum heat and binding the safety valves on the steam boilers shut. Afterwards the pair would proudly declare that they had run a hundred times more risks on those riverboats than during their crossing of the Atlantic: 'Thirty of them exploded or sank during the first six weeks we were in the United States.'

Finding themselves on the Ohio River in 1831, they were struck above all by the contrast between the well-tended landscape of 'free' Ohio on one bank and the neglected land of the slave-state Kentucky on the other. The divide between the puritan, hardworking, forward-looking North – which was increasingly shaping the 'national' culture of America – and the quiet, slave-owning and nostalgic South was deepening in those years. They visited the elderly John Quincy Adams and the three men spoke about the risk of such differences ultimately resulting in armed conflict, which of course is what happened thirty years later.

The two friends were astonished time and again by the passion with which public debate was conducted. There were still no clearly defined political parties. The Republican Party as we know it today was founded in 1854, as a protest against huge concessions made to the Southern slave owners under the Kansas–Nebraska Act. The Democrats were then still known as the Democratic Republicans, a populist grouping that had split from Thomas Jefferson's Republican Party. All politics, Tocqueville wrote, was reduced to 'a question of men – those who have power and those who want it; the ins and the outs'.

A similar wilfulness could be felt with regard to religion. Something known as the Second Great Awakening was occurring, as millions of Americans withdrew from the Christian denominations of the Old World. They increasingly laid an emphasis on passion and spirituality, sought new certainties in all kinds of sects – such as the Shakers – and mixed traditional Christianity with other traditions and folk wisdom. From this popular movement a series of typically American religions arose with theologies all their own, in which American exceptionalism often featured large. They formed the basis for, to take one example, the rise of Mormonism.

Before the revolution, America consisted, as Gordon Wood puts it, of 'a collection of disparate British colonies composed of some two million subjects huddled along a narrow strip of the Atlantic coast – a European outpost whose cultural focus was still London'. After the war of 1812 these European outposts grew to become one huge republic of more than ten million inhabitants, with a territory that covered almost half the continent and a population that was doubling every twenty years – twice as fast as in Europe. Within ten years the young state of Ohio changed from a wilderness into a region with a higher population density than most of the original colonies. In a single generation the Americans occupied more new land than in the 150 colonial years that had gone before – at the cost of the lives of hundreds of thousands of Native Americans.

By about 1815, the way Americans saw the world and themselves had changed fundamentally. This transformation took place before industrialisation, urbanisation and all the other developments generally associated with the Industrial Revolution of the nineteenth century. Change was increasingly regarded by Americans as a virtue in its own right, something that should be valued and pursued in perpetuity. Europeans were more attached to the status quo, and the differences between Europe and

America became even greater after the fall of Napoleon in 1814 and the subsequent restoration of the old aristocracy and conservative regimes. Europe, especially France, was no longer in any sense a source of inspiration.

America 'laughs at their folly and shuns their errors', wrote the justice of the peace and schoolmaster Noah Webster, shortly after independence, of his country's attitude to Europeans. 'She sees a thousand discordant opinions live in the strictest harmony . . . it will finally raise her to a pitch of greatness and lustre, before which the glory of ancient Greece and Rome shall dwindle to a point, and the splendor of modern Empires fade into obscurity.'

Webster watched his new country taking shape and developing a language of its own. Slowly the American idiom started to diverge from the British in tone, rhythm and especially vocabulary. The words buck, dough, small change, flat broke, deadbeat and blizzard all came into use after 1800. Pronunciation changed too: pretty became 'priddy' and butter was pronounced 'budder'. Words were switched: trousers became pants, biscuits became cookies, holidays became vacations, shops became stores, 'to walk away' became 'to make tracks', and so on. British travellers frequently complained that those weird Americans couldn't string a proper sentence together. It didn't occur to them for a second that this new world needed a new language to suit its needs and conditions, and indeed its new society.

Shortly after the revolution, Webster began to compile 'spellers', or guides to spelling. They were still entirely British in content. In 1828 he published the first dictionary of American English, the *American Dictionary of the English Language*. It was the first in a classic series of Webster's dictionaries, and an important piece of historical heritage. For the first time, American English was being treated as a language in its own right. It was a language of space, and of openness towards newcomers; its courteous yet direct tone distinguished it in a whole range of ways from British circumlocution. It was also the language of a thoroughly egalitarian society. Everyone was a lady or a gentleman, and an accent indicated only where you were from, saying nothing about your rank or station in life. British writer Charles William Janson once described slipping up by addressing a waitress as 'servant'. 'I'd have you to know . . . that I am no *sarvant*,' she snapped back. 'None but *negers* are *sarvants*.' She was, she said solemnly, a 'help'.

European visitors who came to take a look at the New World on the other side of the ocean often regarded America as a perfect example of regression, of cultural deterioration in comparison to civilised nineteenth-century Europe. In 1832, after a failed business venture in the United States, British writer Frances Trollope published a book called *Domestic Manners of the Americans*, a derisive travel account that describes the American lifestyle. She worked through the entire list, from that damnable class equality, through the spitting of tobacco to the ownership of slaves. In the view of Charles Dickens, most Americans were brutes who spat, boozed and blasphemed. Others, Rudyard Kipling among them, admired precisely the unpolished nature of the New World's inhabitants. They saw it as a form of strength, in contrast to a weakened and decadent Europe.

Almost all visitors criticised the hypocrisy of Americans, who made much of their proudly held principles of equality, yet at the same time allowed their Southern economy to rely to a great extent on the work of slaves. Gijsbert Karel van Hogendorp, later to become a Dutch statesman, spent six months in the new country in 1783. He pointed out to Thomas Jefferson the incompatibility between slavery and liberalism. In 1815 America was still governed largely by slave owners. President James Madison, the speaker of the House of Representatives, ministers at the State Department and at the Treasury, most members of Congress and the Supreme Court, the senior ambassadors – they all owned slaves.

Not even free 'Negroes' were regarded as equal. In around 1830, French traveller Michel Chevalier noted that 'an American of the North or South, whether rich or poor, ignorant or learned, avoids contact with blacks as if they carried the plague'. Black people were not allowed into hotels, and in theatres or on steamboats they were forced to stay within certain areas; business life was closed to them and they were refused access to stock markets and banks.

Europe had not abolished slavery anywhere at that point, in fact in the Dutch colonies it continued until 1863, when it was ended in response to considerable international pressure. But in practice slavery had died out in almost all regions of Europe, and Europeans had to confront it directly when they visited the United States. Without exception they reacted with bewilderment – which actually says something about how they looked at America, no longer as a colony but as part of the Western world in general.

In a collection of eyewitness accounts I found a report from 1829 about the detention by the Royal Navy of an American slave ship in the southern Atlantic. It shows how the slave trade worked at that particular time. The ship had taken 562 slaves on board at the African coast, 336 men and 226 women, 'and had been out seventeen days, during which she had thrown overboard fifty-five'. The slaves had been branded like cattle. They were stacked under grated hatchways between the decks, so low that they sat between each other's legs and so close together that they couldn't lie down or change their positions during the day, let alone at night. 'The heat in these horrid places was so great, and the odour so offensive, that it was quite impossible to enter them, even had there been room.' After the slaves had briefly been allowed the 'unusual luxury' of fresh air, some water was brought for them. Suddenly it was as if the extent of their suffering had been exposed. 'They all rushed like maniacs towards it. No entreaties or threats or blows could restrain them; they shrieked and struggled and fought with one another for a drop of this precious liquid, as if they grew rabid at the sight of it.' The British could do nothing more, since the ship did not fall under their jurisdiction. They had to let it sail on.

It was the notion of America as a historical experiment that held the greatest appeal for the imaginations of proponents and opponents alike. The Declaration of Independence, as a political manifesto quite apart from anything else, had caused deep shock right across Europe. It was a major source of inspiration for the French Revolution, and nationalist movements in Greece, Germany, Italy and Eastern Europe drew upon it, as did political reformers elsewhere, including in Britain.

'The entire society seems to have merged into the middle class,' wrote Alexis de Tocqueville, four days after arriving in New York. It's no accident that he gave his two-part description of the United States, published in 1835 and 1840, the simple title *Democracy in America*. As a freethinking aristocrat, democracy was what fascinated him most about the young

America. Above all, he was curious about its effect on American citizens: were they really becoming different people?

On the first page he comes to the point straight away: 'the equality of conditions', in other words the absence of class and station in American society, was in his view 'the fundamental fact from which all others seem to be derived, and the central point at which all my observations constantly terminated'. A little later he gives a series of examples: 'Mark, for instance, that opulent citizen, who is as anxious as a Jew of the Middle Ages to conceal his wealth. His dress is plain, his demeanor unassuming; but the interior of his dwelling glitters with luxury, and none but a few chosen guests whom he haughtily styles his equals are allowed to penetrate into this sanctuary. No European noble is more exclusive in his pleasures, or more jealous of the smallest advantages which his privileged station confers upon him. But the very same individual crosses the city to reach a dark counting-house in the centre of traffic, where every one may accost him who pleases. If he meets his cobbler upon the way, they stop and converse; the two citizens discuss the affairs of the State in which they have an equal interest, and they shake hands before they part.'

Tocqueville idealised such relationships, incidentally, as did the Americans themselves. In New York at the time there were already hundreds of families who enjoyed fabulous wealth, even by European standards. Half of all property in America was in the hands of four per cent of the population. The belief that everyone in the United States had earned his own fortune was no longer true by 1831: only a few were self-made men; a considerable majority of rich New Yorkers had been born rich, and they were becoming more and more wealthy for that reason alone.

The American ideal was of course predicated upon the absence of a solid aristocratic top layer, combined with the presence of huge stretches of land that were there for the taking for anyone willing to roll up his sleeves. Rich and poor lived side by side, as they did in Europe, but the poor of America had no intention of staying poor. Not that they wanted to take the place of the rich, like the revolutionaries of the Old World – no, they wanted to be rich alongside them.

The South was a different matter. The 'national' American ideals of courage, hard work and enterprise had only really caught on in the North. Many Southerners were sceptical. Hard work was for slaves, and they idealised the elegant lifestyle of the Spanish and French aristocracies of the eighteenth century, while Northerners fastened eagerly upon the future. The South had considerably fewer schools, roads, businesses, banks, doctors, schoolteachers and engineers; taxes were lower there, and the quality of education, roads and public services correspondingly poor.

Southerners also had different ideas about the rights of the individual states, known as 'states' rights', and the role of the federal government. They were of the opinion that the United States was a voluntary union, and if the central government exceeded its limited powers then every state had a right to declare the offending law invalid. One of those states' rights, the South claimed, protected the property of slave owners, no matter where those who escaped might have fled. The North believed that the law allowing escaped slaves to be retrieved by their masters from anywhere in the United States, the Fugitive Slave Act, was incompatible with their own states' rights. Northerners were also in favour of a stronger federal government.

All these differences of opinion lay at the root of a conflict that in 1861 would culminate in the Civil War. The Confederacy of eleven Southern 'slave states' attempted in those years to secede from the Union of twenty Northern 'free' states (plus the five 'border states' which still practised slavery). The Union advocated an extension of the democratic rights and freedoms achieved by the American Revolution, and in 1863 slavery was officially abolished there. The Confederacy wanted to preserve certain elements of the old European class-based society. In the words of historian and Civil War specialist Gary Gallagher: '[The] slaveholding aristocrats who established the Confederacy . . . posed a direct threat not only to the long-term success of the American republic, but also to the broader future of democracy.'

It became a life-and-death struggle, a harbinger of the industrial slaughter in Europe of the First and Second World Wars. On the Southern side, some three-quarters of available men were mobilised, on the Northern side around two-thirds. More than a million American men were wounded or killed. Fighting in serried ranks, some regiments lost three-quarters of their troops in a single day. The three days of the Battle of Gettysburg resulted in more American casualties than the twenty-first-century conflicts in Afghanistan and Iraq, which went on for more than a decade. The social dislocation was huge. One in three Southern soldiers didn't live to see the end of the Civil War; three times the proportion in the North.

On 10 May 1865 the Southern president Jefferson Davis was taken prisoner. It was 'the night they drove old Dixie down', as Robbie Robertson of The Band memorably described the drama a century later. From that night on – 'and all the bells were ringing' – the power and wealth of the South were gone for good. It took more than a century for the wound to heal, and to this day certain cultural and political clashes within American society can be traced back to the principles fought over at that time: individual and state autonomy, the scope of the federal government, the power to raise taxes and, not least, the principle of equality.

In a sense the rest of America emerged from the conflict stronger than ever before. Union troops had gone to war under the flags of different states, each of which had its own colourful uniform. At the victory parade on 23 and 24 May 1865 they marched through Washington as a single army, in blue uniforms, a vast column twenty-five miles long, over-whelming evidence of new unity and power.

America's egalitarian ideal prevailed for much of the twentieth century. I remember seeing television pictures of President Obama, on his first visit to Westminster, warmly shaking the hand of the police officer on duty in front of 10 Downing Street. To Gordon Brown, the Labour prime minister in Britain at the time, the policeman might as well have been made of thin air. A meal comes to mind at which the contrasting table manners of the Europeans still said something about their social back-grounds, whereas most of the Americans, rich or poor, ate in the same way, with their forks, using the knife purely to cut meat. I recall a street scene, on one of those sunny mornings after I landed in America for the first time. A street sweeper got talking at the traffic lights with the owner of a white Cadillac convertible about how much a car like that cost, how much gas it consumed and what he thought of it. The rich car owner responded openly and seriously to each of those questions. The street sweeper was convinced that one day he would own something like it. Yes, this was truly another world.

One of the greatest differences between Europe and America was, and remains, the way people deal with failure. In Europe a bankrupt is branded for life, whereas an American will pack up whatever he has left and try again somewhere else; 'Go West, young man!' This frontier ideology, as it's known, combined with the promise of self-made wealth, gave American society an extraordinary dynamism compared to Europe, where you all too often found yourself in the hands of fate. In America you could always pick yourself up again.

I have written those last two sentences in the past tense deliberately. The flag of equality is still held high in American society, whatever the reality. Americans do not regard those with few means of subsistence as poor but rather as underprivileged. The same attitude emerges from sociological research. People think of themselves as part of one big middle class, whether they have an annual income of 20,000 or a 150,000 dollars. Yet if there is one aspect of the American self-image that requires revision, then it is the ideal of – perhaps I should call it the mission to achieve – equality.

When Steinbeck drove around America, social relations were still largely determined by the New Deal, that ambitious response by President Franklin Roosevelt to the crisis of the early 1930s. Kennedy and Nixon could argue all they liked, but on certain political subjects, including poverty and social equality, there was still a high degree of consensus in 1960. In the America of the time there were probably more rich people than ever before, but as Steinbeck wrote in *America and Americans*: 'Far from boasting of their wealth they live almost like fugitives, secret and shy.'

It was the continuation of a trend towards greater equality that had started during the Second World War. The rich had made significant sacrifices with all their extra war taxes, while ordinary workers earned good wages in the munitions factories. On top of that came a phenomenon that many Americans actually regarded as un-American, but that improved their quality of life enormously: the rise of what is still known as 'social security', the first social safety net in American history. The social programmes introduced by Roosevelt in the 1930s were always controversial. They did not put an end to the Great Depression – that came only once the war economy was fully up and running after 1941 – but they introduced an atmosphere of hope and optimism in those difficult years, and voters showed their gratitude by re-electing Roosevelt in 1936 with an overwhelming majority.

Later the social safety net was expanded, just as it was in post-war Europe. Even a man like Dave Lee in Sag Harbor, who wanted nothing to do with socialism, was full of praise for the GI Bill that treated millions of discharged soldiers to all kinds of public provision. 'The GI Bill was fantastic. It paid for my brothers to study. What am I saying; three-quarters of the people I know got their academic qualifications thanks to that GI Bill!' Americans even began to get used to it. What was seen in the 1930s as an eccentricity had by 1960 come to be regarded as a right.

Since the 1970s that system has been slowly dismantled. Democrat president Jimmy Carter provided the initial impulse; in 1978, under his administration, the top rate of income tax was reduced from forty-eight to twenty-eight per cent. In 1981, Ronald Reagan – who incidentally increased countless taxes – introduced new bonuses and reductions, and under his successors George H. W. Bush, Bill Clinton and especially George W. Bush, tax cuts became the new article of faith for millions of American voters. Surrounded by flags and other patriotic symbols, one president after another recited the Taxpayer Protection Pledge, that expensive oath that taxes would never, ever again be raised by so much as a dollar.

In reality, Americans have for a long time had little to complain about as far as taxes are concerned. They pay considerably less than citizens of most other developed countries. Much state support in America takes the form of tax breaks rather than subsidies, from child benefits to those mammoth exemptions for producers of ethanol.

Yet there remains that same eternal, intense revulsion felt by so many Americans against any form of taxation. The presidency of George W. Bush illustrated this most starkly. The hugely expensive free Medicare drugs for elderly people, the launching of two wars simultaneously, the introduction of a vast anti-terrorism bureaucracy under the name 'Homeland Security', the huge and rapidly increasing cost of pensions, the billions spent stemming the economic crisis of 2008 – none of it was allowed to cost the taxpayer one additional cent. In fact taxes were reduced yet again. Before a cheering crowd of supporters, Bush promised that his tax reductions for 2001 would benefit all Americans. In reality,

fifty-one per cent of the gains went to people with the top one per cent
of incomes.

What some American economists later concluded is correct: the essence
of so-called Reaganomics, from which Bush's policy flowed, was not a
fairer tax system but a massive transfer of income from the poor to the
rich. Behind it lay a characteristically puritan theory: whoever is blessed
with earthly goods spreads those blessings around him. In other words,
money is not simply a reward for hard and creative work, it also inspires
further hard and creative work. If the rich earn more and are allowed to
pay lower taxes, the thinking went, then they will make more of an effort
and thereby contribute more to the American economy. The government
will then be able to manage with lower tax revenues, and further cuts
will produce even greater efficiency. The benefits of all this will trickle
down to the lower-income groups and eventually everyone will be better
off. That was the theory.

The consequences of the politics of tax reduction have been dramatic.
The national debt, which in the 1960s hovered around 270 billion dollars
and in 1980 around a trillion, exploded to more than sixteen trillion by
2011. This gigantic debt was a particularly heavy burden because America's
trade balance was seriously out of kilter. Year after year, America produced
less than it consumed. In practice, total government expenditure was barely
reduced at all. There were cuts in the social sector, certainly, but expenditure on defence and security rose dramatically year on year, not to mention
the billions spent on supporting business after the crisis of 2008.

The transfer of prosperity from the top to the middle class did not
eventuate. In fact between 1980 and 2005 more than eighty per cent of
the increase in national income went to the richest one per cent of the
population. In 1960 that same one per cent received one dollar out of
every ten earned in the country. The figure is currently one in four.

The imbalance between rich and poor prompted a remarkable letter
to the New York Times in 2011 from Warren Buffett, then the third-richest
man in the world. He was responding to an appeal by American politicians for 'shared sacrifice' in the economic crisis. He had been spared,
which he found odd. When he asked his mega-rich friends what their
expectations were, he realised they had noticed no increase of any kind
in their tax burden.

Buffett asked around among his employees, too, and to his amazement he was forced to conclude that of all the people in his office he, the super-rich boss, was paying by far the lowest percentage of his income in tax. He thought the government ought at last to take seriously the notion of 'shared sacrifice': 'Billionaires like me should pay more taxes.'

When it comes to inequality in wealth and income, American statistics are reminiscent of a Latin American banana republic. 'Imagine a giant vacuum cleaner, looming over America's economy, drawing dollars from its bottom to its upper tiers,' writes political scientist Andrew Hacker. He estimates that since 1985, the bottom sixty per cent of American households have missed out on four trillion dollars in total, and most of that sum has ended up in the hands of the top one per cent. The combined wealth of the richest 400 Americans is currently greater than that of the poorest 150 million.

The consequences have been devastating. Not so very long ago, families belonging to the lower-middle class could put aside enough money to send their children to college. Those buffers are no longer there, so millions of students are being saddled for years to come with repayments on extremely expensive student loans. The question is whether they can or will continue to pay. Children of the upper classes have no such problem, so in theory they can choose whatever course of study they like.

According to a UNICEF report called 'The Children Left Behind', of the thirty-four highly developed OECD countries, the United States is at the bottom of the list when it comes to equal opportunities for every child, rich or poor. Moreover, one in thirty Americans is either in prison, on parole, or has a suspended jail sentence hanging over him. These proportions take you, in an economic sense at least, close to the class-based society of the eighteenth century, from which the American revolutionaries freed themselves with such difficulty.

> Ill fares the land, to hastening ills a prey,
> where wealth accumulates, and men decay.

That was the theme of the swansong of the great British-American historian Tony Judt. Shortly before his death in 2010 he wrote *Ill Fares the Land*, in which he warns from beginning to end against this rapidly increasing inequality, against the continuing erosion of the egalitarian ideal of the American Revolution. Equality was a principle that powered the dynamism of American society relentlessly in the past, and growing inequality will make American society more and more rigid.

With the help of a series of graphs, Judt compares countries with major disparities in income – the United States and, to a lesser extent, Britain – with countries where those differences are relatively small, such as Norway, Sweden, Finland, Denmark, Germany and Canada. The opportunities offered by each society become clear from these graphs if you look at mobility between the generations. America comes last in that respect, rather than first. According to the latest statistics, a mere eight per cent of American young people feel they have a chance of making the leap from the bottom social layer to the top. In Europe the figure is a good twelve to sixteen per cent. Judt writes: 'In contrast to their parents and grandparents, children today in the UK as in the US have very little expectation of improving upon the condition into which they were born. The poor stay poor.' In other words, if a boy or girl with a paper round wants to become a millionaire, then the place to be these days is Stockholm, not Chicago.

The graph representing fathers and sons is revealing. It indicates the average percentage of the income of the sons that can be explained by the income of their fathers. In other words it shows how much those children achieved for themselves and how much of their success is attributable to their parents. In the America of 1960 the figure was barely more than ten per cent, which accords with the classic American ideal. In 2000 it was almost thirty-five per cent, a figure more appropriate to a traditional class-based society. Then there are the striking differences in how long people live. 'We spend vast sums on healthcare, but life expectancy in the US remains below Bosnia and just above Albania.'

America is getting used to this. That's the worst part. Just as in Tocqueville's America the idea of equality became common currency within a few decades, just as the Americans of the 1960s quickly got used to food stamps, Medicare, Medicaid, the Head Start Program and other 'European-style' provisions, so the opposite is now taking place. As Judt writes: 'Conversely, thirty years of growing inequality have convinced the English and Americans in particular that this is a natural condition of life about which we can do little.'

In a newspaper I picked up later in Minneapolis and St Paul, I could see the effect. In the richest suburbs of the twin cities, average life expectancy is eighty-three years or more, in the poorest districts it is between seventy and seventy-five. 'This is a society of haves and have-nots.' I used to hear that kind of fatalistic comment only in Europe. Now it's heard here too. And the bitterness is growing.

Three

CANADA IS VIRTUOUS, for mile after mile. It has girls so perfect, so beautiful and unblemished, so completely flawless, that all desire is smothered by banality and predictability.

We're driving on Highway 3, close to the northern shore of Lake Erie, an endless farm road featuring miles and miles of maize and wheat, occasionally a farmhouse, a towering silo, a barn like a red cathedral and then another three miles of bare, wet fields. The farm labourers' dwellings are modest. The agricultural enterprise comes first; the reverse would be unthinkable. At house after house, everything is combed, trimmed, manicured, the blemishes smoothed away, permanently in its Sunday best. Dutch names are everywhere, a perfect fit with the neatness of the landscape: Ted Hessels, John Dekker, Richard Dijkstra.

It's a neat and respectable country. There are just as many guns floating about here as in the United States, yet the proportion of fatalities caused by firearms is more or less the same as in Europe, between 1 and 1.5 per 100,000 inhabitants. In America the figure is 5.3, four to five times as many. I still clearly recall the images captured by American documentary maker Michael Moore, who nipped over the Canadian border from Flint while investigating the use of guns. An hour away, people suddenly turned out to have no locks on their doors and to use their weapons purely for the purpose intended: for killing game, not people.

It's getting dark and the rain doesn't let up. Tillsonburg. A murky motel with a sweet Vietnamese woman at reception. We walk into the little town. On Broadway Street there is no one to be seen. In the distance the sound of yodelling blares across the silent asphalt. It's a Swiss family restaurant, empty other than one slowly chewing couple. They are Swiss themselves, and local residents. Once homesick, always homesick. We chew along with them, wordlessly.

The next morning the hotel's breakfast room is dominated by the television. A sun-drenched scene unfolds: a dusty village street, a white house with ivy, and a man who steps forward to sing a song. It must be somewhere in Central Europe. Halfway through, an elderly matriarch appears at a window and wipes away a tear. Next scene: a family at home. Large sofas, elderly uncles and fathers, another prominent maternal figure, the same melodious singer, sighs, silence broken by the occasional sob. Next image: the kitchen. The cook, who must also be well over sixty, prepares a typical local dish and the singer appears again, with another rosy song. So it goes on, from one tear to the next, this Macedonian heritage hour, canned nostalgia in daily doses for a world that vanished long ago.

I can't help thinking of General Patton. His orders on 10 July 1943, when Allied troops set foot in occupied Europe for the first time, on Sicily, left no room for ambiguity: 'When we land, we will meet German and Italian soldiers, whom it is our honor and privilege to attack and destroy. Many of you have in your veins German and Italian blood, but remember that these ancestors of yours so loved freedom that they gave up home and country to cross the ocean in search of liberty. The ancestors of the people we shall kill lacked the courage to make such a sacrifice and continued as slaves.'

For all their theatricality, Patton's remarks were not far from the truth. Most of his men were from European families and most of their parents or grandparents – because usually it didn't go back much further than that – had consciously opted for an American lifestyle and cast off their European ballast. Many had escaped from an oppressive world, where they were exploited by landowners and faced pogroms, discrimination and persecution. A few exceptions aside, they did not feel the need to replicate with any accuracy the lifestyle of home. They realised they were now in a completely new situation, in a whole new country.

It was different in Canada, a colony with its origins in two nations rather than one: Britain and France. Canadians have an instinctive respect for all possible distinctions between the two. At the same time they have a down-to-earth attitude to immigrants; love and work must come from both sides, from Canadian society but also from the immigrants themselves. In that respect they resemble Americans. This was illustrated by the results of a study carried out in forty-four countries by the Pew Research Center in 2002–2003, which looked at the most important rules to live by. One of the statements presented to participants ran: 'Success in life is pretty much determined by forces outside our control.' The Europeans were in agreement at least to some degree, whereas the Americans, along with the Canadians, rejected the assertion out of hand.

Canadians, however, combine that attitude with elements of the European welfare state – something to which the Americans have a growing aversion. To that extent the paternal, caring ruler is still present. Affairs are well organised. In the crisis of 2008, when banks in America and Europe tottered, Canadian banks, well regulated and disciplined, were barely affected at all. The police officer is a national symbol here, Robert Kaplan decided during his travels. Canadian heroes are more often groups – such as the builders of the transcontinental railway – than individuals. As Kaplan puts it, 'Canada never had a "Wild West" because the Royal Canadian Mounted Police got there first.'

Canadian author Margaret Atwood once compared the great idea behind America (the Frontier, that ever-advancing western border) and the idea behind Britain (the Island) with the central theme of Canada: Survival. 'Our central idea is one which generates, not the excitement and sense of danger which the Frontier holds out, not the smugness and/or sense of security of everything in its place, which the Island can offer, but an almost intolerable anxiety. Our stories are likely to be tales not of those who made it but of those who made it back, from the awful experience – the North, the snowstorm, the sinking of a ship.'

At first sight London, Ontario, seems to exude the same sense of sadness as the American towns we saw earlier: a desolate access road, endless high-tension cables, car breakers' yards to right and left, warehouses and fast-food chains, and behind them a treeless plain. Then a city centre full of holes, empty spaces, here and there an old fleapit hotel, and right nearby a handful of gleaming office blocks and a brand new shopping mall: two worlds lying no more than a hundred paces apart. In the centre of town, outside Starbucks, is one of those groups of small-town homeless you find all over the United States, gabbling endlessly, eating and drinking: coffee, cans of Coca-Cola, chicken drumsticks, hotdogs and greasy cakes.

In a café I leaf through the London Free Press. A survey by the London Community Foundation has just been published, showing that things are not going too badly for the city after all. The proportion of children growing up below the poverty level is 5.6 per cent here, and slightly under 1 per cent of residents make use of the food bank, a mere fraction of the usual percentages in the United States. Moreover, practically everyone in London has access to excellent education and healthcare, and the sense of community is strong. 'We are truly multicultural,' the newspaper declares proudly. There is one angry letter writer: 'I had to wonder how smuggled illegal Tamils can land on our shores where they receive the best medical treatment this country can offer, endless financial help at taxpayer expense, but we as a country refuse to properly look after our own?'

One of the homeless has meanwhile entrenched himself in the café and fallen asleep, and he's refusing to get up. A slight rustling sound can be heard and then two Canadian police officers arrive, don smart pairs of white Canadian gloves, take hold of the man, lead him back out onto the wet Canadian street, remaining polite and friendly throughout, and then remove their gloves.

We get up as well, climb into our Jeep, and drive out of the city centre, across the railway tracks and through endless neat residential neighbourhoods. No, nothing the matter here.

Chatham, Tilbury, and then finally the prim and proper avenues of Windsor. We drive straight towards the Detroit River and on the far bank America is within reach again. Into the river tunnel, which has a small border post at the exit where an American official asks us, with a chuckle, why in heaven's name we wanted to visit Canada, and we're in the heart of the metropolis that is Detroit. The traffic lights change from red to green and back again without a car passing. An old newspaper blows across the broad city street. Here and there I can see a light behind the dark glass of the office and hotel tower blocks. Occasionally a monorail train rumbles past above our heads, but other than that it is deathly quiet.

Four

ON ARRIVAL IN DETROIT IN 1945, John Gunther requested an interview with the great Henry Ford. The legendary automotive pioneer was still alive; he died two years later. Sure enough, Ford was prepared to receive the travelling journalist. Gunther had spoken to him several years before at Ford's private office in Dearborn, a suburb of Detroit to which he, along with his manufacturing empire, had moved in 1927. The powerful old man was sitting behind a practically empty desk, but the windowsill was lined with the little toys – rubber dolls, stuffed animals – that he would hand out to local children during his walks. There was a table covered in watches. Henry Ford had remained a lover of mechanisms, of carefully dismantling clockwork, of playing with time and speed.

Ford had always paid his workers well. In 1914 he was the first to introduce a minimum daily wage of five dollars. His competitors thought he was crazy. But anyone he didn't like had to leave at once, and unions were banned. His political beliefs were no less extreme. His generous support facilitated the translation and marketing of the classic anti-Semitic pamphlet *The Protocols of the Elders of Zion*. As his employee, the Episcopalian minister Samuel S. Marquis, wrote: 'If only Ford himself were properly assembled! If only he would do in himself what he has done in his factory!'

On his second visit, after the war, Gunther found a milder Henry Ford and a more relaxed atmosphere in the factories. The intimidation and the gangsters had gone, relations with the unions had been more or less normalised, and the elderly gentleman at the helm was now concentrating his formidable powers mostly on his intellectual legacy.

His company was by this point a gigantic concern, an early example of globalisation. Ford was already, as Gunther notes, a kind of government in its own right, often more powerful than a real government, with an annual turnover three times the entire state budget of Brazil. Even when compared to those vast enterprises, Ford had something resilient about it. Until after the war it remained a family company, based on a family fortune of more than 800 million dollars. 'Ford has no outside stockholders to satisfy, no banking interests to appease, no interlocking directorates to keep in order,' Gunther writes. He saw Henry Ford as the last of the flamboyant, stubborn and unpredictable American individualists. 'If he suddenly lowers the price of his cars, as happened without warning in early 1947, the rest of the industry lurches with dismay because, whereas Ford can do this, they may not be able to do so – or rather, even if they can, they may not want to.'

Henry Ford talked with Gunther mainly about his museum initiative. He was making grandiose plans to bring the American past back to life in his native Greenfield Village, a few miles from Dearborn. He wanted to replicate the America he knew as a child. The problem was that, as Gunther rightly remarks, he had done more than anyone to destroy that America. 'Now, in his old age, out of some kind of psychological displacement or nostalgia, he tinkers with his fingers in a blacksmith shop and looks for old-style locomotives that go puff-puff. The man who made the Model T allows no automobiles in Greenfield Village, except in the museum.'

The museum plan was an exercise in extreme manipulation. He could build and sell all kinds of things, so why not reconstruct time, turn back the clock, be the boy next door he once was, polish up the apple from his lost paradise and hang it back on the tree? The museum was intended to take the visitor home, or to the home of a boy called Henry Ford, to the 'good', rural, hardworking America of his youth. This was indeed nostalgia, presumably arising from the same kind of unease about the new America that motivated John Steinbeck, but experienced and interpreted in an entirely different way.

Henry Ford had been working on his museum plans for years when he received John Gunther, and a good deal was already in place: a sixteenth-century Cotswold cottage, brought over from England stone by stone, plank by plank, and restored down to the tiniest detail; the building in which Abraham Lincoln practised law; the garage in which Ford built his first car; the original laboratory used by Ford's great hero Thomas Edison, including the test tubes and retorts he used for his experiments and the original hawker's basket he used as a boy to sell newspapers and bananas. It was all plucked out of the country and out of history by Ford the magpie.

The complex is now the size of a large amusement park. Trains and vintage cars travel around it, and you can take a look at the workshop used by the Wright brothers. I understand that the collection now even includes a vial said to contain Thomas Edison's last breath.

The Henry Ford Museum next to the village is a doll's house filled with historical gems, including an original copy of the Declaration of Independence. You can gaze upon the upholstered rocking chair from Abraham Lincoln's box at Ford's Theatre, the very seat in which he was assassinated on 14 April 1865, five days after the capitulation of Confederate commander Robert Lee. You can walk past George Washington's camp bed, a drinking fountain from 1954 inscribed 'whites only', and the gleaming Lincoln Continental in which John F. Kennedy was being driven on that fateful November day in Dallas. You can even climb aboard the GM bus with the license plate 'Alabama 2609' in which black secretary Rosa Parks was sitting on 1 December 1955 when she refused to obey the driver's order to stand up for a white passenger, the moment that led to her arrest and thereby prompted the Montgomery Bus Boycott, the first major act of Martin Luther King's civil rights movement.

Historical bits and pieces like these form only a small part of the exhibition. The rest of the complex is full of machines, hundreds of them in all shapes and sizes, an enormous collection of cars, tractors, pumps and threshers, not forgetting the trains. They include not just passenger trains but goods trains, refrigerator cars, coal wagons, even a metres-high snowplough from Canadian Pacific. What energy, what power it all repre-sents, in the battle between man and the elements.

This is the world in which Henry Ford, mechanical genius, grew to become one of the greatest of American icons. The Declaration of Independence and that theatre seat of Lincoln's are all very fine, but I could stand and look endlessly at the Allegheny steam locomotive built in 1941, the iron monster of the Chesapeake and Ohio Railway that until the 1960s pulled coal trains several miles long through the mountains, hissing and whistling, sometimes with more than 160 wagons, so big and powerful that you could park two normal steam locomotives in its boiler alone.

Yes, the machine too is America, and in his 'mechanical thinking' Ford was a typical American. It was a worldview that made nineteenth-century America increasingly different from Europe. When people and organisations were spoken of in America, the usual image was not of nature, not of a tree with roots, not of growth, but of the machine, of action and creation. Ford's assembly line turned the human being into a kind of machine and Americans accepted that, even praised him for it. The way Ford dealt with materials was no less revolutionary.

Uncertain as American men can be regarding their fellow men, anthropologist Geoffrey Gorer writes, they are self-assured, serene, bold and creative in their relationship with materials. 'The American completely dominates his material . . . His vision, his plan, comes first; if nature does not provide the requisite materials, then he will do his utmost to improve and invent materials which will realize his vision.' That was Henry Ford all over.

Steinbeck believed that the remarkable inventiveness of Americans arose from pure necessity. It would be impossible to survive on the lonely prairie without it. 'Who among us has not bought for a song an ancient junked car, and with parts from other junked cars put together something that would run?' In earlier American literature, too, this phenomenon was regularly identified and described. 'The American taken randomly,' Alexis de Tocqueville wrote as far back as 1832, 'will be ardent in his desires, enterprising, adventurous, and above all an innovator.' In the margin of his manuscript he developed the point further: 'Nothing prevents him from innovating. Everything leads him to innovate.'

Poet and essayist W. H. Auden believed that mechanical thinking was closely connected to the unique power of imagination with which Americans were blessed. In America, work and industry were regarded as civilisation, so myths were not being dismantled here but created. George Santayana went a step further, believing that Americans think in two completely separate worlds. With one half of their brains they see the real world and with the other half a 'moral world', a world as it ought to be, a dream world but one that, or so they believe, is within reach. This explained the average American's focus on the future and his optimism, in contrast to the often rather fatalistic inhabitants of the Old World. 'Were he not imaginative he would not live so much in the future.'

In that same tendency lies the implicit but deeply rooted idea that to a great degree every individual holds his life in his own hands. *You Learn by Living* is the title of one of Eleanor Roosevelt's books about the 'good life', and the same was implied by dozens of titles of contemporary publications. For many Americans, life is not a natural thing but rather an activity that has to be filed and polished continually, a capability you need to train, as if preparing for an examination, something in which you start out as an amateur and can rise to great heights, becoming a professional in the art of living.

That too is part of the legend of the man who carried on tinkering with watches until his last breath, ultimately trying to bend even time to his will.

Five

DETROIT SEEMS TO BE SLEEPING when we drive into it on 7 October 2010. It looks like half past eight on a Sunday morning, but it is a Thursday morning at half past eleven. That is a measure of the disaster that has struck this city. It has become a contemporary ghost town, the postmodern Chernobyl of the United States.

From the window of our high hotel room I gaze out on what looks like a park, green and full of trees. Block after block, street after street, the lots on which houses used to stand are now largely empty, and vegetation is reclaiming them. The homes that remain are often isolated, like Hansel and Gretel houses in what is fast becoming a forest. The factory buildings are falling apart, their roofs collapsing, with trees growing out of their loading platforms and large holes burnt into their facades. Everything in the inner city was built and equipped for three times the number of people as live there now. The basic facilities are still intact, the headquarters of General Motors and the Renaissance Center hotel dominate the city centre with their luxury glass towers, but the sidewalks are empty, the ordinary shops and hotels boarded up, the office blocks squatted, the parking garages forgotten.

Just one type of person is present in abundance: the private security guard. Along the river a pleasant boulevard has recently been laid out, with space for half the city to stroll in the evening twilight, but there are only two joggers and a handful of security people. Classical music sounds continually from loudspeakers, to keep the junkies calm. The atmosphere is reminiscent of the banks of the Volga at Volgograd – the former Stalingrad – city of heroes, where I once spent a few days in transit and where everything was permeated by battles of old and stirring martial music.

Detroit is a textbook example of a metropolis that both sprang up and met its ruin with a single type of activity and the handful of men who dominated it. In the nineteenth century the city still had exactly the right formula for steady and balanced growth: a well-educated population and a multitude of small businesses. But in the twentieth century major success suddenly hit its streets. Detroit became 'Motown', America's 'Motor City', with more than 200 factories producing cars, engines and auto parts; a world where everything and everyone lived in the shadow of three giants: Ford, Chrysler and General Motors.

The men and women who lived in Motown were mostly workers on the assembly line, able to do one or two things well but lacking any vocational training. It made Detroit an ideal place for immigrants, especially black workers from the Southern states, who moved to the city in their tens of thousands from the First World War onwards. It was not so wild as Los Angeles, Chicago or New York; you couldn't grow rich so quickly here or make a big show of yourself, but Detroit did offer fortune hunters the security of a good job, a modest house, a car and a future for their children.

In November 1935 Ernie Pyle passed through a Detroit so big, busy, filthy and smoky it was almost frightening. At the same time it was a city with a personality, and it had already miraculously recovered from the Depression. 'Prosperity is definitely back. The auto plants are going full-tilt,' Pyle noted. 'The streetcars are crammed with workmen, lunch pails on their laps. The cocktail lounges are overflowing with rich-looking people. Theaters, many of them closed for years, are jammed to the hilt. Detroit is happy again.'

During the war the area around Detroit became the centre of the American munitions industry. In Willow Run, some thirty-five miles south of the city, the Ford Motor Company threw up a gigantic factory complex, producing not cars but B-24 Liberator bombers. Forty thousand people worked there, and at the height of production a B-24 rolled off the assembly line every hour. By the end of the war the American munitions factories had produced – along with millions of bombs, shells and guns – 7,400 ships, 300,000 aircraft, 88,000 tanks, 635,000 jeeps and 2.4

million trucks, largely manufactured in the industrial region in and around Detroit.

John Steinbeck drove past Toledo and nearby Pontiac in October 1960, then on to Flint, where General Motors' huge Buick and Chevrolet factories were located. He avoided Detroit itself, just as he avoided most other major cities. His notes were brief, he was in a hurry, eager to get to Chicago to meet up with Elaine. He was amazed at the fabulous size of everything he saw, and at the impossible chaos that seemed to prevail. It was as if the air was full of electricity, he wrote, so much energy was produced by this part of America. 'No matter what the direction, whether for good or for bad, the vitality was everywhere.'

At that point Detroit, with its population of two million, was one of the five richest cities in America. Now, half a century later, it's the country's poorest. According to the latest census, some 700,000 people still live here. Of those, twenty-eight per cent are unemployed, and for the black population that figure is fifty per cent. More than twice as many families as in the rest of America – thirty-eight per cent – live below the poverty line. Between 2000 and 2010 the city lost a quarter of its population, a demographic catastrophe.

Right now around 60,000 of the houses are empty, a third of the total. The average price of a house here in 2003 was 98,000 dollars; by the end of 2009 it had fallen to 15,000 and with a bit of luck you can get hold of a place for a thousand. The city has a budget deficit of 200 million dollars. Since 2005 almost seventy schools have closed. Less than a quarter of the city's pupils graduate from high school.

Behind the glass walls of the Renaissance Center none of this is in evidence. A congress is taking place about Christian Leadership. 'Isn't it great, being here together from all different countries,' a lady says by way of introduction as we swish down in the lift. 'From India, Nebraska, Kansas, wonderful, wonderful. God bless.' And she's gone, leaving us with her smell of fresh soap.

In the lobby I find that day's Detroit News. 'Grocer shot dead', 'Carjack – by a boy of ten this time. "He could barely reach the pedals," said the car's owner, laughing nervously.' On the inside pages I come upon a report about the trauma department at the Henry Ford Hospital, a grim indicator of the city's malaise. Cities like Miami and San Antonio make do with a single trauma centre. Detroit has four. 'If you are going to be a trauma surgeon', says the head of trauma and critical care surgery Pat Patton, 'Detroit is the place to be. Few see as much knife and gun stuff as we do.' A handful of cases at random on a typical evening: a woman weighing 200 kilos who, because she has no insurance, put off visiting a doctor until a virus had eaten clean through her intestines; a boy hit by a car, fortunately not too badly, whose mother refuses to pick him up, so he has to take the bus; a man shot through his ankle as a 'friendly reminder' that he's in arrears. There are men Pat Patton and his seven colleagues see on the operating table year after year with knife or gunshot wounds. Patton is forty-six and has worked like an army surgeon on the battlefield for two decades now, almost without a break.

On the riverside terrace the voices continue to babble and the wine sparkles as it always has. The waiter smiles. He's always lived here. 'One good way to deal with a problem, of course, is to go and stand with your back to it.'

Albert Speer, Hitler's favourite architect, loved to philosophise along with his boss about the 'ruin value' of their projects. What would the vast Nuremberg complex look like in, say, a thousand years? Even after it had collapsed and become overgrown, the glory of the Third Reich must still be clearly visible, like the glory of Rome today. Speer, with his sketches of ruins, would have been delighted by Detroit. There are other enthusiasts too. On the internet you can take a virtual walk through the city on websites like the 'Fabulous Ruins of Detroit', where the home page draws a comparison with ancient Ephesus, Athens and Rome.

The full passenger trains seen by Pyle and Steinbeck came to a halt in 1988. In 2010 the huge, square-looking Michigan Central Station, eighteen storeys high, with its once widely admired Beaux-Arts classical interior, stands alone in an empty field. The entire station district, with its once-busy offices, hotels and restaurants, has been completely erased. From a distance the building is reminiscent of the palace built by the Romanian dictator Nicolae Ceauşescu. For years it was the domain of squatters, junkies and disaster tourists, but now it's been securely cordoned off with razor wire that glitters in the sun.

Outside the centre, old Detroit was largely a wooden city. What now remain are mostly stone buildings, concrete complexes and innumerable underground parking lots with not a car to be seen. The timber has largely gone. Here and there you find a hotel, partly collapsed, partly burned out, sometimes still with a few half-smashed neon signs: 'AIR CONDITIONING, COLOR TV'. There are dozens of ruins of nineteenth- and twentieth-century schools, offices and factories, still in the process of falling down, with holes burned in them and with trees growing out through the windows and doorways. Office blocks are surrounded by timber structures to protect passers-by from falling rubble – thirty storeys or more, completely empty. The magnificent auditorium of the city's main theatre, where Frank Sinatra and other greats once performed, is now in use as car-parking space.

Six o'clock. Rush hour. We take a ride through the city centre on the People Mover, the virtually empty monorail, and get out on Broadway, at the Opera House, where Daniel, who runs a small bar, has put a few plastic chairs and two small tables out on the sidewalk opposite. He's playing draughts with Charles, who also lives around here. The Opera is shut. The orchestra has been on strike since yesterday over a pay cut of thirty per cent. Heated debates are going on at the bar. 'They used to bring *Nabucco* here with a sixty-strong choir. Now we do it with thirty-two.' 'But we still have to eat!'

Outside, part of the bar's terrace has been closed off. Here, too, rubble might fall from the buildings above. One car passes. Birdsong echoes down the street. The men calmly make their moves, exchanging a few words now and then. A black man cycles past with a heavy loudspeaker on the luggage rack; soul music is still audible long after he disappears around the corner. 'This is a really great spot,' says Charles. 'I always like sitting here. It's peaceful and quiet. Broadway! We could never have imagined that, either.'

What it reminds you of, they both decide, is the epilogue to a disaster movie.

In her epic work *The Warmth of Other Suns*, Isabel Wilkerson, the first black journalist to win a Pulitzer Prize, describes a wave of migration that for many years received less attention than it deserved from mainstream American historians. It has become known as the Great Migration, the mass flight of millions of Southern blacks who moved to the free North. Wilkerson tells her story from the perspective of three main characters: Ida Mae Gladney, a working housewife who moved from a poor rural district of Mississippi to Chicago in 1937; George Starling, an irascible and combative worker who swapped Florida for Detroit in 1943 and later moved to Harlem; and Robert Foster, an army medical officer who left Louisiana in 1953 to build a career for himself in Los Angeles. In all three cases they made a decision that every black person in the American South had to make sooner or later: whether to stay and knuckle under, or create a life of freedom elsewhere.

It was a silent exodus that began during the First World War, when the North was crying out for workers. Between 1914 and 1918 the black population of Detroit rose from just over 5,000 to more than 40,000. It continued to grow in the 1920s and 1930s, reaching new peaks during the Second World War when, as the black immigrants put it, the aircraft factories in and around Detroit paid 'dollars per hour' rather than 'pennies per box', and it continued right into the 1960s, when the 'WHITES ONLY' signs in the South finally started to come down.

In around 1910, just ten per cent of the black population of America lived outside the South, by 1970 it was almost half. In the intervening sixty years a total of six million black people left the plantations, villages and small towns of the South 'as though they were fleeing some curse'. They sought a new life in big cities like Chicago, New York, Detroit, Los Angeles and Philadelphia. The New York district of Harlem became the unofficial capital of black cultural life, Oakland in California became an important outpost of Louisiana, and Chicago and Detroit became places where you could find a steady job and start a family.

These were not immigrants who had entered the country through the famous Ellis Island, Isabel Wilkerson points out. They were already citizens, 'but where they came from, they were not treated as such. Their every step was controlled by the meticulous laws of Jim Crow, a nineteenth-century minstrel figure that would become shorthand for the violently enforced codes of the southern caste system.'

The Jim Crow regime, as it was known, was a system of written but

above all unwritten rules that every black person was expected to obey.
It was these Jim Crow laws that Rosa Parks was rebelling against when
she refused to stand up for a white passenger on that December afternoon
in 1955. As she would say later, you never knew what would happen if
you didn't obey those rules, but people knew enough to make sure they
never got into trouble.

For the first few decades after slavery was abolished, race relations in
the South were less troubled. In 1880 there were still mixed schools here
and there, and until 1891 everyone sat next to everyone else on the trams.
In 1877 at the end of the Reconstruction Era, as it became known, Federal
troops withdrew from the Southern states under strong pressure from
the Democrats. Southern whites remained grateful to the Democratic
Party for decades as a result, and even in Steinbeck's day the South was
a vital Democrat bulwark. The black population was left to its fate. On
paper, former slaves had the same rights as other Americans, but when
there were no longer any Federal troops around to enforce those rights,
they became virtually meaningless. Jim Crow would poison relations in
the South for almost a century. Everything in that system was aimed at
keeping black people in the position of slaves and outcasts, without them
being such in any formal sense. Meanwhile the Democratic North looked
the other way, fearful of losing votes – until the situation became
untenable.

Although the 'Negro problem' was the great social and political issue
of the United States at the time, weighing on the conscience of every
right-thinking American, in his work as a whole John Steinbeck paid
little attention to it. One incident does return repeatedly in his writing,
however, *Travels with Charley* included. On a winter's day he was standing
at dusk at the window of his house in Manhattan. The streets were icy.
The black man who worked for him came round the corner just as a
tipsy white woman emerged from a bar and fell flat, tried to get up and
fell again. She screamed melodramatically, but the black man declined to
lift a finger to help and stayed as far away from her as possible.

'Why didn't you give that woman a hand?' Steinbeck asked when the
man came in.

'Well, sir, she's drunk and I'm Negro. If I touched her she could easy
scream rape, and then it's a crowd, and who believes me?'

'It took quick thinking to duck that fast.'

'Oh, no sir!' he said. 'I've been practicing to be a Negro a long time.'

In the South the reality was a good deal grimmer until well into the 1960s. There were black and white waiting rooms, black and white ambulances, black and white public toilets for men and women, black and white cafés, bars and restaurants. Swimming pools and amusement parks had different opening times for blacks and whites, trains had separate carriages for 'colored people' – usually right behind the engine, uncomfortable, dirty and unsafe – and buses and trams had separate seating areas. The slightest interaction with a white person could get a black person into serious trouble: talking back, overtaking on a highway, failing to give precedence, even shaking hands without being asked.

Black men always had to be on their guard. Even a glance could impugn a hysterical white woman's honour, and on the rumour mill such an incident could easily grow into rape. According to the annual Lynch Report from the Tuskegee Institute, between 1882 and 1959 a total of 3,446 black people were lynched, 154 of them women. Three-quarters of those lynchings took place in the South, quite often for trivial reasons or for offences in which the victims were entirely uninvolved. Crowds stood by laughing; photographs of the hanged were sold as postcards. Every time another wave of violence swelled somewhere in the South, it would be felt even in the North. Black school principals in Philadelphia, for example, could tell from the sudden influx of new immigrants from specific regions of the South that something had happened there.

Isabel Wilkerson relates the story of Eddie Earvin, a young day picker at a plantation in Mississippi. While cutting spinach he sliced his finger. After three days he could no longer avoid going to the doctor, a walk of six miles, and on his way back he was stopped by the boss: '"Don't you know you don't go nowhere unlessen I tell you to?" the boss man said. He pulled a Winchester rifle out of the truck. "Maybe I ought to kill you right now," he said. The man put the rifle to Eddie's head. "You don't go nowhere unlessen I tell you to go," he told him.' In 1960, things like that were still happening.

In American literature it's often suggested that the Southern blacks moved north for economic reasons, mainly because the introduction of the cotton-picking machine meant there was no longer any work for them. Nothing in Wilkerson's research – and she interviewed hundreds of migrants – points to that. Most didn't work in cotton at all, and anyhow millions of black people left the South before the first machines arrived in the fields; in fact their introduction was, if anything, speeded up by a shortage of manpower. Whites tried by any means possible to prevent the mass exodus: train carriages were uncoupled, tickets torn up, black passengers arrested on departure. But black families continued to leave and their motives had everything to do with a lack of human dignity and, yes, with that American promise of equality.

So Jim Crow caused a wave of migration of historical magnitude and significance. Wilkerson writes: 'The Great Migration would become a turning point in history. It would transform urban America and recast the social and political order of every city it touched. It would force the South to search its soul and finally to lay aside a feudal caste system. It grew out of the unmet promises made after the Civil War and, through the sheer weight of it, helped to push the country toward the civil rights revolutions of the 1960s.'

It did not stop there. The Great Migration broke open the old America in a cultural sense too, influencing language, clothing, cuisine and dance, creating new musical genres – jazz, rhythm and blues, soul, hip hop – and signalling the birth of a broad black middle class. The first black mayors of the major cities all, without exception, came out of the Great Migration: Tom Bradley in Los Angeles (1973), Coleman Young in Detroit (1974), Harold Washington in Chicago (1983), David Dinkins in New York (1990) and Willie Brown in San Francisco (1996). Brown had started out as a cotton picker in East Texas.

Every black person knew the boundaries of Jim Crow territory: El Paso to the south, Washington to the north, the Ohio River if you were on your way to Detroit. These were the places where the illuminated signs saying 'COLORED' above the doors to the carriages were turned off and for the rest of the journey everyone could sit where they liked. This new freedom was usually recorded immediately by the immigrants in the form of a proud photograph. Isabel Wilkerson describes how as a little girl she found photos of such a moment in a drawer, featuring her mother and father. She was already at an expensive, predominantly white school by then, enjoying an education of which her parents could not even have dreamed.

Her classmates talked about ancestors who had arrived from Ireland or Scandinavia without a cent to their names. She mixed with children of recent immigrants from Argentina, Nepal and El Salvador and realised increasingly that she too was a typical child of migrants, with overly anxious parents, a circle of friends made up largely of 'fellow immigrants', cuisine from 'home', gossip from 'home', and a father who would have liked to see her engaged to a boy from 'home'. That was the origin of the fundamental realisation that lay behind her project: the exodus of black people from the South was also a wave of migration, with all the successes that accompany such a phenomenon, and all the social problems too.

'The migrants had been so relieved to have escaped Jim Crow that many underestimated or dared not think about the dangers in the big cities they were running to – the gangs, the guns, the drugs, the prostitution. They could not have fully anticipated the effects of all these things on children left unsupervised, parents off at work . . . Many migrants did not recognize the signs of trouble when they surfaced and so could not inoculate their children against them or intercede effectively when the outside world seeped into their lives.' Unlike in the South, there were no grandmas, aunts, brothers, ministers, cousins, sisters, grandpas, uncles, doctors, neighbours and family friends, no village of kindly souls surrounding them, day and night.

'Detroit is a sociological disaster story,' Joseph Amato told me later. A story of three disasters combined, a perfect storm. 'One: an economic base that concentrated on a single product. Two: a stream of immigrants that was too much for the city, families, churches and other social networks to cope with. Three: a housing market that eventually collapsed, robbing people not just of their homes but of any remaining financial security.'

Amato grew up in Detroit in the 1950s, and he saw the decline for himself to some extent. 'In my youth it was still a small version of Chicago, a nice town, and despite all the factories there was a lot of green space. The city had beautiful parks and good schools. But when my father became elderly he could no longer even walk round the block in his own neighbourhood – it was far too dangerous.'

The decline of Detroit began, as he saw it, at the end of the 1950s. The city's economy started to suffer setbacks, and when car manufacturing was automated, human hands were increasingly replaced by robot arms. Then there was the arrogance of General Motors, that conglomeration of automobile companies – Cadillac, Oldsmobile, Pontiac, Chevrolet and their suppliers – which after the war grew into the biggest car producer in the world. In some years, the company produced more cars than all its competitors combined.

Henry Ford, with his assembly line, was the first mass-producer. For years he made just one model, in just one colour. The first car for the ordinary man, the Model T Ford, was above all a solid, utilitarian product. At General Motors the designers took the era of the automobile into a second phase. From the late 1920s their cars were increasingly presented as status symbols, and the countless Americans who were doing all they could to fight their way up into the middle class were extremely suscep- tible to marketing ploys of that kind.

Whether it's a matter of the contents of our bookcases or the type of car we drive, our possessions say something about us, but rarely as much as they said about twentieth-century Americans, with their cheerful notion that you could always start again. Americans, some critics claimed, tried to recreate themselves primarily by purchasing things. The acquisition of the latest model of car was a statement. To underline the message, new features were added as the years went by – chrome strips, striking colours, tail fins – and, as in the clothing industry, new trends and fashions arose. By continually bringing out new models, a different one each year, a kind of restlessness was created among car owners: Isn't it time for a new car again? Am I falling behind?

Criticism gradually emerged, even within the automotive industry. Form has taken over from content and function, warned one of the most important designers, Raymond Loewy, in 1955, and he compared the latest models to jukeboxes on wheels. What went on under the hood was no longer a priority. Insiders felt that the spiral of innovation for innov- ation's sake contained the seeds of its own destruction. But no one listened. In 1956 more than half the cars sold in America came from General Motors, and some three-quarters of those cars were Chevrolets.

In his book *The Fifties*, David Halberstam writes that Chevys definitely belonged on the shortlist of things guaranteed to be American, things that could have originated nowhere else: Coca-Cola, a World Series baseball game, a grilled hamburger in the backyard, and sketches by Normal Rockwell in the *Saturday Evening Post*. The 1958 model was marketed through a TV commercial about a handsome young blond man who – surprise, surprise – suddenly finds a brand new Chevy with its roof down outside his front door. It's his high school graduation present. A secret kept by dad (wise and good-natured), mom (rather more strict) and sis (a little bit naughty). 'It is all clear: this is a great kid, a great family, a great car.' In the background the Chevy tune of the time is playing: 'See the USA in your Chevrolet.'

In Steinbeck's day General Motors seemed such a natural part of America that hardly anyone raised any questions when, for example, Charles Erwin Wilson, the most important man at GM, suddenly moved into one of the most important positions in government, as secretary of defense. When he was asked about potential conflicts of interest he replied: 'For years I thought what was good for our country was good for General Motors, and vice versa.' Those last three words were particularly telling.

General Motors was America, even when the downturn came. For decades the company had little trouble with foreign competition. Like the rest of the American automotive industry, it ran on cheap oil, easy government money for new highways, and an abundance of land and water for all those new suburbs where you couldn't live without a car. But the cars themselves, with all their stress on appearance and image, gradually fell behind technically. Meanwhile the unions had managed to negotiate excellent terms and all those obligations eventually grew into a heavy financial burden. General Motors was such a gigantic concern that for years its size alone concealed its inefficiencies.

In the 1960s the decline set in. Consumer activist Ralph Nader revealed that American cars, especially the Chevrolet Corvair, were unsafe. Their roadholding was notoriously bad. During the oil crisis they also turned out to be gas guzzlers. By this point Volkswagen was showing that an economical and well-built alternative was possible, namely the VW Beetle, which changed hardly at all over time. It was 'an honest car', as *Popular Mechanics* put it, and it sold well because 'it doesn't pretend to be anything it is not'. Japanese makes of car were also reliable, economical and technologically advanced, and their sales shot up year after year. An increasing number of American consumers drew the obvious conclusion: their Chevys, Fords and Chryslers were out of date.

An acquaintance of mine once told me that in 1976, as a young employee of General Motors, he proposed at a meeting that the company should start producing smaller and more economical cars. The response from the directors was immediate: 'We don't do things like that and we never will.' 'I thought, this is the beginning of the end for you,' the former employee told me. 'You're blind to the rest of the world. You refuse to adapt, but there will come a time when the world stops taking you seriously. I left.'

On 1 June 2009 General Motors was forced to file for bankruptcy protection. With assets of a little over 82 billion dollars, it had debts of 172 billion. The company was saved from bankruptcy only by an injection of billions in government money.

Much has improved since then. General Motors is once again the largest car manufacturer in the world, with more than 200,000 employees, and with factories in more than thirty countries. In a technological sense, however, the carmakers of Detroit are still lagging behind the Japanese and Europeans. According to figures from the Environmental Protection Agency, in 2010 US manufacturers were still near the bottom of the list when it came to the average fuel consumption of their products. Of the four bottom places, Detroit occupied three. At the North American International Auto Show in Detroit, once a highlight of the car world's calendar, hardly anything new can be found these days. All the innovation is coming from Europe and Japan, experts have told the New York Times. Attention has shifted. All eyes are now on the Frankfurt Motor Show.

For the workers of Motown the decline has been catastrophic. In 1970 General Motors employed 468,000 people in America, many of them in or near Detroit. By 2010, no more than 52,000 employees were left.

Detroit stands at an intersection at which the great social and economic problems of the twentieth century have come together with disastrous results: mass migration, a turnaround in economic fortunes, globalisation, and on top of all that the breakdown of old sources of social cohesion, such as neighbourhoods and families. The city represents the culmination of the problems John Steinbeck anticipated, which were part of what spurred him to go on his America expedition. He rarely expressed himself on the subject in public. In *Travels with Charley* some of those feelings are hinted at but later, in *America and Americans*, he ended, despite everything, with a hymn of praise to the strength of this country, 'wide open, fruitful and incredibly dear and beautiful' – precisely the kind of thing his readers wanted to hear from him. In reality, as is clear from his letters and certain things he said, he was extremely concerned about America's future.

He was not alone. A debate was underway among journalists and intellectuals about the mission of America in the new world of 1960. In its purposefulness it was a typically American question: What is our country really after, now that such an incredible amount has been accomplished? 'The critical weakness of our society is that for the time being our people do not have great purposes which they are united in wanting to achieve,' wrote columnist Walter Lippmann. 'We talk about ourselves these days as if we're a completed society, one which has achieved its purpose and has no further great business to transact.'

Presidential candidate Adlai Stevenson was worried as well. 'Why are so many Americans fearful that we have lost our sense of national purpose? . . . Why is there a slackness about public problems and a wholesale retreat to the joys of private life?'

Life magazine published a collection of articles under the alarming title *The National Purpose: America in Crisis: An Urgent Summons*, with contributions from Adlai Stevenson, Walter Lippmann, Billy Graham and James Reston. John F. Kennedy's New Frontier rhetoric can be traced back in part to the debate. Even President Eisenhower believed that a problem was starting to emerge. He appointed a special Commission on National Goals.

A few months before Steinbeck set out, something of his pessimism emerged. In the March 1960 issue of *Coronet* magazine, Adlai Stevenson describes visiting the writer in the old cottage in Somerset where he was working on his adaptation of the King Arthur story. Surrounded 'by all the ghosts – Druid, Saxon, Roman, Norman, English', Steinbeck talked endlessly about the legend of King Arthur and about the ever-recurring need for moral authority and a compass in times of confusion and doubt. He spoke about the meaning of that legend for the present day, about the eternal struggle between simple goodness and cunning wickedness and about the hunger, when such a period of corruption of the human spirit had passed, for purity and noble aims.

In November 1959, after Steinbeck had returned from Europe and read some of the American newspapers – the TV quiz scandal was at its height – he wrote Stevenson that disturbing letter about everything being rigged. Two things had struck him on his return. First, he talked about 'a creeping, all pervading nerve gas of immorality which starts in the nursery and does not stop before it reaches the highest offices both corporate and governmental'. Second, he felt he had identified 'a nervous restlessness, a hunger, a thirst, a yearning for something unknown – perhaps morality'. Then there was the violence, the cruelty and hypocrisy, symptomatic of a people that possessed too much. He believed the country could not survive on that basis. 'What we have beaten in nature, we cannot conquer in ourselves.'

Steinbeck did not foresee that all these problems would occur on a small scale as well, within the family. American family life was starting to change radically. There were more two-income families and more divorces, while neighbourhood and family ties were weakening. These problems were most acute among the black population. By 1960 the statistics were already troubling: more than a fifth of black babies were born to a single mother, often a teenager. Twenty years later, in 1979, the figure was more than half and it has since risen to almost three-quarters of black children.

These were statistics that pointed even then to enormous social problems within the black community. The sociologist, and later senator, Daniel Patrick Moynihan wrote in what became known as *The Moynihan Report* (1965): 'The family structure of lower class Negroes is highly unstable, and in many urban centres is approaching complete breakdown.' Moynihan was not thanked for that conclusion, least of all in progressive circles, but for countless neighbourhoods it was an inescapable reality.

There are two important comments to be made on this, one of a moral nature and the other practical. Firstly, black people were the only American population group that had not migrated of their own free will, whether from Africa to America or from the American South to the North. On the first occasion they were taken as slaves, and on the second it had been made virtually impossible for them to carry on living where they were. That past takes away none of the responsibility each person and each population group has for the way life is lived in today's world, but it remains a fact that these disasters are the consequence of the misery once caused by a specific group of white people, who were acting purely in their own interests, based on prejudice and a sense of superiority, without any scruples at all.

The second thing to note, of a practical nature, is that in contrast to what is generally believed, it was not the black immigrants personally who caused the greatest problems in cities such as Detroit. Isabel Wilkerson quotes a series of more recent surveys demonstrating that first-generation immigrants to the North were more likely to remain married than the black people who were already living there. They more often raised their children in stable households, were more likely to be in work, earned more, and fell into poverty or relied on welfare less often. The researchers say it was not the immigrants who caused trouble in the cities, in fact it was the reverse.

'In cases where things went awry, it turned out that the longer the migrants were exposed to the northern cities, the more vulnerable some became to the troubles of the preexisting world they had entered,' Wilkerson writes. At the same time, she continues to point to the quiet success stories of many ordinary migrants, such as Ida Mae Gladney in Chicago. Ida Mae always worked, never resorted to welfare or got into trouble in any way, went to church all her life and paid taxes, and through it all 'remained her true, original self'. Because of its fixation on the black underclass, Isabel Wikerson writes, America has completely ignored the huge achievements of all those millions of Ida Maes.

In Detroit, the first major street riots to involve blacks attacking whites took place during the Second World War, in the summer of 1943. It was the first time black people had broken out of the ghettos in such numbers to fight against white people and harm their businesses. In previous race riots, whites had always attacked and looted black districts. Now the blacks fought back. The rioting was terrible; it lasted a week, and thirty-four people were killed and over a thousand wounded.

After that, tensions gradually increased, as did criminality. In the 1950s half a million white residents left the city. The exodus accelerated after another week of major riots, arson attacks and looting in the summer of 1967. Joseph Amato described to me what happened: 'It got completely out of hand. The authorities were forced to deploy tanks, machine guns were fired in the streets, it was a mess. From that point on the whites left en masse. Their houses lost value, and the city too. That was the start of a fresh tragedy, since for Americans a house may be their only capital, their pension, their investment for their old age. If the house isn't worth anything any longer, that's a disaster in itself.'

When Steinbeck passed through Detroit, seventeen per cent of its residents were white. Ten years later it was the blackest city in America, an important black cultural centre with a black mayor and a robust black middle class. It was just that people were earning less and less, the city was becoming poorer, the police more corrupt and the criminals more powerful and violent. 'In my old neighbourhood, shop owners were robbed by children of twelve or fourteen, with those fat handguns in their small fingers,' said Joseph Amato. 'In the end the only ones who dared run a shop in my old neighbourhood were refugees from Iraq. They were used to that kind of violence and they shot robbers without mercy, even if they were only boys of fourteen.'

Detroit, with its record total of more than 10,000 unsolved homicides, became the murder capital of America. Dereliction leads to arson, and Detroit was no exception. In the disastrous 1980s and 1990s, fires were an everyday occurrence. In 1983, on Devil's Night, the eve of Halloween, more than 800 buildings were set alight. Not until after the start of the new century did the chaos slowly abate – on Devil's Night in 2009 the city had only sixty-five fires, a negligible number by Detroit's standards.

Anyone who has watched The Wire, a television series about ghetto life in a major American city, and who then drives through Detroit, will see the place in a quite different light. You do have to think about your own safety – a Dutch colleague of mine recently had a gun put to her head at the traffic lights and lost her car – but you see it all: the little drug dealers on street corners, the waiting, the punters driving slowly past, the clearly delineated territories. Beyond the next intersection you may suddenly find yourself in a smart neighbourhood, house after house with white fences and manicured lawns. Another block and you're taking your life in your hands again.

The Wire is about the fifteen to twenty per cent of the population for whom America has no use, who know it, react to it, and at the same time do all they can to survive. You come upon them everywhere. But it's about more than that too. Where Steinbeck wrote of the 'all pervading nerve gas of immorality', the creator of The Wire, David Simon, talks of 'the death of work'. He means not simply the loss of jobs, but the loss of the self-worth and integrity that would normally be features of a working community: the pumping-up of statistics, the pleasing of superiors rather than honestly saying what's going on, the concentration on scores, the performance assessments, and the substitution of form and appearance for quality.

The city government in Detroit fell prey to all that when the downturn first set in. It wasted years believing that new offices, industrial areas, roads and tunnels, subways and other transport systems, recreational facilities and prestigious buildings could turn the tide. Eventually the city switched course and accepted, like other declining regions, that shrinkage is a fact.

Now, slowly, in the emptiness and silence, a new urban culture is emerging, made up of a thousand and one small and ingenious initiatives. Above the MexicanTown Bakery in the south-west of the city you'll find SOUP, a simple place where you can get a bowl of soup and a plate of salad for five dollars. Every month the customers vote on which neighbourhood project should receive the proceeds this time, so that a tiny park can be laid out, a couple of security cameras mounted, that kind of thing. There's Bizdom, a huge 'startup accelerator program' aimed at entrepreneurs who have spotted new opportunities in Detroit. Plenty of cheap space is available. City farms are springing up in the urban prairies – sometimes little more than a football field with some vegetable plots and a few untidy-looking polytunnels, but it's an interesting initiative. A few people make a living as urban hunters. I hear about a retired truck driver who is doing good business with raccoon meat. His recommended marinade is composed of herbs, spices and vinegar. Rabbits and squirrels are particularly tasty in stews.

A new art world is emerging, too, including an international collective called the Detroit Unreal Estate Agency, a group that focuses on the new ways of living together that are emerging in this 'post-apocalyptic city'.

Then of course there's the internationally famous project on Heidelberg Street, a rustic backstreet in East Detroit where disintegrating telephone cables trail along the ground and packs of wild dogs prowl about. Artists are turning the entire street into an artwork, and the project now attracts tens of thousands of visitors each year. The houses have been painted orange and bright blue, or covered in dolls and teddy bears; a car stuffed with doll flesh is gently rusting away, and in one garden dozens of Father Christmases meditate. There are tall wooden structures, a sculpture in a cage, and one white-painted house is covered simply with numbers: 60, 4, 20, 13A, 375, 1000 . . . I even spot the Dutch 'Ban de bom' cartoon by Opland – 'Kick the bomb habit!'

On the corner is a half-buried Hummer, the gas-guzzling luxury armoured personnel carrier that General Motors manufactured and sold in the 1990s. Where the engine used to be is a tiny flower garden and on a purple sign a kind of motto: 'Ashes to ashes, dust to dust / We bury a Hummer here to rust. / And from these ashes we recreate / A world of peace, an end to hate.'

Small vegetable plots grow along the side streets, a neighbour has started keeping chickens, and here and there you see someone calmly cycle past. The city has returned to the village. There's an odd kind of peace, an acceptance of fate. Home. Home again, always.

PART FOUR

Michigan – Chicago – Illinois – Wisconsin – Minnesota

'I'm still a man. Damn it!'

JOHN STEINBECK
1960

One

WITHIN TEN MILES DETROIT IS ERASED from the landscape, gone
without a trace, forgotten like a bad dream. Just fifteen minutes out and
the highway rises and falls through the undulating cornfields of Michigan
as if nothing has happened. The company names sound respectable again
and, to a Dutchman, familiar: Hoekstra, Ritsema, Van Deck. A billboard
shouts: 'A family that prays together stays together.' Along the roadside,
dead animals are strewn like shreds of a car tyre, except for one raccoon
lying intact on its back, paws folded, as if asleep.

Steinbeck was enjoying himself here. He, too, noticed how abruptly
the teeming industrial areas came to an end, disgorging him onto a quiet
country road with trees on either side, fenced fields and cows everywhere.
He writes that he circled northwards slightly, 'through or near' Pontiac
and Flint, ending up beside a lake of clear water in northern Michigan.
In his disposable aluminium pans he prepared 'improbable dinners' and,
sitting on the step outside Rocinante's back door, he tried to get his
thoughts in order about all the things he had seen. He watched the arrows
of ducks and geese flying south high above him.

As planned from the start, he avoided the hubbub of cities. He had
noted down a few generalities about them and it was only now that
the real, unspoilt America began for him. In that sense he was following
in the venerable tradition of Thomas Jefferson, for whom the ideal
America was an agricultural country, a democracy of independent
farmers living off the produce of their own land. 'Those who labour
in the earth,' said Jefferson, 'are the chosen people of God if ever he
had a chosen people.'

The result of Steinbeck's policy, however – and this was something of which I was increasingly conscious – was that in his travel account he deliberately excluded a large part of America. It was a reticence I was drawn into along with him, despite myself. The eternally rejuvenating America, the America of the suburbs and the dynamic inner cities of Detroit, Chicago, Seattle and – for example – San Francisco, were largely omitted from Steinbeck's account. To that extent he had something in common with the elderly Henry Ford; his America was ultimately the America in which he grew up, the rural and small-town America he brought to life time and again in his books.

There was something equivocal about it, that avoidance of cities, and Steinbeck admitted as much. Should his readers follow his route after him, they might encounter a quite different America. 'On the long journey doubts were often my companions,' he wrote. 'So much there is to see, but our morning eyes describe a different world than do our afternoon eyes, and surely our wearied evening eyes can report only a weary evening world.'

Steinbeck made himself out to be a traditional American, most at home amid the eternally silent folk of the open country. That does tally with what Arthur Miller wrote about him: 'A shackled giant of a man fit for sun, water, and earth and not sidewalks and smart people.' In practice, however, he was as much a modern city dweller as Miller, with an apartment in New York and a busy social life, frequently taking long trips to Paris, London and other European cities. That inner conflict, hidden within *Travels with Charley*, was characteristic of Steinbeck, and it seems very likely that his large American readership were all too eager to recognise themselves in this rural America, whether or not such a self-image reflected reality.

Steinbeck's musings beside that Michigan lake were disturbed, he writes in *Travels*, by an angry-sounding employee of the owner of the land. He managed to placate the young man with a cup of coffee and a glass of whisky. They went fishing for pike together and, as they talked, a friendship grew up between them – for a day, anyhow.

The 'guardian of the lake' had a wife, Steinbeck wrote, who found her only companionship in the magazines *Charm* and *Glamour* and who, by exerting gentle pressure, was sure to persuade this man of nature eventually to move to the city, where he would live the rest of his life dissatisfied, although he didn't know it yet.

They caught not a single pike.

That evening we find ourselves in a large family villa built of timber in Queen Anne style, stately blue-grey, all turrets and dormer windows, surrounded by a big, leafy, old-fashioned garden. The town is called Kalamazoo, meaning 'boiling water' in the language of the Native Americans who were still to be found ranging abroad here in 1820.

The further west you go, the shorter history gets, in European eyes at least. When Alexis de Tocqueville and Gustave de Beaumont travelled the region in 1831 it was covered in endless forest, aside from the occasional felled area with tree stumps still sticking out of the ground. Detroit was 'a fine American village' of 2,500 residents, Pontiac a settlement of twenty houses, Chicago a trading post, and as for Washington, they wrote that it 'offers the sight of an arid plain, burned by the sun, on which are scattered two or three sumptuous edifices and the five or six villages composing the town'. They dined with John Quincy Adams, on a riverboat they ran into Sam Houston – the man who would declare independence for the Lone Star Republic of Texas four years later – and it was only for lack of time that they passed up a meeting in Virginia with the eighty-year-old James Madison, one of the Founding Fathers of the Republic.

I experienced the brevity of history here on a trip through Texas several years ago. An elderly farmer told me that his mother, born to pioneers, had spent her childhood in a dugout, a kind of hole in the ground, the sort of dwelling you come upon in descriptions of seventeenth-century New Amsterdam. Yes, she was still alive; she lived with him and was almost a hundred. I saw a small, wrinkled woman standing by the kitchen counter, whisking ice-cold milk for us in a large red blender. So much history in one milkshake.

The same applies to the house we are staying in. To a European it's not particularly old, dating from 1886, but it represents practically all the local history there is to be told, from beginning to end. It was built by the owner of the *Kalamazoo Gazette*, and at its heart is a large hall with an open spiral staircase and doors to at least ten rooms: a drawing room, dining room, smoking room, study with library, and upstairs five or more bedrooms. It was skilfully restored some twenty years ago, and the builders discovered that the original design used a different kind of wood for each room: pine, beech, oak, fir, ash, cherry.

'Michigan was the centre of the nation's timber industry in those years,' says Chris, the current owner, as he stands juggling things on the stove. 'You can still see how well built the house was.' It offers bed and breakfast now, and all the guests tend to come together in the kitchen. It has become his life's work, this house, and he and his wife Dana cherish every sash window and every dormer as a work of art.

He fetches *A Pictorial History of Kalamazoo* from the library, a family album full of old photographs. We skip through a century and more. First there is Main Street in about 1900, with its own horse-drawn tram, rows of shops to left and right, the awnings low against the sun, a few carriages and carts, and the sidewalks crowded with pedestrians. Then the hardware store owned by the Kersen family, on a summer's day in 1896. Arend Bos' smithy in 1908, when everyone still met everyone there. The harsh winter of 1918, when even the train got stuck in several metres of snow. Arnold van Loghem's saloon in 1915 and Jan Brink's bread factory in 1920. Helen van der Kolk at the edge of town in 1923 – 'Speed limit 15 miles per hour. Thank you!' Nelly Grace and her father, listening to the radio together in 1930. 'Bomber queen' Lorraine den Boer, who was accorded the privilege of christening a B-17 that the town had collected money to build in 1943. Then, once again, the wide shopping street at the corner of Michigan Avenue and North Burdick Street, which is now all high-rises and large display windows, full of cars and shoppers.

I recall a journey through this area a few years ago, past villages called Holland, Zeeland, Overisel, Borculo and Vriesland. I saw graveyards full of Dutch names; in Grand Rapids I passed the huge Van Andel Arena, and in the *Grand Rapids Press* I read all the Dutch preacher names and saw all the hard Reformed Church faces still locked in typically Dutch theological disputes, as if nothing had changed since 1950.

Next morning a fresh copy of the *Kalamazoo Gazette* is waiting for us in the kitchen. The Kalamazoo Singers have a new conductor, another of the town's war casualties will be buried on Tuesday – Anthony Matteoni, leaving a young wife and an unborn child – and the letters page features a discussion about the blessings or otherwise of the major retail chains: 'The big stores such as Walmart and Meijer are pushing mom-and-pop stores out of business.'

At breakfast a lively discussion breaks out about the old phenomenon of the date, a North American ritual performed by girls and boys that is found nowhere else in the world. It may have started because all those immigrants had different customs at home, so a need arose for new but firm rules.

Tocqueville and Beaumont were barely twenty-five when they made their American journey, and in their letters, among all the serious-minded observations, you regularly come upon remarks about the many blue eyes and other charms of the young women they met. They were astonished even in those days by the freedom and independence of American girls, and by their flirting, which was combined with an overt prudishness. It totally confused the young French travellers. 'Can you believe, *mon cher ami*, that since our arrival in America we have practised *the austerest virtue*. Not the slightest swerve. Monks – I ought to say, good monks – could not have done more.'

'Does the dating ritual actually still exist?' I ask. Geoffrey Gorer, who described Americans the way an anthropologist might an indigenous tribe, devotes many pages to the custom, which he finds exotic. A good date, he writes, is comparable on the one hand to a formal dance and on the other to a contest, a game of chess, accompanied at all times by the whispered commentary of spectators. It is a combination of show, flattery, wit and lovemaking, and there are many unwritten rules. The boy and girl have to spend most of their time together in a public place and the girl is nearly always offered food. What finally happens in the car on the way home depends on the dynamics of negotiations between the pair, but it is not the primary objective. An easy lay is not a good date, and vice versa.

Gorer describes the date as it still existed in the 1950s, the ritual that we Europeans have witnessed in countless films and books. But does it still happen? Chris and Dana shake their heads: no, that was before their time. Carol, one of the guests, is a university lecturer who happens to be a specialist in this kind of research. When she tells her students about rituals like dating they look at her, wide-eyed. 'They do everything in

groups now, they don't get attached so quickly, they mess around a bit
first.'

She believes the phenomenon of the kiss to be far more interesting
than the old-fashioned date. 'If an anthropologist from Mars landed here,
he'd certainly want to make a study of the kiss. It's such an extraordinary
human activity. Think of all the variation you see. The Pentecostals are
crazy about the full body hug, whereas the Methodists are terrified of it
and just shake hands. In New Hampshire and Vermont people are even
less likely to start kissing and hugging. They keep their distance. But you
should see California!'

She laughs ebulliently.

The following morning it's time for a short trip around town. First we
explore older parts of the central district, the streets laid out between
1900 and 1940. Among the biggest builders was one Henry van der Horst,
a Dutch orphan who wound up in Kalamazoo in 1891 and made his
fortune here. His classic timber houses are all over the town, with bay
windows and dormers, and always a large porch where everyone can sit
and talk in the evening. Children are playing with a wheelbarrow full of
leaves in the warm autumn sun; you can hear their squeals of pleasure
half a block away. This is still the world of Norman Rockwell, the artist
who became a household name in the years around the Second World
War with his covers for the *Saturday Evening Post*. Week after week he depicted
America as a small-town utopia, inhabited exclusively by polite pedestrians, pleasant neighbours, a few shopkeepers and well-bred mischievous
children, a world that would never change.

We pass the big town square, which features a huge First Presbyterian
Church, made of neo-Gothic concrete, and a handful of other houses of
God – the Reverend Matt Loney will be preaching tomorrow on the
subject of 'When money buys happiness' – and then we set off in search
of the shopping street in the old photographs we saw.

It is actually quite hard to find the right place half a century later. On
the corner of Michigan Avenue and Burdick Street I manage to orientate
based on a frontage further along and the odd detail, but the rest has
changed beyond recognition. Most of the old Burdick Street has been
demolished and replaced by an enormous Radisson tower and its adjoining

catering complex. The street is pedestrianised, trees have been planted, and the impression it gives is that of the umpteenth shopping mall in a random suburb – identical from Spokane to New Orleans.

Steinbeck wrote with some alarm about that hotel where absolutely everything was wrapped in plastic. Well, here an entire town centre has been wrapped in plastic. The facades, ridge boards and ornaments once had a clear function and conveyed their own message. They told the story of previous generations and created a sense of solidarity across the years. They've been reduced to pointless embellishments, fripperies with nothing to say. The rhythm of the street and the frontages, the streetscape, has been completely eradicated by that gleaming Radisson colossus.

Every historical building says something not just about the past but about our civilisation, the context of our lives, even in the relatively young towns and cities of America. In Kalamazoo, the function of all those fine and idiosyncratic frontages from the first half of the twentieth century was far more important than their mere appearance. The builders and developers were interested, often unconsciously, in the town as a whole, in creating an environment in which classic citizenship, *civitas*, could continue to flourish. That was characteristic of the towns Steinbeck passed through. Now we see only the remnants of it.

Kalamazoo does what it can to preserve the *civitas* of the town. Established, wealthy families have clubbed together to reverse the decline with an eye-catching campaign. Every young person who graduates from public high school in Kalamazoo can attend college free of charge for four years, their tuition fees paid by the Kalamazoo Promise fund. The fund keeps families in the town and it even attracts newcomers but, 'Promise' or not, here as in so many similar places the local economy has largely vanished, and the characterful town centre has been surgically removed with all too much skill.

Sunday in Kalamazoo. I go to church again, the Netherlands Reformed Congregation, founded by Dutch immigrants but English-speaking for the past hundred years or more, since otherwise no one would come, let alone any young people. Churches in Europe are settled institutions, with strong ties to a place and the land, quite often bound up with the authorities and the established order. In America almost all churches were established from the bottom up, on the initiative of churchgoers who came together voluntarily to form congregations. They differ greatly from place to place and all have to pay their way, which explains why the members, and especially the clergy, always devote so much attention to fundraising. Researchers speak of a 'lively market', complete with 'religious entrepreneurs', continual 'product development' and 'competing' congregations. A strong progressive movement exists alongside all those conservative and reactionary denominations. In their films for new members, these more liberal churches present themselves as offering a broad spectrum of activities, from soup kitchens and clothing distribution to programmes for drug users, orphans, veterans, vagrants and prisoners.

Such groups are not at all happy that the Republicans have more or less set themselves up as the party for believing Christians. In 2008, in a document headed 'An Evangelical Manifesto', evangelical leaders from major American educational institutions and religious denominations, including the National Association of Evangelicals, voiced resistance to any fusion between biblical truths and Republican beliefs. Believers would do better to distance themselves from all party politics, the signatories wrote, since otherwise 'faith loses its independence, the church becomes "the regime at prayer", Christians become "useful idiots" for one political party or another'.

There is little evidence of any such irritation at this church, and certainly no sign of 'product development'. It belongs to the Netherlands Reformed Congregations of North America, which has some 10,000 members: American yet thoroughly Dutch. As I drive up I see my fellow churchgoers pouring in as if on their way to a funeral, the men in dark suits, the women with (in some cases elegant) black hats, and many of the young girls wearing straw boaters.

In the doorway stands the verger, a hearty Rotterdammer who emigrated to these parts fifty years ago. 'It may take a while this morning; we have Holy Communion, but there's a sermon first,' he whispers. 'It's a fairly strict congregation here. Don't be alarmed.'

I step into a robust and intimate church with a small but jaunty steepled tower. Apart from the enormous parking lot – all members without exception are blessed with opulent earthly bodywork – none of this would look at all out of place in Zeeland or on one of the islands of South Holland. There's no cheerful welcome here as there was from the Baptists in Camden; at best, people peer furtively at the stranger. In their house of God they focus on serious business and the preacher gives a sermon stiff enough to stand a spoon up in. You can count on that, you old sinner!

We sing in semibreves, heavy and slow. Wasn't it on the island of Urk that I last heard this kind of singing, forty years ago? The elders get to their feet, a black-clad block, and the pastor begins to pray for us all, 'wretched hell-deserving sinners'.

In front of me sits a young couple, she with a straw hat, he in a stiff suit, and she presses herself discreetly to his black sleeve.

Now for Holy Communion. I'm suddenly back in the Pelikaankerk in Leeuwarden, in 1950. The pastor begins to recite an endless service, precisely the same as sixty years ago, only this time in English. It's clear that none of those who go up to the Lord's Table are adulterers, frequenters of whores, thieves, murderers, drunks, or interesting sinners of any other kind: 'If they come to the Table, they will be all the more harshly punished in the afterlife.'

The children sit twisting in their seats. Nothing new there, either.

The wife of the verger, with an encouraging nod, slips me an extra Wilhelmina peppermint.

Where exactly am I?

Two

IN THE AFTERNOON WE DRIVE TO CHICAGO. All along the verges we see roadkill, this time even a deer. You could eat every night from the highway here, in fact I've heard of people who do. The conduct of our fellow motorists has been extremely easy-going up to this point, especially on the back roads. Manoeuvring around gas station parking lots, restaurants and motels was all very amiable. Whopping great trucks and four-wheel drives slid silently and slowly into their parking spaces, like languid cows returning to their stalls. Everyone was polite. You rarely saw any cutting-up or tailgating. Reduce speed when you're being overtaken, move out if someone has stopped at the side of the road, give priority to pedestrians: the American traffic rules encourage all these things. You're expected to wait for others at crossroads and stop behind stationary school buses. Perhaps it has something to do with the availability of space. No need to jostle for position.

As we approach Chicago, all that courtesy suddenly goes out the window. The atmosphere on the interstate becomes more turbulent, you can feel the energy building; high-tension cables appear, major intersections, subway lines. A goods train joins us, with four locomotives, at least a mile long. In the suburbs the highway becomes a mincing machine, with sharp turns onto slip roads, unexpected flyovers, a mass of vehicles, and no one gives a damn about any speed limit.

Then suddenly we're all at a standstill. It's the day of the annual Chicago Marathon, which treats us to a traffic jam lasting half an hour or more.

A pause for breath, to grow accustomed to the city.

Hog Butcher for the World,
Tool Maker, Stacker of Wheat,
Player with Railroads and the Nation's Freight Handler;
Stormy, husky, brawling,
City of the Big Shoulders.

After New York and Los Angeles, Chicago is the third-largest city in the US, and nowhere else is so thoroughly American. Carl Sandburg, who wrote the above lines, adored the place, but Rudyard Kipling hoped never to see it again: 'It is inhabited by savages . . . and its air is dirt.'

New York is perhaps more of a 'world city', John Gunther writes, but Chicago gives a sense that 'America and the Middle West are beating upon it from all sides'. Gunther was hardly objective. He had spent his childhood in Chicago and to him it was the city with 'the most intense vitality and energy' of all those he had lived in:

The icy wind screaming down snow-clogged boulevards; the sunny haunch of Lincoln Park near the yacht moorings in torrid summers; the automobilelike horns on the Illinois Central suburban trains; the steady lift of bridges, bridges, bridges; holes and bumps and mountains and earthquakes and yawning pits in the streets; the piercing whistles of angry traffic cops; the marvelous smooth lift of the Palmolive Building and how the automobiles seem to butt each other forward like long streams of beetles; the tremendous heavy trains of the North Shore whipping like iron snakes through the quivering wooden suburban stations; the acrid animal smell from the stockyards when the wind blew that way, and the red flush of the steel mills in black skies – all this is easy to remember.

Chicago – its name is derived from the Native word for 'wild onion' or 'wild garlic' – was founded as late as 1830. It was initially little more than a fort plus a few neighbouring buildings. Someone who passed through in 1833 described it as three muddy streets with a group of huts accommodating some 350 souls. Less than sixty years later, a million people were living at that same spot. There are now not far short of three million. In the second half of the nineteenth century it was the fastest-growing city in the world, a fact closely connected with the advent of two new means of transport that were crucial to the opening-up of the continent and to the American success story: the railway and the steamboat. Chicago's location made it ideal for both.

Between 1830 and 1880 America changed so radically and at such a pace that it astonished even the Americans. The population grew by 400 per cent, compared to 17 per cent in France, for instance. Between 1850 and 1880 industrial production rose by 600 per cent – three times faster than in Great Britain.

The territory of the United States took shape in those years. The Americans had bought Louisiana from the French back in 1803 and Florida from the Spanish in 1819. In 1836 the pioneers of Texas, under the leadership of Sam Houston, rose in revolt against the Mexican authorities and in 1845 Texas became the twenty-eighth American state. A year later the settlers in California rebelled against rule by Mexico; the US Army intervened and their state officially became part of the United States in 1850. A large stretch of wilderness in the north-west – including what would later become Washington, Oregon and Idaho – was acquired from the British, then in 1853 another piece of Mexico was purchased and in 1867 the US took over Alaska from Russia. All this gave the United States of America roughly the size and shape it has now.

Illustrative of the great zest of nineteenth-century America were the many inventions on display in 1851 at the Great Exhibition in London's Crystal Palace. American machines, one visitor said, could 'stamp out nails, cut stone, mold candles – but with a neatness, dispatch and tireless reliability that left other nations blinking'. By about 1880 there were more miles of railroad track and telegraph wire in America than in all of Europe put together. So much power, so much vitality; the country was truly blessed. Abraham Lincoln described it as 'the last best hope of earth'.

This was the period in which Chicago grew to become a world city. The era determined its character, since its dynamism inevitably created huge social and political tensions. In 1848 the city was connected to the rail network for the first time, and in that same year the Illinois and Michigan Canal was opened, a new transport artery between the Great Lakes and the Mississippi River that provided Chicago with the largest inland harbour in the world.

The whole place was an example of American serendipity. Because the houses kept sinking into the mud, the city government decided in 1856 to raise the entire urban area by more than a metre. Briggs House, five storeys high and made of stone, was jacked up – it continued to function as a hotel throughout the operation. When a third of the city was burned to the ground in a massive fire fifteen years later, leaving a hundred thousand people homeless, Chicago made a virtue out of necessity. New fire-resistant construction methods were developed, using steel frames, stone floors and terracotta cladding.

Partly for that reason, and because of the invention of the lift, the first tall office blocks and skyscrapers appeared in 1880. They would shape the look of downtown Chicago, and of American city centres in general. In 1885 the Home Insurance Building became the first skyscraper, ten floors high. Two years later the construction of the Auditorium Building began, also ten storeys. Completed in 1890, its magnitude was unprecedented: 136 offices and shops, a 400-room hotel, a sixteen-storey tower at one corner and a concert hall that could seat 4,200, making it the largest building in the world. In a cultural sense, too, Chicago had taken centre stage.

Skilled artisans moved to the city from the start, especially furniture makers. Architects and engineers were given a chance to make their wildest plans a reality, and to this day much of the architecture in Chicago is of the highest standard. Butcher Gustavus Swift combined his meat-processing plant with a refrigerated boxcar and started the first national meat-packing company in 1885. One of the reasons why Chicago became such an important railway hub was that it had access to an astonishing amount of ice. Suddenly it became possible to transport vegetables, fruit, meat and other perishable goods by train from coast to coast. As far as their markets went, farmers were no longer dependent on their immediate surroundings. When canning became popular, these developments accelerated dramatically. In no time the huge cattle herds of the Midwest had made the city the world champion at canning meat. Between 1899 and 1905 alone, American food production rose by forty per cent, and Chicago became the unrivalled centre of all that abundance.

The city was a magnet for immigrants. In 1900 more than three-quarters of its population were newcomers or the children of newcomers, mainly

Irish, Poles, Swedes, Germans and Italians. Most ended up in poorly maintained apartment complexes. Dwellings designed to accommodate one family were quite often inhabited by five or six. As early as 1874, 20,000 unemployed workers marched through the city demanding 'bread for the needy, clothing for the naked and houses for the homeless'.

It was the central hub linking the country's East and West. Chicago, a city of warehoused people, railway sidings and meat-packing plants, the Rome of the Railroads.

John Gunther was a typical product of the city. He was a phenomenal reporter, one of the founders of modern journalism. His travel account *Inside U.S.A.* is one of the most accurate descriptions of America in the middle of the twentieth century. So determined was he to give a comprehensive account that he ended the book with a summary of all the things he had left out.

Gunther started his career as a reporter for the *Chicago Daily News*. The editorial office was next to the city hall, and through its dirty windows you could see the 'L' trains on their high steel girders thundering above the streets, with teeming crowds of immigrants, traders and labourers beneath them. In the office itself all that activity came together in a cacophony of ringing telephones, rattling telexes and typewriters, and through it all repeated calls for a messenger boy to rush yet another item to the typesetting room. Gunther's heart, he later wrote, lay with literature, but he reported on whatever was happening in this bubbling cauldron: fires, robberies, homicides or politics.

In 1924 Gunther left for London as a foreign correspondent and for twelve years he ranged across Europe, from Rome, Berlin and Madrid to London, Paris and Moscow. He knew Churchill and Roosevelt personally. Hitler put him on his hit list.

Whenever he was back in America he immediately threw himself into city life again. An article for *Harper's* begins with the sentence: 'I have lived in Chicago off and on for twenty years, and I have never seen a murder.'

That sounds implausible. Up to and including the 1930s, Chicago was one of the most notorious cities in America, the domain of Al Capone and Frank 'The Enforcer' Nitti. But rarely if ever was an innocent bystander killed. Murder in Chicago was expensive, costing at least fifty dollars. The more important the victim, the higher the price. As Gunther wrote in his article for *Harper's*: 'To kill me, a newspaperman, would probably cost $1,000. To kill a prominent businessman might cost $5,000, a prominent city official $10,000. To kill the president of a large corporation, or a great power magnate, would cost a great deal more, probably $50,000.'

In that article he names hardly any known criminals. Instead he writes mainly about the criminal system that had held the city in its grip for decades. Suppose you have a small business selling car tyres and batteries. A gangster comes along, accompanied by hired thugs, and asks for $100 a month. You pay him, of course. Otherwise you'll either end up shot or have your shop set on fire. Police? A share of the proceeds is channelled straight to the cops, who are part of the system. Politicians? The activities of the gangs are tolerated everywhere, merging seamlessly with the widespread political corruption that has been in place for far longer.

During prohibition – from 1920 to 1933 not a drop of alcohol could legally be sold in America – Chicago quickly became the centre of the illegal drinks trade. There were vast fortunes to be made. According to Gunther, in those years the annual turnover of a man like Al Capone amounted to some hundred million dollars. Of that hundred million, Capone paid out at least thirty million in bribes.

Chicago's gangster empire ultimately collapsed because its sources of income dried up. Prohibition ended and the Depression set in, so there was little money left to extort. Pressure from the FBI steadily increased and Chicago's big businessmen decided to act; the city had become so degenerate and corrupt that it was impossible to do business. City politics still had certain peculiar features decades later.

John Gunther, like most Americans then and now, had little faith in the honesty of politicians. 'Politics in the United States is a profession out of which most politicians expect to make money,' he wrote. But hardly anywhere did they go to such extremes as in Chicago.

In 1960, when everyone was wondering who would win, Kennedy or Nixon, the legendary mayor of Chicago, Richard Daley, rang Kennedy to give him a reassuring message: 'With a little bit of luck and the help of a few close friends, you are going to carry Illinois.' All too soon it transpired that there had indeed been irregularities. Anomalies were found in ten per cent of voter lists. Some voters were supposedly living on empty building sites, while others had moved away years before and several had died. In one district the list showed only twenty-two voters, but seventy-seven votes were cast, a large majority of them for Kennedy.

Robert Blakey, a member of Kennedy's Organized Crime and Racketeering Section, said later: 'In my judgement . . . enough votes were stolen – let me repeat that – stolen in Chicago to give Kennedy a sufficient margin that he carried the state of Illinois.' As it was, Kennedy won the presidential election by a tiny majority.

Politics here still stinks at least as badly as the cattle market. In 2006 a former governor of Illinois, Republican George Ryan, was convicted of bribery and extortion. In 2009 Democrat governor Rod Blagojevich was removed from office for having in effect put up for sale Barack Obama's Senate seat, which fell vacant when Obama was elected president. It had proved possible, in 1970, for a secretary of state to be found dead in a hotel room in Springfield, Illinois, and for 900,000 dollars to be found in a suite at another hotel, where he had been living, packed into shoe-boxes. In the last three decades of the twentieth century, twenty-seven sitting or former Chicago aldermen were prosecuted for corruption.

When a proposal was made in 1999 to reduce the pension age for aldermen from sixty to fifty-five, alderman William Beavers (whose hands were lily-white, incidentally) declared: 'If you can survive twenty years without going to jail, then you need a pension and you should have it.'

Just as some places in New England still generate a nineteenth-century atmosphere of egalitarian public spiritedness, Chicago represents the tough years that followed: the wild capitalism of the railroad magnates, steel manufacturers and other great industrialists of the years around 1900; the fierce battle fought here, as elsewhere, between labour and capital.

Lawyer Clarence Darrow, born in 1857, wrote in his memoirs that in his youth a person in gainful employment could count on respect wherever he went. It was not uncommon for him to receive an invitation to dinner at his employer's house, to join him at church on Sundays or to court his daughter. There was little money, Darrow writes, 'and nobody had a monopoly of either riches or poverty'.

In the years that followed he watched that sense of equality between boss and employee quickly disappear. Big companies increasingly set the tone, wages were lowered again and again, anyone who protested was sacked (there were enough immigrants to get the job done), and anyone who tried to organise workers into a union found himself up against gangs of heavies and private armies sent by the magnates. Within a few decades Chicago had a penniless industrial proletariat. There was no way out, since the old American escape route, the trek further westwards, was no longer a realistic option after 1890.

When the British ambassador to the United States, James Bryce, took a close look at the phenomenon of America half a century after Alexis de Tocqueville's trip, he encountered a society changed almost beyond recognition. The egalitarian character that had so frequently astonished Tocqueville was largely gone. 'Sixty years ago, there were no great fortunes in America, few large fortunes, no poverty,' Bryce wrote in The American Commonwealth (1888). 'Now there is some poverty . . . and a greater number of gigantic fortunes than in any country of the world.'

In the spring of 1886, Chicago's tensions erupted. Strikes for better working conditions were called and on 3 May, not for the first time, fighting broke out between strikers and strike-breakers in front of the gates to the tractor factory run by the McCormick Harvesting Machine Company. This time the police opened fire on the strikers, killing four and wounding many more. The workers were furious. The following evening a bomb went off during a protest meeting on Haymarket Square, right in the middle of a police detachment. Sixty-six officers were wounded and seven died.

Since those responsible could not be found, the police arrested the city's eight most prominent anarchist leaders. There was no actual proof; in fact not one of the leaders was present that day on the Haymarket – except for the man who was giving a speech when the bomb was thrown. Although the indictment was based purely on their ideas and their writings, seven of the eight were sentenced to death. In the end, four were hanged and a fifth blew himself up in his cell by putting a stick of dynamite in his mouth.

The case caused great agitation, in Europe as well as America. Protests

were staged in Russia, Italy, Spain, the Netherlands and Britain. A petition
with 60,000 signatures led to a new investigation and the three surviving
prisoners were eventually pardoned. The Haymarket martyrs were famous,
and they were commemorated year after year. The real bomber was never
found.

In Chicago, Clarence Darrow was one of many for whom the Haymarket
case was a personal turning point. He supported the movement that took
up the suspects' cause and gradually became a figurehead in the fight to
preserve personal freedom and dignity. 'The marks of battle are all over
his face,' the prominent journalist H. L. Mencken wrote of Darrow. 'He
has been through more wars than a whole regiment of Pershings. And
most of them have been struggles to the death, without codes or quarter.'

Darrow's speeches during court cases in defence of the underdog,
whoever he might be, were legendary. They sometimes went on for two
or three days, and they were often so emotional that by the end tears
were running down his cheeks, many of his listeners were sobbing, and
even the judge had to wipe an eye. Americans needed men like him to
help them maintain their faith, despite everything, in their country's
principles of honesty and fairness.

Darrow's life story reads like a relentless assault on that agglomeration
of wealth and political power that had come into being in the late nineteenth century. In 1902, for example, he successfully defended the miners'
union in its battle with the coal and railroad magnates.

The miners were slogging away for a little over a dollar a day, often
in extremely dangerous conditions. The abundance of cheap child labour
provided by the miners' families was exploited to the full. Daughters
were taken out of school at an early age so they could work in the textile
factories that were set up around the mines. The boys pored over the
conveyor belts from the age of twelve, picking out impurities from the
lumps of coal, a particularly horrible job. Ten workers were dying per
week in those days, in Pennsylvania alone.

For *Chicago's American*, Darrow wrote a series called 'Easy Lessons in Law':
about John Swanson, for example, a worker who lost his right hand to
an industrial saw because of the absence of proper safety measures; about
Pat O'Connor, an Irish railroad worker who was made to do dangerous
work on a night train because of his union activities and was decapitated

by a low bridge; about James Clark, a metalworker, who fell to his death from a half-finished skyscraper and ended up 'a limp, shapeless bundle of flesh and blood and bones and rags'. His widow received no financial help at all.

Even the Roman emperor Trajan demanded that acrobats in the circus be given a safety net, wrote Darrow, 'but this was before Christianity and commercialism'.

All these dramas were played out around local communities in which, despite or perhaps because of such hard-heartedness on the part of employers, social cohesion was firm. The same went for all American cities in the first half of the twentieth century. In 1967 Studs Terkel, the well-known radio reporter, published a book called *Division Street: America*, a collection of dozens of interviews with residents of Chicago – young, old, rich or poor, without distinction. It was a portrait of Chicago, but in fact it portrayed all of America. In the life stories of people who grew up between 1910 and 1930, one common element leaps to the fore, namely the atmosphere of solidarity that still characterised city and neighbourhood life in those days.

'Chicago was a big city before and yet it was pretty much like a small town,' one elderly construction worker said. 'Neighborhood after neighborhood, you know, were like small towns themselves. People integrated, relatives visited, you had more friends, you talked more, you got to know each other. You know what I mean? You miss this. There was more music, homemade music, you understand. You were able to develop yourself to a far greater extent.' At weddings half the neighbourhood would turn up, and everyone brought food and drink, often home-made. 'People seemed to have more time,' said an elderly woman. 'They used to get out more, sit on their front porches and talk with the neighborhood.'

Life was tougher then, she said, but simpler too.

The black population of Chicago originally lived in one long, narrow strip of the city, the 'Black Belt', and any black person who dared to move into a house outside that overpopulated ghetto faced the worst problems imaginable. Between 1917 and 1921 white militants carried out bomb attacks on almost sixty houses where black newcomers were living. In the summer of 1919, fierce riots broke out when a black swimmer drowned after stones were thrown at him for coming too close to a white beach. Whites dragged blacks out of trams and black snipers shot at white messenger boys.

Nevertheless Chicago, like the rest of Illinois, was regarded as liberal. It was Lincoln's state; blacks had been able to vote there since 1870 and racial segregation in schools was forbidden. Like Detroit it was one of the final destinations during the first Great Migration from the South. Between 1916 and 1920, 50,000 black people took the train – the 'Fried Chicken Special' – from the Mississippi Delta to Chicago. Everywhere on station platforms in the South, black train staff distributed the Chicago Defender, the weekly paper of the free black community in Chicago since 1905. It published lines like: 'I hear you calling me, and have boarded the train singing "Goodbye, Dixie Land".'

The Defender was the face of the strong, self-confident black community in the city. The paper was already suffused with the atmosphere of freedom that would later have such an influence on figures like Jesse Jackson, who grew up in South Carolina, Oprah Winfrey from Mississippi, who was pregnant at fifteen, and the city's first black mayor, Harold Washington, whose election in 1983 people had thought impossible. 'Everybody owes something to Harold Washington, because his election was something they never thought could happen,' Lou Ransom, editor of the Defender, explained later. A switch had been turned. 'If Harold can be mayor, what can't we do?'

That victory was one source of the 'audacity of hope' that made Barack Obama and his supporters think: Why couldn't a black man or woman become president of the United States one day? Obama had a photograph of Harold Washington on the wall of his office when he started his career as an associate at Davis Miner in 1993. He was plunged straight into the countless intrigues of political Chicago. One of his first cases was Barnett vs Daley, in which several black plaintiffs argued that in 1991 the city had been divided into electoral districts in such a way that whites were in the majority, however slim, everywhere, even though black residents had outnumbered white residents citywide since 1990. Several years later they won their case and the map was redrawn.

The young Obama dealt with various cases of this sort – he filed a group lawsuit against a bank for systematically refusing to give loans to people from a black neighbourhood, for instance – and through his work as a lawyer he soon became involved in politics. Meanwhile he was writing *Dreams from My Father* (1995), which he first read out to a handful of acquaintances in the back room at 57th Street Books and which soon became a major success, with rave reviews in the *New York Times* and the *Washington Post*.

In that same year he began seriously considering a political career. A chance came his way when one of the established politicians got involved with a sixteen-year-old girl. Obama campaigned successfully for the seat that came free in the Illinois Senate – his old university friend Jesse Ruiz organised a small fundraiser at his girlfriend's apartment that brought in a thousand dollars – and the rest of the story is familiar to us all. Except for one thing. When Obama first revealed his plans for a political career in a private conversation with Ruiz, he did not consider the presidency for a second. He aimed to start off in the state Senate, and the ultimate goal of his career would be his election as mayor of Chicago. He wasn't out to become a second John Kennedy. His dream was to be a second Harold Washington.

Obama's early career shows what a struggle it was to secure civil rights, even in the late twentieth century, even in Chicago. As black people said among themselves: 'In the South, the white man doesn't care how close you get, as long as you don't get too high. In the North, he doesn't care how high you get, as long as you don't get too close.'

On the shop floor in the early years of the century, a similar battle raged. Chicago's employers quite commonly reacted to strikes by deploying armed militias. Militant union activists, for their part, sometimes resorted to what can only be described as campaigns of terror. In the steel industry, more than a hundred bomb attacks were carried out between 1908 and 1910 against companies and workplaces where unions were banned. The militants learned their bombing techniques from their comrades in the mines.

Clarence Darrow remained a pivotal figure in the struggle, but he grew more cynical as he got older. He resigned himself to many things because he needed money and the unions paid him well but, in his own way, he was still passionate and independent. In 1920, he supported the American communist Benjamin Gitlow, even though he didn't agree in the least with communist ways of thinking. Gitlow had been arrested purely for publishing the Left Wing Manifesto, in which he predicted that one day the workers would rise up against the capitalist order – he was not calling on them to revolt.

Darrow defended him with élan, pointing out that Gitlow was purely an intellectual, with beliefs that fell within the American tradition. George Washington had been a revolutionary too, Darrow declared to the jury. As had Jesus Christ. And indeed Lincoln, who talked about the 'revolutionary right' of Americans to overthrow their government.

Gitlow was sentenced to five to ten years in Sing Sing and served two, during what became known as the 'Red Scare', the turbulent years of 1919 and 1920 when left-wing militants, inspired by the Russian Revolution, rose in rebellion. A bomb was placed on the front steps of the house of Attorney General A. Mitchell Palmer; parcel bombs were sent to members of the Cabinet and to senators; there were race riots in Chicago and Washington, and mass strikes in the mines and steelworks.

In the years that followed, through protracted and painful struggle, the unions gained a place for themselves in American society and in some cases a powerful one. In 1934 and 1935 especially, the years of the Great Depression, wildcat strikes swept across the country like forest fires. In the spring of 1934 the dockworkers, with the support of the transport unions, went on strike all along the west coast. San Francisco was shut down for weeks. In the South around 300,000 textile workers took strike action that autumn, and around Detroit the Goodyear and Firestone tyre factories were brought to a standstill. Sit-down strikes were held at General Motors, and even the black agricultural labourers in the South set up a union along with their white fellow workers, the Southern Tenant Farmers' Union. The bosses hit back. More than 2,500 American businesses were defended by armed militias and by spies of the famous Pinkerton National Detective Agency.

President Roosevelt responded in 1935 by recognising the right of workers to join a union of their choice, on condition that in future all labour conflicts were first put before a national mediation body, the National Labor Relations Board. This Wagner Act – along with the introduction of a minimum wage, a forty-hour week and other measures that were part of the New Deal – brought a degree of calm to the labour market. For the unions it marked a huge step forward; they finally had an opportunity to organise themselves properly in all sectors of industry.

Many employers capitulated surprisingly quickly, although Republic Steel, one of the three largest steel companies in the United States, categorically refused to permit union activities. During a strike at one of its factories in Chicago, on Memorial Day 1937, a crowd a thousand strong, including many women and children, marched to the steel mill led by a handful of union leaders to set up pickets. They carried a large American flag to show that they had rights now too, but they ran up against a police cordon.

'You got no rights,' some nervous police officers called out. 'You red bastards! You got no rights.' Someone threw a couple of branches. The cops opened fire. Ten people were killed, seven of them shot in the back, and thirty were injured. No police officer was ever prosecuted; in fact there were no disciplinary measures at all, although a year later Republic Steel was punished severely by the National Labor Relations Board. Seven thousand sacked union members had to be reinstated and their lost wages paid to them in full. In 1942, unions were finally permitted at Republic Steel.

Clarence Darrow died in March 1938, exhausted, sick and destitute. He had sometimes defended strange and distasteful cases purely for money, and he never had any qualms about bribing a judge or a jury member if it suited him, yet there was something grand and epic about his fierce resistance to all those 'inexorable oppressive forces', as his biographer John Farrell writes. 'Americans drew strength watching Darrow rage against the machine.' As Darrow put it himself: 'If the underdog got on top he would probably be just as rotten as the upper dog, but in the meantime I am for him.'

Three

JOHN STEINBECK STAYED at the Ambassador East on North State Parkway. Rocinante, with all his tools, guns and other survival equipment on board, was left in a garage. Charley was put into kennels. In Chicago, Steinbeck was briefly a man of the world again. In *Travels* he describes stumbling into his hotel in 'wrinkled hunting clothes', with a thin layer of dirt all over, unshaven, and bleary-eyed from driving for much of the night. Here he would be meeting Elaine, who was coming over for a long weekend. It was early in the morning and the room he had booked was not yet available, but after being quietly insistent he was allowed to take a bath and to rest in an unprepared room that had just been vacated by the previous guest.

The Ambassador East stands in a peaceful, leafy district, near the corner of Goethe Street. It still has that atmosphere of the 'elegant and expensive pleasure dome' that Steinbeck wrote about, and it's easy to understand why being there made his urban alter ego feel good. The lounge is dominated by huge crystal chandeliers and a striking green marble floor. Lavish brass gleams and flashes wherever you look: banisters, lamps, even the lift doors.

We are only just in time. Another two months and all this will be ripped out as part of a thorough renovation. On the walls of the Pump Room, the hotel's restaurant, are hundreds of portraits of famous people who have enjoyed a stay here, from Frank Sinatra to Nixon and the Kennedys. There is no trace of John and Elaine. The manager shrugs: 'We've got another eight hundred or so pictures down in the basement; I'm sure they'll be among those. But we like to keep it reasonably topical.'

In his book Steinbeck describes the condition in which he found the hotel room, and he makes a nice bit of detective work out of it, writing a brief biography of 'Lonesome Harry', as he calls the previous guest. From discarded laundry tags he deduces that the man is from Westport, Connecticut. He must be on a business trip, Steinbeck concludes from a piece of paper he finds in the bin. 'Darling: Everything is going OK . . . I'm writing this while I wait for C. E. to call. Hope he brings the cont . . .' It's the start of a letter to Harry's wife. But instead of a phone call, Harry was actually waiting for a woman with pale lipstick – still visible on the cigarette ends in the ashtray and on the edge of a highball glass – with whom he drank a whole bottle of Jack Daniel's, although she didn't stay the night ('second pillow used but not slept on').

And so it continues for several more pages of *Travels*. It's almost too neat and tightly structured to be true. Years ago the critic Alfred Kazin wrote of Steinbeck's characters that they 'are always on the verge of becoming human, but never do'. This is a case in point. That remark by his son John, bluntly declaring that his father had probably made up everything in *Travels with Charley*, begins to trouble me again. Now that this expedition is well underway, a problem is starting to emerge: to what degree can I trust the reports of my fellow traveller of half a century ago? I have already alluded to the fact that his itinerary makes no sense. He drove at such a pace that he could hardly have had the time for calmly looking about him, let alone for in-depth conversations, and he was definitely not the best of observers, being so tired and tormented. None of the delights of *Cannery Row* can be found here. Rarely if ever do people in *Travels* laugh. As one perceptive reviewer remarked early on, he may well have been travelling not just with Charley on the front seat next to him but with the bear of depression as well.

I'm reminded of that odd situation surrounding the ghost motel in Lancaster, when Bill Steigerwald and John Woestendiek suddenly came into the picture, the other two men taking a trip with the ghost of John. If Steinbeck's account is accurate, then he was in Lancaster twice, once on his way to Deer Isle, when he camped with a local farmer and had a conversation about politics, and once in the ghost motel. Both Steigerwald and Woestendiek found Jeff Woodburn at home, the local historian whose name I was given to no avail, and it turns out that a motel of the kind described in the book did exist, the Whip o' Will. But when Woodburn, a great admirer of Steinbeck, went looking for the farmer who allowed our hero to stay, he failed to find anyone for miles around who even came close to fitting the description.

He did discover something else. Steinbeck seems to have spent at least one night at the Spalding Inn, an expensive hotel further up in the hills. Several witnesses, including the son of the then owner, remember Steinbeck's stay very clearly, since he was turned away at first because his clothes were so dirty. After he made his identity known, he was of course received with great respect. So much for camping in Rocinante. That's not all. Of the two nights spent near Lancaster that Steinbeck describes in *Travels*, with the wise farmer and at the motel, only one can actually have taken place.

It seems likely that Steinbeck made up the dialogue with the farmer, presumably basing it on several conversations he'd had. These incongruities fascinate Bill Steigerwald in particular. He writes that he is not trying to blow the whistle, in fact he quite likes 'the old guy', but his journalistic hunting instinct is now fully aroused. As he travels on ahead of me, I watch his blogs focus increasingly on separating fact and fiction within *Travels with Charley*.

Is it serious, this tarnishing of Steinbeck and *Travels* that's unfolding right under my nose? No, and yes. Steinbeck was a born storyteller and he liked to exaggerate. Jackson Benson, who encountered Steinbeck's exaggerations time and again, reached a mild verdict: 'He sought to give his life drama.' Above all he wanted to write a good book, with an irresistible story. Just take the way he describes his great friend Ed Ricketts in his books: as an eternal bachelor, solitary and romantic, the life and soul of the party and at the same time always the man to console whores and failures. Well, Ed Ricketts did do all those things, but he was primarily a hardworking and reputable biologist. Not only that, he lived as a family man for years. His wife left him only later and his son regularly came to stay. Hardly the eternal bachelor.

Or take Steinbeck's fieldwork for *The Grapes of Wrath*. He gave the impression that he'd driven all the way from Oklahoma in his pie wagon, following in the wake of all those destitute migrants. In reality his trips to the reception centres probably never took him out of California. At first he merely smiled when friends and acquaintances made references to his Oklahoma expedition, but after a few years he took to telling them about his journey out of Oklahoma with the migrants as if it had actually happened. He'd begun to believe his own myth.

As a writer of stories and novels, Steinbeck could do whatever he liked. That is the freedom of the fiction writer. But he and his publisher presented *Travels with Charley* as the account of a journey actually undertaken, as non-fiction. Faced with so many 'invented' facts, the journalist in me begins to mutter: to what extent can I still rely on him? Did Steinbeck actually camp in Michigan and spend a whole day fishing with that nice young 'guardian of the lake'?

A glance at his tight schedule makes that meeting seem highly improbable. He spent barely two days covering the more than 900 miles from Niagara Falls to Chicago, which leaves no time at all for a quiet spot of fishing. It wouldn't surprise me if he actually drove straight along the boring old US 20 and the recently built Indiana Toll Road to Chicago, where Elaine was waiting for him.

Later in his life Steinbeck said on several occasions that often, in retrospect, he no longer knew the difference between all the things he'd made up and the things that actually happened. He wished any future biographer luck disentangling fact from fiction. The question is, does that matter very much in the end? Steinbeck was a writer, not a journalist. He refused to drag along with him the ball and chain of verifiability and endless fact checking that is every journalist's lot. In his own way he was searching for a specific truth, the reality of America as he experienced it during his trip, and *Travels* says a great deal about the American nation in 1960. It presented Americans of the time with new insights and gave them a fresh perspective on their country and society. It was a reality they recognised. The book was a huge success.

Once you know how Steinbeck went to work, his biographer wrote, you begin to understand. 'He loved the words, the shape, the sound, the history of meaning; he delighted in the magical properties of language; he even got satisfaction from the touch of pencil and paper. Behind nearly everything that he wrote there is a man enjoying himself, surprised and delighted that words work the way they do.'

Today is 10 October, and it's as warm as August. The whole of Chicago turned out earlier this Sunday afternoon for the marathon and now, with evening coming on, the parks and sidewalk cafés are full of families, friends and lovers. We're seeing the city in one of its rare moments of relaxation: a city of pedestrians, children at play, short trousers and summer dresses, with a central district that for all its magnificence has achieved human scale again. I can feel the atmosphere of the Midwest already. The pace is slower than in New York, the breathing calmer.

Sitting outside at one of the cafés we get talking with a couple at the next table. Geoffrey and his wife Sarah were born and raised in Chicago and they never want to live anywhere else. We talk about the climate, about these summery temperatures. When Steinbeck left Chicago in mid-October he could already feel the frost. Tomorrow, precisely half a century later, the temperature is expected to reach thirty degrees Celsius, yet another record.

Despite heavy snows in North America and Western Europe, 2010 turns out to have been the warmest year since records began. The average temperature on earth is 1.12 Fahrenheit (0.62 Celsius) higher than the average for the twentieth century. Twelve record-breaking years have occurred since 1997. Alaska, Canada and the high North have been abnormally warm. We felt the tail end of it in Maine, and now here in summery Chicago.

Most Americans are remarkably relaxed about these statistics, despite all the alarming documentaries and books, and despite the fact that per person they expel twice as much greenhouse gas into the earth's atmosphere as Europeans. Climate change is seen here mainly as a technological challenge and a stimulus to innovation, not as a warning to change their behaviour. Politicians and commentators have been celebrating the miracle of shale gas in recent years: no energy shortage any longer. An end to dependence on long pipelines and strange regimes – who wouldn't sign up for that? The accompanying problems – an increase in carbon dioxide emissions, immense chemical pollution and water wastage, the chance of a second Dust Bowl – are brushed aside.

'Yes,' says Geoffrey. 'Energy saving and restrictions simply don't fit with our attitude to life. Abundance and excess are things we take for granted, and many people are perennially distrustful of government and of know-it-all scientists.' He runs a national website aimed at the rodeo world. 'Those people really do believe everything they see on Fox News. Because it was on TV, right? It's all far worse than ten years ago. There was a lot more common sense then. My own brother . . . I love him, but don't let's talk politics! They never concede a point, those conservatives.'

In every city he came to, the first thing John Gunther asked himself was: Where does power lie here? His account of his travels is therefore in some ways a concise encyclopaedia of 1940s American politics. Power usually lay with the various local party machines. That is still true of Chicago, Geoffrey tells us, and here the party machine has a huge amount of influence at a national level, too, even if the system is getting a little rusty, like everywhere else.

All the corruption scandals and FBI investigations have made it slightly less a matter of course to 'buy' political support by doling out government jobs and promotions. Geoffrey says that the city 'has been ruled since the very beginning by the Combine, a complex clique made up of Democrats, Republicans, big business and the mafia. The power of the mafia is far less than it used to be, but the closed system of deals and compromises is still intact.'

'What about Barack Obama, then?' asks my wife. 'Didn't he manage to make his way to the top here as a clever community organiser?'

'Please,' says Geoffrey. 'It was more the other way around. The party apparatus chose Obama as "their man" for the coming few years and poured all its energy into him.' He was lucky, too, Geoffrey goes on, because in normal circumstances it would have been almost impossible to break through in the Chicago political system. An opening was created unexpectedly by that sex scandal with the politician and the young girl.

'Change?' he sneers. 'Don't give me that. In exactly the way that Bush was a product of the Texas Combine and Reagan of the California Combine, Obama was and is entirely a product of the Chicago Combine. And if there's one thing that never changes, and won't tolerate any real change, then it's the party machine in Chicago.'

Obama is regularly compared to Kennedy, and rightly so, according to this couple. They believe that, like Kennedy, he's a great talker with a huge rhetorical talent but nothing more. 'It was here in this city that Obama became a politician, which helps to explain his strong tendency to compromise – in Chicago you've got no other choice.' But as a product of the Combine, he has never completely lost that artificiality, Geoffrey believes. 'He's an extraordinary man, but he's still a construct, made by himself and by others. He's manufactured out of bits of his own history, out of ideas and out of words. But real? No, not for me he's not.'

Halfway through Travels with Charley, Steinbeck describes how, before he set out, he was spoken to and instructed by all kinds of friends and acquaintances. They included a well-known and widely respected political reporter who was bitter about politics and had a feeling the country was sick. He set Steinbeck a task: 'If anywhere in your travels you come on a man with guts, mark the place. I want to go to see him. I haven't seen anything but cowardice and expediency. This used to be a nation of giants. Where have they gone? You can't defend a nation with a board of direc-tors. That takes men. Where are they?'

Steinbeck didn't find any men with guts. True, he saw real men fighting, twice in fact, 'with bare fists and enthusiastic inaccuracy', but in both cases over a woman. Nothing political.

As for me, I think for a long time about that cheerful exchange of views and preconceptions at a sidewalk café on a warm October evening in 2010. Indeed, where are the men with guts nowadays? How pure and natural American democracy must have seemed to eighteenth-century Europeans and travellers like Tocqueville, who back on their own continent were watching the decline of a decadent aristocracy and a corrupt ruling class. But now?

Although Steinbeck was disturbed a century and a half later by how politics worked in practice – 'It is our national conviction that politics is a dirty, tricky, and dishonest pursuit and that all politicians are crooks,' he wrote in America and Americans – he still admired the political system as such. After all, it had ensured that despite all the tricks and dirt, good and capable people generally rose to the top. It often seemed, he wrote, as if Americans were 'watched over by a kindly and humorous deity'. American democracy was 'at once flexible and firm'. He went on: 'It has been proof not only against foreign attack but against our own stupid-ities, which are sometimes more dangerous.'

I have to say that Steinbeck was right. Anyone who has read The American Future: A History by British historian Simon Schama will recall how it opens in Des Moines-West, with a simple caucus in the first round of the 2008 presidential elections. Schama describes in meticulous detail a meeting of neighbours whose children go to the same schools but who rarely, if ever, talk to each other about politics. Now they are doing so, in a clear and surprising fashion. Despite differences of opinion there's an atmosphere of consensus. This caucus is an act of right-minded citizenship. People literally vote, calling out one by one. 'Thus the vox populi of Des Moines sounded,' Schama writes. 'Elderly aunts; high school tenors; gravelly taxi drivers; sonorous lawyers.' Ever since then he has known precisely when American democracy, after long years of despair, came back from the dead: '7:15 p.m. Central Time, 3 January 2008, Precinct 53, Theodore Roosevelt High.'

The entire political history of America is steeped in villainous tricks and corruption scandals. The deployment of massive flows of funds (whatever their source) in order to gain or improve a political position is entirely normal. Anyone entering politics motivated by ideals alone, like Adlai Stevenson for example, is actually regarded as suspect in some circles. But no one who has ever watched an American election campaign from close proximity – the rounds of phone calls, the door-to-door leafleting, the dedication and enthusiasm of all those hundreds of thousands of volunteers, the intense debates – will underestimate the vitality of American democracy.

Does that 'kindly and humorous deity' of Steinbeck's still exist? Is that equilibrium, are those checks and balances still in place?

For years Americans have been in the grip of two cast-iron coalitions, conservative and progressive, against which the established parliamentary system is powerless. Faith in Congress in general has not been so low since the New York Times first started polling on the subject in 1977. The system's utter paralysis is new, and to some extent that has to do with the way it's designed.

The Founding Fathers believed above all in the power of local politics. A country as big as America was best governed by local communities, which is why the election meeting Simon Schama experienced was so impressive; it represented the core of the American system. Unlike many European states, America was not built around an existing power structure such as a royal dynasty. To this day the consequences for Washington are considerable, especially now that the United States can and must operate far more as a single country as regards foreign policy, economics and infrastructure than it did in the past. Whether under Abraham Lincoln, Franklin D. Roosevelt, Ronald Reagan or Barack Obama, political battles come down to the same question: What is the status of the federal government?

A state like Wyoming, with half a million inhabitants, has the same number of seats in the Senate as California, with thirty-seven million. Of the hundred senators, it takes only forty-one to quash a bill completely by means of a filibuster, the final resort available to any member of a minority who wants to delay or block a majority decision. All those senators are daily assailed by extremely well-organised interest groups. The number of registered lobbyists in Washington is approaching 5,000, almost ten times as many as at EU headquarters in Brussels. The total sum spent on lobbying in Washington each year is estimated at upwards of nine billion dollars. The richest county in America is to be found not in Silicon Valley or thereabouts, but close to Washington DC: Loudoun Country, Virginia, the most rapidly growing suburb, home town of American lobbyists.

Two factors, the home constituency and money, are decisive in Washington's laborious decision-making process, in which the government of the nation as a whole sometimes threatens to get bogged down.

First, the voters back home. Whereas in most European countries a parliamentarian's term in office (by-elections aside) is at least four years, the 435 members of the House of Representatives have their seats for only two years. This means that a representative needs to work on getting re-elected right from the start of his or her term. Many members of the House are almost continually campaigning for re-election in their home states, and they focus most of their attention on that task. Their voters demand no less: What will this candidate do for us in Washington? What is he going to bring back for us from there?

The entire country is therefore peppered with projects that serve purely to safeguard someone's seat in Congress. One famous example is the Gravina Island Bridge in Alaska, which was granted funding of 233 million dollars – until it became generally known that Gravina Island has barely fifty inhabitants. In the end the project did not go through. Or take John Murtha airport in Johnstown, Pennsylvania, where hundreds of millions were thrown away purely to oblige a handful of passengers a day. Representative John Murtha (Democrat) happened to be chairing an influential congressional committee and no one was prepared to offend him. Or look at Senator Richard Shelby (Republican) from Alabama, who frustrated the new Obama administration by blocking no fewer than seventy nominations. He was demanding an FBI laboratory for his state – even though the FBI had no use for it – plus a contract for the manufacture of a new tank by Northrop Grumman. The list of examples is endless.

One notable phenomenon is what is known as 'gerrymandering': the systematic manipulation of the boundaries of electoral districts. The Republicans in particular have grasped every opportunity over recent years to create safe seats in this way, by ensuring there are districts where the Republican candidate will always win. Wherever they've seen the chance, Democrats have done the same. As a result, in 400 of the 435 electoral districts it's more or less obvious beforehand which party will win. So much for democracy.

The effect of all this, however, is that primaries have become increasingly important, since whoever wins at that stage is almost certain to be elected. In primaries the tone is set by more radical party activists, rather than moderate, 'ordinary voters'. As a consequence the number of extreme and radical members of Congress has increased enormously. They are free to take the daftest of standpoints knowing they are nevertheless certain to be re-elected. The Republican leadership is gradually beginning to curse this gerrymandering, since local radicals are becoming a threat to its own position. Here lies the most significant source of extreme polarisation in American politics.

The tendency to put local interests above all other considerations also has to do with the sums that need to be spent these days to secure re-election. The price of American democracy has increased spectacularly. Kennedy and Nixon's presidential campaigns in 1960 cost a total of 24.2 million dollars, or 176 million in today's money. In 2008 the combined cost for the Democrats and Republicans reached more than a billion, an almost sixfold increase.

Congressmen always set out to please their electorates and their sponsors. According to an estimate from Americans for Campaign Reform, in 2008 a prime seat in the House of Representatives cost around 700,000 dollars. A total of 2.6 billion was spent on all the campaigns put together, compared to 1.7 billion in 2004.

As a result, many representatives live in social and political isolation. In Washington they give themselves little chance to form coalitions or even friendships that cross traditional party boundaries, even though such relationships used to be common. This alone makes the system far more liable to become polarised than it once was, since it's no longer lubricated by normal human interaction or any sense of togetherness. It's becoming harder and harder for a statesman or stateswoman to rise above those divisions. As representative Tim Griffin (Republican), fresh in from Arkansas, told the New York Times: 'A lot of us feel that we're here on a mission, and the mission is now, and we are not that concerned about the political consequences.'

Then there is the second factor: money. 'A forum for legalized bribery,' is what columnist Thomas Friedman calls Congress today. In 1974, just three per cent of politicians leaving office became lobbyists. Nowadays fifty per cent of senators and forty-two per cent of members of the House of Representatives take that step.

By far the most powerful lobby on Capitol Hill is Wall Street. The consumer website OpenSecrets.org has calculated that the financial industry, including mortgage insurers, spent 2.3 billion dollars on campaign contributions between 1990 and 2010. After Silicon Valley and Hollywood, Wall Street was for years the main financier of the Democratic Party. In 2008 it contributed eighty-nine million dollars to the Obama campaign, which goes a long way towards explaining Obama's obvious hesitancy about tightening regulation of the banking sector.

The interdependence of Goldman Sachs and the US Treasury is particularly striking. Goldman Sachs, in a similar way to the FSB in Russia, provides a continual succession of key figures to run America's finances, and they determine policy.

Similar pressures could be seen during debates about reform to the American healthcare system. It was clear that something had to be done. According to a report compiled by Harvard University in 2009, some 45,000 Americans were dying every year purely because they were unable to afford health insurance. Lobbyists representing insurers and the pharmaceutical industry spent about 1.5 million dollars a day in 2009 and 2010 in their

efforts to influence the proposed legislation in order to make it more favourable to their own interests. In 2009 a total of 3,300 lobbyists were registered
in the healthcare field, six for every member of Congress.

PhRMA (the Pharmaceutical Research and Manufacturers of America),
which lobbies on behalf of the pharmaceutical industry, had forty-eight
lobby firms working for it at its peak. Eventually a deal was done with
the White House that conceded so much to the pharmaceutical companies
– there would be no negotiation on the price of many medicines, for
example – that they promised to broadcast a hundred million dollars'
worth of TV advertising in support of the reform. Had they not got so
much of what they wanted, the White House would probably have experienced the opposite: a bombardment of negative ads.

'The United States has far higher health costs than any other advanced
country, and very low taxes by international standards,' writes American
Nobel Prize winner Paul Krugman. 'If we could move even part way toward
international norms on both these fronts, our budget problems would be
solved.' Why does that remain such an elusive goal? Because the American
political lobbies – in this case those of the medical industry and various
coalitions of rich taxpayers – are so big and powerful that they can
completely derail the normal democratic decision-making process.

On the left of the political spectrum, powerful lobbies representing the
unions play a similar role. The American public-service workers' union for
example, the American Federation of State, County and Municipal Employees,
has managed to secure excellent terms for its members. People working for
the fire service or the police department are sometimes able to retire before
the age of fifty, and their pensions place an increasing burden on the budgets
of cities and states. Many employees in the public sector are very difficult
to fire, so the unions are able to block reorganisations indefinitely, even
those that are sorely needed. All this makes government-run services in
America unnecessarily inflexible and expensive. A place like Buffalo still has
as many people on the government payroll as it did in 1950, even though
the city's population has shrunk by about half since then.

All kinds of things are decided by the powerful lobby system. Are
cities and states where people are allowed to carry firearms safer or less
safe? It is an obvious question to ask in the debate about gun ownership.
Yet proper research has never been done. The National Rifle Association,

one of the most powerful of all lobbies, has made sure that the budget for research into the consequences of the prevalence of firearms is only a fraction of what it was in the 1990s. The tobacco industry similarly managed for years to obstruct research into the dangers of smoking.

Isn't there an urgent need to change the way banking is regulated? Although most economists are in favour, the powerful banking lobby sabotages almost every step in that direction. Do people pay too much tax? A company like General Electric has such a mighty lobby that, because of all kinds of well-defended loopholes in taxation law, it paid not one cent of tax in 2010 despite making a total profit of 14.2 billion dollars (5.1 billion of it within America). The company actually received income from taxation to the tune of 3.2 million dollars.

Or take another, more delicate question: Is America's pro-Israel policy actually in its own interests? Even to ask the question is sacrilege in the eyes of the deeply Protestant electorate and a proportion of Jewish voters. Anyone who supports the Israeli leadership no matter what it says or does will receive millions from certain billionaires, and anyone who expresses any criticism had better watch out, since there's hardly a politician anywhere who can afford to lose the support of the American Israel Public Affairs Committee.

The impact of such forces is increasing, and its distorting effect emerges time and again in polls. The priorities that shape the political debate sometimes turn out not to correspond in the slightest with the beliefs that prevail in contemporary American society. Yet opportunities to influence politics with larger and larger sums of money are growing all the time. Those in favour see the financing of political parties in this way as an essential aspect of freedom of expression. The Supreme Court shares that opinion. In 2011 it decided that legal entities have exactly the same right to free speech as real people, which means that large concerns can put just as much money as private individuals into campaigns by their favourite candidate, via political action committees or Super PACs. In the words of philosopher of law Ronald Dworkin: 'The Court has given lobbyists, already much too powerful, a nuclear weapon.'

'There used to be a thing or a commodity we put great store by,' said the political reporter who issued Steinbeck with travel instructions. 'It was called the People. Find out where the People have gone.'

So how are they doing today, the People? Among American voters, profound changes are taking place. The first shift is a matter of demographics, something that most of us outside America are only just starting to take in. The percentage of voters who have a European background is falling year on year, whereas the share of the electorate that has its origins in, for example, Latin America or Asia is steadily growing.

Today, two-thirds of the population is more or less European in origin; in 2050 less than half will be. Americans with some other background or ancestry, in many cases Latin American, Chinese or African, will then constitute a majority. Europe is already less of a priority in American foreign policy. This shift in attention and frame of reference may have major consequences in the long run. Since today's minority groups generally vote Democrat – eighty per cent of them voted for Obama in 2008 – the effect on party politics will be considerable as well.

The second change, which can also be seen in Europe, has to do with the mentality of voters. The demand for equality of opportunity is increasingly being replaced by a demand for equality of status. We, the voters, want to feel equal to those we elect. They are our fellow citizens, no more and no less. This is a normal democratic principle, but for Americans who time and again follow the latest populist figure to emerge, the principle of equality of status is uppermost: he – or she – is one of us. They regard the fact that 'you can drink a beer with him' or that she's 'an ordinary housewife' or 'just like the girl next door' to be among the most attractive of attributes, and the candidates naturally do all they can to exploit that attitude.

Of course as the writer of a recent letter to the *New York Times* correctly points out, choosing a national leader on the basis of his or her 'ordinariness' is about as sensible as choosing a dentist based on 'ordinariness' rather than professional skill. 'Good dentists are not like "normal people".' When it comes to their president, however, tens of millions of Americans arrive at a different conclusion.

It's all largely based on the menu served up for Americans day after day by Fox News and other television broadcasters. The internet is rapidly developing into a vast democratic counterweight, but the influence of the media giants remains overwhelming. Up to a point they function as privatised parliaments, since they decide who gets to participate in the public debate and who is excluded. Their main concern is not the public good or the democratic debate but the programme's ratings, since that's all their sponsors – again those same large corporations – look at. Prejudices are confirmed and reinforced; the personal and emotional are central; the viewer must be enthralled and entertained at all costs. As with Twenty-One, that fraudulent quiz show of the 1950s, showmanship and the techniques of the theatre are of overriding importance.

Television broadcasters like Fox News are drawing upon an old American tradition. The country always had thoroughly partisan news media. In the 1930s, when Steinbeck was living and writing in California, the Los Angeles Times was one of the game's main players. The paper supported the big bosses of Southern California through thick and thin in their battle with the emerging trade unions. Any form of social legislation was described as a serious threat and anyone who disagreed with the paper would be denied even a millimetre of space or attention. David Halberstam called it 'a manifestly unfair newspaper' that continually reinforced the ignorance and prejudice of its readers. 'The Times was not an organ of the Republican Party of Southern California, it was the Republican Party. It was intensely, virulently partisan.' The Los Angeles Times could make or break politicians. It even produced a president: Richard Nixon.

As far back as 1958, Ed Murrow, the legendary old stager of radio and television at CBS, castigated this political media complex. 'If there are any historians . . . a hundred years from now and there should be preserved the kinescopes for one week of all three networks, they will find recorded, in black and white or color, evidence of decadence, escapism and insulation from the realities of the world in which we live,' he declared in a passionate speech to radio and television news directors in Chicago. 'If we go on as we are then history will take its revenge and retribution will [catch] up with us.'

Shortly after that speech he broke with CBS, and CBS with him.

Four

IN CHICAGO JOHN SPENT A FEW DAYS of contentment with Elaine, 'a resumption of my name, identity, and happy marital status'. They stayed for one night with Adlai Stevenson, in Stevenson's pleasant country house in Libertyville. It's still there, and Bill Steigerwald even managed to find Steinbeck's Sag Harbor telephone number in the address book on the desk of the perennial candidate for the presidency.

The pair must undoubtedly have exchanged fascinating thoughts about the state of America, rotten or otherwise, and about Stevenson's rival, Kennedy, a real bed-hopper according to Steinbeck. Yet Steinbeck barely refers to any of this in his account of his travels, since it would only interrupt the flow – and, I would add, detract from his tale of solitude and hardship.

He had left Charley in kennels – the animal 'cried out in rage and despair' – but now they resumed their journey together. They had to get used to each other again. The dog was angry at having been abandoned, but he was also glad to be off and tremendously proud of his appearance, since during his weekend in Chicago he'd been groomed and clipped and washed, and after such treatment he was always, Steinbeck writes, 'as pleased with himself as is a man with a good tailor or a woman newly patinaed by a beauty parlor, all of whom can believe they are like that clear through'.

It was 10 October 1960, a sunny autumn day. They drove northwards along Highway 12 into Wisconsin, and Steinbeck was delighted by what he saw. Because of all the dairy products that come from this state, he had imagined the landscape as 'one big level cow pasture' and he was totally unprepared for the beauty and variety of its fields, hills, forests and lakes. 'The land dripped with richness, the fat cows and pigs gleaming against green, and, in the smaller holdings, corn standing in little tents as corn should, and pumpkins all about.' Then there was the light. 'The air was rich with butter-colored sunlight, not fuzzy but crisp and clear so that every frost-gay tree was set off.' It was a 'magic' October day.

Fifty years later, in the same week of autumn, it is downright hot. The air is heavy and slightly misty. Now too the maize harvest is in full swing, but the fields are endless, the patchwork of farms gone. Combines sweep everything up, and when they are done a haze of yellow and brown hangs over the hills, the landscape looking damp and tired. The road is quiet and dead straight. The farmland rolls mile after mile beneath our wheels, without much history, without old buildings, roads, paths or ditches. Everything here is the first to arrive.

A long Canadian Pacific freight train shuffles beside us. At the Pine Cone bakery the chocolate chip cookies are the size of breakfast plates, so big that they make you feel like a child standing at the counter, like Alice in Wonderland. Further on the landscape gradually grows more charming. Then we see Wisconsin Dells up ahead, in Steinbeck's time still a weird, dreamlike place of lakes, woods and marshes, 'the engraved record of a time when the world was much younger and much different'. Today Wisconsin Dells calls itself the 'Waterpark Capital of the World', and to many Americans the area is popular above all for its Noah's Ark Waterpark, with Jungle Rapids, the Bermuda Triangle, Black Thunder, Time Warp, Curse of the Crypt and forty-five other resounding attractions. Somewhere it must still be possible to find the old charm of the Dells, but certainly nowhere near here.

Steinbeck spent the night in Mauston, still in Wisconsin, as is clear from a letter he wrote to Elaine that night. Where he must have parked up is immediately obvious: at the edge of a broad arm of a river, a charming, quiet place surrounded by trees. In Travels he describes an evening walk during which, on the far side of a hill, he came upon a valley whose entire floor seemed to move and to breathe. Going to investigate he found turkeys, thousands of them, 'a reservoir for Thanksgiving', waiting 'to lie on their backs on the platters of America'.

In his account he turns two nights into one. There is no turkey farm in Mauston and there never was, but the following day, according to his letters, he camped in Frazee, in Minnesota, between the trucks in turkey country. 'Just below this hill the earth is black with them.'

By then he had covered another 400 miles.

I find those 400 miles disturbing. Despite all his jubilation at 'a noble land of good fields and magnificent trees', only one conclusion is possible: after Chicago, Steinbeck set off again at a sprint. In *Travels* he hints at his motives. After parting with Elaine he had to 'go through the same lost loneliness all over again'. It was no less painful than at the start of the trip. 'There seemed to be no cure for loneliness save only being alone.'

In all kinds of ways, that weekend in Chicago forms a watershed in *Travels with Charley*. Steinbeck's increasing agitation from Chicago onwards comes through loud and clear. When he arrived he had already reached the halfway point in his book, but he wasn't even halfway through the outward journey; he still had three-quarters of his expedition ahead of him.

His attention shifts as well. Before Chicago he still allocates plenty of space and time to personal interaction, but after Chicago he concentrates mainly on the landscape. Americans excite him less and less. 'John got awfully lonely on that trip,' Elaine admitted later to Steinbeck's second biographer, Jay Parini. 'That was the main problem, I think, though it doesn't really come out in the book much. He was homesick most of the time.'

The letter he wrote to Elaine from Mauston indicates his confusion. He is absolutely determined to go to Fargo, simply because if you unfold a map of the United States, Fargo is always right at the crease. 'Maybe this whole trip is just as silly,' he acknowledges. He stresses once again the personal motive behind it, perhaps as a sequel to a conversation they had, for the umpteenth time, in Chicago. He refuses to go the way of many American men of a certain age who, after an illness, simply allow people to take care of them. 'You see, I *can* read a map. I *can* drive a truck, I *can* make do. And I *can* stand the loneliness as you can.'

'I'm still a man,' he wrote to Elaine. 'Damn it!'

We spend the night in the Days Inn at Black River Falls, near just the kind of truck stop Steinbeck would have used to park Rocinante. In the parking lot are six lonely semi-trailers. A cold wind gets up. Most of the drivers leave their engines running while they take on sustenance at the all-you-can-eat ('$9.99') restaurant opposite.

Steinbeck described the long-distance truck drivers he came upon on his journey as 'a breed set apart from the life around them'. They had fixed places along their routes where they knew the mechanics and waitresses and met up with each other from time to time. 'In some town or city somewhere their wives and children live while the husbands traverse the nation carrying every kind of food and product and machine. They are clannish and they stick together, speaking a specialized language.' Small though his own truck was, they were kind and helpful to him.

That atmosphere still prevails among the long-distance truckers we come across. There's a lot of laughter, every familiar face is greeted with jubilation. They are mostly men, although here and there you see couples who have opted for this nomadic existence now that the children have left home.

'Husband–wife team sell printing business to see the US in a truck,' is the headline in the latest edition of their most popular magazine, The Trucker – the truck-driving fraternity has been discovered as a valuable target audience – and they are not the only ones.

Everyone is asking for drivers. The magazine is full of recruitment ads: Southern Refrigerated Transport specifies an average of 1,200 miles per trip, with ninety-nine per cent no-touch freight; CRST offers a bonus of 1,000 dollars on signing up; Con-way promises 'the reliable home time you need' and 'the best pay packages in the industry'.

Here in Black River Falls, however, none of that buoyancy is in evidence. In the restaurant – a large room with dark beams, a big American flag against the wall and widescreen television in every corner – you could cut the loneliness with a knife. The place is empty aside from six drivers, each of them silently and separately chewing through their $9.99. One by one they stand up to fetch dessert: thick blancmange, ice cream, cheesecake, chocolate tart – a treat.

Meanwhile the television screens are showing a slimming competition. At a training camp, extremely fat men and women are being relentlessly tormented – 'Come on, more, more!' – until they fall to the ground whimpering. It looks like a penal colony for fatties, led by miserably supple, firm and young disciplinarians. We all sit watching in silence, breathless, each at his own table.

At breakfast the next morning I meet William, an elderly man with a lined face and bony shoulders under his brown chequered shirt. His family came from Ireland, all of them farmers, but nearly everyone has given that up now. 'By heaven, we saw a few things: accidents, tuberculosis, some of us died young.' A cousin took over the farm from William's parents, and later the farms belonging to his uncles and other cousins as well, before he too called it a day. Everything was bought up by an even bigger farmer. William himself never had any intention of staying down on the farm. He worked at a sawmill for years and later became a concierge, which meant he could do a lot of reading. Fantastic, that was.

And now? I ask. How are he and all those Irish cousins doing? 'As long as things were going okay and we could pay our bills and our mortgage, we didn't care too much I guess. Of course we all knew politics was a mess, always favouritism and corruption, you know what I mean. But now that things are going so badly, yes, it makes you think. That they let this happen . . .'

But did he vote for those same established politicians, the ones with plans that weren't in his interests at all? William is silent, resigned. Is he angry with them? 'Yes, everyone is a bit. But I'm angry with myself too . . .' He's not the only one. According to the latest polls, at least half of all Americans are angry with politicians. Of both parties.

William shows me his vitamins: six brown pots.

'These keep me going.'

The conversation with William reminds me of discussions I once had in the breakfast room of a cheap hotel in San Diego. It was one of those hotels that also functions as an old folks' home and nursing home. Almost all the guests were single men and women struggling to get by on tiny pensions that were just enough to cover a hotel room and three meals a day. The radio was always playing songs from the time when their children were growing up and their houses were still full of life.

I was there to report on the 1994 midterm elections. In California a fierce battle was raging that year between Democrat old stager Dianne

Feinstein and the Republican candidate for the Senate Michael Huffington, a millionaire's son who was trying to buy a Senate seat with tens of millions of dollars.

The men and women I interviewed were all thoroughly warm-hearted, and despite their reduced circumstances they retained their dignity and their sense of humour. They had every imaginable opinion about the world and about politics, yet without exception they were going to vote for Michael Huffington.

I remember how surprised I was by that, time and again. After all, the plans of their favoured candidate – which included reducing welfare payments and social provision, and imposing a strict ban on the hiring of illegal workers – wouldn't exactly improve their insecure existence. If he was elected they'd be the first victims of cuts, and they'd no longer have any nice Mexican girls to fry their eggs and make their beds. The answer came down to the same thing every time: 'That's not the point. Huffington is a real man, someone who stands for the family and for America, who has the same norms and values as we have, a guy you can trust.'

It's not a new phenomenon. Steinbeck saw it on his trip through America. In *Grand Expectations*, a wide-ranging study of the years 1945–74, historian James Patterson describes many white workers in New York even back in 1960 grumbling about the existence of welfare and other forms of social support. Yet in the 1930s they had benefitted enormously from such public spending, some of them using welfare to bridge the gap between jobs. As soon as possible they got back on their own two feet, whatever it took.

'Welfare helped us, and it was right and just that it did,' one New Yorker remembered. But afterwards 'we could shift for ourselves'. In other words, the norms and behavioural codes of those workers had a far stronger influence on their political beliefs than any economic or financial interests they might have.

In the early years of the twenty-first century, journalist and historian Thomas Frank posed the question again: How come so many Americans act against their own social and economic interests at election time? You see it happening all over the world, but it is particularly striking here. Frank took Kansas as an example, the state in which he grew up, once a left-wing Democrat bulwark, now largely conservative. Not so very long ago his old neighbours and acquaintances would have reacted to the crisis with a simple 'make the bastards pay'. Their response would have been just as predictable as what happens if you touch a match to a puddle of gasoline, he wrote. Nowadays it is very different. All their concerns and discontents pull them in one direction: to the right. 'Strip today's Kansans of their job security, and they head out to become registered Republicans. Push them off their land, and next thing you know they're protesting in front of abortion clinics. Squander their life savings on manicures for the CEO, and there's a good chance they'll join the John Birch Society.'

What's the Matter with Kansas? is the title of Frank's much-discussed book. In it he paints a political panorama every bit as crazy in places as a painting by Hieronymus Bosch: 'Of sturdy blue-collar patriots reciting the Pledge while they strangle their own life chances; of small farmers proudly voting themselves off the land; of devoted family men carefully seeing to it that their children will never be able to afford college or proper health care.'

He traces the problem largely to the Great Backlash, the failure of a Democratic Party that, in seeking votes from the 'rich and self-righteous' centre, abandoned the working class. Many of his old neighbours and acquaintances in Kansas were people who felt allied to the Democratic Party because of their economic situation, even though on moral issues – family values, abortion, gay marriage – they were closer to the Republicans. In the past, economic interests were always decisive, but New York and Silicon Valley are a long way away from Kansas, and when the Democrats became increasingly foreign to them they turned to the Republicans en masse. There at least they felt spiritually at home.

It's a common pattern. Rapid social change leads to a sense of in-security that creates an increasing need for predictability and a wealth of pseudo-certainties. The more unrest there is in society, the more people tend to reject everything that's new and different. The established path, your own country – they're all that counts.

Every statistic and every bit of sociological research demonstrates the same trend. For American conservatives there are indeed plenty of grounds for concern. Take that focus of so much discussion: the family. In the 1930s one in ten babies was born out of wedlock; in 2008 the figure was four in ten, the highest proportion ever. The majority of Americans have no moral objection to one-parent families any longer, and three-quarters would not ban divorce. It would be strange if they thought otherwise, since of all adult Americans who have been married, a third have at least one divorce behind them, evangelical Christians included.

In 1960 cohabitation was still regarded as a major problem. In 2000 half of all American couples lived together before marriage. The influence of Church and faith is declining, despite all the rhetoric. The number of Americans who want to give religion a greater say in society has fallen by a fifth since 2001, and the number who want to restrict that influence has risen by half.

The numbers do vary a great deal according to level of education, income, place of residence and race. In 1960 there were poor and rich neighbourhoods, but the differences were nothing like as extreme as half a century later. Disparities in income had not yet led directly to major disparities in behaviour. Almost all men between the ages of thirty and forty-nine, rich or poor, were in work. Their families often lived in the same neighbourhoods and their patterns of life looked much the same.

In that respect the transformation is complete. America, more so even than Western Europe, has become a country of social tribes that have broken free of each other. Some authors talk of the emergence of 'Super Zips', rich enclaves around almost all the big cities, from Chicago and New York to Houston, Los Angeles and Seattle. Anyone born in a Super Zip will probably go to school there, marry in a Super Zip and start a family in one, and he will probably stay there for the rest of his life. Within those enclaves – which account for around twenty per cent of the American population – seven per cent of children are born out of wedlock, whereas in the poorest thirty per cent of America, forty-five per cent of births are to unmarried mothers. It's the same with every other aspect of life in the Super Zips: a far higher level of education, more work, less crime, a more stable family life. Their inhabitants are not necessarily liberals – many Super Zips vote Republican – but most have lost contact with ordinary America.

In 2008 a provocative study appeared under the title *Red Families v. Blue Families*. Drawing upon a range of statistics, its authors demonstrated that after the sexual revolution of the 1960s the professional middle class, 'Blue America', found a new balance one way or another. Blue Americans often have a liberated lifestyle; they are not quick to marry, they have fewer children than average, but they work hard and have a relatively low rate of divorce and extra-marital births. Nevertheless, their lives, according to the statistics, are closer to the traditional norms than those of people living in most of America.

The rest of the country, 'Red America', has been left behind, according to this study at least. It has clung to the old norms and values, but it lives in a chaotic reality, with early marriage, a high rate of divorce, and more and more children born out of wedlock. The attitude of the conservatives, with their refusal to countenance abortion and contraception, and their unrealistic stress on abstinence, only encourages these developments. Young people get pregnant early and often, marry in haste and quickly divorce. Their family life, their 'home', is under serious threat.

Many American sociologists therefore believe that something contradictory is going on around religious and political fundamentalism. Fundamentalist movements do not in fact signify a revival of conservative values. They arise precisely because traditional norms and values have been eroding rapidly over the past few decades. It's a decline that is spurring traditionalist Americans to unprecedented activity as they throw everything into the struggle to defend their threatened lifestyle.

Who is the enemy here? During my trip I've been listening regularly to demagogue Rush Limbaugh and he is crystal clear: we have 'professionals' and 'experts' to thank for all this misery, including 'the medical elites, the sociological elites, the education elites, the legal elites, the science elites . . . and the ideas this bunch promotes through the media'.

Limbaugh and his countless supporters are building upon the aversion that conservative America has traditionally felt towards intellectuals. That sense of distaste goes back to the Shakers, the evangelical Protestant churches and all those emotional American religions in which direct communication between God and man was central. Such believers wanted nothing to do with professional theologians, who were always analysing everything to death. As Thomas Frank writes, 'critical thinking merely gets in the way of holiness'.

This was a seedbed on which a profound abhorrence gradually developed towards a professional middle class that, with research and policy advice, was able in the words of political essayist Barbara Ehrenreich to exercise 'non-violent social control' over ordinary men and women. In the past few decades, people have been subjected to a deluge of 'commands, diagnoses, instructions, judgments, definitions – even, through the media, suggestions as to how to think, feel, spend money, and relax'.

It was above all conservative Republicans who capitalised on the fretting and bitterness. They presented themselves as the party of anti-intellectualism, posing as 'ordinary housewives' and 'honest farm boys', even though quite often, like George W. Bush, they were from the highest social circles. Moderate, middle-of-the-road types, still in abundance in Steinbeck's day, are heard less and less often, especially within the Republican Party.

The two most important traditions in American thought – the pious pursuit of purity seen in the Pilgrims and the Enlightenment ideals expressed by the Founding Fathers – seem to be locked in a life-and-death battle. Both sides have a sense that 'their' America is being taken away from them, and those two Americas no longer resemble each other in the slightest.

We drive along Highway 10 into Minnesota, across mile after mile of rich, dark earth, the most fertile soil in the world. It's a landscape of gently rolling hills, once yellow with wheat, now given over to maize and soybeans. The farms are small, the barns weathered by storms and cold – the money is clearly made elsewhere. Strange installations appear alongside the road, processing plants where all those bountiful harvests are turned into ethanol, a biofuel. It's actually a kind of Kuwait, but the installations, oddly enough, smell of precisely that which is no longer produced here: bread.

This is lobby country, where lobby money is sown and harvested. The American ethanol lobby has managed to arrange substantial subsidies for itself, and the oil companies are obliged to buy huge amounts of ethanol. Since 2010, every litre of gasoline must have a ten per cent ethanol content. It adds up nicely, since Americans are still consuming petrol in vast quantities. It's not really in their nature to economise. Until recently there were high tariff barriers, designed to block imports of cheap Brazilian sugarcane ethanol.

The effect of all these measures is bizarre. Ethanol meets only eight per cent of America's energy requirements, but its production consumes no less than forty per cent of the American maize harvest. Of the 400 million tons of corn harvested in America, 120 million go to the ethanol distilleries. Hardly any attention is paid to efficiency. Brazilian ethanol produces eight units of energy for every one unit of energy invested in it; for American ethanol the figure is only one and a half.

Main Street in Red Wing looks as if nothing has changed in the past half-century, apart from the people that is: the streets are as quiet as a Sunday afternoon. We mail a letter at a post office beside the highway, a little square building flying an American flag. Inside are a counter, a handful of pigeonholes and a stern lady with a pencil and a stamp – an oasis of federal order, a modest but powerful expression of a shared identity. Throughout the afternoon that follows we drive past fields of maize for at least 200 miles. The trees are bare, but the Indian summer is still with us. Halloween dummies stand or hang in front of the houses, sometimes filling the garden.

Two greasy and dusty locomotives travel alongside us, hauling a mile or more of freight cars over the hills. 'America Building' it says on some of them, but more often Hyundai or China Shipping. The farms are visible only as islands in the oceans of maize. Everywhere in the fields large combines are harvesting. I see a farmer stop, get out and pull a maize plant from the ground before inspecting a cob minutely, counting the exact number of grains. A farmer is still a farmer, whatever the technology.

From time to time we see a cloud of dust on the horizon as a car comes towards us along a dirt road, the only change of scene in ten or twenty miles.

John Steinbeck travelled through St Paul and Minneapolis. He had pored over his maps in preparation but, nevertheless: 'As I approached, a great surf of traffic engulfed me, waves of station wagons, rip tides of roaring trucks.' He lost all sense of direction, the diesel fumes burned his lungs, Charley had a coughing fit, and for hours he drove around blindly until he found himself on a road with signs saying 'Evacuation Route'. It was a while before he realised what they meant; this was the planned escape route from the bomb that even now has not been dropped, 'a road designed by fear'. In the end he saw nothing at all of the Twin Cities.

Just before reaching Minneapolis we turn off onto a different route, taking Highway 19 westwards for Redwood Falls. Ours is a journey without planned meetings, with one exception: I want to talk to my old friend Joseph Amato, the great local historian of the Midwest. And I want to see Marshall, population 13,680 – at first sight just a small town in the middle of the plains, but under Joseph Amato's magnifying glass a world in itself.

Amato is a broad man who loves to talk, a passionate researcher bursting with ideas and energy. He's an audacious thinker who has written a great deal about village communities but also, for example, a book that recounts the history of dust. 'Local historians have to think things through,' he says. 'When you describe the earliest settlement you inevitably come up against the question of what went before it, and the price that was paid for the spread of European civilisation across America.'

You might write a history of prairie grass, or of grain, maize and soybeans, or perhaps bears and bison – both extinct in Minnesota since 1860 – and wolves. In Marshall, the last bounties on wolf kills were paid out in 1894. Or you might for a change look at history from the point of view not of those who laid out the railroads and small towns but of the landscape, of the Redwood River, as Amato does.

We've only just arrived and already he's whisking me off to the town archives in the racks of a room at the university. 'Look, the *Tax Assessment Book* from nineteen hundred and one. There was a fair amount of prosperity, as you can tell from the cattle, the pianos, the sewing machines, the jewellery, the number of pieces of furniture. And there must have been small farms everywhere on the prairie, you can see that just from all those wells and springs.'

He hands me a red, oblong book, the *Jail Record* of 1909 to 1939. Most of the offences concern drunken or disorderly behaviour, but I also see references to 'abandonment, wife' and to bigamy. Among all the immigrant names I spot only three that are Dutch: John Hennen served sixty-one days in 1921 for attempted robbery, and Fred Leschen and Frank van Althorst received sentences for drunkenness, in 1920 and 1931 respectively. You can see that over those thirty years the people detained become more American. At first they were mostly born in Belgium, Norway, Germany or Denmark, but after 1920 almost exclusively in Minnesota, Ohio or Kentucky.

Marshall lies to the south of an area that forms the watershed of almost all the great rivers of the United States. Flowing southwards are the Mississippi and the Missouri, northwards the rivers that empty into Canada, the Great Lakes and the Hudson. For centuries, rivers and lakes were the main transport arteries across the American continent. The routes travelled by Native Americans were closely linked to all those watercourses, which formed a network connecting everyone in this wilderness with the rest of the world. Tocqueville and Beaumont travelled mainly on that river network in 1831, using what were then ultra-modern steamboats. The rivers were natural lines of communication and they gave shape to early America.

The first harbingers of major change were, as they always are, the mapmakers and surveyors. Taking their cue from the Land Ordinance of 1785, in the late eighteenth century hundreds of cartographers and surveyors began to move into the still largely unknown West to measure and map everything in sight. The surveyors worked in teams and used special measuring chains that were exactly 660 feet long, one-eighth of a mile. It was a huge project, astonishingly ambitious. One hundred and forty years passed before all of the West was divided up into those familiar squares of 160 and 320 acres (the equivalent of 64 and 128 hectares). In the early years of the twentieth century, the surveyors were still at work in the prairies of Montana.

In 1860, railroads were laid through this landscape. The Homestead Act of 1862 enabled anyone to claim 160 acres of uncultivated land and develop it, which made the region extremely attractive to all kinds of immigrants. In accordance with the mapmakers' imaginary lines, the prairie was divided into sections of 640 acres each, and through them came dead-straight roads with a village or small town every six miles, complete with a school, a courtroom and a few other buildings. An inescapable grid was thereby laid on top of the landscape, awkwardly at odds with the old paths and river routes.

No line was ever drawn so sharply across the landscape as that of the railroad. Alongside the tracks, the rail companies founded a railroad town every few miles, and in this region the distance between them, based on all kinds of calculations, was set at seven miles. Many of the rail bosses actually decided what the towns would be called, and they often named them after their children, which explains why so many have elegant girl's

names such as Lorain, Alice, Marion or Ismay (a combination of Isabel
and May).

Everything was uniform: the houses, the street plans, even the names
of the streets. The buildings looked like wooden shoeboxes and every
Main Street had a post office, a hotel, a saloon and a general store. The
bank was invariably on the corner of First and Main. The earliest church
buildings usually went up somewhere near Third Street.

Despite this uniformity, most residents quickly came to regard their
town as the best and most attractive place for many miles around. They
built grand town halls and courthouses, embellished their Main Street in
every possible way, firmly believed in the growth and success of their
own particular town and, as Amato writes, 'persisted in denying that they
were small fry in a big game'.

In Marshall, history began in the summer of 1872, when a group of
settlers arrived at the bend of the Redwood River, the place where the
Winona & St Peter Railroad had chosen to found a new town. 'In every
direction was a seemingly endless expanse of undulating prairie, green
with a verdure which a hand of man had never disturbed,' one of them
would later say. That is what the landscape of the Midwest looked like
until the mid-nineteenth century. As in seventeenth-century Deerfield, the
noises of the time were simple: the river, the wind across the prairie,
the cries of a few wading birds, and in winter the howl of blizzards that
lasted for weeks.

Barely three months later, on 12 October, the shrill whistle of a steam
locomotive sounded across the plains for the first time. The bridge was
ready, the first train arrived and there was even a hotel – where half the
village would fall through the floor a week later, during a lively dance.
It was a constant coming and going of pioneer families. 'A family will
arrive in town on the evening train,' the same settler said, 'and next
morning charter an ox team and stock, then start out across the prairie
to find a piece of government land.'

A year later, on 11 October 1873, the little town had four shops, four
hotels, two mills, two hardware stores, a smithy and a printing works
where it even produced its own newspaper, the *Prairie Schooner*. Another
year later, according to the tax estimate for 1874, Marshall had 524 (male)

voters, 498 horses, 2,690 cattle and 365 carriages and carts. That same year, wooden sidewalks were laid on Main Street.

The long winter nights were still filled with the howling of wolves. In 1874 large packs of them surrounded the town, coming to within a mile of the first houses. Even after the introduction of telephone lines (1881 onwards) and the establishment of the Marshall High School Band (1889), an annual Decoration Day Parade (in about 1895), three banks, five hotels and seven churches (around 1900), Marshall still remained an open community on a silent plain. A visitor in 1905 wrote that from the station the cry 'All Aboard' resounded for miles across the prairie.

Marshall then followed the course taken by all small American towns. The extent of individual choice increased. With just an ordinary family radio you could listen to anything you liked in the evenings. The boys had to serve in the army and sometimes they saw a lot of the world: Europe, later Korea and Vietnam. They didn't automatically come back home. The GI Bill made it possible for them to start a new life in the big cities. Those who did stay gradually brought the advantages of the city into the town, including good doctors and a good hospital, good schools, a university, and later swimming pools and green golf courses.

That was how Steinbeck saw all the Main Streets he passed through: at the high point of their existence.

Joe Amato takes us with him to nearby Ghent, a town established in 1881 by twelve Flemish farming families who, galvanised by their priest, had come to the New World to found Catholic settlements.

None of the settlers felt American. They were Norwegians, Dutch, Belgians and Germans transplanted onto a strange open plain. As soon as they had the means, they did their best in those early years, with something close to desperation, to create reminders of the old fatherlands. In 1897 the German settlers of New Ulm built a scaled-down copy of the Hermann Monument near Detmold, mounted atop an attractive cupola. Hermann the German, as the monument is popularly known, has had a hard time of it. During the First and Second World Wars the Teutonic warrior was targeted by trigger-happy patriots, and only in recent years have the bullet holes been patched.

The first thing the Belgians of Ghent did was to build a parish church,

St Eloi's. Then they started an *estaminet*, a cheery Flemish watering hole. The Silver Dollar Bar in Ghent still has a homey smell of Flanders, with a long bar, a gleaming beer tap and behind it a carnival of sparkling glass. They hold *rolle bolle* championships, a version of boules imported from Belgium. We walk around the graveyard, where you can read history in the names: Blomme, Van Keulen, Claes, Van Uden, Stassen, Rogge, Olieslager. Nowhere do we see a neglected grave; this is still a tight-knit community.

In Minnesota the reciprocal prejudices of the Belgians and the Dutch have been turned on their head. Here it is the Belgians who are thought of as clever and ultra-frugal, as reflected in sayings like 'No one works harder than they do – not even God during the six days of creation', 'Who is shrewder than a Belgian farmer? Another Belgian farmer', 'Why do all Belgians paint their houses and barns the same colour on the same day? They got a good deal on the paint.'

The Belgians lived soberly and thriftily, with 'big barns and little houses' as they say here. And they became rich. At one point you could walk the full thirteen miles from the village of Cottonwood into Marshall without having to step off land belonging to a Flemish family by the name of Louwagie.

One of them didn't make it; homesickness paralysed him. I heard the story of a Belgian who kept climbing up into a windmill, sometimes in the searing cold, to stare out across the plain, as if frozen rigid, towards his far-off, beloved Flanders.

Joe once showed me a documentary about Ghent, made more than twenty years ago by the Belgian television network BRTN. It shows those large Catholic farming families in all their glory, the traditional ideal of a family working the land, trusting in God, answerable only to Him. 'Every new child is a surprise,' says the mother of one of the large broods of children. 'We're happy with each one of them. They find their way alright.'

High prices after the Second World War meant that the children and grandchildren of the first settlers did well out of farming, but in the 1980s tough times arrived. One of the grandchildren says: 'When I started out as a farmer all the family businesses were still running at full capacity. Half of them have stopped now.' In the years that followed, the old family farms merged into bigger and bigger units, increasingly anonymous and large-scale. All production was concentrated on maize and soya, used for cattle feed, ethanol and industrial food production in a thousand forms and flavours. Marshall is now above all the town of the frozen pizza, the headquarters of one of the biggest producers in the world, the Schwan Food Company.

Amato knew almost all the farmers BRTN interviewed in the late 1980s. 'They all live in the city now, apart from one family.' The 1980s spelled the end for small-town America. However you measure it, in influence, money or the number of residents and regulars, the result was the same almost everywhere: the smaller provincial towns fell into decline and the small traders disappeared. 'The Midwestern town can be pronounced stone dead,' says Joe.

In the archives I saw how many wells and springs remained around here in 1960, how many houses, how densely populated the plains still were. At least two-thirds of residents have left in the past half-century. Fifty years ago the school in the St Eloi parish still had at least 200 pupils. By around 1990 the proud building was in use by thirty at most. Now it is boarded up.

The Silver Dollar is for sale too. 'We used to get about two hundred and fifty people in here for *rolle bolle*,' the owner tells me. 'And it would go on until deep in the night. Now we're happy with forty.'

We're her only customers. She refuses to charge us for the coffee. 'Nice that you're here, that you listen to us.'

Again we drive across the plains, mile after mile. In the distance a dust cloud rises. That must be it. Jerry Louwagie, one of the last remaining Belgian farmers, is standing in front of a house built of glaring white synthetic materials. He waves. You can smell the soil of the fields. The barn, big as a cathedral, is completely empty. 'This used to be a mixed farm. In nineteen sixty we were one of the largest cattle breeders in the entire district; we had two hundred cows in this barn. Now all that's left is maize.'

His farm has nothing in common with that of his parents and grand-parents. 'When I started, in nineteen sixty-five, you still had those little pioneer farms of a hundred and sixty acres. Twice the acreage was better, but six hundred and forty acres was big, really big. Now you need at least three or four thousand acres to make a living.' All his maize is genetically manipulated. 'Thirty years ago I got a hundred bushels off an acre, now it's getting on for double that.'

I hear that in Chicago record prices are being paid for maize at the moment. The ethanol lobby in the agricultural states has performed miracles. World food prices have been driven up further as a result. And Jerry is able to keep his place going.

The maize harvest began ten days ago. He has another five days of twelve to fourteen hours on the combine. 'Climb in for a bit.' We drive in straight lines through the forest of maize. The cabin looks like a cockpit. There's a screen on which you can immediately see the probable size of the crop as it pours in.

'A hundred and ninety thousand, two hundred bushels. Very good. A nice harvest,' Jerry mumbles. 'The moisture content is fine too.' He points to where the ethanol plant is proudly emitting its scent on the horizon. 'Yep. That's where it's all going.'

'What's your view on that, if you're honest?' I ask.

Jerry thinks for a moment. 'It pays well. We have to do it. But of course I'm not producing food.' He shakes his head. 'This isn't why I became a farmer.'

That evening we have a visitor, Calvin, a former student of Amato's. We talk about the problems Europe is facing. 'At least we still have immigrants here, and we're good at making most of them into first-rate Americans within one or two generations,' Joe and Calvin announce cheerfully. Then we turn to the differences between American states. 'Here in Minnesota things are going really well, the prices for produce are sky high. But then there are the problem states, like California, Illinois and Florida; they're America's Greece, Spain and Italy.'

Such contrasts should not be underestimated. That much has been clear to me for some time. To the outside world the United States manages to maintain with some vigour the image of unity that Steinbeck painted. Internally, the solidarity of the nation is reaffirmed time and again with flags, pledges and other rituals. Nevertheless the differences are immense.

Maine is rather like Ireland. New Mexico is half-Spanish. Alaska has the climate of northern Scandinavia. Nevada and Arizona are largely desert. Florida is ageing rapidly. Texas and Southern California are remarkably young. Alaska still has Russian mission churches. And that's without even mentioning the immigrant groups that have brought their own traditions with them, from Poles and Italians to Mexicans, Japanese and Chinese. Until the end of the nineteenth century there were churches along the Hudson where sermons were delivered in seventeenth-century Dutch. Fifty years ago, in the hills of Kentucky, people still spoke a kind of Elizabethan English.

In the spring of 2010 the American Human Development Project published *A Century Apart*, a detailed study of the life of the average American. It confirmed once again that America is anything but a melting pot. In the north-eastern states, for example, there are many 'high trust areas', as they are known, where people have a reasonable amount of faith in each other and in the government, where the average level of education is high and where state provision is relatively good. In the South especially, by contrast, there are regions where people trust their fellow citizens and the government far less, and where the average level of education is astoundingly low.

All this produces differences in lifestyle comparable to the gap between, say, the Polish countryside and a Paris suburb. An American of Asian origin in New Jersey lives an average of twenty-six years longer than a Native American in South Dakota, and is eleven times as likely to have been to university. It's a similar story if you compare a white American in Connecticut to a black American in Arkansas.

On his journey Steinbeck was astonished time and again by the fact that America, despite all these differences, still exists. 'Four centuries of work, of bloodshed, of loneliness and fear created this land,' he wrote in *America and Americans*. 'Then, in a little, little time, we became more alike than we were different – a new society; not great, but fitted by our very faults for greatness.'

E pluribus unum, 'Out of many one.' It remains an aspiration rather than an accomplished fact. In Joe's living room that evening a debate arises not unlike the one going on in Europe: Why should we, in Minnesota, have to pay higher taxes just because California is badly governed? Must we go on putting up with their theft of our water? They've even set their sights on the Great Lakes now. How can it be right that because of the new national healthcare system we suddenly have to start paying for all those illegals in Arizona who don't contribute a cent? And that's despite the fact that in Minnesota our own healthcare is perfectly well organised, with good hospitals and excellent doctors, and not even all that expensive.

The further you go from Washington, the more often you notice that the United States are just that, united states, a collection of sovereign nations where, although they form a union, the centre of gravity remains with the state. Of course in elections the distinction between Democrats and Republicans makes a great deal of difference, but for most people it's mainly a question of which man or woman will be sent to Washington as a senator on behalf of Minnesota, to serve the interests of this state.

In that sense America looks more like our own divided Europe than I ever suspected. Like most Americans, the people I talk to hate having government at any level tell them what to do, but they reserve their deepest loathing for federal rules and regulations, and they complain in exactly the same way about Washington as Europeans do about Brussels. 'The Federal Government is . . . the exception; the Government of the States is the rule,' wrote Tocqueville, and for most Americans that remains the case.

'We're ruled from Washington by the best and the brightest,' says Joe. 'They think up the cleverest plans and they're firmly convinced they're right. But are they really producing the best plans? No, because they're not familiar with the daily reality on the ground. It's true of our wars in distant countries, but it applies to all the things they get up to here as well, in fly-over country, an indeterminate, endless expanse they know only from an airplane seat, from five miles up.'

I recall a map of America published by the *Economist* in 2009, in which every state had been given the name of a country elsewhere in the world with an economy of a comparable size. California was Italy on the map, Texas was the equivalent of Russia, Louisiana became Israel, Florida the Netherlands, Michigan Taiwan, Ohio Belgium.

So now we're travelling through Thailand.

Tomorrow, on towards Uruguay, Lebanon, Sudan and Greece. And then, via Pakistan, to Italy at last.

PART FIVE

Minnesota – North Dakota – Montana – Washington – Seattle

'Uncle Sam sends you an invitation . . .'

PAMPHLET SOLICITING FOR EUROPEAN
IMMIGRANTS
C. 1910

One

A COOL MORNING SUN HANGS over the land. In the breakfast diner Fox News takes up its old bombastic refrain. Terrorists are threatening the United States. The new healthcare system violates the US Constitution. An autumn storm is about to hit the east coast. Everything is dangerous. Everything is deployed to keep adrenaline levels high.

The left–right conflict comes into play less than I've always assumed. Another antithesis is increasingly prominent: between local and national – plus the rest of the world. There is a continual effort to make the intangible tangible again, to reconquer a world that has slipped out of the hands of the ordinary man or woman. For Fox the truth, or rather the search for the truth, is completely irrelevant. A story going around here, to give just one example, is that in the liberal Netherlands older people are being murdered wholesale, that at least half of all cases of euthanasia are involuntary and elderly Dutch people who want to live for a while yet wear wristbands saying 'No euthanasia please'.

The people you speak to are firmly convinced this is true. They didn't make it up. It's fallout from all the nonsense with which certain American mass media inundate the public, whether it has to do with the murderous propensities of Muslims, the president's birth certificate, 'weapons of mass destruction' in Iraq, the 'socialism' of Europe or the euthanasia policy of Dutch doctors.

It's a bombardment of factoids, as Norman Mailer once called them, fabricated truths that serve purely to buttress the prejudices of the average viewer and to strengthen and embellish those prejudices with a constant stream of new and appetising stories.

*

We aim to pick up Steinbeck's trail again at Sauk Centre, a morning's drive northwards. First we call in at the local Jeep garage, since our aerial has snapped, which hasn't done a lot for our radio reception. As foreigners we're greeted with immense hospitality; everyone engages with our little problem and eventually the professor on the team – glasses, tiny screwdriver, biting his lower lip – manages to remove the remains of the old aerial.

'What on earth brings you here?' the professor asks. 'No one ever comes to this town.'

There is much telephoning back and forth. In Detroit Lakes, a couple of hundred miles further on, a new antenna will be waiting for us tomorrow. They've spent at least half an hour helping us but no, of course it won't cost us anything. What are we thinking of? 'Nice that you were here.'

Then we make up the miles. We pass Clara: thirty houses, a large ethanol plant, a funeral home, immense silver silos, a pipe out of which pours a thick, unbroken, yellow river of maize. Next comes another dead-straight road with a cluster of houses every fifteen or twenty miles, followed by the plains again.

After a few hours a town appears on the horizon: Sauk Centre, the mother of all Main Streets, birthplace of Harry Sinclair Lewis, who wrote the classic novel Main Street, a hilarious yet sad portrait of small-town America at its most stifling. When the book was published in 1920 it caused a sensation. Since then Gopher Prairie, as Sauk Centre is called in the book, has come to symbolise something far broader. 'Main Street is the climax of civilization,' Sinclair Lewis wrote. 'What Ole Jenson the grocer says to Ezra Stowbody the banker is the new law for London, Prague, and the unprofitable isles of the sea; whatsoever Ezra does not know and sanction, that thing is heresy, worthless for knowing and wicked to consider. Our railway station is the final aspiration of architecture. Sam Clark's annual hardware turnover is the envy of the four counties which constitute God's Country. In the sensitive art of the Rosebud Movie Palace there is a Message, and humor strictly moral.'

In 1930 Sinclair Lewis won the Nobel Prize for Literature, the first American to do so, but he'd better not show his face in Sauk Centre for a while. That was probably the reason why Steinbeck devoted a couple of lines to him: 'I had read *Main Street* when I was in high school, and I remember the violent hatred it aroused in the countryside of his nativity. Did he go back? Just went through now and again.' Steinbeck had experienced a similar hatred in his native region, where in the summer of 1939 *The Grapes of Wrath* was removed from schools and libraries. Enraged landowners publicly threw it onto the pyres as 'obscene in the extreme sense of the word'. He would never again feel at home there.

Steinbeck and Lewis had lunched together a couple of times in New York. Steinbeck noted that Lewis didn't drink a drop and he ate without enjoyment, 'but now and then his eyes would glitter with steel'. Sinclair Lewis was a good deal older, but they were both outsiders in the literary world, never having completely managed to wrest themselves free of the provinciality they so despised. Lewis died in 1951. By then he'd become the town's great hero and there was even talk of changing the name of Sauk Centre to Gopher Prairie.

'The only good writer was a dead writer. Then he couldn't surprise anyone any more, couldn't hurt anyone any more,' Steinbeck wrote of his old colleague. 'And now he's good for the town. Brings in some tourists. He's a good writer now.'

Today's Sauk Centre has a Sinclair Lewis Avenue, a Sinclair Lewis Park, a Sinclair Lewis Campground and even a Sinclair Lewis Museum. Lewis himself lies under a small, grey stone in Greenwood Cemetery. Yes, he did go back.

The heroine of *Main Street* is Carol Kennicott, an enterprising young woman who, after her college years in St Paul, hastily marries Sauk Centre's country doctor. Her husband belongs to the town's upper middle class, to circles that include the bank manager and the most prominent retailers, and she tries to introduce more life, beauty and culture into that community.

Lewis describes Carol going to do some shopping on Main Street on the first morning after her arrival, to kill time. She walks past Dyer's Drug Store with its greasy, marble soda fountain, the Rosebud Movie Palace – film of the week: *Fatty in Love* – the blood-soaked window display of Dahl and Oleson's Meat Market, the Bon Ton Store for gentleman's fashions, and Billy's Lunch with its oniony smell. The street is 'cluttered with

electric-light poles, telephone poles, gasoline pumps for motor cars, boxes
of goods'. Directly beyond it lies the open prairie.

'When Carol had walked for thirty-two minutes she had completely
covered the town, east and west, north and south; and she stood at the
corner of Main Street and Washington Avenue and despaired.'

Carol would not have recognised any of today's Main Street, except
for the Corner Drugstore and the old bank building. Even when John
Gunther visited the place in the 1940s, little was left of it. The frontages on either side were at least half as high again, all the shops had
been expanded and rebuilt, and everyone had cars and money. The
1940s were good years for American farmers. Gunther writes that Dr
Kennicott would have been amazed by the standard of living. 'Remember
how he charged one of his country patients $11.00 for an operation,
and told him he could wait till next year to pay up – if his crop was
good enough? Today the mortgages and "barnyard loans" are largely
paid off.'

In 2010 fragments of the world of Carol Kennicott, Ole Jenson and
Ezra Stowbody can be found only in the small town museum, a collection of junk assembled with care and dedication, a place full of uniforms,
tableware, sewing machines, toasters, evening dresses and rusty tools.
One photo is worthy of more than superficial attention, a shot of the
corner of Main Street and Sinclair Lewis Avenue in about 1960, showing
a lively shopping district with sturdy-looking shops and offices, plus the
Corner Drugstore. Even the most archetypal Main Street in America has
had its day. The men's fashions store is still there, the cinema and Palmer
House Hotel Café are bravely carrying on, but the bakery is boarded up,
the First National Bank building now houses a gift shop and the Corner
Drugstore is up for sale.

Carol Kennicott bears some resemblance to Madame Bovary, Gustave
Flaubert's heroine, the doctor's wife buried away in a French village along
with all her dreams and aspirations. Except that Carol is far more active.
She introduces new literature to the library, joins several clubs, debates
social problems and makes friends outside of the predictable little circle
– friends who are taken from her, one by one, through all kinds of
manipulation. Carol has launched herself into a classic American endeavour:

the bringing of urban civilisation to the wilderness, and the preservation of it there.

Life on the prairie was a rough and lonely struggle for survival, and brawls – up to and including Congress – were a regular occurrence, but from the start there was a cultural counter-movement. Despite the sometimes harsh conditions of life, the eighteenth-century inhabitants of colonial Deerfield, then still the back of beyond, bought expensive luxuries like coffee and tea, owned paintings and sets of crockery, and used fashionable toiletries. From an inventory dated 1774 it is clear that even among the poor, four out of every ten households had a proper tea set. As a contemporary wrote: 'For the pleasure of taking tea in the parlor, more than a few families were content to continue pissing in the barn.'

Tocqueville too was struck by the drive to elevate the quality of life through luxury and culture of every kind, preferably European. 'When you've traversed a sort of wilderness on a frightful road and reach a habitation, you're astonished to encounter a more advanced civilization than in any of our villages,' he wrote to his mother in the summer of 1831. 'The farmer takes pride in his appearance, his dwelling is perfectly clean, and his first concern is to talk to you about politics.' One pioneer he met immediately started asking him questions about the relative strengths of the various French political parties.

Ever since 1800, an excellent postal service had existed throughout America, supported by Congress, which meant that newspapers and magazines were read in the most remote parts of the country. Pianos and French teachers arrived with the riverboats. The first fur hunter to settle in Minnesota in about 1830, Joseph Laframboise, sent his daughters to a boarding school on the east coast as soon as he could. In Detroit, still a village in the wilderness in 1831, Gustave de Beaumont came upon advertisements for the latest French fashions.

From the second half of the nineteenth century onwards, that process of civilisation advanced rapidly in extent and significance, and Carol Kennicott's initiatives should be seen in that light. The immigrants brought their own traditions and rules of etiquette with them. They founded churches and schools, and demanded that everyone abide by their rules even out here in the wilderness. The pioneers learned to wash more often, like respectable city people, to shout, fight and spit less, and above all to keep better control of their anger and other emotions.

Often it was the women who, like Carol, kept the flag of urban culture flying at village level. In a local museum I once saw the dress worn by a great-grandmother during something called the Oklahoma Land Run of 22 April 1889, a madcap race in which some 50,000 settlers took part, attempting to claim the best stretch of land in that undeveloped territory. I found it deeply touching. The woman – her name was J. B. Cobbs – had evidently taken part in that ferocious contest wearing her best clothes: a long black frock with dark-grey dots and a black chequered collar; simple but extremely elegant. Civilisation.

Phil Graham, who became the great man behind the *Washington Post*, grew up in a houseboat in the swamps of the Everglades. Even in the harshest of circumstances his mother, a former teacher, kept up her subscription to the *New Yorker* and *Time*. Steinbeck's mother, Olive Hamilton, was made of similar stuff. She taught, involved herself in a hundred and one social activities, and created a home atmosphere in which poetry was recited, books were read, classical music was played and stories were told.

In small-town communities, the influence of older women in particular increased as the twentieth century went on. 'This is a very unusual social phenomenon,' writes Geoffrey Gorer in his study of 'the American' of the 1940s and 1950s. In almost all societies, whether primitive or complex, European or Asiatic, older married women who do not work are of little importance on the social scene. Their power lies in the domestic arena. In America, by contrast, 'this group is one of the most active and influential bodies of citizens, as well as one of the most conspicuous'.

'American women reach their greatest social influence from the time they near the menopause,' Gorer writes. So don't laugh at these middle-aged women, he warns, with their 'eager seeking after knowledge and wisdom, their dogged clinging to stylishness and a falsely youthful appearance, their naïve approach to the arts and to gracious living (a key phrase), their façade of almost excessive self-assurance so often a protective front to the deepest uncertainty and humility'. They are a source of both culture and money, and when serious local abuses are addressed, the initiative comes in many cases from the women's clubs. 'They are our chief bulwark against chaos.'

Madame Bovary, Flaubert's heroine, takes arsenic. Carol becomes trapped as well, in the sour provincialism of Gopher Prairie. She flees to Washington, DC, but eventually returns to her husband and child and accepts her fate. She keeps her head held high to the very last page: 'I do not admit that Main Street is as beautiful as it should be! I do not admit that Gopher Prairie is greater or more generous than Europe! I do not admit that dish-washing is enough to satisfy all women! I may not have fought the good fight, but I have kept the faith.'

Twenty years later, when John Gunther travelled through Sauk Centre, she would probably have grown into a strong American woman after all, with more informal power and influence than she could ever have foreseen. Gunther watched as outward appearances began to change in the 1940s. On Main Street he spotted sixteen-year-old girls in short trousers. The bar of Palmer House, once a male bastion, was now there for everyone: young or old, male or female. The masculine conviviality within the walls of the lodges and clubs was cracked open and replaced by cinema going, motoring trips, lunches and other outings in which women could take part.

There were already developments that worried him. The automobile and the chain stores had changed Sauk Centre 'from a village into a metropolis'. This new type of store would never truly become part of the local community, was the fear. The managers of such stores tended to move on after six months or a year, so they never became 'a real ingredient in the life of the community'. As a result, people told Gunther, the chain store 'undermines civic spirit'.

In writing this he touched upon an important point. That same civic spirit is now, as ever, the basis of American politics. Steinbeck's circle of friends in Sag Harbor was one small example: its members often differed vehemently in their opinions on all kinds of political issues, especially with 'red' John, but they talked every day, they came together to arrange for new street lamps and better sewers, and they respected each other.

The American nation originated in enthusiastic local associations like these, which emerged right across the country. They formed the foundations of political life. Tocqueville described time and again the political 'tumult' he encountered everywhere, the 'confused clamor' that 'rises up on all sides' and the 'thousand voices' that reached his ear. Main Street, with its clubs and lodges, but also with its local newspapers and all its casual meetings, produced a lively social intercourse that could be built upon. American friends of mine value the warm school and church communities that have emerged everywhere in the suburbs, and on the internet too, of course. 'The internet will become the new, virtual Main Street, just you wait and see,' they say. I have my doubts. The dynamism of Main Street was spurred by its universal character, by the fact that everyone did business with everyone else, whatever their political or religious persuasion. One characteristic of the internet is that people can separate themselves, close themselves off, limit all communication and information to certain groups and ways of thinking. Main Street connected people. The internet does that as well, but it also feeds a tendency to individualisation and polarisation.

Yes, I know, there isn't just one Main Street but thousands in America, with major differences between them. The downfall of almost all those Main Streets, however, is a universal phenomenon, with huge political consequences. Even banker Ezra Stowbody would now have to admit that Main Street has moved on beyond the 'climax of civilization'. This problem goes further than a boarded-up bakery and a bank building put to new use. Main Street has lost its emotional power and therefore its political role.

'All politics is local', as the saying still goes in Washington. Members of Congress are steered by their home constituency, which determines what they do to an overwhelming degree. But the foundations of that constituency are disappearing. The political 'tumult' that Tocqueville observed everywhere, the 'thousand voices' of Main Street USA, the civic spirit of Steinbeck and friends in Sag Harbor has fallen silent or evaporated. And no one can explain to me what has taken its place.

We are on our way to Fargo, in North Dakota, the town right at the central fold of the map of America. I've tried it out and it's true. On many maps, because of the crease, Fargo has actually worn away. Perhaps for that reason it is a town whose very existence is questionable, a place the elements are always conspiring against. To Steinbeck, from early

childhood, it was a magical place. On a cold day Fargo was guaranteed
to be the coldest town on the continent. Whenever it was hot, or snowing,
or raining, Fargo broke all the records. In Steinbeck's memory, at least.

Steinbeck spent the night in Frazee, some sixty miles short of Fargo,
probably in a loading and unloading area for trucks, an experience he
shifted back to Mauston along with his description of turkey country. He
was tired. He had taken the same route from Sauk Centre as we took,
the US 71 and the US 10, driving through the same landscape of meadows
and woods, and he'd no doubt seen the same powerful coal trains and
freight trains passing as they hauled their way howling across the plains
– on one occasion I counted five locomotives pulling ninety-two wagons.

In *Travels* Steinbeck describes seeing himself reflected in the windscreen,
'a lean and shriveled face like an apple too long in the barrel, a lonely
face and sick with loneliness'. The tone of the letters he wrote to Elaine
is cheerful and relaxed, however. He is grilling sausages, he writes from
Frazee, and he's had a fruitful day. There was much talk about local politics, but Washington is far away. One man who saw his license plates
said: 'Clear from New York.' He's been listening to local radio stations all
day, which mostly play the same music as at home: '"Pure Apple Princess",
"My Baby Has Brown Eyes".'

The next day Steinbeck wrestled his way through Fargo, a town that
was 'as traffic-troubled, as neon-plastered, as cluttered and milling with
activity as any other up-and-coming town of forty-six thousand souls'.
He found peace again only when he reached Alice, some forty-five miles
beyond Fargo, on a narrow side road on the banks of the Maple River.

We travel in his wake, driving through Fargo with similar haste, past
hundreds of identical housing complexes, tacky but comfortable, of the
kind that are spreading insidiously all over the earth. Then, after Fargo,
the true emptiness of America suddenly opens up, the endlessness of the
Great Plains, the desert of brownish grass in the heart of this country.
The landscape is gently hilly, and somehow or other everything has a
certain orderliness to it, although we rarely see a farm or a settlement.
The road is one long strip of concrete leading to nothing and nowhere.

According to *Travels*, Steinbeck must have camped somewhere here on
the Maple River. He did his washing in an ingenious way, in an empty
garbage bucket that shook as he drove along, and he hung the clothes

over the bushes to dry. Among some rubbish he found a discarded court order – overdue alimony – and contemplated loneliness and politics. Another car stopped a short distance away, with a caravan attached, and it turned out to be the home of a stage actor – 'Good afternoon . . . I see you are of the profession' – who travelled to all the rural gathering places with a Shakespeare monologue, borrowed word for word from a record made by Sir John Gielgud. They settled down to drink together and Steinbeck stayed there by the river for the rest of the afternoon and evening.

Eventually we do indeed cross the Maple River, and sure enough there is a turning for Alice (then 164 souls, now 40), which lies some ten miles from the main road. I can well imagine Steinbeck taking a break here. The Maple River is a friendly little brook, in fact it's the only pleasant place in this mostly bare infinity.

'The night was loaded with omens,' he wrote. 'The grieving sky turned the little water to a dangerous metal and then the wind got up – not the gusty, rabbity wind of the seacoasts I know but a great bursting sweep of wind with nothing to inhibit it for a thousand miles in any direction.'

That same evening, however, his letters reveal, he slept in a motel room more than 300 miles further on, in the village of Beach. He rang Elaine, took a bath and talked with a couple of men at the bar for a while about deer hunting. That was all he found worthy of mention. A good fabrication always carries a germ of truth. He did wash a few shirts that night. In the bathtub.

A little further on from Alice, in Tower City, there's a new diner at the side of the road, the only one for miles around. Five men in chequered shirts are sitting looking at enormous omelettes with hash browns, rösti they call them here, the speciality of the house. They eat with their forks, with great concentration, their left hands, large and callused, resting in their laps.

Not a lot happens here. The fines imposed this week by the local magistrate are described in detail in the newspaper: Evan Luhr, 10 dollars for speeding; Gary Scott, 25 dollars for driving through a red light; Harry Blozonski, 250 dollars for drink-driving. This is the America of solitude. Thirty out of the fifty American states have fewer inhabitants than Denmark. The population density of European countries like Britain and

Germany hovers around 250 per square kilometre, whereas in the United States the average is thirty-three. Four-fifths of Americans live in a town or a suburb. What remains is this, here.

Empty land.

The *Bismarck Tribune* reports on a meeting of the local Tea Party movement, with slogans such as 'Russia called. They want their socialism back.' In the Theodore Roosevelt National Park, elk reduction teams are at work. Parts of the park are closed, because out of 950 wapitis, around a third must be shot. The meat will be shared out among Native Americans and charitable organisations. The international news is dominated by French students, who are smashing everything in sight because in forty years from now their state pensions will be less generous than those of their grandparents. In the American commentary, whether from left or right, mild astonishment can be detected at this European 'decadence'.

An exuberant commercial recommends a dietary supplement called Bactium, a pill that rids the colon of worms and damaging bacteria, thereby driving out most diseases: the end of all medication. 'This tiny pill could put your doctor out of business by 2012!'

My wife gets talking to an older couple. They join our table and are keen to chat, telling us how glad they are that this diner has reopened. 'Everyone around here loves coming; at last we get to see each other again.' They live some fifty miles from the road and they drive here regularly, just for a cup of coffee. 'Otherwise we'd never speak to anyone.'

They've always had a farm. Both are natives of these plains. They were born fifty miles to the west and now they live fifty miles to the east of here. 'Right, we haven't gone far, but we've had a great life.'

We talk about the emptiness of the country and whether you ever get used to it. The man, a little melancholy, tells the old story: there were once farms in these parts, here and there, and everyone knew everyone else. 'You know, it used to be that if you were on the road and found yourself in a blizzard you never had to worry. You could always find someplace, there was shelter all over. Now you can drive fifteen or twenty miles without passing a single house. It's become unfriendly country.'

We drive on, the next hundred miles, out of one local radio station and into another, all of them playing the same homogeneous mix of soft rock and country music that spurred Steinbeck along in his day.

Now and then the asphalt shines in the sun like a big puddle of water. Sometimes we sail through strange patches of dust that hang in the air, thin and still, like banks of fog. Now I understand why Steinbeck fitted Rocinante out as a ship. After a while you no longer drive through this space; it becomes a sea that you sail upon. We grow increasingly silent in the rise and fall of our Jeep.

We pass Bismarck. When Ernie Pyle drove this way at the time of the Dust Bowl, in July 1936, he saw a completely ruined land, populated by bankrupt farmers and tradesmen, the once-green hills where huge herds used to graze in complete freedom 'now parched and cramped and mishandled by man'. In 2010 I keep on along smooth highways, through a few well-fed suburbs, and then it's behind us. Later in the afternoon, white cirrus clouds gather in the sky overhead, with streaks of pale blue and pink. A flight of geese makes its way through the emptiness.

I'm reminded of what British author Jonathan Raban wrote about the ravaged landscape of the Midwest, about the snowstorms and plagues of grasshoppers, and about the piety of the people who live here. The more often he came here the better he understood why the Protestant God of America was so much more fierce and temperamental than the calm English God he'd grown up with. 'A land of earthquakes, deluges, hurricanes, lightning-strikes, forest fires and grotesque extremes of heat and cold deserves a God in keeping with its wrathful climate.'

I once got hold of the first volume of the Left Behind series, Christian science fiction that fascinated me right from the opening pages. Pilot Rayford Steele, on his way from Chicago to London Heathrow in a full Boeing 747, receives a disturbing message from the cabin crew halfway across the Atlantic. A large number of passengers have suddenly disappeared, leaving all their clothes behind, neatly folded in their seats. He makes contact with the control tower. People have disappeared everywhere, en masse. No one can understand it. Everyone is in a panic. Rayford is ordered to fly back to America and from above O'Hare airport he sees the chaos with his own eyes: driverless cars are caught in the crash barriers; trains have derailed; aircraft lie in pieces on the ground; all around are the blue and red lights of police cars and fire trucks.

The stewardess comes over to him. 'Sir, we lost every child and baby on this plane . . . All of them! Not one was left.' The television screens at the airport show footage from all over the world. There are pictures of a birth, with the baby and a maternity nurse dissolving into thin air, and of a funeral at which the deceased and most of the cortège suddenly vanish.

At first I couldn't understand what all this was about, brought up though I was with the Protestant doctrine, but suddenly I realised what was going on. This was the Rapture, the beginning of the end times, the central theme of a typically American version of Christianity. Here, many people believe that the biblical prophesies found in the books of Daniel, Ezekiel and Revelation — wars, hail, plagues of locusts — are coming true. The Rapture is close at hand, when Christ will return and all true believers, living or dead, will go straight to heaven.

All this happens in the first few pages of the thriller. Signs of the end times can be seen everywhere, believers say, with the growth of a strong central government, the increase in the number of international organisations, and the rise of a superstate led by an apparently benevolent figure who will later turn out to be Satan, the Antichrist. After the Rapture of the holy, the rest of humanity will face great tribulation, the Messiah will return to earth, and Satan will be defeated and locked away in a bottomless chasm. After a thousand years, a millennium, the Antichrist will return. He will gather Gog and Magog around him, two peoples at the far ends of the earth. The Messiah will appear once more, and after a horrific final battle — Armageddon — Satan and all those who followed him will be engulfed by the eternal fires of hell. That final battle will take place in God's 'favoured city', Jerusalem.

This version of Christianity was popular in the 1930s. Stalin and Hitler were widely seen as foreshadowing the Antichrist, and some even saw satanic tendencies in President Franklin D. Roosevelt, with his dreams for the United Nations. The faith has been kept alive, sustained with great fervour by conservative evangelists and media personalities like Billy Sunday, Billy Graham and Jerry Falwell. In the Lincoln News, a local weekly in Maine, I came upon an angry article by the activist group Take Back America that opposed the creation of a national park simply because it was part of a United Nations nature conservation programme. The headline read: 'The Betrayal Continues'. Here you see cars with bumper stickers like 'Warning: In Case of Rapture, This Vehicle Will Be Unmanned' – and I suspect those inside truly believe it.

'This is Armageddon' has become common parlance. Whether the problem is a banking crisis or a particularly heavy snowfall, you'll soon hear the commentators announcing: 'This is Armageddon!' In the Left Behind series, God and Satan are the central characters. Satan is immediately recognisable by the fact that he speaks more than one language, clearly comes from a big city and has dedicated himself to the work of the United Nations. In other words: anyone who is not a fanatical nationalist delivers himself up to evil. More than sixty-five million copies of the books in the series have been sold. And with his charisma and his international background, no one fits the part of the Antichrist so perfectly as President Barack Obama.

Every landscape inspires its own religious feelings. I know this from the Netherlands, where fear of a biblical flood has always set the tone in the low-lying polders, and under the grey skies a melancholic and mystical faith prevails. This landscape evokes the same kind of feelings, a sense of the smallness and vulnerability of humanity under the all-seeing eye of the Almighty. 'Had I been born to this,' Raban admits, 'I think I might listen to the end-time evangelists with something more than the mixture of alarm and scorn they now provoke in me.'

In Bad Land Raban investigates the history of a forgotten farm belonging to Ned Wollaston, established in about 1910, and the nearby settlement of Ismay, later renamed Joe. The American cattle farmers were traditionally ranchers, using methods adopted from the Spanish. From spring onwards, when the calves were born, they let their cattle and sheep roam more or less freely across the immense prairies. Every animal bore the brand of its owner. In the autumn the cowboys would drive the young cattle back towards the ranch to winter there. The older animals were driven to market, or in later years to states like Kansas, Nebraska or Wyoming, where they were fattened up for slaughter. In around 1870, herds several thousand strong moved back and forth across the plains of the Midwest. In spring they made for the grassy meadows of the North and in autumn, as an old rancher once told me, they would 'turn their asses to the wind and walk south, sometimes for thousands of miles; there was no stopping them'.

The rancher, the lonely cowboy and the nomadic life they led became the ultimate romantic symbols of the eternally forward-marching American. In reality the heyday of the cowboy lasted only twenty years or so. By about 1890 it was over. They were displaced by two thoroughly prosaic inventions: barbed wire and the small metal windmill. Cattle ranchers used barbed wire to fence off their territory and windmills to irrigate even the driest patches of land from deep wells, making it fertile. Large parts of the Midwest that had been regarded as desert in the middle of the nineteenth century could now be farmed.

Meanwhile the railroad companies were placing advertisements all over Europe and distributing pamphlets. Writers and artists depicted the most beautiful landscapes, a new American Garden of Eden, with the slogan 'Uncle Sam sends you an invitation . . .' So the pioneer families came, in their hundreds of thousands, experienced farmers but also city people who had never held a spade. They were given land for almost nothing, especially after a new Homestead Act in 1909. Then the real work could begin: collecting timber, sawing thousands of posts, stringing barbed wire.

Barbed wire, rather than laws and regulations, created order in prairie society, and a new sense of citizenship. 'Fencing along a common boundary, watched from a distance by a rancher riding his high horse, neighbouring homesteaders became friends and allies,' Raban writes. 'Barbed wire belongs to the iconography of war, which was how the ranchers saw it; but putting up a fence together was, for the settlers, a fine way of bridging their different languages and social classes.'

All that barbed wire could even function as a telephone network, long before the Bell Company appeared on the horizon. You had to yell, reception was far from perfect and anyone could listen in, but across the barbed-wire telephone you could share news good or bad with neighbours and friends, whether of sudden illness or a stray cow.

By the autumn of 1911 most of the fences in Ismay were ready, and Raban describes how the prairie became scattered with houses, huts and other structures, each a mile from the next: those stone bothies built by the Scots, the log cabins of the Americans, English farm cottages,

Norwegian huts with sod roofs. At night you could see the electric lights of the nearest settlement on the horizon. The howling of wolves had stopped. The children in the farmhouses went to sleep to the whistle of a train as it died away amid the hills, and from time to time the ringing of a barbed-wire telephone.

The earth seemed rich and generous. In fact the topsoil was far too thin and repeated ploughing proved disastrous. The pioneers were all nearly killed twenty years later by the storms of the Dust Bowl, but no one foresaw such calamities. Everything was new, spacious and severely geometrical, and the inhabitants were immigrants from all corners of Europe, chancers and hard workers.

'This was no longer mere land,' Jonathan Raban writes, 'it was a land-scape; and it was an American classic.'

The Wollaston family, which plays the central role in Raban's book, invested every scrap of energy in the ideal of a farm of their own, but in the late 1930s they were forced to capitulate like everyone else. In the 1980s, along with a grandson of Ned Wollaston, Raban tried to find the old homestead. It took them all morning. It seemed that as few traces were left of Ned Wollaston after half a century as of a stone-age farmer. In the end they found the spot with the help of a topographical map, an old photograph and what was left of the fence. Out of the grass a handful of other silent witnesses came to light: the rusty lid of a milk churn, the bumper of a Model T Ford, a lightning conductor, the remains of a child's sledge.

There was one human memory of this patch of earth, the only one Wollaston's father had ever spoken about: a mother on her knees, day after day, begging God for rain.

Two

IT'S SUNDAY. Yesterday, towards evening, we drove into the only real Badlands. I'd heard and read about the place, yet it still came as a surprise. Almost without any transitional stage, the earth tore open and rock faces appeared, crevices, a rough landscape rising up out of the ocean of the prairie as if a spell had been cast. We eventually found ourselves in Medora, the only little town for miles around. In summer it's overrun by tourists, but now only one hotel was open. Everything else was shut, ready for winter. The trees were bare. The first snow might fall at any moment.

Steinbeck compared the Badlands to the work of an evil child, a world that does not welcome people. 'Such a place the Fallen Angels might have built as a spite to Heaven, dry and sharp, desolate and dangerous, and for me filled with foreboding.' He describes the groaning of Rocinante's suspension as he struggled across this bleak landscape. He met a taciturn farmer and an elderly woman who suffered from homesickness, but when evening fell the light was so beautiful that he stopped near a thicket, 'trapped in color and dazzled by the clarity of the light'. The night he spent there was full of stars and was more lovely than he had ever expected. 'My fire made a dome of yellow light over me, and nearby I heard a screech owl hunting and a barking of coyotes.'

In reality, though, as it turns out from his letter of 12 October 1960 to Elaine, Steinbeck drove on at a good pace and slept that night in Beach. He found the Badlands 'moody things – really as though someone were being bad', although he could imagine how a person might fall in love with them. The road was rough and the wind high. That was the bald truth of it.

*

But now it's the Lord's Day. Medora is deserted and the only church in the area is locked. Today, like millions of Americans, we'll have to worship through the television. There's no other option. So first we listen for half an hour to Joyce Meyer, a battle-axe of a preacher with tight corners to her mouth who has just one message to deliver: 'Never, ever, ever argue with me.' She talks about 'the battlefield of the mind', words like 'sin' and 'peace' rain down upon us, and a choice has to be made, here and now, between a good life and a bad life, between heaven and hell.

After the sermon there's a minute-long advertisement for the book *The Battlefield of the Mind*. A useful purchase, I'm given to understand. It will teach me how to wash my soul clean of the stains of evil. I'll receive the book and a pious CD free of charge if I make out a cheque for ninety dollars or more to Joyce Meyer's ministry. I click on her website. It's nothing but business and Bible texts: Lourdes, American style.

Quickly over to the Lakewood Church in Houston for *A Night of Hope* with Joel and Victoria Osteen. Heavens above, a packed stadium. And what a creep that Joel is, with his sleek black hair, his sharp suit, his purple tie and quick eyes. He preaches about miracles. 'Anyone who speaks words of faith can move mountains' is the subject he returns to time and again. He tells a story about a mother with terminal cancer. 'She went home, prayed and spoke to the cancer: "Go out from me."' I quickly note down all Joel's claims. 'Say: be gone, sickness. And the sickness will disappear. Be gone, earthly cares. And the cares will disappear. It may take time, it won't just happen. The moment that you speak in the name of Jesus or God, something happens in the unseen world of heaven. God sends his angels. God does for you, in a supernatural way, what you can't do for yourself.'

My parents were good Christian people, and part of that was their faith in the power of prayer. I sometimes think it got them through the war and the concentration camps. I'll never make fun of it. But something is happening here that I don't like at all. This stinks of marketing and magic, and countless Americans allow themselves to be stupefied by it, every Sunday.

I remember zapping between television channels years ago and happening upon a mass church service in California. The minister delivered a short but fiery sermon on Mark 10:30, which amounted to: 'Give and you shall receive back a hundredfold.' Songs were sung and then the preacher, surrounded by some forty swaying ladies, called on each of his viewers to write out a cheque for ten dollars twenty-nine cents, payable to his church. Within a month they would receive back, miraculously, a hundred times as much. The women confirmed this with a series of personal testimonies, followed by more singing, organ music and devotion. The church was located somewhere in Florida, but it was pure magic.

'Positive' mega-churches are the new trend. These days you won't often come upon the kind of fire-and-brimstone preacher Steinbeck listened to in Vermont. Even a cross is rare. The divine message has become purely materialistic: 'You *can* have a new car, because a God who loves children will give them everything they want.' The norm for a mega-church is a congregation of at least 2,000, but there are now around fifty 'churches' with a capacity of between 10,000 and 50,000. These positive mass churches no longer pray for forgiveness and mercy. Their prayer meetings are sometimes more reminiscent of whining children at a birthday party: 'I want my stuff – RIGHT NOW!' And then a choir: 'YEAH, I WANT MY STUFF RIGHT NOW, TOO!'

Between 2001 and 2006, churches of this kind doubled in number to more than 1,200, with a combined congregation of around 4.4 million. The reach of the new holy message is far greater still, however. Evangelists like Robert Schuller and Oral Roberts have been promoting the lavish lifestyle of the 'prosperity gospel' since the 1950s. Schuller became world famous with his *Hour of Power*, broadcast from his fabulous Crystal Cathedral in California. Roberts claimed he could conquer even death with his 'positive' powers, and in 1987 his son Richard told *Time* magazine that he had watched with his own eyes as his father brought a dead child back to life. They faced competition from Jimmy Swaggert (who fell prey to sex scandals), Pat Robertson and Jerry Falwell, but the faith flourished.

In 2006, according to a poll published in *Time*, seventeen per cent of all Americans saw themselves as adherents of this 'prosperity gospel'. At its heart are not faith, piety, heaven or hell, but your stance in life. 'It's especially important to maintain a positive attitude', says Joyce Meyer on her website, 'because God is positive.' She's doing well out of it herself. Her fortune amounts to hundreds of millions.

Joel Osteen, whose broadcast I happened upon immediately after hers, took over the religion business from his father. He has seven million viewers, 300 brothers and sisters working for him, and a turnover of a million a week. His books sell in print-runs of four million or more.

Oral Roberts said it over and over: God wanted him to be rich. One day, in 1947, when he'd just wrecked his car, his Bible fell open at a verse that promised him prosperity and well-being along with the good of his soul. He bought an expensive Buick and God continued to bless him. All his life he preached along those lines. He was the inventor of the phenomenon I saw on television: every dollar contributed to the Oral Roberts Evangelistic Association – 'Amex, Visa, whatever the Lord leads you to do' – would be returned to the giver a hundredfold. His mail-order business, which among other things sold 'healing' handkerchiefs he had prayed over, brought him a good income too. When in December 2009 Roberts left this earthly vale of tears at the age of ninety-one, his annual income stood at some 120 million dollars.

God as Father Christmas, or Father Christmas as God. It's the last resort of the eternal American – and Western – positive thinking: when you no longer know what to do, when everything is a vast chaos, then there's always the miracle that will enable you to bring order to your existence. However mechanically and rationally Americans often think, they are remarkably receptive to magical solutions. Whether it's the miraculous supplement Bactium that drives out all sickness, the magic box marked 'tax reductions' that will melt away all economic problems, President Reagan making the Berlin Wall collapse with his 'Mister Gorbachev, tear down this wall!' or the missionary work of 'success coaches' like Mike Hernacki with books like *The Ultimate Secret to Getting Absolutely Everything You Want* (New York, 1988), Americans continue stubbornly and enthusiastically to believe in their exceptional powers.

In 2008 *Time* suggested, rightly, that prosperity preachers like Joel Osteen were among those who laid the foundations for the mortgage crisis, which was after all caused by self-delusion and magical thinking on a massive scale. People with low incomes were encouraged Sunday after Sunday to accept a mortgage sent by God, even though they couldn't afford it: 'God blinded the bank so that it didn't see my low credit score and blessed me with my first house.'

The American desire for a world that can be shaped by human effort is as insatiable as ever, even though they know better. Magical thinking has gradually spread out from the religious world into business circles. An entire motivation industry has grown up with an annual turnover of at least ten billion dollars, offering books, readings, coaching, diets, DVDs and the like, all of which substitute 'affirmations' or 'declarations' for the ritual of prayer. Barbara Ehrenreich wrote a penetrating analysis of the phenomenon called *Smile or Die*, in which she picked out countless examples of the new magic. Take coach T. Harv Eker, who in *Secrets of the Millionaire Mind* advises his clients to put hand on heart and say:

'"I admire rich people!"

"I bless rich people!"

"I love rich people!"

"And I'm going to be one of those rich people too!"'

Eastern religions are hugely popular as well. Concerns such as AT&T, DuPont, TRW, Ford and Procter & Gamble buy 'spiritual experiences' for their senior personnel as if they're tickets to the circus, including shamanic healing sessions, Buddhist seminars and exercises in 'deep listening'. Problems among junior staff are drowned out in a similar way. Redundancies are defined as 'releases of resources' or 'career-changing opportunities'.

The downside of this magical positive thinking is cruel. If things don't turn out too well after a 'career-changing opportunity', or if you become ill or your business goes bankrupt, then ultimately you have only yourself to blame: you simply didn't try hard enough, you didn't have enough faith in your own success. Yet the popularity of such thinking is rising relentlessly, perhaps precisely because reality and dream are growing further and further apart and only a miracle can bridge the gap. In 1962, twenty-two per cent of Americans said in a survey by Gallup that at some point or other they'd had a 'religious or mystical experience'; by 2009 the percentage was almost fifty.

'Americans believe in evil, but we're uncomfortable with tragedy,' writes columnist Ross Douthat. 'We accept that there are wicked people in the world, with malice in their hearts and a devil whispering in their ears. But the idea that many debacles flow from choices made by decent, well-intentioned human beings is more difficult for us to wrap our minds around.'

Many Americans remain fiercely loyal to their vision of eternal abundance, of the Good Country that gives every possible blessing to those who live a virtuous life, working the land or making the most of their talents.

In the Badlands, rather than in Washington, lie the roots of modern American foreign policy, the basis for America's interference in the rest of the world. It was here that the model emerged for America's approach, in the twentieth century, to the Badlands of Europe, Asia, Arabia, Africa and Latin America.

In 1884 Theodore Roosevelt, Republican president from 1901 to 1909, withdrew to this region to recover after the loss of his first wife. He started a ranch, the Elkhorn. He was still young then, twenty-five years old, and that harsh episode placed its stamp on the rest of his life – and indeed on his image. The Badlands he discovered were a deathscape, scattered with the bones and skulls of bison, the valleys often concealing quicksand in which animals and people simply disappeared. Here and there, steam, sulphurous fumes and other traces of underground volcanic activity hung in the air.

He didn't care about any of that. He was living his own Western. 'I wear a sombrero, silk neckerchief, fringed buckskin shirt, seal skin chaparajos, alligator-hide boots,' he wrote in a letter home, 'and with my pearl-hilted revolver and beautifully finished Winchester rifle, I shall be able to face anything!' He ejected the local troublemaker from the saloon with his fists, went after a trio of villains and caught them at the end of a lengthy chase, massacred the local wildlife, and two years later returned invigorated to the political jungle of Washington.

Roosevelt made his way up to the position of governor of New York and then, in 1901, became vice-president under William McKinley. When the president was shot by an anarchist the following summer, Roosevelt abruptly found himself in the job. He was forty-two, the youngest president in American history.

The influence of his presidency would reach far further than the two terms that were granted him. With his flamboyant personal style, his theatrical manner towards the 'real' America, his close contacts with writers and journalists, the instinctive way he had of getting issues resolved and the obvious pleasure he took in it all, he set an example to the presidents who came after him. To his distant great-nephew Franklin D. Roosevelt, Democrat president from 1933 to 1945, 'Uncle Teddy' was an unmatched source of inspiration and the same went, directly and indirectly, for John F. Kennedy and Lyndon Johnson in the 1960s, for Ronald Reagan in the 1980s and even, in his own way, for George W. Bush at the start of the twenty-first century.

Now the Badlands have been tamed. We have two routes to choose between, both of them smoothly asphalted roads that weave across the landscape like pretzels. Prairie dogs scrabble about on the slopes, small marmot-like animals that have built entire cities, their heads peeping up out of holes in the sand all over the place. The hills make me think of enormous heaps of cinders, cathedrals from the beginning of time. It's a grey afternoon, but occasionally there are bursts of sunlight that make all sorts of colours suddenly glint off the rocks: fiery orange, amber, blue.

In the distance is a herd of bison, grazing peacefully. These days the total number of bison in America is estimated at no more than 15,000. In 1800, when hardly any white people lived here, some eighty million roamed the plains between Canada and Mexico, and in 1830 artist George Catlin noted that in places the bison gathered in such numbers they turned the prairie black for miles on end. One immense herd was 'in constant motion; and all bellowing . . . in deep and hollow sounds; which, mingled together, appear, at the distance of a mile or two, like the sound of distant thunder'.

It was around this time that the great slaughter of bison began. Professional hunters shot them by the thousands for their hides. Native Americans now had firearms, so they could hunt far more effectively than before. In around 1830 the Comanches and their allies alone shot some 280,000 bison a year. During a long train journey, a herd of bison was a pleasant diversion; passengers picked them off like clay pigeons, purely for fun. The railway companies and the farmers encouraged the bison hunt, since herds sometimes damaged the locomotives and the farmers wanted their cattle to have priority on the plains.

The federal government put not the slightest obstacle in the way of the hunters. The bison were the Native Americans' primary source of food, and without them they could not continue their old way of life. That was precisely the point. They would have to withdraw to the reservations.

The frontier, the boundless West, was for years the heart of the American story, but suddenly it was all over. From Dickinson 200,000 bison hides were sent to the east coast as late as 1882, and in 1883 another 40,000 followed. When Theodore Roosevelt moved to the Badlands, in 1884, one more wagonload of hides was dispatched. That was the last. The wilderness in the West, wrote Owen Wister in 1902, was 'a vanished world . . . The mountains are there, far and shining, and the sunlight, and the infinite earth, and the air that seems for ever the true fountain of youth – but where is the buffalo, and the wild antelope, and where the horseman with his pasturing thousands?'

Historian Frederick Jackson Turner described the end of the frontier as a turning point in American history. The frontier experience had brought individualism and democracy, and immigrants from all parts of Europe had shared its joys and sorrows. With that phase now over, he feared democracy would be replaced by privilege and hierarchy, individualism by conformism, ethnic harmony by a Tower of Babel. His theory struck a chord, as it does to this day.

Teddy Roosevelt, to whom Wister dedicated the novel that contains the above lines, was unconcerned about any of that. He dressed as if the traditional West was still the same as ever, and he behaved accordingly, the first president to make nostalgia his trademark. 'Theodore Roosevelt was a classic American sissy,' Gore Vidal wrote in one of his essays, a weakling 'who overcame – or appeared to overcome – his physical fragility through "manly" activities of which the most exciting and ennobling was war'.

Roosevelt thereby created a tradition that continues to this day. A perpetually recurring feature of American films and literature is the trip undertaken by father and son who spend a weekend together hunting and fishing. It's an indispensable element that even turns up in Travels, when Steinbeck spends the day fishing with the young estate keeper in Michigan.

In the spring of 2010, half of America swooned as it watched Sarah Palin's *Alaska*, in which the once-so-promising lady climbed rocks, paddled rivers and took on the breathtaking landscape of Alaska in all sorts of other ways. In previous years we had been able to enjoy, time and again, President George W. Bush's photo sessions at his 'ranch' in Crawford, a pale imitation of the festive cowboy shows Ronald Reagan served up from Santa Barbara. Every right-wing politician plays at being Theodore Roosevelt in his own way, and that includes supporting the cult of the gun and the constitutional right of every American to accumulate, should he or she wish to, a large arsenal of weapons.

Steinbeck drove hard with Charley all the way around America mainly to prove he was no sissy. 'Attached to his love of weapons was some measure of boylike play acting,' wrote Jackson Benson, 'of adolescent daydreaming, and of a tough façade'. In reality, the belligerent faces he learned to put on made him look 'twice as tough as he acted', as Budd Schulberg recalled. In *America and Americans* Steinbeck wrote that his fellow Americans always dream of being great hunters, trackers, trappers and marksmen. 'And this dream is deeply held by Americans who have never fired a gun or hunted anything larger or more dangerous than a cockroach.'

So what about Theodore Roosevelt himself? 'Teedie' or 'Teddy' had been an asthmatic, sickly boy, raised by home tutors in a wealthy and protected environment. But did he really deserve the label every macho American fears more than any other?

There is a small museum near Medora where Roosevelt's memory is cherished, with his original clothes in a couple of glass cases and a likeness of him mounted on a large wooden horse. At the door everyone is invited to celebrate his 152nd birthday, on Wednesday 27 October at a quarter past two.

They are grateful to him here, and with good reason. His love of this wilderness was not just for show. As soon as he became president, in 1901, he set up the US Forest Service, and under his administration five national parks were created and more than fifty nature reserves. He was one of the founders of American nature conservation. It represented a break with the American frontier philosophy of boundlessness and eternal abundance, of endless space and a freedom that entailed no responsibility.

Theodore Roosevelt's life, as his biographer Henry Pringle writes, was the dream of every American boy. He fought in a war, hunted bear and other big game, lived as a cowboy, became president and got on the wrong side of the pope. In countless respects he was also an innovator. He resisted the belief held by the great industrialists and railway magnates of his day that the laws of the market were all-important and that the government was there mainly to clear the way for them and remove all obstacles.

Roosevelt's father, a devout Christian, had always dedicated himself to the Social Gospel. An America that abandoned itself to consumption and materialism would be throwing its future away. The president believed in those same norms and codes of behaviour, and Steinbeck and his associates emphasised them afresh more than half a century later, except that Teddy Roosevelt sought a solution in the past. In the struggle of nations to secure their own future, America could survive only by continuing to cherish the fighting qualities it had developed on the western frontier.

Roosevelt hated socialists of all stripes. At the time of the Haymarket affair in 1886 he wrote from his ranch in the Badlands that it was a shame his cowboys hadn't been around to try out their guns on the crowd. 'My men shoot well and fear very little.'

At the same time he detested the excesses of the predatory capitalism of his day, fulminating against big business and refusing to accept the vast differences between, as he put it, 'the men who possess more than they have earned and the men who have earned more than they possess'. He welcomed the rise of trade unions – it was just that they must not be allowed to become too powerful.

Order – a balance between the various powers within America and those in the rest of the world – that was his goal. It need be no threat to the freedom of the American individual, in fact Roosevelt was eager to protect that very freedom. 'The sphere of the State's action,' he believed, 'may be vastly increased without in any way diminishing the happiness of either the many or the few.'

The decisions he made concerning this balance of power were remarkable. He quickly gained the honorary title of 'Teddy the Trustbuster' since he did everything he could to break the power of the big cartels, whether they were railroad companies, coalmining companies or banks. When the United Mine Workers of America brought the entire coal industry to a standstill in the summer of 1902, with the mine owners determined not to give an inch but to starve the strikers back to work, Roosevelt intervened, threatening to nationalise the mines and mobilise the army. The employers were furious, but they backed down.

His Republican Party was then still a broad party of the people. He was a fanatical moderate. He said so himself: 'I am a man who believes with all fervor and intensity in moderate progress.' In Roosevelt's worldview there was certainly room for industrialists, but also for trade unions, farmers and even black people – he invited Booker T. Washington, author of Up from Slavery, to lunch at the White House, for instance. When he campaigned for office again in 1912, he put forward ideas that were already very much like those of the New Deal: social security, equal rights for women and a National Health Service.

The Roosevelts belonged to the American patriciate. They were the descendants of a family from the Dutch province of Zeeland who had sailed across the Atlantic Ocean in the seventeenth century and made their fortune on the American east coast. In meetings with Dutch people, Teddy Roosevelt always took pride in being 'a Hollander'. In reality he had far more in common with his slightly younger British contemporary, Winston Churchill. Although they did not like each other, they were remarkably similar, cut from the same cloth. As historian Paul Johnson puts it, both were the 'romantic-intellectual-man-of-action-writer-professional-politician'.

Both were also a typical product of the closing decades of the nineteenth century, a period when everyone in the Western world had to learn to deal with large-scale industrialisation and modern city-living. It was a period of innovation, yet also one of nostalgia. Germany's Wilhelm II filled his capital city with statues and replica cathedrals, the British gloried in an empire on which the sun never set, the Dutch built brick museums and stations shaped like neo-Gothic castles, in Rome a pseudo-Roman wedding cake arose to the greater glory of Italy, and everywhere collective fantasies of national greatness flourished.

It was no different in America. Historian Jackson Lears speaks of 'a widespread yearning for regeneration and rebirth'. 'Conversion' and 'purification' had always been part of the Puritan tradition, and Americans expanded them into an eternal optimism, a sense that you could always make a fresh new beginning, start over and reinvent yourself.

The nostalgic dreams of Theodore Roosevelt and others played an important part in the search for authenticity. Central to the shared fantasy was the heroic and recurring battle between civilisation and the barbarians. Losers had no place in it. Native Americans, poor immigrants and the foreign victims of military adventures did not count. They were written off from the start.

Lears extrapolates this into the twenty-first century, into the regime of George W. Bush and Dick Cheney and the way in which their war on terrorism 'revived all the old, destructive fantasies – the belief in America's capacity to save the world; the faith in the revitalizing powers of combat; the cult of manly toughness in foreign policy'.

Teddy Roosevelt was a phenomenon. To the Europe of his day he was the personification of the dynamic, unexpected, great and at the same time earthly character of that strange country America that was preparing itself for a powerful role in the twentieth century. He dragged diplomats and politicians off with him on strenuous walks through the woods around Washington, took them swimming in the Potomac in winter, or raced them on horseback through outlying districts of the city. When the Dutch ambassador came to pay his respects, Roosevelt demonstrated a couple of jujitsu holds on him that he had learned shortly before.

He was squat in build. Whatever megalomaniac fantasies he may have had about himself and the American nation, he was certainly no sissy. During his 1912 campaign a mentally disturbed man in Milwaukee shot him in the chest. He calmly climbed the podium, bloodied as he was, pulled the fifty sheets of paper with his speech on them out of his pocket and began telling his story. Only when he looked more closely at the stack of papers and saw the bullet hole was he startled – more by that than by the blood running down his fingers. He spoke for an hour before allowing himself to be taken to hospital. The bullet, close to his heart, was lodged in a rib, having been slowed by his metal spectacles case and the interminably fat speech.

If anything Roosevelt actually had excessive machismo, and an accompanying disdain for anyone lacking such theatrical masculinity, which he mistook for courage. 'Aunties', he called opponents with more nuanced views, 'sublimated sweetbreads' or 'circumcised skunks'. He was one of the first politicians to smear those who opposed him by using the term 'un-American'.

Roosevelt's machismo came to the fore in his foreign policy in particular. He arranged for the digging of the Panama Canal, which necessitated – after a failed attempt to buy the zone from the corrupt Colombian government – staging a coup and setting up a puppet regime. The troops of the Colombian garrison at Panama were bought off for fifty dollars a man. The officers received 10,000 dollars, the general 30,000.

It was a formula the Americans would use on subsequent occasions. Roosevelt realised that in the nineteenth century the United States had become a world power without most Europeans noticing, and it now had international responsibilities. At first America used the Monroe Doctrine of 1823 as a guide to foreign policy. The interests of democratic America and feudal Europe were fundamentally incompatible, it was generally believed, and every new colonial adventure by a European state in North or South America was to be regarded as an act of aggression. America, for its part, would not intervene on the European continent.

Even in the nineteenth century, America did not keep itself to itself. An overview published in 1962 by the State Department shows that the United States intervened in the affairs of other countries no fewer than 103 times between 1798 and 1895, with initiatives ranging from military action in Argentina in 1852, aimed at protecting American interests during a revolution, to the installing of a satellite regime in Hawaii in 1893.

From 1880 onwards, American farmers and exporters increasingly pressed for a foreign policy that went further. Overseas markets were essential. 'We must have a place to dump our surplus,' wrote the United States Export Association. No one wanted to establish new colonies like the Europeans did – that would be against all America's ideals – but both businessmen and politicians were keen to end American isolation and believed the American fist should be felt rather more often.

There were attempts to make headway in China, partly by setting up mission posts. In 1887 Hawaii gave the United States the right to build a naval base in Pearl Harbor, and in 1893 the archipelago was annexed. In 1887 a fierce dispute arose with Britain over Venezuela, and Irish-American veterans soon started to organise their own regiment for a renewed attack on 'perfidious Albion'. That crisis was resolved at the last moment. In 1898 a war with Spain broke out over self-determination for Cuba, during which the American navy destroyed the Spanish fleet at Manila and brought the Philippines into the American sphere of influence.

Roosevelt fought bravely in Cuba, where he led the legendary attack on San Juan Hill with a bunch of cowboys and intellectuals known as the 'Rough Riders'. He later claimed to have killed a Spaniard with his bare hands, 'like a Jack-rabbit'. Within three years he was president of the United States.

Never would the Americans, product of a grim struggle against colonialism, use the word 'empire' themselves. They find that difficult to this day. Yet from the classical edifices they built among meadows in the young Washington – an immense Capitol, a second Roman Forum – it is clear that some Americans were dreaming even then of the imperial greatness of a new Rome.

At the start of the twentieth century those dreams became more concrete. Now that democratic thinking was more firmly established in Europe as well, it would be the mark of a wise government, Roosevelt believed, to act based not on interests that conflicted, as in the Monroe Doctrine, but instead on a shared democratic ideal. In that battle America would need to seek allies, in Europe and elsewhere. Like any other civilised nation, America had the right to intervene in foreign countries in support of that cause, just as it had the right to intervene to tackle wrongs at home. In a ferocious conflict in 1902–3 over Venezuela's debts, for instance, when France, Britain and Germany blockaded that country, Roosevelt mediated successfully. The American navy, already the third largest in the world, would be inimitable in the role of international policeman, he believed. This was to become the fundamental philosophy behind countless American interventions all over the world, from the European wars fought in the years between 1914 and 1945 to Vietnam and, in the 1990s, the conflicts in the Balkans.

Despite all the talk about 'exceptional' and 'exemplary' America, the foundations Roosevelt laid for the new American empire were hardly a revelation. All too often the Americans presented things that were in their own interests – such as control over Cuba – as being in the interests of the whole world. This was true above all of their superior civilisation and attitude to life. In that sense they were no different from the European colonisers, except in the force of the almost religious conviction they had, and in many cases still have, of their superiority.

The popularity of Ronald Reagan and especially George W. Bush was partly a result of the messianic power of their central message: America is the most sublime example in this world of democracy and human rights, and the country therefore has a duty to disseminate its values all over the world. It is fortunately in a position to do so, with God's help. As George W. Bush put it in 2005, in his second inaugural address: 'History has an ebb and flow of justice, but history also has a visible direction, set by liberty and the Author of Liberty.'

At the same time those grand pretentions stood in the way of America from the very start. It's not easy to export a message of freedom, democracy and human rights if your hands are dirty, if you have supported and continue to support dozens of corrupt dictatorships and if, as now, there is still a Guantánamo Bay. The mess left in Iraq by that 'Author of Liberty' will not be forgotten in a hurry.

As early as 1900, Mark Twain castigated America's messianic attitude in a furious polemic aimed at Roosevelt. 'Shall we go on conferring our Civilization upon the peoples that sit in darkness, or shall we give those poor things a rest? Shall we bang right ahead in our old-time, loud, pious way, and commit the new century to the game; or shall we sober up and sit down and think it over first?'

In a sense the American empire is second-hand. It was created in the latter years of all the other empires, so it had to pay the price not only for its own faults but for those of its predecessors. Before the Americans became involved, the French had already made a complete mess of Vietnam, the Russians of Afghanistan, the British of Iraq, and everyone had already worn themselves out in the Middle East.

A further handicap is the orientation of American democracy. A quick way for a politician to make himself vulnerable is to point out that in some respects things are going better elsewhere than in the United States, or that America might be able to learn from other countries. He or she will immediately be accused of lacking 'national pride' and of 'apologising for America'. Only a 'sissy' would do such a thing.

They are doing it all for a Higher Ideal, a National Religion, nothing less, but also nothing more. Most Americans still deny that their country is imperialist, because that reality directly contradicts the ideal of an exceptional nation striding on ahead of the rest of the world on the road to Freedom. In any case, American voters do not want to be lumbered with the huge costs of these messianic expeditions, let alone all the investment needed after a war ends, in Afghanistan and Iraq for instance. Which explains why American governments now do all they can to gloss over the costs of reconstruction, by contracting out much of the dirty work to private companies. 'Aunties!' Roosevelt would cry, with that catch in his high-pitched voice.

The United States was successful for decades at organising alliances. NATO is a good example. But in settling conflicts it made one mistake after another. As a result America is unstable in certain respects as a world power. It can easily be provoked to irresponsible acts and then has a tendency to withdraw into splendid isolation once again. It takes the initiative in setting up international bodies such as the League of Nations and the United Nations, but it cannot mobilise sufficient political support to enable such institutions to grow to full stature in the longer term.

Comparisons with, for example, the Roman Empire or the British Empire are misleading for that reason alone. The American empire still has neither colonies nor, as the Romans did, provinces. The Americans station their troops everywhere – unconfirmed figures suggest there are more than half a million men in some 120 countries – but it is not their intention to create relationships that could last forever, unlike the British and the Romans.

Illustrative of this is the way in which almost all American troops are quartered, even in Europe, in completely segregated worlds where everything is flown in from the United States, right down to the cutlery in the canteen and the brownies next to the checkout. Their stay depends entirely on the prevailing wind in Washington; if a military presence becomes too costly, or loses popularity, then it stands a good chance of being abruptly terminated. So for America, in the words of political essayist John Gray, 'long-term alliances with local ruling classes of the kind that enabled empires to endure for centuries in the past are seldom possible'.

American politics has, in short, a tendency to resist the notion that all parts of an empire need continual care and attention. Many politicians are blind to the fact that their empire has to function in the twenty-first century, a new era with problems – climate change, money flows, arms races – that can be resolved only with the help of international rules and cooperation. In essence they still have a nineteenth-century worldview. Their hero, if in a version both embroidered and distorted, remains Teddy Roosevelt.

Theodore Roosevelt was a tempestuous tyrant who insisted on being at the centre of attention. His daughter Alice once said: 'He wants to be the bride at every wedding, the corpse at every funeral and the baby at every christening.' That was the power of his presidency, but it was also his downfall. In 1912, angry that the Republican nomination for a third term had passed him by as a result of all kinds of manoeuvring behind the scenes, he stood for election as an independent. He easily beat the official Republican candidate, William Taft, but he was no match for the united front of the Democrats. Woodrow Wilson became president. The split lost the Republican Party much of its progressive wing. So began the conservative Republican Party as we know it today.

Even then his recklessness knew no bounds. When America finally intervened in Europe to part the two sides in the First World War – at least, that was how many Americans saw it – Roosevelt begged President Wilson for a regiment of his own, like the one he had led in the Cuban War. He was almost sixty. His request was denied. He sent his two sons to France, where the younger of them died in an air battle.

The death of his favourite son was a huge blow. The Rough Rider, who had so often glorified and romanticised war, was hardly able to bear it. 'What made this loss so devastating to him,' writes his biographer Edmund Morris, 'was the truth it conveyed: that death in battle was no more glamorous than death in an abattoir.'

Three

BEACH, THE PLACE WHERE STEINBECK FINALLY SPENT the night, consists of a crossroads and a handful of houses. The Westgate Motel is still there, with its beautiful wooden verandas and 'clean rooms, low prices'. They could put up a sign: 'John Steinbeck slept here on 12 October 1960.' He had a long telephone conversation with Elaine, and it was probably then that he decided on the title for *Travels*.

Elaine would say later in an interview that Steinbeck called her, that they talked about his letters to her, which he wanted to use as the basis for his book, and that she said it reminded her of Robert Louis Stevenson's *Travels with a Donkey in the Cévennes*. She had the nineteenth-century travel story about south-central France in her bookcase. 'That's it!' Steinbeck exclaimed. 'What?' she asked. 'My title! You've just given me my title: *Travels with Charley*.'

We drive on along the Interstate 94. The old road that Steinbeck took has been absorbed in places into the new highway, but often it runs parallel to ours: two numbing lines stretching away to the horizon. There is practically no traffic. The land is slightly hilly, the grass scorched brown with some grey tussocks, and so it goes on, mile after mile. The radio crackles out country music; we hear the market prices of wheat, maize and cattle, and then comes a Christian Scientist to tell us that Nietzsche was a sinner and that the Western world is nearing its end.

In the late morning the Badlands are suddenly behind us. Montana unfurls in all its loveliness. A river meanders slowly across the landscape, a railway line winding alongside it. Somehow or other the endless, sluggishly labouring freight trains fit the rhythm of the country. Steinbeck called this part of his journey a 'love affair', and I understand what he meant. 'It seems to me that Montana is a great splash of grandeur. The scale is huge but not overpowering. The land is full of grass and color, and the mountains are the kind I would create if mountains were ever put on my agenda.' If Montana was on the coast he would move there immediately, 'and petition for admission'.

Like Steinbeck, we take a detour south. On Highway 38 a couple of factories suddenly rise out of the plains in the distance. Colstrip, the place is called, a jumble of giant installations, pipelines and conveyor belts, and next to them a settlement of synthetic houses and caravans for the workers, a couple of warehouses, then solitude again. Further on across the plains is the occasional house, often little more than a collection of huts surrounded by four, six, ten cars and car wrecks. These are the original inhabitants of this country, the 'Indians' of 2010.

Steinbeck took a short detour to visit the battlefield at the Little Bighorn, the place where on 25 June 1876 the last major battle took place between the original America and everything that came after it. Thousands of Native Americans, led by their legendary chief Sitting Bull, made short work of a small army unit that had set out on a punitive expedition. Of the central column of the 7th Cavalry Regiment, led by the popular general George Armstrong Custer, not one man returned alive.

The news reached the rest of America on 7 July 1876, when festivities to mark the first centenary of the glorious republic were at their height. At first no one could believe that 'their' Custer, 'their' soldiers and 'their' nation, blessed by God, could have suffered such a devastating defeat at the hands of 'savages'. America, even America, really was vulnerable. The Battle of the Little Bighorn was almost as traumatic for American society as Pearl Harbor in 1941 or 9/11 in 2001 – a tragedy but also an event with a message, a story full of hidden symbolism.

Characteristic of America, and of being American, is choice, free will. Being Dutch, Spanish or Polish in Europe is in most cases a matter of fate, something that happens to you. Having American nationality denotes an act of will, a conscious choice in favour of immigration and integration that may have been made in the distant past but which is made afresh over and over again and which still works through into current generations. There are two population groups to whom this does not apply: black people, whose ancestors were dragged here against their will and who, if for that reason alone, regard the American story of triumph with a degree of irony and ambivalence; and Native Americans, who always lived here and likewise had no choice in the matter.

It is striking how little Americans copied from the original inhabitants of this continent. Spanish, British and Dutch colonials, despite their own sense of superiority, almost always adopted certain elements of the native cuisine, adjusted native inventions for use in the construction of their houses and took note of local techniques of cultivation. In present-day America, aside from certain maize dishes and a few place names, the native influences are barely discernible. That says a great deal. Native Americans, after all, did not fit the image of the New World that was created here. They did not have the will; things simply happened to them; they were not real Americans. They did not belong in this great historical experiment. They weren't really supposed to exist at all.

At the start, when a majority of the colonists still lived on the coast, white people had every reason to want a cooperative relationship. Beaver pelts and other trade goods had to be brought from further inland, and to secure those trade routes they were dependent on Natives. Almost two centuries after the arrival of the first colonists, the Americans still did not know exactly what their continent looked like, which ways the rivers ran, where the mountains were. Their maps still had many blank patches, especially in the far West. Only Native Americans, using their own networks, could find their way.

In 1803 President Thomas Jefferson set up a Corps of Discovery, and in 1804 thirty soldiers and Native scouts set off from St Louis, led by Meriwether Lewis and William Clark. Their task was to seek a trade route from the eastern seaboard to the west coast and, if possible, a northern passage for shipping to Asia. They were also ordered to investigate opportunities for economic exploitation of the west of the continent.

In total they covered 8,000 miles, straight across a barely inhabited desert of man-high prairie grass, thick forests, icy wastes and untrodden mountain passes. In *Travels* Steinbeck takes his hat off to them. He writes that it took them two and a half years to make their way across that wilderness – 'only' one man died, one deserted – and we 'fly it in five hours, drive it in a week, dawdle it as I was doing in a month or six weeks'.

The expedition was a great success. On 7 November 1805 Lewis and Clark reached the Pacific Ocean at what is now Oregon. 'We had not gone far . . . when the fog cleared off, and we enjoyed the delightful prospect of the ocean; that ocean, the object of all our labours, the reward of all our anxieties.' On their return in 1806, the explorers reported that the land beyond the Mississippi should be regarded as 'mostly desert, incapable of cultivation, unfit for white people'. They had, however, made contact with dozens of previously unknown Native tribes that turned out to have trading links with the 'civilised' east coast through roving white fur trappers.

Their discoveries gave the politicians an idea. The indigenous peoples, an increasing source of annoyance to the trappers and pioneers in the West, could be pushed back into this western desert, into a Permanent Indian Country, where no one would have any more trouble from them. In 1825 President James Monroe began the deportations, a form of ethnic cleansing that took off on a large scale under President Andrew Jackson, after the passing of the Indian Removal Act in 1830.

As late as the summer of 1831, Tocqueville and Beaumont crossed the forests of Michigan with the help of a couple of Native guides, who jumped effortlessly over every obstacle and found their way without faltering in woodland where no routes were marked. The two Europeans felt blind in this environment. 'It was a singular spectacle to see the scornful smile with which they led us by the hand like children until they brought us close to the object they themselves had seen for a long time.' They also came upon a group of painted Natives who performed a dance for them, 'jumping like devils', for a little money. 'We give them a shilling. It is the War-dance. Horrible to see. What a degradation.' Elsewhere Tocqueville wrote: 'The nations I have mentioned formerly covered the country to the sea-coast; but a traveller at the present day must penetrate more than a hundred leagues into the interior of the continent to find an Indian. Not only have these wild tribes receded, but they are destroyed.'

In 1834, under the Indian Intercourse Act, a boundary was devised to the west of the Mississippi, behind which the Native peoples could live in safety. This was not yet a reservation; it was simply a line on the map. Whether or not an individual was an 'Indian' was determined by the blood quantum laws, a system in use since the eighteenth century that looked at parents and grandparents in order to determine how much 'Indian blood' someone had in his or her veins. White people were forbidden to travel beyond the line without a special permit. President Jackson promised the 'Indians' in 1835 that the new territories would always remain theirs, 'secured and guaranteed'. By 1840 the operation was complete.

That is the history as it appears on paper. Tocqueville and Beaumont caught a glimpse of it in practice, from their riverboat on the Mississippi at Memphis in late December 1831. Casting off from the bank, sixty Choctaw came towards them. They were being taken across the river into Arkansas by a federal official, under the Indian Removal Act. There they would begin their long journey to Indian Territory, in present-day Oklahoma. It was one of the coldest winters for years. The snow lay frozen hard on the ground and ice flows moved with the current. The people had neither tents nor wagons, and their entire families were with them, including newborn babies, the sick and the elderly. 'Their property consists of very little: a horse, a hunting dog, a gun, a blanket – and that's the fortune of the wealthiest,' Beaumont wrote. It was a definitive departure from their ancestral lands. In *Democracy in America* Tocqueville describes what he saw. 'No cry, no sob was heard amongst the assembled crowd; all were silent. Their calamities were of ancient date, and they knew them to be irremediable. The Indians had all stepped into the bark which was to carry them across, but their dogs remained upon the bank. As soon as these animals perceived that their masters were finally leaving the shore, they set up a dismal howl, and, plunging all together into the icy waters of the Mississippi, they swam after the boat.'

In the decades that followed, the line was moved further and further west. In 1838 15,000 Cherokee were deported from Georgia to Indian Territory in the same way. More than 4,000 died on that 'Trail of Tears'.

The line remained a thoroughly porous boundary. White settlers, gold seekers, trappers and wandering army veterans paid no attention to it, and the same went for Natives who, often out of pure necessity, moved with the herds of bison and other animals they hunted. So around 1850 another new policy was introduced. For the different indigenous peoples and tribes, pieces of ground were marked off as 'reservations' or 'colonies'. There they could learn farming and other accomplishments of the white man, and they would not be in the way of the settlers or the railroad companies. Partly by violence and partly by means of so-called treaties, many tribes were removed to these territories.

Some refused. The Lakota Sioux had done well for themselves back in the eighteenth century. By trading with the whites they had secured horses and firearms, which increased their range as bison hunters considerably. They conquered large stretches of territory from other indigenous peoples. As time went on, their society concentrated increasingly on hunting and war. Warriors were highly respected, and by about 1825 they commanded a large part of the Great Plains. They formed an alliance with the equally powerful Cheyenne.

Other tribes kept escaping from the reservations, partly by force of habit, partly from dire need: bison were becoming scarce and there was often little else to eat. In August 1862 a group of starving Dakota Sioux raided a food depot in Minnesota, an incident that ended in a horrific slaughter of settlers. Almost 500 men, women and children lost their lives. It was the first large-scale retaliation against the politics of deportation and persecution.

A month later the Native warriors were defeated by a military force of 1,500 men. The day after Christmas, thirty-eight Dakota Sioux who had been sentenced to death were led to the gallows. It was the biggest mass execution in American history. The condemned Natives sang and danced atop the square scaffold, which swayed under their weight. 'It seemed that the purpose of the singing and dancing was only to sustain each other in their last ordeal,' an eyewitness wrote. 'As the last moment rapidly approached, they each called out their name and shouted in their native language: "I'm here! I'm here!"'

After that, hostilities became frequent. The soldiers built fortifications, the Native peoples developed all kinds of guerrilla tactics, and the fighting escalated. In 1866 a young army captain, William Fetterman, who shortly before had boasted that he could ride through Sioux country with no trouble at all, was ambushed and killed along with eighty inexperienced recruits.

In 1874 a conflict arose with the Lakota Sioux over part of their territory: the Black Hills, in what is now South Dakota. It was holy ground to the Native Americans and a potential goldmine for the whites. Moreover, the Northern Pacific Railway wanted to extend the track from Bismarck westwards into the Montana Territory. Negotiations proved fruitless, gold seekers arrived in the Black Hills in increasing numbers, and eventually the American government decided to force the troublesome Cheyenne and Lakota Sioux into submission. That marked the start of the Great Sioux War of 1876. The punitive expedition by Custer's 7th Cavalry Regiment took place during that campaign, in June 1876. It was, in retrospect, a textbook example of the arrogance and blindness for which the gods punish powerful nations.

There is much that repeats itself in history, the Battle of the Little Bighorn included.

'We expect to go after Sitting Bull and his cutthroats,' one of the soldiers wrote to his sister, 'and if old Custer gets after him he will give him the fits for all the boys are spoiling for a fight.' Custer and his fellow commanding officers set out with far too few troops. Custer's regiment consisted of no more than 750 men, and they were up against at least 3,000 superbly trained Sioux and Cheyenne. More than a century later, just to take one example, precisely the same error was made in 1993's disastrous Operation United Shield in Somalia: far too few troops in a big, complex and dangerous country. The same goes for the Iraq War in 2003, when hostilities were started on the basis of incorrect information, the CIA had hardly any agents in the country and detailed knowledge was almost entirely lacking.

George Custer went into battle with that same overconfidence of the ignorant. A few months before the fatal encounter, in the spring of 1876, he had declared during a talk to New York businessmen – he was a popular public speaker – that his 7th Cavalry Regiment 'could whip and defeat all the Indians on the plains'. When he first caught sight, from a hill, of the enemy camp, he realised there were more of them than he had ever seen together before, and a great deal of activity was going on among women, children and hundreds of warriors. His troops were in mortal fear and his most important scout and interpreter, Mitch Boyer, half-French, half-Lakota, warned him not to proceed any further: 'If you go down that hill you'll never come back.' But Custer refused to be deterred. He cheerfully called out to his men: 'Boys, hold your horses! There are plenty down there for all of us!'

He didn't know the terrain; too late he realised that his men would have to clamber across all kinds of ravines and rock formations before they could join battle. Nor did he have any idea of the actual number of Sioux and Cheyenne who had gathered at the bottom of that hill: over three times as many as the troops at his command. So he was utterly surprised when, as if out of the ground, hundreds upon hundreds of warriors suddenly appeared.

Custer was known as an excellent officer and a great 'Indian hunter', but his troops were trained to fight orderly battles and had no tactics for countering the Natives' guerrilla warfare. Nor were his soldiers seasoned heroes out of a Western, in fact forty per cent were not even born in the United States – twelve per cent were from Germany, seventeen per cent from Ireland and the rest represented the American melting pot of their day: Brits, Poles, Swiss, Spaniards, Italians, Norwegians, Swedes, Danes, Canadians and Russians.

The sheer determination of the Native population and the quality of their weapons were seriously underestimated, again as happened in later wars. Both the Sioux and the Cheyenne were excellent archers, and their warriors had concealed themselves so well that no one could see where the arrows were coming from. No gun smoke gave them away. If a thousand men each shot ten arrows during the battle, then it amounted to 10,000 arrows, some forty per soldier. As for firearms, they were barely any less well equipped than the regular army.

Yet it was not the Native peoples who opened the engagement but the daredevil Custer, without authorisation from his superiors. The consequences were inevitable.

In *Travels* Steinbeck leaves Custer's heroism intact, but in a letter to Elaine he was more honest: 'I shed a tear for Custer (the dumb bastard).' He was right. Custer had actually split his troops into three units. The military engagement at the Little Bighorn was therefore made up of three battles around Sitting Bull's camp. All three ended in defeat, but it was Custer's own troops who were slaughtered to the last man, even including the embedded reporter for the *Bismarck Tribune*, Mark Kellogg – and of course Custer himself. Most of the men in the other two units managed to get away.

As tends to happen, Custer's defeat was soon transformed into a myth. In his account of his trip, Steinbeck refers to the famous painting *The Last Stand* by Frederic Remington, which shows Custer standing proudly on a hill surrounded by his fighting and dying troops: 'I removed my hat in memory of brave men, and Charley saluted in his own manner but I thought with great respect.' It is the ultimate story of martial courage: the last men alive, who, despite knowing it to be futile, make a final stand against an overwhelming enemy. Anyone facing defeat in such a manner wins immortal fame. George Custer, fearless, eternally young, became the James Dean of the nineteenth century.

How the battle actually went, no white man lived to tell. There is one bit of testimony from a soldier, Peter Thompson, twenty-two years old, who escaped because his horse was lame. He dismounted when his spurs came loose, but his fingers were trembling so much with fear that he was unable to tie a knot. It suggests a great deal about the mood of the average soldier under Custer's command.

Captain Frederick Benteen, who sought out and inspected the battlefield two days later, could see no pattern at all to the positions in which the more than 200 dead were lying. 'It was a rout, a panic, till the last man was killed. There was no line on the battlefield, you can take a handful of corn and scatter it over the floor and make just such lines.'

Archaeological research confirms this impression. By using metal detectors to hunt out bullets and cartridge cases, then linking them to the weapons used by the troops, it is now possible to reconstruct fairly accurately the movements of many of the men on the battlefield. In a few places there are signs of organised resistance, but in general everyone ran for his life. It was all over far more quickly than the Custer legend would have us believe. The entire battle may have lasted no more than twenty minutes.

These findings correspond with the stories told by Native Americans who fought on the other side. In the 1920s, Thomas Marquis, a doctor who worked among the Cheyenne and had learned their language, interviewed dozens of elderly veterans. His conclusions also contradict the epic tale. Most of Custer's soldiers were in a blind panic; some committed suicide to avoid falling into enemy hands. 'These soldiers became foolish, many throwing away their guns and raising their hands, saying "Sioux, pity us; take us prisoners" . . . None were left alive for even a few minutes.' Others fired into the ground, into the air, maddened by fear. Some seemed paralysed and could barely operate their weapons.

For the Native warriors the legendary Battle of the Little Bighorn was more like a bison hunt than anything else, an image so shocking to the rest of America that in 1934 Marquis failed to find a publisher for his manuscript. More than forty years passed before it was finally published in 1976.

These days Americans drive to the old battlefield in huge camper vans and buses. In the distance the Interstate 90 drones on. The places where dead soldiers were found are marked with white stones, as if in a war cemetery – the bodies were laid to rest elsewhere. There is a small museum, with rusty rifles and pistols found buried in the earth, as well as several of the hundreds of horse skulls.

Some of the human skulls have been studied, and attempts have even been made to reconstruct a few of the soldiers' faces. One of those reconstructions precisely matches a photograph of the explorer and interpreter Mitch Boyer, who warned Custer not to advance. The teeth show signs of intensive pipe smoking, and Boyer was a fanatical smoker. Unlike his commander, he never felt he stood much chance of surviving the expedition. If he had to die, he said, then he was comforted by the fact that he'd sent so many of his Lakota opponents to the other world that his enemies would never be able to replenish their numbers. His skull was found as recently as 1983, in the gulley where the last of Custer's soldiers were slaughtered.

The drama can be read clearly from the white stones on the hills. Some are close together; further along the brown valley is a thinner trail of stones, and up on the ridge are two more. You can see roughly what happened, how more and more men ran frantically over the low hill and through the little valley behind it, falling one after another, most of them butchered at its deepest point. A few slipped away, only to be killed higher up on the slope.

At the edge of the road is one small, red marble stone commemorating the dead Lakota warriors: 'They fell here while defending the Lakota way of life.'

Sitting Bull, the Lakota warlord, became a hero of sorts. The Great Sioux War petered out after a year with negotiations and a few minor skirmishes. After that he settled down in the south-west corner of his reservation, on the Grand River, travelled a few times to the cities on the east coast and in 1885 even took part in Buffalo Bill Cody's Wild West show, the climax of which was a re-enactment of Custer's Last Stand. The bison, meanwhile, had almost become extinct. The people on the reservation tried to feed themselves by growing crops, but in December 1890, after years of drought, their supplies ran out. One after another they started to succumb to starvation or sickness, including one of Sitting Bull's children.

A medicine man appeared, called Wovoka. He predicted that a great wave of earth would roll across the world, burying the white man forever. Then the bison would return, along with some of the most beloved of the ancestors. His followers believed they needed to speak to the dead, by means of the Ghost Dance. Wovoka preached non-violence, but the authorities feared the worst.

Rumours suggested Sitting Bull was on the point of joining the movement. An arrest warrant was issued for him, and a group of Lakota policemen – the nation had its collaborators – forced their way into his hut one evening. Fighting broke out in the dark between them and his supporters. Sitting Bull was killed by a bullet to the chest and then his face was beaten to a pulp by a vengeful Lakota police officer.

On 28 December 1890, two weeks after the murder of Sitting Bull, a group of Ghost Dancers of the Miniconjou tribe, part of the Lakota Sioux people, surrendered at the camp at Wounded Knee to a US Army detachment, part of the same 7th Cavalry Regiment to which Custer and his men had belonged. The following night a number of officers and men from the regiment, blind drunk, started interrogating and torturing their prisoners. They asked just one question: Which of them had been present at the Battle of the Little Bighorn? The Natives said they knew nothing about it.

The next morning the troops surrounded the captives, many of whom were women and children. The men were ordered to hand in their weapons before being led away. A rifle went off by accident and the soldiers immediately started shooting. Within a few minutes, more than eighty Miniconjou warriors were lying dead on the ground. The women and children fled, but the soldiers caught up with some of them. A certain Captain Edward Godfrey, a veteran of the Little Bighorn, came upon a small group that had hidden in the woods. He suspected they were women and children, but when he called out and received no response he ordered his men to open fire. They heard screams, and when they went to look they found a woman and two girls in their death throes. A boy was still alive, so they shot him in the head. In total more than 150 Sioux were killed. It was the white man's revenge for the heroes of the Little Bighorn. For his courageous deeds, Godfrey was promoted to the rank of major.

Of all those who once spoke the language of the Sioux, barely 6,000 are left. Their average age is around sixty-five. The blood quantum laws are still applied, but by the Native Americans themselves, to determine who can or cannot share in the vast profits of the casinos that have sprung up everywhere on the reservations.

The battlefield where Custer and Sitting Bull fought is a tourist attraction by day and a haunted place by night, with frequent reports of supernatural phenomena: the ghosts of warriors and soldiers, cold spots and unexplained voices. It was a battle that, it seems, needs to be fought time and again.

Four

AT THE LARIAT COUNTRY KITCHEN IN HARDIN THEY'LL do you
French toast, mashed potatoes, fried chicken, pancakes, spare ribs, scrambled eggs or potato soup from early morning to late in the evening, and
all in unimaginable quantities. This is the town's living room. All the
customers are white. At breakfast the workers sit spread about the place
as they do everywhere; the farmers, some six of them, at one table. They
keep their Stetsons on while they sit heavily in front of their eggs and
potatoes. Not a great deal is said.

'How are you doing today?'

'Good.' Sombre expression, silence.

'Going away then, this winter?'

'Israel.'

One of the farmers walks over to a bunch of young men. They drive
too rough. Everyone complains about it. It was even in the paper. It can't
go on. The boys say nothing and stare outside.

A Native American girl serves us, big and clumsy. The farmers leave,
one of them staggering under his own weight as he crosses the diner,
only just making it to his car. The girth of many Americans is a sore
point; British historian Niall Ferguson was once castigated for daring to
make a few comments about it, but it remains a phenomenon that strikes
any non-American immediately.

It's an old problem. In one of his first letters to his mother, Tocqueville
expressed his amazement at the enormous quantities of food that
Americans 'somehow stuff down their gullets'. Several times a day you
come upon people who are so fat they need two chairs, a degree of
obesity rarely seen in the rest of the world. In Europe, fifteen per cent

of people are overweight; in America the proportion is almost double that.

It has to do with too much sugar in the bread, too much fat in the meat, too many mouth-watering adverts by the side of the road, too much encouragement to keep stuffing away all day long, but it's also a result of the unbounded eagerness with which Americans set their teeth into everything that comes in sight. The further west we drive, the larger the portions our fellow diners shovel into themselves for breakfast. It's astonishing what the human body can take.

Outside, in the dazzling sunlight, it's freezing. Not far away begins the reservation of the Crow, eternal enemies of the Lakota Sioux. There are still some 11,000 Crow, 8,000 of them in this area. Many people have romantic ideas about Native American life, but the everyday reality is equally sad every time you see it: poverty, rust, beaten-up caravans, tax-free casinos, alcoholism, heaps of rotting cars.

We take a road straight across an endlessly rolling grassy plain, dusty and bare. There is no one to be seen. In the settlement of St Xavier the doors to the abandoned houses rattle in the cold wind. Officially, sixty-seven people still live here. The proud building of the St Xavier public school, erected in the 1950s to propagate the American Dream even in this place, stands empty. The schoolyard is overgrown with weeds, the windows smashed. In its large gym, once the scene of so many festivities and ceremonies, the ceiling is hanging down, the lockers are half-open and birds flap off in panic.

We cover more long lonely miles. After half an hour, three horse riders pop up, travelling along with us at a distance. They turn off when we drive into a kind of Badlands again, a moonscape of cinder chunks where not even a goat can live. Our electronic guide Sandy seems bewitched. She pilots us along one impossible unsealed road after another, suggests routes that don't exist and ignores the presence of roads that are right in front of our noses. Halfway across a couple of stubbly fields a row of simple dwellings appears, washing on the line, a small health centre, a Catholic mission school, a gathering of wild dogs, and at the end of the village a wrecked caravan with at least twenty loose horses around it, some of which race along beside us for a while. This must be Pryor.

At last we find ourselves in Edgar, in a warm, white room at the far side of the reservation called the Edgar Bar. No film stars or old village faces on the wall here but photographs of combines, bulldozers, mowing machines, each more imposing than the last. In the corner are a few fruit machines and by the door a sign saying 'Danger. Many illegal activities in progress. Enter at your own risk.' At the central table are twelve farmers and two women. Not a man without a Stetson here, but other than that the conversation is no different from the buzz at the central table in a café in the Dutch province of Friesland on the other side of the world: bullshitting, laughter, and the finalising of plans for the weekend, when the village band will be playing again.

Like Steinbeck we make for Yellowstone Park. The pass is closed, snow threatens, and at this time of year only a small area of the park is accessible anyhow. Steinbeck was lucky; he took the right entrance. In Yellowstone he discovered that Charley was a great bear hunter, who growled and barked and flung so many insults at a passing bear that it would have attacked Rocinante if Steinbeck hadn't intervened. We get the picture and turn back.

Then a scene opens up that is burned into the souls of countless Americans. A blue sky with white clouds. An endless plain. And beyond it, in the distance, a great wall suddenly appears that cuts right across the country: the Rocky Mountains, with snow-covered peaks full of challenge and promise and beyond them everything the Far West could offer a group of tired settlers in their worn-out covered wagons. It was this scene that in 1893 inspired teacher Katharine Lee Bates to write the hymn 'America the Beautiful'.

Next to the road flows the Yellowstone River and on both sides are grassy meadows and stands of trees: greenish-yellow along the riverbank, higher up the dark outlines of pine forests. It's all so lovely that I can imagine even Steinbeck being lifted out of his depression. He thought of things he needed to buy, he wrote, 'to make [himself] linger: in Billings a hat; in Livingston a jacket; in Butte a rifle'. It's unclear where he slept that night, perhaps in a motel in Livingston where, according to a crossed-out passage in his manuscript, he watched the third televised debate between Nixon and Kennedy, or in a freezing cold truck stop in Bozeman, as he wrote to Elaine.

We stay in Livingston, where Main Street looks practically the same as on the cold autumn day when Steinbeck bought his jacket. The trains issue as melancholy a call as they did then. The shops almost deserve a preservation order, every one of them built in the rich years around 1900. The nature of their trade is less durable: a great many souvenirs, drink, second-hand goods, pawnshops. One is called 'Action Pawn, Take II'. No newspapers are on sale here apart from the *Bozeman Daily Chronicle*. No *New York Times*, no *Wall Street Journal*: 'They won't come over the mountains for us,' says the newsagent. At the far end of Main Street an attempt has been made at creating a new development in retro style, but it's almost completely empty. Since the crisis of 2008 no buyer has dared to risk burning his fingers.

The trains set the rhythm of all these little towns. Their presence is unavoidable. They slowly pass gardens and housing blocks, tendrils miles long of coal wagons and containers, pulled by four or five locomotives that whistle and toot at every level crossing before finally vanishing into the distance with a few howling blasts. Their coming and going penetrates to the farthest rooms in the Murray Hotel, every hour, day and night. You learn to live and sleep with it.

Everyone is now under the spell of Halloween, the great American ghost festival, the ritual transition to darkness, cold and death, and at the same time an exorcising of them. The *Bozeman Daily Chronicle* features a whole page about ghost houses and how to hunt ghosts yourself. 'Phantom music from long ago or the lingering smell of an old perfume could mean a ghost is present.' The Murray Hotel has spared no expense. Dusty rags and cobwebs hang across the windows, on the sofa the skeleton of a lady in black nineteenth-century clothing makes inviting gestures, another corpse speaks cheerfully to passers-by near the stairs, from under the piano the legs of a third dead body protrude. Rats are scattered here and there, and as you walk upstairs you see yourself approaching on a screen that makes you look as transparent as a ghost.

Snow is forecast, yet the next morning the sun is still shining, cheery and hot.

Onwards, then, on the endless Interstate 90. Steinbeck once again put his foot down. He must have driven along here at a fairly reckless speed half a century ago. It seems his love for Montana wasn't as great as all that.

Michael Savage, a popular talk-radio host, speaks to us. 'I've studied fascism and I've studied totalitarianism, and I can tell you: where this is leading to, this Obama administration, it's precisely the same. Don't forget, Hitler also came to power by democratic election.'

In what he is saying I can hear the grim voice of Ayn Rand, a refugee from the Soviet Union and author of the futuristic 1957 novel *Atlas Shrugged*, a counterpart of sorts to George Orwell's *Nineteen Eighty-Four*. She describes an America governed by socialists, a society in which all productivity, creativity and intelligence is outlawed. In Rand's worldview there are just two groups: creative people, the Atlases, and parasites. Socialism, like any sort of public provision, forces the Atlases to share the fruits of their enterprise with less talented and hardworking people. In her view that was a huge injustice; it is morally reprehensible to make people share their money and possessions with others.

During her lifetime even staunch conservatives found her beliefs too crazy for words and she remained on the margins of public debate. Today they think the world of Rand. During meetings of the Tea Party her story is the chorus to every speech. They adore her.

Michael Savage is her prophet for these times. He has a beautiful, warm voice and his sentences roll on and on. He's a first-class preacher. Now he's discovered that Obama pronounced the term 'Declaration of Independence' slightly hesitantly in a speech. He plays a recording of it. 'Hear that? This is typical of liberals, but they only occasionally admit it. They don't actually believe in our Declaration of Independence.'

In Butte, Steinbeck bought a Remington bolt action .222 with telescopic sights. He had to wait for the sights to be mounted, so in the meantime he got to know everyone in the shop and all the customers who came in. He wrote that he spent a good part of the morning there, mainly because he wanted to stay. 'But I see that, as usual, love is inarticulate. Montana has a spell on me.'

It's a very different story from that told by John Gunther, who visited Butte – 'the richest hill on earth' – some twenty years earlier. He called the Butte of his day the 'toughest, bawdiest town in America', and one of the ugliest places he'd ever seen. It was one big mining camp, with thousands of men below ground, mountains of slag everywhere, hardly any vegetation, poisonous fumes, all brightly lit at night by large, copper-coloured lamps. The town revelled in being called 'the only electric-lit cemetery in the United States'. Part of Butte, a strip 600 yards wide and a mile long, was suffering subsidence in Gunther's day because of all the tunnels and mine shafts, but none of the house owners dared to sue the Anaconda Copper Mining Company for compensation. No jury in the county had dared to return a verdict against Anaconda in forty years.

We drive through. Butte is still a rather messy affair, but little is happening here now. Anaconda has gone. The ground is still full of lead, cadmium, zinc and arsenic. The number of residents has practically halved. Butte is now mainly known for its Evel Knievel Days, a mass gathering of motorcyclists from all over the world in memory of the famous stunt man Evel Knievel, the highlight of which comes when a group of dare-devils jump over several trucks simultaneously, fireworks are lit and the fanfare 'God Bless America' is played.

You can still tell that the place has been through hard times. It's clear from the kind of women you come upon on the street and in the shops: robust creatures who know their own minds, civil and not unfriendly, but with the traces of a tough childhood deep in their eyes.

Now the only newspaper at the filling stations is the Montana Standard. It reports the discovery of a human skull at Maney Lake, the arrest of an eleven-year-old boy for possession of marijuana, and the opening of the hunting season next Saturday: 'Chance to fill the freezer good in Southwest Montana.' Farmers are complaining about the price of meat. They often receive only one offer from the buyers, since it all goes to the few big companies who run the show. It's been that way for years, but now they earn so little that one after another they're stopping farming. Since 1996 some 11,000 ranchers have given up, a fall of more than a quarter in fourteen years. 'There's no market anymore, no supply and demand, it's all dead,' one farmer says. 'You accept what those guys offer you or you get nothing at all.'

There's now a hard frost. The weather is on the turn. The roads grow increasingly quiet. It's not at all easy to find a room for the night here.

A lot of the motels are closed for the winter, but many more are up for sale. It's about half and half. The crisis is visible everywhere; vacations are the first thing people economise on. In a saloon in the town of Drummond, a man is playing guitar. An old farmer sits at the bar listening. Everything else is empty. Outside the train whistles.

We drive into the mountains the following morning. It's cold and misty. To the right of the road, stretching for miles, are burned and blackened forests. Somewhere here Steinbeck stayed in a lonely motel attached to a gas station, where he claims to have sorted out an argument between the owner and his son. The father was a burly American hunter. The son liked fashion, wanted to be a women's hairdresser and regularly read the New Yorker. Steinbeck sided with the son. I believe it was actually a conversation about homosexuality, but the subject was still taboo.

Just before Lookout Pass we fill the tank. Both in Travels and in his letters Steinbeck wrote about 'a burning desire to go' that he saw in the eyes of the people who stood looking at Rocinante, wherever he went. 'They spoke quietly of how they wanted to go someday, to move about, free and unanchored, not toward something but away from something.'

Half a century later, nothing has changed in that respect. Most working Americans have little time or opportunity to take long journeys. I see the eyes of waiters, gas station attendants, hotel staff, even border officials start to gleam when I tell them about this project, this trip, our Jeep.

'How much do you pay for a gallon in Maine?' a young man had asked at a pump in North Dakota. 'Oh, you come from Amsterdam. Sweden! And how much do you pay there? You're joking! Then you guys have a big problem.'

The man at the cash register here broaches the subject as soon as I see him. 'Wow! I've only been over beyond the Mississippi once. When I was in the army. Yep, that's life . . .'

On the far side of the mountains the trees are still in leaf: bright red, yellow, green. In Idaho and Washington it's autumn again. We spend a night in Spokane, where Steinbeck rushed to find a vet because Charley had suddenly fallen ill. We stroll back and forth along a riverside footpath with rustic benches and a bit of greenery, but it does nothing to distract us from the town's great distress. All the life in its centre has been sucked out by the shopping malls and suburbs on the outer edges. The bookstore has not survived the onslaught. There, too, the windows are dark and bare.

The next day it rains. The countryside is almost maternal now, with grassy curves that must look as beatific in spring as a *Teletubbies* landscape. It had other associations for Steinbeck. He could smell the Pacific for the first time, the great ocean of his youth, and there was no stopping him now. It came subtly, he wrote, that distant smell of sea rocks and kelp and churning water, but to him it was electrifying. 'I found myself plunging over the roads of Washington, as dedicated to the sea as any migrating lemming.' A sentence in the manuscript reveals that he had another reason for driving hard: Elaine. He would be seeing her again in Seattle. 'In a word: I was lonesome for my family.'

If Steinbeck had stuck rather more firmly to his original plan of describing the country, he would undoubtedly have devoted a passage to some of the surreal landscapes he passed: the worn banks and crusty bed of an inland sea that dried up thousands of years ago, waterless waterfalls as big as Niagara, left by one of the greatest floods ever to ravage the earth. He would certainly have taken a couple of hours out to visit the Grand Coulee Dam, which aside from the Hoover Dam is the most famous barrage in the United States, the country's biggest hydroelectric power station.

On its completion in 1941, the dam was the largest in the world, almost a mile long. It was part of an enormous irrigation project, and at the same time its power plants produced an astonishing amount of electricity. During the Second World War the Grand Coulee Dam powered the aluminium smelters for the aircraft industry and the shipyards, as well as plutonium production for the top-secret Manhattan Project that made the first atomic bomb.

The dam must have stunned everyone when it was first built. Deep poverty prevailed in the region and suddenly this huge structure arose, taller than the Great Pyramid of Giza, a beacon of hope in bright-white concrete surrounded by the buzz of a community of builders and engineers, a brand-new town where thousands of people lived and worked.

The dam still looks impressive, but the shine has gone. The concrete is covered in an itchy rash. In Coulee City a few of the huts occupied by the original builders remain, but most of the houses are now constructed out of clean, twenty-first-century synthetics. They've managed to scrape together a small museum. In a glass case is a jackhammer, plus a few measuring instruments, and you can hear personal statements from the workers. One of them says: 'When you leaned into the rock face with a drill like that, every muscle in your body seemed to vibrate along with it. After five minutes you felt like a milkshake.'

Then there is the specially built wheelchair in which Franklin Roosevelt was pushed around when he visited the giant building site in August 1934. Roosevelt was deeply impressed. He gave permission to make the dam higher than the original budget allowed and eventually made the project the showpiece of his New Deal programme.

The comparison with the Great Pyramid is understandable. Except that what was conquered here was not a foreign nation or the people, but nature.

We have by this point passed hundreds of bridges, viaducts and other structures that, to judge by the architectural style, must have been built in the 1930s and 1940s. We have driven for thousands of miles along the imposing interstate highways of the 1950s and 1960s, continually face to face with the effects of the enormous quantities of money, energy and imagination America invested in the public sector in those years.

Now we are seeing the reverse. The New York Times reports that even the building of the sorely needed new railroad tunnel under the Hudson between New York and New Jersey has been cancelled for lack of money. Planning had been going on for twenty years. The current rail connection, around a century old, simply cannot cope with commuter traffic any longer. It would have been a big, expensive job, but for such a large conurbation certainly not a luxury project. All over the Western world, tunnels of a similar kind are being built.

'This is a railroad tunnel we're talking about,' writes Times columnist Bob Herbert, enraged. How is it possible that a nation that built the Erie Canal and the Hoover Dam, that laid railroads right across the continent, is no longer able to build a tunnel? 'We're not trying to go to the Moon. This is not the Manhattan Project . . . What is the matter with us? The Chinese could build it. The Turks could build it. We can't build it.'

Right. Why not?

The July issue of the magazine Holiday in which Steinbeck published the first excerpt of Travels in 1961 also featured a story about the best train trips you could take in America. The piece had a slightly nostalgic tone, because even then the heyday of the railroad was over. In 1911, for example, a special luxury train travelled between Chicago and Los Angeles once a week, and for an extra twenty-five dollars it offered the services of a total of seventy people, including a barber, a manicurist, a secretary and a nanny. There were baths and showers on the train; the passengers had access to a library, as well as telegraphed news reports and ticker tape from the stock exchange; when it began to get dark, stereoscopic images of the landscape were projected in the compartments.

In 1961, of all those glorious trains, only the Broadway Limited was left, the luxury connection between New York and Chicago, its seventeen or eighteen carriages painted Tuscan red and gold. It was lightning fast and punctual to the second, 'rushing through the night in a torrent of glittering privacy and superb public apartments'. Now you run into abandoned railway tracks and forgotten stations all over the American landscape. Anyone flying into San Francisco, for example, will see the remaining evidence of a tragedy beneath them: a huge, rusty, half-open rail bridge over the southern part of the bay, the straight route of the old railroad to Oakland that is still clearly visible among houses and weeds. It's no different elsewhere.

We once took a six-week train trip around the United States, from New York to New Orleans, then via Houston along the southern border to Los Angeles, on to Oakland and then back via the Rocky Mountains and Chicago. With a little improvisation it can still be done, although on some stretches the service is sporadic. In a silver, double-decker Amtrak Superliner we slid slowly across the country for thousands of miles. From time to time the world of rails and trains looked like a bomb site, a corridor of ghostly buildings, rusty rail yards, half-collapsed bridges, and goods wagons overgrown with weeds.

The masses of people who once used this system left visible traces everywhere, but they themselves had disappeared. In the station at Ottumwa the roof was hanging down and swallows flew in and out. Burlington, which used to see dozens of trains arriving and departing every day, now accommodated a total of two. In Oakland, a former hub, no one under thirty could tell me where the station was. Los Angeles railway station had on display a photograph from the 1940s, when the place was packed with soldiers and sailors on the way to the front or returning home. Now that same stunning concourse has been restored like a cathedral, but almost all the ticket windows are closed.

During the Second World War the American railroad was still operating at its peak. Petrol and oil were rationed, car traffic was limited, and at the same time troops needed to be moved all over the country in their tens of thousands. Trains carried ninety-seven per cent of all passengers and ninety per cent of all freight, making profits not seen since the beginning of the century. The station was once again the centre of the community, with photographs in the papers of workers handing out cigarettes to departing soldiers, or reading matter for the journey. Trains were, for a short time, wildly popular.

Immediately after 1945 the roles were reversed. On the face of it the railroads were in a better position than they had been for years, but in contrast to nineteenth- and twentieth-century Europe, where a properly functioning rail network was seen as a valuable public asset (partly for military reasons, of course), they were not state-owned or partially state-owned. Successive American administrations, under pressure from a powerful car lobby, supported the railroad companies' competitors, the road builders and car manufacturers. Compared to the automobile and the aircraft, the railroad was seen as belonging to the past.

The lucrative freight trains kept running, rattling endlessly along all those nineteenth-century tracks, but after the war most of the passenger routes were soon in the red. Beautiful new trains were being developed, such as the California Zephyr, and there were carriages with viewing domes for the passengers, such as the Chesapeake and Ohio's lounge car, silver and streamlined like planes. None of this could halt the downward trend.

As Stephen Goddard writes in his epic story of the decline of the American railroad: 'Gone were the days when a Chicago and a Northwestern train to Omaha could offer travellers thirteen entrees, six kinds of game and twenty-five desserts. Conductors now watched Kaisers and Studebakers speed by on parallel highways at twenty-six cents a gallon and driven by the millions of long-time rail commuters seduced away from the rails.'

Between 1947 and 1957 no less than a third of all American railroad tracks were abandoned. By about 1960 barely half of the more than 230,000 miles of track in place in 1916, the high point of the American railroad, was still in use. On 1 May 1971 the US government signed what remained of the passenger lines over to Amtrak, the National Railroad Passenger Corporation. Since then, ten per cent – at most – of the once so vast rail network has been used for passenger transport.

The last great American passenger trains have their idiosyncrasies, and during our round trip by rail we soon got to know them. We learned all about the gaps in the system of seat reservation, about the unavoidable delays (a quarter of trains arrive late), about comfort (watch out for the afternoon sun!), defective seats (make sure you get leg rests for night-time travel), and the paradox and tragedy of Amtrak was increasingly brought home to us: oldest is invariably best. The oldest carriages had the best toilets, the oldest seats had the most legroom, the oldest conductors were the most attentive. The Amtrak network seemed more and more like one great heritage line.

I recall a conversation with a train conductor one afternoon, labouring through the dusty desert of Arizona. 'When I'd just started this job there were ten or twenty trains a day between New York and New Orleans,' he said. 'Now there's just one. Same on the classic east–west line between Chicago and San Francisco. Nowadays you actually have to do the last stretch by bus; the train doesn't go beyond Oakland now that the rail bridge is out. And on the New Orleans to Los Angeles route they only run three times a week.'

Of course I know there are exceptions, such as the many commuter trains for a start, and the Acela Express, the high-speed connection between Washington and Boston that handles a large proportion of local passenger traffic. To European eyes these are perfectly normal trains. While the French TGV has for decades raced between Paris and Lyon at close to 200 miles per hour, even the Acela rarely manages to average more than eighty. The rails are not suitable for much higher speeds. As columnist Thomas Friedman wrote: 'If all Americans could compare Berlin's luxurious central train station today with the grimy, decrepit Penn Station in New York City, they would swear we were the ones who lost World War II.'

Amtrak trains use the same ancient railroad infrastructure as the freight trains, which seldom go faster than fifty miles an hour. That alone makes the service fairly slow. Normal passenger trains achieve a maximum of about seventy miles per hour, but they are often slower than that. While China is putting the finishing touches to a network of high-speed lines, just one passenger train a day rumbles back and forth between the great population centres of the American west coast, San Diego and the Bay Area, whistling and ringing its bells at level crossings as if nothing has changed since 1910. There are plans for thirteen high-speed lines, including connections between New York and Buffalo, Los Angeles and San Francisco, and Chicago and Detroit – but it will be years before any of that becomes a reality, if it ever does.

In some respects, self-satisfied stagnation has prevailed here over the past few decades. We are familiar with that in Europe, but in dynamic America it comes as a surprise. What's more, most Americans have no idea how far behind they are in some fields because they've never set foot outside their own country. So their self-satisfaction remains firm as a rock.

One morning in North Dakota I took a quick look under the hood of our brand-new Jeep, just to check the oil. It was a strange experience. All kinds of electronics have been added over the past fifty years, of course, and everything is smoother and more comfortable, but in essence what I saw was still more or less the same as what Steinbeck must have seen in his Rocinante: a heavy engine, heavy cylinders and dynamos, a machine capable of surviving almost anything, but slow, with a voracious appetite for fuel and parts.

On a larger scale, things happen much as they do under the hood of my Jeep. On my monitor the emails roll in like slow freight trains. When it comes to internet speed even the largest American cities are way down in the world's league table. After a long list of South Korean, Japanese, Chinese and European cities, the fastest place in America in this respect – San José – comes fifty-seventh. In South Korea an internet connection of one gigabyte per second is available to almost all households.

As for the quality of its infrastructure in general, the United States is in twenty-third place, according to a 2010 report by the World Economic Forum, coming between Spain and Chile. Traffic congestion around the major cities is far worse than in Western Europe, with more than a third of urban roads regarded as extremely problematic. One in every nine bridges is 'structurally deficient'. Roads serving cities like Los Angeles are very similar to the crumbling motorways of the former Eastern Bloc.

All over the country another problem occurs that's familiar from the old Eastern Europe. Ancient and rusty water pipes can burst at the oddest moments, creating small fountains. Water supply systems come right at the bottom of the infrastructure grades handed out by the American Society of Civil Engineers, receiving a D-minus. Their spokesman says: 'We're relying on water systems built by our great-grandparents, and no one wants to pay for the decades we've spent ignoring them.'

In an increasing number of cities, a third or more of the streetlights have been turned off to save energy. On television you see pictures of firemen in Los Angeles collecting money in the street to enable them to continue their work. Americans like to fly, but more and more large airports are becoming notorious for frequent delays caused by having too few air-traffic controllers, inadequate capacity and insufficient new investment.

'Public poverty' was how economist John Kenneth Galbraith described this phenomenon in his 1958 book *The Affluent Society*. Even then, in the late 1950s, he was watching American society slip more and more off balance. The shops were stuffed with luxury innovations for private use, while attention to everything that belonged in the public realm was visibly declining. He described a future outing by an American family. In their mauve and cerise car with power steering and air conditioning, they drive through towns with potholes in the streets, mounds of rubbish, dilapidated buildings and above-ground phone and electricity cables. 'They picnic on exquisitely packaged food from a portable icebox by a polluted stream and go on to spend the night at a park which is a menace to public health and morals. Just before dozing off on an air mattress, beneath a nylon tent, amid the stench of decaying refuse, they may reflect vaguely on the curious unevenness of their blessings. Is this, indeed, the American genius?'

Galbraith and Steinbeck were good friends, and in both *Travels with Charley* and *America and Americans* Steinbeck described, with increasing unease, that same disjunction.

Many economists believe that a country will sooner or later run into serious problems if the national debt rises above ninety per cent of the gross national product, since it then has to put so much energy into interest and repayments that there is virtually nothing left over for growth and modernisation. In some southern European debtor countries this is already happening, and America is approaching the tipping point. It is the consequence of a campaign against public affairs and civil administration in general that has been underway since the 1980s. Conservative groups within the Republican Party, television syndicates such as Fox News and radio talk shows like Michael Savage's set the tone, and gradually the effects are becoming visible everywhere.

During the presidency of Republican Dwight D. Eisenhower, business provided a quarter of tax income, and the very richest Americans paid a top rate of ninety per cent. That was how America could afford to build its Interstate Highway System, pay for social security, forge a lasting alliance with Western Europe through military and economic aid, finance schools and universities, maintain roads, bridges and national parks, and send Armstrong, Aldrin and Collins to the moon. Now tax revenues have fallen dramatically. Only 2.4 per cent of gross domestic product goes on roads and the water supply, less than half the percentage spent in Europe and a third of the figure for China. Of America's federal government there will eventually be little left other than, in the words of Paul Krugman, 'an insurance company with an army'.

Many Americans today, influenced by campaigns that draw upon the work of Ayn Rand, are heedless of all this. In a recent Gallup poll, two out of three Americans agreed with the statement that big government rather than big business is the greatest threat to their country. To such people, taxes are pure loss of income. It rarely occurs to them that they receive countless collective goods and services in return, from roads and schools to street lighting and airports, from garbage collection to the fire service, and on top of it all the most powerful military apparatus in the world.

It's not just a question of money but of a lack of imagination. In the time when the Grand Coulee Dam was built, American thinking was to a great degree focused on public affairs, public services, public works. As historian Henry William Brands writes: 'The dreams of 1945 had been collectively ambitious but individually modest; those of 2010 were collectively modest but individually ambitious.'

The America that put more than sixteen million troops in the field during the Second World War is having difficulty maintaining a force of a few hundred thousand men in Iraq and Afghanistan. The economic powerhouse that bent the world economy to its will at Bretton Woods is now dependent on the central bankers of China and Japan. Proud industrial cities like Detroit and Buffalo are a shadow of what they once were. At the same time, Brands writes, the lifestyle of individual baby boomers, with their houses, cars, computers, travel and cappuccinos, puts that of their parents in the shade. 'Bretton Woods, the Marshall Plan, the Great Society – those were dreams of another age; the nation in 2010 could aspire to nothing so grand.'

That bizarre family picnic described by John Kenneth Galbraith is slowly becoming a reality.

PART SIX

Oregon – California – San Francisco – Monterey

'We may be brothers after all. We will see.'

CHIEF SEATTLE
1854

One

TRAVELS WITH CHARLEY was once called In Quest of America. That was the working title, and it was also the title of the series of prepublications in *Holiday*. In the end the subtitle became In Search of America. The difference is subtle but nevertheless important, since a quest is a long, meandering journey with a view to accomplishing a feat, whereas a search is a focused investigation. Steinbeck's original intention was indeed to perform a search. Along the way it became a quest, with all the accompanying vacillation, but that was something he didn't want to stress too much to the reader. In the final version it became a search once again. A hero must have a clear purpose in mind.

Something similar applies to our journey, half a century later; our search is gradually becoming a quest. Just take all the problems you encounter if you try to reconstruct, as accurately as possible, Steinbeck's expedition and the writing of *Travels with Charley*. Where are the necessary documents? Many of Steinbeck's letters were left to Stanford University by Elaine, and a good deal more material is available at the National Steinbeck Center in Salinas and in the library of San José State University, but the rest is spread out across the country. Fragments of the writer's life have been filed away in universities and libraries all over the place, as if after his death the summerhouse in Sag Harbor exploded, sending its contents flying in all directions.

The galleys of *Travels* ended up in Salinas, the letters – which also served as travel notes – are in Stanford, and the manuscript can be found in New York, in the Morgan Library & Museum. Steinbeck wrote by hand, usually on yellow legal pads, and part of the manuscript is a kind of diary. On the first page he wrote: 'This will be page 52 of the report which has the working title *In Quest of America*.'

It's always interesting to compare the manuscript a writer sweated over with the published version. You get to know a little more about the writing process, about the problems the author wrestled with, about his later interventions – often at the urging of editors, agents and other readers of the manuscript version – and the way in which he gradually moulded his experiences and ideas into a book.

The manuscript of *Travels with Charley* consists of several stacks of paper, some of them stapled together, and one leather-bound notebook, which has part of the text of the book (pages 45 to 104) on the right-hand side and on the left the occasional diary entry, running from 3 February to 3 March 1961. Then there is a typed version edited in pencil, although it's not clear whether the annotations are by Steinbeck himself. The number of corrections increases as the book goes on, and in places entire passages are crossed out. Instructions for the typesetter have been inserted here and there, in red ink.

In the first part of the journey, between Sag Harbor and Seattle, there are few differences between the manuscript and the book. In the manuscript Steinbeck is less of the tough guy, openly admitting that he 'paused' no fewer than five times during his journey, not just in Chicago but in Seattle, San Francisco, Amarillo and Austin. He is also far more outspoken politically. The election campaigns by Kennedy and Nixon get his full attention, the presidential debates are followed keenly, and John and Elaine's preference for the Democrats is plain for all to see.

That was all largely scrapped, and the reasons are clear. In the book Steinbeck needed to remain a lonely hero, and he could not afford to scare off his broad readership by expressing too many party political opinions, which were in any case of only short-term relevance.

After Seattle, however, a minor revolution takes place. In the manuscript Steinbeck's travel account changes radically in both tone and content. It is a stylistic discontinuity that knocks his whole story off balance. A long series of corrections erased all that and set things straight again, but it remains indicative of the confusion that took hold of Steinbeck the more his America project went on.

I write 'John and Elaine', because that is the most important change. Whereas in the final version of Travels our protagonist takes a walk on the 'narrow streets and cobbled surfaces' of the desolate old centre of Seattle and then goes off on his lonely way with Charley at his side, in the manuscript he does something else entirely. He drives to the airport and checks into one of the stainless-steel hotels there to wait for Elaine.

'It was a triumph of the modern,' Steinbeck writes. 'In my room, one whole side of which was glass, everything was built in. My big bed withdrew into a wall in the daytime as a snail slides into its shell. The bedside cabinet was a mass of buttons and little lights controlling radio, television, telephones and a great many other conveniences I never penetrated.'

In the manuscript version he describes his fantasies: how he intends to treat Elaine – after her rapid and luxurious journey by ultra-modern jet from New York – to a delicious dinner in the hotel restaurant before they explore the city together. Events take a different turn. Elaine is unable to get a ticket and doesn't arrive in Seattle until three days later, after a tiring journey via San Francisco.

They are described spending some three weeks together. First they travel south along the Pacific Coast Highway, then they stay in a luxury hotel suite in San Francisco, where they paint the town red with their friends for days on end. There is no more sleeping in Rocinante. Elaine, often dubbed 'Queenie' or 'Madame', is the boss.

The whole story is a complete break with everything that goes before it. The lonely wanderer John Steinbeck is magically transformed into a lazy tourist, one half of a presentable, harmonious couple. He no longer writes about the cloudscapes, the silence and the few lonely souls he meets but instead about the hotels he sleeps in and misunderstandings between him and the staff. Charley vanishes into the background. You can barely hear his distant whining.

Exactly how and why the abrupt transition came about is unclear. Perhaps these lines were intended as an ode to Elaine. Or perhaps they were an attempt to make a link with modern America and with the estrangement from his old friends that he experienced later on the route. It may also be that with this version he had the readers of Holiday in mind, who were after all mainly interested in America's tourist spots. It also happened to be true. What he describes is what took place. It's just that it doesn't fit into the story.

The California passages starring Elaine did not make it into either *Holiday* or the published version of *Travels*. A few critical remarks by Steinbeck's literary agent Elizabeth Otis were probably enough, and maybe even those were unnecessary. Steinbeck was too professional an author and storyteller to ignore such a stylistic aberration. The 'we' was systematically crossed out and replaced by 'I' or 'Charley and I'. Elaine and her nice little restaurants disappeared. Charley resumed his position of pride on the front seat.

In Seattle the rain is bucketing down. Even the locals are impressed, which is quite something for a city universally known for sucking up all the moisture in the surrounding region like a sponge. Seattle and rain are practically synonymous. The city centre looks like San Francisco, with steep streets, the ocean a constant presence and a cheerful fish market on the waterfront. But this weekend everything is drowning, the alleyways and gutters choking in the flood, and even the ocean is hiding. The only sign of it is the ferries honking somewhere in the fog.

People born and bred in Seattle pay little attention to any of this. The city was originally built as an outpost of Alaska. Fish and timber kept the economy ticking over and beyond that the residents had to look out for themselves. They built their own houses, laid their own railroad and even organised deliveries of potential brides from the east – many Civil War widows among them – to alleviate the shortage of women.

On the coast, where our hotel stands, Ernie Pyle visited a Hooverville, as the crisis districts built during the Depression were known: a shanty town of shacks made of old crates and driftwood. He spent an afternoon there in 1937 with Jesse Jackson, the 'mayor' of Hooverville, a thin man who put the fear of God into people. Alcohol abuse was strictly banned, and children and young women were forbidden to live in the town, since they only caused disquiet. The men, all of them jobless, scraped a living by combing the beach for washed-up timber and collecting the trash from shops and hotels. 'We're mostly lumberjacks and seamen and fishermen and miners,' Jackson said to Pyle. 'We're used to a hard life. We build our own huts here. When you've got a roof over your head, the battle's three-fourths won, you know.'

Nowadays Seattle is one of the richest and most popular cities in the United States, the city of Boeing (since the Second World War), Jimi Hendrix (since 1942), Starbucks (since 1971), Nirvana and Pearl Jam (since the late 1980s), and Microsoft (since the company moved here from Albuquerque in 1979).

The hills where Jackson's men earned a few dollars picking fruit every summer are now full of the country houses and cottages of twenty-first-century American workers. Their neighbourhoods have charming names like Edgewood Park and Bellevue, and the leafy lanes breathe the freedom of the old Deerfield. Here the boss stands next to the doorman once more in the rain on the local sports field, as their sons and daughters come marching in like army detachments; here America once again has all the self-confidence it needs.

John wanted to show Elaine the old Seattle, but he barely recognised the place. He remembered it as 'a town sitting on hills beside a matchless harborage – a little city of space and trees and gardens, its houses matched to such a background'. That was over. In the 1930s Seattle had more than 300,000 residents, by the 1960s almost twice as many.

John quickly lost his way in the suburbs. 'Along what had been country lanes rich with berries, high wire fences and mile-long factories stretched, and the yellow smoke of progress hung over it all.' Eight-lane highways now ran 'like glaciers' through the disturbed hills, and the traffic raced across the city 'with murderous intensity'.

The entire dockside of the old port had been beaten into submission by the huge concrete pillars of the Alaskan Way Viaduct, set down there in the 1950s, a detail Steinbeck does not mention. The thing still stands, and it very much reminds me of a plan a developer came up with in the 1960s for Amsterdam, with flyovers and motorway viaducts all over the place, above the houses and canals. Most of the old districts of the city were to be sacrificed to it; that was precisely the point. Amsterdam narrowly escaped a wave of demolition. In Seattle, the poor old inner city bore the brunt.

The rain keeps on. We hang around for a bit in our hotel room, just like Steinbeck. What else can we do in this weather? On television is a film about a divorced man whose daughter takes a trip to Europe. He lives in one of those Super Zip neighbourhoods, but years ago he fulfilled his duty to his country as a secret agent in dangerous lands and now he's worried about the trip his beloved daughter is making. 'You, with your houses and your staff, you've no idea what the world's like out there!' he tells his ex and her new husband.

Sure enough, everything goes wrong. Barely an hour out of Paris, his daughter and her friend are kidnapped by a bunch of unshaven Russians and Arabs. The father rushes out to find the two girls, aided in his search by a French former colleague who works for the secret service. Eventually he has to finish the job himself, since his French ally – oh, duplicitous cheese-eaters! – turns out to be part of the plot.

Silly rich girls in the big bad world, trapped in decadent and perfidious Europe, and a dynamic dad who comes to their rescue with a huge amount of violence – so the plot unfolds. In the end the father manages to save his daughter from the filthy clutches of a sheik just in time, at the cost of about fifteen human lives. Her American purity remains intact, although it's a close-run thing. 'Oh, daddy!'

Once, with Grace Kelly in it, Europe was still comfy and cosy. Every American wanted to see Paris at least once in his life. That's all over, as was made abundantly clear to us on a soaking wet Sunday afternoon in Seattle.

The city was named after Chief Seattle, who for much of the nineteenth century was the chief of the Duwamish. In 1854 he transferred owner-ship of his land to the white settlers with a legendary speech of which a few snatches have been preserved and translated. There is naturally some doubt about the accuracy of the text, but according to tradition he said something like this: 'It matters little where we pass the remnants of our days. They will not be many . . . A few more moons, a few more winters, and not one of the descendants of the mighty hosts that once moved over this broad land or lived in happy homes, protected by the Great Spirit, will remain to mourn over the graves of a people once more powerful and hopeful than yours. But why should I mourn at the untimely fate of my people? Tribe follows tribe, and nation follows nation, like the waves of the sea. It is the order of nature, and regret is useless. Your time of decay may be distant, but it will surely come, for even the White Man whose God walked and talked with him as friend to friend, cannot be exempt from the common destiny. We may be brothers after all. We will see.'

We make our way southwards along the Interstate 5, between the mountains and the coast, towards Portland. The peace of Montana and Western Washington is behind us. Steinbeck, driving hard, is almost a week ahead by this point, and now that he's off touring Route 101 with Elaine we pick up the pace a little ourselves. The clouds hang heavy and grey against the Cascade Range. The weather is stormy; gusts of wind shake our Jeep and at regular intervals a fresh downpour rattles the roof. We keep on through a thick fog of raindrops, with the rear lights of the vehicle in front as our only compass. Towards four it's already dark. We spend the night in a kind of sleeping factory in an industrial zone, or rather a refreshments zone, because they have those here too, all the standards: a Subway, a Kentucky Fried Chicken, a Dairy Queen and our Super 8 Hotel.

The next morning we drive into Oregon. It's the same story as yesterday: squally rain hammering on the roof, steaming semi-trailers beside us, eyes fixed on the rear lights of the car in front. Rush Limbaugh on the radio tries to keep us awake. Our enemies have one great plan, he tells us, and it lies at the root of all that they do. Look at what Obama has in mind with his reorganisation of healthcare: socialism and euthanasia. That's what it's all about. That's his plan. A series of ads and then the next speaker, this time about changing your life today and having a total makeover. Everything is malleable and plannable. Our lives need a clear goal and they are short. Which is why we're in such a hurry.

Just past Eugene we turn onto the 38, heading for the ocean. The rain and noise stop immediately. The road rolls between green hills, along a broad river. The forests are dark with pine and larch, and the bright yellow and orange of autumnal, deciduous trees is interspersed between them. Oregon is one long surprise. We stop on a side road, simply because it's so beautiful.

It's a chilly autumn day. The trees sough, the grass is fragrant, the sun shines in between the retreating clouds and suddenly travelling is a treat again. One final shower. In the meadows beside the river, brown cattle

stand with their rumps in the rain. Further away is a herd of elk. Above
the hills are the remaining shreds of fog and cloud, and from time to
time everything lights up in a brilliant ray of sunlight. Then we're in
another endless pine forest and at last, at Winchester Bay, we see the
ocean again.

We spend the night at Port Orford. You could hardly call it a harbour.
It's a large concrete platform on stilts sticking out into the ocean with
dozens of boats parked on top. Anyone wanting to leave has himself
winched down, and when you get back you're immediately hoisted up
again. 'The ocean swell is so powerful that if you tie up alongside here
for the night your boat will be gone by morning,' says the owner of
Griff's on the Dock, the harbour restaurant. For most of his life he worked
on a tug. Then he took over the restaurant. It's not much more than a
cosy wooden shack on the quayside. He likes it that way. 'At least in Port
Orford you still have weather. Twice a year or more we get a raging storm
and our guests have to come in through the back door in the foam from
the waves, but they're happy to do that. In California everything is always
perfectly calm, clear, blue and sunny.'

The cod on our plates just swam in, the best in the world. There are
a few benches and tables and everyone chats with everyone else. 'By
October the tourists have gone,' says one of the customers. 'Then the
storms start and the harbour and the sea are all ours again.' Unemployment
in this part of Oregon is approaching twenty per cent, 'but we gave up
on politicians a long time ago'. They promise things, our fellow diners
say, but they don't do them.

It's the same conversation every time, as if the political debate is taking
place in a different atmospheric layer. The Democrats we speak to are
disappointed in Obama, and the Republicans apologise for the extremists
in their party. Often relations are so polarised that Republicans and
Democrats have decided not to discuss politics. It only leads to trouble
and arguments. Everyone is embarrassed by the pointless political uproar,
by the state of the country.

The next day is composed of greys, whites and blues. Above the coast
the sky is open; further out, heavy showers hang over the sea with the
sun bursting through. Above the hills is a grey mist and in front of it

little white clouds against the lightest of blue. So the day begins. A few seagulls screech. *Desert Storm* and *Max* are lowered into the water, small but solid fishing boats. These are all one-man craft. The captain of *Max*, as weather-beaten as his boat, stands on the deck in orange fisherman's overalls calling out instructions to the man working the hoist. Engines throb. Waves boom against the concrete. Salt is everywhere.

It's a world of its own, that concrete dock: a few fishermen and their wives, two hoists, the man who lowers the boats, the man who operates the towing trucks, the big man and the little woman at Griff's, the washer-upper, the rocks, the seagulls and the sea. The wife of the captain of *Max* stands at the dock rail. 'I love you!' 'I love you too!' She blows her husband a kiss and then the boat is lowered into the waves, far down below the dock. 'He's going to catch twenty salmon today,' the woman calls out to the man at the hoist. 'No, twenty-one,' the man calls back. 'One extra for me.'

The captain's wife counts it out on her fingers: 'Now he catches salmon, then the whole winter it's crab and from January cod again. Everything's laid down in the quota.' Does it pay? 'You're joking. If you've got four or five boats you might make a small profit. Everything gets scooped up by the big industrial ships.'

With a sweeping gesture she points to the fishing boats parked in the dock: OR 511, *Top Gun*, *Tiburon*, *Belle*, and twenty others. 'They all have to sit and wait. They're allowed out only once a week. We've become as dependent as the farmers, with thousands of rules. We can't do anything ourselves any more. We're all consumers now.'

Right next to Griff's is a small monument to all the fishermen who never came home. There have been eleven since 1959; the last four drowned only four years ago, on 16 December 2006. 'Twenty salmon. Today!'

A few hours later we reach the California border, a proper state line this time. Serious-looking officials glance at our Jeep and ask probing questions about the presence of apples, pears, salad and harmful insects. Shortly after that, forests full of the legendary redwoods loom up, giant sequoias from primeval times that are found only here. The trees are sixty to a hundred metres tall, often 1,000 years old, sometimes 2,000, the oldest living organisms on earth aside from certain fungi. All proportions are wildly out of kilter. The forest is suddenly as big as in a fairy tale, we and our Jeep grow smaller and smaller, and Highway 101 turns into a tiny, mouse-sized footpath. Bright patches of sunlight flicker between the tree trunks. Further on it grows steamy, as the treetops disappear into the cold fog rising out of the ocean.

They spent two days here. To Charley every tree, a thousand years old or not, was simply a thing on which he could lift his leg. To John and Elaine everything was fascinating: the hush, like in a cathedral, the greenish-gold sunlight between the trunks, the flash of a passing bird, the deep darkness at night. 'And there's a breathing in the black, for these huge things that control the day and inhabit the night are living things and have presence.' John felt dreamy and protected here, although he could imagine why the place gave other people a sense of unease. 'It is not only the size of these redwoods but their strangeness that frightens them.'

We limit ourselves to a walk through the dripping woods. Among the trees there's a silence you could cut with a knife. It isn't frightening exactly, but these giant organisms do have a presence. They're silent, powerful and possessed of an astonishing dignity. That tree over there was standing when Charlemagne was crowned, and that one was already a giant when printing was invented, when the Pomo people ruled this region and when the Portuguese Juan Cabrillo became the first European to sail along this coast in 1542. Every tree in this forest saw what came after that.

They're a stern lot, these trees standing here for a thousand years. Their trunks are impossible to lean on, unlike a cosy old oak or a friendly plane. You're a stranger in this world and always will be. Everything tells you that you're a little ant who happened to show up here for a few minutes one wet autumn afternoon in 2010. Leave us in our centuries and our silence. Leave us.

The 101 is the most beautiful highway in America. It's starting to get dark and we twist and turn endlessly through tall pine forests. The road has been cut into the hills in places and it's as if we are twisting our way deeper and deeper into the land like a corkscrew. Midway a clearing emerges between the trees, with the ruin of a dark-red house. Next to it are the remains of a truck, rusty, flat on its old worn tyres, the same model of GMC as Rocinante. In the last of the daylight the ocean appears again, the foam on the waves bright white. We're in for more rough weather.

Yes, this is undoubtedly California, along with Texas the most headstrong state in America. It really belongs to the ocean, not to the continent, and here and there we can already detect the taste of Asia. Some people who live on the coast actually take that notion literally, believing that when the predicted Major Earthquake tears open the San Andreas Fault – the huge split in the earth that runs through and alongside California – the state will have its original nature restored, once again becoming an island far out in the ocean.

Such fantasies are evoked by the sparkling light, the sea and the high coast, and by the fact that California is the endpoint of the eternal trek westwards. Here you can't go any further. So this must be the Promised Land, the American Dream's utopia fulfilled.

Extraordinary things do indeed happen here. California is among the ten most important economies in the world and the most populous state in America, with more than thirty-seven million residents. Despite all its problems, Los Angeles is still one of the most vigorous of American manufacturing centres, and Hollywood is the most important location of all for the entertainment industry.

As well as having a lengthwise divide in its geography, California is culturally divided across its width by a line that passes, roughly speaking, through San Francisco. Northern California differs in mentality from Southern California at least as much as, say, Denmark from Italy. Those differences are reinforced by the climate. The north is relatively cool and wet, the south dry and hot. Water has a huge impact on the relationship between the two. It's the oil of the Californian economy. Three-quarters of the state's water comes from the north, while four-fifths of the total is used in the south, mostly in agriculture.

Cities like Los Angeles are completely dependent on water that has to be fetched from elsewhere by means of complicated and expensive transport systems. In the past there was fierce speculation with water rights – without extra water the city would have been unable to grow – and in the 1920s a full-on Water War broke out between Los Angeles and rebellious farmers in nearby Owens Valley. The city was drawing so much water from their land that agriculture had become impossible.

The shortage of water causes perpetual friction between the north and the south of the state. The south, with its great concentrations of population, has all the power; the north feels it's being sucked dry. That tension is a permanent feature of Californian politics. I recall a departing governor once saying to his successor something like: 'Pray for rain. A few wet summers and anything's possible. If it stays dry, forget it, there's nothing you can do.'

Perhaps because of the eternal water problem, California is more aware of environmental issues than the rest of America. Whereas many American states don't give a damn about environmental norms, California, on the initiative of a Republican governor, is trying to reduce its output of CO_2 to its 1990 level by 2020. New cars have to comply with increasingly stringent standards, air pollution caused by businesses is being cut and solar energy is making great headway. In parking lots from time to time you'll even see those elegant 'solar trees' that automatically turn their panels to follow the sun.

As far as new technology is concerned, the state is way ahead of the rest. Silicon Valley, the former Santa Clara Valley to the south of San Francisco, is famous the world over. With America moving in one direction, California is seeking a different course.

At the same time, this progressive state balanced for years on the edge of bankruptcy. The countless ways of blocking any bill involving taxation were used all too eagerly by citizens and lobby groups, and the consequences became obvious. For months the Interstate 5 from San Francisco to Los Angeles, the state's central highway, was reduced to its left-hand lane for dozens of miles. Around Los Angeles I see potholed motorways such as I have seen only once before: shortly after the fall of the Berlin Wall, in the bankrupt East Germany.

In some ways California could be described as the most democratic state in the world – with all the disadvantages that brings with it. Voters can force any elected politician who fails to satisfy them to step down early by petitioning for a recall election. This is sometimes done by a pressure group, but it's just as likely to be initiated by a lobby with a great deal of financial backing. On 31 August 2010 the mayor of the small town of Livingston, Daniel Varela Sr, was removed from office amid scorn and derision. As the New York Times put it: 'His crime? He had the temerity to push through the small city's first water-rate increase in more than a decade to try to fix its ageing water system, which he said spewed brownish, smelly water from rusty pipes.' Varela's own explanation: 'We were trying to be responsible.'

It's a pig-headedness typical of an outlying district, a part of the continent in which the great powers of the day showed little interest for centuries. California was initially home to just its 300,000 or so Native Americans, who lived by hunting, fishing and a little agriculture here and there. The main colonial powers of the seventeenth and eighteenth centuries regarded the western edge of America as a wilderness. They saw no future in it. For Europeans it was simply too difficult to reach.

In the eighteenth century the greatest interest in these parts was shown, remarkably enough, in Saint Petersburg, at the court of the Russian tsar. Just as the Europeans sailed west and, having landed, moved on into the continent, so progressive Russian aristocrats organised expeditions to the east, to the farthest regions of Siberia and then on along the totally unexplored north-west coast of America.

Expeditions were mounted in 1729 and 1741, both led by the Danish naval officer Vitus Bering – after whom the Bering Strait is named – and his Russian lieutenant Aleksei Chirikov. In their wake came various groups of trappers, and in 1784 the first Russian settlement was established in Alaska. The local inhabitants, the Aleut people, paid the price. After a few years only one in ten were left, the rest having fallen victim to hunger, sickness and violent conflict.

The Russians managed to keep their American adventures quiet for a long time. All were top secret. Not until 1760 did the Spanish ambassador in Saint Petersburg get wind of the expeditions and he immediately warned his government in Madrid. The news caused great commotion. Although no Spaniard had ever set foot there, the Spanish king regarded the entire west coast of the North American continent as his territory. At the same time, reports reached him about British fur traders who were operating out of the East and venturing closer and closer to the Pacific.

Perhaps the Russians, possibly even the British as well, would reach the gates of Mexico, then known as Baja California. That must be prevented at all costs.

An expedition was sent north to Alta California, today's California. Since hardly any ordinary Spaniards could be persuaded to undertake such a dangerous journey across unexplored territory, priests were sought. A series of mission posts would be set up to convert the natives to Christianity, thus retaining the region, without too much trouble or manpower, for the Spanish throne. Captain Gaspar de Portolà de Rovira accompanied the priests, with orders to use this opportunity to seek out the best harbours along the coast and establish colonies there.

The expedition set out in 1769. In the early spring the first mission post at San Diego was consecrated and in the summer the men moved on to Monterey where, according to plan, they built a second mission post with a fort attached. They chanced upon an excellent natural harbour, in a large bay beyond the hills, which they baptised with the name of Saint Francis: San Francisco. Spanish ships had sailed past the Golden Gate long before, but because of the perpetual fog hanging over it, the relatively narrow access the strait afforded to the bay had escaped the notice of the explorers every time.

It all remained small and simple for many years. In 1774 the entire colonial population of California was made up of some 180 souls. But slowly the mission posts multiplied until there was one every thirty miles, or a day's ride on horseback. Many are still standing. The simple, white adobe chapel of Mission Dolores, for example, built in about 1776, can still be found in the heart of San Francisco, even though it looks a little out of place these days amid the office blocks of the Mission District.

The mission posts were connected by El Camino Real, a 'Royal Road' that ran all the way from the San Diego mission to the Mission San Francisco Solano in Sonoma in the north. The road is still used intensively, and the 101 now follows it in part.

After the mission posts, from the late eighteenth century onwards, the *ranchos* were established, huge estates on which cattle and horses were raised. This was the origin of the Californian landed gentry. The land was taken from the Native Americans with little ceremony. In Northern California the Russians, too, made plans for new settlements. In about

1810 their seal hunters were at work as far south as San Francisco, and about a hundred miles north of the city there is still a Russian River. Nothing came of all Russia's ambitions, however. It was simply too far away. California remained a marginal region for many years, a long strip of forgotten land in the far north-west corner of the old Spanish Empire.

As for the 'Indians', the Native peoples of the coast between San Diego and San Francisco amounted to more than 70,000 souls at the start of colonisation in 1769. In 1821, only 18,000 were left. As a Franciscan missionary said: 'They live well free but as soon as we reduce them to a Christian and community life . . . they fatten, sicken, and die.'

However small their numbers, the influence of the Native Americans on the original landscape of California should not be underestimated. It can be clearly seen in Yosemite National Park, a region of forested mountains inhabited for centuries by the Ahwahneechee and not 'discovered' by white people until 1851. The earliest photographs, taken not long afterwards, show a charming and richly varied landscape, with many meadows, patches of open woodland, and here and there a large solitary tree. It was the result of the forest fires lit by the Natives with great regularity to clear away dry undergrowth, a technique that enabled them to improve their hunting grounds considerably.

After 1851 the traditional forest burning of the Ahwahneechee was forbidden, and later photographs show the results. The park became overgrown, the forests increasingly thick, and the balance between woodland and meadow was lost. The Ahwahneechee disappeared. As the saying went, after 1851 'they didn't make Indians anymore'. In the few photographs that remain, you can watch them grow steadily older. The last of them died in 1931.

Every nation is an 'imagined community', runs a theory proposed by anthropologist and political scientist Benedict Anderson, and the same goes for each of the diverse states of the American federation. California is particularly wayward because its imagined community is still so young.

The story of the original state flag with its walking bear, star, red stripe and the words 'California Republic' is telling. It was hastily sketched on a piece of raw cotton. The American settlers who rose against Mexican rule on 14 June 1846 in Sonoma – Mexico had gained its independence in 1821, including Alta California – needed to be able to fly a flag. The small group of rebels was forced to hold out for just three weeks. The Mexican–American War was raging and regular US troops were happy to take over the government of California, with their own stars and stripes. The Bear Flag vanished into the museum, along with the California Republic.

At that point no more than 5,000 colonists were living in California. Eight years later there were 300,000. San Francisco was a sleepy harbour-side town until 1848. As a result of the gold rush, within three years it was the largest port on the American west coast. Los Angeles, too, was transformed at an astonishing rate from a provincial town into a metrop-olis. In 1884 it had 12,000 residents, in 1886 there were over 100,000.

Links with the rest of America improved rapidly. The first mail to be carried overland from St Louis reached San Francisco on 19 October 1858, at half past seven in the evening – the letters had taken 'only' fifty-five days to cross the Great Plains. Three years later the Pony Express – a meticulously organised chain of ponies and couriers that kept up its relay race day and night – covered the 1,670 miles from St Joseph in Missouri to Sacramento, California, in eight days. The service was extremely expen-sive, the letters had to be ultra-light, but everyone was exceedingly proud of it. Mark Twain made a special stop on a journey to see one of the pony riders flash past, 'like a belated fragment of a storm'.

When the first transcontinental railroad was completed in 1869, that phase came to an end. No pony could compete with the train. Eventually there was a shortened sea route, too, between the east coast and the west, after the first ship steamed through the Panama Canal from the Atlantic Ocean to the Pacific in 1914.

In the years following the Second World War, California grew to become one of the richest states in America. Everything looked extremely prom-ising: the top-class universities, the modern irrigation systems, the flour-ishing agricultural enterprises, the hundreds of films made there every year, the thousands of miles of highway built in the 1950s and 1960s, and the new schools that were opening week after week. California was not merely a state, it was a phenomenon, a dream, the grand finale to the Great Migration, that classic American trek to the paradise of the Far West, which began beside the Atlantic Ocean and didn't stop until it reached the Pacific coast.

Steinbeck was unimpressed. In *Travels* he grumbles, mostly, whether about the 'four-lane concrete highways slashed with speeding cars' or all the modern amenities that in his view were destroying his beloved California. He had never resisted change, he said, 'even when it has been called progress', yet he felt 'resentment toward the strangers swamping what I thought of as my country with noise and clutter and the inevitable rings of junk'.

No, he preferred the redwoods. They were the true natives, 'grown trees when a political execution took place on Golgotha'. They were approaching middle age when the Roman Empire fell. 'To the sequoias everyone is a stranger, a barbarian,' he wrote. 'Could that be why the sequoias make folks nervous?'

Two

IT'S POURING WITH RAIN AGAIN, rattling the roofs of Mendocino, one of those historical tourist towns on California's northern coast, a friendly hotchpotch of wooden houses, pleasant little shops, and restaurants serving only organic health food. Everything looks fresh and cheerful in yellow, pale blue and white, the colours of this little town. High Culture is the order of the day here. No diners selling steak and eggs but instead bistros playing French *chansons*. No one with a four-wheel drive out front but plenty with a Toyota Prius. No shops selling hardware and soup from a can but stores artfully displaying organic potato chips and cheeses and wines from all over the world. No 'drill, drill, drill' from the oil lobby but every week a new high-profile project: electric cars, solar parks, measures to tackle light pollution, bicycle-hire schemes.

This part of California, without intending to be, is a commentary on the rest of America: this is the end of the continent; we can't go any further; we'll have to make do with what we have, but it'll be comfy and clever.

We alight on The Moosse Café. It's a morning for reading newspapers. Amid all the sensible self-indulgence, the *San Francisco Chronicle* reports the latest bad news. For many of the thousand-year-old sequoias, this century may well mark the end. One of the first effects of global warming will be to disperse the coastal mists, the famous Californian early-morning fogs. The survival of this particular species of tree is at stake. Whatever these giants may have put up with over all those centuries, they are utterly dependent on fog.

The author of a letter to the *Press Democrat* of Santa Rosa is no less sombre: 'We are seeing the example of how great the European societies do with socialism. They are all melting down, right in front of us, as we also are.'

We read away the time, but soon we become distracted by two couples who have settled down to the right of us. We can't make out what they're saying, but their facial expressions are interesting enough. The men are clearly peeved. The rain has played havoc with their plans. They're probably from somewhere further inland, not from here. They have firm jaws, taut faces, pointing fingers – clearly go-getters. The women's gestures, by contrast, express a high degree of helplessness. They smile all the time, and whenever they want to ask something they put on a childish voice; the youngest of them consistently flapping her hands as she talks, especially when she becomes excited about some issue or other. Everything they do is aimed at deflecting aggression.

'Those are quite different types from the staunch ladies we came across in diners all over Montana and the Dakotas,' my wife whispers. Pioneer women – and their daughters and granddaughters – were always famous for their self-reliance and independence. Where has that gone?

Almost every European travel writer of the nineteenth century remarked upon the freedom of action enjoyed by American women. In their view it was remarkably far-reaching. Even young girls, for example, could undertake long journeys unescorted – unthinkable in the France of Tocqueville and Beaumont. That independence perhaps had to do with the demands of colonial existence, and later the ways of the pioneer. It was often a lonely life, which meant that social norms were less significant here, and everything was so tough and complicated that all hands were needed, for every task, whether it was a question of altering clothes or driving a wagon. They simply couldn't permit themselves to pay too much heed to prescribed roles for men and women.

In later times, during the great waves of immigration, the position of women was further reinforced, since on arrival they could often find work more quickly and easily than the men. In the twentieth century, American women were increasingly well educated, they were given the vote, and a range of household appliances enabled them to spend more time on things other than housework.

After the Second World War, all this came to an abrupt end. In the American suburbs, a new image of womanhood was created. Gone were the years of robust pioneer wives, of women who kept the factories running during the war and who, as Steinbeck wrote, manned huge articulated trucks on the highways. He commented: 'My god, they must have been Amazons.' That sort of thing was believed to be men's work. Women, especially married women, did not need paid employment. Within two months of the end of the war, some 800,000 women were dismissed from their jobs in aircraft construction, and a comparable number were forced to leave the auto industry and other manufacturing sectors. By 1946 more than two million working women had become unemployed.

In the prosperous post-war years a new definition of the ideal American woman emerged. First of all, she should not work. If she did she would be competing with men, which would make her tough and aggressive. Instead she should devote herself to her family, support her husband and keep herself attractive, eternally positive, not a hair out of place. Her house in the suburbs must be perfect. It was the centre of that universe, the family, around which everything revolved. Roles in this new play – for that is what it tended to resemble – were rehearsed day after day in films and television soaps. The father was the leader who each morning marched off into the rugged outside world to hack out a living in the jungle of business and office. The myth of Teddy Roosevelt had been transplanted wholesale to the second half of the twentieth century. The mother did the caring.

Women like Betty Draper, tragic wife of office macho Don Draper in Mad Men, which is set in the 1960s, took that task extremely seriously. Despite all the washing machines, lawn mowers, televisions and other blessings of the 1950s, life was not easy. In the suburbs, family and friends generally did not live nearby and, like their pretty houses, the women had become detached from the old centre of town. Their husbands expected a wife to be dependent and subservient. But what changed above all was the place of the child.

Under the influence of childcare specialists such as Dr Benjamin Spock, in post-war America and to a lesser degree in Western Europe the emphasis came to be placed on the child's own potential. Roles were reversed. It was no longer the environment that made demands and set boundaries, instead the child was central and the environment had to adjust itself accordingly.

Spock would never have become so popular if his theories had not been rooted in pre-existing American values such as individualism and a powerful desire for self-fulfilment. American children had long been seen as wayward. In one collection of letters by travellers in America, a man who later became a pioneer of the European Community, Max Kohnstamm, a young student at the time, complains vehemently after staying with friends about 'America's public enemy number one: progressive education' and about 'the pandemonium, tyranny and guerrilla war' it produced. 'Like shy, timid shadows, adults totter through the houses where the almighty child-dictators reign.'

That was in 1938. Spock's bestseller, Baby and Child Care, was still several years from publication, but existing theories reinforced the tendency and by doing so pushed American women yet more deeply into their domestic role.

Until the 1950s, childrearing was not regarded as a full-time job anywhere in the world, America included. Women and mothers had their hands full with other things; in the often poor and time-consuming households of the time they had no choice in the matter. In post-war America that changed. The raising of budding little miracles now had to occupy all a woman's attention, and no trouble or expense was to be spared in enabling the little geniuses to flourish.

It's a development that has continued in America to this day. I recall a long conversation with an old acquaintance, a Dutch woman living in a Californian suburb with her American husband. They had two growing children. In her circles, she told me – and on the east coast it's no different – the children had to be perfect. They must be excellently educated and broadly oriented; pre-selection for the best universities began at around the age of ten. Most children therefore took piano or violin lessons at four years old and they really ought to be doing ballet as well by then. From the age of six they started courses in Chinese, sports of every description, and of course charitable activities too.

'Our son has already worked in a soup kitchen for the homeless,' she told me. All very nice, but she wasn't wholly content with those endless demands. After all, you were given no chance to discover the world in an ordinary, childlike manner of your own. 'I'm not sure whether focusing entirely on such a curriculum makes you happy.'

It was no accident that Betty Draper, sitting at home in the evening waiting for her adulterous husband, had women's magazines like *Ladies' Home Journal*, *McCall's* and *Redbook* within reach. They told her how life was to be lived in a completely new and extremely complicated women's world. 'When Jim comes home,' says a wife in a 1954 advertisement for prefabricated houses, 'our family room seems to draw us closer together.' And who is ultimately responsible for togetherness if not the wife?

There was another Betty. In the summer of 1942 one Betty Goldstein graduated summa cum laude from the prestigious Smith College, which admitted only women. Many of her fellow students received that same designation, 'with highest honour', since Smith College offered some of the best university-level education in America.

Betty became a journalist in New York, threw herself heart and soul into the campaigning life of the time, and five years later married an attractive and charming veteran, Carl Friedan. They had a child, then she became pregnant again and to her astonishment was fired from her job. Newspaper editors did not want women with children. The union had no desire to take up her cause since her pregnancy was her own 'fault'. Deeply disappointed, she withdrew to one of the New York suburbs, like so many women of her generation.

In the summer of 1957 there was to be a Smith College reunion. Betty had a plan. She wanted to use the opportunity to interview her fellow students, the class of 1942, and one question would be central: What had become of their ideals and expectations, fifteen years on? She presented the idea to the women's magazine *McCall's*, and everyone there was enthusiastic. It might form the basis for a cheerful story about the ways in which a good education had enriched these women's lives. The working title was 'The Togetherness Women'.

Betty was not easily satisfied, however. She asked questions such as: What difficulties have you found in working out your role as a woman? What are the chief satisfactions of your life today? What are the chief frustrations? She also asked what else they would like to have done. Then something unexpected happened. Instead of cheery tales, a flood of bitterness and frustration was released, with one story after another about isolation, about children for whom they had no affection, about husbands who seemed like visitors from another planet. The women felt humiliated and tucked away out of sight. Betty Friedan spoke about the 'suburban syndrome' to which she, her former classmates and millions of other American women had fallen prey. 'Is this all?' was a question that kept recurring.

During that reunion she also spoke to the new generation of women students, the class of 1957. When Friedan asked those young women about their future, they looked at her with empty eyes: marriage of course. Children. Above all, to give up working. She was profoundly shocked. This is happening in Smith College, she thought, a place that was full of life for us fifteen years ago, full of intellectual excitement. What can possibly have had such a terrible effect on this generation?

Betty's project initially seemed destined to fail. McCall's suddenly lost interest. Ladies' Home Journal wanted to publish the article, but the editors rewrote the story so that it ended with precisely the opposite conclusion. Redbook turned it down. In the end Betty Freidan wrote a book called The Feminine Mystique, which was not published until six years later, in 1963. It became one of the most influential books of the twentieth century. Soon more than three million copies had been sold and it was the starting signal for the second feminist wave, in both America and Europe.

The Feminine Mystique was not the first crack in the country's idealised image of itself. Further truths emerged in that America of the 1940s and 1950s. Several major sociological studies were published that held a mirror up to Americans: How much truth was there in all those stories they told themselves and broadcast to the rest of the world? Was America really the Promised Land? What went on behind the scenes, in the shadows?

In An American Dilemma (1944) Swedish economist Gunnar Myrdal made short work of the American principle of equality. His book was a no-holds-barred description of how the black population, almost a century after the abolition of slavery, was still discriminated against and browbeaten. Four years later America's puritan morality came under scrutiny when, after conducting thousands of interviews, biologist Alfred Kinsey published Sexual Behavior in the Human Male, a detailed report on the sex life of the average American man. Within ten days it had sold 185,000 copies and reached the top of the bestseller lists. Among its conclusions: eighty per cent of successful American businessmen are unfaithful to their wives. That same sexual twilight world was described in the novel *Peyton Place* by Grace Metalious (1956), a sequel of sorts to *Main Street*. There was a great sense of recognition and excitement; within nine months, six million copies had been sold.

In the same period as *The Feminine Mystique*, books appeared in other fields that were to have an equally powerful impact on American public opinion. In 1961 Jane Jacobs published *The Death and Life of Great American Cities*, which set its seal on approaches to cities and to urban regeneration worldwide. A year later Michael Harrington shook the country out of its slumber with his description of the poverty that still prevailed everywhere, despite all the affluence. *The Other America* marked the start of President Lyndon B. Johnson's War on Poverty. Black homosexual essayist and novelist James Baldwin, meanwhile, in *Notes of a Native Son*, *The Fire Next Time* and other books, described his personal quest in a society full of racial and sexual tensions. In 1965 Ralph Nader, with *Unsafe at Any Speed*, presented a pitiless analysis of the dangerous design faults of many American cars. It was the start of the consumer protection movement.

In 1962 marine biologist Rachel Carson published *Silent Spring*, in which she described the consequences for the food chain of the increasing use of pesticides. Birds would be affected first, then ultimately all life on earth. It was partly because of her book that one of the most powerful insecticides, DDT, was banned in the United States in 1972. Her warning is now generally seen as the beginning of environmentalism.

In short, an atmosphere of anxiety and dissatisfaction hung in the air during those years, and it was with the arrival of books and reports of this sort that such feelings crystallised. It did not stop there. James Dean, who had played the central role in the film version of Steinbeck's *East of Eden*, was immortalised in 1955 by his performance in *Rebel Without a Cause*, the story of conflicting generations and value systems. That same year he was killed in a car crash, and so he remained the young hero forever. The film touched upon something quite new, something many young people felt but couldn't yet put into words.

Two years later a new trendsetter arrived with the publication of Jack Kerouac's *On the Road*, the free-ranging account of a trip across America by two wild young men, Sal Paradise and his buddy Dean Moriarty. Steinbeck's *Charley* project was vaguely reminiscent of it, but the aim was totally different. Whereas Steinbeck stressed asceticism and austerity, Kerouac's book was typical of a new generation that emphasised consumption. For Kerouac, travel was no longer about a purpose or a goal but purely about the journey itself, about being rootless, about not giving a damn about anything.

In his letters and his account of his trip, John Steinbeck said not a word about this new movement, even though it was to turn large parts of America upside-down barely five years later and have a massive impact on his own family. To the extent that he noticed it at all, he saw it mainly as yet another expression of the decadence to which 'his' America had fallen prey.

The appeal of figures like James Dean and Jack Kerouac had everything to do with the traditional American instinct for self-fulfilment, the duty to make something of your life that Steinbeck continually held up before his children and that emerges again in the demands made of the offspring of my Californian friend. Opinions differed only about how this self-fulfilment was to be achieved. In that sense, a deep gulf existed between generations.

For the generation that grew up during the Great Depression and the Second World War, peace, work and a degree of material prosperity were marvels in themselves. Unprecedented educational opportunities, modern business and the new life in the suburbs were challenges involving more than enough adventure for most adult Americans in the 1950s. For the post-war generation it was different. Hunger was a problem hardly any of the Kerouac-influenced baby boomers in America, or indeed in Europe, had ever known. A steady job, a house with a garden and a two-car garage, a sound marriage – to them that was all just more of the same and not the reason they were on this earth. Work, many felt, must be meaningful and interesting; the home must be part of a life lived to the full; a relationship must be an eternal flame of fierce emotions – nothing less would suffice. The term 'beat' already existed in the drugs scene, where it was applied to people who'd been robbed of their dope or were emotionally exhausted. Kerouac made it a key word for the new generation, or rather for the part of it that was setting the tone and the trends.

He derived the term from 'beatific' as a way of describing the mood of the beatniks, of all those who stood up to the tide of materialism and self-enrichment.

Lawrence Wright, a journalist at the *New Yorker*, described in his 'baby boomer memoirs' how in the 1950s he and his parents gradually found themselves in an era of 'no-iron shirts and no-wax floors', a time of Formica and polyester, Whirlpool and General Electric. Whatever remained of poverty and injustice would inevitably dissolve into this flood of prosperity; even diseases would disappear, even unhappiness.

All the same, 'to grow up in this heaven on earth was rather like living inside a plastic bag,' he wrote. 'There was a suffocating sense of confinement and of breathing one's own air. Too much order, too little risk, made life anxious and trivial, and yet this was supposed to be a world of freedom and opportunity. This would be the big surprise to my parents' generation. In their minds we were living in an idyll they had created for us, but instead of growing up grateful we grew up angry, confused, and rebellious.'

Berkeley became one of the most important centres of this rebellion, and Telegraph Avenue, close to the university, was a place you simply had to be in those years. In Cody's Books, all the world's brainwork was for sale. Caffe Mediterraneum, the oldest coffee house in the city, was the American counterpart to Café de Flore in Paris. Allen Ginsberg, one of its regulars, wrote his legendary poem 'Howl' there in 1956, a lament for the fate of the 'other' America that was to have at least as much influence as Kerouac's book:

> I saw the best minds of my generation destroyed by madness, starving hysterical naked,
> Dragging themselves through the negro streets at dawn looking for an angry fix . . .

Supporters of Black Power gathered at the café, and the Free Speech Movement – the germ of the international student movement of the 1960s – was invented at its tables. It was, briefly, the eye of the storm.

Driving along Telegraph Avenue today, little is left of all that. True, there's still a row of stalls selling hippie antiques and wild punk para-phernalia to the last of those in search of an angry fix. Some of the doorways house rough sleepers, permanently it seems. Shop windows are boarded up. Cody's Books is for sale. Only Caffe Mediterraneum has managed to keep going despite years of decline, a large airy space with a perpetually raging cappuccino machine, dozens of customers buried in newspapers or notebooks, and the odd table off to the side where some-thing beautiful is flourishing, the way it does in any good coffee house.

This was once the world of my American mother Edith. The green avenue in old Berkeley where she lived with Lou, all gardens and rustic timber houses, is as peaceful and silent as ever, but their house, with its pungent smell of wood, coffee and dusty paper, is now up for sale. The last of the stock of their second-hand bookshop, a garage full of the wisdom of Marx and Marcuse, has been cleared away. The garden, where they so often sat debating with old comrades, is fast becoming a wilderness.

Their son Aron was one of the last beatniks of Berkeley – at least, so he claims. He once explained to me the difference between the beatniks of the 1950s and the hippies that came after them. 'We were individual-ists and non-conformists; we raced off in all directions. The hippies were typical herd animals. We concerned ourselves with the future, we explored modern life; the hippies were nostalgic, withdrawing into the warm and safe past. Above all, we were anti-bourgeois, whereas the hippies just created a bourgeois mentality of their own.'

'It must have been hard to rebel when your parents were already such rebels,' I said. Aron was by then a respectable lawyer with two growing children. He smiled rather shyly and started telling a story about how Edith hadn't even wanted to go out driving with an old friend who'd come to call for her in a car she regarded as too expensive.

My American mother's other son is called David. He has stuck to his principles. For the past thirty years he's been a teacher at the most difficult schools you can find, first Beaumont High School in Oakland – better known to colleagues as the 'Killing Fields' – and now Oakland Technical High School. As a featherweight boxer he can still keep his classes under control, handguns and knives are still confiscated from his pupils every week, the boys and girls still make a tremendous racket because, as they say themselves, 'if there's silence, something bad will happen', and he is still standing. 'If I can no longer get my classes to quieten down, if I no longer have a reasonably good relationship with my students and their world, then I might as well stop.'

I spend half a school day with him, just as I did in the 1990s. Then he was still working in an old barracks and most of the pupils looked shabby. I remember him calling out the names on the absentee list: 'Ill.' 'Arrested.' 'Don't know.' 'Ill.' 'Jail.' 'Ill.'

His current pupils are again almost all black, but the building in which he teaches these days looks fine, the classroom has big electronic screens, and the students no longer shout at each other but send texts instead.

The king of the class is a strikingly well-dressed boy. He sits at the front of the central row and comes over to shake my hand firmly on behalf of everyone. The queen sits in the middle, broad, radiant, with an ultra-tight pink sweater and large gold earrings.

David is trying to teach the class the basic principles of statistics. One girl sits sleeping ostentatiously with her head on her bag, but he ignores her. With his jokes and his questions, he drags most of the children through the tedious lesson material and at first they are all fairly alert. When their attention begins to flag he starts to explain what blood pressure is and how it says something about the condition of your heart. Suddenly everyone is listening again; this is about them, and about their families. He jumps back to the importance of statistics. It's because of all kinds of statistical data that we know how important blood pressure is.

The minutes pass and the class grows restless again. David carries on teaching and questioning, sometimes generally, sometimes picking out one particular student. He implores the class: 'Stay with me! Don't put your pencils down!' Afterwards he tells me that out of this class of thirty-five students, no more than half will go on to college. The rest will probably have a tough life. 'For a child in these neighbourhoods there are only a few options: compete in the race for a high school and college diploma, or subside into the circuit of throwaway jobs at Walmart, or teenage pregnancy, or the army.'

It's not getting any better. The Californian public school system, once the pride of the state, is being subjected to savage cuts like everything else. California's universities are still among the best in the world, and because of endowments and sponsorship they have a lot of money at their disposal, standards are unprecedentedly high, the facilities are fantastic and everyone works terribly hard; 'excellence' is not advertising talk here but the reality. The reverse is true of the rest of the education system. In 1960 the most innovative state in the country devoted around 5.6 per cent of its tax income to education. The figure is now only 3.5 per cent. Every year less than 8,000 dollars is spent per pupil – as against an average for America of around 11,000.

'Build schools and you can close your prisons,' was the slogan of the nineteenth-century idealists. Here precisely the opposite is happening. Since 1980 twenty-one jails have been built in California, and one college campus. In 2011, 9.6 billion dollars was spent on the prison system and just 5.7 billion on higher education. It's a problem right across America, but here it's particularly stark. In the United States as a whole, with its 760 prisoners for every 100,000 inhabitants, seven to ten times as many people are in prison as in other developed countries. Even in the context of American history, these numbers are unprecedented. In 1980 there were 150 prisoners per 100,000 Americans, so the figure has increased fivefold since then.

It's a new development. Under the pretext of the war on drugs, and at a phenomenal cost, an underclass is being created of people who will spend a large proportion of their lives inside or in the shadow of a prison system of a monstrous size: mass detention as an alternative to good schools.

Of course the American education system had serious problems in the past too, and they were to a large extent overcome. In the 1900s schools were inundated by the children of immigrants from Eastern and Southern Europe who didn't speak a word of English. In the 1950s and 1960s the Civil Rights Movement was united in opposition to the 'institutionalised racism' of having separate schools for black and white pupils, and from the 1980s onwards there was increasing criticism of the 'mediocrity' of American education.

In the early years of the twentieth century, when Steinbeck was a boy, less than ten per cent of American children gained a high school diploma. Now the figure is almost eighty-five per cent. In Steinbeck's day only two per cent went on to college, whereas sixty-five per cent do today, although the level of college education has no doubt fallen. All in all, things have improved hugely, but still most schools are in practice either white or, like David's, largely black. In inner city areas of, for example, New York, Chicago and Oakland, the amount spent on schools can be as little as one-third of the amount that goes into education in rich suburbs.

The Spellings report, as it's known, a 2006 analysis commissioned by Secretary of Education Margaret Spellings, concluded that in the standard of its higher education, America has fallen to twelfth place in the ranking of developed countries. As in Britain or the Netherlands, most politicians and major financiers place all their faith in school tests, as if a handful of figures can tell the whole story of families torn apart, teenage pregnancy, drugs, or children running households by the age of twelve. It's easy to reach a judgment on that basis; clearly the fault lies with lazy teachers, bad schools and egotistical unions.

Talking about this after his lessons are over, I watch David turn into one solid lump of sorrowful anger. 'For many of my students, school is the centre of their existence, the only fixed point in their lives. It's an anchor that holds them. Now that's under serious threat, but many politicians are blind to the fact. And nothing is being put in its place.'

If good test scores become the only goal of his work, then he might just as well go off and train chimpanzees. There's something else, too. Students who score below average – and among them, inevitably, are a disproportionate number of poor and socially disadvantaged children – are labelled for the rest of their lives as 'stupid' and 'losers'. It puts paid to any chance they had. The public education system is slowly being replaced by a vast network of private schools, with fees that David's pupils can't possibly pay. Yes, David growls, his union is resisting tooth and nail – and being slowly strangled.

'Stay with me!' But even for the king and queen of the class, life will be tough.

When I used to visit regularly, in the 1980s and 1990s, Telegraph Avenue was long past its heyday, but Berkeley was still one of the most important centres of alternative America. The bulletin board in Edith's kitchen spoke for itself. I check my notes from that time.

Sunday: Benefit Recital To Stop Nuclear Weapons Testing.

Monday: Day Tabling by Pacifist Mothers on the theme of 'Resisting Apartheid'.

Tuesday: Fundraiser for Latin American refugees.

Wednesday: Discussion Meeting held by Radical Elders.

Thursday: Benefit Performance for the Women's Construction Brigade in Nicaragua.

Saturday: Meeting about Socially Responsible Investments.

And so it went on, week after week. Progressive and right-thinking America kept itself pretty busy in those days, with ambulances for Nicaragua, shipments of medical supplies to Vietnam and Cuba, help for refugees from Central America, lawsuits on behalf of homeless people and prisoners with AIDS, marches against the bomb and referendums on environmental protection. At that time there were at least 3,000 anti-war movements spread across the country, and they had an effect. In 1983 an unprecedented proportion of Americans believed too much money was being spent on defence. A *New York Times*/CBS study put the figure at no less than forty-eight per cent.

The activists were not all left-wing liberals. 'The movement couldn't exist without the Church,' I heard from everyone in those days. Whether socialists, Maoists, communists or heretical anarchists, they all pointed to the Church. 'Those nuns, they have the most fantastic names, Sisters of the Bleeding Heart, but if you ring them they come right away. The soup kitchens for the homeless, the peace movement, they all largely depend on the Church.'

Edith and Lou were strictly orthodox. Wealth was theft; everything you owned you must share. Their bookshop served as a refuge for young drifters, and you were never obliged to buy a book. The story in the family was that Lou once had the chance to make a fantastic deal, a huge transaction involving surplus army supplies, shortly after the war. He refused. He didn't want the money, it would taint his family. I remember once arriving back with a couple of bunches of grapes, not realising that some kind of strike was being staged by Mexican grape pickers. It was as if I'd brought home a copy of *Mein Kampf*. Edith exploded. The grapes were red with blood. 'Never, ever do this again!'

We debated communism daily. To Edith, the Soviet experiment was a fascinating alternative to everything that was wrong in America. I never managed to convince her that people like Lou and herself would probably have been locked up almost instantly in the Soviet Union of the time. They were Jewish intellectuals, they were far too honest and, above all, they were born dissidents irrespective of which country they lived in.

Many of the other participants in opposition movements of this kind, I soon noticed, didn't carry nearly as much ideological ballast. They drew their motivation from traditions of which America can be proud: a warm heart, a profound sense of justice, a hatred of politics and a readiness to help the neighbours at any time. As one of them once said to me: 'Our committees and activist groups consist mostly of decent people who want nothing more than to see other people treated decently too. But they can get incredibly angry if that doesn't happen.'

That's still the case. Such groups, however small, should not be underestimated. These are the sort of people who did the legwork in the election campaign that brought President Obama to power in 2008.

One aspect of this 'other America' strikes every outsider immediately, namely how fragmented it is. Whether it's a matter of the environment, the wars in Iraq and Afghanistan, repression in Central America or help for the homeless and illegal immigrants, in the Bay Area alone dozens of groups are active. There are umbrella organisations, but even they have little idea of exactly what they're bringing together. It's often impossible to find anyone who can provide concrete information on either the number of participants or the outcome. The informal network is strong, and with all the new possibilities offered by the internet it's often extraordinarily effective, but the various groups are like loose sand, eluding any attempt to get a grip on them.

At election time, volunteers from all these groups support the campaigns of their favourite candidates, in exchange for certain political commitments on their part, of course. So although the people manning the local campaign offices are generally a mixed bunch, it's rare for a broad alliance of liberals or progressives or whatever they call themselves to emerge. Even alternative America is ultimately thoroughly American, as individualist as all those farmers who plough their own fields.

A sense of solidarity did once exist, at least to some degree. Lou told me about his childhood on New York's Lower East Side in the early 1920s. His world was no bigger than five buildings to the left and five to the right, with a Polish block around the corner, an Italian block next to it and the Jewish block in the centre. The streets were full of carts, horses and pedlars. Sometimes two musicians came by with a trumpet and a violin and they would call up from the street: 'Mom, may I have a dime?' The women would open the windows and throw a coin down. 'There's no place that has produced so many journalists and politicians as the Lower East,' Lou would say proudly. 'There we learned what people can do to each other. Bad and good.'

He'd remained true to his ideals, experiencing at first hand the history of the 'other America', from protests against evictions during the Depression, the boycott of Germany and Japan in the 1930s – dates with girls wearing Japanese silk stockings were taboo – right up to the Civil Rights Movement and the Vietnam protests of the 1960s and 1970s. His brother brought him up on stories about the Haymarket Martyrs, about the legendary campaigner and singer-songwriter Joe Hill, the great strikes of the 1910s, and the dreamland on the other side of the world, the Soviet Union. He learned the whole repertoire of the American workers' movement:

> That's the Rebel Girl. That's the Rebel Girl
> To the working class she's a precious pearl.
> She brings courage, pride and joy
> To the fighting Rebel Boy.

Lou's great friend throughout those years was Milton Wolff, who was jailed at a young age for tearing up a swastika flag on a German ship. During a meeting of the League of Young Communists in 1937, an unknown young man asked which of those present wanted to go and fight with him in Spain. Milton was the only one to put up his hand. He eventually became the last commander of the American volunteers, the Abraham Lincoln Brigade. During the Second World War he worked for the Office of Strategic Services (the OSS), forerunner to the CIA. One of his jobs there was to act as liaison with the communist resistance in Italy and France.

The American workers' movement bears no comparison to that of Europe. Collective action was seen by most people as un-American, inappropriate in a nation of individualists. The 'reds' were fiercely opposed. Yet people like Milton and Lou were certainly not alone. The American Communist Party, including all its splinter groups, had between 60,000 and 70,000 members. Even after the war, Fifth Avenue in New York was always packed with demonstrators during the 1 May procession, and filled with music and red flags. Ten years later there was hardly anyone left who dared say he'd ever been a member of a left-wing party of any kind. You could belong to a union, but that was the limit of it. When I interviewed a number of older activists in the 1980s, nothing had changed in that respect. At best they used words like 'sympathiser' or said they'd been 'close to' some movement or other.

'According to the history books, the Cold War began in nineteen forty-eight,' Milton told me. 'But for me it all started in nineteen forty-five. Franco was allowed to do as he liked, but people like me, who had opposed him, were thrown out of the military as soon as the war ended. Our army files were stamped "PA" – Premature Anti-Fascist.'

He soon became estranged from the Communist Party, as did Lou some years later. They were too self-willed for such a rigid organisation. Nevertheless they were affected in all kinds of ways by the McCarthy witch hunts of the 1950s.

'They didn't need to lock us all up,' one of their friends once said to me. 'It was enough that for years we had to pour all our energies into simple questions like: How can we stay out of jail? How can we keep our families together? A gap was created, a whole generation wide, and we didn't know how to bridge it. That was the great achievement of McCarthy and co. We never did manage to recover.'

Three

IN NEARBY ORINDA, WHERE WE STAY WITH FRIENDS, another class struggle is underway in the autumn of 2010, the war against leaf blowers. Orinda is a hilly dormitory town of 20,000 or so residents, about ten miles north-east of Oakland. The houses – with an average sale price of 1.3 million dollars – are spread out among ancient oaks, sequoias and larches. The children go to excellent schools, the parents are prosperous and well educated, and in the daytime all you can hear is the birds, a few children shouting and a distant car. Then suddenly there are the leaf blowers. The whole neighbourhood is filled with a blaring din as one garden after another is meticulously blasted clean by Mexican maintenance teams. It goes on all afternoon. The day after tomorrow it will be the turn of the other side of the avenue. Next week they'll be back.

One of the residents, furious about the noise and the dust that drifts down onto his organic salad plot, has started a campaign: No Blow. As in several other Californian towns, the campaigners are asking for a ban on leaf blowers. 'It's an aggressive and obnoxious purification ritual. You're getting rid of all the waste on your property and sending it over to your neighbors.' They have produced official estimates; a grandmother with a rake and a broom takes only twenty per cent more time to clear the leaves off a lawn than a gardener with a leaf blower.

The gardeners and libertarians think that's nonsense: leaf blowers are far quieter now than they used to be, and anyhow all those respectable people who complain still want their vast lawns to be immaculate, 'manicured like in a magazine'.

The blower war touches a nerve. The *New Yorker* points out that the

conflict has led to a kind of referendum about the meaning of the word
'neighbour' in a modern suburb. Do you and your neighbours form a
community, or do you merely tolerate each other? Meanwhile the Mexican
maintenance teams are hitting back. They've gone on strike and occupied
the sidewalk outside the town hall. A ban on blowers would cost jobs.
Class war!

Our friends take us along to a remarkable site not far away, the Crosses
of Lafayette. It's a simple war memorial, and its simplicity makes it all
the more impressive. We see merely a slope where thousands of white
wooden crosses have been planted, with two American flags at the top
and a large sign saying 'In Memory of Our Troops'. Every Sunday new
crosses are painted and added to the rest, one for every soldier killed the
previous week in the Iraq War. The total since 2003 now stands at more
than 4,000.

Most of the crosses are anonymous; sometimes a name has been painted
on: 'Keith Jesse More, 1978–2006'. 'Until we meet again. Mom, Dad.' One
has a crutch leaning against it. 'We will not forget you.' Other crosses
are surrounded by flowers. Occasionally there's a Star of David instead
of a cross, even in a few cases a crescent moon. 'Denison' – his cap hangs
over the cross. 'Days of pain for a lifetime of pride, Mom, Dad' – another
crutch. 'Thank you for serving.' 'May God bless you, Jake Yelner.'

This sea of crosses, without any commentary, elicits responses of
profound intensity. Parents and other family members come to lay flowers,
sobbing, but from passing cars there are sometimes volleys of abuse:
'Filthy traitors!' One elderly couple even began a lawsuit, determined to
have their daughter's cross removed. It's all very ambiguous, as are the
feelings of most of the people around here. This is an ode to the dead,
and at the same time one big anti-war monument, a slope covered in
grief and loss and at the same time a field full of protest because it makes
the price of the American war cult horribly visible.

The reality is hard to face. There are of course some honourable exceptions, but no traveller who follows the daily news on Fox and KSFO in
the diners and breakfast rooms will have the impression of travelling
through a country caught up in two wars simultaneously. There's a lot
of enthusiastic flag-waving, a great deal of theorising, and of course the

inevitable pictures, but to an even greater extent than in Europe, the reality of the fighting in Iraq and Afghanistan is kept out of the news on the main popular stations. These are two separate worlds.

In Steinbeck's time, half a century ago, the army was still very much part of society. The average soldier in the Second World War was what was called an 'American Everyman'. The vast majority of GIs were conscripts, and they were the personification of American patriotism, prepared to risk their lives for their country in that Good War. It was 'our army', Americans said, simply because it was made up of 'us'. Which also meant that after the war, everyone picked up their ordinary lives again. The army was consigned to the background, a trend further reinforced by the isolationist tendencies of many politicians of the time.

As recently as 1948, Geoffrey Gorer described the majority of Americans as anti-militaristic. Not because they disliked fighting but because they had an aversion to authority, and any military apparatus will inevitably demand a high degree of discipline and obedience. He came to that conclusion after a series of conversations with GIs who had recently returned from the war. Most had deeper grievances against their own officers than against the enemy.

In the 1960s everything changed. Flag and fatherland, values about which a silent consensus existed in the 1950s, became loaded and confusing concepts. According to some – and they later included Steinbeck – the soldiers defending South Vietnam from communism were exactly the same kind of patriots as the GIs during the Second World War. Others claimed it was the conscientious objectors, those who respected the moral values of America, who were the real heroes. President Richard Nixon eventually decided to end conscription and since the mid-1970s America has had an army composed purely of professional soldiers. 'Our army' became 'them'.

This had huge political, social and indeed psychological consequences. One in ten Americans had some sort of combat role in the Second World War. More than sixty years later, the country finds itself fighting the two lengthiest wars it has ever been involved in, yet only one in 200 Americans has had anything directly to do with either of them. As Sergeant Todd Bowers, a veteran, told the Washington Post: 'It's very common to sit in a room of 100 people, and none of those individuals has ever met an Iraq or Afghanistan veteran.' In 1975, three out of every four members of Congress had served in the armed forces in one way or another. Currently the figure is just one in five. Only a few have sons or daughters in uniform.

In the words of the then defense secretary, Robert Gates, in a recent speech he gave to Duke University: 'For a growing number of Americans, service in the military, no matter how laudable, has become something for other people to do.' The ties between the American nation and those who actually fight America's wars are loosening. 'To most citizens, this war is an abstraction,' Gates warned, 'a distant and unpleasant series of news items that do not affect them personally.'

That gap between political slogans and personal reality is widened even further by the fact that no war has been fought on American soil for almost a century and a half. For those who still claim that Europeans are from Venus and Americans from Mars, here are a few figures, for comparison. In the First World War alone, 1.3 million French soldiers died, more than twice as many as the total number of American dead in all the wars the United States has fought from 1776 to the present day. During the Second World War, 420,000 American troops were killed, but among American civilians, in the two world wars put together, the figure is less than 2,000. The number of civilian deaths in Poland alone during the Second World War was close to 5.5 million. The Vietnam War, which lasted fifteen years, cost almost 60,000 American soldiers their lives. The toll on the Vietnamese side was between fifteen and fifty times as great, with estimates ranging from one to three million, most of them civilians.

Whereas the lives of generations of Europeans and Asians in the twentieth century have been defined by war and its aftermath, the vast majority of Americans – with the exception of refugees and veterans and their families – have no personal experience of war these days, or hardly any, even at second or third hand. I recall a trip through Germany in the spring of 1999, when the NATO bombing of Belgrade had just begun. Wherever I went – in bars, in transport cafés – everyone was talking about their own wartime experiences, and the stories they'd heard from their parents and grandparents. It all came to the surface again.

That would be unthinkable in America. The horrors of the Civil War are history, the millions of GIs who served in the Second World War have also more or less left the stage, and everyone prefers to ignore the begging and homeless Vietnam veterans. War has become increasingly abstract, too, and therefore easier. With unmanned aircraft, drone pilots can carry out precision bombing in Afghanistan from a base in Arizona without any risk to themselves. To many Americans today, the message of the twentieth century is that war works, or at least that it's an option worth considering. The soldiers and veterans know better, but who listens to them?

Now that the army is no longer 'us' but 'them', countless loud, patriotic symbols are deployed to shout across that increasing distance. In New England especially, at the start of our trip, practically every village was hung with the stars and stripes, as if every morning marked the start of another national holiday. The presidency used to be a civilian office; the nation was led by one of its citizens. Now a president is only truly credible if he plays the role of commander-in-chief with verve.

The few hundred thousand Americans on active service – and it is largely the poorest who do the job – are praised to the skies at every opportunity. They are living proof that America is still a country worth dying for. Those killed are quite often given a hero's funeral, with hundreds of people lining the streets. 'Supporting the troops' is an expensive duty. In a 2010 Gallup poll, only seven per cent of those questioned believed that the American military is 'stronger than it needs to be'. In other words, ninety-three per cent of Americans want no tampering with their current military superiority. A politician who expresses any doubt at all about the value of using armed force is instantly pilloried: Appeaser! Isolationist! Sissy!

All that patriotic rhetoric, all those symbols and all those sacrifices by 'our troops' bind this fragmented nation together over and over again, and the need for that imagined community grows as domestic tensions mount. A slope with thousands of white crosses does not fit within such a story.

In a military sense, America is still the most powerful country in the world. Every other nation counts its missiles in the dozens, whereas the Pentagon clusters them into batches of a thousand. The US Navy has around ten carrier strike groups active at any one time. Each group comprises military units of 7,500 men, sixty or seventy aircraft and its own aircraft carrier, a huge floating airbase that can be deployed at a moment's notice anywhere in the world. Other countries have one at most. In the late 1950s the United States had around 150 military bases worldwide. It currently has some 900 – the exact number, like their size and location, is secret.

Experts have calculated that if the next twelve countries in the military world ranking were to join forces, America would still be the most powerful. Yet it has been in a virtually permanent state of fear and war for the past seven decades, ever since 1941. Victory in 1945 did not bring real peace. On the contrary, intense feelings of insecurity remained. Every emergency, every declaration of war in the world was a fresh danger signal.

That perpetual fear seems all the more remarkable given that America, from a strategic point of view, is in an extremely safe geographical position, bounded by two oceans. Some believe the Japanese attack on Pearl Harbor in December 1941 and 9/11, sixty years later, were hugely traumatic events for precisely that reason. America really did seem to be within reach of a foreign enemy.

Others argue that their country's safe location has created unrealistic expectations of security. Many politicians and ordinary citizens nowadays have the idea that this 'great' and 'unique' nation need never accept even the threat of aggression. A 'preventive war' or the suspension of treaties, constitutions and civic freedoms – such things are permissible in their eyes if there is even the slightest threat to national security.

Still, putting aside for a moment all the fine talk about security, freedom and democracy, it's undeniable that in the second half of the twentieth century there were strategic reasons for America to maintain a huge military apparatus. As diplomat George Kennan said to his bosses at the State Department in 1948, in a burst of candour: 'We have about 50 per cent of the world's wealth but only 6.3 per cent of its population.' The challenge for American policymakers, he believed, was 'to devise a pattern of relationships that will permit us to maintain this disparity'. Kennan was thinking above all of diplomacy. Most American politicians, however, believed that the main resource it had for preserving America's special status was its military power.

This led to an unusual combination of power displays, involving a permanent presence of American troops on hundreds of bases spread all over the planet and a demonstrable preparedness to intervene militarily, whether openly or in secret. That would safeguard international stability, guarantee American access to markets and resources, and increase American power and influence.

In Japan, South Korea, Indonesia, parts of the Middle East and post-war Europe this formula worked. Elsewhere, particularly in Cuba, Vietnam, France, Latin America and later in Iraq, Afghanistan and Pakistan, the results were dubious, even catastrophic.

So after 1945 there was none of the disarmament that had, as a rule, taken place after earlier wars. By late 1950, American troops were deeply embroiled in the Korean War. The defence budget shot up from thirteen billion dollars in 1951 to fifty billion in 1953, while the US nuclear arsenal increased from 300 atomic bombs in 1951 to 1,300 in 1953.

When China came to the aid of North Korea in October 1950 and the Americans were driven further and further back, General Douglas MacArthur actually asked President Truman for permission to deploy atomic weapons on the battlefield. The chief of staff of the US Air Force, General Hoyt Vandenberg, went a step further: why not launch a pre-emptive nuclear strike against the Soviet Union? Truman refused. 'I could not bring myself to order the slaughter of 25,000,000 non-combatants,' he wrote later in his memoirs. 'I just could not make the order for a Third World War.'

After the Second World War, to a greater degree than anywhere else, a national security state arose in America – a powerful complex of businesses, institutions and political interest groups that derived their position, financial resources and privileges primarily from a permanent atmosphere of crisis and insecurity. It was one big feedback loop that, in the words of a military historian and former teacher at West Point, Andrew Bacevich, 'transformed tax dollars into appropriations, corporate profits, campaign contributions and votes'. Countless think tanks, publications, television stations and lobby groups fattened the monster further by continually warning of new dangers and then thinking up military solutions for them. It continues to grow.

In his description of America in 1960, Steinbeck was not conscious of where the military apparatus was headed. 'It is a strange thing how Americans love to march when they don't have to,' he wrote in *America and Americans*, and he describes the army as a community of citizen soldiers, with a small core of professional troops, who grudgingly do their duty and then, as veterans, endlessly dredge up memories of the 'best time of their lives'. Yet, barely a month after his trip with Charley ended, on 17 January 1961, the term 'military–industrial complex' was used for the first time, and it was not a pacifist or a left-wing Democrat who launched the concept but the incumbent president.

As commander-in-chief of US troops in Europe, Republican Dwight D. Eisenhower had seen from close proximity how the American armaments industry grew beyond all recognition during the war years and how, after the Second World War, it proved impossible to put the genie back in the bottle. Above all he was deeply worried by the permanence of the system. Military forces, he said, ought to grow or shrink as the need arose. Subtly inverting the biblical metaphor, he said: 'American makers of plowshares could, with time and as required, make swords as well'.

It became the main theme of his valedictory speech. He was laying down the responsibilities of office, he said, with a real sense of disappointment. There was no lasting peace in sight, although 'happily, I can say that war has been avoided'. In his speech he focused on the ever-growing number of manufacturers that were wholly or partly involved in the production of armaments. 'This conjunction of an immense military establishment and a large arms industry is new in the American experience.' He recognised the urgent need for these developments but warned of the consequences: 'The potential for the disastrous rise of misplaced power exists and will persist.'

Eisenhower's diaries and private notes reveal that his words were prompted in part by worries about the economy. The arms race, with its accompanying hazards of overspending and inflation, might in the long run stifle the nation. 'To amass military power without regard to our economic capacity would be to defend ourselves against one kind of disaster by inviting another.' He ground his teeth as he watched the 1958 military budget, under the influence of 'missile gap' hysteria, grow to more than half of all federal spending.

To Eisenhower it was not just a matter of expense, however. He feared above all 'the total influence – economic, political, even spiritual' of the complex he had identified, an influence that was felt 'in every city, every State house, every office of the Federal government'. His warning had no effect. Even though the percentage of its budget that America officially spends on defence has fallen since 1961 – in 2010 it amounted to twenty-eight per cent of income from federal taxation – actual spending has continued to rise, by sixty-seven per cent between 2000 and 2010 alone. What's more, the army is now increasingly using 'contractors', in other words private companies and mercenary units, and outgoings of that kind are quite often invisible.

Still more military expenditure is hidden within other budgets. The CIA, for example, carries out thousands of Special Access Programs (SAPs) annually: undercover activities that range from spying to sabotage and the use of paramilitary violence. The Pentagon is obliged to send Congress a list of such operations every year, although not everything needs to be mentioned. In 2010 alone there was a file more than 300 pages thick. Experts believe that at least 1000 government agencies operate in this twilight zone, along with a similar number of private firms. Since 9/11 their budgets have doubled to an estimated seventy billion dollars a year.

It has been estimated that in total around half of American federal tax revenues are spent on the military–industrial complex, or more than 2,000 dollars per annum for every American. (By comparison, France and Britain spend less than 900 dollars a head, the Netherlands some 750, Germany and Italy less than 600.) For the annual cost of one American soldier in Afghanistan, twenty schools could be built. The Iraq adventure alone cost 12.5 billion dollars a month, and that figure doesn't include the billions in disability pensions that will have to be paid out to veterans over the coming fifty years. This is to say nothing of the most important aspect, the human tragedy: the estimated hundreds of thousands of Iraqi dead, the 30,000 American wounded (5,000 killed), and the state of total devastation and chaos in which Iraq was ultimately left.

These wars were not just financial disasters, they absorbed a huge amount of political attention. During the first decade of the twenty-first century the centre of gravity of the world economy began to move from the West to Asia, a shift that will have major historical consequences. Yet America focused its political energies on two places on the globe where it was entangled in a war of its own choosing: Iraq and Afghanistan. In short, in the words of historian Ira Katznelson, America has developed into 'a crusading state', with 'a permanent war economy'.

All the same, something remarkable has happened in recent years. More and more criticism is coming from the military apparatus itself. Andrew

Bacevich, quoted earlier, made a career with the army, fighting in Vietnam and teaching at top military academies, but eventually he grew sick of all the patriotic talk about 'supporting our boys'. Precisely because of his experience as a soldier he knew as well as anyone that his fellow Americans were grossly overestimating the usefulness of the army and the positive impact of military intervention. It was often possible to achieve far more by diplomatic means.

Romanticised images of war in films and television series, Bacevich wrote, along with the average American's lack of war experience, gave the American people a highly unrealistic and even dangerous idea of what fighting and military life actually involve. In other words, Custer's mistake at the Little Bighorn was being repeated again and again. In March 2007 Bacevich was more specific than ever, describing the strategy of 'preventive war' as 'immoral, illicit and imprudent'. Two months later his only son, a first lieutenant in the US Army, was killed in Iraq.

The message put out by Robert Gates in the latter years of his time as secretary of defense was essentially the same. 'Be modest about what military force can accomplish, and what technology can accomplish,' he said in 2008 to students at the National Defense University in Washington. 'Never neglect the psychological, cultural, political and human dimensions of warfare, which is inevitably tragic, inefficient and uncertain'.

In 2010 Gates explicitly repeated Eisenhower's warning: 'Does the number of warships we have and are building really put America at risk when the US battle fleet is larger than the next 13 navies combined, 11 of which belong to allies and partners? Is it a dire threat that by 2020 the United States will have only 20 times more advanced stealth fighters than China? These are the kinds of questions Eisenhower asked as commander-in-chief. They are the kinds of questions I believe he would ask today.'

Half a century on, and nothing has changed.

Four

TO JOHN STEINBECK, SAN FRANCISCO was the only place in America that deserved the honourable title 'the City'. It was his great lost love. 'It had been kind to me in the days of my poverty and it did not resent my temporary solvency,' he wrote. He had spent his 'attic days' there, 'fledged there, climbed its hills, slept in its parks, worked on its docks, marched and shouted in its revolts. In a way I felt I owned the City as much as it owned me.'

San Francisco is a city of rapidly changing moods: one minute the sparkling Californian sun, the next those ever-recurring fogs that make the hilly streets vanish like ghosts that are sure to return. In the past fifty years many American cities have shot upwards, and all those silvery towers have given the urban landscape a quite different face. That is particularly true of San Francisco. The hills had always determined its look, with the city lying like a nice bumpy carpet laid over them. High-rise construction tore that fabric to pieces. For over a century San Francisco was an archetypal City on the Hill. That time has gone.

Steinbeck's description reads like a renewed declaration of love. In 1960 it was the old, relatively low-rise San Francisco that unfurled before his eyes, without the glistening Transamerica Pyramid, without the hefty concrete tendrils of the freeways and without the Manhattan of Market Street. Large passenger ships bound for China and Japan still tied up at the piers around the Embarcadero, and fishing boats still bobbed next to Fisherman's Wharf. Close to the Golden Gate Bridge, 'the necklace bridge over the entrance from the sea that led to her', he stopped at a parking spot to look at San Francisco 'rising on her hills like a noble city in a happy dream'. A city built on hills always has an advantage over flat places, he wrote, 'but this gold and white acropolis rising wave on wave against the blue of the Pacific sky was a stunning thing, a painted thing like a picture of a medieval Italian city which can never have existed . . . Over the green higher hills to the south, the evening fog rolled like herds of sheep coming to cote in the golden city.' It had never looked more lovely.

In *Travels* Steinbeck writes that he immediately travelled on to Monterey, another half-day's drive south. In reality he and Elaine stayed in San Francisco for five days, eating and drinking with old friends and visiting relatives. Steinbeck spent a lot of time with Barnaby Conrad – former secretary to Sinclair Lewis, old-fashioned adventurer and a real Steinbeck man. Conrad was one of the few American bullfighters to have performed in the arenas of both Spain and Latin America. Two years earlier he'd been seriously wounded. His book *Matador* was chosen by Steinbeck as the best of its year.

In the autumn of 1960, Conrad had his hands full with the filming of one of Steinbeck's short stories, 'Flight', but production was proving difficult. When John and Elaine visited him in San Francisco, the money had almost run out. To refloat the enterprise, Steinbeck offered to narrate certain scenes. Conrad, who had never dared to ask, naturally leapt at the proposal. He described later how they sat together on the terrace outside Enrico's café, Charley big and obedient in the corner near their table. 'Look at that dog over there,' Steinbeck said. 'Yesterday in Muir Woods he lifted his leg on a tree that was fifty feet across, a hundred feet high and a thousand years old. What's left in life for that dog after that supreme moment?'

Together they drove to Monterey, and after looking around for a while they found a beautiful place, close to the ocean, where Steinbeck could tell his story. He did it all for friendship's sake. He hated this kind of performance and kept forgetting the words, but he pushed on through it somehow.

'He looked very tired,' his sister Beth Ainsworth said later. After the film work, John and Elaine stayed in Beth's house on 11th Street in nearby Pacific Grove. In the 1930s and 1940s he'd lived there himself, roaming these neighbourhoods with his old friend Charlie Chaplin, who was fascinated by Steinbeck's books and the places his stories were set. But since his marriage to Elaine he'd not been back.

The simple cottage at number 147, painted red, is still there, a little way back from the road and entirely focused on its small, intimate garden. Music carries across from one of the neighbouring buildings and someone along the street is cooking a tasty stew. There is a lot here that reminds me of Steinbeck's house in Sag Harbor. The place has the same atmosphere, the trees are just as strongly scented, and here too an ocean roars, breathing like a sleeping giant.

The coast is three blocks away, a sheer cliff with boulders strewn in the water below. The waves crash against the rocks, seagulls screech as they go about their day's fishing, and amid the heaving seaweed basks the occasional sea otter, sunning itself on its back like a sleepy cat. The foam flies up from the surf, making rainbow after rainbow, violet and red and everything in between. It's a magical place. You don't ever want to leave.

All his life Steinbeck remained a would-be marine biologist. He and his great friend Ed Ricketts had a lot in common and it's no accident that Ricketts made his living here. Since warm and cold currents come together at Monterey, this part of the coast has a remarkable diversity of marine fauna, a treat for any biologist. Near a headland a little way off, a large family of seals is sunbathing on the sand, at least fifty of them, young and old together, the great patriarch highest up the beach. Near the ruins of a public swimming pool, the Grill at Lovers Point has been pluckily plodding on through the decades since 1936. 'I don't care if not many people come,' the owner says. She cooks fries, fish and hamburgers for a handful of guests and spends the rest of the time looking through her telescope. 'Here you've always got the ocean.'

A local journalist, dispatched by the *Monterey Peninsula Herald*, found Steinbeck while he was mending his sister's front gate, dressed in corduroy trousers and a shapeless green shirt. 'I haven't got the right tools,' he grinned. 'That's always my excuse.' Then, surveying the result: 'It won't stay and it won't come off. That's the way I make things.' The two men had coffee in the back garden along with an old acquaintance. Steinbeck was asked whether he might ever come back to the Monterey Peninsula to live. He bowed his head, thought for a moment and said: 'No. I don't know anybody here anymore. Not many people, anyway. I used to walk down the street and know everybody I met. Now I'm a stranger.'

In the *San Francisco Chronicle* of Sunday 6 November 1960 a more substantive interview appeared in which Steinbeck recalled 'his' old San Francisco. 'In the Twenties and Thirties it was a crime to be poor anywhere, except in Europe or San Francisco. Here it was mostly fun. If you had clean fingernails, a little spit polish on your shoes, and four silver dollars in your pocket you could have a wonderful time.'

As a journalist he'd actually seen plenty of misery here. In the 1930s, one of the editors at the *San Francisco News* had got wind that 'over in the valley' some people were starving and asked: 'Do you want to go over and see what it is all about?' Steinbeck went and was deeply touched by the plight of the migrant workers driven out of the Midwest by the dust storms. That experience became the basis for *The Grapes of Wrath*.

In the *Chronicle* article, however, he talks mainly about the things that concerned him at that moment, about King Arthur, about his next book, *The Winter of Our Discontent*, and about the subject that was increasingly occupying his thoughts: immorality, which he defined as 'taking out more than you are willing to put in'. He repeats his pessimistic view of the country. 'The American people are losing their ability to be versatile, to do things for themselves, to put back in. When people or animals lose their versatility, they become extinct.'

The following Tuesday was the day of the presidential election and Steinbeck, as an 'ardent and veteran Democrat', did not mince words. He believed that thanks to the Eisenhower government it was 'socially fashionable to be stupid'. Present-day America, he felt, needed a King Arthur.

In a medieval guise, he was harking back to a myth created by Teddy Roosevelt. As Steinbeck saw it, the American Western was a direct successor to the Arthur stories. 'The King is the man who solves everything with a gun,' he said. 'The Western has its Guinevere and Gawain, all the characters. Arthur did not originate in England; all peoples have their Arthur, and need him. He is created out of a need, when they are in trouble. America's Arthur is coming because the people need him.' He predicted a resounding victory – whoever the winner might be.

The Sunday edition of the *Chronicle* in which the interview was published opens with a report about a group of a hundred men, women and children who, at the request of the Office of Civil Defense, were to spend two days in a nuclear shelter that weekend to test it out. 'I brought lipstick, homework and my Kennedy button,' fifteen-year-old Anne McQuilling declared. 'I'm here to convert a couple of Nixon fans.'

The paper's 'question man' asked random passers-by whether they thought America's defence was fit for purpose. Clarence Gibby agreed with Kennedy: 'This country is in a bad shape. Let's not kid ourselves; the Russians have the lead.' Elinor Magee put her faith in the effectiveness of the new American missiles: 'That's good enough for me.' There was speculation as to when, following mice, dogs and monkeys, the first human would be blasted into space. Soon, the journalist felt. He was right.

The rest of the paper is full of election news. Adlai Stevenson was in the city too, and he used the budget deficit they'd left after eight years as a stick to beat the Republicans with – eighteen billion! Nixon spoke in Oakland and said, hoarse after giving so many speeches, that in the past few days, millions of voters had sided with him. 'The tide is running in our direction', was his slogan. 'My friends,' he said in conclusion, 'it is because we are on the side of right, it is because we are on God's side that America will meet this challenge.' Despite the pouring rain, his cheerleaders, the Nixonettes, flapped all around him with iron-clad jollity.

In Ohio a girl had tried to throw a tomato at Kennedy. In New York the Democratic candidate had announced that he didn't simply want to go down in history as a president who prevented war, but as a president of whom the historians would say: 'He not only laid the foundations for peace in his time, but for generations to come as well.' In Chicago, within an hour of each other, two men were arrested for running behind Kennedy's car with automatic weapons under their coats. They claimed they were carrying them purely 'for their own protection'.

Steinbeck could not escape the election. He almost immediately found himself at loggerheads with his Republican sisters. 'Each evening we promised, "Let's just be friendly and loving. No politics tonight." And ten minutes later we would be screaming at each other. "John Kennedy was a so-and-so—" . . . "Father would turn in his grave if he heard you." "No, don't bring him in, because he would be a Democrat today." . . . "You talk like a Communist." "Well, you sound suspiciously like Genghis Khan."'

Compromise was impossible, forbearance out of the question. If a stranger had heard them, Steinbeck wrote, he 'would have called the police to prevent bloodshed'. He generally had a good relationship with his sisters, but when it came to politics his sister Esther in particular could get very emotional. She was extremely conservative; she didn't want to know about John's glamorous existence and she distrusted everything he was involved in.

It's one of the few moments in *Travels* when Steinbeck openly declares his political preferences. He was a popular writer, and if he wanted to remain one he couldn't afford to flaunt his political beliefs too often. But here he couldn't resist. Rightly so. A portrait of America without fierce political debates is unthinkable, and however much Steinbeck restrained himself, he was unable to avoid including them. Kitchen-table arguments are part of American democracy and have been from the very beginning. Way back in the eighteenth century, endless debates between the Hamiltonians and the Jeffersonians, supporters of Alexander Hamilton and Thomas Jefferson, were rife in the young republic.

The Hamiltonians focused on the big cities. They stood for industrialisation, modernisation and a strong central government. The Jeffersonians were distrustful of all those urban influences. Their ideal was the small-town community of trust, over which a central government had only limited authority. Jefferson advocated 'a wise and frugal government' that would concern itself with peace and order, and aside from that let everyone go their own way, a government that 'shall not take from the mouth of labor the bread it has earned'.

To this day many political debates in America can be traced back to that particular difference of opinion, even though the parties switch sides from time to time. Sometimes it is mainly the left that propagates Jefferson's point of view – in the 1960s, for example – and sometimes mainly the right, as now.

Whenever economic problems arise, all sorts of populist movements pop up in between the two, and they are based, in various ways, on a radical kind of individualism: the right to make your own choices in many different fields, in the face of the power of the state and big business. In the late nineteenth century, for example, there was the People's Party, which opposed big business and the gold standard. During the

Great Depression, a number of popular movements emerged that opposed the power of the banks, inflamed in part by radio talks by the anti-Semitic priest Charles Coughlin. The 1960s saw the formation of the John Birch Society, which opposed the United Nations, the communists and above all Supreme Court Judge Earl Warren, a true liberal. In our day the Tea Party is all the rage, with its determination to be rid of Wall Street, taxation, immigration, 'socialist' Europe and established politics in general.

The 'Red Peril' is a classic theme. In *Travels* Steinbeck describes a cheerful conversation in a village store at an intersection somewhere in Minnesota. He bought dog biscuits and a tin of tobacco there, and tried to engage in a conversation about the elections, but the shopkeeper didn't really want to talk about politics. He had to do business with everyone and 'could not permit himself the luxury of an opinion'. But he had a twinkle in his eye, so they broached the subject after all and talked about emotions and the disputatious conversations of his customers.

The Russians were the ideal scapegoat, the two men agreed. 'Hardly a day goes by someone doesn't take a belt at the Russians.' Yet no one there had ever met a Russian. 'That's why they're valuable. Nobody can find fault with you if you take out after the Russians.'

It reminded the shopkeeper of the people who'd blamed Franklin Roosevelt for everything in the 1930s. 'Andy Larsen got red in the face about Roosevelt one time when his hens got the croup.' Now it was the Russians who had that cross to bear. 'Man has a fight with his wife, he belts the Russians.'

All the same, the way that dissatisfaction was expressed, the tone of those debates, was then generally less extreme than what we have become used to in America today. Franklin Roosevelt was in profound conflict with his Republican opponents ideologically, but in practice his cooperation with Republican members of Congress and governors usually went smoothly. Four of the most important posts in his first administration were filled by Republicans.

Extreme political polarisation was avoided because Hamiltonians and Jeffersonians had roles to play within both the major parties. In 1960 there were still quite a few liberals in the Republican Party, and in the Democratic Party quite a few conservatives. One important reason for this lay in the distant past. During the Civil War the Republicans had been at the forefront of the struggle against the South, and the Southern whites had never forgiven them for it. Generation after generation of Southerners voted Democrat as a result.

The Republicans in turn became dominated by wealthy, well-educated city dwellers in the Eisenhower years – conservative in some respects but progressive on social issues. Eisenhower had an excellent working rela- tionship with the Democrat majority in Congress, and under his admin- istration a start was made on huge public works such as the construction of the interstate highways and the St Lawrence Seaway.

Few judges have devoted themselves to civil rights and the abolition of racial segregation with such intensity as the Republican chief justice of the United States, Earl Warren. Sam Rayburn, Democrat speaker of the House of Representatives between 1940 and 1961, was a close friend of the Republican Joseph William Martin, who replaced him as speaker in the few of those years in which the Republicans had a majority (1947–49 and 1953–55). In his 'Board of Education', as his private club was known, friends from all parties would come together after sessions were over, to play poker, drink and, yes, to practise politics – together, the way it's supposed to be in Main Street USA.

So it's no surprise to find that Kennedy and Nixon, during the three television debates, were fairly close ideologically. Nixon's later proposals for changes to the healthcare system were very like the highly contro- versial plans implemented by Obama some forty years later. Most Americans, for all Steinbeck's grousing, had a remarkable amount of faith in their government until the mid-1960s. In 1965, for example, almost half of all Americans believed that Johnson's War on Poverty really would 'help wipe out poverty', as the president promised – a vote of confidence unimaginable half a century later. And even though Johnson thought his Republican opponent Barry Goldwater was 'as nutty as a fruitcake', in public he was always polite during the 1964 campaign.

In 1960 sociologist Daniel Bell went so far as to announce 'the end of ideology' in a much-discussed essay collection of that name; he predicted that the great ideologies of the nineteenth and twentieth centuries were exhausted, and that future political issues would be worked out in an increasingly professional manner. Among Democrats and Republicans after all, or so he believed, a high degree of unanimity had developed over the fundamental questions surrounding foreign policy and the relationship between state and individual. Ideological issues belonged to the past. Political debates would in future concentrate mainly on practical questions about the 'management' of the country.

How wrong he was. Beneath all the apparent unanimity, something was brewing right across the country, left and right. Except that it was about very different sentiments from those Bell had in mind. In his memoirs Lawrence Wright describes the Dallas Citizens Council, of which his father became a member in 1960, as 'a collection of dollars, represented by men'. No doctor or lawyer was a member, let alone a woman. The tone was set by major business leaders and by large companies. They chose the men nominated to be judge, sheriff or mayor; they decided what was good or bad for the city, without giving a moment's thought to the voters or elected representatives. Dallas was full of distrustful Protestants. They fulminated against Kennedy, who was still merely a candidate for the presidency. 'The election of a Catholic as president would mean the end of religious freedom in America,' preached Pastor W. A. Criswell of the First Baptist Church.

According to Wright a cloud of adolescent bitterness hung over the country, a premonition that betrayal might occur at any moment, a tendency to see conspiracies lurking around every corner. Arthur Schlesinger reflected this state of mind. 'The mood was one of longing for a dreamworld of no communism, no overseas entanglements, no United Nations, no federal government, no labor unions, no Negroes or foreigners – a world in which Chief Justice Warren would be impeached, Cuba invaded, the graduated income tax repealed, the fluoridation of drinking water stopped and the import of Polish hams forbidden.'

With the unexpected Republican candidature in 1964 of a charismatic senator from Arizona called Barry Goldwater, all these sentiments were given a voice. The conservatives began a fresh offensive against the New Deal and the liberal elite that, in their view, had taken over America. In the South, the Democrats lost their natural supremacy when President Johnson signed the Civil Rights Act on 2 July 1964. It was a historic act,

putting an end to the legalised racism of the South, that profound injustice
and centuries-old curse. Johnson was aware of the price he was paying.
After he'd put his signature to the Act, one of his assistants asked why
he looked so sombre. He sighed. 'Because I think we just delivered the
South to the Republican Party for a long time to come.' Sure enough,
many Southern Democrats defected to the Republicans in the years that
followed, or became floating voters.

Still, the Republican liberals, most of whom lived on the east coast, could
not go along with the politics of conservative Republicans who joined
Goldwater in aiming to reverse the New Deal and everything that had flowed
from it. They in turn switched to the Democratic Party. The effect of all this
was that both parties became more homogeneous. They expended less energy
on internal debates and had an increasing tendency to reinforce political
polarisation by becoming wholly focused upon their opponents.

Yet Daniel Bell was right in some ways. Voters did feel less attached to
the old ideologies, which made it harder for the political parties to
represent them – a development seen all over the world in democratic
societies. In America the crisis of confidence was compounded, more
than anywhere else, by the media, by the way in which elections were
hijacked by tycoons, by increasing individualism and the collapse of Main
Street USA.

Victory margins shrank, which further stoked the flames of electoral
battle: in 2000, 2004 and 2008, George W. Bush and Barack Obama won
with majorities of a mere one to three per cent. Then there were the
increasing differences on the subject of religion that led people to side
with one or other party. Fundamentalist Christians were embraced more
and more by the Republicans, liberals and non-believers by the Democrats.

Meanwhile a major crisis of authority was developing. Opinion-poll
data presents a shocking picture. In 1966, fifty-five per cent of Americans
had faith in senior managers; by 2010 the figure had dropped to fifteen
per cent. Doctors: from seventy-three to thirty-four. University professors:
from sixty-one to thirty-five. Congress: from forty-two to eight. In a
study by the *Economist* and YouGov in February 2010, twenty-four per cent
of Democrats, fifty-two per cent of independents and sixty per cent of
Republicans were downright angry about government policy.

Mutual distrust was, and still is, cunningly manipulated and nourished by some politicians and advisors. 'Always be the instigator,' popular strategist Tom Tancredo (representative in Congress for Colorado, presidential candidate in 2008, a popular guest on Fox News and at one time an advisor to Dutch populist leader Geert Wilders) told Dutch journalist Tom-Jan Meeus. His message? Make sure people get mad at you. If you can rouse a bit of anger, then you'll prove to your supporters that you're important. Put irresolvable problems on the agenda. Suffer defeats – they'll confirm the citizens' suspicions. People distrust the government and each other. They have the idea that America is slipping through their fingers. You need to appeal to that.

It's obvious every day in Congress just how much relations have hardened. Between 1955 and 1961 there was just one attempt to prevent a vote by the use of a filibuster. In 2009 and 2010 alone, eighty-four attempts were made to sabotage normal voting procedure by endlessly dragging out the debate.

Linguistic usage has changed accordingly. In the years of George W. Bush's presidency the opposition could sometimes be fairly fierce, but those outbursts were nothing compared to the warlike language used against his Democrat successor after 2008, even by the establishment within the Republican Party. John Boehner, for example, the Republican speaker of the House, described the passage of Obama's healthcare legislation as 'Armageddon'. In his book *To Save America* (2010), prominent Republican Newt Gingrich writes that the 'secular-socialist machine' of Obama and his supporters is as great a threat to America as Nazi Germany or the Soviet Union were in their day. Gingrich claims that Muslims want to impose sharia on America – and who is more likely to go along with them than 'Imam Obama', as demagogue Rush Limbaugh habitually calls 'America's first Muslim president'?

All this belligerent rhetoric has not been without effect. A significant proportion of the American electorate is convinced, despite all the evidence to the contrary, that their president is a Kenyan Muslim who faked his American birth certificate – a foreigner, and a black president too, a combination that remains unacceptable to them. 'Kenyan' is code for 'Negro' in their jargon. 'Muslim' stands for 'foreigner'.

Just occasionally, unalloyed racism surfaces, for example when

Republican activist Rusty DePass of South Carolina said that he was sure
a gorilla that had escaped from a zoo was one of Michelle Obama's
ancestors. Usually such sentiments remain submerged. 'You're lying!'
shouted congressman Joe Wilson, a native of that same South Carolina,
from the back of the House during one of the first speeches by the newly
elected Obama. 'You're lying!' he roared, and what he really meant to
say to the black president, as one commentator convincingly wrote, was:
'You're lying, boy!'

In 1960 there were not yet so many scores to be settled. The weather was
beautiful on 8 November, the day of the presidential election. The turnout
was overwhelming, eleven per cent more than at the previous election.
Even back then, computers were used to generate prognoses – two
whacking great things, one from IBM and the other from RAC. At the
start of the evening on the east coast they calculated that Nixon was well
out in front, with 459 electors to Kennedy's 68. Then the results started
to shift in the direction of the Democrats and by half past ten both
computers were predicting a clear victory for Kennedy.

Viewers on the east coast turned off their television sets and went to
bed. Jacqueline Kennedy whispered to her husband: 'Oh Bunny, you're
president now!' No, he said, it's far too early. The first results from Los
Angeles looked fine too – California was up for grabs.

Then something unexpected happened. From the middle of America,
results came in that were far worse for Kennedy than for his Democratic
predecessors Truman and Stevenson, even though people had been
expecting the opposite trend. Kansas, South Dakota, North Dakota,
Nebraska: all over the place solid majorities had opted for Nixon. Kennedy's
lead was visibly shrinking. At three in the morning it was a close race.
If Nixon could claim the last four states he'd have won. He got only two.
Next morning, at half past nine (of all the Kennedys, only Robert was
still awake) the Republicans threw in the towel.

'Boy, there's a lot of them,' mumbled one of the special agents on the
security team that stationed itself at the Cape Cod holiday home where
the Kennedys were staying. A reporter for United Press International
described standing on the top of a dune and seeing Jacqueline Kennedy,
heavily pregnant, exercising on the beach while the new president kicked

a ball around with a friend, their dog Charlie racing back and forth with another ball in his mouth. John's father Joseph Kennedy was starting his morning walk, and the other Kennedys wandered in and out of the house or sat talking on the sunny porch while Robert worked through dozens of phone calls with campaign staff. The neighbours started practising, giggling a little – from now on it was no longer 'Jack' but 'Mr President'.

In the end it turned out that Kennedy had won with a tiny majority of 112,881 votes, no more than about 0.1 per cent. By comparison, Kennedy's hero Franklin D. Roosevelt had beaten Republican Herbert Hoover in 1932 by almost seven million. Texas and Illinois – Chicago! – were abuzz with rumours about ballot boxes full of fake ballot papers and other irregularities, but Nixon acknowledged defeat and the battle was over.

Nixon withdrew to California, profoundly disappointed, especially since the result was so close. As historian and journalist Rick Perlstein writes in his portrait of the era, *Nixonland*: 'Every last errant decision, each missed opportunity, every break that had it tumbled this way instead of that would have made Richard Nixon the hero instead of the lonely man who spent the first half of 1961 alone in a Los Angeles apartment eating meals from soup cans as his girls finished out the school year back East – this torture of retrospection Richard Nixon would rewind for the rest of his life.' All those dreadful memories – an ill-judged remark, his sweaty forehead during the first televised debate – tormented him for years.

He was going to have to start again from scratch.

The political arguments between Steinbeck and his sister Esther did not spoil their relationship in the long term. However stormy, their conflict was nothing like as charged as the political debates of half a century later. They remained one family.

Political debate in America has gradually gone off the rails. Old stagers in politics, from left and right, are increasingly concerned about the culture wars that are steadily undermining the workings of national government by blocking decision-making on all kinds of practical issues, such as routine appointments or technical problems concerning the budget. It has become almost impossible to make normal agreements; every compromise is regarded as treachery. More and more voters simply refuse to accept any representative or president who doesn't subscribe to their principles 100 per cent.

The layout of the battlefield is simple. On one side, in the inimitable terms of humourist Dave Barry, are the 'ignorant racist fascist knuckle-dragging NASCAR-obsessed cousin-marrying roadkill-eating tobacco-juice-dribbling gun-fondling religious fanatic rednecks'. On the other side are the 'godless unpatriotic pierced-nose Volvo-driving France-loving left-wing communist latte-sucking tofu-chomping holistic-wacko neurotic vegan weenie perverts'. The American 'unity in diversity' that Steinbeck applauded in *America and Americans* – 'The American identity is an exact and provable thing' – seems to have gone.

To return to anthropologist Benedict Anderson, with his nation as an 'imagined community', it seems as if in the case of America no such thing exists any longer, or rather it has been divided up into several communities that have no contact at all with each other.

In San Diego I was once given a hamburger lesson by Jay, a mild-mannered, rotund man who was making a valiant effort to stay off the drink. How on earth do you consume a great big fat hamburger without making a mess? Jay told me how. Using a knife and fork was ridiculous; first cover yourself with napkins, then flatten the whole thing and you'll be able to slide even the fattest of hamburgers into your mouth. 'And you start by biting, a really good bite; you fight it inside.'

Jay was fresh out of jail, where he'd served a year and a half for a drunken brawl, and now he had a suspended sentence hanging over him. That meant he wasn't allowed to vote. 'Thank God,' said his friend. 'Otherwise that jerk Bush would be guaranteed another vote.' 'That's right,' replied Jay. 'I'm a conservative. I believe in values and principles.'

Jay was a confirmed and practising homosexual, he was working himself to death in construction for a pittance, had little if any insurance, didn't own a house, and when it came to his political preferences he barely paid any attention at all to his own social and economic interests. 'George W. Bush fights terrorism, and he shares my values. That's the most important thing for me.' Jay reiterated this several times and then we had nothing more to say to each other about politics. We went on to have a great night.

In recent years things have been moving in precisely the opposite direction to that predicted by Daniel Bell. Even practical discussions about concrete problems turn into heavily ideological or even quasi-religious arguments. Conservative and liberal voters alike, including pleasant and kind-hearted people like Jay, tend to express their political views in combative terms: us against them; good versus evil.

The 'Volvo-driving France-loving' liberals regard the New Deal and the modern welfare state it produced, for example, as a great thing – a view the Republican Party of the 1950s shared, of course – whereas the 'gun-fondling rednecks' believe that people have the moral right to keep what they've earned and that all taxation is a form of theft. For one part of the nation, reform of the tax system to the detriment of the richest is a matter of social justice, whereas the other half sees it as an attack by arrogant bureaucrats on all those free spirits with the courage to run a business. They also see gun control as an attack, especially on the rural ideal of many Americans.

The theory of evolution is another subject about which opinions are diametrically opposed. In the eyes of one America it's an accepted scientific explanation that everyone should know about, to the other America it's a diabolical doctrine that undermines not only the basic principles of the Bible but also those of the American nation. After all, if everything is down to chance and not the result of a divine Plan, then what is the Higher Goal of project America?

So it goes on. Subsidised healthcare: one group sees it as a moral necessity, the other as an attack on the basic right of every American to spend his money however he likes. Climate change: three-quarters of Democrats are sincerely concerned, whereas most Republicans refuse to believe all those alarmist stories. Time and again, even during our conversations over breakfast, the same questions arise: How much influence should the federal government have on our lives? How much power are we prepared to yield to Washington, to 'the Union'?

Moderate politicians are having a hard time, especially within the Republican Party. In the past there were always unifying figures such as Gerald Ford in the Republican ranks, acceptable to all the different groups within the party, from social conservatives and free-market libertarians to neo-conservatives. That balance has been lost. Conservative supporters are making increasingly radical demands, and it's not a matter of either/ or but of both/and. Things are gradually getting to the point where a Republican candidate who wants to have any chance at all needs to embrace an entire package of conservative values, without any conditions or qualifications.

Politics and religion are effortlessly combined. At a conservative mass picnic in the summer of 2010, Becky Benson from Orlando, Florida, announced to a reporter from the *New York Times*: 'We believe in Jesus Christ, and Jesus would not have agreed with the economic stimulus package, bank bailouts and welfare.' Pocket editions of the US Constitution are distributed like pocket bibles, and in certain circles it has the same status as the Ten Commandments, holy and immutable. The men who framed the Constitution in the summer of 1787 fully realised that all things were relative, including this crucial document; in fact Benjamin Franklin, when called upon to vote, gave a short speech about the need for flexibility, 'even on important Subjects', yet any change is regarded in these circles as high treason.

In a study carried out in the summer of 2010, eighty-six per cent of Americans questioned said that the Constitution 'has an impact on their daily lives'. At the same time, seventy-two per cent admitted they had never been able to read it to the end. 'This is my copy of the Constitution,' said John Boehner, addressing a Tea Party rally in Ohio that summer. 'And I'm going to stand here with the Founding Fathers, who wrote in the preamble: "We hold these truths to be self-evident . . ."' Except that those words are not in the Constitution. They are the start of the second sentence of the Declaration of Independence.

All those pledges and perennial promises, all that idolisation, all those outward shows of unity create a smokescreen. Behind all the slogans, conservative America is deeply divided. The American concept 'conservative', just like 'liberal', is wide-ranging and almost impossible to define. It encompasses the traditional, thoughtful conservatism that warns against reckless plans and ideals, but also the modern neo-conservatism that attempts to bend history to its will, the religious conservatism of the Christian fundamentalists, the libertarian conservatism of the defenders of absolute individual freedoms, the anti-federal conservatism of the opponents of taxation, and the nationalist conservatism of the defenders of the flag and the armed forces.

There are also deep, if rarely articulated, differences of opinion within the conservative movement about various issues that include cuts to the army, the bailout of Wall Street in 2008 and taxation of the very rich. Republican activist Rusty DePass can say what he likes about Michelle Obama's forebears without altering the fact that to Glenn Beck, hero of the Tea Party, Martin Luther King is actually a great example to follow. Neo-conservative intellectuals like Niall Ferguson eagerly advocate an active American empire that defends Western civilisation all over the world, while the isolationists of the monthly *American Conservative* fly into a rage at the very thought. Religious conservatives abhor gay marriage; the libertarians of the Cato Institute would like nothing better.

Political scientist Mark Lilla writes that you can indeed see present-day political America as a battle between two tribes, one 'Volvo-driving' and the other 'gun-fondling', but you must never forget that within those two tribes are all kinds of clans that propagate more radical or moderate versions of the same outlook. Currently it's the right that is causing most of the agitation in American politics, because of the fast-changing force field between its various clans. Lilla goes on to say that the influence of the conservatives who derive their vision from social and political reality is waning. The gap they have left is now being filled by a new kind of conservative, the populist reactionary who is guided mainly by ideology and an aversion to the past – in this case primarily the 1960s.

In the eyes of these populists, American history has taken a disastrous turn – so disastrous that doom-mongering has become central to their way of thinking. Apocalyptic ideas have always been part of the landscape, on the left as well as the right, but among many Republicans the apocalypse has become a fundamental assumption. Public affairs, concern for the future – they no longer care about any of that. This is new. This is where the *Left Behind* science-fiction series goes to the heart of politics.

At some point in the 1980s, Mark Lilla writes, neo-conservative thinking became clouded. The big question was no longer how conservatives ought to deal with the limitations of politics and democracy but how to cast off the cultural revolution of the 1960s, which in their eyes had caused so much misery: drug use, broken families, pornography, the collapse of bourgeois culture. The problem, in other words, was no longer how to cope with history but how to throw it into reverse. That too was new, for conservatives anyhow.

What makes these groups most angry of all is that history cannot be changed. They can only dream of revenge. As Lilla puts it: 'People who know what kind of new world they want to create through revolution are trouble enough: those who only know what they want to destroy are a curse.'

That bitterness was reflected in the election results of 2 November 2010, half a century after the sunny November day on which Jack Kennedy was elected president. Americans seemed to have forgotten that it was only two years since they once again placed all their hopes in a newcomer, a King Arthur who was going to change everything: Barack Obama. You could hear the jubilation everywhere then. In every city centre, people danced in the streets.

Now the Republicans are back. The election results for the House of Representatives spelled disaster for the Democrats. Young voters, who supported Obama en masse in 2008, were deeply disappointed. Half of those who voted for him two years ago stayed home. For nineteen countries, 2010 was the warmest year ever recorded, with the Greenland ice caps melting at an unprecedented rate, dried-up grain fields in Russia, and rain causing serious flooding everywhere, especially in Asia. Most Americans paid little if any attention; only the economy mattered to them.

Four out of ten voters told exit pollsters that their families were worse off financially than two years before. One in three said someone in their family had faced unemployment since 2008. In both the House and the Senate, the Democrats lost dozens of seats. It was the biggest loss for any party since 1938.

Was it deserved? Where do all those economic and social problems come from? Was it not the previous administration, led by George W. Bush, that drove up the national debt with irresponsible tax breaks, that allowed the banks to run amuck, that saddled the country with two costly wars and left it in a deep economic crisis? Surely everyone knows that Obama was faced with having to clear up the mess. Do the voters and commentators have such short memories?

Asking these questions seems futile. Many American voters no longer care. They are furious. With everyone. They have no fondness for the Republicans, they tell exit pollsters; they were simply keen to teach Obama a lesson.

'They want America to stand alone on top again,' writes philosopher Ronald Dworkin in response to the election result. 'They want politicians to tell them that it can, that God has chosen us but false leaders have betrayed us.'

Those voters have lost their country. They have lost their story.

Five

NO PLACE IN THE WORLD MEANT MORE to John Steinbeck than this bit of California, the peninsula of Monterey and Pacific Grove and the rolling hills at its back, the area around his native town of Salinas. He grew up here, spent more than half his life here, and he recreated it in his stories as an almost mythical land. His most important books, *The Grapes of Wrath* and *East of Eden*, are set in the Salinas Valley, and the west bank of the Salinas River is the setting for *Of Mice and Men*. All the action in *Cannery Row* and *Sweet Thursday* is centred on the quaysides, the piers and the canning factories of Monterey.

'Cannery Row . . . is a poem, a stink, a grating noise, a quality of light, a tone, a habit, a nostalgia, a dream.' With that sentence, Steinbeck tears back the curtain of his theatre and immediately introduces us to the decor of his small, heroic saga: the Row as it was in the 1930s, grimy and smelly, the beaches covered in flies and fish offal, usually deserted.

Most of the time it was so quiet there that you heard only the wood of the piers heaving and creaking in the ocean swell, until the fishing fleet appeared on the horizon. Then the factories began to stamp and whistle, the workers and packers rushed out of the hills to the canneries, and everyone was busy for days packing the 'silver rivers' of sardines into thousands of cans. 'The canneries rumble and rattle and squeak until the last fish is cleaned and cut and cooked and canned and then the whistles scream again and the dripping, smelly, tired Wops and Chinamen and Polacks, men and women, straggle out and droop their ways up the hill into the town and Cannery Row becomes itself again – quiet and magical.' The fleet set out once more, silence fell over the quayside again and all you could hear were a few seals barking in the distance.

In the early 1930s Steinbeck lived close to this tin-can clamour with his first wife Carol, and his existence was framed in part by that rhythm of peace interrupted by sudden commotion. The atmosphere recalled the Hooverville in Seattle in the same period: everyone was poor, people lived on a little bread and a few bottles of cheap wine, but there was always something going on. He was part of a group of close friends of whom Ed Ricketts – nicknamed 'the mandarin' – was the central figure. 'There were great parties at the laboratory, some of which went on for days,' Steinbeck wrote later. 'There would come a time in our poverty when we needed a party. Then we would gather together the spare pennies. It didn't take many of them. There was a wine sold in Monterey for thirty-nine cents a gallon.' At the end of the evening Ed Ricketts would do his 'tippy-toe mouse dance'.

Close by was Carmel, already a flourishing artists' colony in those days, described by Ernie Pyle as the 'Greenwich Village of the Pacific', although by 1940, when Pyle passed through, it had been pretty much ruined by 'rich dilettantes'. Monterey was still unspoilt and Cannery Row was still called Ocean View Avenue. In those days John often went to a diner called Maria's to talk with the fishermen, the day labourers, the prostitutes and the local indigents. A few years later they all became world famous – like it or not – because of the novels *Sweet Thursday* and *Cannery Row*: Mack and the boys at the Palace Flophouse, the warm-hearted madam Dora Flood and her girls at the Bear Flag Restaurant, Doc and his lab, the Chinese grocer Lee Chong, and Mr and Mrs Malloy, who live in a huge, empty boiler and rent out bits of sewer pipe as sleeping quarters for single men.

Fiction or not, most of Steinbeck's main characters in Monterey really existed, and most of the events in *Cannery Row* actually took place. A big frog hunt had been held to provide Ed Ricketts with laboratory specimens, and people really did live in old pipes and boilers that had been left to rust next to the factories. The novel is in that sense the opposite of *Travels with Charley*: largely non-fiction, packaged as fiction. According to the local police chief, there was no exaggeration at all in the descriptions of Mack and the other residents of the Palace Flophouse: 'I've had them all in the cells, year after year.'

Dora Flood's real name was Flora Woods (she was born Julia Silva), an impressive woman, universally loved and a model of generosity. Every year she had Christmas hampers delivered to fifty poor families, stuffed so full of food that they could live off them for weeks. Her Bear Flag Restaurant was in reality the Lone Star Café, directly opposite Ed Ricketts' lab. Ed and John often went over to visit, without entering into any intimate relationships with the girls. On 2 July 1941, the Lone Star Café was closed unexpectedly on the orders of the Californian judiciary. Ricketts wrote to one of his friends that week: 'Everything was moved out, including, of course, all the beds – and, boy, were there a lot of them.' Flora died of a heart attack on 1 August 1948.

Lee Chong was based on a Chinese man called Won Yee, although the character also includes elements of his son Jack Yee, who took over the business after his father's death in 1934. Won Yee called his shop 'Wing Chong', meaning 'glorious, successful'. It closed in the mid-1950s. The figure of Mack, the leader of the boys at the flophouse, is based on the cheerful alcoholic Gabe Bicknell, a good friend of Steinbeck's. He led a nomadic life, and died in a fire in the winter of 1954. And in the lively Mary Talbot in the book, who knew how to make a party out of nothing, there was a great deal of Carol, a source of immense comfort and support in Steinbeck's penniless early years as a writer.

Ed Ricketts' lab was in reality the Pacific Biological Laboratories, a well-known source of biological specimens for universities and scientific institutions. As Ricketts was making his way home in his noisy old Packard at dusk on 7 May 1948, he drove, as always, over the unguarded railroad crossing at the corner of Drake Avenue and Wave Street. This time he failed to notice the onrushing Del Monte Express from San Francisco. He died four days later, at the age of fifty-one. He left a legacy; partly because of his work, Monterey now has one of the best marine aquariums in the world.

After the war, Steinbeck dreamed for a while of buying a piece of land and returning to Monterey. In the end he decided against it. He wrote to his old friend Toby Street that the Monterey he knew no longer existed. Toby wrote back saying that was certainly true, but that today's Monterey consisted of real people, unlike Steinbeck's dream world. In a later letter,

Steinbeck said, 'I never want to have roots again.' Toby drew his friend's attention to that little word: 'again'.

John Steinbeck initially suffered the same fate in Monterey as Sinclair Lewis had in Sauk Centre. Local citizens were far from happy with the image of their little town created by *Cannery Row* as one big repository of tramps, whores and other down-and-outs. But with the success of the book, all that changed, even more so than in Sauk Centre. The real-life Ocean View Avenue was renamed Cannery Row and over the years the place became the author's depiction, reality adapting itself to his imagination.

Decline set in fast at the fishery and the canneries after 1946. In 1945, the year *Cannery Row* was published, the seventeen canneries reached their absolute peak, producing 237,000 tons of canned sardines. In 1946 the catch suddenly fell to 146,000 tons, and in 1947 there were only 31,000 tons. Everyone wondered where on earth all the sardines had got to. Ed Ricketts offered the simplest explanation: 'They're in cans.'

Steinbeck's novel saved the Row. Dozens of visitors wanted to see the lab, Lee Chong's shop and the Bear Flag Restaurant with their own eyes. 'How charming!' the ladies would exclaim to Ed Ricketts if he happened to be mounting one of his specimens. 'What's that, Mr Ricketts?' 'Oh that's the foreskin of a whale,' he would invariably reply.

The last cannery, which canned squid, closed in 1973. More and more factories and piers were converted into restaurants and amusement arcades. The railway was removed and a footpath laid in its place. Shiny new hotels were built, shops selling antiques and souvenirs appeared, until everything matched the needs, dreams and nostalgic fantasies of the modern tourist.

In today's Cannery Row a photograph is on display of the street as it looked in the glory days of Mack, Dora, John, Doc and Lee Chong. I find one house I can orientate by, clearly recognisable from its heavy, angular frontage. On an empty patch of land are a few rusty tanks – so the vacant lot where Mack and his boys always hung out is still there. Further along I can see Lee Chong's, or rather Won Yee's grocery store, now full of souvenirs, T-shirts and cakes. Diagonally opposite, lonely amid all that clamorous tourism, is Ed Ricketts' sober, brown wooden lab. Meticulously restored, it's the only structure that remains unchanged, without

signboards or smooth talk. The concrete yard at the back, featuring rows
of rectangular troughs in which Ricketts once kept his catch, looks as it
always did, weather-beaten and deserted.

In November 1960 John and Elaine, along with Barnaby Conrad, took a
walk just as sentimental as our own. Elaine was delighted by everything
she saw, Conrad later told Jackson Benson. It seems she had never been
there before and she was hugely curious to see the piers, houses and
other places she'd heard so many stories about. 'Oh, isn't that Ed's lab
over there?' 'Is that where the Chinese grocery store was?' 'Look! Look,
there's a movie theater called the John Steinbeck Theater. Can't we go in
and see it?'

John, shy as he was, walked beside her, moaning with distress. No,
he didn't want to go into the movie theatre. No, he didn't really want
anything to do with any of this, in fact he barely wanted to look, and
he involuntarily put his hand over his face. Everything had changed, he
told Elaine, except that 'the sea never changed, the light never changed
over the water'. He'd never have imagined that the poor but happy world
of his young days would be converted into a tourist attraction – the
process was well underway in 1960 – and he thought it was all perfectly
terrible.

'The place of my origin had changed, and having gone away I had
not changed with it,' he writes in *Travels*. 'In my memory it stood as it
once did and its outward appearance confused and angered me.'

He had to admit that the Monterey Peninsula had been thoroughly
smartened up since the 1930s. The canneries used to put out a 'sickening
stench'. The beaches once 'festered with fish guts and flies'. Now everything was clean and neat. 'They fish for tourists now, not pilchards, and
that species they are not likely to wipe out.'

As for Carmel, it had got completely out of hand. If the founders of
the little town, the 'starveling writers and unwanted painters', were to
return they would 'be instantly picked up as suspicious characters and
deported over the city line . . . What we knew is dead, and maybe the
greatest part of what we were is dead. What's out there is new and perhaps
good, but it's nothing we know.'

Monterey forms the definitive turning point in *Travels with Charley*.

Steinbeck's pessimism, ever present beneath the surface, bursts out into full view. Everything in this chapter of *Travels* concerns modernity, progress and change, both the desirability and blessings of change and the loss that it always brings. The days of pure American optimism were over.

Steinbeck was a doom-monger. He had no time for the apocalyptic religious theories that were doing the rounds in some circles even in his day, but his worries about American society would be recognisable to many a present-day conservative. 'If I wanted to destroy a nation,' he'd written a year earlier in his letter to Stevenson, 'I would give it too much, and I would have it on its knees, miserable, greedy, and sick.'

Steinbeck had started out on his Operation Windmills with the last of his optimism. Along the way he'd lost his hope and his illusions, even if he would not be quick to admit it. The way in which his old Monterey had been rebuilt as a theme park was illustrative of everything he had seen on his journey through America: the hollowing-out of political debate, the restlessness of Americans, their drive to consume, their blindness to waste, their forfeited ideals.

'You can't go home again.' In *Travels* Steinbeck dealt with that feeling in two ways: first of all by describing a dramatic meeting with his old compadres in Johnny Garcia's bar in Monterey, with 'tears and embraces, speeches and endearments' in the *poco* Spanish of his youth. 'The years rolled away. We danced formally, hands locked behind us.'

The atmosphere soon soured. Nothing and no one, after all, was the same. 'I guess maybe you're too good for us,' said his old friend, Johnny the barkeeper. Steinbeck faced him down, and for the first time he gives the real names of his heroes of *Cannery Row*: '"Where are the great ones? Tell me, where's Willie Trip?" "Dead," Johnny said hollowly. "Where is Pilon, Johnny, Pom Pom, Miz Gragg, Stevie Field?" "Dead, dead, dead," he echoed.'

Steinbeck continued on through the list: '"Ed Ricketts, Whitey's Number One and Two, where's Sonny Boy, Ankle Varney, Jesús Maria Corcoran, Joe Portagee, Shorty Lee, Flora Woods, and that girl who kept spiders in her hat?" "Dead – all dead . . . It's like we was in a bucket of ghosts,"' said his old compadre, who had been one of the bearers at Flora Woods' funeral.

'No. They're not true ghosts. We're the ghosts.'

It was Steinbeck's farewell to a way of life. *Cannery Row* was more than an enjoyable, well-written novel. As Benson rightly observes, it was in some ways an experiment: 'Nearly every element – language, form, imagery, and characterization – expressed a non-teleological view of the world.' It was one great ode to an aimless existence, to life for its own sake – and that rejection of Great Aims made it an extraordinarily un-American, perhaps even an anti-American, book. Steinbeck abandoned all of that when he pulled the door of Garcia's bar shut behind him.

His second reaction to going home was almost biblical. He writes in *Travels* that he climbed the solitary, rocky summit of Fremont Peak. It was his way of taking leave of California, with a last look at what had once been the Promised Land.

In many of his books he wrote not just about California but about the Californian myth, the American Garden of Eden. Not that he had any sympathy for the traditional story of America's heroic trek westwards. In his view it was a dangerous myth that had made many Americans unable to see the true nature of the country of which they, from east to west, had taken possession as if by right.

To Steinbeck the western edge of the continent meant something else. He saw it as the ideal place to investigate in detail, time and again, the paradise of America – both the dream and the reality. In all his writing he asked questions about the effect this Garden of Eden had on the people who lived there, and about the myth that kept endlessly driving Americans west until they reached the coast and could go no further.

'In Steinbeck's fiction, the American myth, with its Old Testament reverberations, and the Quest of the Arthurian legends with which he had a lifelong fascination become one impulse pushing toward the "Garden of the West",' wrote Louis Owens in a lengthy essay about the image John Steinbeck had of his own country.

Steinbeck was thereby associating himself with a classic and irresolvable conflict in the American intellectual tradition: on the one hand a deep longing for a pastoral New World and on the other an increasing awareness, throughout American history, that violence and depravity will follow people always, the world over, no matter where they settle. The lost paradise – living 'off the fatta the lan', to quote one of its central characters – is the great tragedy of the novel Of Mice and Men, for example. The location is cleverly chosen: 'a few miles south of Soledad', a town that does exist in California and, dull and bland as it is, fully lives up to its name, which means 'loneliness'.

'Eden,' Louis Owens writes, 'proves to be corrupted, its fruit of scientific knowledge rotting in fields and orchards, its lands lying fallow in the ownership of corporations and millionaires, its people frightened and dangerous.'

As far as that goes, Travels is again to a great degree a variation on an old theme. Owens thinks, however, that it differs in one essential respect from the classic American tradition. Steinbeck switches things around. In his book it's in the 'ideal' West that ruin and death predominate; he believes he has managed to discover remnants of the idyllic, traditional communities in the gently rolling hills of the East.

On the high rocks of Fremont Peak in 1960, Steinbeck was able to reconcile himself with California, with Monterey, and to a certain extent with himself. Anyone who winds up all those hairpin bends still has a breathtaking view of the ocean, the hills and the Salinas Valley, but what claims the attention most of all is a plain full of gleaming hothouses, businesses, supermarkets and parking lots, with rivers and a green patch of woodland here and there, and, squeezed in between the suburbs, the old Salinas.

Steinbeck looks with the eyes of his youth, and he tells Charley about it: in that little valley he fished for trout, over there his mother shot a wildcat, that dark patch is 'a tiny canyon with a clear and lovely stream bordered with wild azaleas and fringed with big oaks', forty miles away is the old family ranch where they faced starvation. 'In the spring, Charley, when the valley is carpeted with blue lupines like a flowery sea, there's the smell of heaven up there, the smell of heaven.'

It is still absolutely silent, apart from the tapping of a woodpecker. The sky is clear blue with just a few wisps of white. In the distance the ocean sparkles. Indeed, this is the ideal place to say farewell to that 'permanent and changeless past'.

'You can't go home again.' Steinbeck was deeply disappointed, in himself most of all. The best times of his life were behind him. He'd tried everything to keep himself going as a writer and he had immense difficulty admitting that it was all over. For him, as for so many who made the great trek westwards, California was the finishing line.

The previous summer he had fiercely defended his Charley project to Elizabeth Otis. His illness, he wrote to her, had turned him into an invalid, a 'stupid, lazy oaf who must be protected, led, instructed and hospitalized'. He balked at that. 'Between us – what I am proposing is not a little trip or reporting, but a frantic last attempt to save my life and the integrity of my creative pulse.'

Now he had lost even that motivation. His 'frantic last attempt' had failed. He'd been intending, the letter to Elizabeth makes clear, to drive along quiet back roads and carry his house with him. 'I can invite a man to have a beer in my home, thereby forcing an invitation from him.' That was the reason he'd chosen a truck, 'a respectable and respected working instrument'. Any remaining suspicion among those he spoke to would vanish as soon as they saw his equipment: 'If in my truck I have two fishing rods, two rifles and a shotgun, there will never be any question of my purpose.'

That was how he envisioned it, his reunion with America: rural, peaceful, in proud isolation. In practice only the first week went to plan. After that, tormented by homesickness, he'd picked up the pace more and more. He'd virtually skipped whole sections of his expedition. What he wrote about the new interstate highways, that they would make it possible 'to drive from New York to California without seeing a single thing', now applied to him.

His dependence on Elaine had become abundantly clear during those weeks, and now he gave up. Elaine caught a plane and flew ahead of him to her family in Texas. John stayed for a few more days in Monterey, contracted food poisoning in a restaurant with his sister Beth, and revised his plans. He would inspect two more regions – Texas and the Deep South – and then call it a day. All the images in his head were starting to get muddled together, was the excuse he gave to the readers of Travels. In reality he was worn out.

In a passage from the original manuscript that was omitted from the book, Steinbeck described trying in vain to find his way back to his hotel in San Francisco, the city he knew so well. Later it would happen again, when he returned to the other big city he'd lived in for years, New York. The gist was the same each time; even in his 'homeland' he no longer knew the way. In San Francisco he tried once more to act as a guide for his wife, but he couldn't manage even that. He and the world had changed too much.

It is striking that in *Travels* he uses terms about himself that evoke disenchantment and decomposition, just as he did in the description of America he sent to his publisher after the trip, with its memorable 'gasses in a corpse'. He would have loved to discover the truth about his country. Then he could have leaned back satisfied when he got home. 'But what I carried in my head and deeper in my perceptions was a barrel of worms.' He goes on: 'This monster of a land, this mightiest of nations, this spawn of the future, turns out to be the macrocosm of microcosm me.'

In the end he tied, with his own hand, the knot that bound everything together, rightly or wrongly: the decline of his country and his own tragedy, California and Steinbeck, America and Americans.

PART SEVEN

California – Arizona – New Mexico –
Texas – Louisiana – New Orleans

'I Can't Believe I Ate the Whole Thing.'

ALKA-SELTZER ADVERTISEMENT
1972

One

'MY DEPARTURE WAS FLIGHT,' Steinbeck wrote at the end of his stay in California. He liked to dramatise a little. The National Steinbeck Center in Salinas has preserved the recording of an interview in which Toby Street relates with relish what actually happened. An extract from my notes:

John appeared. I didn't know he was coming. Suddenly there he was. Something to do with his family, I don't know what. It turned out he was here only for a short time. I said: 'Shall we throw a party?' He said: 'Good idea.' My wife was away, all our friends still lived in the neighborhood and everyone came, the whole house was full. He brought his camper with him. The party got completely out of hand and John said: 'I have to go to Texas and visit Elaine's family, why don't you go with me?'

The house was a real mess by then, and I said: 'Okay, but let's leave early.' So we drove off at eight-thirty, Charley in between us. At a certain point we thought it must be lunchtime, so we decided to drive through San Juan and have lunch in the Bishop's Palace. No sooner said than done. But John ordered something that took an hour to make, cannelloni or something like that. When it finally reached our table he was so hungry he immediately ordered another portion. As a result of all that, we didn't get any further than Tulare the first day.

We had to keep stopping to let Charley out. He might run right off into the desert to pee. All in all we went so slowly that I called it a day in Flagstaff. I really did need to get back to work. I had to wait all night at a small airport for a flight home; they had nothing

there at all, not even a chewing-gum dispenser. That thing had such
a rumble, you couldn't hear a voice. And Charley was there . . .
Then John would say something and Charley would beg a bit as
an answer.

We follow John and Toby's route through the scorched Californian hinter-
land. It's a hot day. The tachometer stands at 6,710 miles. Steinbeck was
barely halfway, yet there's a sense that his journey was over. That first day
with Toby he was still taking it easy. Then he really floored it, in order
to join Elaine again as soon as possible.

In San Juan Bautista, an hour's drive from Monterey, we decide to
lunch at exactly the same place. We'll order cannelloni, in memory of
our illustrious predecessors. The eighteenth-century mission post in San
Juan where it all started is still intact, an imposing white building
surrounded by cool corridors. It stands on a large, dusty square, with
what remains of the richly decorated houses, inns and saloons all around
it. It's as if the shouting, shooting and laughing in these nineteenth-
century timber structures could start up again at any moment, even
though it's deathly quiet here now, aside from the clucking of a few
wandering chickens. The Bishop's Palace is nowhere to be found. We ask
around a bit and eventually arrive at two women and a young man who
are standing waiting their turn near an ATM at the local bank. Steinbeck?
Yes, they know him. But cannelloni? Bishop's Palace? They fall silent and
look at each other.

Suddenly the young man bursts out laughing. 'You mean the Bishop!
Well, that's been closed for years. But it wasn't a restaurant, it was a
knocking shop.'

He reveals to us the history of San Juan. The town was famous for its
brothels; it was little more than a mission post with a few saloons and
fourteen whorehouses. 'That was the main business here. I'm sorry, but
you'd have had a hard time getting cannelloni at the Bishop. They usually
served up something else.'

So off for a sandwich among the local young people at the Mission
Café – 'No, we don't talk about politics any more. In 2008 Obama was
cool, but that's a long time ago now' – and then back on the road,
through the hot, lush Salinas Valley. We pass Fremont Peak. Toby made

no mention of the climb and I wonder whether they really did take that detour, especially given the distance the pair covered that day.

We drive eastwards past Los Banos, then onto Highway 99 heading south. The forests and brown hills give way to the productive landscape of the San Joaquin Valley: cotton, then apples and cherries, then garlic. The land is as flat as Friesland, but here an evil god has eliminated all loveliness – trees, barns, villages – and then lit a fierce hellfire underneath.

It's starting to get dark, and the scents of this Californian landscape drift into our Jeep: cattle, dung, a factory for processing garlic, pigs, garlic again, some animal body odour that permeates everything, and then we're in Tulare.

In the Days Inn on Memorial Highway they speak only Spanish. Mexican migrant workers are sitting outside their rooms drinking and playing cards. Some sing a song while others, down below, are fixing up their cars for tomorrow's trip further north. Radio voices blare through everything. In the restaurant a stray Amish family is settling up, a father with two large sons, the mother dignified behind them. Two younger children, a boy in dark-blue trousers with braces and a girl in a long dress and white bonnet, are feasting their eyes on a display of sweets and toys. They are quiet, just staring. For a moment, the eighteenth century collides with the twenty-first.

Steinbeck drove out of California by the shortest possible route, via Los Banos, Fresno and Tulare to Bakersfield – that way you leave Los Angeles off to your right – and along Route 58 and Interstate 40 into the Mojave Desert. He was to meet up with Elaine again in Amarillo, Texas, where they would celebrate Thanksgiving with friends.

We follow his trail. Highway 99 is one endless procession of steaming trucks, the land-bound ships of this continent, a parade of immense silver radiators, puffing exhaust stacks, improbably long trailers, and cabins in which the drivers sit enthroned like kings. They haul vast amounts of stuff ever onwards: milk, furniture, parcels, tree trunks, bales of cotton, heaps of scrap, cars, chemicals, fruit, sewer pipes. The road is ugly, the land is ugly; this is the scullery of California.

Eastwards, along Route 58, into the heat. In California you sometimes have the illusion of driving through almost all the climates and landscapes

of Europe in barely a day, from the grey ocean cool of Trondheim via
the vineyards of northern France to the dry heat of the Spanish plateau.
Yesterday we were in sweaters as we sat on the beach, now we're driving
through a desert, a landscape of jagged boulders, fractured rock and
cracked earth as far as the eye can see.

The Mojave, Steinbeck wrote, used to be a sort of endurance test, with
its frightening desolation, as if nature wanted to check you were tough
enough to get to California. In 1960 you saw regular stopping places and
air-conditioned service stations, but still it was a demanding drive through
the desert. Rocinante, like almost all trucks in those days, was without
air conditioning and Charley in particular felt the heat. He panted as if
he had asthma, his body jarred and his tongue hung far out of his mouth,
'flat as a leaf and dripping'. Steinbeck stopped in a narrow gulley to give
the dog a drink and to throw water from his tank over them both to
cool them down a little. He then sat in the shade of Rocinante, on his
kitchen steps, with a can of beer.

In his youth it was different. Steinbeck remembers how he and his
friends prayed as they drove across this desert of rocks, bushes and cacti,
their ears peeled for any unusual sounds from the labouring old engine,
plumes of steam rising from the boiling radiator. If you broke down you
were in real trouble. 'I have never crossed it without sharing something
with those early families foot-dragging through this terrestrial hell, leaving
the white skeletons of horses and cattle which still mark the way,' he
wrote.

Now we merely have to follow the four-lane 58, pleasantly cool. The
occasional preacher or rock musician drifts in through the radio. The
route of the old 'way of sighs' Steinbeck wrote about is clearly visible
from the taut telephone and electricity cables, which stride alongside us
across the plain a short distance away. Some of the gas stations he passed
are still there too, or the remains of them − solitary, rusting and very
much of the 1950s.

To Steinbeck the Mojave was 'a sun-punished place'. He vividly
described 'the conspiracy of life in the desert to circumvent the death
rays of the all-conquering sun' − the water-retentive properties of the
plants, the animals' armoured exterior (I've read about large tortoises
that can live for a year without drinking), the techniques by which every

living being finds or creates shade. The desert, he wrote, seems in its
desolation to have freed itself of 'parasitic man'. Seems, because in fact
it has not. If you follow a double line of wheel tracks across the sand
and rocks you will find a habitation somewhere, 'with a few trees pointing
their roots at under-earth water, a patch of starveling corn and squash,
and strips of jerky hanging on a string'.

We put it to the test. At Barstow we take the Interstate 15, straight
across the desert, and after about forty miles we turn off onto a narrow
road in the hills to look for somewhere to sleep. We find ourselves at an
old railroad junction called Nipton: a few trees, a pond, a dozen houses
(some boarded up), a rusted water tank, a few caravans, a café with its
windows smashed in. You are welcomed by the Nipton Trading Post and
next to it an old boarding house where, for a few dollars, a bed awaits.
And a rocking chair on the porch.

Until 1940 Nipton was a flourishing little town that even had its own
school. Now just sixteen people remain. The woman at the trading post
is looking forward to the cool of evening – yes, the cooler season is on
its way again. She comes from Alaska. 'We're very much on our own,
yes,' she says. 'But we're very close, too. Anyone who lives here wants
peace and quiet.'

We're the only guests. In the café they cook for us: steak, chips and
salad. The place is run by a couple. There are a few randomly placed
tables and chairs, there's a pool table, and in the middle of the café is a
multi-coloured plastic swing and in it a child with a contraption that
chatters and squeaks every time the child moves, a mass of little lights
flickering. That is the only sound.

We get talking. She calls herself Angie and his name is Steve. She's
from China. She studied English and was sent to the United States as part
of preparations for the Olympic Games in Beijing, to get used to looking
after American guests. There she met Steve.

Some people like extreme places and perhaps couldn't live anywhere
else. Steve is also from Alaska. As a professional soldier he fought pretty
much everywhere, but during his last mission in Iraq he was made a
prisoner of war. He'd been in a cell for eighteen hours when he and his
men saw a chance to escape. That's when it started. It got steadily worse,
especially the noises. That short period of imprisonment kept coming

back to him in his dreams and it wouldn't stop. The doctors advised him to look for somewhere quiet, which is how he ended up in Nipton. He has to stick it out here for another year, but he can't wait to get back to Alaska. 'You can see for two hundred miles, clear as glass, that's what life's like there.'

We sit on the porch all evening. The sky is black, with a dizzying abundance of stars. An intense silence hangs over the earth and the hills. High above us, barely audible, a plane makes its way between the stars. Half an hour later, just for a moment, we hear the sound of a backfiring motorcycle. It quickly dies away. A dog wakes up – a couple of barks. Every sound is separate.

Then all at once the silence is torn to shreds. Bells start ringing, there's a roar in the distance and within a few seconds, on that apparently deserted railroad in front of our door, three bright lights appear. Three heavy, double locomotives emerge from the darkness of the desert. A howl of lament resounds across the plain and then they thunder past, at least a mile long, these container wagons, refrigerated wagons, timber wagons, coal wagons and whatever else Union Pacific hauls around the world. The train has to get up the hill; the locomotives labour and snort, slower and slower. This is one of the places where tramps and stowaways jumped on or off. They made Nipton into what it once was.

Steinbeck wrote: 'There is a breed of desert men, not hiding exactly but gone to sanctuary from the sins of confusion.'

Those desert men are still around.

A classic anecdote about Tolstoy. In 1877, when his novel *Anna Karenina* had been holding half of Moscow spellbound as a newspaper serialisation for four years, the author stormed into the English Club one evening, utterly bewildered. 'Gentlemen, gentlemen,' he cried. 'Now Anna Karenina has gone and thrown herself in front of a train.'

Every writer or storyteller knows how it goes; you can invent all sorts of things, but at some point the story runs off with you rather than you with the story. Anna Karenina slips out from under your fingers. There's no stopping her, and suddenly it's all over.

That's what travelling is like too. Every journey has a personality, a temperament of its own, as Steinbeck wrote in the introduction to *Travels*, and whatever your plans may be, you're no match for it. 'We find after years of struggle that we do not take a trip; a trip takes us.'

We are having the same experience. Of course this is our trip, our carefully thought-out project, our intellectual property. But the opposite is also true. Along the way this journey has taken possession of us and carried us into a maelstrom from which we cannot escape.

We drive for days past rocks and dried grass. Near the Colorado River, on the border with Nevada, we come upon a gambling city, Laughlin, a mini Las Vegas in the middle of the desert, and there we eat a cheerless sandwich in a huge replica paddle steamer. The casinos are full of old ladies, the hundreds of fruit machines sing their song and from time to time spit out money with a great burst of rattling and jubilation. The regular sound of cheerful chinking makes everything carefree and bright, as if the gates to heaven are about to open.

In Kingman, Arizona, we rejoin Steinbeck's route. After the Colorado, the Interstate 40 begins its ascent. We drive across the 'huge tilted plain' back up onto the 'backbone of the continent', which here means the Aquarius and Juniper Mountains, and then on to Flagstaff. Semi-trailers pass us, each of them carrying one giant wing, like an enormous dinosaur bone, followed later by turbines: they're building a whole windmill park.

A strong wind has got up. The towns have names like Ash Fork, Two Guns and Canyon Diablo. Often they are little more than settlements of stationary caravans and plastic prefabs, jumbled together among the bushes, with a handful of shops and a bank at the centre. Beside the road an Indian Trading Post announces itself, with gold nuggets and meteorites for sale – 'Two T-shirts, Five Dollar!' – then another hour of nothing but yellow-brown loneliness and in the far distance the straight line of a train.

It's 8 November 2010, a bleak Monday afternoon. The radio provides classical sounds, or rather an endless piece of orchestral music, pink blancmange out of a packet that goes on dripping from early morning until late at night. It's getting colder fast now; the desert is behind us and the wind is turning northerly.

We drive into New Mexico. In Gallup we eat an omelette at Maria's Restaurant. Maria is geniality itself. She urges us to be careful. 'Thursday it's going to snow and it can get pretty bad around here.' Through her front window we look out onto the cinema, the optician's and a handful of pawnshops. Main Street is empty and abandoned, aside from three men standing there to talk.

Steinbeck must have camped somewhere near here, in the same bright cold. This part of *Travels* says a lot about the exhaustion that overcame him after he dropped his friend Toby in Flagstaff. For the first time in weeks he was alone again, and at last he acknowledged what he had been refusing to admit: 'I was driving myself, pounding out the miles because I was no longer hearing or seeing. I had passed my limit of taking in or, like a man who goes on stuffing in food after he is filled, I felt helpless to assimilate what was fed in through my eyes.'

As we drive into Albuquerque with evening coming on, it starts to drizzle. The city is cold and empty. There's hardly anyone about, even in the old Mexican centre. The next morning, the men of the breakfast club at the Village Inn start talking about the snow that's on its way. It's fairly normal for this time of year, I hear them say, except that they've had it so warm here for so long that people are no longer used to it.

An old man wearing a Marines cap comes to sit at our table and joins the conversation. He was born and raised in these parts, he says. 'My family was already living here before the Pilgrim Fathers had ever heard of America.' He knows the climate well. 'We always had fiercely cold winters, with a good bit of snow. You haven't seen that in years and you won't again. I'm no fan of those environmentalist types, but the climate is changing here, that's for sure.'

My new friend doesn't hold back: eggs, sausage, roast potatoes, pancakes and a big slice of apple pie. He's on his own, his pension is good, ex-military; why shouldn't he have a bit of pleasure in life? He tells us about his Spanish forebears, a family that emigrated to Mexico centuries ago and ended up in the north, in the part of Mexico that was later annexed as the New Mexico Territory and in 1912 finally became the 47th State of America. 'My family changed nationality three times even though they stayed living at the same place.'

He was a career serviceman with the US Navy, which for a simple lad was one of the few ways to build a career and see something of the world. Korea, yes, that was tough, but from then on he had a quiet time of it, mostly stationed in Hawaii. They didn't want him for Vietnam. He took early retirement.

When he returned to his home town, everything had changed beyond recognition. I ask him about the difference between 1960 and now. He points to a letter in that morning's paper, the *Albuquerque Journal*. 'Surprise: of the twenty-seven children who knocked on my door on Halloween, just three spoke English. Same story with their parents. Nice to be able to share these celebrations with someone!'

Up to a point he understands a letter like that, but then again he doesn't. 'Millions of Mexicans have come over the border in the past few decades. They're all here illegally, but they're also hard workers. It's pushed wages right down. The employers think that's great, but for the ordinary worker there's not a penny to be made around here any longer. That's the main difference between now and fifty years ago. There's a lot more poverty. And the mood is bleak. No one knows where we go from here.'

We order another slice of apple pie. 'It's strange,' says our fellow diner. 'If you think about it, those illegal Mexicans everyone sneers at are immigrants only on paper. In reality this has always been Mexico.' He has a good grasp of history, and we pass the rest of the morning talking about it, about the Spanish colonisation of California, about Florida and Mexico, about empires that come and go, rise and fall. 'That's the rhythm of history,' he says, with something close to resignation. 'It's all going to be different in the next hundred years. That's inevitable. Our grandchildren will see it.'

As we drive away, the first flakes fall.

Two

TEXAS. SUDDENLY IT'S WRITTEN on all the car bumpers: 'God Bless Texas', or 'Don't Mess With Texas', or 'American by Birth, Texan by the Grace of God', or 'Texas Born, Texas Proud'.

Texas is a land apart. A Texan will never say he comes from America. He's from Texas. In May 1945 John Gunther saw a slogan in Fort Worth designed to encourage the buying of war bonds: 'Buy Bonds and Help Texas Win the War.'

'Texas is a state of mind,' Steinbeck wrote. 'Texas is an obsession. Above all, Texas is a nation in every sense of the word . . . A Texan outside of Texas is a foreigner.' That attitude is a product of Texan history. The Texans fought single-handedly against the Mexicans for their freedom; between 1836 and 1845 they even had their own Lone Star republic, the Republic of Texas, before they joined the United States.

Texas is, first of all, huge. From Amarillo in the north to Laredo in the south is a journey of at least two days. It's roughly the same size as France. There are a few beautiful mountain ranges, but mostly it's a brown dusty plain, hammered flat under a steel-blue, celestial dome.

Texas is astonishingly hot. It can also be freezing cold – snow is falling as we cross the border – but Texans call Houston 'Los Angeles with the climate of Calcutta'. Mexico is right nearby. You can recognise Texans immediately by their speech, with that sing-song drawl of theirs. They say 'shit' as if smearing it on bread, in long syllables with lots of 'y's in the middle. Their manners are coarse yet they have a Southern gallantry.

When Texans go for a night out they keep their jeans and boots on. It's their national costume. Still, those sharply cut pants cost 400 dollars, the boots 700, and I don't dare ask the price of their Stetsons. There is

something German about Texas as well. As recently as 1945, a sixth of
the population had German origins, San Antonio had a Sauerkraut Bend
– once the Kaiser Wilhelm Strasse – and Gunther described the rural
areas as still scattered with villages and towns that were almost as German
as the villages and towns of Bavaria.

Texas is rich, or rather Texas is nouveau riche. It's the only confederate
state that became seriously wealthy, resulting in what John Gunther
described as 'a remarkable fusion of old "southern" characteristics, plus
big money'. When Gunther travelled around here just after the war, oil
had been found in four-fifths of the state, production was in full swing
and many people, even the poorest tenant farmers, were overwhelmed
by 'vast and instantaneous wealth', as Gunther put it. 'That there should
be a cultural lag was inevitable; that plenty of the newly rich should have
done crazy things was inevitable; that the wave of wealth should have
produced some obscurantism was inevitable.'

Steinbeck travelled through Texas fifteen years after Gunther, and his
account is in the same vein, culminating in his description of a typical
Texan 'orgy' – 'showing men of great wealth squandering their millions
on tasteless and impassioned exhibitionism'. That phase of easy pickings
is over now. There's still a great deal of money in Texas, but people work
and pioneer hard for it.

Steinbeck wrote about the 'boundless and explosive' energy of Texans,
and those adjectives still apply. AT&T, Dell, Texas Instruments, Exxon Mobil
– they all have their origins in Texas. Dallas/Fort Worth is the country's
third-biggest airport and Houston its second-busiest harbour. Almost
three-quarters of the country's increase in employment in 2008 was
attributable to Texas, especially the densely populated triangle of Houston,
Dallas and San Antonio that is known as the 'texaplex'. Illustrative of the
pull of Texas are the rental costs of a U-Haul removal van. Anyone wanting
to move from Los Angeles to Houston pays three times as much as
someone moving from Houston to Los Angeles.

Texas is above all big. Very big. The first place we stop at, just before Amarillo,
is the Big Texan Steak Ranch, a bright-yellow timber building where you
can buy all the things that Texas is big in: hats, boots, rocking chairs and
of course meat, in vast quantities. Inside is a dark-brown-panelled dining

room with a wooden gallery above it. There's room for at least 200 diners, the tables are spread with cowhides, and on the walls are stags' heads, guns and bison skulls. The Christmas decorations are already at full glare. Dozens of different beers are available, a reminder of the German side of Texas.

The menu recommends the eighteen-ounce jubilee steak, commemorating the Ranch's fiftieth anniversary: over a pound of meat, 'a tribute to man versus food'. Anyone who feels up to it can order the seventy-two-ounce steak, more than two kilos, free to any customer who manages to consume the whole slab. 'Many have tried, many have failed.' The research bureau Harris Poll announced in 1999 that Americans were 'the fattest people on Earth' and 'getting fatter every year'. Nothing has changed since then.

Alka-Seltzer once caused a furore by using the slogan, 'I Can't Believe I Ate the Whole Thing.' Columnist David Wilson claims it applies to the entire nation, which with five per cent of the world's population manages to consume a quarter of all the available energy. Per head, that's one and a half times as much as the Netherlands or Sweden, six times as much as Mexico or China, and fifteen times as much as Tanzania.

We've seen it all along our route south: desert in every direction but also big golf courses, parks and avenues with green lawns, huge fountains, and the frothing sound of sprinklers day and night. There's no end to it. All that water is from elsewhere – in Arizona they're even dreaming of bringing water down from the 'great green sponge up north' that is Canada – all of it laboriously brought here so that, with great exuberance, improper use can be made of it. This is no longer a matter of carelessness and waste, it's more than that, it's a strange kind of triumphalism: look what we can do!

'Man against nature.' The patio heaters are burning fiercely, even though it's twenty-three degrees in the shade.

Molly Ivins, a witty and astute columnist for the *Texas Observer* and the *Dallas Times Herald*, claimed that no one in Texas is interested in the impression he or she makes on others. It is 'an un-self-conscious place . . . Reactionaries aren't embarrassed. Rich folks aren't embarrassed. Rednecks aren't embarrassed. Liberals aren't embarrassed . . . Lobbyists, loan sharks, slumlords, war profiteers, chiropractors, and KKKers are all proud of their callings.' But, she warned, Texas is not a civilised place. 'Texans shoot one another a lot. They also knife, razor, and stomp one another to death with some frequency. And they fight in bars all the time. You can get five years for murder and 99 for pot possession in this state – watch your ass.'

She's dead now, cheerful old Molly, but how crazy about Texas she was. Especially Texan politics, although that was something she saw as a worrying aberration. 'Good thing we've still got politics in Texas – finest form of free entertainment ever invented.'

I once interviewed her about the Bush family. I can see us now, sitting on a bench outdoors in Austin, laughing away. But I also remember how she suddenly became serious: 'Never, never underestimate the Republican machine, never underestimate their political skills, their immense network, the campaigning techniques, their capacity to pull off the most improbable tricks. You laugh at their show, not believing for a moment that people like that could ever run the world. Well, forget that. Don't underestimate them.'

The 'Texan orgy' Steinbeck wrote about took place on Thanksgiving Day, at the house of friends of John and Elaine. The tireless Bill Steigerwald managed to find the precise location after much searching: Bitter Creek Ranch near Clarendon, east of Amarillo. The house is still there, he discovered, in the middle of land belonging to a medium-sized ranch. A good many things have been modernised, but other than that it exactly fits Steinbeck's description. According to Steigerwald, 'it is not your typical cabin in the woods'; in fact he found it more 'like a little motel, only in 1960 the regular guests were usually members of Texas' richest cattle families'.

Steinbeck studied them closely, these rich people 'concealing their status in blue jeans and riding boots'. The talk was about hunting, riding and cattle breeding, the jeans appropriately faded and frayed, the boots 'salted with horse sweat', while the bar 'consisted of a tub of ice, quart bottles of soda, two bottles of whisky and a case of pop' and 'the smell of money was everywhere'. He remembered what an old odd-job man had once said to him, refusing to go out onto the street in his dirty working clothes: 'You got to be awful rich to dress as bad as you do.'

John and Elaine remained at Bitter Creek Ranch for about a week before travelling on to Austin, where they stayed with Elaine's sister. From there John set off alone again, heading for New Orleans.

As for ourselves, we have little to detain us here: no friends, no ranch, no Thanksgiving. We spend the night just beyond Amarillo and breakfast in a gas station on weak coffee and soft, cellophane-wrapped muffins, sell-by date around 2020. Then off across the plains again, eastwards along the Interstate 40. In the clear morning light the horizon looks at least a hundred miles away and there's not a house, not even a tree between us and all that infinitude.

This is the old wagon trail, US Highway 66, better known as Route 66, the legendary road that first skirts Chicago and then cuts straight across the heart of America, through Texas and Arizona, eventually reaching the ocean at Santa Monica, near Los Angeles. When Steinbeck drove to Texas in Rocinante in 1960, he took the US 66 almost all the way. Only later was it largely replaced by the Interstate 40 and other highways. These days at best you'll find fragments of it, in all shapes and sizes: a bit of the old 66 through the centre of a city, a short detour of a few miles, an empty stretch of asphalt parallel to the interstate, a gas station rusting away, an abandoned motel in the middle of the desert.

The US 66 was not just a romantic road through the most isolated parts of America, it was one of the more important transport arteries, running diagonally across the country. Every day, thousands of dusty trucks carried everything imaginable and unimaginable along the 66: farming machinery from Detroit to Houston, fruit and vegetables from the Salinas Valley to Chicago, farming families from Oklahoma to Fresno, tanks and troops from the Midwest to the ports on the Pacific coast, hippies from Illinois and Texas to San Francisco.

The route symbolised the country's eternal restlessness, the trek westwards that was inextricably bound up with the great milestones of twentieth-century America: the wild 1920s, the Depression of the 1930s, the war years, the beginnings of tourism in the 1950s, the Civil Rights Movement and youth revolt of the 1960s – again and again the US 66 blazed a trail through history.

The Grapes of Wrath, the story of desperate farmers from Oklahoma fleeing the storms of the Dust Bowl, is largely set around Route 66. 'All of these people are in flight, and they come to the 66 from the tributary side roads, from the wagon tracks and the rutted country roads. 66 is the mother road, the road of flight.'

In the little towns along the way, stories are still told about the 'Arkies' and the 'Okies', the refugees from Arkansas and Oklahoma who drove past in an endless stream of chugging Model T Fords. 'We'd classify the poor people as first class or third class depending on how many mattresses were on top of the car,' Joseph Smith told journalist Susan Croce Kelly, who describes the history of the road in detail in her book *Route 66*.

Smith's father had a gas station in Santa Rosa, New Mexico. 'Sometimes you couldn't see the car for all the stuff tied on. Sometimes they would try to pawn things like furniture or spare tires for gasoline, but we didn't take it. When my dad first went into business, he tried to help some of those people who didn't have any money, but he couldn't afford it and finally got hardhearted.'

Bill Nelson, son of a garage owner from Tucson, Arizona, recalled how the Okies came out of the Midwest 'like flies', with cars that might give up the ghost halfway. 'Some would even come and leave their cars and go walking off.'

After war broke out, the US 66 looked totally different. Ford built thousands of aeroplane wings in Detroit in those years, and huge trucks drove them to the assembly works in St Louis. The same went for tank parts and even the huge gliders that were used in the Normandy landings. All kinds of things were lugged back and forth along the 66.

Hundreds of thousands of conscripts from the Midwest, who had travelled along Route 66 to the California coast for the first time in their lives, could imagine nothing better than to stay there after 1945. As soon as they were demobbed they raced back along the 66 to find their home-town sweethearts, got married, then left as soon as they could to return to perpetually sunny California. In total some 3.5 million men and women moved to the west coast in the post-war period.

One of those departing GIs was pianist Bobby Troup, who in 1946 headed westwards with his wife Cynthia along Route 66 to try his luck in Hollywood as a composer. It took them ten days in an old Buick. They found themselves in Amarillo in a nocturnal blizzard, were astonished by the silent beauty of the Mojave Desert, messed around a bit along the way with the lyrics for a new song, and by the time they got close to Los Angeles they had the refrain, a brainwave of Cynthia's: 'Get Your Kicks on Route Sixty-Six.'

> Well, if you ever plan to motor west,
> Travel my way; take the highway that's the best.
> Get your kicks on Route Sixty-Six.
> Well, it winds from Chicago to LA
> More than two thousand miles all the way
> Get your kicks on Route Sixty-Six.

'I finished the song with a map after we got to Los Angeles,' Troup said later. 'I wasn't aware of what a great lyric I had written. I do remember it was possibly the worst road I'd ever taken in my life.'

It became the favourite of all those restless drivers, and thanks to the swinging rhyme by Cynthia Troup, no road in the world is as famous.

The decision to build this 'Main Street of America' had been taken in 1926. It was to be a completely new federal highway, from Chicago to Oklahoma City, then on via Amarillo, Flagstaff and Barstow to Los Angeles. The number '66' was chosen because it sounded good. Here and there it followed old roads and trade routes, but the new highway mainly crossed endless empty plains, rough and barely cultivated land where white settlers had lived perhaps only since the beginning of the century.

Large parts of the US 66 were not even sealed at first. Steinbeck wasn't exaggerating when he described the strenuous journey from California across the Mojave Desert that he undertook as a young man. That whole stretch consisted of a narrow track running past the telegraph poles standing in the open landscape in a lonely line. Not until 1934 was the asphalt complete on the section between California and New Mexico. By 1938 you could drive straight from Lake Michigan to the Pacific, a five-day journey past small towns, villages, forests, prairies and deserts to the edge of the ocean.

It was then that the US 66 took on another role, becoming a lifeline for thousands of shops, gas stations, hotels, diners and garages. All those passers-by gradually built the economic foundations for countless villages and towns, hundreds of Main Streets that grew and flourished. A couple would start selling gasoline, then a simple diner appeared, a few cabins were built for people to spend the night, a neighbour started fixing broken-down cars, someone further on set up a stall selling fruit and souvenirs, a few Native Americans sat at the side of the road with their pots and baskets. It went like that all the way along. Close to Route 66 anyone could earn a few dollars, even during the Great Depression.

The road – in reality little more than a simple two-lane highway – was notorious for its many accidents. People talked about the 'Bloody 66' and the 'Two-Lane Killer'. In Arizona and New Mexico it was the 'Camino de la Muerte', and there were sections with names like 'Devil's Elbow', 'Death Alley' and 'Blood Alley'. Every little town had one or more wreckers, mechanics with tow trucks who specialised in pulling crashed cars apart and sawing the casualties free. Within about twenty years the US 66 was starting to become the victim of its own success.

The road was simply too full and too busy. In 1946 alone, Detroit manufactured around 2.1 million cars. Between 1946 and 1952 the number of passenger vehicles increased by more than half, and in 1960 there were about four cars on the road for every ten Americans. From the 1930s onwards car producers, oil companies, tyre manufacturers and road builders formed a powerful coalition, the National Highway Users Conference.

It was all about the 'freedom' of the American road, the lobbyists claimed, and they pointed to the 'threats to automobility' posed by the railroads. In 1965 the American Road & Transportation Builders Association even published a special prayer for American highway construction teams:

Oh, almighty God, who has given us this Earth and has appointed man to have dominion over it, who has commanded us to make straight the highways, to lift up the valleys, and to make the mountains low, we ask thy blessing. Bless these, the nation's road builders, and their friends.

When I travelled across America by train, I heard the same story any number of times: the fantastic American rail network fell victim to a vast conspiracy of road builders, oil companies and the auto industry. They bought up shares in the railroad companies and their competitors, then destroyed them.

That is indeed what often happened to the extensive networks of local trams that had been built around large American cities. They were put out of business in the 1920s and 1930s with great determination, often with the help of the car industry. But with the railways other factors came into play. Of course pressure from the powerful motoring lobby made it impossible for the rail companies to hold on to a reasonable share of passenger transport, but behind the scenes many of their directors heaved a sigh of relief. After a brief revival in the war years, passenger transport was above all a source of anxiety and financial loss for them. Only with freight was there still good money to be made.

President Eisenhower was speaking from the heart when he advocated improvements to road transport. During the war, as supreme commander of the Allied forces, he'd become familiar with the German autobahn network. He was deeply impressed. America must have something like it, a system of highways on which troops and materiel could be moved from one side of the continent to the other at great speed. The threat posed by Russian atomic weapons was another important catalyst. In a crisis it would take days to evacuate the major cities using only the antiquated road networks. To Russian bombers, New York, Chicago and Philadelphia were sitting ducks. Such military considerations did a great deal to persuade those members of Congress who had been wondering whether this was really a task for the federal government.

So the motoring lobby won on all fronts. In 1956 Congress showed how dynamic it could be by deciding to build an Interstate Highway System, mainly with federal funding. Of course Americans were starting to fly more and more, and in the 1960s the plane took over from the train to a great extent when it came to long-distance passenger journeys. In the mid-1950s Elaine would have caught up with Steinbeck by train. In 1960 she flew everywhere. As for transport over shorter distances, with the Federal-Aid Highway Act of 1956 America clearly opted for the car and for roads. Car ownership was further stimulated by low taxes and remarkably cheap fuel. Congress deliberately allowed that other transport system, the railroad, to wither. The loser was ultimately the general public, which was deprived of all choice. Large parts of the country have had to manage ever since without any decent public transport at all other than by air, a situation unique in the developed world.

Moreover, with the Federal-Aid Highway Act the means – a road, a car – became an end in itself. The interstates, the auto industry and everything they brought with them provided one-sixth of American jobs, and that machinery had to be kept running at all costs. Stephen Goddard spoke of a 'highway-motor complex', a system comparable to the military sector, a permanent feedback loop of further expansion, as if no conceivable alternative ever existed.

The American interstates differed in one respect from the German autobahns: they were intended not just to join cities together but to reshape them and create new urban areas. In the early twentieth century, America was still largely an agrarian society, and for some decades car makers and road builders did everything they could 'to get the farmer out of the mud'. From the 1920s onwards, attention increasingly switched to the cities. There, after all, was where most voters lived. That was where most of the money was.

The stores of Main Street USA, where you did your daily shopping on foot, were replaced by huge, anonymous shopping malls on the edge of town, where you parked your car and could find everything you needed under one roof. That spelled the end for countless typical mom-and-pop stores, and with them the classic entrepreneurial capitalism that had set the tone for the first two centuries of America's existence. The car was the force behind a huge revolution that took place in silence, or at least with no more than a whisper.

McLean, some seventy miles east of Amarillo, was one of the last towns on Route 66 to be connected to the new interstate network, in 1984. We end up there by chance when trying to find a bit of the old US 66. First Street is elegant and deserted. There are two museums, a local one and a barbed wire museum called Devil's Rope, and both are still open.

'Route sixty-six went straight through town and we had all the shops you can imagine,' Billie Kingston, selling tickets at the McLean Museum, tells us. 'We were the watermelon capital of the world, we had a pharmacy, a newspaper, cafés. Until well into the Seventies there were at least

ten motels here and about twelve gas stations. The new Baptist church
built in 1960 was full every Sunday, with a congregation of a good 400.
Now it's barely fifty.'

We look at the exhibits, which include the old barbershop, the windmill that generated electricity (six volts), the printing press that used to
produce the McLean News, Ruth Smith's 1927 Model T Ford, the McLean
Volunteer Fire Department's fire truck, and the wedding dress worn by
the grandmother of June Woods in 1897. In the folders of photographs
we walk through the little town's entire history: the ladies who in 1943
treated soldiers in transit to home-made cookies; the camp where German
prisoners of war were held; the legendary dust storm of Sunday afternoon,
14 April 1935; the failed attempt by shopkeepers to secure a location next
to the new Interstate 40; Jimmy Hill, who refused to relinquish his Phillips
gas station on Route 66 until the government had paid him enough
compensation: 'I ain't leavin' it . . .'

'You should talk to Archie Cooper, the oldest man here,' says Billie.
'He's seen it all.' She takes us to his house, where we are given the
warmest of welcomes. Archie is ninety-eight. He still works as an evangelist, and embedded in the pale skin of his face are two deep, clear eyes.
Now that his wife has died he spends all his time renovating his attic
– 'Praise the Lord!' – and maintaining the Ten Commandments Monument
that he – 'Praise the Lord!' – saved from the hands of unbelievers when
it had to be removed from the courthouse in Alabama. We admire both
projects in detail and then he is more than willing to tell us about the
Dust Bowl.

'Christ conquered our hearts, that's how simple it was at the start.
When I was still a bachelor I travelled around. Sometimes there was an
empty building and we'd use it as a church. Before we married my wife
ran the Sunday school. When there was no money I worked as a carpenter,
just like Jesus and Joseph.

'In the spring of nineteen thirty-five I was working for a farmer near
here and on Sunday fourteenth of April we had a job to do on the land
that couldn't wait. Suddenly we saw an inky black cloud rolling towards
us. It was coming real fast, soundlessly. "Run," the farmer shouted. "Get
home!" A hard rain started up; mud poured down on us.

'Then the storm struck. Everything went black. Our team of horses stopped immediately. What were we supposed to do? I tried a little test. I held my hand in front of my nose and I couldn't see that hand any more. For us it didn't last very long, but I heard that people thought it was the end of the world. A faint sun was visible in all that darkness, like a red ball.'

The great drought had begun in the early 1930s, in the middle of the years of economic crisis, when some two million Americans were already roaming the country, hungry and jobless, hopping on and off moving freight trains. The first great dust storms came in 1933 and the Dust Bowl period lasted until the early 1940s. The black storms swept through Colorado, Kansas, Oklahoma and northern Texas. The dust fell as far away as Chicago and the Pacific Ocean.

It was a natural disaster caused by the hand of man. The Midwest regularly sees long dry periods, but this was something else. The topsoil of vast areas of agricultural land was completely blown away. The earth had been regularly ploughed and loosened, so there was no longer any thick vegetation to hold the soil in place. When the rain finally came, it bucketed down, which made everything even worse. The soil that had not been taken by the wind was simply washed away.

For many farmers there was no choice but to pack up all the possessions they had left and go off in search of shelter. In total some two and a half million people fled. Some found new employment along Route 66; others tried their luck in California, where they often ended up in federal migrant camps. Entire towns in Oklahoma emptied – for the lower middle class there was even less chance of earning a living. Half a million people became homeless. When John Gunther travelled through here in 1945 the dust dunes still stood alongside the roads, houses were still buried under the blown soil and he saw abandoned farms everywhere.

In August 1936, on behalf of the *San Francisco News*, Steinbeck visited the camps and settlements where fleeing Okies had taken shelter. He wrote about a family living in a hut made of willow stems, the gaps plugged with grass, old paper and flattened tin cans. Husband, wife and three children were sleeping on the ground under an old carpet. The youngest, a child of three, severely malnourished, had no clothes other than a gunnysack.

'He will die in a very short time,' Steinbeck wrote. 'The older children may survive. Four nights ago the mother had a baby in the tent, on the dirty carpet. It was born dead, which was just as well because she could not have fed it at the breast; her own diet will not produce milk. After it was born and she had seen that it was dead, the mother rolled over and lay still for two days. She is up today, tottering around.'

Archie Cooper stayed where he was. 'The dust storms came over us almost every day. As far as possible we hung wet sheets and towels over all the cracks, day after day. And we kept on sweeping. We swept whole washtubs full of dust off the floor.'

He shows me a collection of clippings and diary entries. The station-masters warned each other of the next approaching storm by sending telegrams: 'My God, here it comes!'

A farmer wrote: 'Leaving for the east. Our families will suffocate otherwise. We saw thirty-six trucks loaded with furniture on the US 66.' Another wrote: 'More than a hundred families from our area have already left. We have to leave too, for a place where our children can at least live.' And one wrote simply: 'We bath . . . and we bath . . . and we bath again.'

It is a history that will not be repeated in a hurry. Far less ploughing is done, and far more cautiously. Care is taken to prevent overgrazing, and a huge number of trees have been planted and groundcover plants introduced to give the soil more firmness and structure.

The economic refugees Steinbeck described can still be found everywhere, although now they come from Mexico and Latin America. Government estimates suggest that over eighty per cent of American agricultural labourers are Hispanic, and at least half – according to some experts the figure is as high as ninety per cent – are illegal.

Their precarious existence differs little from that of the Joads in The Grapes of Wrath. They pick strawberries and grapes from early in the morning until late at night and often earn barely enough to eat. A bit of bad luck and they turn up at the right place at the wrong moment, when the harvest is already in. Then the family has to sleep on the streets until other work can be found. A bit of good luck and they can pick grapes under a swelteringly hot cover of leaves, and if they stand up for a moment to stretch their backs the pesticides drip into their faces. They have a strikingly high rate of cancer and miscarriage.

It's difficult and risky these days to cross over from Mexico surreptitiously. If you're not caught and sent back by the American border guards you may well be robbed by the Mexican gangs that prowl around. Almost all the stories told by immigrants involve three or four failed attempts before they managed to cross the border – fearful wanderings, sometimes with children, often lasting for several days, until one final effort brought success.

The American newspapers report that more and more corpses are being found in the border area: 'crossers' who died on the way. Border security is getting tighter all the time and the people-smugglers are looking for more outlying routes. The trip is increasingly dangerous. The mortuary in Tucson is completely full. In the summer of 2010 alone more than fifty bodies were brought in, and the river of dead is unending. Refrigerated trucks have been rented to store the bodies of illegals who died on the way. Often they are already mummified. Sometimes all that remains is a few bones. It usually proves impossible to give them back their names.

Yet the American Dream continues to draw them.

Three

WE TAKE US ROUTE 70 TOWARDS CLARENDON, then pass Memphis and Childress as we head south on Route 83. The soil is red, the grass yellow-green, and in the fierce midday sun a brownish-red glow hangs over the endless plain. Here and there the ground has been torn open. There are visible gullies and even a small, dried-up canyon left by the floods that once ravaged this region. Again, dead animals lie all along the sides of the road: roebucks, prairie dogs, badgers, racoons, cats – the verges are draped with wretched furs.

Clarendon, where Steinbeck stayed, is a green oasis in the hard landscape of the Texas Panhandle, all woods and golf courses. There are even whole deer at the roadside now, two of them within fifteen minutes. Then nothing but the chestnut-coloured plain again, and the occasional caravan, rusty watermill or tumbledown timber farmhouse. Billboards beside the road say: 'Real Texans don't litter.' A few miles further on, the day of judgement is announced for a date in May 2011. The white flakes of the first cotton fields appear. The harvest is largely in and we see big white bales from time to time. Gradually, more nodding donkeys appear in the landscape. Here the farmers are slowly pumping themselves rich.

The radio is full of voices. Every third station has someone giving good advice, telling stories about what to do and what not to do, sharing experiences with the listener all day long. A father, sometimes a mother, speaks words of wisdom and warning. Whether it's a matter of the Fall of Man or the budget deficit, everything comes in the guise of a staunch sermon; rhythm, accents, silences – all the rhetorical devices of the pulpit are loosed upon us. Faith, politics and social etiquette all meld together into an endlessly rolling meatball of words and admonitions.

Towards evening we drive into the little town of Paducah. The Hunters Lodge Motel lives up to its name. The other guests are here purely to hunt and they don't talk about anything else. Signs have been stuck up near our beds saying 'Do Not Clean Guns On The Towels' and 'Do Not Clean Game In The Rooms'. Outside there's not a soul to be seen. In the last of the daylight we walk down old Richards Street. The only sounds are from the sparrows in the bushes and a lonely truck in the distance. Between the buildings are patches of grass and bare earth, like gaps in a row of teeth: here was once a shop, a business, a family.

Suddenly we're standing in a large open space called Courthouse Square. At the centre, like intransigence turned into a great block of stone, is the huge courthouse, towering over everything else. It's a temple, no less, and above the door is the Great Commandment, 'To no one will we sell, deny or delay justice.'

Around it stands a wide range of shops: a bookstore, a hardware store, a florist's, a drugstore, Dick Norris Furniture, the Variety Store, Paducah Parts and Co., the Palace Barbershop, the Zana and Palace cinemas – a lively collection. But it's as if an evil wizard waved his wand over them all in about 1968. The windows are grey with dust, the doors boarded up, the neon lights extinguished, the iron ornamentation bare and rusty. The once-fashionable Cottle Hotel looks like an abandoned factory. It's as if the entire centre of town was immobilised at a stroke. Lights are burning in just one building, on a corner; the local paper is still extant, the *Paducah Post* (since 1903).

Back at the hotel I buttonhole the skinny night porter. 'What on earth happened here?' He tells a story that is gradually becoming familiar. The oil and the cotton stopped making money and those were precisely the two things the town ran on. 'We used to have thirty schools in this neighbourhood. The whole region was full of small independent farmers, and they made a good living, but they didn't have enough to invest in modern machinery and that did for them. Only the largest are left. The young people left for the big city . . . Sir, this town is dead, stone dead.'

The next morning I walk into the offices of the *Paducah Post*. At the desk is the Most Beautiful Girl in Town, 1956. Her name is Jimmye Taylor, now seventy-three, and she's still a real Texas beauty. She is the owner, as well as the editor-in-chief and editorial secretary, and nowadays she puts out the paper all on her own. Circulation has fallen from 20,000 to 1,400. She greets me warmly and then settles back into her chair.

First, the good news. 'They opened up the drugstore on the corner again this summer, the old soda fountain has been completely restored. You really should go see it.' She tells me that the chambers of commerce are now mainly trying to attract older people. 'The countryside around here is beautiful, the hunting's great and there's hardly any crime. Last year we had zero murders, assaults and rapes. And I can assure you the centre of town will soon be added to the National Register of Historic Places.'

She comes from a poor farming family. 'I worked just as hard as the boys. I drove the tractor even when I was a young girl. On Saturday afternoons we were allowed to go to Courthouse Square. My parents did the shopping and we watched a film. It was our only outing. On afternoons like that you could barely put one foot in front of the other it was so busy. There were people everywhere. Not anymore.' Yet the sense of community is still strong, she believes. 'We greet one another, we help each other if someone gets sick or dies, we make sure there's food for the funeral, that hasn't changed.

'This is a poor town, a very poor town. The headmistress earns more than anyone else, I think. We've always provided a lot of boys for the army, in World War Two, Vietnam, now Iraq and Afghanistan. Only we don't have all that many young people left.

'Sometimes I wonder how the town can survive, it has so little tax revenue. There's a beautiful swimming pool; we have Roosevelt to thank for that. Whatever you say about the man, he did what he promised. He got us through the last depression.' Her parents adored him. 'He was almost God. Now we know he was halfway to being a socialist.'

This was once a Democrat bastion. Nowadays almost everyone in the town votes Republican, but, says Jimmye, 'we don't trust anyone any more, not even our own members of Congress. We're all poor people, and poor people depend on really concrete things. If those fail to materialise, they become fearful and insecure.'

I've been in this region before, years ago, in Lubbock (a bastardisation of Lübeck), where I was shown around by Bob Gibson, the leader of a group of protesting cotton farmers and a loyal fan of Roosevelt. Gibson was an excellent storyteller, especially on the subject of the most memorable event of his childhood: the visit by Eleanor Roosevelt to Lubbock on 9 March 1938.

The president's wife did five things, if we are to believe Bob and local legend. She opened a new library, accepted a huge bouquet of roses, examined the New Deal housing project for new farmers where little Bob Gibson lived with his parents, took the salute at the annual parade of mothers-in-law (in which more than 600 took part on that occasion) and visited Dole Smith's toilet.

From that moment on, poor Dole was the target of hatred, envy and jealousy. Why visit him, when there were far better houses and bathrooms to be seen? He eventually took refuge in Oklahoma.

Bob Gibson still lives in the district that Eleanor Roosevelt travelled around like a fairy godmother in 1938. There's a famous photo that shows her talking to a man who is just putting the finishing touches to a water tower. He's hanging half out of the tower and in the background is his house, modest but handsomely painted. His wife and children are standing beside it, and above them is the beaming sun of Roosevelt's New Deal.

'It is hard for Americans today to realize what a power the Roosevelts exerted not only in our politics but in the public's imagination,' wrote Gore Vidal. From the moment in 1898 when Teddy Roosevelt stormed San Juan Hill during the Spanish–American War, right up to 12 April 1945, when Franklin Roosevelt died, the Roosevelts were centre stage – a period of nearly fifty years, and for almost half that time a Roosevelt was president.

Theodore and Franklin Delano Roosevelt were only distantly related. They were both descendants of Claes Maartenszen van Rosenvelt, from the Dutch province of Zeeland, who emigrated to America some time in the seventeenth century, but the two branches of the family grew apart. One Roosevelt was a Republican and the other a Democrat. Ties were restored when Franklin married Teddy's favourite niece Eleanor, his younger brother's daughter. Theodore was a witness at their wedding and Franklin was allowed to call the president of the United States

'Uncle Ted'. They were also related politically, in a sense. To quote Paul
Johnson, 'TR was a radical conservative whereas FDR was a conservative
radical.'

Franklin always modelled himself on 'Uncle Ted'. He radiated the same
cheerfulness and vitality as Theodore, his treatment of the press was
light-hearted and amicable, and he managed to form a bond with the
nation over the heads of his opponents. Like Theodore, he believed it was
his job to help the country to rebuild itself morally as well as in every
other way. At the same time he adored the political game. That was another
thing they had in common, their obvious pleasure in holding office.
Franklin was known as the 'gay reformer', at a time when 'gay' simply
meant merry.

There was one major difference in that Franklin was seriously disabled.
In the summer of 1921, when he was thirty-nine, he'd contracted polio,
an incurable disease against which there was no vaccine in those days.
He spent months helpless in bed, then used a wheelchair and finally,
with great persistence, learned to get around to some extent on crutches.
He poured all his energy into regaining a normal life. It took seven years,
most of the 1920s.

Some polio patients managed a fairly reasonable recovery, and Roosevelt
did all he could to give the impression he belonged in that category.
Prior to important public appearances he rehearsed endlessly, like an actor,
the walk and movements of a more or less normal man. He was determined not to leave anyone in any doubt as to whether the presidential
candidate, and later the president, was healthy enough to run the country.
There was soon a tacit agreement with the press: no one was ever to
hint that he was an invalid and at awkward moments they would look
away. 'No pictures, boys!' They all stuck to it. The president had to look
good.

Roosevelt's disability was severe. To walk at all, he needed two heavy
braces on his legs, from his feet to his hips. One foreign reporter,
Dutchwoman Jo van Ammers-Küller, decided she need pay no attention
to local codes of honour. Under the headline 'My lunch with Roosevelt'
she described in detail in De Telegraaf of 29 November 1939 how the president made his entrance. 'Two strong young men carry him in between
them. He sits on their linked hands with his arms around their shoulders.

While he is carried across the large room to an armchair near the fireplace, no one greets him; everyone pretends, as implicitly agreed, that he is not yet here. Only at the point when he is put down in his armchair is he present, and from that moment on he is naturally the unrivalled centre of attention.'

At the same time his disability worked in his favour. Until the 1920s Franklin Roosevelt was widely seen as a cheerful lightweight without much experience of life, despite the fact that he'd held the title of Assistant Secretary of the Navy from 1913 to 1919. A different image emerged from his heroic – and apparently successful – struggle with major disability. No one was able to claim he was merely Teddy's spoilt great nephew. If he could rebuild his life with such tenacity, why not the country too?

This attitude enabled him to become governor of New York, and in 1932 he announced his candidacy for the presidency. His opponent was the gruff and tight-lipped Herbert Hoover. The crisis was at its height, banks were failing all over the country and much of the financial sector was on the point of bankruptcy. According to official figures, a quarter of all breadwinners were unemployed; the reality was probably closer to a third. Newspaper reports included coverage of a demonstration in Chicago by 500 skinny and ragged schoolchildren who wanted school meals, crowds of several hundred jobless who surrounded a restaurant on New York's Union Square demanding a meal, and a buffet lunch in Boston that was raided by twenty-five starving children – two police assault vans were needed to chase them away.

Roosevelt won by an overwhelmingly convincing margin of more than seven million votes, and the Democrats achieved large majorities in the House of Representatives and the Senate. It meant he had a free hand – even with a filibuster the Republicans could not stop him.

On 4 March 1933 he gave his famous inaugural speech: 'So first of all, let me assert my firm belief that the only thing we have to fear is fear itself – nameless, unreasoning, unjustified terror which paralyzes needed efforts to convert retreat into advance.' He kept his word. Looking back it is astonishing to see what his administration achieved in its first hundred days. The day after his inauguration he declared a 'bank holiday' and all the banks were forced to close. When they reopened a week later America had left the gold standard and the banks had access to as much federal money as they needed. Capital was flowing again.

Roosevelt imposed rules on stockbrokers for the first time in history, to prevent excesses on Wall Street. He ended prohibition. He saved the famers by buying up their surpluses. He established a Civilian Conservation Corps that created jobs for three million young people, as well as the Federal Emergency Relief Administration and the Works Progress Administration, which between them gave support and work to seventeen million Americans. He set up the Home Owners' Loan Corporation to save the collapsing housing market. He initiated major infrastructure projects to get the economy moving again by building roads, bridges and huge hydroelectric power stations. He started his fireside chats, those famous radio talks in which he explained to all of America what he was planning to do and why. In the words of his biographer Arthur Schlesinger Jr, it was 'a presidential barrage of ideas and programs unlike anything known to American history'.

Roosevelt 'included the excluded'. It was one of his greatest achievements. He gave the poor and minority groups the feeling that 'America is ours too, and we count just as much as everyone else'. Tens of thousands of people shared their concerns and expectations with the president. The White House was inundated with letters – something that had never happened before – and they came from the black population as well as the white, partly because of Eleanor's pioneering work. In the Roosevelt years the black electorate crossed over to the Democratic Party, where it has remained ever since.

From the start there was harsh criticism: the New Deal was the Red Deal. Roosevelt was said to have turned the White House into 'the Kremlin on the Potomac' and adopted Karl Marx as the patron saint of the Democratic Party. In reality the New Deal was no ready-made blueprint for tackling the crisis, it was more a matter of continual searching and exploring, trial and error. Some measures were contradictory; others came too late or too soon. It became possible to rectify those errors only after the economy was boosted by American participation in the Second World War.

It was a long time before anyone could see which approach and which projects were successful. Historian Richard Hofstadter writes: 'At the heart of the New Deal there was not a philosophy but a temperament. The essence of this temperament was Roosevelt's confidence that even when he was operating in unfamiliar territory he could do no wrong, commit no serious mistakes.' What else could he do but radiate optimism? When he took office, America was facing a completely new situation in which the traditional methods could offer no comfort. Only a leader who was prepared to experiment, prepared to engage in that painful process of exploration, would be able to find a way out.

In 1934 Martha Gellhorn, who at the time of the New Deal was a young journalist travelling through North Carolina to report on the Depression, wrote to her boss, Roosevelt's right-hand man Harry Hopkins, that she had not found a hostile atmosphere among the jobless workers, nor even any bleak despair. 'I found a kind of contained and quiet misery; fear for their families and fear that their children wouldn't be able to go to school. ("All we want is work and the chance to care for our families like a man should.") But what is keeping them sane, keeping them going on and hoping, is their belief in the President.'

They said things to her like: 'You heard him talk over the radio, ain't you? He's the only president who ever said anything about the forgotten man. We know he's going to stand by us.' Or: 'He's a man of his word and he promised us; we aren't worrying as long as we got him.' Or: 'The president said no man was going to go hungry and cold; he'll get us our jobs.'

Bob Gibson told me similar stories. Almost half a century after the event, he drove me to the water tower where Eleanor had herself photographed in 1938 with such a cheerful look. The structure had rusted away, and the New Deal house next to it was an empty ruin with no glass in the windows, with shrubs growing out of the roof and the floor of the porch. Once it had been a pretty little wooden house with a living room, a kitchen, two bedrooms and a useful attic, a product of the New Deal's Home Owners' Loan Corporation, which meant that even poor farmers and agricultural labourers could finally have homes of their own.

We squirmed our way around some clumps of thistle to get inside and almost fell through the floor. Everything was covered with a layer of red dust at least a centimetre thick. Bob showed me a shaft with ventilation grids that ran from the cellar to the roof. 'Look how cleverly designed these houses are. This shaft somehow allowed the cooler air from the cellar to circulate all through the house. A kind of simple air conditioning.'

He explained to me in detail how ingeniously the whole project was financed, and he told me how as a boy he watched week by week from the school bus – also new – as houses went up all over this poor neighbourhood, shiny and brightly painted. He described the atmosphere of hope and expectation in those years, when a new school was built for them. 'And there was mains water! And electricity!'

In the context of the United States, what Roosevelt did was groundbreaking. The New Deal created a totally different relationship between government and citizen. When he came to office, America was still a country in which the independent businessman was of prime importance. It was generally felt that the government existed merely to maintain a few basic facilities and create the most favourable climate possible for business.

Roosevelt introduced a broader aim for the federal government, and with it a new concept of citizenship. He had no doubt that Americans bore responsibility for fellow citizens in need. Theodore Roosevelt had already provided the initial impulse, arguing for more active government, but FDR went far further, saying it was the task of government to intervene where private enterprise failed.

In his first hundred days, with a barrage of crucial federal initiatives that helped to put the country back on its feet, he laid the basis for modern America. At the same time, however, he sowed the seeds of the deep ideological rift that would shape American politics for the rest of the twentieth century: for or against state aid; for or against federal intervention.

From that trip with Bob Gibson I recall the graphs on the wall of his office: bankrupt farmers, bankrupt banks, threatened farmers, threatened banks. It was in the mid-1980s, the Reagan years. The little yellow blocks representing statistics from the 1960s and 1970s became great yellow columns during that presidency. In a single year, more farmers had been ruined than in all the bankruptcies since 1949 put together. 'I've lived here all my life,' Bob said. 'In all those years not a single one of my farming neighbours went bust, but the past two years there's suddenly been a flood of bankruptcies, twenty-four of them, mostly families that have been farming here for three generations, the grandchildren of the first pioneers. And the government still won't lift a finger to help.'

Bob Gibson acknowledged that the American farmer was 'the most capitalist animal in the world', independent to the point of being 'stubborn as the mules our grandfathers used to plough the land'. But he was also the victim of that same capitalism, because the large industrial agricultural corporations had an increasingly tight grip on farming. All the same, few farmers were inclined to make a stand. They continued to vote Republican, they hated any kind of government intervention and they despised Roosevelt's 'socialism'. 'If my neighbours have problems then it's the fault of the weather, or unfavourable prices, or a bad supplier. They're still refusing to recognise the situation we've all ended up in.'

During those same Reagan years Russell Baker, a universally respected journalist, once asked a Republican senator friend what the Senate would be doing that afternoon. 'We're killing the New Deal again,' he was told. As Baker wrote: 'George Bush was still at it a quarter-century later as his term ran out.'

Franklin Roosevelt was certainly no typical war president at the start, even if the New Deal was an unintended dress rehearsal for the huge mobilisation of national resources that America set in train in 1941. As late as 1940 the Democratic Party Platform spelled out how things stood: 'We will not participate in foreign wars, and we will not send our army, naval or air forces to fight in foreign lands outside of the Americas, except in case of attack.'

It was not just a matter of strategy but of capacity. When Hitler annexed Austria in 1938 and there was talk of a growing threat of war in Europe, the US Army had only 185,000 men. In the league table of military powers, the United States held eighteenth place. America had bravely come to the aid of Britain and France during the Great War but for all its sacrifices it had gained nothing. After that disillusionment America was seized by a powerful urge to withdraw behind the wide Atlantic

Ocean and leave the Europeans to their own devices. The Americans had troubles enough of their own.

Roosevelt realised early on that a Europe ruled by Adolf Hitler would in the long run pose a huge threat to America, and that all the democratic forces in the world were going to have to unite against German aggression. Senior French diplomat Jean Monnet, a future founding father of the European Community, described in his memoirs how he was sent on a secret mission to Roosevelt a week after the notorious Munich Agreement of September 1938, and was received with great warmth at the president's rather chaotic residence on the Hudson.

Even at that early stage, Monnet and Roosevelt, in the deepest secrecy, came to various agreements about American support for Europe. They calculated that in order to defeat Germany some 70,000 aircraft would be needed, and America would have to produce between 20,000 and 30,000 of them. Plans were made to start building three aircraft factories in the United States immediately.

Roosevelt, interestingly enough, wanted to have the planes assembled in Canada. That would enable him to get around any weapons embargo imposed by Congress. He had to walk on eggshells to avoid endangering his re-election in November 1940. As late as September that year, eighty-three per cent of Americans wanted to avoid being drawn into a European war, even though most expected they would be. Almost everyone has forgotten how isolationist America was then, and how much effort it took to persuade the Americans to get involved in another world war. Until late in 1941 many in Congress wanted nothing to do with it, in fact some prominent figures even advocated cooperation with the 'misunderstood' Nazis, among them Henry Ford, Joe Kennedy and Charles Lindberg. The aid Roosevelt gave the British after May 1940 – exchanging fifty US destroyers that were surplus to requirements for access to a number of British naval bases, and later supplying weapons and ammunition through the Lend-Lease Act – was therefore limited and cautious. It didn't amount to much.

In early August 1941 the president met with Winston Churchill in the greatest secrecy, on board the battleships USS *Augusta* and HMS *Prince of Wales* off the coast of Newfoundland. Together, under pressure from Roosevelt, they compiled a policy statement called the Atlantic Charter.

Before the United States entered the theatre of war, the president wanted to make clear to the world that for the Americans this was all about moral principles, about freedom and democracy, and nothing else. In contrast to the First World War, no new territories would be seized by the victors. Borders would be altered only with the agreement of the peoples involved and every nation, including those ruled by colonial regimes, had a right to self-determination.

The Atlantic Charter, although never officially signed, was a political masterstroke. Without making any concrete promises, Roosevelt had persuaded a desperate Churchill to recognise the right to self-determination of all peoples, including those living under British rule. It meant, in effect, the end of the British Empire, a final victory for the American revolutionaries.

Significant support for democratic Europe became a reality only after the Japanese attack on the American naval base at Pearl Harbor on 7 December 1941, and the German declaration of war against the United States that followed. America then became what Roosevelt had promised it would be: the 'Arsenal of Democracy'. With one major proviso: the Americans would help the British to defeat Hitler, but not to keep their empire intact.

Roosevelt was engaged in a splendid deception. He did all he could to look like a spry, healthy man with a slight disability. But he drank heavily, smoked a lot and had more and more health problems after 1941. His blood pressure was excessively high and he suffered from a heart condition and shortness of breath. John Gunther, who was on good terms with him, was deeply shocked when he saw him again after several years, at a reception around the time of the inauguration to his fourth term on 20 January 1945. 'I could not get over the ravaged expression on his face. It was gray, gaunt and sagging, and the muscles controlling the lips seemed to have lost part of their function,' he recalled. 'All the light had gone underneath his skin.'

Three months later, on 12 April 1945, FDR had a stroke. Within two hours he was dead. His death came as a great and unexpected blow to ordinary people everywhere; Roosevelt had kept up appearances to the last and the vast majority of Americans had no idea he was in such a bad way. The same went for the rest of the world. Steinbeck heard the news in Mexico, in the attractive and pleasant Cuernavaca, where he was staying to work on a film script. There, too, the general feeling was of grief at Roosevelt's death, he wrote to Elizabeth Otis. When a man at the hotel made a feeble joke about it, a Spanish woman who had overheard what he said gave him a slap in the face. The German capitulation, by contrast, excited no one in the Mexican city. If any rejoicing went on, it was at home. Steinbeck wrote: 'The people who got drunk are the ones who get drunk every day anyway.' There was no official celebration. 'We had one toast and that was all.'

Roosevelt's influence was immense and long lasting, and it can be seen in his successors. John F. Kennedy imitated FDR's relaxed and easy interaction with the press and adopted elements of his language. Kennedy's New Frontier was directly derived from the New Deal, and one of his advisors and speechwriters was Roosevelt's biographer Arthur Schlesinger Jr. He even adopted Roosevelt's 'splendid deception'. Like the forerunner after whom he modelled himself, John Kennedy radiated great strength and vitality even though he was in fact seriously ill: his back caused him constant pain and he could barely move without wearing a tight, corset-like back brace. In the Senate and on other occasions he had to report sick time and again, yet he managed to keep his physical infirmities a secret.

As a young man Ronald Reagan was a great admirer of Franklin Roosevelt. His speechwriters studied Roosevelt's speeches minutely and often fell back on the tone and rhythm of 'the most presidential of all presidents'. Reagan took a similar attitude to life, relishing power and remaining eternally optimistic, convinced every story had a happy ending.

The Texan Lyndon Baines Johnson was in a category all his own. Of all presidents, he was the greatest Roosevelt fan. As soon as he got into the Oval Office he had Roosevelt's desk installed there. Roosevelt's enemies – Joseph Kennedy, for example – were his enemies as well. Johnson was too much his own man to imitate Roosevelt outwardly but the content of Roosevelt's legacy was essential to him.

On 4 March 1933, when Johnson was a young student, he witnessed Roosevelt's inauguration. He decided he wanted to stand there himself one day. Four years later, at the age of twenty-eight, he was elected to the House of Representatives as the member for Austin. 'He came on like a freight train,' said Roosevelt later about his first meeting with Johnson, and the young member of Congress kept hurtling ahead. He won a seat in the Senate, worked his way up to the position of Democrat majority leader, and became renowned for his shrewd political performances. In the 1950s he was known as the second most powerful man in Washington.

Johnson was notorious for his 'treatment'. If he wanted to get a fellow senator to do something he would push him into a corner with his enormous bulk and then let loose an overwhelming flood of emotions and words: flattering, accusatory, reconciliatory, convincing, sometimes with a real hint of threat. Such sessions might last ten minutes, but sometimes they could go on for hours. Two journalists described the effect in 1966, saying it was an 'almost hypnotic experience . . . Its velocity was breathtaking, and it was all in one direction. Interjections from the target were rare. Johnson anticipated them before they could be spoken. He moved in close, his face a scant millimeter from his target, his eyes widening and narrowing, his eyebrows rising and falling. From his pockets poured clippings, memos, statistics.' It left the victim shattered.

Johnson gave up that legendary position of power in 1960 to become vice-president under Kennedy. His reasoning was on the face of it a mystery. He had focused all his ambition on winning the presidency and been forced to watch, grinding his teeth, as the young senator beat him with ease in the contest for the nomination. In Washington, the office of vice-president was generally seen as a sleepy position with a great deal of status but little substance and practically no power. The joke went: a mother had two sons from whom no one had ever heard anything more. One had been lost at sea; the other became vice-president.

Then there was the hatred and contempt Johnson had felt for Joseph Kennedy ever since his Roosevelt years. He thought him a cowardly bungler and made no secret of the fact. As for John Kennedy, Johnson continually repeated the refrain: 'The boy cannot win.' With Robert Kennedy he was at war from the start. As a young assistant to Joseph McCarthy, Robert, loyal to his father, had initially refused to shake Johnson's hand when they met. It was the start of what Johnson's biographer Robert

Caro called 'perhaps the greatest blood feud of American politics in the twentieth century'.

Why the Kennedys, despite all this, allowed him to join their court is no mystery at all. Without Johnson and 'his' Texas it would be impossible for them to win the election. Kennedy's margin was so tight that he would never have made it without Johnson's support. Johnson's motives were more complicated. He could not refuse – that would lose him a great deal of support in the Democratic Party – and anyhow, if he ever wanted to gain the highest office he needed a national platform. He explained to close friends that it was the only way a Texan could ever become president.

There was another factor. Caro and others have convincingly shown that Johnson's staff made a thorough study of Kennedy's illness. They discovered he had Addison's disease, a rare and serious disorder of the adrenal cortex that can have a devastating impact on the sufferer's performance, especially under stress. They even revealed this information – to the fury of the Kennedys – during the campaign, saying Kennedy would not be alive but for regular doses of corticosteroids.

They had made a calculation. Five out of eighteen presidents over the past century had died in office. The vice-presidency was only a heartbeat away from the presidency, all the more so with a man as sick as Kennedy. As Johnson said to the wife of Henry Luce, Clare Boothe Luce, in the VIP bus on the way to Kennedy's inaugural ball: 'Clare, I looked it up: one out of every four Presidents has died in office. I'm a gamblin' man, darlin', and this is the only chance I got.'

With that for a starting point, their collaboration could hardly be what you might call inspiring. The president kept Johnson – pushy and over-powering as he was – at a distance whenever possible. In 1963 the pair met in person just once, for barely two hours. Robert Kennedy humiliated Johnson whenever he could and their hatred grew insidiously. The rest is history. Kennedy was shot dead on 22 November 1963 and suddenly Johnson was the 36th President of the United States.

Like FDR, LBJ began his hundred days with a torrent of projects and plans. Almost immediately he added to Kennedy's agenda a new and crucial element: the War on Poverty. 'This administration,' he said in his State of the Union address on 8 January 1964, 'today, here and now, declares unconditional war on poverty in America.'

His sequel to the New Deal was called the 'Great Society' and he managed to fulfil much of it: better education, support for house building and urban development, Medicare and Medicaid (cheap healthcare for the elderly and the needy), old age and invalidity pensions, an ambitious road-building programme; and so it went on. His vision was to make America into a land of 'abundance and liberty for all'.

That now explicitly included the black population. Johnson made history with his Civil Rights Act of 1964 and the Voting Rights Act of 1965, in which discrimination in elections was strictly forbidden. For the first time, millions of black people in the South were able to vote.

The great tragedy of Johnson's presidency was that his real ambition, the continuation and completion of the New Deal, was sidelined by a war he had inherited from Kennedy and neither could nor wanted to end: Vietnam. It lost him the support of the liberals he needed so badly for the social projects of his Great Society. Many of his ambitions became bogged down in the phase of planning and good intentions. His War on Poverty was laughed offstage, even though it certainly had an effect: between 1964 and 1969 the percentage of Americans in poverty fell from 24.1 to 14.4. (The percentage is now back at the 1964 level.)

Johnson knew from the start that the Vietnam War was a hopeless business. Back in the 1950s General Matt Ridgway had calculated on President Eisenhower's behalf that continuing the French war in Indochina would cost America at least eight divisions and eight years. According to estimates by Senator Richard Russell, one of Johnson's most important advisors for several decades, it might be fifty years.

Nevertheless, in the first few days of his presidency, in deepest secrecy, Johnson decided to step up American military operations in Vietnam. In the summer of 1964 he allowed the war to escalate further after what became known as the 'Gulf of Tonkin Incident'. The US Navy reported that one of its destroyers, the USS *Maddox*, had been attacked by several North Vietnamese torpedo boats. The president responded with bombing and troop deployments. (An internal historical study by the National Security Agency, released in 2005, suggests that in reality it was the *Maddox* that opened fire first and the North Vietnamese were merely defending themselves. A second supposed assault, two days later, did not take place at all: 'No attack happened that night.')

The Gulf of Tonkin Resolution of 7 August 1964 gave Johnson, at his request, the opportunity to use all the force he thought necessary to defend his allies in Southeast Asia, without any formal declaration of war. It was a dramatic moment. To his assistant and later biographer Doris Kearns Goodwin, he once said: 'If I left the woman I really loved – the Great Society – in order to get involved with that bitch of a war on the other side of the world, then I would lose everything at home. All my programs . . . All my dreams . . .'

Yet that is exactly what had happened that summer.

Johnson's intervention in Vietnam was inspired mainly by domestic political motives. It was a way of stealing a march on his belligerent rival for the presidency, Barry Goldwater, who was threatening to deploy nuclear weapons, and at the same time a way to keep a grip on his own military leadership. But the genie was out of the bottle. By June 1965, 75,000 troops had been deployed to Vietnam, hundreds of thousands were on the point of leaving, and hundreds of thousands more would follow in 1966.

Johnson had overplayed his hand. Vietnam would become America's 'longest war', a traumatic episode, primarily for Southeast Asia but for the United States as well. The war lost the country much of its hard-won prestige. Johnson was brought down by it, opposition to his policy culmin-ated in a youth revolt and by the end he was barely able to show his face in public.

It took eleven years and millions of casualties – cautious estimates range from two to three and a half million dead on the Vietnamese side – before Nixon and Ford saw a chance to withdraw from the conflict.

Johnson left politics in January 1969, tired, sick and disillusioned. Demonstrators all across the country were chanting, 'Hey, hey, LBJ, how many kids did you kill today?' That was how this driven idealist would go down in history. He didn't dare enter the battle for the nomination in 1968. He would almost certainly have lost to the popular Robert Kennedy, and that thought alone was unbearable to Johnson. The hatred remained. On 5 June 1968 Robert too was murdered, shortly after a campaign meeting at the Ambassador Hotel in Los Angeles. Johnson's hostility was so extreme that he initially refused permission for Robert to be buried next to his brother in Arlington Cemetery.

Four years later, Johnson died of a heart attack at the age of sixty-four. His Vietnam policy had split the Democrats to the core.

It was the great opportunity that Richard Nixon had been waiting for.

Four

DURING THE SAME AUTUMN CAMPAIGN IN 1960 that brought Johnson the vice-presidency, the Democrat speaker of the House, Sam Rayburn, decided to take a short trip abroad. The elderly Texan representative was in El Paso, on the southern border of Texas, for an election rally. John Kennedy (whom he distrusted) and Johnson (his protégé and great friend) were both scheduled to speak that evening, but it was still lunchtime and Rayburn had a whole afternoon to kill. So he nipped over the border for a drive in a foreign country, Mexico.

Sam Rayburn was approaching eighty, yet in both Texas and Washington he was still the man who pulled all the strings behind the scenes. He'd been a member of Congress since 1913 and his authority was legendary. At crucial moments his vote had decided the course of American foreign policy, but there was one thing he lacked: experience in the field. During almost half a century on the front lines of American politics he'd been out of the country just once when, as a young member of Congress, he'd visited the Panama Canal. True, he was supposed to have been present at some kind of dedication ceremony in Mexico, but uncertainty surrounds that story.

With his guides – who included a certain Larry King, then assistant to a representative from El Paso, later a world-famous radio and television presenter – he drove to nearby Ciudad Juárez and looked around rather aimlessly before travelling back across the Rio Grande in the late afternoon. So, that was abroad.

The expeditionary party was stopped at the American border checkpoint. David Halberstam describes the incident that followed. Sam Rayburn did not have a passport. The border guards asked his nationality and

Rayburn, who was hard of hearing, thought his name alone was sufficient: 'Sam Rayburn.' The border guards grew angry and shouted: 'Declare your nationality!' Rayburn, with the same ferocity he'd displayed in shouting down demonstrators at innumerable Democrat conventions, yelled at them, 'Sam Rayburn! Sam Rayburn!' That was how he shouted his way back into America. His identity was his nationality. It had never occurred to him that he might need a passport. He would never set foot outside America again.

I was reminded of that story by a DVD we borrowed at a motel earlier in the week called Charlie Wilson's War, a 2007 film by Mike Nichols starring Tom Hanks, Julia Roberts and Philip Seymour Hoffman. Beautifully made, but what a strange version of history. The film begins with a ceremony. It is the early 1990s. In a large hangar, the CIA is awarding Congressman Charlie Wilson the highest honour given by the secret service, that of Honored Colleague. On the back wall hangs a large banner: 'Charlie did it!'

'The defeat and breakup of the Soviet Empire, culminating in the crumbling of the Berlin Wall, is one of the great events of world history,' one of the speakers begins. 'There are many heroes in this battle, but to Charlie Wilson must go this special recognition. Just thirteen years ago the Soviet Army appeared to be invincible. But Charlie, undeterred, engineered a lethal body blow that weakened the communist empire. Without Charlie, history would be hugely and sadly different.'

What had Wilson done? Along with a rich and fiercely anti-communist Texan lady and a rogue CIA agent, with the aim of saving Afghanistan and inflicting on the Soviet Union such an overwhelming defeat that communism would collapse, he had set up an elaborate secret mission to provide the Afghan resistance with billions of dollars' worth of military support year on year. In the film there is a great deal of messing about with women at parties and in jacuzzis, and Wilson travels to Afghanistan a couple of times to spend a day or so there. In a refugee camp he wipes away a tear, in the corridors of Congress he makes a handful of deals, and then the dollars begin to flow. The Mujahideen receive excellent training and generous amounts of the most modern weaponry, one Soviet helicopter after another is brought down and, sure enough, in 1989 communism collapses.

That is the story told in the film. The bizarre thing is that, aside from the final conclusion, it reflects the actual course of events. There was a real-life Charlie Wilson (he died in 2010). He was the Democratic representative for Lufkin in East Texas and according to Molly Ivins was a typical 'gonzo politician', a disorderly bruiser with the charm of a four-teen-year-old, an astonishing sexist who at the same time voted as a progressive and a pro-feminist. He was re-elected twelve times, but Ivins claims most voters in Lufkin had no idea what 'their' Charlie got up to in Washington. 'There is far greater tolerance for eccentricity and human frailty in small Southern towns than most folks who live in great cities have any notion of.'

Wilson was mad keen on the theatre of war, especially as an observer. Israel against Egypt, Nicaraguan dictator Anastasio Somoza Debayle against the Sandinistas, the Afghans against the Soviet Union: all over the world he took intense pleasure in performing his Rambo act. Later he generally preferred the role of Lawrence of Arabia, riding on a big white horse across the dry plains of Afghanistan, cartridge belts across his chest, surrounded by the rebels in whom he was inculcating the steely Texan battle cry, 'Kill the commie cocksuckers!'

In Washington in 1979, representative Wilson did indeed, as in the film, put in place secret funding for the militant Muslims in Afghanistan. At the instigation of his Texan girlfriend Joanne Herring, and supported by CIA agent Gust Avrakotos, he managed to stump up at least 400 million dollars for the acquisition of the most up-to-date Stinger rockets. The trio's efforts grew to become Operation Cyclone, the biggest covert CIA operation ever. With Pakistan and Israel as intermediaries, at least three billion dollars' worth of weaponry was eventually smuggled into Afghanistan – some sources speak of ten billion or more.

In Charlie Wilson's War the story seems simple: the courageous Davids of the Afghan resistance make short work of the communist Goliath, needing only a few good rifles and rocket launchers to finish the job. The reality on the ground was rather more complicated.

The Soviet war in Afghanistan certainly contributed to the fall of the Soviet Union, although it was not decisive, and the intervention by our hero, his Texan girlfriend and the CIA undoubtedly helped the resistance. That resistance, however, was less favourably disposed towards America than the couple and their associates assumed. It was mainly made up of Taliban fighters. The Americans had loosed an untameable monster. An entire generation of Afghan jihadists became exceptionally well armed and trained, and the way was paved for the atrocious Taliban regime that terrorised Afghanistan from 1996 to 2001.

Millions of Afghans fled, a powerful Islamist bulwark was created in north-west Pakistan, making that nuclear-armed nation increasingly unstable, and Osama bin Laden was provided with plenty of space to prepare and launch his attacks. America is still searching for the Stinger missiles it once delivered to the Afghan Mujahideen, many of which were never used. They would be extremely effective against US troops.

Since 2001 the United States has been trying to bring the region to heel, to some extent at least. So far that effort has cost several tens of thousands of lives, some 500 billion dollars, and a further deterioration of the worldwide authority of the United States that was built up so carefully over the years. Thank you very much, Honoured Colleague Charlie Wilson.

So why make a film about it? The story of Charlie Wilson, like Teddy Roosevelt's Wild West and George Custer's Last Stand, encompasses a theme that pops up repeatedly in the American story: a simple boy takes on injustice, pushes aside the bureaucrats and appeasers, supports the good and destroys the bad and ultimately brings universal peace and freedom.

The problem is that the majority of Americans by far – including members of Congress – have little idea of what is going on in the rest of the world. It's the flipside of exceptionalism. If we're the best country in the world, blessed by God like no other, then foreign countries can't possibly be better. In fact, when it comes down to it, they're not even worth the trouble of studying in any detail.

Many things escape the Americans. I have seen American friends utterly astonished on encountering Western European infrastructure, with its rail networks and other public transport provisions, with its social safety net and all kinds of things we find perfectly normal. They had been expecting to find themselves in a romantic but badly neglected old world, rather like London in the mid-1950s. As for China, most Americans know about its rapid modernisation only from the occasional rumour.

Americans continue to come up with spectacular successes – Google, Apple, Amazon and Facebook are the icons of the early twenty-first century – but that bright light blinds them in some ways. Just as Britain lived off its nineteenth-century glory well into the twentieth century, continuing to run on coal and steel, so America is stuck in the twentieth century in several vital sectors, especially energy, the environment and infrastructure, while in the rest of the world the twenty-first century is well underway. Most Americans fail to realise this because they are never confronted with the reality of it.

In that sense America has two faces. In the 1920s the *Chicago Daily News*, John Gunther's paper, had a network of more than a hundred part-time correspondents, plus foreign bureaus in London, Paris, Rome, Berlin and Peking. Its reports, analyses and in-depth coverage were sold to thirty-nine other American papers, as well as London's *Daily Telegraph*. Large networks like CNN and newspapers like the *New York Times* still work in this tradition.

American diplomats are among the best in the world, the country has outstanding information systems, its army is capable of anything, its universities and the State Department have brilliant strategists and political analysts at their disposal, and American businesses operate all over the world. The United States has had a hand in countless peace negotiations, often bringing them to a successful conclusion. Presidents Wilson and Roosevelt took the initiative in setting up a whole range of international institutions that, despite all kinds of problems, have brought the beginnings of order to international politics and the world economy.

In the twentieth century the United States saved Europe at least four times: from a war it had locked itself into, from the Nazis, from Soviet power during the Cold War, and then in the 1990s from the wars in former Yugoslavia, which the EU failed to resolve. Meanwhile it pumped billions of dollars into European economies – motivated by its own economic interests, but still. It was America that inspired Western European countries and prompted them to engage in their own great peace project, the European Community.

Something similar happened during post-war reconstruction in Japan, which transformed itself under American leadership into a modern, Western-oriented nation, a success that tempted the United States to try something similar in Vietnam and Iraq, with disastrous consequences. America did all that, as ever, for reasons of its own – a grown-up super-power, it had every interest in seeing a degree of order and stability in the world – but idealism was part of it. America once again had a mission to fulfil: the American Creed must be disseminated all over the world.

Publisher-editor of *Die Zeit*, Josef Joffe, wrote in 2009 that America was 'the twentieth century's indispensable nation'. It is no less so today. 'The United States is the default power, the country that occupies centre stage because there is nobody else with the requisite power and purpose.'

All the same there is something awkward about America's attitude to the rest of the world, as if the country keeps contradicting itself. It has a perpetual tendency to turn inwards, to be isolationist. In 1959, when someone applying for a job at the politics desk of the *Los Angeles Times* voiced an ambition to work as a foreign correspondent, the boss there at the time, Kyle Palmer, said: 'Listen, we've got one man as it is in Switzerland and he costs us forty thousand dollars a year, and he doesn't bring in a single ad.'

Now, more than half a century later, that attitude turns up over and over again. In many respects America is an empire in denial, lacking essential knowledge (some specialists and a well-informed elite aside) about areas of the world over which it exercises enormous power. Charlie Wilson is typical of a phenomenon we see time after time. Important decision-makers live in a bubble in Washington, or in Charlie's case Texas, and they interpret their world according to simple diagrams charting good and bad with hardly any idea of the complexity of the situation on the ground. America has produced countless astute observers. All too often they have been shouted down by the Charlie Wilsons of their time.

There is no shortage of examples. Towards the end of the Second World War, more and more Americans were rightly concerned about the European expansion of the Soviet Empire. After Franklin Roosevelt's death, reproaches poured in: a sick man, he made far too many concessions to Stalin at Yalta in 1945. Why didn't we push on to Berlin? Why didn't we save Warsaw from the communists? As a Democrat, he was far too soft on communism – and just look where that leads.

Those domestic critics refused to recognise that British and American troops were simply not up to it. They had enormous problems with their supply lines and it took them until the spring of 1945 just to cross the Rhine. The critics were even less willing to acknowledge that, from a military point of view, the war in Europe was not won by the Americans so much as by the Soviets. The Americans won the war in the Pacific. In Europe it was mainly the Russians who slowly but surely destroyed Hitler's armies.

After the war, Americans continued for years to dream of rollback, of successfully implementing a policy of pushing back the Iron Curtain, by military means if necessary. Legendary Soviet expert George Kennan was one of the few Americans to recognise the bitter European reality. When he was asked in 1946 how Soviet expansion could be contained he said: 'Sorry, but the fact of the matter is that we do not have the power in Eastern Europe really to do anything but talk.' That was simply how things were. Many Americans, convinced of their superiority, refused to accept this. They bravely looked away.

Kennan was acutely aware of the Charlie Wilson syndrome. The weakness of American foreign policy, he believed, lay in its overly simplified 'legalistic-moralistic' approach to the world. Americans applied their own concepts of good and evil uncritically, paid little heed to the effects of their policies on other nations and were poorly prepared for the possibility that their plans might be thwarted by unforeseen developments. America, in short, acted as if it could predict the future. As Kennan put it: 'The cultivation of these utopian schemes, flattering to our own image of ourselves, took place at the expense of our feeling for reality.'

American policy remained strongly anti-colonial – the Americans supported the young Indonesia in its conflict with the Netherlands, for example – until the anti-communists gained the upper hand. Most American politicians and commentators, Steinbeck included, saw communism as a single massive bloc, a perfectly coordinated conspiracy against 'the free world'.

President Reagan called the dictator of Guatemala, Efraín Ríos Montt, a great democrat, for example, 'a man of great personal integrity and commitment'. In reality entire families were executed under his rule, villages burnt to the ground, babies beaten to death, girls raped until they fainted. (Ríos Montt, president from 1982–83, was eventually sentenced in his own country to eighty years in jail. The conviction was later overturned, but the trial will resume in 2015.)

The notion that all those rebels in Cuba, Argentina, Chile, Guatemala, Nicaragua and El Salvador – in the latter three countries alone an estimated 200,000 people were killed in the 1980s – might have motives of their own, aside from anything to do with communism, occurred to hardly anyone. The same went for the huge differences between Vietnamese, Chinese, Russian and, say, Italian communists – they were hardly ever mentioned. The communist threat, that grand conspiracy against 'the free world', was the guiding force behind foreign policy after 1945.

Illustrative of this way of thinking was American policy on China, the consequences of which were far-reaching. From the late nineteenth century, America showed a great deal of interest in China and it was a recurring theme in foreign policy. The United States had opposed attempts by Britain, France, Russia and Japan to divide the weakened Chinese empire up into colonies and protectorates. Instead the Americans advocated the Open Door Policy, which meant that China would remain one nation and all countries would be free to trade with it. Meanwhile China continued to fragment, until in 1911 the emperor was deposed and a republic declared that had little to say for itself. A communist rebellion arose, among farmers in particular, and quickly gained support.

The Americans congratulated themselves on having saved independent China. This was of course a misconception, and after that, one misconception followed another. Politicians in Washington were receiving their information almost exclusively from American evangelists and missionaries, or from the Christian communities that had slowly grown up all over China. Those circles had considerable stores of knowledge about Chinese languages and Chinese culture, but their information was one-sided. The Christians wanted nothing to do with the 'godless' communists, so they ignored their presence as far as possible and stressed their own role, despite making up only a small minority of the population.

In the 1930s, when China was ravaged by a civil war between Chiang

Kai-shek on one side and the communists under the leadership of Mao Zedong on the other, the Americans were convinced that Chiang, a Christian, had the larger following by far. Dissident voices were stifled. To this day it is painful to read how Time magazine's China correspondent Theodore White risked his life travelling around the country to uncover the other side of the story. He was barely able to get any of his reports about Mao's huge following in rural areas published in his own magazine. Embittered, he hung up a sign in his office in Chungking that read: 'Any resemblance to what is written here and what is printed in Time magazine is purely coincidental.'

Along with the photo magazine Life, Time was extremely influential in America in those years. There was still very little television. Time and Life were practically the only national media, and Time in particular shaped conversations around Sunday dinner tables right across the country. Its owner Henry Luce was as wild an amateur diplomat as Charlie Wilson and Joanne Herring. He was thoroughly charmed by Mrs Chiang, so China was portrayed in his magazines as a plucky, pro-American country, ruled by an attractive, Western-looking couple. As for stories about the influence of the communists and the threat of a civil war – all that was greatly exaggerated.

Even in 1950 – when the facts spoke for themselves and the communists had the entire Chinese mainland in their hands, with Chiang driven out onto the island of Formosa (later renamed Taiwan) – Luce, like many other Americans, refused to look reality in the face. To him there was just one China from that moment on: Formosa. The rest of China had become communist not because of all the mistakes made by Chiang or because of deep historical tensions that had culminated in a revolution, but purely because of a 'red' conspiracy. The Americans, for whom China was a strange, opaque country, believed him and his magazine.

White did not want to be part of this any more. Time had misled America, he would say later, and the consequences were huge. If Henry Luce had been willing to look into the reasons why the inefficient, authoritarian and deeply corrupt Chiang regime collapsed, and why communism gained the upper hand among the Chinese, America might have escaped the McCarthy witch hunts and the Korean War. Instead, China became the Americans' greatest foreign trauma. The congenial,

westernised China of Chiang Kai-shek and Henry Luce had been transformed overnight into a vicious empire of 600 million angry communists.
Only a handful of explanations were credible: Conspiracy. Evil. A stab in
the back.

There is another example, a success story this time but based on the
same misconception: the fall of the Berlin Wall. To this day the event is
traced back in countless American publications to the appeal made by
Ronald Reagan on 12 July 1987 at the Brandenburg Gate: 'Mr Gorbachev,
tear down this wall!' Behold, like Jericho in the Bible the wall collapsed
two years later. There is even a highly readable book in which a similar
role is attributed to Ronald Reagan as that played by Charlie Wilson, *Tear
Down This Wall: A City, A President and the Speech that Ended the Cold War.*

In reality a whole range of causes led to the fall of the Wall: Gorbachev's
reforms, the impending bankruptcy of the GDR, a steep fall in oil and
gas prices in the late 1980s that cast the Soviet Union into major financial
difficulties, support by Polish pope Karol Wojtyła and the Church for the
trade union movement Solidarność, and last but not least the hard, painful
struggle by hundreds of thousands of courageous Polish, East German,
Hungarian, Bulgarian, Romanian, Albanian and Czechoslovak dissidents.

The Americans paid little attention to any of that. The CIA, despite
warnings from one of its experts on the Soviet Union, William Lee, had
no conception of the Soviets' rapidly mounting financial difficulties. The
then secretary of state for defense, Dick Cheney, expressed a belief that
Gorbachev's reformist policies 'may be a temporary aberration in the
behavior of our foremost adversary', and the serving president, George
Bush Sr, had little fondness for all those strange, bearded Eastern European
dissidents.

Many Americans were completely blind in that sense, and often they
still are. The simple diagram, the magic of American exceptionalism, is
good enough for them. Fair enough. It's a phenomenon seen all over the
world. It does become a problem, however, when a world power is
governed on that basis.

Self-deception reached rock bottom on 1 May 2003. The war in Iraq had
been underway for barely a month and a half. The first phase was over,

dictator Saddam Hussein had been ousted and President George W. Bush decided that was it. He organised a spectacular television show in which, dressed in combat gear, he landed on the deck of the aircraft carrier *Abraham Lincoln* – not anywhere near Iraq but just off the coast near San Diego – and allowed himself to be cheered by the crew under a huge banner reading 'Mission Accomplished'. He then gave a 'victory speech'. It would be another eight years before the last American troops left Iraq.

Yet in his bizarre speech Bush did say something interesting: 'Other nations in history have fought in foreign lands and remained to occupy and exploit. Americans, following a battle, want nothing more than to return home.'

According to Niall Ferguson, that is precisely the problem. In *Colossus*, his book describing the rise and fall of the American empire, Ferguson depicts America as a disposable empire. Far too few Americans, he says, are prepared to help build and maintain their empire, to spend a major part of their lives in other regions of the world and to be educated and trained to do so. Picking up on the catchphrase 'Don't even go there', he writes: 'Americans have little interest in the one basic activity without which a true empire cannot enduringly be established. They are reluctant to "go there" – and if they must go, then they count the days until they can come home. They eschew the periphery. They cling to the metropolis.'

British by birth, Ferguson has a tendency to reproach the Americans for not being British. As a concept, the British Empire was integrated into everyday life; in its glory days it was an inseparable part of Britain's imagined community, and countless Brits were prepared to devote their lives to the maintenance of the Pax Britannica all over the world. Twentieth-century Great Britain was still 'officially' a coloniser; between 1900 and 1914, 2.6 million British people left for other parts of the world, most going to Canada, Australia or New Zealand, but many to less comfortable destinations. There was a high level of education among them. More than seventy per cent of the Indian Civil Service in those days was educated at Oxford or Cambridge.

The American power bloc that came into being after the Second World War looked nothing like previous models. It was a loose, 'informal' empire, and in many respects a reluctant one. The average American is still an isolationist at heart, with no real desire to interfere in the rest of the world. He has his hands full with his own country. When Paul Bremer was acting as temporary 'governor' of Iraq, only three of his staff spoke fluent Arabic. For years the CIA had no one at all who could even read Korean (that vacancy has since been filled). A tiny fraction of Americans live outside America, often for no more than a couple of years. Of those graduating from Harvard and Yale, few choose a career abroad.

Let's be clear. In the European empires of the nineteenth century and the first half of the twentieth, huge blunders were made, and if you asked British schoolchildren precisely where India was they would often get it wrong, just as their American counterparts would later. A great deal of the world's misery – Iraq, Afghanistan, Pakistan, Central Africa – can be traced back to lazy decision-making by leaders of the British, French and other empires of the nineteenth century. But they did pay more attention to the insights and experiences of those in charge on the ground. They had to, since communication with the mother country was far slower than it is now. Those colonial rulers often spent many years in the colonies. They knew their countries of residence reasonably well and put a huge amount of time and energy, quite often over several decades, into creating a reliable caste of native administrators. Often, if far from always, this meant that the greatest of follies were avoided.

In America that counterweight of solid local knowledge is lacking. The result, as Dutch journalist and Asia specialist Karel van Wolferen writes, is that foreign policy all too often falls prey to an array of impulsive moves by Washington, up to and including wars. There is also a strong tendency to overlook and ignore complications. In that sense too, Charlie Wilson was typical. The entire US policy on Afghanistan and Pakistan was turned upside down purely because Wilson and his girlfriend spotted a chance to have a go at the communists.

As a journalist in Vietnam, Van Wolferen saw exactly this kind of thing happening. The knowledge acquired by American specialists about local conditions, such as it was, might be waved aside as the result of some quirk in Washington. He believes this was in fact the cause of the debacle: 'The American military is effective when it can follow rules of frontally engaging a force using a predictable strategy. But it is wholly incompetent as a coloniser having to deal with ever-changing situations that require a capacity to respond in ways that cannot be reduced to rules covered in a handbook.'

Some commentators say that the American empire increasingly suffers from the 'dog and car syndrome'. A dog fantasises endlessly about chasing cars, but once it has sunk its teeth into a back bumper it has no idea what to do next. That happened in Vietnam and was repeated in Afghanistan and Iraq. The credit America enjoyed all over the globe in the first few months after 9/11, and that includes in the Muslim world, was systematically forfeited. The invasions of Muslim countries that followed sowed more hatred than Osama bin Laden could ever have dreamed of.

Everything those Charlie Wilsons could possibly do wrong came together in the Iraq War. Before the Americans began their attack, their knowledge of Iraq was minimal. Later investigations suggest that the spies sending information from enemy territory could be counted on the fingers of one hand. No one listened to the few experts who were available. Politicians, commentators and most policymakers – the best among them excepted – lumped the entire Islamic world together: 'the Muslims'; 'the Muslim countries'.

President George W. Bush accused Iran, for example, of supplying the Taliban with arms without having any idea of the virulent hatred that existed between the Iranian Shiites and the Sunni fundamentalists of the Taliban. Most Americans would surely not have been so ready to believe that Saddam Hussein was behind the attacks of 11 September if they had paid more attention to the irreconcilable differences between the Salafist suicide squads of al-Qaeda and the secularist Ba'athists of Saddam Hussein's Iraq.

This is to say nothing of Saddam's supposed weapons of mass destruction – the immediate cause of the war – that were nowhere to be found. The Iraq War culminated in one huge private enterprise, run by companies ranging from oil giant Halliburton to countless paramilitary security firms, an astonishing number of which were connected to the circle of friends surrounding President Bush and Vice-President Dick Cheney.

That show carried on even under Obama, albeit with different main players and in a different light. Critics still justifiably complain that the main aim of the American government is not to take strategic decisions but to satisfy domestic public opinion. There has always been a degree of rivalry between the White House and the State Department, but the State Department usually had the last word, simply because of its vastly greater experience. Under the presidency of George W. Bush those roles were reversed, a development that continued under Obama. Four of the president's aides, 'Obama's Four Horsemen', in effect took charge of foreign policy and set priorities, all too often expressing them in military terms, which after all get through to the public easily and clearly. The real problems – in the case of Afghanistan, for example, the dual role of Pakistan and immense corruption – remain in the shadows. It continues to be a policy of hit and run.

As I have already said, the foreign policy of the United States, even more than that of other major powers, is the outcome of domestic political contests, domestic debates and priorities, domestic lobbies and funding streams, and domestic opinions. The result, especially in the long term, is a tendency to lurch back and forth.

The attitude of Americans to international organisations is telling. Andrew White, Andrew Carnegie and Woodrow Wilson were present at the birth of the Permanent Court of Arbitration – the forerunner of the International Court of Justice – and of the League of Nations, but their fellow Americans vilified both as soon as their country seemed in danger of losing its grip on them.

It was an American president, Roosevelt, who in late December 1941 thought up the term 'United Nations' and with it the organisation bearing that name. (It was during a visit to the White House by Winston Churchill. Roosevelt, excited about his new idea, wheeled himself into the guest room just as the British statesman was drying himself, in Roosevelt's words, like a 'pink cherub'.) More than twenty years later, in 1963, Texas passed a law making it illegal to fly the UN flag. A small country can permit itself such inconsistencies, whether or not it loses authority and face as a result. An empire, in the long run, cannot.

American missionary zeal, American naivety, the American craving to be loved by everyone, the tendency of Americans to see the world in their own image: in 1955 a novel appeared that bore these themes within it

like no other. *The Quiet American* was based on British author Graham
Greene's experiences as a war correspondent during the collapse of the
French regime in Indochina between 1951 and 1954. The Americans were
intensely involved behind the scenes; more than three-quarters of the
French military force was financed by the United States. The book had
an almost prophetic character, especially given the subsequent American
intervention in Vietnam.

At the centre of the novel is American Alden Pyle, a Harvard graduate
and a serious young idealist from a good family. He bombards his British
friend Thomas Fowler – an older, experienced, sometimes deceitful journalist – with theories and bookish knowledge, without knowing much
about the actual situation on the ground. They both have a complicated
relationship with a Vietnamese woman, Phuong, who eventually opts for
a life with the much younger Pyle.

Tragedy results. The young American, out of a combination of self-
confidence and ignorance, becomes hopelessly entangled in Vietnamese
politics. He is absolutely determined to put a stop to 'communism' and
ultimately doesn't fight shy of even the most violent means. Fowler warns
him in vain: 'We are the old colonial peoples, Pyle, but we've learnt a
bit of reality, we've learned not to play with matches.'

The dialogues between the Brit and the American speak volumes.

Fowler: 'You and your like are trying to make a war with the help of
people who just aren't interested.'

Pyle: 'They don't want Communism.'

Fowler: 'They want enough rice. They don't want to be shot at. They
want one day to be much the same as another. They don't want our white
skins around telling them what they want.'

Pyle: 'If Indo-China goes . . .'

Alden Pyle's idealism is sincere. That's what makes it all so complicated.
America was genuinely striving for peace, democracy and freedom, all
over the world. But the American imperial philosophy had another face
too, the face that George Kennan showed in that analysis he sent to the
State Department: 'We have about 50 percent of the world's wealth, but
only 6.3 percent of its population.' There was a need 'to devise a pattern
of relationships that will permit us to maintain this disparity'.

*

Reinhold Niebuhr was another writer who predicted future developments. In his 1952 book *The Irony of American History*, he invented an appropriate term for the attitude to life shown by Alden Pyle and Charlie Wilson when he wrote of 'our dreams of managing history'. He believed those dreams arose from a uniquely American mixture of arrogance, hypocrisy and self-deception, and that they might constitute a potentially fatal threat to the continued existence of the United States.

Niebuhr recalled with approval the words of John Adams: 'Power always thinks it has a great soul and vast views beyond the comprehension of the weak; and that it is doing God's service when it is violating all His laws.'

In his book Niebuhr investigates the dilemmas that American society faced after the country emerged from the Second World War as a world power. Instead of crowing, he confronts his compatriots with several worrying qualities that lay at the root of a number of historical errors in the decades that followed. He describes, among other things, American exceptionalism and all the arrogance that a myth of being special brings with it, the spurious enticements of the simple solution, the country's impatience with the course of history and its refusal to acknowledge that power, even American power, has its limits.

In particular he warns of the dangers of the American pretence of eternal innocence, of the 'deep layer of Messianic consciousness in the mind of America', of the good intentions of the quiet American. No nation in history has ever had such difficulty putting into perspective its position of power in the world, he writes. 'We do not think of ourselves as the potential masters, but as tutors of mankind in its pilgrimage to perfection.'

That innocence and that missionary zeal blinded the Americans both to the temptations of power and to the complexity of the real world. The debacle of Vietnam in the 1960s and 1970s made this devastatingly clear. In April 1965, Lyndon Johnson said in a speech at Johns Hopkins University: 'We must fight if we are to live in a world where every country can shape its own destiny.' But Assistant Secretary of Defense John McNaughton had written a month earlier in an internal memo that three-quarters of the reason for fighting in Vietnam was 'to avoid a humiliating US defeat'.

By that point Operation Rolling Thunder was underway. It involved the aerial bombardment of North Vietnam and the Ho Chi Minh trail with more than a million tons of bombs, napalm and missiles. And, oh, how cheap those non-American lives were. 'The Oriental doesn't put the same high price on life as does a Westerner,' said General William Westmoreland. 'Life is plentiful. Life is cheap in the Orient.' Around two million Vietnamese were killed, and many times that were maimed for life.

The Vietnam War was above all else a huge blow to the American dream of superiority and benevolence, of innocence and God's blessing. That, for Americans, was the real trauma of Vietnam.

Five

'MY DEPARTURE WAS FLIGHT,' John Steinbeck wrote, and in fact that applied to his whole expedition. He was fleeing Elaine's nannying, fleeing the infirmities of age, fleeing the modern city and fleeing himself, the successful author.

His longing for the simple life was great, as he continually stresses in *Travels*. Elaine pulled him more towards the worldly side, where he felt comfortable and flattered but uneasy at the same time. He distances himself when describing the 'Texan orgy', as if he's betraying his earlier, less complicated life. It's an interlude that doesn't really fit with the story he wanted to tell.

After Amarillo he picked up the thread again, for the last time. In late November 1960 the newspapers were full of a bizarre race riot, a disturbing piece of theatre that was repeated day after day. It was all about the admission of a seven-year-old black girl, Ruby Bridges, to the William Frantz Elementary School in the Ninth Ward of New Orleans, and of three other black pupils to the McDonogh Elementary School two miles away. They were among the first black children in the South whose parents sent them to white schools.

The schools were obliged to accept black pupils after a pronouncement by a federal judge who, in accordance with a judgement by the Supreme Court, had determined that segregation in education violated the Constitution. But as soon as Ruby Bridges walked up to the door of William Frantz Elementary as its first black pupil, white parents started keeping their children home en masse. Of the 575 white pupils, within two days there were only two little girls left.

Press attention was attracted above all by a noisy group of women, referred to as 'mothers', who stationed themselves in front of the school every morning to shout abuse at the three remaining pupils and their parents. A number of them became so proficient at it that they were known as the 'Cheerleaders', and a crowd would gather to applaud their performance.

It awoke the journalist in Steinbeck. Before setting course for home he wanted to visit New Orleans to see this strange drama for himself. 'It had the same draw as a five-legged calf or a two-headed foetus at a side-show,' he wrote, 'a distortion of normal life we have always found so interesting that we will pay to see it, perhaps to prove to ourselves that we have the proper number of legs or heads.'

It turned into a difficult phase of the journey. As he headed south and then eastwards, winter came on, with freezing rain and sleet. He had left Elaine behind in Austin. Charley sat upright beside him again on the front seat, or curled up to sleep with his head on Steinbeck's lap. Texas was 'achingly endless' and they drove relentlessly, stopping only to fill the tank and for Charley to relieve himself. They slept briefly at stopping places before heading on into the icy night.

In Beaumont, close to the Louisiana border, he stopped at a gas station. The man filling the tank for them, his fingers blue with cold, looked at Charley and laughed, saying: 'Hey, it's a dog! I thought you had a nigger in there.' Steinbeck was to hear that remark at least twenty times. 'It was an unusual joke,' he writes, 'always fresh – and never Negro or even Nigra, always Nigger or rather Niggah. That word seemed terribly important, a kind of safety word to cling to lest some structure collapse.'

In late November 1960 this was still the country of Jim Crow. The South, where scenes featuring Lena Horne, one of the most beautiful women in the world, were systematically cut from films because she was black. The South, where NBC TV stations switched to old films whenever black writer James Baldwin appeared on the *Today* show. The South, where mixed couple Mildred and Richard Loving, who had married elsewhere, were roused from their beds by the sheriff and his deputy because their cohabitation was an affront to 'the peace and dignity of the Commonwealth'. They were given a choice: a year in jail or exile. They chose the latter but later returned, living for years by meeting in secret.

In the Second World War, 1.2 million black American soldiers had fought just as hard as white troops, if in separate units. At home that no longer counted. The former Buffalo Soldiers had to resume their subordinate position within the image of a cheerful, dynamic America where everyone was equal in theory.

In their case that was obviously a lie, and everyone knew it, black and white. Segregation was not confined to the South. Black people were excluded even from modern suburbs like Levittown. The Levitts feared they would scare off white house buyers. In the 1950s almost everyone regarded the colour bar that ran right across America as entirely normal.

Yet change was coming and it was reflected in conversations Steinbeck had, invented or not, with the three hitchhikers he picked up, and in the aggressive theatrics around the William Frantz school in New Orleans that he witnessed.

The experience of war shared by white and black GIs had left its mark despite everything. Soon after the war ended, the colour bar was cautiously broken for the first time. Black baseball players – often the best – had for decades been forced to play in their own Negro Leagues, but from 1947 onwards Jackie Robinson was allowed to play with the Brooklyn Dodgers, as the first-ever black member of the team. Suddenly Dodgers fans saw what they'd been missing all those years.

At least as important was the building of musical bridges. In the late 1940s Charlie Parker and others experimented with combinations of jazz bands (mostly black) and string bands (mostly white). Then came 5 July 1954, when an unknown schoolboy, Elvis Presley, performed for the first time at the Sun Studio in Memphis. After a few respectable songs he suddenly broke into 'That's All Right (Mama)', a brilliant number by the black blues singer Arthur Crudup.

When the recording was first played on local radio the telephones rang off the hook. The disc jockey invited young Elvis Presley to the studio for an interview, talked a little about his style and then suddenly asked him which school he attended. Humes, said Elvis, which in the local code meant: I'm a white boy. But he played black music, in a new way that made it his own.

Most experts see it as the moment rock 'n' roll was born. But that was not all. In the words of rock expert Jan Donkers: 'The musical colour bar, which had already become rather diffuse in some respects in the South, was formally broken.' It was the start of a cultural landslide.

Something similar occurred a year later in politics when first Claudette Colvin (who was the first to be arrested for refusing to stand up for a white bus passenger) and then Rosa Parks in Montgomery triggered the first initiatives by the Civil Rights Movement. The still little-known preacher Martin Luther King took the lead. In 1957 a large number of non-violent civil rights activists came together at the Southern Christian Leadership Conference, a grouping that at first concentrated mainly on mobilising the black churches and later became the driving force behind countless sit-ins, demonstrations and other mass expressions of civil disobedience.

It is important to see the confrontation in New Orleans in that light. Whites were panicking. In 1954 the Supreme Court had found that the segregation of schools contravened the Constitution. President Eisenhower wrote to supreme court judge Earl Warren that he could imagine how worried white Southerners must be, now that their 'sweet little girls' were going to be forced to sit at school desks beside 'some big, overgrown Negroes'. By 1960 the painful process of desegregation was well underway all over the South. The newspapers that autumn regularly featured reports about incidents large and small surrounding the admission of the first black students to high schools and universities.

What made New Orleans special was the age of the children – this was all about girls of six or seven years old – and the obscenities they faced. Indeed, the word 'nigger' was used again and again as something to cling to, 'lest some structure collapse'. Which is exactly what happened. In those years the old slave country fell apart.

I found a telling letter in the Thanksgiving edition of the *Atlanta Journal-Constitution*, one of the most important Southern newspapers, dated 24 November 1960. Amid all the ordinary news – 'Kennedy Celebrates Thanksgiving in Washington', 'Eichmann Confesses', 'New Orleans: Mass Switching of Schools by Whites', 'Negro Arrested in Bus Issue. Woman in Montgomery Tried to Sit next to White' and a cheap Thanksgiving recipe, 'Cost per portion around 35 cents' – there is suddenly a cry from the heart, sent in by an anonymous reader.

He asks whether there is any reason to look back on Thanksgiving with gratitude. This typical Southerner had after all felt scared, more than anything else, over the past year. He'd been scared to vote Republican, since his grandfather, of the old Confederation, would have turned in his grave and cursed him. He'd been scared to vote for Kennedy, since his family doctor would foam at the mouth at the socialisation of healthcare, and anyhow he would be giving the pope far too much power. He was scared of saying openly that it didn't matter to him in the least who sat next to him in a bar, since his closest friends would make him out to be a traitor to the Southern way of life. He was also scared, he wrote, 'of declaring himself a do-or-die segregationist, ready to padlock the schools and sit it out, for the next century, for fear his liberal friends will point him out as an anachronism – a pterodactyl among the jets'. Signed: 'Scared to sign.'

November 2010 brings neither snow nor freezing rain to Texas and Louisiana, and Thanksgiving is celebrated without a fear of mixed schools, a coup by the pope or a successful television appearance by a black actress or intellectual. The word 'niggah' has gone underground. The mixed neighbourhood is a completely normal phenomenon. Of the roughly 70,000 American neighbourhoods, an estimated 0.5 per cent are pure white. Weddings between white and black people have become common-place, and a majority of people, even of Southerners, have no objection any longer. The White House is occupied by a president born of such a marriage.

But, still, around a third of black children live in poverty. Of black people in their twenties, one in nine males are in custody. Of black women aged between thirty and forty-five only a third are married, although most have children. The figure in 1970 was two-thirds. Less than a fifth of black and Hispanic families have built up any form of pension, compared to almost half of white families.

Whichever statistics you look at – housing market, jobs market, schools, incomes – black Americans are always a good deal worse off than the rest. There are all kinds of reasons for that, many of them complicated, but racism is definitely among them. Shortly before he became a house-hold name nationwide, Obama said to a television reporter who asked whether his skin colour was still relevant in any way: 'When I leave this interview and go out on the street and attempt to hail a taxi, there is no question who I am.'

John and Elaine had spent a few days in Austin before he travelled on to New Orleans, and we do the same. We visit the Lyndon Baines Johnson Museum there, including its replica of the Oval Office on the top floor. We admire the desk from which the president dealt with affairs of state, as well as regularly giving secretaries and other passing women a 'treatment'. Few American presidents have been well-behaved family men, but Johnson, like Kennedy and Clinton, was an extreme case, to the point of mania. He claimed to have had 'more women by accident than Kennedy had on purpose'. He regarded women as the spoils of war; they went with his power and his victories, and according to one of the women involved he was not the least bit embarrassed about using the furniture in the Oval Office for the purpose.

We attend church in Austin the following morning, the Wesley United Methodist Church, where the Reverend Sylvester E. Chase is concerned mainly about the accounts. 'Today we need to raise ten thousand dollars; reach into your pocket and give to the Lord!' Collection plates are passed round and we're invited to fill out a Pledge Card so that a monthly contribution can be paid by direct debit. Even during the prayers sums fly about your ears. 'Count your blessings!'

In the evening we go out, to the venerable Continental Club, where only the best blues and rock 'n' roll is on offer and only the best dancers dare to try a few steps, the rest of those present standing beneath their Stetsons listening in silence. Morry Sochat, the king of the Chicago Blues, plays there regularly with The Special 20s, slowly thumping away like the heartbeat of the factories and the combines in the fields, like the pistons and valves of one of those crazy Allegheny steam locomotives, sounding its shrill whistle as it heads on and on out across the plains.

Then we're off again. After Austin the landscape acquires a certain charm, with rolling meadows and here or there a beautiful old tree. We have lunch at the Key Truck Stop restaurant, just outside Houston. It's full of truck drivers, trousers hanging sloppily around their midriffs, shirts grimy and tired. Everywhere there is laughter, on the bar is a pot with donations for a colleague, a driver who was stranded here last week with a heart complaint and needs to get back to Arizona. The giving is generous.

We spend the night in Lake Charles, just over the border in Louisiana. The city lies on the edge of a lake, and on its waterfront an enthusiastic property developer has laid out a long, straight boulevard to which all the big hotel chains have contributed, block after block after block: America's Best Suites, Comfort Inn, Days Inn, Holiday Inn, Oasis Inn and so on. In the evening twilight the high voices of cheerleaders float across from a schoolyard in the old city centre where they are practising for the game this coming Saturday. At the lakeside there is complete silence and not a soul to be seen.

Beside the rippling water the lawns all look neat, the slabs of the sidewalks are sturdy and straight, but nowhere is there even an ice-cream stall to be found, let alone a diner or a local café. In this little slice of the world, dominated by hotel chains, property developers and real-estate entrepreneurs, all forms of normal private enterprise seem to have been swept away.

Over a bridge made of tens of miles of concrete, across an endless region of swamps, creeks, dying vegetation and rotting life, we drive into New Orleans the following afternoon. The city is an island, surrounded by water, engorged with wetness and repeatedly ravaged by floods.

New Orleans is regarded as the least American city in America, and its residents agree. The French Quarter, the central and most touristy part, is mainly Spanish in structure and layout, and the whole city is a confusing mixture of French and Spanish influences. It came into American hands only in the nineteenth century. Until 1862 half its schools still taught all their lessons in French. Until the mid-twentieth century you might have come across old Creole women here who didn't speak a word of English. I talked to someone whose grandfather always called passing tourists 'the Americans' – as far as he was concerned, he and the other residents of New Orleans were not Americans at all.

New Orleans is a city where death lies rotting at the gates, and where life has to be enjoyed for that reason. 'The people of New Orleans believe devoutly in their right to drink, dance, gamble, make love, and worship God,' noted Ernie Pyle when he visited the city in the spring of 1936.

'People care a little less in New Orleans. They're born to a what-the-hell attitude. They grow up to take a chance. They have a heritage in them, and they're hardly conscious of it. They have a heritage of hot blood mixtures, of warm weather and great rainfall, of pirates and buccaneers and revolutionists, of great wealth and great poverty, of battles and heroes and grand ladies, and balconies and iron lace and ships from far corners, and haughtiness and dignity and carousal.'

Steinbeck too had good memories: the black duck he once ate at a friend's place, 'a darkened house where the shades have been closed at dawn and the cool night air preserved', and the melodious toast to welcome him, 'in the singing language of Acadia which once was French and now is itself'. But this time he would flee the city. His 'body churned with weary nausea' in response to what he had seen and heard. 'I was in New Orleans of the great restaurants,' he wrote, but 'I could no more have gone to Gallatoir's for an omelet and champagne than I could have danced on a grave.'

Half a century later Ruby Bridges, the little black girl all the fuss was about, has not been forgotten. Those events are recalled at length in the newspapers, and Ruby Bridges, now a dignified lady in her fifties, is being interviewed and celebrated all over the place. The famous drawing by Norman Rockwell is regularly on show, a little girl going to school escorted by a pair of huge US marshals, past a wall spattered with rotten tomatoes and the word 'nigger': The Problem We All Live With.

Official segregation is a thing of the past; the sharp contrast between the races has gone, ostensibly at least. New Orleans now has a problem at least as great, one that unites and at the same time divides it: the city's own physical survival.

Ernie Pyle, John Steinbeck, Ruby Bridges and the Cheerleaders – everything they experienced took place in the old New Orleans, the city that existed before 29 August 2005, before Hurricane Katrina struck, the rickety dykes broke and most of the city disappeared under water, mud and silt. That New Orleans no longer exists.

The number of residents has since fallen by more than a quarter, from almost 485,000 in 2000 to 355,000 in 2010. Three-quarters of all the houses in New Orleans were damaged or destroyed. Some neighbourhoods had electricity restored fairly quickly; others were not reconnected to mains supplies for several years. There are still some 53,000 unoccupied addresses – houses and apartments that were demolished, irreparably damaged or simply abandoned by their owners. Of the 274 public schools open in 2005, seventy-seven are functioning today.

By the time we walk through New Orleans, five years after the disaster, most of the debris has been cleared away. The elegant Spanish city centre looks as if nothing has happened and around it, in all their glory, are the shady avenues and old dream villas. No, those terrible events are long forgotten here. But a mile further out and suddenly whole streets have disappeared and there are gaps all over the place, houses eroded to nothing. Everywhere, from the lamp posts to the walls of the buildings, you can still see the subtle stripes in green and grey, the marks of the water that stood here, sometimes a mere forty centimetres deep, sometimes almost two metres. People immediately start talking about what happened. They all carry their own personal watermarks, indelibly printed on their hearts and their memories.

'It wasn't Katrina, y'know,' says the deeply tanned taxi driver who takes us to a local restaurant. 'It was the levees that broke, that's what put the city under water.' He got out alive, he was glad enough of that. 'I lost everything I'd ever owned in my life, but I'm good and healthy. There are people who came out of it a lot worse off.'

We drive no more than four or five blocks; a taxi is a must at night if you don't know the city. 'Look,' says the driver. 'Here on this stretch you can walk just fine. But after the traffic signals over there it's really risky. That lasts for two blocks. Then, on the Esplanade, it's reasonably safe again. The whole city is like that.'

New Orleans is known as the murder capital of the United States, with some seventy murders a year per 100,000 inhabitants. For the sake of comparison: in the major cities of the Netherlands the average is less than four per 100,000. On the wall of the Saint Anna's Episcopal Church they are keeping track of the score for 2010 on two large boards covered in names. Next to most of them it says 'shot', sometimes 'beaten', 'burned' or 'strangled'. Number 169 is the last so far: Rodnika Hall, seventeen, stabbed to death. Yet everywhere in the city there's miraculous optimism: we're not giving up, we won't be beat, we're going to get our New Orleans back, whatever it takes.

The next day we see it all with our own eyes. The collapsed houses, which are now finally being cleared away at a great rate. The doors marked by the search teams: an 'X' with the date above it, to the left the mark identifying the rescue team, to the right the number of dangerous situations inside, and at the bottom the number of bodies found. Next to the X are notes and warnings: 'To room 258', '1 dead in kitchen', 'Do not demolish'. There's a huge mound of washed-up yachts, some of which were left hanging from trees, and streets with nothing but empty green fields to the left and right where entire rows of houses were swept away.

We inspect the old sea defences, which consist of a kind of concrete wall on top of a narrow dyke, a structure you'd expect to see in a developing country, not around a modern American urban area. They're working hard to build new levees, which look a good deal more solid, but as a Dutchman you rub your eyes with astonishment when you see that some of the gaps in the structure are being filled – temporarily, I assume – with nothing more than heaps of sandbags. One hurricane that gets a bit out of hand and the city will be under water again this fall.

Almost eight miles of flood defences were washed away. Actually, a large stretch simply subsided after the storm was over, as a result of sloppy construction, design faults, lack of investment and a general absence of interest in infrastructure of any sort. Whole stretches of the levee along the 17th Street Canal were made of peat on top of a weak clay layer that had not been reinforced. The construction of concrete flood defences on land of that nature was, as an engineer warned back in the 1990s, comparable to 'putting bricks on Jell-O'.

The real disaster came in two phases. First there was the hurricane itself, which caused devastation that Sunday night in an area as large as England, including a tidal surge that poured between six and twelve miles inland. The second disaster was quieter and slower. The city is built on the shores of Lake Pontchartrain, and there the levees held, but the flood tide pushed its way into several secondary drainage canals with levees that were not built to take it. They promptly broke and the water slowly but surely filled the city, until some districts were almost five metres under.

Ivor van Heerden, who was at the crisis centre in his capacity as a hurricane expert, later said that on the Monday evening after the storm, when everyone thought it was all just about over, he was suddenly asked why an old folks' home in St Bernard Parish was flooding. 'Well, it shouldn't be flooding,' Van Heerden said. 'The surge is over.' He thought it must be rain damage or something like that.

He heard afterwards that several people in authority knew by the start of that Monday afternoon that some of the levees in the drainage canal had given way. 'Why didn't they tell the media? We could have warned the hundreds of people who died in their attics.' Not until two in the morning did CNN broadcast the first vague reports of new breaches of the levees. Van Heerden had no idea of the full extent of the problem until he saw ultra-sharp satellite images that a French company made available on the Wednesday.

In the end, four-fifths of the city flooded. More than 1,500 people died, many of them elderly. They were mainly the very poorest, those who had no means – money, cars – of leaving the city in time. The rest of the population fled, many of them for ever. Bodies are still being found. Recently two were discovered under a pile of debris out in the swamp.

Many of the people we talk to start venting their exasperation spontaneously. 'The army said the levees could withstand a class three hurricane. No one told us they'd broken. We went to bed calmly on the Monday night. The city was pitch dark but the sky had cleared. We've got through it, we thought. When we woke at three in the morning there was a foot and a half of water in our house. All we could do was go to the attic. If you were in a wheelchair you had no chance at all.'

'We had an elderly neighbour, a nice old lady. That evening she noticed her carpet was suddenly wet. Ten minutes later she was standing on a chair, with eighteen inches between the surface of the water and her ceiling. She went on standing on that chair for the next twenty-five hours.'

'It was baking hot in the attic. You immediately start trying to make a hole in the roof, through all that thick insulation, otherwise you'll suffocate. Okay, heads outside. Now they can find you and rescue you, you think. That was on the Tuesday morning. The US Army turned up on the Friday.'

'The first group of rescuers to get here were from the Royal Canadian

Marine Search and Rescue. Everyone around us was in their attic or on their roof but our government was nowhere to be seen. The Canadians had to rescue us.'

'Our doctor told us he'd gone around all day in his boat getting people off roofs. At the end of the afternoon he found a whole family on a rather isolated roof. He ferried them to a big boat belonging to FEMA, the Federal Emergency Management Agency, our official American relief workers. They didn't want to take them. It was five o'clock; they were closing for the day.'

'Our whole family fled. Only my brother-in-law stayed, with his sixteen-year-old son. They sat out the storm together and then spent three days going around by boat to rescue people and bury the bodies. When we finally came back to look at our house weeks later, everything was covered with a thick black layer of silt and oil. Nothing was usable any more. I had two shirts with me, a pair of pants and some underwear. That's all I had left. By the end of the week my nephew had become a man.'

'In the two months after Katrina I attended more wakes than in my whole life up to then. And they weren't direct victims of the disaster but mainly indirect. So many people, especially the elderly, couldn't deal with it, collapsed, gave up.'

Every major disaster is a test of the established order, and a tough test too. The approach of Hurricane Katrina, the evacuation, the subsiding of the levees, the flood, the inadequate relief effort, the slow reconstruction, the fortitude of New Orleans residents – it has all been described in great detail in dozens of books and documentaries. It says something about America's powers of recuperation in the twenty-first century, and in New Orleans in particular. It also says something about the quality of the American public sector after twenty years of neo-liberalism. In that sense, New Orleans makes for an alarming story.

Ten years before Katrina, in 1995, the Japanese city of Kobe was hit by an even greater disaster, a powerful earthquake. Four times as many people died as in New Orleans, around 6,000, and entire districts were flattened. Roads, railways and bridges were badly damaged. Japan was going through a severe economic crisis at the time, yet after barely three years, in 1998, the last of the evacuees were able to return to the city. By 2000, five years after the earthquake, urban life in Kobe had largely returned to normal.

In New Orleans, an important city in the most powerful and wealthy country in the world, nothing like that has happened. The story about the doctor is no exception. Time and again I am regaled with astonishing examples of FEMA bureaucracy. Five years after the flood, many districts still have no street lighting. Many of the original residents are still displaced and large areas of the city have not been rebuilt. The disruption remains extreme.

Fierce debates are going on between 'innovators' and 'conservatives'. The latter want to restore New Orleans to the way it used to be and bring back as many of the old residents as possible. The 'innovators' want to use this opportunity to thoroughly modernise the city: no more housing projects for the poor; no policy of rebuilding every district; private education to replace the public schools. They have the wind in their sails, if only because poor families, who usually have little insurance, cannot afford to return to their old city to build something new.

Skin colour is a factor here, if only under the surface. White journalist and historian Nicholas Lemann, who comes from New Orleans, writes that black distrust of the 'innovators' is not entirely unfounded. After Katrina he heard quite a few conversations in the white living rooms of the city. He saw no sign of a specific programme, but he did keep noticing the old, ever-present fear among whites of a black insurrection. 'There was a palpable longing for New Orleans to be reconstituted as another Charleston or Savannah, smaller, neater, safer, whiter, and relieved of the obligation to try to be a significant modern multicultural city.'

Some therefore see the neglected levees, the disaster and the inadequate relief effort as part of a grand conspiracy: at a stroke the demographic and political balance of the city – once two-thirds black, one-third white – could be adjusted. Whether it's true, or whether it could possibly be true, is a good question. Three-quarters of the dead were older than sixty, and it was above all the older poor white people who did not survive the disaster.

If unconscious discrimination did occur, then it was based rather more on a profound contempt for everyone who was poor, who hadn't made

it, who hadn't managed to pluck the fruits of this country with all its
God-given blessings. That disdain could be detected everywhere: in the
systematic looking away by Washington; in the astonishing failure to give
out information; in the way the very poorest were driven together in the
Louisiana Superdome, packed in tight and forced to survive for days with
hardly any food, water or sanitation; in the way in which crates of food
were flung down from army helicopters tens of metres up; in the eagerness with which the National Guard immediately started hunting 'street
criminals and gangs' because, in the words of Commander Steven Blum,
that rendered 'a huge success story'.

The most effective relief effort in the weeks after the disaster was
mounted by churches and private aid organisations rather than the US
government. The rebuilding of the levees – a government task if ever
there was one – has yet to be completed, after all these years. It's the
flipside of individualist America, the America of few taxes and no great
public works, the neo-conservative America that ruled the roost in the
years of the George W. Bush presidency.

Forty years earlier, in September 1965, New Orleans was hit by
Hurricane Betsy. Then too, neighbourhoods such as the Upper and Lower
Ninth Ward were hard hit. President Johnson hastened to the city and
walked straight into a shelter full of evacuees. It was dark in there, with
no electricity, and everyone was nervous and fearful. Johnson picked up
a flashlight, pointed it at his face and thundered: 'My name is Lyndon
Baines Johnson. I'm your goddamn president and I'm here to tell you
that my office and the people of the United States are behind you!'

Compare that to the visit to New Orleans by President George W. Bush
in September 2005. Five days had passed by the time he arrived. He spent
one day in the city all told, accompanied by a group of local politicians
that included Democrat senator Mary Landrieu, and his visit attracted
many journalists and many cameras. The whole gathering was taken to
see a breach in the levee on the 17th Street Canal, where a huge amount
of activity was going on, with cranes, diggers and the Army Corps of
Engineers hard at work closing the breach. Despite all the misery, it was
a promising scene.

Next morning Senator Landrieu happened to fly over the same stretch
of levee in a helicopter. She couldn't believe her eyes. Everything had

gone. It was totally still, aside from one lonely crane. Landrieu said later: 'I could not believe that the president of the United States had come down to the city of New Orleans and basically put up a stage prop . . . They put the props up and the minute we were gone they took them down . . . At that moment I knew what was going on.'

Six

I EAT BREAKFAST WITH JARVIS DEBERRY, one of the city's most famous black journalists, editor of the *Times-Picayune*. He believes most Americans don't really know how to handle New Orleans. It has always been a maverick city. Perhaps that's one reason for the Bush administration's lax and hypocritical attitude: New Orleans doesn't really belong among 'us', the American family.

Race relations were always different in New Orleans compared to the rest of the South, which may help to explain the vast amount of attention paid in the national press to the race riots of late November 1960. The fierceness of the conflict was at odds with the relatively smooth relationship between the races that had always been the norm here.

From the eighteenth century onwards, slaves in New Orleans had a right to buy their freedom, and when the city came into the hands of the United States in 1803 there was an entire district, called Tremé, where four out of every five houses were owned by black people. Mixed marriages were completely normal. The rich whites in the mansions on Esplanade Avenue had huge houses built across from them for their black and mixed-race mistresses. In the daytime they lived on one side of Esplanade, at night on the other. Their children, whether white or brown, could pursue any course of study they chose.

Tocqueville and Beaumont, who visited this 'Babylon of the West' in January 1832, were astonished by these relationships. They did notice a firm division in status. At the opera they attended, the white men were at the front, the 'mulatto' women ('very pretty') behind them and the black women up in the gallery. 'Strange sight,' Tocqueville wrote. 'All the men white, all the women colored, or at least with African blood.'

'Of course race was always an issue,' says DeBerry. 'New Orleans was the centre of the slave trade. I can point the slave market out to you. It's a tourist restaurant now. The heavy bars are still there. But in a certain way it was more free, too, less suffocating.' The sharp racial division in the South, he insists, started only in the nineteenth century. A clear distinction developed between different districts and neighbourhoods. 'I grew up in Mississippi. I had a white history teacher there who told me that when he was a child he never saw black people. They lived on the other side of town; they simply didn't exist.'

New Orleans remained an exception in that sense, retaining the old atmosphere of laissez-aller. In neighbourhoods like the Ninth Ward, white, black and mixed-race people lived side by side. DeBerry tells me: 'That's the ironic thing about the segregation riots Steinbeck witnessed. In 1960 some people acted as if the world would come to an end if the schools integrated. But eighty years earlier there were integrated schools all over New Orleans, it was perfectly normal.'

Only with the further 'Americanisation' of New Orleans in the twentieth century did the principle of segregation creep in. Louis Armstrong grew up here in the early years of that century and then travelled widely. In 1949, at the Mardi Gras street carnival in New Orleans, he was given a hero's reception as 'King of the Zulus'. He hadn't been back for years, and he was deeply shocked by the New Orleans he encountered: so much more distrust, so much more segregation than when he was a child.

The hurling of abuse that John Steinbeck witnessed was the low point of that process. His account in Travels belongs in a long line of classic descriptions of riots, in the same tradition as, for example, Gustave Flaubert in Paris in 1848 and Joseph Roth in Berlin in 1920.

All the ingredients were present. First of all, the crowd. Then the passion for sensation, 'like people going to a fire after it has been burning for some time'. Then there was their informal leader – in this case a full-busted lady of about fifty with a 'ferocious smile', gold earrings, a fake fur coat and a voice like 'the bellow of a bull'. And finally public attention, the news clippings that were read out 'with little squeals of delight', the ever-present media that lifted everything and everyone up out of normal life for a moment.

The object of all this popular rage was the one thing that was exceptional in this case: the smallest black girl Steinbeck had ever seen, dressed in 'shining starchy white', with new white shoes, the whites of her eyes gleaming 'like those of a frightened fawn'. Surrounded by big, square-chested security men, she walked slowly up the steps to the school, and because the men were so big they made the child look even smaller.

'Then the girl made a curious hop,' Steinbeck writes, 'and I think I know what it was. I think in her whole life she had not gone ten steps without skipping, but now in the middle of her first skip the weight bore her down.' He was almost right, but in fact it was worse. As a small girl, Ruby Bridges had picked up the frenzied mood of the crowd, but the aggression that went with it failed to get through to her at first. She thought it was Mardi Gras, she would often say afterwards, and when she got out of school she even taught a friend a new skipping rhyme she'd learned that day: 'Two, four, six, eight, we don't want to integrate.'

The climax in that kangaroo court came a little later that day, however, when a white man appeared who dared to bring his white child to that same school, 'a tall man dressed in light gray, leading his frightened child by the hand'. His body was stiff with tension, 'a man afraid who by his will held his fears in check as a great rider directs a panicked horse'.

This must have been Methodist preacher Lloyd Foreman and his five-year-old daughter Pamela Lynn, or perhaps James Gabrielle, an assistant meter-reader for an energy company, and his daughter Yolanda. The Gabrielles had refused to take Yolanda out of school along with the other white children. Yolanda was very fond of her infant teacher and her parents were completely confident that she would arrange for the one black girl to be integrated into the class without any problems. The irony was that the girls weren't in the same class, not even in that empty school. Yolanda Gabrielle, now a therapist on Rhode Island, told the Times-Picayune that she saw Ruby Bridges just once, through a slightly open classroom door: 'That's the irony of this: we were still kept segregated.'

Neighbours came to warn Yolanda's mother, Daisy, to stop this at once. Yolanda might get 'their diseases'. When Daisy said she wasn't concerned about that, they stared coldly at her. 'Daisy, we never knew you were a nigger-lover.' The next day the threats started; their house was pelted with stones and James was sacked from his job. A month later they moved to

Rhode Island. The Foreman family was terrorised for months, even threatened with bomb attacks and forced to flee from one friendly parsonage to the next. No hotel in the South was willing to let them in.

Jarvis DeBerry did not have to go through all that. He was born in 1957, and when he started school as a black boy his classes were already mixed. Something else did happen, though. 'When I stepped into the classroom on my first day, it was still full of white kids. By the time I left school they'd almost all gone.'

As soon as segregation was banned, white parents started sending their children to private schools. Officially these schools were for everyone too, but Jarvis can't remember a black child being admitted to one during his school years. Official segregation was over, but actual segregation remained largely in place.

The statistics tell the same story. Half a century has passed and still almost three-quarters of black children in America attend a typical 'black school'. In New Orleans the public school system – where ninety-three per cent of pupils are black – was practically bankrupt even before 2005. According to the Louisiana Department of Education's school performance scores, standards at 47 per cent of public schools in the city were 'academically unacceptable', and another 26.5 per cent were at the level of 'academic watch'. Those are the two lowest categories. And that was before Katrina.

'The riots around the William Frantz school were indeed historic,' Jarvis tells me. 'They marked the start of the great exodus of white families from public education. Public schools are black, private schools are white – that's how it's been ever since. The system has never had a chance to show what truly desegregated education could mean. That's the real tragedy.'

I take one more look at some archive photographs of the rioting outside William Frantz Elementary. Sure enough, most of the Cheerleaders are sturdy ladies in robust headscarves and raincoats. They are holding up signs with slogans such as 'Integration is a Mortal Sin' and 'God Demands Segregation'. But among them are a good many nicely dressed, attractive women, not at all the kind of embittered mothers Steinbeck describes, and they are shouting just as loudly. In all the memorial articles and archive documents, I come upon little if anything about their motives, although these would of course be just as interesting: how on earth do you get it into your head to carry on like that, as a 'mother', against a seven-year-old girl?

There is a world-famous photograph of a similar situation, taken on 4 September 1957, when teenager Elizabeth Eckford became the first black pupil at the Little Rock Central High School in Arkansas. As she entered, she too was shouted at by a white crowd: 'Lynch her! Lynch her!' 'No nigger bitch is going to get in our school!' Here a prominent 'Cheerleader' was one Hazel Bryan. In the photo she is shown yelling, mouth wide open, at the dignified Elizabeth, who is dressed in white. Fifty years later, *Vanity Fair* journalist David Margolick tracked down both women and wrote about their lives. Elizabeth Eckford had taken part in commemorations and documentaries. She stayed angry and proud for many years, but four decades after the event she was finally prepared to meet Hazel. Hazel Bryan was full of regret. After just a couple of years she'd traced Elizabeth and rung her up, sobbing, to tell her so, but in the end she'd felt too embarrassed to say very much.

She was still very young herself when the photo was taken, just fifteen, although she looked a lot older. The only black person she knew was a woman who sometimes came to her house to do the ironing, whom she thought very nice; when she was little she sometimes pretended to be ill so that she could be with her. She hadn't intended to protest, she said, but it was such fun: all those people, the reporters, the boys in uniform, the theatre. 'The mouth was mine,' she admitted.

In New Orleans the riots were less spontaneous. Behind the scenes the women were being egged on by the local Democrat boss Leander Perez. It was he who had arranged for a building in nearby St Bernard Parish to serve as a temporary school for the white children. Perez was a corrupt, violent and racist demagogue who described the Civil Rights Movement as the work of 'all those Jews who were supposed to have been cremated at Buchenwald and Dachau but weren't, and Roosevelt allowed two million of them illegal entry into our country'.

On this occasion he voiced his objections with fervour again. 'Don't wait for your daughter to be raped by these Congolese,' he said at a meeting of the White Citizens' Council. 'Don't wait until the burrheads are forced into your schools. Do something about it now.' Five thousand local people cheered him to the rafters.

Those same neighbours assailed Pamela, Yolanda and Ruby the following day with a torrent of abuse. Steinbeck makes it sound like call-and-response singing: 'A shrill, grating voice rang out. The yelling was not in chorus. Each took a turn and at the end of each the crowd broke into howls and roars and whistles of applause.'

Exactly what the Cheerleaders shouted remained unclear. The newspapers used terms like 'indelicate' or 'obscene' and on television the sound was deliberately muffled. In the final version of *Travels* there are only vague descriptions: 'bestial', 'degenerate', 'carefully and selectedly filthy', 'a kind of frightening witches' Sabbath'. In the manuscript Steinbeck does quote the Cheerleaders word for word and I found the text in the Viking Press proofs that are held at the Steinbeck Center. On page 155, a firm hand has deleted the final paragraphs. A piece of paper has been stuck over them, bearing the text that was printed in the book.

The original, however, is still easily legible. Those sentences read: 'I don't know how the sick sadness of this morning can be felt without those words. I am going to write down the exact expressions screamed in banshee voices, voices in which hysteria was very near the surface. The texture of the morning cannot be experienced without them. You mother-fucking, nigger-sucking, prick-licking piece of shit. Why, you'd lick a dog's ass if he'd let you. Look at the bastard drag his dirty stinking ass along. You think that's his kid. That's a piece of shit. That's shit leading shit. Know what we ought to do? Strip down them fancy pants and cut off his balls and feed them to the pigs – that's if he's got any balls. How about it, friends?'

Steinbeck had encountered problems before with obscene language in his books. *Of Mice and Men* was on the blacklist at many libraries for years, as was *The Grapes of Wrath*. In Buffalo, New York, *Grapes* was actually burned for being 'full of filth'. A letter from Steinbeck to his friend Robert Wallsten in January 1962 shows that there were worries about this part of *Travels* causing fresh problems. Steinbeck had known it all along. 'Those words will go to *Holiday* on this manuscript, and there is not a chance in the world that my readers will see them,' he wrote explicitly in a prepublication piece, and he was right. After that sentence comes an editor's note: 'Mr Steinbeck is right. The Cheerleaders words were a string of unrelieved filth and had to be deleted.'

Viking Press initially wanted to stand its ground, but eventually it caved in, probably for legal reasons. Steinbeck felt tired and ill, and he wrote: 'I have been so bloody weak that I just don't give a damn. It seems to me that everybody in America is scared of everything mostly before it happens. I finally sent word that what reputation I had was not based on timidity or on playing safe. And I hope that is over.'

'We knew it wasn't right. We knew it was wrong. I still remember being a little white boy sitting in a bus when a black boy was thrown off. When I was thirteen, the first black girl was admitted to the Catholic school I attended. It caused a huge protest. A priest walked alongside the girl holding up a cross to protect her. The mothers of my classmates spat and shouted the most terrible things. I was deeply shocked.

'We all have our own memories. The public drinking fountains in the city were strictly segregated – imagine what would happen if a black man drank from a white fountain! There was an amusement park with three different swimming pools, strictly separate according to race and skin colour. When they were forced to integrate they closed down. The swimming pools sat there without water for half a century.'

I spend my final morning with John Biguenet, playwright and guest columnist for the *New York Times*. Like his fellow authors in New Orleans, after Katrina he threw aside everything he was working on. In a short period he wrote three new plays: *Rising Water*, *Shotgun* and *Mold*.

'After the disaster we all had a powerful sense of transience. At the same time we were almost ecstatic: this isn't the end of the world, it's the beginning of something totally new. At one point there were only about fifty thousand of us in a city where almost half a million people used to live. We reorganised our schools, the police, politics, everything. The public schools were shut for a year. Everywhere little groups of mothers broke the buildings open and started giving lessons themselves. At last we were with our own kind, the real people of New Orleans, that's the feeling we had. It was an impossible situation, but anything is possible when there's nothing left.

'New Orleans is the place where the future arrives first,' John says. 'If you don't pay any attention to the environment, to infrastructure, to poverty, to education, to integrity in politics, then you get New Orleans. All the evils of America came together here.' He starts to sum them all up, counting them off on his fingers.

One. Contempt for public life and public affairs; the idea that it doesn't matter who's in charge. FEMA, the federal organisation for emergency relief, was headed by a completely inexperienced acquaintance of George W. Bush. Of the ten top people at FEMA, five had no experience of disasters of any kind.

Two. Bush himself, one of the most incompetent presidents in American history. When a powerful earthquake hit San Francisco in 1906 and the city was largely destroyed, a catastrophe comparable to Katrina in many ways, President Teddy Roosevelt immediately issued orders for as many trains as possible to travel west. Within twenty-four hours the federal government had the city under control. 'I can assure you, leadership counts. Especially in these kinds of situations.'

Three. The distortion of reality by the propaganda machines. Politics based on lies. The Army Corps of Engineers insisted for a year that the water had come over the top of the levees, that their levee constructions had worked, that the army couldn't be blamed for anything. That was the first story their PR machine came out with, and it stuck. Most Americans think Hurricane Katrina was to blame.

'We had no time back then to rectify that nonsense and afterwards it was too late. The attack on the republic of New Orleans began almost immediately: it was all the fault of the black leaders; the city was full of riff-raff and looters. The Republican speaker of the House proposed that New Orleans should be "bulldozed". No one here was in a position to respond. We were too busy surviving, while a completely false story was made up about us.

'At first we, as writers, had no shape to give to our own story. What on earth was happening to us? Now I can say something about it, but then we were all searching. This city is so beautiful, but so earthy as well. It's very difficult to imagine how dangerous it is. I had to turn to European literature, to Heinrich Böll, Günter Grass and other Europeans, to find a way to describe this falling away of all certainties.

'In the end what matters most are stories that are deeply embedded in the mythology of the country. So eventually I came back to New Orleans, to the stories of the city itself: water, dreams, death, life.'

I drive to the place where it all happened, where Steinbeck stood half a century ago, watching in disgust: the William Frantz Elementary School at 3811 North Galvez Street in the Ninth Ward. A sign announces major restoration work, but for now the building stands as a lonely, empty, grey colossus. It's deserted and deathly quiet. The nearby houses have been propped up in places as they gently subside; in some cases all that's left is a heap of timber or an empty lot. In the distance I can hear the highway and for a moment the call of a train. A high fence of barbed wire runs all around the school, windows have been smashed, ceilings hang down, everything is brownish and weather-stained.

I immediately recognise the entrance from the photographs, that vast front door that gobbled up the tiny Ruby Bridges. But now it has a big 'X' daubed on it, with the familiar codes inside: 9/13, IFW, Y162, 0.

Searched on 13 September. Zero dead.

Epilogue

'You can't go home again.'

THOMAS WOLFE

1940

One

STEINBECK'S JOURNEY WAS LOPSIDED in time. As he said himself, his expedition began long before he left and it was all over before he returned. The unravelling of Operation Windmills began in Chicago and accelerated after Seattle. By Monterey, Steinbeck had more or less abandoned the project.

Steinbeck tells his readers that he brought his quest to a close in Abingdon, Virginia. Halfway through the long stretch back to New York his journey suddenly left him one afternoon, without warning. The trees became 'green blurs', the people lost their faces, the road was 'an endless stone ribbon'.

We too went home. After New Orleans there was no more to investigate; Steinbeck had nothing appreciable to say about those final miles. It was over and done. We gathered our things, my wife spoke words of gratitude to our faithful Jeep for the last time at New Orleans airport, I put our suitcases onto the luggage belt, and together we disappeared across a jetway, back to the old continent. We became observers again, distant nephews and nieces of our American family.

Our fellow travellers went on their way too. After taking a quick look at the William Frantz school, Bill Steigerwald had headed home, grumbling at the roads of New Orleans and the crazies that populated Louisiana, as he saw them. After forty-three days he'd had enough, and he'd also had his fill of that half-fantasist John Steinbeck.

John Gunther, partly because of money troubles, worked himself to death. As well as his popular *Inside* series (he made a couple of similar journeys through Russia and Africa), he wrote several novels and biographies, on subjects including Roosevelt and Eisenhower. He became famous above all for a moving book about the death of his teenage son from a brain tumour in 1947. Gunther himself was dead by 1970.

Ernie Pyle went to war. He grew to become a legendary war reporter, working for more than 300 American newspapers, always among the troops, loyal to the last. Right towards the end, in April 1945, he was killed on an island in the Pacific. At the request of a press agency, Steinbeck wrote an obituary for his friend. It was never published. By the time it reached the newspaper Pyle's death was already 'no longer news' to his former colleagues. 'He had done everything with the soldiers except this last thing,' Steinbeck wrote. Now even the corpse of the utterly exhausted Ernie was added to the great heap.

As for Tocqueville and Beaumont, they travelled on to New York and set sail on 20 February 1832 for France, arriving back there in late March. Tocqueville soon entered politics, becoming a member of the Assemblée nationale. In 1849 he was even foreign minister for a brief time, with Beaumont as his ambassador in Vienna. His next major work, about the French Revolution, was never completed. He died in 1859 at the age of fifty-three. Beaumont died seven years later.

One final postcard to Elizabeth Otis, sent on 2 December from Pelahatchie, Mississippi, tells us that John Steinbeck travelled north at a cracking pace via Natchez and Vicksburg. From Pelahatchie his route took him along the US 11, bound for New York. 'It's been a long haul.' Charley had had enough too. He went to sleep, stopped looking out of the window and didn't say 'ftt' once. It was one long dash, a hypnotic droning dream, 'but at the end of it was the one shining reality – my own wife, my own house in my own street, my own bed'.

He got lost for a moment, for the umpteenth time, in the evening rush hour in his own home city. He pulled up to the curb, his hands shaking from 'road jitters' and started laughing uncontrollably. He'd travelled the entire country with Rocinante and Charley, through all those mountains, plains and deserts, and right close to his home at 209 East 72nd Street he completely lost his way.

'And that's how,' he ends, 'the traveler came home again.'

It was probably 5 or 6 December 1960. Steinbeck had driven almost

10,000 miles. He'd seen thirty-three of the fifty American states and the trip had taken almost eleven weeks.

The world had not stood still in the meantime. As Steinbeck was covering his final few miles, the Soviet Union launched another experimental satellite, this time with two dogs on board. They were called Pchyolka and Mushka, 'Little Bee' and 'Little Fly'. Two specialists at Dartmouth College in Hanover, New Hampshire, had invented an education machine, a complicated affair with cards for correct and incorrect answers. New York was mesmerised by a new hit film starring Marilyn Monroe, *Let's Make Love*, in which she danced and sang 'My Heart Belongs to Daddy'.

Luxury was the order of the day that Christmas season. The latest TWA Superjet could fly from New York to San Francisco in five hours and thirty-five minutes. The west coast had never been so close. Meanwhile United States Lines were drawing attention to the restful nature of a sea voyage: 'Relax your way to Europe. And there is plenty of luggage space for what you want to take with you, and what you buy to take home.' The soft colours of the Buick Special, the Oldsmobile F-38, the Chevrolet Corvair and the Pontiac Tempest beamed from the pages of magazines. American Optical presented its sunglasses for 1961 – red, with big white wings.

The original manuscript of *Travels* includes a final chapter of more than four pages – 'Envoi' – which was omitted from the published version. Rightly so, even though its remarkable mix of politics and domestic cosiness gives a special twist to the book. His story begins with a storm, Steinbeck writes, and he will end with one too. He describes how, after his arrival back, his 'lady wife' Elaine sees in the newspaper, to her amazement, that they have been invited to John F. Kennedy's inauguration on 20 January 1961. They travel to Washington, staying with friends in Georgetown, and Steinbeck describes the huge snowstorm on the day before the ceremony. What looks as if it might end in chaos instead turns into a party. 'Even republicans who had seen in the weather Divine wrath at a democrat victory began to have fun.'

On the day itself the sun shone, the main thoroughfares were cleared of snow by the army, and John and Elaine, far too early, sat shivering in the cold. From Benson's biography we know that they spent the whole day with the Galbraiths. John Kenneth Galbraith was an important advisor to Kennedy, and it was he who'd thought up a telling sentence of the president's inaugural speech: 'Let us never negotiate out of fear, but let us never fear to negotiate.'

All day the two couples were followed by the television networks. 'We might presume that when the producer wanted beauty, he cut to Janet Leigh,' Benson writes. 'But when he wanted irreverence and relief, he went to Galbraith and Steinbeck.'

They enjoyed themselves greatly, and on television the two men were a prominent presence. Some journalists even assumed that Steinbeck would be offered a post in the new administration. Steinbeck later wrote a thank you note to Kennedy, saying he'd been profoundly moved and felt the inaugural speech 'had that magic undertone of truth which cannot be simulated'.

'And so, my fellow Americans, ask not what your country can do for you – ask what you can do for your country . . .' Meanwhile Steinbeck spent the entire ceremony with Elaine's cold feet in his lap. 'With every sentence of the interminable prayers, I rubbed,' he writes in the manuscript. 'And the prayers were interesting, if long. One sounded like general orders to the deity issued in a parade ground voice. One prayer brought God up to date on current events with a view to their revision. In the midst of one prayer, smoke issued from the lectern and I thought we had gone too far, but it turned out to be a short circuit.'

They were also invited to the grand ball that evening. Everyone in the house where the Steinbecks were staying was getting ready for the party. Outside, the traffic was jammed tight because of all the snowdrifts. They decided not to go, letting the storm rage without them this time. They made sandwiches, had a few drinks and watched the celebrations on television. And when people later asked what the ball was like they said: 'Loved it. Remarkable. Wonderful.'

The manuscript ends: 'And in the morning the snow was past and so was the journey.' Then comes a ten-word line that has been crossed out, followed by the final words: 'I do know this – the big and mysterious America is bigger than I thought and more mysterious.'

In an old copy of Holiday I happen upon a full-page photograph of John Steinbeck with Charley, taken shortly after the trip. It was the overture to the first episode of his travel account, published in July 1961. The photo was taken in the bare winter garden at Sag Harbor. The poodle looks dapper, but how old Steinbeck has become! He gazes wearily at me, his hair thin, his beard grey, his eyes heavy and swollen.

'Life without travel is only half living,' was *Holiday*'s motto. In the pages of adverts, Avion Travel Trailers shows off its latest models of caravan, streamlined and silver like rockets, with hot and cold running water, a bath and a shower. 'Even in the barren wilderness, you'll live on the top of luxury.' The country depicted in the pages of *Holiday* is full of pastel colours, and Steinbeck's rough way of travelling looks a little strange next to it – or perhaps not, since it makes his lonely voyage in a sober truck seem all the more exotic.

Steinbeck must have started to write that January. His journal entries in an exercise book make clear that he continued to work hard even during a holiday in Barbados – in February 1961 he filled almost sixty pages. The first instalment of the 'In Quest of America' series needed to be ready for publication in the July issue of *Holiday*. Parts two and three would be published in December 1961 and February 1962.

Steinbeck had an excellent memory. He took few if any notes. He seems to have written nonstop; his handwriting is steady and firm, without the slightest hesitation, rolling on and on; corrections are rare and minimal – in part one at least. He had his letters to Elaine to go on and he probably wrote the rest from memory. After an untroubled start, however, he ran aground in parts two and three.

The poor reviews that greeted *The Winter of Our Discontent* in June 1961 greatly unnerved him, and his despair comes through in the manuscript. The corrections become steadily more numerous and substantial. The breakpoints in the book correspond precisely with the beginning and end of the three instalments in *Holiday*. The first part runs smoothly all the way to Chicago; the second, via Seattle to Monterey, is more problematic; the third, from Monterey to New Orleans, is full of repressed pessimism – the journey is actually already over.

In the summer he wrote to his publisher Pascal Covici that he was having great trouble getting back 'the rhythm and flow of the *Travels* piece' – he probably means the first *Holiday* instalment. At night he lay awake, trying to resolve one difficulty after another. Aside from the geography and the unity of time, he felt it was 'a haphazard thing'. He referred to *Travels* as a book full of disconnected memories, shapeless and aimless. 'The mountain has labored and not even a mouse has come forth.' Every morning he got up at five, and he was dead tired. 'I think I've overworked my engine.'

Travels with Charley was published in July 1962. It was received with huge enthusiasm. The *New York Times* called it 'pure delight, a pungent potpourri of places and people interspersed with bittersweet essays on everything from the emotional difficulties of growing old to the reasons why giant Sequoias arouse such awe'. The paper appreciated above all Steinbeck's determination to rise above 'stubborn regionalism' and seek a shared American national character. *Newsweek* found it 'vigorous, affecting, and highly entertaining'. The *Atlantic Monthly* compared *Travels* to the best work of Henry David Thoreau. Other reviews were in the same vein. Not for years had a book by Steinbeck received such fulsome praise.

Time alone was distinctly negative. Henry Luce had never forgiven Steinbeck for publishing *The Grapes of Wrath* and his magazine described *Travels* as 'one of the dullest travelogues ever to acquire the respectability of a hard cover'. Nonetheless, the book held firmly to its place in *Time*'s own top ten for at least a year.

Steinbeck was less than delighted despite all the praise. In another letter to Covici he poured out his feelings, saying he was extremely uncertain about his future as a writer and wondered whether he'd ever write another book. *Travels* was indeed his last major work.

Now that it's all over and done, I do of course read *Travels* differently. It remains an engrossing travel account, robustly set down in one masterful paragraph after another. Excellent craftsmanship, all of it, as we would expect from Steinbeck, and it makes you want to set out on a journey of your own. If you read it carefully, however, you can see the composition gradually disintegrate, just like the project itself. Towards the end you can feel the haste with which he wrote the final pages.

That time pressure was real. Steinbeck had decided to take a classic 'grand tour' of Europe with Elaine and his two sons (then fifteen and seventeen), lasting almost a year. A special teacher for the boys would travel with them, Terrence McNally, later a renowned playwright. On 8

September 1961 the group was to leave for England from New York on the *Rotterdam*, a ship of the Holland America Line.

That was the firm deadline Steinbeck had set himself for the writing of *Travels*, and he only just made it. To him, *Travels* was above all the three articles for *Holiday*. After that he would see.

To be honest, Steinbeck was not always a pleasant travelling companion. He promised to show me America, and he did, if in a rather different way than I imagined as we were packing our bags. He was often moody, hasty and unreliable, and on top of that he fantasised too much. He turned out to be anything but the compass to guide you on a trip around America. I often found I was much better off relying on John Gunther and Ernie Pyle.

But in his good moments – and there were plenty of those – Steinbeck was a fantastic observer and a shrewd thinker. He painted with words, creating one beautiful watercolour after another until an inimitable picture book emerged of people and landscapes, memories and visions of the future. That is what makes *Travels* so enchanting.

Steinbeck could never have predicted that questions would be raised about the veracity of his account. No one would dare to do anything like it today, but in 1960 an author could still imagine himself to be reasonably unobserved. Only after the 1960s did literary studies develop a need to analyse an author's entire writing process, using methods that hold every letter, every note, every snippet up to the light. He could never have suspected that half a century later his work would be put under the microscope by a tenacious journalist like Bill Steigerwald.

Elaine did feel uneasy, however. She never said anything about all those miles and days when it was she rather than Charley who sat in the front seat next to John. In the published collection of Steinbeck's letters she claims that John stopped writing to her after Montana because she joined him 'for a few days at a time along the way'. In reality, if you add it all up, the voyage lasted two and a half months and John and Elaine were together for at least half of it. Parini, who spoke to Elaine on several occasions while researching his Steinbeck biography, told the *New York Times* that the whole business had surprised him. 'She never mentioned that. She made a big deal about how painful it was for them to be

separated and how she insisted that he take the dog along for company.'
By contrast Bill Barich, another writer who more or less retraced
Steinbeck's journey, in 2008, was not surprised at all: 'I'm fairly certain
that Steinbeck made up most of the book.'

Reactions showed that many Steinbeck fans were not happy with this
series of discoveries. They were sad and angry, feeling their hero had
been defiled. Somehow or other Steinbeck was part of the collective
fantasy of a huge number of Americans about their country and their
history. It was an image they themselves had worked hard to create and
the spell must not be broken.

Yet it is impossible to describe *Travels* as serious non-fiction. Far too
many of the meetings are of dubious veracity, too many facts are wrong,
too many dialogues – such as those with the three hitchhikers towards
the end of the book – are clearly invented. As John Jr wrote in his autobiography, they are caricatures of conversations. No one talks like that.
Twenty years earlier he'd come to the same conclusion as Bill Steigerwald:
his father was far too shy to engage in the kind of conversations he
describes in *Travels*. He couldn't have coped with so much interaction. 'So
the book is actually a great novel.'

Does that matter? Steinbeck's other son, Thomas, compared his father's
way of working with that of the young Da Vinci, who was always
wandering the streets of Florence, sketching the faces of passers-by as
material for his great works. However much Steinbeck may have been
spinning yarns, however much he may have whipped together everything
he'd heard and beaten it into stories of his own, he remained an excellent listener. He loved conversations in drugstores and diners with any
Tom, Dick or Harry, whether they were factory workers and crab fishermen
or travelling salesmen and truck drivers. His readers had a sense of
recognition – he was, after all, describing their world.

Bill Barich points to Steinbeck's depression, and his poor health: 'By
that point he was probably incapable of interviewing ordinary people.'
He has the same explanation for Steinbeck's pessimistic view of America.
Yet Barich found a lot of what Steinbeck wrote about America significant.
'His perceptions were right on the money about the death of localism,
the growing homogeneity of America, the trashing of the environment.
He was prescient about all that.'

The New York Times was harsh in response to Steigerwald's revelations. 'Books labeled "nonfiction" should not break faith with readers. Not now, and not in 1962.'

Steigerwald's own conclusion is milder, and after all those months travelling with Steinbeck and him, I share his conclusions. Steinbeck did not make up stories in an attempt to mislead his readers or to achieve a political effect. It was a last resort. In just a few months he had to write three long pieces of reportage for Holiday about his headlong dash around America, and he'd made hardly any notes. He also needed to turn it into a book, which his publisher would then market as undiluted non-fiction. As Steigerwald wrote in the libertarian magazine Reason: 'At crunch time, as he struggled to write Charley, his journalistic failures forced him to be a novelist again.'

Four months after Travels was published, on 25 October 1962, Steinbeck heard that he had been awarded the Nobel Prize for Literature.

Two

WHAT WOULD STEINBECK HAVE MADE of today's America? I've asked myself that question again and again. What would he have felt if he'd made the same trip again in 2010, from affluent and orderly Deerfield to the chaos of New Orleans? As for me and my fellow Europeans, is America still our future, the way it was in the 1950s and 1960s? Is it still that same irresistible world of gloss, glitter and soft pastels, populated by a superior and innately relaxed species of human being, the world of *Disneyland Dream* and 'Hey-Ba-Ba-Re-Bop'?

'There are, at the present time, two great nations in the world which seem to tend towards the same end, although they started from different points: I allude to the Russians and the Americans,' wrote Tocqueville in 1835. 'Both of them have grown up unnoticed; and whilst the attention of mankind was directed elsewhere, they have suddenly assumed a most prominent place amongst the nations; and the world learned their existence and their greatness at almost the same time. All other nations seem to have nearly reached their natural limits, and only to be charged with the maintenance of their power; but these are still in the act of growth; all the others are stopped, or continue to advance with extreme difficulty; these are proceeding with ease and with celerity along a path to which the human eye can assign no term.'

How do things stand with those two peoples now – or, to take a rather broader view, with the two worlds separated by the Atlantic Ocean? In both systems people did indeed set out with great optimism, but their paths diverged markedly. Until well into the twentieth century, Russia and Europe had great difficulty adjusting to modern society and the new power relationships that went with it. The old continent was tormented for decades by mass murder, state terror and horrific wars. America, with great reluctance, was forced to intervene several times and eventually the Soviet Empire collapsed. In the 1950s the rest of Europe began a political experiment that bore some resemblance to what America had begun two centuries earlier, the creation of a power that, like the United States, would stand above the different states: the European Union.

Americans immediately embraced the achievements of the modern era and, despite all its problems, that 'ease and with celerity' can still be felt. They also discovered something important, without even fully realising it: how it is possible to live in reasonable harmony and even build up a sense of being one with a huge number of other people who have totally different backgrounds. Now as ever they choose to be Americans, and they stand by that.

Just compare their attitude to the mentality of the residents of a Russian or European city. The place where they live is a firm fact and many of the walls have been standing for centuries. It's a similar story with citizenship; most Europeans don't have to do much if anything to achieve it, and neither did their parents or grandparents. Their nationality was never a matter of choice. It is their fate.

Most Americans, whether of the left or the right, are sincerely proud of their country, or rather of their country's dynamic culture. If their happiness machine falters, the disappointment is all the greater; anyone today following Steinbeck's route around America will feel that. Here and there you come upon islands of prosperity, but in between are oceans of anguish and poverty. That divide is the most striking aspect. It's mainly the centres of production that are in decline, the factory cities, the agricultural towns, the places where things are made and produced. Everything is still going well in the places where things are consumed, the shopping malls. America, more than it realises, has become a land of consumers, a buy-now-pay-later republic.

From 1914 onwards, for almost the whole of the twentieth century, America was unquestionably the most powerful economy in the world. The American consumer was for decades the engine of the world economy. That time has gone now. Both America and Europe are lugging a mountain of debt around with them, and it's proving harder and harder to manage. The cost of pensions and social security is rising steadily. Whatever growing pains may be afflicting the emerging economies, especially in Asia, they are predominantly youthful and energetic, and hundreds of millions of people are on the point of joining the middle class. To some degree at least, they will set the world's course and determine the rules of the game.

In the first decade of the twenty-first century, a shadow fell over the eternal optimism of the Americans. For the first time they recognised, so all kinds of sociological research tells us, that their children will probably be less well off than they are. In Western Europe the same kind of change in mentality is taking place and there too the decline of the middle class will have huge consequences, but for America its effects are especially drastic, because the expectation that things will always be better in future was an essential part of the national philosophy, the American Creed.

Despite a perceptible decline, Americans and Europeans still have it relatively good. Half a century ago people worked equally hard and long on both sides of the Atlantic. After the 1960s the Europeans converted their increasing productivity mainly into free time, while Americans opted instead for property and affluence. Even education and healthcare, taken as a whole – public and private provision combined – are no worse in America than in Europe, and in some respects considerably better. Where the two continents differ is mainly in the distribution of money and services across the various population groups.

Most Europeans have an aversion to extremes of social inequality. That is one of the reasons why the services provided by their welfare states – at least until recently, certainly in Western Europe – give the average citizen a sense of security unthinkable for the average American. Americans judge the need for a strong safety net very differently. The contrast has to do with America's ethnic diversity, since states with a more homogeneous population often have rather greater social solidarity, and with the type of political system.

Countries with multi-party systems, such as are common in continental Europe, afford minority groups more space than places like America that have a two-party system, and the political basis for all kinds of social provision is often broader and firmer. In any case, services provided by the state do not sit easily with American individualism. Americans like opportunities; Europeans prefer certainties. Only a quarter of Europeans think poor people are lazy, for example, compared to two-thirds of Americans.

Then there is another issue: the Western world is ageing. It's one of the reasons why we have problems with debt. Europe, which once accounted for around half the world's productivity, is now responsible for no more than a fifth. Population prognoses speak volumes. The expectation is that in 2050 the average person in Europe will be over fifty. If nothing is done, the working population will have fallen by more than a third. Italy will have only one worker for every two retired people, and in France half of all incomes will come from pensions.

The rising cost of care and pensions is not just a problem for European countries, it's one of the causes of the rapidly increasing national debt in the United States. The American economy, as one commentator puts it, looks as if it has just emerged from an exhausting war, but demographic prognoses for the United States are a good deal better than those for Europe, or indeed for Japan and China. The average age of Americans in 2050 will be around thirty-five. That's the result of something the country has excelled at for centuries: integrating newcomers, wherever they come from.

Whereas Europe keeps immigrants out and sees migration primarily as a problem, America plucks its fruits. The United States still admits a million immigrants every year and, for all the innumerable difficulties that result, those newcomers bring great dynamism and vitality. An analysis by the State Department speaks of immigrants as 'living links back to their home countries', links that ensure reciprocal flows of people, products and ideas worldwide. This kind of global connectedness is the key to success in today's world, more so than money or status.

Immigrants make a major contribution to the success of Silicon Valley and other centres of innovation, and they keep America young. Immigration will affect the composition of the population markedly in the long run. Of Americans over the age of sixty-five, four-fifths are white, of children under five barely half. This represents a considerable generational shift that will have major cultural and political consequences. The America of Steinbeck, largely white and focused on a white, Europe-oriented world, will change over coming decades into a truly mixed society, with completely different political and cultural preferences.

It's been several years, therefore, since Americans saw Europe as central to their foreign policy, although Europeans are having great difficulty getting used to that fact. America's attention has switched from the Atlantic to the Pacific and beyond, from the old continent to Japan and the rising economies of India, Korea and China. This is clear from research by the German Marshall Fund. In 2004, more than half the American public still felt that European countries were of greater strategic importance than Asian countries. By 2011 the centre of gravity had shifted: half had come to believe that China, India and other Asian nations were of vital importance, with only a third still firmly attached to Europe.

In the *International Herald Tribune*, columnist Roger Cohen described visiting the White House to speak to the chief of staff of the National Security Council, Denis McDonough. On the wall was a clock showing different times in crucial places around the globe. Not long ago you would have been able to see, roughly speaking, the time in London, Paris, Berlin, Moscow and Tokyo. In 2011 the times shown were those of Kabul, Baghdad, Jerusalem and Tehran. A display like that is to some extent play-acting, but what interests Cohen is something else. 'What is striking, just two decades after the end of the Cold War,' he writes, 'is the absence of a single European city. Europe, for the first time in hundreds of years, has become a strategic backwater. Europe is history.'

As I write these final lines, an advert is circulating on the major television networks for the latest Audi A6. It opens with images of a potholed American road as a sombre voice intones: 'Across the nation, over 100,000 miles of highways and bridges are in disrepair.' No problem, it goes on: Audi's outstanding road holding and other features enable it to cope just fine. The Old World comes to the aid of the New.

To be honest, our experiences on this trip were less dramatic. In many states, especially in the North, the roads were in excellent condition. In California and close to the major cities it was another story. Roads and bridges cried out for repair; public poverty was in evidence everywhere.

The situation is symptomatic of political deadlock in the United States, where it has become impossible to reach a compromise, even on the means to keep streetlights burning and bridges maintained. It seems as if American politics is approaching the limits of what a popular democracy can handle. Instead of discussing 'the national goal', the debate is now about national unity, or rather the question of whether the American nation is cohesive enough to continue playing a prominent role in the twenty-first century.

Europe has similar problems. However much peace, freedom and prosperity European unification may have brought, the euro crisis has unsparingly revealed everything that is amiss: the flaws in the design of the monetary union, the ungovernable nature of such a fragmented system, the rigidity of the countless rules and treaties, the immense differences in political culture, especially between northern and southern Europe, the decline in public support, and the impossibility of sustaining democratic principles above and beyond the national level.

Democratic society, which Tocqueville found so innovative and interesting, is in crisis on both continents. Within the European Union, far-reaching power structures are being built, out of sheer necessity, that are outside any kind of democratic control. The public responds with indignation, voters increasingly opt for extremes of left and right in national elections, and moderate parties in the nation states, with which the EU is used to conversing, are crumbling rapidly. There is increasing polarisation.

In America something similar is going on. The problem there too is the democratic process. Rather than being thrown into confusion, as in Europe, it is being corrupted. Decision-making in America can be influenced to a great degree by means of gifts and donations, and the scope for doing so has been expanded significantly in recent years by the Supreme Court.

The rich are not only getting richer, they're getting more powerful too, and on top of that they're being given more and more opportunities to protect their wealth and extend it further. The opposite is happening to the poor and to large sections of the middle class.

Sociologist Katherine Newman speaks about 'the missing class', the 'near poor', that large group of Americans – a fifth of the population – who earn too little to belong to the middle class and too much to be counted among the poor. These are households in which the breadwinners cannot even manage to pay the minimum sum due on their credit cards (one in nine), are in mortgage arrears (one in eight), or are either unemployed or working at jobs below the level for which they are qualified (one in five).

Although the egalitarian ideals of the American Revolution are still fervently professed, American society is slowly turning into the kind of class-based system the Founding Fathers rebelled against with such passion in the eighteenth century. Since the 1970s the equilibrium has been lost. As Newman sees it, rich and educated America has continued on its upward trajectory while the remainder of the population has not.

She stresses the importance of the American popular myth, the idea that everyone can make it, saying that while it gives many people a sense of power, at the same time it makes those who haven't yet made it feel they are powerless. Of the many unemployed people she spoke to, it turned out to be those with the firmest faith in the American Dream who felt most hurt, believing themselves responsible for their fate.

In the past few years, with the assent of all parties, the term 'culture wars' has become common parlance. Steinbeck's political argument with his sister Beth got completely out of hand, but it was child's play compared to the frustrations that dominate the debate now, half a century later, and block the political process. Yet today's opinion polls produce figures that give a more subtle picture. Around one in five Americans regard themselves as liberals, two out of five are conservative and the rest say they are moderates. Without the support of that large group in the middle, neither side has any chance at all.

Moreover, time has an important effect. Beliefs shift, slowly but surely. In 2010 many liberals were a good bit less dogmatic than a generation ago, and many contemporary conservatives have beliefs about racial equality, sexual freedom and the emancipation of women that would have horrified conservatives in 1960. The electorate is shifting too. Within about thirty years, white voters of European origin will be in a minority compared to voters with an African, Asian or South American background. If for purely electoral reasons alone, this means that America will pay even less attention to Europe. That will not be the only effect. The domestic consequences are sure to be enormous. Hispanics and Asians may, for example, be able to build important bridges across the polarised political landscape. Both groups, after all, have a reputation for adhering to conservative values, like the Republicans, while at the same time their beliefs about the role of the state and the purpose of taxation are assumed to fit better with the outlook of the Democrats.

The striking thing about America, according to British political scientist Anatol Lieven, is that although it is an inseparable part of global capitalism in the twenty-first century, it has large communities that are still rebelling against the twentieth. He claims this has to do with the fact that the cultural and sexual revolutions most Western countries went through in the 1960s and 1970s have yet to be accepted by a large proportion of the American population.

In Europe, the right has been winning the political and economic battle since the 1970s, while the left has been winning the cultural and sexual battle. This is more or less accepted by Europeans as a matter of course. In America, Lieven believes, much of politics is still cultural politics. Elections are still about abortion, gay marriage, evolutionary theory and appointments to the Supreme Court. Thirty or forty years on, that page still cannot be turned.

'The Sixties', that series of explosions that Steinbeck did not foresee but did feel coming, have not settled down even now.

Shortly before I left America, the newspapers started to publish a series of secret official papers and reports from the Pentagon and the State Department. The website WikiLeaks had been handed a treasure trove of internal documents, about the wars in Afghanistan and Iraq in particular, and it was mined extensively. The documents were not exactly top secret, nor did they give a complete picture, and anyone expecting spectacular stories about conspiracies and hidden agendas will have been disappointed, yet they did offer an intriguing look at the way in which America has attempted to rule its empire.

Some of the documents suggested a high degree of self-confidence and an unswerving faith in the American Creed. Behind countless official papers you could sense diplomats who were good at their job, shrewd observers making sensible appraisals who could often write extremely well. But in the background to all those thorough reports you could also see, in the words of British journalist and historian Neal Ascherson, 'an evening landscape', an empire in decline that had lost its way. Of course most diplomats still had complete faith in America's wealth (even though the country was reliant on Chinese banks) and in the superior military power of the United States (even if that power might not be a great deal of use in the complex guerrilla wars of the twenty-first century), but they were noticeably less self-assured when it came to the goal and direction of American policy.

'When communism collapsed, the US expected to become the unchallenged global superpower,' Ascherson writes. 'But instead the US instantly lost control of countless nations and movements stampeding away from cold war discipline. Paradoxically, it was in those cold war years that America had been in charge of most of the world, mostly by consent, and knew why it was in charge. Now that world has burst into a thousand pieces: all sharp, many of them unstable, some of them fearfully dangerous. And the certainty of mission has gone.'

From time to time John Steinbeck suffered from a typically American complaint: declinism, the tendency to see symptoms of decline everywhere, first of all in America itself. He spoke of a 'haunting decay' of the nation, even if beneath it lay the message: 'If we all do our best, everything will come right.' It is the unavoidable counterpart to that eternal American optimism and exceptionalism, that tendency of Americans automatically to see their country as the most privileged and special in world history. With expectations so high, there will always be a fear of falling.

In the 1950s that pessimism was compounded by Russian successes in space exploration, in the 1970s by the oil crisis, and in the 1980s by government deficits and the closure of more and more factories in the great industrial regions.

Nowadays Steinbeck would point to the budget deficit and the excesses indulged in by the banks. He would clutch his brow if he heard that barely sixty per cent of federal spending is covered by federal taxation – the rest has to be borrowed, a situation that previously arose only in time of war. He would describe the political trench warfare that blocks every possible solution. He would point to the waste of resources, a problem he touched upon even half a century ago. He would write about poverty, about the inadequate education given to those at the bottom of the social scale, and about the ever-increasing dependence on credit from China and the Chinese. Young Americans are down in twentieth place in international rankings in mathematics and physics, and more than half of American patents are now granted to non-Americans.

He would also let Americans speak for themselves. In 1964, according to polling by Pew, more than three-quarters of the public had every faith in the government and the course the country was taking; in 2010 the average American, or two-thirds of those asked, believed the United States was in decline.

Might Steinbeck and his pessimistic soulmates be proven right after all? In 1960, even though in some ways they had considerable foresight, they were wide of the mark. After 1960 America experienced decades of immense prosperity. The Soviet Empire, that terrifying enemy that occupied minds so intensely, disappeared thirty years later. Great advances were made in all manner of fields, not least civil rights, healthcare, combating poverty and the expansion of the Interstate Highway System.

Steinbeck had an inkling, especially after the quiz scandal, of both the potential and the danger of television, but he had no idea what the new phenomenon would really mean. It brought the Vietnam War right into American living rooms, it made and broke presidents, it bound the nation together more than ever before and at the same time divided and manipulated opinions in unprecedented ways. He could not possibly have foreseen what would happen in the latter years of the twentieth century – a digital revolution, led by America, that would link up the entire world and usher in a new historical era.

Half a century later, the number of worried commentators has increased markedly, on both left and right, and with good reason. The statistics are hardly encouraging. In the rankings of the World Economic Forum the position of the United States continues to plummet year after year. In terms of competitiveness the American economy is now in seventh place, as regards its infrastructure in fourteenth place, for primary education and healthcare in thirty-fourth place, and when it comes to its macro-economic condition – yes, that enormous national debt – in one hundred and eleventh place. For a long time America and Europe regarded the developments they were going through as universal and natural. Modernisation, the free market, democratisation, human rights: these were all part of an irreversible process that the rest of the world would pass through as well, sooner or later. With the American banking crisis of 2008 and the euro crisis of 2011, with the success of new economies such as India and Brazil, and above all with the lightning rise of China to become the second-largest economy in the world, that immutable certainty that the West knows best has been undermined. On top of that comes a loss of moral authority over recent decades. Even in the most remote corners of the world, people have seen reports about Abu Ghraib and Guantanamo Bay, about support – albeit not uncritical – for Israeli hardliners and about execution by drone in Afghanistan and elsewhere. None of this will be forgotten.

The Bund, the famous boulevard in Shanghai so impressively lined with banks and offices, was once one of the most powerful outposts of the British Empire. Now it's a museum, a historical monument, firmly in Chinese hands. In fact even the British parent companies of those proud bank buildings are now owned by the Chinese. Expert opinions differ only as to exactly when China will overtake the United States economically: 2050, 2040, perhaps even by about 2025.

Russia is on the move again. After the collapse of the Soviet Empire it wants to start making history once more, and how! Old myths about Russian greatness and the Russian soul are being dusted off. Borders are being redrawn, spheres of influence determined by force – it's as if we're back in the nineteenth century, complete with rigid and short-sighted tsarism. Russians have a sense that the Western world, including Western values and Western ways of thinking, are no longer paramount.

In this new situation, Europe is vulnerable, at least in the short term. The continent is divided and susceptible to blackmail because a number of European countries have become highly dependent on Russian gas. Defence has been neglected since the end of the Cold War; NATO has expanded its territory without strengthening its own armed forces; most European countries have implemented severe cutbacks and a common European defence policy remains a distant prospect. After decades of peace, America's traditional allies represent a serious security problem.

These developments need not necessarily add up to the end of American power and influence. At this point, despite all its problems, the United States is still the largest economy in the world. China, with all its economic and military ambitions, still has a huge amount of ground to make up – its standard of living is currently at the same level as El Salvador's and, like Europe, it is struggling to cope with a rapidly ageing population. The dollar remains, for the time being at least, the world's reserve currency, not the Chinese renminbi. Although over recent years America's military capacity has been reduced to a historically low level, especially when it comes to boots on the ground, its military power remains overwhelming. The US spends almost three times as much on defence as China, India, Japan and Russia put together. American universities have produced a disproportionate number of Nobel Prize winners, more than 200. Many world leaders, present and future, have been educated there, engaging in endless discussions in seminars and lecture theatres, and being profoundly influenced by American norms and values.

So American soft power, although eroded, is very much with us – and I don't just mean the fondness that billions of world citizens have for American music, literature and other cultural manifestations, nor simply the appeal of America's consumer society. Soft power is, at its core, the power of persuasion a state possesses, the power to influence the debate, to set the agenda for world politics.

America has functioned for decades, in Europe especially, as a keeper of order, as world policeman – not to mention all the aid it has dispensed. True, with his eternal messianism, the 'quiet American' has also brought suffering or death to hundreds of thousands of people abroad, and indeed at home, in recent decades. As has happened several times in the past, America seems to be retreating, disappointed, into stubborn isolation. Nevertheless, in large parts of the world the United States is still the 'world's indispensable nation' as Madeleine Albright once put it, the 'anchor', the 'default power'. Although it cannot bend everything to its will, it can set the tone, sometimes for better, sometimes for worse. However the world may change, that is a role neither Russia nor Europe, nor even China, are going to fill in the near future.

Is this state of affairs permanent? I find it hard, just as Steinbeck did, to settle upon an answer after this journey. Every generalisation negates itself, every sweeping statement invites contradiction. That is true of every country, but it would be hard to match the diversity of all those free, headstrong Americans I came upon during this project, from Teddy Roosevelt to the men in Al's Diner, from Joe Amato and his farmers in the Midwest to Angie and Steve in that lonely desert village of Nipton, from Clarence Darrow to my friend David in front of his school class: 'Stay with me . . .' I often find myself thinking of Jimmye Taylor, sitting there in that one place on the rundown town square in Paducah where a light still burned, the offices of the *Paducah Post*. Jimmye remained proud of her paper, her town, her country and her Texas, but her self-image as an American had lost almost all connection with the reality around her.

'A barrel of worms.' 'Like gasses in a corpse.' 'When that explodes, I tremble to think what will be the result.' That was how Steinbeck wrote about himself and his country. During his trip with Charley he was confronted relentlessly, for the first time, with the person he really was: an elderly man who kept shouting himself down, unable either to accept his age or to let go of his youth. As a result he achieved the opposite of what he intended; the partial failure of his *Charley* expedition merely demonstrated how far gone he was. America, as an imagined nation, has developed a number of powerful self-images in the course of its history, and each of them had an important function, but now, to some extent, they get in its way: the idea of America as God's own country, the myth of natural equality and matchless American democracy, the notion that nature is inexhaustible and new conquests are always possible, the illusion that capital and the market always ultimately reflect God's order and justice, and a tendency to see the world purely in America's own image.

America, partly because of its powerful self-image, has always had a tendency to undermine the world order that it is apparently trying to create. Two elements in particular are responsible for this, and in combination they are downright dangerous: the myth of eternal plenty and the myth of exceptionalism.

The myth of eternal plenty creates the impression that everything is a choice, that everything you want is something to which you have a right. Those promises, however, far exceed what the world can physically bear, a fact to which the majority of Americans turn a deaf ear, avoiding even any discussion of the matter. The newly discovered shale gas, which is suddenly raining down over God's people like manna, has only reinforced the myth of inexhaustibility. But it remains a myth.

The myth of exceptionalism repeatedly tempts the Americans to play God. It entices them into foolhardy adventures on foreign territory, into rigging up a Monstrous Ear to detect and record every sigh of every human being on earth, into launching hundreds of drones that cause Fire and Death to fall upon anyone who displeases this Supreme Being.

The American model might, in short, develop into one of the greatest destabilising factors of the twenty-first century. It could be argued that the current state of Iraq shows it has already become exactly that. In the diaries he wrote in his later years, George Kennan stressed this time and again: the great challenge for the United States in the twenty-first century is to rein in not just rival powers and nations but also the overblown ambitions of Americans themselves – plus their self-congratulatory excep-tionalism. Or, in the words of Kennan's old friend, Hungarian-American historian John Lukacs: 'After the end of the American Century, a major problem is not so much the existence of American omnipotence as it is the way millions of Americans and many of their politicians unthinkingly believe in it.'

Three

AMERICA, EUROPE. I WAS REMINDED time and again during this journey of Chekhov's play *The Cherry Orchard*. A family is deeply in debt and a local businessman wants to build dachas on the beautiful old cherry orchard on the estate. The family, in its despair, decides to throw a party. The play is about a world that is slowly disappearing, even though its inhabitants fail to notice. Everything is changing, rapidly, except for the main characters. They carry on acting as if everything will stay the same forever, while their home shakes around them and ultimately succumbs – because, yes, in the end the cherry orchard is ruthlessly chopped down and the family falls apart.

That is exactly what happened to John Steinbeck. The 1960s would break him.

After his great America expedition, Charley had increasing trouble with stiff joints and other infirmities of old age. He died in Sag Harbor in April 1963 of cirrhosis of the liver, a complaint that, as Steinbeck wrote to an acquaintance, 'is usually ascribed to indulgence in alcohol. But Charley did not drink, or if he did he was very secret about it.'

In 1961 Rocinante was sold to a banker, who happened to have seen the truck at the GMC dealership and who became fascinated by Steinbeck's journey. He drove it no more than 15,000 miles and later donated it to the Steinbeck Center. Rocinante is now on show, looking almost new, in Salinas, with barely 25,000 miles on the clock.

When Steinbeck heard in 1962 that he had been awarded the Nobel Prize, his first instinct was to call his sons. He would find himself deeply disappointed in them later. While he was writing *Travels*, in March 1961, they had suddenly turned up on the doorstep of his house in New York. They could no longer stand their mother Gwyn's aggression and bouts of drinking. They wanted to move in with John and Elaine for good.

This was the reason for the European 'grand tour' that Steinbeck organised. The experience was intended to forge them together into a family at last because, as their home tutor McNally said later, 'they hardly knew each other'.

Within a year and a half, by Christmas 1962, all that affection had gone. A huge row erupted during an alcohol-soaked family evening and the boys left. John Jr went back to his mother and Thom ended up at a new boarding school. In the spring of 1964, supported by the two boys, Gwyn even initiated court proceedings against Steinbeck, accusing him of neglecting her sons and demanding considerably more alimony. Steinbeck was deeply hurt, but he defended himself calmly. The judge dismissed the claim: 'Just because this is a very famous and well-to-do man, I will not have him abused.' Gwyn, hysterical, ran to the window of the courtroom and shouted down to where the boys were waiting: 'Nothing! Nothing!'

In 1966 Steinbeck published *America and Americans*, originally planned as a photo book about America of which he would write only the introduction. The project grew into an interesting study and he was able to include many of the observations and ideas he'd been unable to fit into *Travels*. Meanwhile, just as he used to do, he travelled to Russia and Europe and wrote accounts of his trips.

He had by this point become a close friend of President Johnson. The two men got to know each other in late 1963 through their wives, who were old friends from university days. The Steinbecks regularly went to stay at Camp David, as if they were family. According to John Jr, the two men had a lot in common; they were both country boys who masked their insecurity with much bravura, which actually made them – as each recognised in the other – quite vulnerable. 'There is no doubt that they genuinely liked each other.' It made no difference that one was president of the United States, the other a Nobel Prize winner.

Both men were and remained outsiders in New York and Washington, Johnson as a Texan, Steinbeck as a born Westerner. They were close in their political beliefs as well, great admirers of Roosevelt and his New Deal but decidedly conservative in other respects: fiercely anti-communist, extremely suspicious of the Soviet Union and the 'reds' in general.

Steinbeck could not escape Johnson's political role. He co-wrote a number of speeches and gave the president advice, saying for example that he should mount an intensive search for North Vietnamese dissidents and use them to set up a puppet government, 'even if we have to invent it'. In 1965 Johnson wanted to send Steinbeck to Vietnam to report directly to him on what he saw and heard. During the Second World War, Roosevelt had sent the young Lyndon Johnson to the theatre of war in the southern Pacific as his own personal observer, outside all the regular channels. Now Johnson was asking the same of Steinbeck.

Steinbeck refused. He did not want to endanger his independent position. But in late 1966 he went after all, officially as a correspondent for *Newsday* but secretly on behalf of his friend Johnson. By that point both his sons were fighting in the war, which filled Steinbeck with pride. He had introduced John Jr to the president and even given him a beautiful Colt Derringer just before his departure for Vietnam, in a parting that was replete, according to John Jr, with 'manly patriotism, mostly based on John Wayne movies'.

In Vietnam, Steinbeck emerged as a Charlie Wilson *avant la lettre*. Because of his connections in high places, he was allowed to go everywhere, including the battlefront, to the extent that such a thing existed in Vietnam. Dressed in fine-looking army fatigues he even witnessed a small skirmish between John Jr's platoon and the Vietcong. Sixty-five-year-old Steinbeck promptly entrenched himself behind an M60 to cover his son, who was throwing one hand grenade after another at the enemy. Meanwhile John Jr was thinking: 'Who, in God's name, is producing this movie?'

In debates on the Vietnam War, the once so progressive Steinbeck turned into a veritable hawk. Under the title *Letters to Alicia* – named for the deceased *Newsday* editor Alicia Patterson – he wrote at least eighty short reports and commentaries while he was in Vietnam. They are full of sneers at the anti-war demonstrators who, armed with placards, had no idea of the realities of war. 'I think I have more reason than most of them to hate [war]. But would they enlist for medical service? They could be trained quickly and would not be required to kill anyone. If they love people so much, why are they not willing to help to save them? This country is woefully short of medical help. Couldn't some of the energy that goes into carrying placards be diverted to emptying bed pans or cleaning infected wounds?'

In a personal letter to President Johnson he called the American troops in Vietnam 'the finest, the best trained, the most intelligent and the most dedicated soldiers I ever have seen in any army'.

In the opposition to the Vietnam War he saw all the decadence he hated, in America, in his sons and perhaps even in himself. He was deeply shocked at the 'fall-out, drop-out, cop-out insurgency of our children and young people, the rush to stimulant as well as hypnotic drugs, the rise of narrow, ugly, and vengeful cults of all kinds, the mistrust and revolt against all authority − this in a time of plenty such as has never been known'.

The soldiers fighting in Vietnam were in his eyes just as heroic as the GIs in the Second World War, and that was how they ought to be treated. He was therefore deeply shocked when his own son and namesake was arrested for possession of drugs in the autumn of 1968. The case came to nothing, but in the Washingtonian John Jr revealed that American troops were smoking marijuana on a huge scale and that other narcotics were in use as well. His article, entitled 'The Importance of Being Stoned in Vietnam', was intended as a way of exposing the hypocrisy of drug policy, but Steinbeck was furious. 'They should have thrown you in jail,' he snapped at his son. Those were the last words John Jr ever heard him speak.

After his death, Steinbeck's sons discovered he had his own stash of drugs: two large hospital pots containing thousands of amphetamine pills, one partially empty, the other still completely full. 'He'd been soaring and crashing on amphetamines all along,' John Jr wrote. 'But this was a missing piece of information when we were growing up.'

Vietnam would severely damage the reputations of both Johnson and Steinbeck. According to Elaine, Steinbeck remained a liberal to his dying day. She claimed that after his great voyage to Vietnam, in 1967, he admitted to her that he'd made a terrible mistake: the war was wrong. He'd spoken to Johnson about it, she said, and written a memorandum with suggestions. He wanted to write about it, she claimed later in an interview, but when he got home he became seriously ill and nothing came of it. 'That's one of the cruel tricks fate can play with you.'

'He was a good guy, he didn't play games,' said John Ward, Steinbeck's fishing buddy in Sag Harbor. 'He had two sons. He went to Vietnam to see them. The boys had become completely crazy from the drugs there. They'd changed beyond recognition. He returned with a broken heart. He had more trouble from that than anything else. You could see the change in him when he came back. He was a different man.'

Nada Berry confirms all this. 'He was in pieces. His ideas about the war had changed completely too. He didn't write about it, but we noticed. He wanted to be macho, but actually he was very sensitive.' On 27 February he called by unexpectedly. It was his birthday. 'I quickly made a cake for him. He was quite embarrassed, and amazed. It was his last birthday cake.'

At first I struggled with the tone adopted by his son John Jr, who paints a picture of 'the other side of Eden' in an autobiography that was completed after his death by his wife Nancy. There is something juvenile, something of the junkie, in his story about his famous father, as if your parents are eternally responsible for your failures. Yet the book, for all its faults, does give an intriguing insight into the inner world that Steinbeck and Elaine always carefully hid from public view.

There are the childhood experiences of the two sons, for instance, who were left with their mother Gwyn and endured a hell of drinking bouts, abuse and neglect. Then there is the virtuous couple John and Elaine in *Travels*, who in reality often got drunk several nights in a row, with all the inevitable mood swings and fierce arguments that resulted. Then there was Steinbeck's little secret, his addiction to speed, of which John Jr first caught a glimpse in Vietnam when his father, with a meaningful nod, gave him a couple of pink pills that kept him fresh and active all night.

Steinbeck must have been a long-term user of amphetamines. Gwyn mentioned it in a statement she wrote shortly after their divorce back in 1948. It explains a great deal about certain physical problems he had, about his sudden whims and his behaviour towards his sons, and also about his capricious moods, which show through in his treatment of his own country in *Travels*, one moment attentive, precise and affectionate, the next cursory and fleeting.

Travels with Charley was recreated as a television film in 1968, with a replica of Rocinante in the starring role – the real one was not available at that time – and narrated by Henry Fonda. Steinbeck was too ill by then to do anything. He had severe back pains and heart problems, spent weeks in hospital, and worried greatly about John Jr's arrest. Even the Nobel Prize still bothered him. There was a great deal of criticism at the time of the decision to choose Steinbeck, of all American writers, for such an honour. Next to his sickbed lay a cutting from the *New York Times*, an editorial on the subject: 'The award of the Nobel Prize for Literature to John Steinbeck will focus attention once again on a writer who, though still in full career, produced his major work more than two decades ago.'

After *Travels* his old writer's block had returned, as had the accompanying depression. After the Nobel Prize it only got worse. The award shattered him. 'I think he was scared of it,' Elaine said later. He thought he didn't deserve it, but it was fantastic to have it. A 'modest and shy man, he was always afraid of success. But he loved to be read.'

Producer and fellow writer Budd Schulberg went to visit him one autumn evening in 1968, in 'one of those depressingly antiseptic single rooms in an enormous, impersonal hospital on Manhattan's East River'. For the last time they had a drinking session, like in the old days. They quarrelled about Vietnam. According to Schulberg he was still on the side of Johnson and South Vietnam at that stage. Steinbeck continued to worry about America. 'I have never seen a time when the country was so confused as to where it's headed.' He thought the hippies silly and self-satisfied, talkers who never actually came up with anything. 'The proof will be in what they produce – and what kind of next generation they produce.' As for him, he claimed he had nothing more to say but his hands still needed to hold a pencil. 'When you do something for over thirty years, when you hardly think about anything else but how to put your experiences into the right words, you can't just turn it off and go play in the garden.'

John Steinbeck died just before Christmas, on Friday 20 December 1968, in his home in New York. The funeral was held the following Monday, at St James' Episcopal Church on Madison Avenue. It was a grey afternoon. All his friends had come from Sag Harbor, but Nada Barry was surprised to see so few other writers. 'He'd won the Nobel Prize, but it was as if he didn't belong among them.'

The funeral lasted barely twenty minutes. Henry Fonda read a few poems and an appropriate passage from *The Grapes of Wrath*. Elaine pleaded with everyone who offered her their condolences: 'All I ask is – remember him. Remember him!'

> 'Liar,' said Johnny. 'This is your cradle, your home.' Suddenly he hit the bar with the oaken indoor ball bat he used in arguments to keep the peace. 'In the fullness of time – maybe a hundred years – this should be your grave.' The bat fell from his hand and he wept at the prospect of my future demise. I puddled up at the prospect myself.

It went just the way Steinbeck described it in *Travels*; in the end he returned to his native soil. His ashes are buried, next to Elaine's urn and along with those of his parents and his maternal grandparents, Samuel and Lisa Hamilton, in the old Garden of Memories Cemetery on Abbot Street in Salinas. We visited him when we were in Monterey on 2 November, All Souls Day. Half the graveyard was full of flowers, and Mexican families were picnicking beside the graves in a sea of yellow, red, white and pink. For Elaine (1913–2003) there was a plastic aster. John had been given fresh roses and chrysanthemums, and a visitor had stuck a subway ticket between the stones.

In Vietnam John Jr developed into a respected journalist – along with other reporters, he revealed the notorious massacre at My Lai – but at the same time he was engaged in a ferocious battle against drug addiction. He died in 1991. His older brother Thom is still alive and living as a writer in California.

Elaine, with the help of Robert Wallsten, put together a lengthy collection of Steinbeck's most important letters, *Steinbeck. A Life in Letters* (1975), an excellent resource for anyone interested in Steinbeck. She played the role of widow with verve. 'She loved the theatre; she was theatre,' said Nada Barry. 'And she loved men. Let's leave it there.'

All the old ghosts came back one more time. On his death John left everything to Elaine while his sons were fobbed off with 50,000 dollars each. Steinbeck's bitterness, especially after his trip to Vietnam, left its traces in his will. He clearly had no desire to spoil the boys. No mention at all was made in the will of the copyright to his work.

Within a short time of Steinbeck's death, several legal squabbles arose between Elaine and the boys. The feud – including a fresh succession of failed lawsuits – erupted again in full force when it turned out that Elaine had left all her property, including the rights to all Steinbeck's books, to her daughter from a previous marriage, her two sisters and a series of grandchildren.

Not one of the new heirs had any connection with Steinbeck himself. In fact they had little if any interest in him. The house in New York was sold, along with its contents, which included countless books, documents and other personal possessions of the writer.

In the summer of 2010 the final bits and pieces of Steinbeck's life were sold at auction. A sales list detailing the Steinbeck office archive circulated on the internet:

- a small album with 13 photos of the Steinbeck family and homestead in Salinas, c. 1907–1910
- a large group of personal correspondence to John Steinbeck from a variety of friends and notables
- correspondence relating to the conferring of the Nobel Prize including congratulatory correspondence
- a multivolume, limited edition set of RL Stevenson's collected works, published in Edinburgh, 1895
- leather briefcase belonging to Ed Ricketts
- several manuscripts: 'In America we seem to be obsessed with tensions . . .', 'I went to the last automobile show in New York because I like shiny things . . .', 'You ask me to set down some observations about camping . . .'
- first editions of his own books
- small checkbook noted as 'Paris', mostly in the hand of Elaine Steinbeck
- a reference library of approximately 400 hardbound volumes, touching a wide range of subjects including English and American

history, medieval history, Arthurian knights, classics, language,
shells, etc.
- newspaper clippings of reviews, etc.
- file marked 'Europe', including a variety of items, small photos,
letters of introduction
- a group of 16mm films and audio tapes including Mendelson's
Travels with Charley (1968)
- correspondence to John Steinbeck relating to dogs, including
notes from fans of *Travels with Charley*, etc.
- a carbon typed letter to 'Adlai' asking him to write the Nobel
Prize speech 1962
- the pedigree papers of Anky de Maison Blanche (c. 1951)
- a small group of typed letters signed by John Steinbeck regarding
the house in Sag Harbor
- ephemera and correspondence relating to the humorous group
Organized Bastards of America
- envelope marked 'Cars no longer owned'.

Afterword

TIME DOES NOT STAND STILL, especially when it comes to America and American politics. I carried out preparatory research for this book in 2008 and 2009, made my Steinbeck journey in 2010, spent 2011 writing and in the summer of 2012 finally rounded off the project, shortly before the first Dutch edition was published. Two years have passed since then.

A good deal has changed. Steinbeck's surviving son, Thomas, lost his case against Elaine's heirs. The house in Sag Harbor has been sold.

Bill Steigerwald is no longer a mythical figure to me. Following his revelations, he was castigated by many Steinbeck enthusiasts. All the same, anyone who takes the trouble to scrutinise Steinbeck's journey and the manuscript will have no choice but to come to the same conclusion: *Travels with Charley* is more of a road novel than a travel account. In the autumn of 2010 Steigerwald and I were moving along separate tracks, but afterwards a fascinating email correspondence developed. We promised each other that one day we'd raise a glass of Heineken together to our beloved travelling companion John Steinbeck. As indeed we did, on a glorious afternoon in May 2014.

Much has remained the same, too. Despite more droughts, storms and other extreme weather, despite mounting warnings from scientists and politicians, most Americans still refuse to acknowledge that the climate is changing rapidly all over the world and that this process and its fallout will increasingly set the tone for international relations in the twenty-first century. In fact the percentage of American voters who believe there is 'solid evidence' that the earth is warming has actually fallen, according to the Pew Research Center, from seventy-seven per cent in 2007 to forty-four per cent in 2014.

The American democratic debate is as polarised and frozen as ever, with all the inevitable consequences. After considerable difficulties, so-called 'Obamacare' is now in place, and despite all the earlier scare stories the system is performing unexpectedly well. The state of American infrastructure is, however, still a cause for considerable concern. The top ten worst airports in the world according to the Frommer's travel website in 2012, for instance, included no fewer than four in the United States: New York's JFK (Terminal 3) was in first place, with New York's La Guardia (Terminal C) at number seven, Newark Liberty at eight and Chicago Midway at ten.

California is a pleasing exception to all this. The tide has turned since 2012, when California's voters decided the situation was too crazy for words. A large amount of money has been invested in infrastructure and there is even serious talk of building a high-speed rail link between Los Angeles and San Francisco – at least two decades late in comparison with China and Europe, but still. California is also the first state to make a systematic attempt to halt populism. Since 2012 both parties have been obliged to open up their primaries to all voters. Democrats can now influence the choice of Republican candidate and vice versa – a procedure that may perhaps prevent the worst of extremes.

There is also good news from New Orleans. In 2013 the city was named 'fastest growing city in the USA' by Forbes. Almost 380,000 people now live there – 70,000 fewer than before Katrina but twice the number immediately after the disaster. Even more encouragingly, the gloomy prediction that nothing would be left of the 'old' New Orleans is looking wide of the mark. According to the latest figures, eight out of nine residents of New Orleans lived there before Katrina; eighty per cent of new arrivals are former inhabitants of the city who eventually saw a chance to return.

I'm writing these final lines in a summer during which everything has suddenly started to shift in the international arena, with the rapid rise of ISIS, a cruel war on the Gaza Strip, an extremely tense situation surrounding Ukraine, and more. It's hard to draw any conclusions about what it will all mean for the future. The reader of this book probably knows a good deal more than I do at this point.

In my epilogue I wrote that the American tendency to play God all over the world might become one of the greatest destabilising factors of the twenty-first century. That concern remains. Illustrative of the old illusion of omnipotence were the astonishing mass surveillance operations carried out by the NSA, revealed by whistle-blower Edward Snowden in 2013, which affected virtually everyone on earth. Other than that, however, the Charlie Wilsons in Washington were making little headway. Over recent years, America's foreign policy has been dominated by the doctrine of restraint, with an emphasis on bringing the troops home from Iraq and Afghanistan and withdrawing from old international commitments. Even in the chaotic ring of trouble spots that erupted in North Africa and the Arab world – some speak of a new Thirty Years' War – the Americans initially refused to intervene, openly at least. As I write, however, that phase of self-restraint seems to be over. Interventions in the Middle East are starting to take place once more.

Relations are further complicated by recent developments in and around Europe. There, the old order has been thoroughly undermined. The traditional allies feel increasingly threatened by the unpredictable kleptocracy that has set the tone in Moscow since 2012 under the leadership of Vladimir Putin. The hope cherished by many after 1991, that Russia would gradually develop into a relatively normal European partner, has been comprehensively dashed by its annexation of Crimea and the pseudo-invasion of eastern Ukraine. The Russian reaction to the 'Europeanisation' of Ukraine was predictable – imagine if the Panama Canal Zone suddenly fell into Chinese hands – but it is not any less serious for that. In Russian politics, emotions now dominate that arise from a deep sense of humiliation, and they are being expertly exploited by a number of rival elites. There is little regard for rationality. A new populist–nationalist ideology, with Russia setting itself up as the Great Protector of every ethnic Russian anywhere in the world, may have deadly dangerous consequences. At the same time, the old Cold War fanfares are sounding again everywhere in the West, as if the past half-century has been wiped away. Trade relations and forms of cooperation that were in place for years have been ended, and the first shots are being fired in a new propaganda war.

In short, a profound and fierce conflict has arisen between Putin's nationalist–authoritarian system and the more or less democratic West.

At the same time, there is no certainty that the new situation will fully revive the solid old Atlantic alliance. We might wonder, incidentally, whether that would be a good idea. For many years, NATO was an excuse for not thinking seriously about Europe's own role in the world. In that sense, we Europeans lived for too long in the shadow of our own Big Brother.

There is one more thing that has changed, and it is perhaps the most important of all. In 2013 the American Census Bureau reported that between 2011 and 2012, for the first time in history, more non-white babies – including Hispanics – than white babies were born in America. This historic moment marks a development that will have enormous long-term consequences for American politics, domestic and foreign. At home, new majorities from other cultures may be able to get the stalled American democratic system moving again. Abroad, old loyalties – especially with regard to Europe, but perhaps also to Israel – will play less of a role. After all, to what degree will Americans be willing, in this new situation, to open their security umbrella over the European continent? To what extent, in practice, can the old allies still rise above their differences of insight and conviction? Or, to look at it another way, does an uncertain Europe not run the risk of falling prey to the American domestic political game, as has happened before? The enemies of the United States – or of some currents within American politics – are no longer automatically enemies of Europe, and vice versa.

The certainties of the old Cold War no longer exist. The time of great expectations is over. We Europeans, somehow or other, will have to manage by ourselves from now on. The future is more unfathomable than ever.

Amsterdam, August 2014

Acknowledgements

QUITE A FEW THINGS NEED TO HAPPEN before a journey becomes a manuscript, and a manuscript a book. You can easily become bogged down along the way, lose your footing or even get lost altogether. What good fortune it is then, in every respect, to have competent, committed and enthusiastic people around you.

Alfons Lammers read the manuscript critically and encouragingly. All our discussions were a treat, and again and again I was able to rely on his many experiences of America and his abundant knowledge of American history. René van Stipriaan was a careful reader, a discerning critic and a good friend. The people at my Dutch publishing house proved invaluable, as ever: Emile Brugman, Ellen Schalker, Anita Roeland, Jessica Nash, Erna Staal and Marjet Knake. The final text remains of course entirely my own responsibility, but they were of enormous help and my gratitude is immense.

The same goes for all those who were helpful in any number of ways before and during the journey: Jan Donkers and Karel van Wolferen in the Netherlands, Gwen Waddington and Nada Barry in Sag Harbor, Joe and Cathy Amato in Marshall, Steve and Maureen Gilbert in Little River, Catherine Singels in Calistoga, Inez Hollander and Jon Lake in Orinda, David Laub in Oakland, John Biguenet and Jarvis DeBerry in New Orleans.

I felt more than welcome in the American Literature section of the library at Stanford University when researching Steinbeck's letters and other material. Annette Keogh there was helpfulness personified. The same goes for Herb Behrens at the National Steinbeck Center in Salinas and James Spohrer at the Doe & Moffitt Libraries of the University of California, Berkeley. I am also indebted to Frank Ligtvoet in New York for his additional research at the Morgan Library & Museum into the manuscript of *Travels*.

Mietsie, my wife, deserves a special mention. Even in the pouring rain of Maine and on the endless monotonous plains of the Midwest she was the most delightful travelling companion imaginable: loyal, optimistic, always looking and thinking along with me. The same goes for the writing process. It's no fun living for months with a man with a bucket over his head. She always kept her spirits up, which made all the difference in the world.

As I travelled and wrote, I stood on the shoulders of countless predecessors, and made grateful use of their observations and ideas. I drew upon multiple sources: conversations, interviews, reports and opinion pieces in local papers, digitalised local archives, statistical material from countless reports and analyses; plus a bookcase full of books and other printed matter. The most important sources will generally have been named in the text. Anyone wanting to know more can find the relevant information here.

General

The best and most comprehensive biography of John Steinbeck is by Jackson Benson, *The True Adventures of John Steinbeck, Writer*. It is an excellent source. A good second, rather more recent, is by Jay Parini, *John Steinbeck: A Biography*. Then there is the enjoyable if rather brief sketch of his life by Milton Meltzer, *John Steinbeck: A Twentieth-Century Life*. Chaotic and bitter, but nevertheless interesting is the story told by Steinbeck's younger son John Jr, who grew up in the shadow of all this literary prowess: John Steinbeck IV and his wife Nancy Steinbeck, *The Other Side of Eden: Life with John Steinbeck*.

I regularly consulted *John Steinbeck: A Life in Letters*, which includes a wealth of his correspondence, collected by Elaine Steinbeck and Robert Wallsten. An excellent reference work about his entire literary output has been compiled by Jeffrey Schultz and Luchen Li: *Critical Companion to John Steinbeck: A Literary Reference to His Life and Work*. Also useful were *Conversations with John Steinbeck* by Thomas Fensch, and *John Steinbeck: The Contemporary Reviews*, compiled by Joseph McElrath, Jesse Crisler and Susan Shillinglaw. The latter has also put together a fascinating collection of memories of Steinbeck, *John Steinbeck: Centennial Reflections by American Writers*. A book about the condemnation of Steinbeck after the publication of *The Grapes of Wrath* is Rick Wartzman, *Obscene in the Extreme: The Burning and Banning of John Steinbeck's* The Grapes of Wrath.

On Steinbeck's *Charley* project, Barbara Reitt published a now slightly dated scientific analysis in the Spring 1981 edition of the *Southwest Review*, '"I Never Returned as I Went In": Steinbeck's *Travels with Charley'*. Several authors more or less retraced his journey before or after me, including Bill Barich, *Long Way Home: On the Trail of Steinbeck's America*, and German journalist Bettina Gaus, *Auf der Suche nach Amerika: Begegnungen mit einem fremden Land*. Anyone wanting to follow the precise journey described in *Travels* should get hold of the account by Bill Steigerwald, who did an admirable job of hunting out wherever possible the places where Steinbeck slept, bought a rifle or went to church. It was published under the title *Dogging Steinbeck*.

I had other companions too, a couple of older reporters who, each in his own way, offered a great many insights into America and the changes the country has been through over the years. First of all of course Alexis de Tocqueville with his *Democracy in America* of 1835, plus the brilliant notes and letters by him and his travelling companion Gustave de Beaumont that Frederick Brown collected in *Alexis de Tocqueville: Letters from America*. Then there is the astute British ambassador James Bryce, who retraced the pair's journey half a century later in *The American Commonwealth* of 1888.

From the 1930s comes the inexhaustible journalist Ernie Pyle with *Ernie's America*, followed by, among others, John Gunther with *Inside U.S.A.* of 1947, William Least Heat-Moon with *Blue Highways* of 1983 and Robert Kaplan with *An Empire Wilderness* of 1998.

I also derived enormous pleasure from the sharp eye of the British author and broadcaster Alistair Cooke, correspondent for the *Manchester Guardian* and *The Times* from 1947 to 2004, in *Reporting America*. Another useful and inspiring source from time to time was the rather more literary overview of all the states of America put together by Matt Weiland and Sean Wilsey, *State by State*.

As for America, and American history in general, I found a wealth of information in Russell Duncan and Joseph Goddard, *Contemporary America*; Frances Fitzgerald, *Cities on a Hill: A Journey Through Contemporary American Cultures*; Claude Fischer and Michael Hout, *Century of Difference: How America Changed in the Last One Hundred Years*; and, by the same Claude Fischer, *Made in America: A Social History of American Culture and Character*.

For a historical overview of the mid-twentieth century, books I can recommend include *The Glory and the Dream: A Narrative History of America, 1932–1972* by William Manchester and *Grand Expectations: The United States, 1945–1974* by James Patterson. On the Cold War in particular, there is *The Cold War: A New History* by John Gaddis. In his classic *A People's History of the United States*, Howard Zinn offers a highly personal view of American history.

A less detailed but good picture is provided by *Twentieth-Century America: A Brief History* by Thomas Reeves and *An American Portrait: A History of the United States* by David Burner et al. Monumental, of course, are the two books by David Halberstam about the 1950s and about the American press: *The Fifties* and *The Powers That Be*, as well as his brilliant work about the Vietnam War, *The Best and the Brightest*.

Other books I found inspiring were Brink Lindsey, *The Age of Abundance: How Prosperity Transformed America's Politics and Culture*; George Santayana, *Character and Opinion in the United States*; and, in a very different way, Anatol Lieven, *America Right or Wrong: An Anatomy of American Nationalism*.

Also useful were *God Bless America: Zegeningen en beproevingen van de Verenigde Staten* by Alfons Lammers, *The American Future: A History* by Simon Schama and *De tweede Amerikaanse eeuw* by Jan Donkers, as well as *Amerika voor en tegen* and *In Amerika*, both by Maarten van Rossem.

A more anthropological approach is taken by Geoffrey Gorer in *The American People: A Study in National Character*. Something similar, but from the 1970s, can be found in Philip Slater's classic *Pursuit of Loneliness*.

Parts One and Two

The lyrics of 'When the lights go on again . . .' are by Eddie Seller, Sol Marcus and Bennie Benjamin. I was able to find out about the history of Sag Harbor and the life of John Steinbeck in that little town from *Sag Harbor Is: A Literary Celebration* by Maryann Calendrille and *Voices of Sag Harbor: A Village Remembered* by Nina Tobier.

MaryKay Broesder's *The Sounds of a Developing Prairie Town* is all about the aural history of a small town in Minnesota. For early American history I made grateful use of Daniel Richter's *Before the Revolution: America's Ancient Pasts* and Alan Taylor's *American Colonies: The Settling of North America*. The story of the two Indians who helped the Pilgrims and already spoke fluent English comes from William Bradford's *History of Plymouth Plantation*, quoted by David Colbert in *Eyewitness to America*.

The battles in and around Deerfield and events surrounding them were described by, among others, Brian Leigh Dunnigan in 'Those Frenchmen Who Got Themselves Killed in the Open', in *Historic Deerfield*.

For the story of Elisabeth Corse I drew upon the Canadian study by John P. Dulong, published on the internet under the title 'Elisabeth Corse, the Captive'. The tale of the Reverend John Williams was first published in 1707, and it became a classic among American stories of the frontier. The latest reissue is *The Redeemed Captive*, edited by Edward W. Clark.

On the economic conditions experienced by the settlers, the Puritan ethos of hard work, and self-imposed austerity and the friction between it and the consumer society of the 1950s and 1960s, the insights of David Brooks, *On Paradise Drive*, and David Potter, *People of Plenty*, were among those of greatest value. The idea that this attitude was a final attempt to 'resist Adam's curse' comes from Luigi Barzini's *The Europeans*.

On exceptionalism, good sources were Reinhold Niebuhr, *The Irony of American History*, Philip Slater, *Pursuit of Loneliness* and Francis Fukuyama, *America at the Crossroads*. On the Shakers, useful books include Flo Morse's *The Story of the Shakers*. Research data on Americans' belief in heaven and hell are from the Harris Poll of 2008.

The sociological background to the hunt for communists by Joseph McCarthy is excellently described by Anatol Lieven, and by David Halberstam in *The Fifties*. I found a good description – there are others – of the quarrel between the Roosevelts and Joe Kennedy in Gore Vidal's essay on Eleanor Roosevelt in *The Essential Gore Vidal*, edited by Fred Kaplan. Several studies have been published on the electoral contest of 1960. Among those I used were David Pietrusza, 1960 – LBJ vs. JFK vs. Nixon; W. Rorabaugh, *The Real Making of the President: Kennedy, Nixon and the 1960 Election*, and above all Rick Perlstein's compelling *Nixonland: The Rise of a President and the Fracturing of America*.

Figures quantifying the decline of small and medium-sized agricultural enterprises are from *Rethinking Home* by Joseph Amato. The Security Index is borrowed from Jacob Hacker, Philipp Rehm and Mark Schlesinger in *Standing on Shaky Ground: Americans' Experiences with Economic Insecurity*.

The poverty statistics are from the 'US Census Bureau Poverty Report', September 2011. Data on the situation faced by families forced to rely on food stamps come from 'Food stamps: The struggle to eat', Economist, 16 July 2011. Other statistics concerning the growing underclass are from 'New underclass swells as safety net frays' in the International Herald Tribune of 22 February 2010, plus reports in the Economist of 27 February 2010 and 18 December 2010, and especially 30 April 2011.

Part Three

For the concept of 'home' and for life in the suburbs, important sources were The Politics of Home by Jan Willem Duyvendak and On Paradise Drive by David Brooks. I found a number of musings on Niagara Falls in Peter Conrad's Imagining America. Particularly useful was the excellent study of the war of 1812 by Alan Taylor, The Civil War of 1812. Gordon Wood excels at describing the concept of America as opposed to classical Europe in both The Idea of America: Reflections on the Birth of the United States and Empire of Liberty: A History of the Early Republic 1789–1815. On the almost forgotten Loyalists, whom the British government favoured, see Maya Jasanoff, Liberty's Exiles: American Loyalists in the Revolutionary World.

On the emergence of American English as a language all its own I learned a good deal from Bill Bryson, as well as during a number of enlightening conversations with Heather Tess, who teaches the subject in the Dutch town of Vught. On the background to and origins of the Civil War, The Union War by Gary Gallagher proved a good source, as did James M. McPherson's 'What Drove the Terrible War?' in the New York Review of Books, 14 July 2011.

The calculation of average American taxation comes from the Wall Street Journal, 21 September 2011. Figures for growing differences in income are from, among others: Chrystia Freeland, 'To have and to have not. The iPod test', International Herald Tribune, 1 July 2011; Andy Kroll, 'The New American Oligarchy', TomDispatch.com, 2 December 2010; Jeff Madrick, The Case for Big Government and analyses of the American economy in the Economist of 23 January and 20 November 2010. The letter from Warren Buffet was printed in the International Herald Tribune of 15 August 2011. According to official statistics from the Congressional Budget Office, the richest one per cent do in fact pay the most federal tax, at thirty-one per cent as opposed to fourteen per cent for the average American. But that does not take account of all the loopholes and cunning ploys that allow the richest Americans to reduce their tax burden considerably.

Robert Kaplan's description of Canada can be found in the chapter 'Canada the Wild Card' in An Empire Wilderness. The Margaret Atwood quotation is from Survival: A Thematic Guide to Canadian Literature.

Statistical and other facts about Detroit come from sources including: 'Detroit's emptiness: The art of abandonment' in the Economist of 19 December 2009; Tom Ronse, 'Detroit is dood, leve Detroit' in De Groene Amsterdammer of 28 August 2009; and Edward Niedermeyer, 'A Green Detroit? No, a guzzling one', New York Times, 15 December 2010. Experts discuss Detroit's continuing tendency to fall behind in innovation in 'Detroit Sets Its Future on a Foundation of Two-Tier Wages', New York Times, 12 September 2011.

One of the best studies of the mass migration of black people to the North is of course Isabel Wilkerson, The Warmth of Other Suns. My comments on responsibility for the social catastrophe that arose to some extent as a result of it are based partly on what she writes, especially where she cites the wise conclusions of the – white-led – Chicago Commission on Race Relations of 1922 in response to the Chicago Riots of 1919.

Part Four

In Kalamazoo I greatly enjoyed the work of local historians Lynn Smith and Pamela Hall O'Connor, Kalamazoo: Lost and Found, and Roger Kallenberg, Looking Back: A Pictorial History of Kalamazoo. For the role of religion among the migrants, see Hans Knippenberg, Hoe God emigreerde naar Amerika, pp. 19ff.

As for Chicago, the data on American nineteenth-century dynamism are from sources including David Brooks, pp. 259ff. The life of John Gunther is excellently described by Ken Cuthbertson in Inside: The Biography of John Gunther. As for Clarence Darrow, John Farrell has written a fabulous biography: Clarence Darrow: Attorney for the Damned.

The electoral dirty tricks by the Kennedy camp in Illinois during the 1960 election are described in detail by David Pietrusza, 1960, p. 402ff., and by Seymour Hersh in The Dark Side of Camelot. Equally thorough on various other issues is James Merriner in *Grafters and Goo Goos: Corruption and Reform in Chicago.*

For Obama's Chicago years, see his autobiography, *Dreams From My Father,* as well as David Remnick's *The Bridge: The Life and Rise of Barack Obama* and Edward McClelland, *Young Mr Obama.*

The dynastic character of American politics is brought into sharp focus by Kevin Phillips in *American Dynasty.* Especially gripping is *The Age of Reagan* by Sean Wilentz. Figures for payments by the various lobbies were given in the *Economist* of 20 February 2010. Examples of pointless projects carried out in order to secure seats in Congress can be found in Thomas Frank, *The Wrecking Crew: How Conservatives Rule.* The estimates of the cost of a congressional seat are from the *International Herald Tribune,* 22 June 2011. On the healthcare lobby, see the *Economist,* 19 June 2010 and 9 October 2010, plus Michael Tomasky's 'The Money Fighting Health Care Reform', *New York Review of Books,* 8 April 2010.

On the desertion of the Democratic Party by traditional Democrat voters, *What's the Matter with Kansas?* by Thomas Frank remains a classic, as does Naomi Cahn and June Carbone's *Red Families v. Blue Families.* For the growing gap between rich and poor see Charles Murray, *Coming Apart: The State of White America 1960–2010.* Also of interest is Barbara Ehrenreich, especially *Fear of Falling* and *Nickel and Dimed.*

The figures for ethanol subsidies are from the *New York Times* of 12 October 2010 and the *Economist* of 26 February 2011.

As for Marshall (MN), I naturally made grateful use of the extensive historical oeuvre of Joseph Amato, especially *Jacob's Well, Dust, Community of Strangers* and *Rethinking Home.* As I have already mentioned, the aural history of that little town is beautifully described by MaryKay Broesder. Facts about the differences between American towns are from the American Human Development Project, *A Century Apart.*

Part Five

In *Bad Land: An American Romance* Jonathan Raban writes splendidly about the religious character of Americans, especially in contrast to Europeans.

Interesting views on the relationship between America and the biblical story are also offered by Ian Buruma, *Taming the Gods: Religion and Democracy on Three Continents*, and Christopher Collins, *Homeland Mythology*. On magical and religious positive thinking, see *The Positive Thinkers* by Donald Meyer and *Smile or Die* by Barbara Ehrenreich, which was partly inspired by Meyer's book. The scene with 'I want my stuff right now!' can be heard on a DVD from 2000 by a black evangelist called Creflo Dollar.

In describing the life of Teddy Roosevelt, I was helped on my way by two essays in the *New York Review of Books* – one by Tony Judt, 'Dreams of Empire', 4 November 2004, and the other by Christopher Benfey, 'The Age of Teddy', 14 January 2010. Naturally I made grateful use of the excellent three-part biography by Edmund Morris. The analysis of the Golden Age by Jackson Lears is also enlightening, and the same goes for the chapter that Alfons Lammers devotes to Roosevelt in *God Bless America*, as well as *The American Political Tradition and the Men Who Made It* by Richard Hofstadter.

On the rise of the American empire, see Richard Van Alstyne's *The Rising American Empire* and Warren Zimmermann's *First Great Triumph*. Also John Gray, 'The Mirage of Empire', *New York Review of Books*, 12 January 2006, and Anatol Lieven. In describing the fate of the Native Americans I drew upon the already named works by Daniel Richter and Alan Taylor. On Custer and the Great Sioux War, Nathaniel Philbrick's *The Last Stand* is the most informative. No less enthralling is *A Terrible Glory* by James Donovan, and particularly interesting is the almost forgotten viewpoint of the 'Indians' themselves as expressed in *Keep the Last Bullet for Yourself* by Thomas Marquis.

For the decline of the American railroad I made use above all of Stephen Goddard's *Getting There: The Epic Struggle between Road and Rail in the American Century*.

Part Six

For facts about the early history of California, I once again drew heavily upon Alan Taylor. In *Man & Yosemite* Ted Orland describes the changes in the landscape that took place after the Native Americans died out.

Useful information about California is to be found in pieces written by Frans Verhagen for *De Groene Amsterdammer*, especially 'Paradise Lost' of

18 March 2010. Thoughts about the new role of women in the suburbs come in part from *The Fifties* by David Halberstam. For the problems in schools see Diana Ravitch, 'School "Reform": A Failing Grade', *New York Review of Books*, 29 September 2011. The leaf-blower war in Orinda is vividly described by Tad Friend in 'Blowback', *New Yorker*, 25 October 2010.

Lawrence Wright has written a brilliant book about America in the 1960s and since: *In the New World*.

As for the American military, Andrew Bacevich, 'Cow Most Sacred: Why Military Spending Remains Untouchable', TomDispatch.com, 27 January 2011, looks at why American military expenditure cannot be called into question and at its connection with patriotism. By the same author are *The New American Militarism: How Americans are Seduced by War* and *The Limits of Power*. Steve Coll's 'Our Secret American Security State', *New York Review of Books*, 9 February 2010, is informative as well.

John Steinbeck's stay in San Francisco and Monterey is described by his biographers Jackson Benson (p. 887ff.) and Jay Parini (p. 427ff.), and by Barbara Reitt in her essay. For Steinbeck's relationship with California and his pessimism about the state of the country, see Louis Owens, *John Steinbeck's Re-Vision of America*.

The interviews with Steinbeck during the pause in his trip in and around San Francisco appeared in, respectively, the *Monterey Peninsula Herald* of 4 November 1960 and the *San Francisco Chronicle* of 6 November 1960.

I have the digging by local historian A. L. 'Scrap' Lundy to thank for much of the information about the real people behind the main characters in *Cannery Row*, as published in his *Real Life on Cannery Row*. Other descriptions of Steinbeck's life in Monterey are taken from 'About Ed Ricketts', the foreword Steinbeck wrote, after Ricketts' death, for *The Log from the Sea of Cortez*.

The 'culture wars' are analysed in countless studies, each of which takes a different approach. To name a few of them: Arthur Schlesinger Jr, *The Disuniting of America*; Sam Tanenhaus, *The Death of Conservatism*; Tristram Riley-Smith, *The Cracked Bell*; Cory Robin, *The Reactionary Mind*; and Mark Lilla, 'Republicans for Revolution', in the *New York Review of Books* of 12 January 2012.

For the striking faith in Johnson's War on Poverty in the 1960s as compared to the lack of faith now, I borrowed from Marc Hetherington, *Why Trust Matters*. The statistics about trust in doctors, managers and politicians come from *De Grote Amerikashow* by Tom-Jan Meeus. Nolan McCarty, a political scientist at Princeton, has analysed the voting behaviour of the Senate and Congress over the past few decades. My conclusions are based partly on his findings – see also the *International Herald Tribune* of 15 March 2010.

In the *New Yorker* of 17 January 2011, Jill Lepore wrote sensible things about the canonisation of the 'sacrosanct' constitution: 'The Commandments: The Constitution and its worshippers'.

Election day on 8 November 1960 was described in detail by David Pietrusza, W. J. Rorabaugh and Rick Perlstein. Also of interest is William Manchester in *The Glory and the Dream*, p. 884ff. My thoughts on the 2010 result are partly based on the analysis by Robert Dworkin in the *New York Review of Books* of 9 December 2010: 'The Historic Election: Four Views'.

Part Seven

Facts about illegal immigrants in Arizona come from various sources including in-depth reportage by a journalist at the *Economist*, published on 28 December 2010. For the morgue in Tucson see the *New York Times*, 28 July 2010.

Insights into the presidency of Franklin D. Roosevelt are from, among others, Richard Hofstadter, as well as Alfons Lammers' *Franklin Delano Roosevelt*, which also includes a description of the visit by Jo van Ammers-Küller and a detailed look at the influence of Roosevelt on his successors. Roosevelt's Hundred Days and their consequences for contemporary America are described in Adam Cohen, *Nothing to Fear*.

For the Johnson presidency, Robert Caro's biography *The Years of Lyndon Johnson* was an excellent source, especially the first volume, *The Path to Power*, which describes the feud with Robert Kennedy. The description of 'The Treatment' comes from Rowland Evans and Robert Novak, *Lyndon B. Johnson*.

Sam Rayburn's trip abroad is described by David Halberstam in *The Powers That Be*, pp. 12–15. Molly Ivins' portrait of Charlie Wilson is in her *Molly Ivins Can't Say That, Can She?*, p. 70ff.

For the debate over 'declinism' see Josef Joffe's 'The Default Power: The False Prophecy of America's Decline', *Foreign Affairs*, September/October 2009, vol. 88, no. 5, as well as Joseph S. Nye Jr, 'The Future of American Power: Dominance and Decline in Perspective', *Foreign Affairs*, November/December 2010, vol. 89, no. 6.

George Kennan offers a good description of the Charlie Wilson syndrome before Charlie Wilson came on the scene in *American Diplomacy, 1900–1950*. The stance of *Time* on China can be traced in detail in David Halberstam's *The Powers That Be*, p. 106ff. On the American attitude to Eastern European dissidents, see Jeffrey Engel, *The Fall of the Berlin Wall*. Karel van Wolferen writes about the American empire in 'The President And His Generals', a 2009 essay available on his website. For Niebuhr and the myth of innocence see Brian Urquhart, 'What You Can Learn from Reinhold Niebuhr', *New York Review of Books*, 26 March 2009. Very informative about the monopolising of foreign policy by the White House under Obama is Vali Nasr, *The Dispensable Nation*.

There is a seemingly inexhaustible stream of books and essays about Katrina and New Orleans. My main sources include the following: Josh Neufeld, *A.D.: New Orleans na de watersnood*; Chris Rose, *1 Dead in Attic: After Katrina*; Jed Horne, *Breach of Faith: Hurricane Katrina and the Near Death of a Great American City* (New York, 2006/2008), from which comes the story of Ivor van Heerden; Michael Dyson, *Come Hell or High Water: Hurricane Katrina and the Color of Disaster*; Nicholas Lemann, 'The New New Orleans', *New York Review of Books*, 24 March 2011; Bill McKibben, 'In the Face of Catastrophe: A Surprise', *New York Review of Books*, 5 November 2009.

Details of the visits to New Orleans by Johnson and Bush are taken from Greil Marcus and Werner Sollors, *A New Literary History of America* (Boston, 2009).

Facts about the riots surrounding the Willem Frantz Elementary School and conversations in 2010 with those involved are from news clippings and from police reports of the time, to be found in Isabella Taves, 'The Mother Who Stood Alone', *Good Housekeeping*, April 1961 and in Katy

Reckdahl, 'Fifty Years Later, Students Recall Integrating New Orleans Public Schools', *Times-Picayune*, 13 November 2010. The story of the two women in Little Rock was documented by David Margolick in *Elizabeth and Hazel*.

Epilogue

The truth content of *Travels* is discussed in detail in Bill Steigerwald, 'Sorry, Charley: was John Steinbeck's *Travels with Charley* a fraud?' in *Reason*, April 2011. See also Jay Parini's introduction to the latest edition of *Travels with Charley* and, of course, Bill Steigerwald's *Dogging Steinbeck*. Reactions to the affair can be found on Bill Steigerwald's website and in Charles McGrath, 'A Reality Check for Steinbeck and Charley', *New York Times*, 3 April 2011 – with comments by biographer Jay Parini among others. Then there is Rachel Dry, 'Steinbeck's true enough "Travels With Charley"', *Washington Post*, 15 April 2011. Thomas Steinbeck described his father's way of working – like a kind of Leonardo da Vinci – in the foreword to Al Lundy's description of real life on Cannery Row.

The cynical commentary by his son John Jr can be found in *The Other Side of Eden*.

Since the publication of *Preparing for the Twenty-First Century* by Paul Kennedy, shelf upon shelf of books have been written about the decline of the Western world in general and the United States in particular, each from a perspective of its own. Some examples: *Collapse* by Jared Diamond; *Why America Is Not a New Rome* by Vaclav Smil; *Day of Empire* by Amy Chua; *Free World* by Timothy Garton Ash; *Colossus* by Niall Ferguson; and *Why the West Rules – For Now* by Ian Morris.

The quotes from Joseph Joffe about 'The Default Power' come from his article of that name. The term itself was first used by Madeleine Albright on NBC on 19 February 1998. My views on the great potential of the United States, especially those that arise from the country's sense of mutual solidarity, are partly based on Anne-Marie Slaughter's essay 'Connectivity' in *Foreign Affairs* Jan/Feb 2009, vol. 88, no. 1. The shift in beliefs about Europe among the American public is registered by the Marshall Fund in 'Transatlantic Trends 2011'. Remarks by Anatol Lieven on difficulties in coming to terms with America's 1960s are from an interview in NRC Handelsblad of 25 October 2008.

As well as the biographies and the book by John Jr, Thomas E. Barden's Steinbeck in Vietnam: Dispatches From the War is a good source on Steinbeck's role in the Vietnam War and his Letters to Alicia. Budd Schulberg describes his last conversation with Steinbeck in The Four Seasons of Success, 1972, which is included in Thomas Fensch, Conversations with John Steinbeck, on pp. 105 ff.

Neal Ascherson's thoughts on WikiLeaks and American diplomacy can be found in the Guardian of 4 December 2010. The description of Paul Kennedy's soup kitchen is from his column 'The Spike – 80 years later', International Herald Tribune, 25 November 2011. See also 'The eternal US defense dilemma', International Herald Tribune, 16 March 2012, and 'Marching to different tunes', International Herald Tribune, 27 August 2010.

That Used to Be Us: How America Fell Behind in the World It Invented is by Thomas Friedman and Michael Mandelbaum. Katherine Newman's ideas about 'the missing class', that huge group of 'nearly poor', come from her book of that name and from an interview with her that was published in NRC Handelsblad, 2/3 January 2010, under the headline 'Amerika is een angstig land'.

Bibliography

Alcoff, Linda Martin, et al., *The Good Citizen*, New York, 1999

Amato, Joseph, *Servants of the Land: God Family & Farm: The Trinity of Belgian Economic Folkways*, Marshall, 1990

—— *Community of Strangers: Change, Turnover, Turbulence & the Transformation of a Midwestern Country Town*, Marshall, 1999

—— *Dust: A History of the Small and the Invisible*, Berkeley, 2000

—— *Jacob's Well: A Case for Rethinking Family History*, Marshall, 2008

—— *On Foot: A History of Walking*, New York, 2004

—— *Rethinking Home: A Case for Writing Local History*, Berkeley, 2009

Ascherson, Neal, 'WikiLeaks cables are dispatches from a beleaguered America in imperial retreat', *Guardian*, 4 December 2010

Atwood, Margaret, *Survival: A Thematic Guide to Canadian Literature*, Toronto, 1972

Bacevich, Andrew, 'Cow Most Sacred: Why Military Spending Remains Untouchable', TomDispatch.com, 27 January 2011

—— *The Limits of Power: The End of American Exceptionalism*, New York, 2008

—— *The New American Militarism: How Americans are Seduced by War*, New York, 2006

Barden, Thomas E., *Steinbeck in Vietnam: Dispatches from the War*, Charlottesville, 2012

Barich, Bill, *Long Way Home: On the Trail of Steinbeck's America*, New York, 2010

Barzini, Luigi, *The Europeans*, New York, 1983

Baum, Dan, *Nine Lives: Death and Life in New Orleans*, New York, 2009

Bell, Daniel, *The End of Ideology: On the Exhaustion of Political Ideas in the Fifties*, New York, 1962

Benfey, Christopher, 'The Age of Teddy', *New York Review of Books*, 14 January 2010

Benson, Jackson J., *The True Adventures of John Steinbeck, Writer*, New York, 1984

Brands, Henry William, *American Dreams: The United States since 1945*, New York, 2010

Brechin, Gray, *Imperial San Francisco: Urban Power, Earthly Ruin*, Berkeley/Los Angeles, 1999

Broesder, MaryKay, *The Sounds of a Developing Prairie Town: Marshall, Minnesota, 1872–1918*, Marshall, 1991

Brooks, David, *On Paradise Drive: How We Live Now (And Always Have) in the Future Tense*, New York, 2004

Brown, Frederick (ed.), *Alexis de Tocqueville: Letters from America*, London, 2010

Bryce, Viscount James, *The American Commonwealth*, New York, 1888/1959

Bryson, Bill, *At Home: A Short History of Private Life*, London, 2010

—— *Made in America: An Informal History of the English Language in the United States*, London, 1994

Burd-Sharps, Sarah and Kristen Lewis, *A Century Apart: New Measures of Well-Being for U.S. Racial and Ethnic Groups*, New York, 2010

Burner, David, et al., *An American Portrait: A History of the United States*, New York, 1985

Burns, Jennifer, *Goddess of the Market: Ayn Rand and the American Right*, New York, 2009

Buruma, Ian, *Taming the Gods: Religion and Democracy on Three Continents*, Princeton, 2012

Cahn, Naomi and June Carbone, *Red Families v. Blue Families. Legal Polarization and the Creation of Culture*, New York, 2010

Calendrille, Maryann, *Sag Harbor Is: A Literary Celebration*, New York/Sag Harbor, 2006

Camus, Albert, *American Journals*, New York, 1947/1987

Caro, Robert A., *The Years of Lyndon Johnson*, 4 vols, New York, 2012

Chomsky, Noam, 'Is the World Too Big to Fail? The Contours of Global Order', TomDispatch.com, 21 April 2011

Chua, Amy, *Day of Empire: How Hyperpowers Rise to Global Dominance – and Why They Fall*, New York, 2007

Clark, Joshua, *Heart Like Water: Surviving Katrina and Life in Its Disaster Zone*, New York, 2007

Cohen, Adam, *Nothing to Fear: FDR's Inner Circle and the Hundred Days That Created Modern America*, New York, 2009

Colbert, David, *Eyewitness to America: 500 Years of America in the Words of Those Who Saw It Happen*, New York, 1997

Coll, Steve, 'Our Secret American Security State', New York Review of Books, 9 February 2010

Collins, Christopher, Homeland Mythology: Biblical Narratives in American Culture, University Park, 2007

Collins, Gail, When Everything Changed: The Amazing Journey of American Women from 1960 to the Present, New York, 2009

Conrad, Peter, Imagining America, New York, 1980

Cooke, Alistair, Reporting America: The Life of the Nation 1946–2004, London/New York, 2008

Cuthbertson, Ken, Inside: The Biography of John Gunther, New York, 1992

Damrosch, Leo, Tocqueville's Discovery of America, New York, 2010

Davies, Richard, et al., A Place Called Home: Writings on the Midwestern Small Town, Minnesota Historical Society, St Paul, 2003

Diamond, Jared, Collapse: How Societies Choose to Fail or Succeed, New York, 2005

Donkers, Jan, De Amerikaanse droom in Nederland 1944–1969, Nijmegen, 2000

—— De tweede Amerikaanse eeuw, Amsterdam, 2004

Donovan, James, A Terrible Glory: Custer and the Little Bighorn, New York, 2008

Dry, Rachel, 'Steinbeck's true enough "Travels With Charley"', Washington Post, 15 April 2011

Duncan, Russell and Joseph Goddard, Contemporary America, New York, 2003/2009

Dunnigan, Brian Leigh, 'Those Frenchmen Who Got Themselves Killed in the Open', in Historic Deerfield, Summer 2008

Duyvendak, Jan Willem, The Politics of Home: Belonging and Nostalgia in Europe and the United States, Houndmills, 2011

Dworkin, Robert, 'The Historic Election: Four Views', New York Review of Books, 9 December 2010

Dyson, Michael, Come Hell or High Water: Hurricane Katrina and the Color of Disaster, New York, 2006

Ehrenreich, Barbara, Fear of Falling: The Inner Life of the Middle Class, New York, 1990

—— Nickel and Dimed: On (Not) Getting By in America, New York, 2001

—— Smile or Die: How Positive Thinking Fooled America and the World, London, 2009

Elias, Norbert, Studies over Duitsers: Machtsstrijd en habitus-ontwikkeling, Amsterdam, 2003

Ellis, Joseph J., Founding Brothers: The Revolutionary Generation, New York, 2002

Engel, Jeffrey A. (ed.), The Fall of the Berlin Wall: The Revolutionary Legacy of 1989, New York, 2009

Evans, Harold, The American Century, New York, 1999

Evans, Rowland and Robert Novak, Lyndon B. Johnson: The Exercise of Power, New York, 1966

Farrell, John A., Clarence Darrow: Attorney for the Damned, New York, 2011

Fensch, Thomas, Conversations with John Steinbeck, Jackson, 1988

Ferguson, Niall, Colossus: The Rise and Fall of the American Empire, New York, 2004

Fischer, Claude S., Made in America: A Social History of American Culture and Character, Chicago, 2010

Fischer, Claude S. and Michael Hout, Century of Difference: How America Changed in the Last One Hundred Years, New York, 2006

Fishman, Robert, Bourgeois Utopias: The Rise and Fall of Suburbia, New York, 1987

Fitzgerald, Frances, Cities on a Hill: A Journey Through Contemporary American Cultures, New York, 1986

Fossum, John Erik, 'Europe's "American Dream"', European Journal of Social Theory, 2009, 12, p. 483

Frank, Thomas, Pity the Billionaire: The Hard-Times Swindle and the Unlikely Comeback of the Right, New York, 2012

—— The Wrecking Crew: How Conservatives Rule, New York, 2008

—— What's the Matter with Kansas?: How Conservatives Won the Heart of America, New York, 2004

Freeland, Chrystia, 'To have and to have not: The iPod test', International Herald Tribune, 1 July 2011

Friedman, Thomas and Michael Mandelbaum, That Used to Be Us: How America Fell Behind in the World It Invented and How We Can Come Back, London, 2011

Friend, Tad, 'Blowback', New Yorker, 25 October 2010

Fukuyama, Francis, America at the Crossroads: Democracy, Power and the Neoconservative Legacy, New Haven, 2006

Fulbright, J. William, The Arrogance of Power, New York, 1966

Gaddis, John Lewis, The Cold War: A New History, New York, 2005

—— Surprise, Security and the American Experience, Boston, 2005

Galbraith, John Kenneth, The Affluent Society, New York, 1958

Gallagher, Gary W., The Union War, Cambridge, 2011

Garton Ash, Timothy, Free World: America, Europe, and the Surprising Future of the West, New York, 2004

Gaus, Bettina, *Auf der Suche nach Amerika: Begegnungen mit einem fremden Land*, Frankfurt am Main, 2008

Gellhorn, Martha, *The View from the Ground*, New York, 1989

Goddard, Stephen B., *Getting There: The Epic Struggle between Road and Rail in the American Century*, New York, 1994

Gorer, Geoffrey, *The American People: A Study in National Character*, New York 1948/rev. edn September 1964

Gray, John, 'The Mirage of Empire', *New York Review of Books*, 12 January 2006

de Grazia, Victoria, *Irresistible Empire: America's Advance through 20th Century Europe*, Cambridge, 2005

Greene, Graham, *The Quiet American*, London, 1955

Gunther, John, *Inside U.S.A.*, New York, 1947

Hacker, Andrew, 'We're More Unequal Than You Think', *New York Review of Books*, 23 February 2012

Hacker, Jacob, Philipp Rehm and Mark Schlesinger, *Standing on Shaky Ground: Americans' Experiences with Economic Insecurity*, New Haven, 2010

Halberstam, David, *The Best and the Brightest*, New York, 1969/1992

—— *The Fifties*, New York, 1993

—— *The Powers That Be*, New York, 1980

Havenaar, Ronald, *Eb en vloed, Europa en Amerika van Reagan tot Obama*, Amsterdam, 2009

Hersh, Seymour, *The Dark Side of Camelot*, New York, 1997

Hetherington, Marc, *Why Trust Matters: Declining Political Trust and the Demise of American Liberalism*, Princeton, 2005

Hofland, H. J. A., *Op zoek naar de pool*, Amsterdam, 2002

Hofstadter, Richard, *The American Political Tradition and the Men Who Made It*, New York, 1948

Holmes, Richard, *Footsteps*, London, 1985

Horne, Jed, *Breach of Faith: Hurricane Katrina and the Near Death of a Great American City*, New York, 2006/2008

Hunter, Davison James and Alan Wolfe, *Is There A Cultural War?: A Dialogue on Values and American Public Life*, Washington, 2006

Isaacs, Jeremy and Taylor Downing, *Cold War*, London, 1998

Ivins, Molly, *Molly Ivins Can't Say That, Can She?*, Vintage Books, 1992

Jackson, Kenneth T., *Crabgrass Frontier: The Suburbanization of the United States*, New York, 1987

Jacobs, Jaap, *Een zegenrijk gewest: Nieuw-Nederland in de zeventiende eeuw*, Amsterdam, 1999

Jacobs, Jane, *The Death and Life of Great American Cities*, New York, 1961

Jasanoff, Maya, *Liberty's Exiles: American Loyalists in the Revolutionary World*, New York, 2011

Jessup, John, Adlai Stevenson, et al., *The National Purpose: America in Crisis: An Urgent Summons*, New York, 1960

Joffe, Josef, 'The Default Power: The False Prophecy of America's Decline', *Foreign Affairs*, Sept/Oct 2009

Jones, David W., *Mass Motorization and Mass Transit*, Bloomington, 2008

Judt, Tony, 'Dreams of Empire', *New York Review of Books*, 4 November 2004

—— *Ill Fares the Land*, New York, 2010

Kallenberg, Roger, *Looking Back: A Pictorial History of Kalamazoo*, Mozaline, 1994

Kaplan, Fred (ed.), *The Essential Gore Vidal*, New York, 1999

Kaplan, Robert, *An Empire Wilderness: Travels into America's Future*, New York, 1998

—— *Imperial Grunts: The American Military on the Ground*, New York, 2006

Kennan, George, *American Diplomacy, 1900–1950*, Chicago, 1951

Kennedy, James, 'Hedendaags Onbehagen', *De Gids*, 3/2012

Kennedy, Paul, *Preparing for the Twenty-First Century*, New York, 1993

—— *The Rise and Fall of the Great Powers*, New York, 1989

Kerouac, Jack, *On the Road*, New York, 1957

Knippenberg, Hans, *Hoe God emigreerde naar Amerika*, valedictory lecture, Amsterdam, 2009

Kohnstamm, Dolph (ed.), *'Nog is er geen oorlog': Briefwisseling tussen Max en Philip Kohnstamm, 1938–1939*, Amsterdam, 2001

Kroll, Andy, 'The New American Oligarchy', in 'Tomgram: Andy Kroll, How the Oligarchs Took America', TomDispatch.com, 2 December 2010

Kunstler, James Howard, *Home from Nowhere*, New York, 1998

LaHaye, Tim and Jerry B. Jenkins, *Left Behind: A Novel of the Earth's Last Days*, Wheaton, 1995

Lakoff, George, *Moral Politics: What Conservatives Know that Liberals Don't*, Chicago, 1996

Lammers, Alfons, *Franklin Delano Roosevelt: Koning van Amerika*, Amsterdam, 1992

—— *God Bless America: Zegeningen en beproevingen van de Verenigde Staten*, Amsterdam, 1987

Lears, Jackson, Rebirth of a Nation: The Making of Modern America, 1877–1920, New York, 2009

Least Heat-Moon, William, Blue Highways: A Journey into America, Boston, 1983

Lemann, Nicholas, 'The New New Orleans', New York Review of Books, 24 March 2011

Lepore, Jill, 'The Commandments: The Constitution and its worshippers', New Yorker, 17 January 2011

Lewis, Sinclair, Main Street, New York, 1920/2003

Lieven, Anatol, America Right or Wrong: An Anatomy of American Nationalism, New York, 2004

Lilla, Mark, 'Republicans for Revolution', New York Review of Books, 12 January 2012

—— 'The Tea Party Jacobins', New York Review of Books, 27 May 2010

Lindsey, Brink, The Age of Abundance: How Prosperity Transformed America's Politics and Culture, New York, 2007

Lundy, A. L. 'Scrap', Real Life on Cannery Row: Real People, Places and Events That Inspired John Steinbeck, Santa Monica, 2008

Madrick, Jeffrey, The Case for Big Government, Princeton, 2009

—— The End of Affluence: The Causes and Consequences of America's Economic Decline, New York, 1995

Mak, Geert, De goede stad, Amsterdam, 2007

—— In Europe: Travels Through the Twentieth Century, London, 2007

Manchester, William, The Glory and the Dream: A Narrative History of America, 1932–1972, Boston, 1975

Mansfield, Stephen, The Faith of George W. Bush, New York, 2003

Marcus, Greil and Werner Sollors, A New Literary History of America, Boston, 2009

Margolick, David, Elizabeth and Hazel: Two Women of Little Rock, New Haven/London, 2011

Marquis, Thomas B., Keep The Last Bullet For Yourself: The True Story of Custer's Last Stand, Algonac, 1976

Martin, Albro, Railroads Triumphant: The Growth, Rejection, and Rebirth of a Vital American Force, New York/Oxford, 1992

McClelland, Edward, Young Mr Obama: Chicago and the Making of a Black President, New York, 2010

McElrath, Joseph R., Jesse S. Crisler and Susan Shillinglaw, John Steinbeck: The Contemporary Reviews, Cambridge, n.d.

McGrath, Charles, 'A Reality Check for Steinbeck and Charley', New York Times, 3 April 2011

McKibben, Bill, 'In the Face of Catastrophe: A Surprise', New York Review of Books, 5 November 2009

McPherson, James M., 'What Drove the Terrible War?', New York Review of Books, 14 July 2011

McWilliams, Wilson Carey, Redeeming Democracy in America, Lawrence, 2011

Meeus, Tom-Jan, De Grote Amerikashow: Populisme en wantrouwen in een gespleten land, Amsterdam, 2012

Meltzer, Milton, John Steinbeck: A Twentieth-Century Life, New York, 2007

Merriner, James L., Grafters and Goo Goos: Corruption and Reform in Chicago, Carbondale, 2004

Meyer, Donald, The Positive Thinkers: Popular Religious Psychology from Mary Baker Eddy to Norman Vincent Peale and Ronald Reagan, New York 1965/1988

Miller, Arthur, 'Steinbeck', in Susan Shillinglaw, John Steinbeck: Centennial Reflections by American Writers, San José, 2002

—— Timebends: A Life, London, 1987

Monnet, Jean, Memoirs, New York, 1978

Morris, Edmund, Colonel Roosevelt, New York, 2001

—— The Rise of Theodore Roosevelt, New York, 1979

Morris, Ian, Why the West Rules — For Now: The Patterns of History and What They Reveal About the Future, New York, 2010

Morse, Flo, The Story of the Shakers, Woodstock, 1986

Murray, Charles, Coming Apart: The State of White America 1960–2010, New York, 2012

Naipaul, V. S., A Turn in the South, New York, 1989

Nasr, Vali, The Dispensable Nation, New York, 2013

Neufel, Josh, A.D.: New Orleans na de watersnood, Den Bosch, 2010

Newman, Katherine S. and Victor Tan Chen, The Missing Class: Portraits of the Near Poor in America, Boston, 2007

Niebuhr, Reinhold, The Irony of American History, Chicago, 1952

Niedermeyer, Edward, 'A Green Detroit? No, a guzzling one', New York Times, 15 December 2010

Nye, Joseph S. Jr, 'The Future of American Power: Dominance and Decline in Perspective', Foreign Affairs, November/December 2010, vol. 89, no. 6

Obama, Barack, Dreams From My Father: A Story of Race and Inheritance, New York, 1995/2004

Ogden, Dunbar, My Father Said Yes: A White Pastor in Little Rock School Integration, Nashville, 2008

O'Hagan, Andrew, The Atlantic Ocean: Essays on Britain and America, London, 2008

Orland, Ted, Man & Yosemite: A Photographer's View of the Early Years, Santa Cruz, 1985

Owens, Louis, John Steinbeck's Re-Vision of America, Athens, 1985

Parini, Jay, John Steinbeck: A Biography, New York, 1995

Patterson, James. T., Grand Expectations: The United States, 1945–1974, Oxford, 1996

Perlstein, Rick, Nixonland: The Rise of a President and the Fracturing of America, New York, 2008

Pew Research Center for the People and the Press, Views of a Changing World 2003, Washington, DC, 2003

Philbrick, Nathaniel, The Last Stand: Custer, Sitting Bull, and the Battle of the Little Bighorn, New York, 2010

Phillips, Kevin, American Dynasty: Aristocracy, Fortune, and the Politics of Deceit in the House of Bush, New York, 2004

Pietrusza, David, 1960 – LBJ vs. JFK vs. Nixon: The Epic Campaign That Forged Three Presidencies, New York, 2008

Potter, David, People of Plenty, Chicago, 1958

Pyle, Ernie, Ernie's America: The Best of Ernie Pyle's 1930s Travel Dispatches, New York, 1989

Raban, Jonathan, Bad Land: An American Romance, New York, 1996

—— Driving Home: An American Scrapbook, London, 2010

Ravitch, Diane, 'School "Reform": A Failing Grade', New York Review of Books, 29 September 2011

Reckdahl, Katy, 'Fifty Years Later, Students Recall Integrating New Orleans Public Schools', Times-Picayune, 13 November 2010

Reeves, Thomas, Twentieth-Century America: A Brief History, New York, 2000

Reitt, Barbara B., '"I Never Returned as I Went In": Steinbeck's Travels with Charley', Southwest Review, Spring 1981, p. 186ff.

Remnick, David, The Bridge: The Life and Rise of Barack Obama, New York, 2010

Richter, Daniel K., Before the Revolution: America's Ancient Pasts, Boston, 2011

Riesman, David, The Lonely Crowd: A Study of the Changing American Character, New Haven, 1950/1961

Riley-Smith, Tristram, The Cracked Bell: America and the Afflictions of Liberty, London, 2010

Robin, Corey, The Reactionary Mind: Conservatism from Edmund Burke to Sarah Palin, New York, 2011

Ronse, Tom, 'Detroit is dood, leve Detroit', De Groene Amsterdammer, 28 August 2009

Rorabaugh, W. J., The Real Making of the President: Kennedy, Nixon and the 1960 Election, Lawrence, 2009

Rose, Chris, 1 Dead in Attic: After Katrina, New York, 2005/2007

Rossem, Maarten van, Amerika voor en tegen, Utrecht, 2002

—— In Amerika, Amsterdam, 2009

Rovere, Richard, Senator Joe McCarthy, Berkeley, 1959

Santayana, George, Character and Opinion in the United States, New Haven, 2009

Schama, Simon, Landscape and Memory, New York, 1995

—— The American Future: A History From The Founding Fathers To Barack Obama, London, 2008

Schlesinger Jr, Arthur, Kennedy or Nixon: Does it Make Any Difference?, New York, 1960

—— The Disuniting of America: Reflections on a Multicultural Society, New York, 1991

Schlissel, Lillian, Byrd Gibbens and Elizabeth Hampsten, Far From Home: Families of the Westward Journey, New York, 1989

Schultz, Jeffrey and Luchen Li, Critical Companion to John Steinbeck: A Literary Reference to His Life and Work, New York, 2005

Shillinglaw, Susan (ed.), John Steinbeck: Centennial Reflections by American Writers, San José, 2002

Shorto, Russell, The Island at the Center of the World: The Epic Story of Dutch Manhattan and the Forgotten Colony that Shaped America, New York, 2004

Slater, Philip, Pursuit of Loneliness: American Culture at the Breaking Point, Boston, 1976

Slaughter, Anne-Marie, 'America's Edge: Power in the Networked Century', Foreign Affairs, Jan/Feb 2009, vol. 88, no. 1

Smil, Vaclav, Why America Is Not a New Rome, Cambridge, 2010

Smith, Jean Edward, Eisenhower in War and Peace, New York, 2012

Smith, Lynn and Pamela Hall O'Connor, Kalamazoo: Lost and Found, Kalamazoo, 2001

Speerstra, Hylke, It wrede paradys: It ferfolch, Leeuwarden, 2010

Spychalsky, John C., 'Rail Transport. Retreat and Resurgence', *Annals of the American Academy of Political and Social Science*, Sept 1997, vol. 553, p. 42

Star, Kevin, *Golden Dreams: California in an Age of Abundance, 1950–1963*, Oxford, 2009

Steigerwald, Bill, *Dogging Steinbeck: How I Went in Search of John Steinbeck's America, Found My Own America, and Exposed the Truth about 'Travels with Charley'*, Pittsburgh, 2013

—— 'Sorry, Charley: was John Steinbeck's Travels with Charley a fraud?' *Reason*, April 2011

Steinbeck, Elaine and Robert Wallsten (eds), *A Life in Letters*, New York, 1975

Steinbeck, John, *The Acts of King Arthur and His Noble Knights, from the Winchester Manuscripts of Thomas Malory and Other Sources*, New York, 1976

—— *America and Americans and Selected Nonfiction*, New York, 1966

—— *Cannery Row*, New York, 1945/London, 2010

—— *East of Eden*, New York, 1952

—— *The Grapes of Wrath*, New York, 1939

—— *The Log from the Sea of Cortez*, New York, 1951

—— *Sweet Thursday*, New York, 1954

—— *Tortilla Flat*, New York, 1935

—— *Travels with Charley: In Search of America*, New York, 1962/1997

—— *The Winter of Our Discontent*, New York, 1961

Steinbeck, John IV and Nancy Steinbeck, *The Other Side of Eden: Life with John Steinbeck*, Amherst, 2001

Swidler, Ann, 'Cultural Constructions of Modern Individualism', Pittsburgh, 1992

Tanenhaus, Sam, *The Death of Conservatism*, New York, 2009

Taves, Isabella, 'The Mother Who Stood Alone', *Good Housekeeping*, April 1961

Taylor, Alan, *American Colonies: The Settling of North America*, New York, 2001

—— *The Civil War of 1812: American Citizens, British Subjects, Irish Rebels and Indian Allies*, New York, 2010

Terkel, Studs, *American Dreams: Lost and Found*, New York, 1980

—— *Coming of Age: The Story of Our Century by Those Who've Lived It*, New York, 1995

—— *Division Street America*, New York, 1967

—— *Talking to Myself: A Memoir of My Times*, New York, 1973/1995

Tobier, Nina, *Voices of Sag Harbor: A Village Remembered*, New York/Sag Harbor, 2007

de Tocqueville, Alexis, *Democracy in America*, New York, 1835 & 1840 (the original French edition, *De la démocratie en Amerique*, was published in two volumes, as was the English translation in those same two years. Quotations are taken from that first translation, by Henry Reeve, as published in a revised edition in 1899)

Tomasky, Michael, 'The Money Fighting Health Care Reform', *New York Review of Books*, 8 April 2010

Tuchman, Barbara, *The First Salute: A View of the American Revolution*, New York, 1988

UNICEF, 'The Children Left Behind', New York, 2010

Urquhart, Brian, 'What You Can Learn from Reinhold Niebuhr', *New York Review of Books*, 26 March 2009

Van Alstyne, Richard Warner, *The Rising American Empire*, New York, 1974

Verhagen, Frans, 'Paradise Lost', *De Groene Amsterdammer*, 18 March 2010

Wartzman, Rick, *Obscene in the Extreme: The Burning and Banning of John Steinbeck's The Grapes of Wrath*, Philadelphia, 2008

Weiland, Matt and Sean Wilsey (eds), *State by State: A Panoramic Portrait of America*, New York, 2009

Wilentz, Sean, *The Age of Reagan: A History 1974–2008*, New York, 2008

Wilkerson, Isabel, *The Warmth of Other Suns: The Epic Story of America's Great Migration*, New York, 2010

Williams, John, *The Redeemed Captive*, ed. Edward W. Clark, Carlisle, 1976

Wolfe, Alan (ed.), *America at Century's End*, Berkeley, 1991

Wood, Gordon S., *Empire of Liberty: A History of the Early Republic 1789–1815*, Oxford, 2009

—— *The Idea of America: Reflections on the Birth of the United States*, New York, 2011

Wright, Lawrence, *In the New World: Growing Up with America from the Sixties to the Eighties*, New York, 1983

Yates, Richard, *Revolutionary Road*, London, 1961 / 1989

Zimmermann, Warren, *First Great Triumph: How Five Americans Made Their Country a World Power*, New York, 2002

Zinn, Howard, *A People's History of the United States*, New York, 1980 / 2005

Index

JS indicates John Steinbeck.